Moral Psychology

Moral Psychology

Volume 3: The Neuroscience of Morality: Emotion, Brain Disorders, and Development

edited by Walter Sinnott-Armstrong

A Bradford Book
The MIT Press
Cambridge, Massachusetts
London, England

MIT Press books may be purchased at special quantity discounts for business or sales promotional use. For information, please e-mail special_sales@mitpress.mit.edu or write to Special Sales Department, The MIT Press, 55 Hayward Street, Cambridge, MA 02142.

This book was set in Stone Sans and Stone Serif by SNP Best-set Typesetter Ltd., Hong Kong and was printed and bound in the United States of America.

Library of Congress Cataloging-in-Publication Data

Moral psychology / edited by Walter Sinnott-Armstrong.
    v.   cm.
"A Bradford Book."
Includes bibliographical references and index.
Contents: v. 1. The evolution of morality: adaptations and innateness—v. 2. The cognitive science of morality: intuition and diversity—v. 3. The neuroscience of morality: emotion, disease, and development.
ISBN 978-0-262-19561-4 (vol. 1: hardcover : alk. paper)—ISBN 978-0-262-69354-7 (vol. 1: pbk. : alk. paper)—ISBN 978-0-262-19569-0 (vol. 2: hardcover : alk. paper) —ISBN 978-0-262-69357-8 (vol. 2: pbk. : alk. paper)—ISBN 978-0-262-19564-5 (vol. 3: hardcover : alk. paper)—ISBN 978-0-262-69355-4 (vol. 3: pbk. : alk. paper)
1. Ethics. 2. Psychology and philosophy. 3. Neurosciences. I. Sinnott-Armstrong, Walter, 1955–
BJ45.M66   2007
170—dc22   2006035509

10 9 8 7 6 5 4 3 2 1

This volume is dedicated to Mike Gazzaniga and Scott Grafton for their patience, encouragement, support, stimulation, inspiration, and friendliness while helping this neophyte learn about the brain.

Contents

Acknowledgments

Many people deserve my thanks for assistance as these volumes grew. For financial support of the conference that sowed the seeds for this project, I am grateful to several institutions at Dartmouth College, including the Leslie Center for the Humanities, the Dickey Center for International Understanding, the Master of Arts in Liberal Studies program, the Dean of the Faculty, the Department of Psychological and Brain Sciences, the Social Brain Science Project, the Cognitive Neuroscience Center, the Department of Philosophy, and the Institute for Applied and Professional Ethics. For help in making these essays more accessible to students, I thank Cate Birtley, Cole Entress, and Ben Shear, Dartmouth students who served as my Presidential Scholars. I also greatly appreciate the devotion and editorial skills of Kier Olsen DeVries, who worked long and hard to put the essays from these diverse authors into a single form for the publisher. Tom Stone, my editor at MIT Press, also has my gratitude for his spirited encouragement. Last but not least, I thank my family—Liz, Miranda, and Nick—for their love and patience while I spent many nights and weekends on this project.

Introduction

Walter Sinnott-Armstrong

Moral psychology is old. In ancient times, Plato and Aristotle addressed many of the issues that still occupy moral psychologists, such as the conditions of responsibility and the roles of reason, emotion, and culture in moral judgments. In early modern Europe, Hume, Kant, and Mill continued these themes. Hume even used methods that anticipate some contemporary cognitive psychology. Debates about the evolution of moral beliefs, emotions, and actions have been raging since Darwin.

In contrast, the neuroscience of moral belief is brand new. Brain lesions have been studied at least since Phineas Gage, but such lesions are not numerous, controlled, or focal enough to support precise conclusions. Only within the last few decades have noninvasive techniques made it possible to get solid information about how our brains make up our minds.

Brain science concentrated at first on simple mental events and gradually gained the capacity to investigate more and more complex processes. Neuroscientific studies of moral beliefs, emotions, and decisions were not possible until the 1990s. The first brain imaging studies of moral judgments were reported as recently as 2001. The neuroscience of morality is a mere baby.

This baby is growing fast. Today many labs all over the world are planning or executing studies of the neural bases of moral judgment. The chapters in this volume sample the best work in this emerging field. They also display the variety of approaches, including functional imaging, lesion studies, abnormal psychology, and developmental neuroscience.

Some of the earliest brain imaging studies of moral judgment were performed by Jorge Moll in Brazil, who is also the lead author in the opening chapter of this volume. Moll and his colleagues Roland Zahn, Ricardo de Oliveira-Souza, and Jordan Grafman build on previous functional imaging studies as well as clinical evidence to construct a general theory of moral emotions, including guilt, shame, embarrassment, pride, indignation, anger, contempt, pity, compassion, awe, elevation, and gratitude. This wide array of emotions is tied to certain brain regions and is unified by a certain structure. According to Moll and his colleagues, moral emotions have shared and distinctive phenomenological features that are explained by their representational components, aspects, and functions. This representational account of moral emotion raises profound challenges to the traditional dichotomy between emotion and cognition.

Bill Casebeer comments that the representational theory of Moll and his colleagues inevitably depends on substantive moral assumptions and needs to be integrated with both process views of moral emotions and with knowledge of neural reward-processing mechanisms. In her comment, Catherine Hynes argues that Moll et al. need to define which emotions are moral and that an adequate definition will show why moral emotions need to be understood in terms of inhibitory and regulatory processes as well as the propositional content of moral judgments. Moll et al. reply by clarifying their definition of morality and by showing how their representational view might be related to a process view of moral emotions.

Another early explorer, Joshua Greene, came to moral neuroscience through philosophy. In his contribution to this volume, Greene draws philosophical lessons from a broad base of empirical research in moral neuroscience and psychology, including work by Jonathan Baron and Jonathan Haidt.[1] Greene argues that deontological moral judgments and theories, which Immanuel Kant claimed to be grounded in pure reason, are actually moral rationalizations driven by emotional responses.[2] Consequentialist moral judgments and theories, in contrast, are more likely to be cognitive and to involve genuine moral reasoning. Greene claims that if these empirical claims are true, they cast doubt on deontology as a moral philosophy.

In response, John Mikhail shows how his computational theory accounts for Greene's data without giving up on deontological principles based on moral reasoning.[3] Mark Timmons then responds to Greene's four main arguments by keeping deontology but giving up the rationalist assumption that morality is a matter of reasoning. In his reply, Greene criticizes Mikhail's account of the old cases and presents new and independent evidence for his claims. Then he asks Timmons why deontologists should trust emotions that are fickle and contingent.

Our moral judgments can also be illuminated by comparison with moral judgments by abnormal people, including people with psychopathy, acquired sociopathy, and autism. This method is adopted in the chapters 3 through 5.

Kent Kiehl focuses on psychopathy. Psychopaths are often said to lack conscience or morality because of how they act, but, surprisingly, they do not lack intelligence or the ability to articulate verbally appropriate moral judgments about many real-life situations. To understand this baffling syndrome, Kiehl reviews the neuroscience literature and concludes that psychopathy is associated with dysfunction of the paralimbic system. The particular neural regions implicated include the orbital frontal cortex; insula, amygdala, and parahippocampal regions; anterior superior temporal gyrus; and rostral, caudal, and posterior cingulate.

In their comment, Ricardo de Oliveira-Souza, Fátima Azevedo Ignácio, and Jorge Moll report their unpublished work on "true community anti-socials" and ask whether this distinct population fits Kiehl's model, which is based on violent criminals. Jana Schaich Borg then cites her own work as support for her speculation that psychopaths might resemble normals in some moral judgments but not in others.[4] She also questions the dichotomy between emotion and cognition that underlies Kiehl's claim that psychopaths display an intact intellect despite emotional dysfunction.[5] In his reply, Kiehl reveals further complexities both in the distinction between emotion and cognition and in studies of true community antisocials as opposed to criminal psychopaths.

Psychopathy is often conflated with so-called acquired sociopathy, which is due to damage to the ventromedial frontal lobe, but these syndromes differ significantly in some respects that are important to moral judgment. In chapter 4, Jeanette Kennett and Cordelia Fine discuss these differences and argue that psychopaths do not make moral judgments except in an "inverted commas" sense, but at least some acquired sociopaths are able to make third-person hypothetical moral judgments.[6] Where acquired sociopaths characteristically fail is in applying those abstract moral judgments to their own situations in the first person. Thus, contrary to published arguments by Adina Roskies, cases of acquired sociopathy do not refute moral internalism—which Kennett and Fine take to be the philosophical thesis that other things being equal, any fully rational person who makes an in situ moral judgment is motivated to act accordingly.

Roskies responds by clarifying how her prior argument works against the specific form of internalism that was her target and then criticizes Kennett and Fine's counterargument that evidence from psychopathy actually supports internalism. Michael Smith argues that Kennett and Fine weaken moral internalism too much when they restrict its claims to in situ judgments and admit that it holds only "other things being equal," and then

Smith defends his own qualified moral internalism against Roskies's criticisms. In reply, Kennett and Fine argue that both sides in the debate over internalism depend on assumptions about which mental states count as moral judgments, so internalism cannot be disproved by any empirical discoveries alone.

Another abnormal syndrome that has attracted attention from moral philosophers is autism. Jeanette Kennett argued that moral judgments by high-functioning autistics support a Kantian rationalist view of moral judgment and agency. In contrast, here Victoria McGeer argues that Humean sentimentalists can accommodate and, indeed, provide a better explanation of moral judgments by individuals with autism. McGeer cites self-reports and other data to show that autistics' moral judgments are based, not on reverence for pure reason but instead on a passion for order. McGeer concludes that disinterested concern can be rooted in a concern for the well-being of others, a concern with social structure and position, or a concern with cosmic structure and position. These three spheres of disinterested concern or varieties of moral agency are all present in normal humans without autism, and autistics share at least some of these concerns.

Kennett responds that McGeer's evidence suggests that Humeans and Kantians have been talking past each other, so Hume's descriptive account and Kant's normative account can be reconciled. Heidi Maibom then presses McGeer for a better explanation of cosmic concern and supports her focus on social concern with additional evidence from the Milgram and Stanford prison experiments. Next, Frédérique de Vignemont and Uta Frith argue for a different view of autism, in which autistic moral judgment and agency are distinctive not because of a lack of empathy or insensitivity to others' distress but instead because of a lack of interaction between an egocentric view of other people (in relation to themselves) and an allocentric view of other people (as having separate lives of their own). In her reply, McGeer elaborates her speculations on the moral importance of cosmic structure and position, and she argues that Frith and de Vignemont's alternative view of autism needs to be supplemented with a fuller account of moral violations in order to cover the variety of cases.

Additional lessons about moral judgment can be gleaned from developmental psychology and neuroscience. Chapters 6 and 7 adopt this perspective, addressing childhood and adolescence in turn.

Jerome Kagan's chapter postulates a universal sequence of stages in the early development of morality. Infants first learn that certain behaviors are followed by punishments, but soon children display a reluctance to violate standards even when they have not experienced prior punishment for violating that standard. Next, children apply the terms "good" and "bad," followed by feelings of guilt, and then the abstract concepts of "fairness" and the "ideal." Kagan emphasizes that this developing morality depends on social categories that have lost much of their moral power in contemporary culture. He then explains how, within these universal patterns, individual variations result from heritable temperaments, including different degrees of vulnerability to guilt, which he traces to patterns of activity primarily in the amygdala.

In their comment, Nathan Fox and Melanie Killen discuss the role of culture in moral development and some pros and cons of the lost power of social categories. Paul Whalen then explains why more work needs to be done on connections between the amygdala and the ventromedial prefrontal cortex. Kagan replies by agreeing that there are costs when social categories lose power and that more than the amygdala is involved in morality.

Chapter 7 turns to a later stage in development—adolescence. Abigail Baird describes four basic stages: classical conditioning first reduces or encourages behaviors by pairing them with sensory outcomes; then through operant conditioning children internalize mental schemas that represent behavioral standards; then more complex abstract thought emerges; and finally comes the sense of belonging to a larger society. With regard to the development of morality during adolescence, Baird emphasizes the roles of cognition, self-conscious emotion, and the transition from a parent-centered to a peer-centered social world. She argues that the integration of visceral emotion with social cognition during adolescence, which is enabled by the maturation of the prefrontal cortex, is essential for a fully developed moral reasoning that functions with minimal cognitive effort. In her view of moral development, knowing precedes feeling, and over time visceral feelings of wrongdoing become rapid automatic responses.

Daniel Lapsley concurs with Baird's emphasis on automaticity, as opposed to Kohlberg's phenomenalism, but questions several aspects of Baird's four-stage model. Katrina Sifferd then asks what Baird's views on adolescent development imply about the origins of pathologies and about juvenile criminal culpability and punishment. Baird replies by developing her views on pathological disruption in the proposed model of moral development and by explaining how horrific moral transgressions can occur in the absence of any discernable pathology.

Richard Joyce closes this three-volume collection with a sober warning not to become overexuberant in drawing philosophical lessons from empirical findings. Jonathan Haidt and Joshua Greene have sometimes suggested that neuroscience and psychology support emotivism.[7] Joyce denies this suggestion if emotivism is understood as the philosophical claim that people who make moral judgments are expressing, not beliefs, but only desires, emotions, or preferences. Similarly, Shaun Nichols argues that experiments on psychopaths and on folk views of psychopaths undermine psychological and conceptual versions of moral rationalism.[8] Joyce criticizes Nichols's argument and concludes that neuroscience cannot undermine conceptual moral rationalism, much less the claim that moral judgments can be rationally justified. In the end, Joyce agrees that empirical research can be relevant to philosophical moral theory, but not as directly as is often supposed.

Shaun Nichols responds by arguing that conceptual rationalists will have more trouble explaining his experimental results than Joyce admits and then by showing how empirical results can undercut the force of some popular attempts to rationally justify moral judgments. Leonard Katz then outlines a way in which the neuroscience of pleasure and pain, together with other scientific theories, might reveal a source of ultimate and objective normatively justifying reasons. Joyce replies that Nichols's experiments might reveal ordinary opinions without illuminating conceptual content, that justificatory rationalists need not appeal to moral intuitions in the way that Nichols assumes, and that Katz's attempted rationalist justification cannot cross the interpersonal divide and show why facts about pain and other hedonic states give *me* any reason not to cause pain to *you*.

These brief summaries cannot come close to doing justice to the subtlety and depth of the exchanges in this volume. Nor can these exchanges finally solve any of the problems raised in these pages. The most that can be reasonably hoped is that the chapters in this volume and its predecessors in this collection will lead philosophers to become interested in relevant empirical research and will lead psychologists and neuroscientists to do more work on issues related to philosophical problems. Our best hope in moral psychology is for philosophers, psychologists, and neuroscientists to work together. These volumes show that collaboration and discussion among these fields can be fruitful and should continue.

Notes

1. Compare Haidt's chapter in volume 2 of this collection.

2. Greene's claims about the role of moral emotions in moral judgment can be usefully compared with Nichols's chapter in volume 2 of this collection.

3. Mikhail's "moral grammar" approach is a version of the linguistic hypothesis defended by Hauser et al. in their chapter in volume 2 of this collection. That chapter includes further criticisms of Greene's model.

4. Schaich Borg also cites a study reported in the chapter by Hauser et al. in volume 2 of this collection.

5. The chapter by Moll et al. in this volume raises related problems for the dichotomy between emotion and cognition.

6. A new study of moral judgments by patients with frontal lobe damage is reported in the chapter by Hauser et al. in volume 2 of this collection.

7. Compare the chapters by Greene in this volume and by Haidt and Björklund in volume 2 of this collection.

8. See Nichols's chapter in volume 2 of this collection. Compare also the debate among Kennett, Fine, Roskies, and Smith in this volume.

Moral Psychology

1   The Cognitive Neuroscience of Moral Emotions

Jorge Moll, Ricardo de Oliveira-Souza, Roland Zahn, and Jordan Grafman

Humans use significant amounts of effort in assessing the appropriateness of their own and other individuals' behaviors. Moral emotions play a central role in both implicit and explicit moral appraisals, being an essential ingredient for human social cognition (Eisenberg, 2000; Fessler, 1999, 2001, 2004; Haidt 2003b). Nevertheless, the psychological structure and neural organization of moral emotions remain underspecified. Here we describe a framework that relates shared and distinctive phenomenological characteristics of moral emotions to a set of cognitive and emotional components. Based on clinical evidence and functional imaging studies (Beer, Heerey, Keltner, Scabini, & Knight, 2003; Eslinger & Damasio, 1985; Moll, de Oliveira-Souza, Bramati, & Grafman, 2002a; Moll, de Oliveira-Souza, Eslinger, Bramati, Mourao-Miranda, et al., 2002b), we suggest that moral emotions emerge as neural representations from the coactivation of brain regions that code for perception of social cues, event knowledge, and emotion (Moll, de Oliveira-Souza, & Eslinger, 2003). According to this hypothesis, the neural bases of moral emotion, knowledge, and attitudes are better explained by a representational approach, in contrast to the view of neural processes as guiding moral appraisals (Greene, Nystrom, Engell, Darley, & Cohen, 2004; Greene, Sommerville, Nystrom, Darley, & Cohen, 2001). This framework may provide a fertile ground for the development of a neuroscientific counterpart of a "theory of moral sentiments" as conceived by Adam Smith in the seventeenth century.

Background

The belief that human beings are endowed with a repertoire of emotions with a strong moral content is not new. In his classical oeuvre, Adam Smith (1723–1790) referred to them as moral sentiments (Smith, 1759/1976). Yet this idea has remained outside the reach of empirical science until quite

Box 1.1

Categories of moral emotions

> **Self-conscious** emotions are linked to self-assessments (Tangney & Dearing, 2002). They arise from concerns about the opinions of others on self behaviors and on self-identity (Eisenberg, 2000). These emotions can be subdivided into **self-critical** (guilt, shame and embarrassment), which are linked to a sense of reduced social status or self-esteem, and **self-praising** (pride), which elicits a sense of increased self-esteem and social rank (Fessler, 2001).
>
> **Other-conscious** emotions include those that are normally directed to others, and can be divided into three subcategories: **other-critical** (contempt/disgust and anger/indignation), **other-praising** (gratitude, awe), and **other-suffering** (pity or compassion). Other-critical moral emotions promote the punishment of others and the rupture of previous social links (Rozin, Lowery, Imada, & Haidt, 1999), while other-praising emotions drive positive reciprocity and cooperation. Other-suffering emotions play a key role in helping and altruistic behaviors (Haidt, 2003a).

recently. This is particularly true for normal and abnormal behaviors that take place within cultural contexts and which are heavily guided by subjective moral experiences and values (Moll, de Oliveira-Souza, & Eslinger, 2003). If, on the one hand neuroscience has grown up *pari passu* with the investigation of the cerebral substrates of cognitive architectures, on the other hand only in the past few decades have the neural underpinnings of social cognition and human emotions fallen within the reach of experimental science (Adolphs, 2003).

One important breakthrough in this respect has been the growing recognition that moral emotions comprise an essential ingredient of human social behavior. Moral emotions differ from basic emotions, such as fear and happiness, in that they are often linked to the interest or welfare either of society as a whole or at least of persons other than the agent (Haidt, 2003b). Although a final taxonomy of moral emotions has not as yet been completed (Eisenberg, 2000), they typically include (but are not restricted to) guilt, pity, embarrassment, shame, pride, awe, contempt, indignation, "moral" disgust, and gratitude (box 1.1 and table 1.1). As such, they are as instrumental in promoting the care of others, as well as cooperation and reciprocity, as in fostering blame, prejudice, and group dissolution (Moll et al., 2003; Schulkin, 2004). In this chapter, we will use the term "moral" according to its more ample definition—*moralis*, which refers to the laws of proper behavior and customs in daily life (Glare, 1982). In our view,

Table 1.1
Categories of moral emotions (subdivisions)

	Self-conscious		Other-conscious		
	Self-critical	*Self-praising*	*Other-critical*	*Other-praising*	*Other-suffering*
Guilt	•				
Shame	•				
Embarrassment	•				
Pride		•			
Indignation/anger			•		
Contempt/disgust			•		
Pity/compassion					•
Awe/elevation				•	
Gratitude				•	

Source: Modified from Haidt (2003b).

this broader definition provides a better approximation of what lay people consider appropriate or inappropriate in social conduct, in contrast to the more limited definitions employed by western moral philosophy in intellectual and professional circles.

In theory, moral emotions can be sorted into groups, or families, according to the particular type of stimuli or conditions that elicit them (elicitors) and by the specific action tendencies they evoke (Haidt, 2003b). However, these two basic classification criteria should not conceal their structural complexity. For example, although the moral emotions of shame and embarrassment share a general propensity to encourage "proper" behavior, especially in the presence of higher-ranking members of a social group, they can be distinguished in that embarrassment is felt when one violates social conventions, while shame is elicited by one's own attribution of a reduced self-value following a violation of a moral norm (Tangney, 2000b). Such naturalistic observations led to three working hypotheses that have currently occupied a number of researchers.

In the first place, the aforementioned subtle distinctions between closely related moral emotions would require an equally sophisticated cognitive apparatus to decode the often fleeting and concealed social cues from the surrounding social milieu. These cognitive mechanisms are obviously more complex than those employed in decoding basic emotions. Second, despite their neurobiological diversity and dependence on cultural codification, moral emotions have been reliably observed across individuals and societies (Fessler, 2004; Harris, 2003; Tangney & Dearing, 2002). However, what is experienced as a moral emotion is probably the result of the blending of elementary subjective emotional experiences, which are ubiquitous in mammals, with emotional and cognitive mechanisms that are typically human. The precise nature of these structural building blocks of moral emotions remains to be empirically determined and is the focus of this chapter. Third, the cognitive mechanisms and the subtle distinctions that prevail among the components of a given moral emotion, as well as among different families of moral emotions, must find an intimate correspondence to the neural representations that mediate each of them.

Moral Emotions and the Human Brain

Some of the most compelling data relating moral behavior, moral emotions, and the brain come from the remarkable overlap between the brain regions activated by explicit moral judgment tasks in functional magnetic resonance imaging (fMRI) studies and those related to disturbances of social behaviors in lesion studies (Eslinger & Damasio, 1985; Eslinger, Flaherty-Craig, & Benton, 2004; Greene, Nystrom, Engell, Darley, & Cohen, 2004; Greene, Sommerville, Nystrom, Darley, & Cohen, 2001; Heekeren, Wartenburger, Schmidt, Schwintowski, & Villringer, 2003; Moll, de Oliveira-Souza, Bramati, & Grafman, 2002a; Moll, Eslinger, & Oliveira-Souza, 2001; Seger, Stone, & Keenan, 2004; Stone, Cosmides, Tooby, Kroll, & Knight, 2002; Takahashi, Yahata, Koeda, Matsuda, Asai, & Okubo, 2004). Most of these studies employed visual presentation of written material, either simple statements or short stories. Activated regions included the prefrontal cortex (PFC), encompassing the frontopolar (FPC) and orbitofrontal (OFC) cortices, the superior temporal sulcus (STS) region, and the anterior temporal cortex. Limbic regions, such as the amygdala and ventral striatum, have also been shown to be activated, though less consistently (probably owing to intrinsic technical limitations associated with functional magnetic resonance imaging).

The brain regions activated in moral judgment tasks have been implicated in experiencing emotion (amygdala), semantic memory (anterior temporal cortex), perception of social cues (STS region) and decision making—either quick and implicit, based on heuristics, or slow and reflective, based on prospective reasoning (OFC, FPC). Remarkably, a similar brain network is engaged when normal subjects passively view visual stimuli with moral connotations (e.g., abandoned children, war scenes, interpersonal aggression), while brain regions associated with more basic emotional mechanisms (e.g., amygdala, brainstem) are activated both by unpleasant scenes without clear moral implications (e.g., dangerous animals, mutilated bodies) and by moral scenes (Moll et al., 2002b). We have postulated that the coactivation of PFC-temporolimbic networks corresponds to the cognitive-emotional states associated with "moral sensitivity." Moral sensitivity provides a critical mechanism by which humans automatically attribute moral significance to ordinary events and behaviors (Moll et al., 2002b).

These findings show that the PFC and associated regions are spontaneously engaged whether or not decisions or behavioral outputs are required, thereby suggesting that the PFC is not merely manipulating information stored elsewhere, but is actively involved in representing social knowledge. This view stands in contrast to the dualistic notion that the PFC sustains executive processes, for example conflict monitoring or cognitive set shifting, and that these rational processes compete with emotional ones (Greene et al., 2004). Instead, according to our view, moral emotions would neither compete with rational processes during moral judgments, nor result from them. Most likely, moral emotions help guide moral judgments by attaching value to whichever behavioral options are contemplated during the tackling of a moral dilemma.

Evidence pointing to differences in the neural representation of individual moral emotions within the networks mentioned is starting to emerge. Pity, indignation, guilt, and embarrassment activate partially distinct cortical and subcortical brain regions in moral judgment tasks (Moll et al., 2003; Takahashi et al., 2004).

The Integration of Context-Dependent Attitudes with Moral Emotions

Psychologists, clinicians, and philosophers have long assumed that humans share cognitive processes, such as inductive and deductive reasoning, attention, conflict monitoring, and semantic categorization. Inferring cognitive and neural mechanisms from observed behaviors, however, can be misleading (Wilkinson & Halligan, 2004). This issue becomes even more problematic when cultural effects are at play because these are often complex and difficult to control experimentally. In other words, contextual embedding plays a central role in human cognition and emotion. For example, westerners and East Asians differ in their use of logic versus dialectical principles and rules of categorization when they make causal attributions and predictions (Ji, Peng, & Nisbett, 2000; Nisbett & Masuda, 2003). Even if the engagement of a cognitive mechanism, say attention, is required to the same degree to solve a task, the content of the brain representations it helps elicit can be extremely variable.

Moral emotions are elicited in response to departures from implicit and explicit social norms and stereotypes, which code for individual attitudes and beliefs (Nichols, 2002b). The contextual elements linking moral emotions to norms can be quite variable and are to a great extent shaped by culture (Ehrlich, 2000). The PFC is a critical region for learning, storing, and binding social knowledge to contextual elements (Wood & Grafman, 2003). Damage to the anterior sectors of the PFC at an early age seems to prevent the acquisition of moral attitudes and values, leading to gross disturbances of social conduct (Anderson, Bechara, Damasio, Tranel, & Damasio, 1999; Eslinger et al., 2004). In addition, ventral damage to the PFC impairs implicit stereotypes (Milne & Grafman, 2001). Social stereotypes and attitudes are associations of the self or other persons with negative or positive attributes (Greenwald, Banaji, Rudman, Farnham, Nosek, & Mellott, 2002). The word "implicit" means that attitudes may be hidden from public view and even from conscious awareness. Thus, even when they linger outside conscious awareness, attitudes are powerful determinants of behaviors that can be justified by convincing logico-verbal arguments.

Recent evidence (Cunningham, Nezlek, & Banaji, 2004) shows that attitudes toward a wide range of social issues, such as war or abortion, activate partially overlapping brain networks (including the amygdala, PFC, OFC, and anterior temporal cortex), regardless of whether such attitudes are evoked explicitly (subjects required to judge concepts as good or bad) or implicitly (concepts judged as concrete or abstract). It is interesting that activity in the anterior PFC was correlated with scorings of "ambivalence" toward attitudes. In accord with the role of the anterior PFC in prospective evaluations and thinking about the future (Goel, Grafman, Tajik, Gana, & Danto, 1997; Koechlin, Ody, & Kouneiher, 2003; Okuda, Fujii, Ohtake, Tsukiura, Tanji et al., 2003), we have suggested that this region also plays a role in a moral calculus (Moll et al., 2003; Moll, Eslinger, & Oliveira-Souza, 2001). A moral calculus results from the ability to envision a number of action-outcome options in a parallel fashion, and compare their relative weights. While Greene and colleagues have recently espoused this view (Greene et al., 2004), their interpretation differs from ours in a subtle but important way: they hypothesize that the PFC performs a cognitive control function, inhibiting emotionally guided responses and leading to more rational moral choices (i.e., utilitarian outcomes). In contrast, we maintain that the anterior PFC (the FPC, in particular) represents different aspects of social knowledge, which are bound to emotional relevance. These representations would then guide the assessment of social-emotional outcomes associated with behavioral choices.

Moral Emotions from a Cognitive Neuroscientific Perspective

Our approach aims to identify some of the building blocks of moral emotions from a neurobiologically useful perspective. By "useful" we mean a coherent scenario that will ultimately guide the design of experiments to probe the neural mechanisms of human social behavior, both in normal individuals and in selected patients with strategic cerebral lesions. A sound framework should be able to predict the occurrence of each moral emotion from different combinations of basic components. We propose a scheme with six main components that seeks to provide such predictions. These components were defined on the basis of psychological and neurobiological plausibility. The first three (attachment, aggressiveness, and social rank/dominance/self-esteem) correspond to basic cognitive and emotional mechanisms that are widely represented across species. The fourth and fifth (outcome assessment and agency or intentionality) rely on more differentiated integrative systems and have been extensively studied in humans in recent years. The sixth (norm violation) has been attributed to the role of the PFC in sequential and motivationally relevant knowledge of an event (Wood & Grafman, 2003).

We describe each component here and briefly address how they might relate to the moral emotions. Then we address how each moral emotion may emerge from specific combinations of these components.

Attachment
Attachment provides the basic ingredient for interindividual bonding and affiliative behaviors, such as mother-offspring ties. Subcortical and limbic structures, including the ventral striatum, septal nuclei, amygdala, and hypothalamus, as well as hypothalamic-hypophyseal hormones such as oxytocin, have been implicated in attachment (Bartels & Zeki, 2004; Insel & Fernald, 2004; Keverne & Curley, 2004). While its essential aspects rely on primitive neural systems, attachment is generally bound to social cognitive mechanisms, including perception of social cues and inference of the

mental states of others. This combination provides the basis for emotional empathy, which is an affective response that stems from understanding another's emotional state, so that one has feelings similar to those of the other person. This ability arises during development, leading to the differentiation between one's own and others' internal states, and allows the emergence of pity and compassion (Eisenberg, 2000). We hypothesize that attachment is an essential ingredient for the emergence of guilt and gratitude. Guilt is often elicited in situations in which one feels bad for causing harm to another person, to other creatures (including animals and plants), and even to objects and abstract values to which one is emotionally attached. Gratitude in turn is associated with strengthened social bonds and an inclination to repay favors to benefactors, and thus might depend on basic mechanisms of attachment.

Aggressiveness

Experimental research has extensively shown that aggression occurs in disputes regarding sex, territory, and feeding. Dopamine has been implicated in the processing of signals of aggression in social-agonistic encounters in several species, including humans. Accordingly, D2-class receptor dopaminergic antagonism leads to a selective disruption in anger recognition (Lawrence, Calder, McGowan, & Grasby, 2002). Basic aggressiveness, combined with sophisticated social cognitive mechanisms of reputation assessment and representation and violations of social norms, is an essential ingredient of instrumental and moralistic aggression (Arsenio & Lemerise, 2004). The subjective experience of other-critical emotions, such as disgust, contempt, and indignation, is probably dependent on the appropriate functioning of neural circuits supporting aggression. These circuits include the amygdala, septal area, hypothalamus, and cingulate cortex, as well as their temporal and frontal connections (Mega, Cummings, Salloway, & Malloy, 1997; Moll, de Oliveira-Souza, Tovar-Moll, Ignacio, Bramati, et al., 2005a; Volavka, 1999). Although there is a close link between aggressiveness and dominance, they may be dissociable.

Social Rank/Dominance/Self-Esteem

Social animals are organized into hierarchical structures. Displays of submission (decreased eye contact and apparent body size) and dominance (increased eye contact and apparent body size) are widespread in mammals (Haidt, 2003b). Primates possess highly structured dominance hierarchies that regulate access to food resources, mating, and other social privileges (de Waal, 1996). Social status marks one as a good or poor partner for future interactions. There is extensive evidence pointing to the role of dopaminergic and serotonergic pathways in social dominance (Morgan, Grant, Gage, Mach, Kaplan et al., 2002). Though both enhanced dopaminergic and serotonergic action have been related to increased dominance, these neurochemical systems probably exert partially separable effects. Increased serotonergic activity provided by selective serotonin reuptake inhibitors (SSRI) has been linked to a decrease in harm avoidance and hostility and an increase in dominance in social encounters (Brody, Saxena, Fairbanks, Alborzian, Demaree et al., 2000). Serotonin most likely exerts a modulatory effect on social interactions that depend on social status (Edwards & Kravitz, 1997).

Further support for the dissociation between aggressiveness and dominance and self-esteem comes from the observation that higher levels of serotonin promote constructive social interactions by decreasing aggression (Young & Leyton, 2002). Self-esteem is a more complex notion that has been defined as the association of a self-concept with emotional valence (Greenwald et al., 2002). Although these dopaminergic and serotonergic pathways are difficult to circumscribe anatomically, brainstem regions (e.g., the midbrain ventral tegmental area), basal forebrain nuclei, and their projections to the OFC and the subgenual area of the anterior cingulate cortex are probably critical for these mechanisms.

Fessler (2004) has suggested that proto-forms of pride and shame developed to motivate the quest for social dominance, but were refashioned into a new class of emotions that allow one to sense the subjective experiences of other individuals toward oneself, thus extending dominance-striving motives into the cultural world of humans. Shame and pride are chiefly linked to social dominance and self-esteem and help regulate approval seeking and dominance striving. They can facilitate cooperation by physiologically enabling internally motivated states that enhance conformity to social norms (Fessler, 2004). Accordingly, self-esteem is influenced by serotonin metabolism, which regulates the degree of engagement of shame and pride (Fessler, 2001). According to the present framework, pride, shame, and embarrassment require the binding of social cognitive mechanisms (e.g., agency and evaluation of the mental states of others) with core motivational states. Some of these sophisticated social cognitive abilities have been described as "theory of mind," "perspective taking" and "simulation theory" (Gusnard, Akbudak, Shulman, & Raichle, 2001; Happé, 2003; Saxe, Carey, & Kanwisher, 2004a). According to the formulation presented in table 1.2, perspective taking supports the ability to perceive that one is being observed, which plays an important role in the elicitation of pride, shame, and embarrassment.

Outcome Assessment

The ability to predict long-term outcomes is uniquely developed in humans and is tightly linked to the development of the PFC circuits. Different functions have been ascribed to the PFC: attention control; monitoring; and adjustment of task scheduling, switching, and planning. A common denominator is the role of the PFC in dealing with events. The structured event complex (SEC) framework (Wood & Grafman, 2003) provides a unifying mechanism to explain how the PFC stores information in event complexes through sequential binding and integrates contextual information under the influence of factors such as familiarity and predictability. In certain situations, moral emotions are tightly linked to the ability to assess outcomes. When humans contemplate a behavioral option linked to short-term rewards, they often estimate (implicitly or explicitly) the possible desirable or undesirable long-term outcomes of that action. This ability is ascribed to the anterior PFC and its role in representing structured event complexes with a long duration (Wood & Grafman, 2003) and in assigning values to future rewards (Tanaka, Doya, Okada, Ueda, Okamoto, & Yamawaki, 2004). When such predictions take place in social contexts, they can influence the occurrence of certain moral emotions prior to or after carrying out an action (e.g., one considers attaining a selfish, short-term reward, but feels guilty and refrains from acting upon foreseeing that the act would make another person suffer; or one acts in the first place but then realizes the possibility of adverse consequences to others).

Agency and Intentionality

Humans often attribute agency and intentionality to others. This is a pervasive cognitive mechanism that allows one to predict the actions of others based on spatiotemporal configurations and mechanical inferences, and on their putative internal states, goals, and motives. Although a high degree of overlap may exist between attributing agency and intentionality, they are not the same thing. If you bump into an object and it falls and breaks, you are the agent of a mechanical action. But if you throw it against a wall, in addition to being the agent, you performed an intentional action. Agency and intentionality can hardly be considered as basic modules of the human mind, however. These abilities draw on evolved brain circuits that are able to link current appraisals of actions and motivational states of the self or of another person to ongoing events.

Brain regions that have been implicated in agency and intentionality include the parietal cortex, the insula, and the motor cortex, as well as the

Table 1.2
Predicted relationships between moral emotions and putative neurocognitive components

	Attachment	Aggressiveness	Social dominance attribution				Outcome assessment				Intentional action (self)	Intentional action (other)	Agency		Social norm violation
			Self by another	Self by oneself	Other by oneself	Being observed by another	Bad, self	Bad, other	Good, self	Good, other			Self	Other	
Guilt	•			→				•					•		•*
Shame			→	→		•	•								•
Embarrassment			→	←		•	•						•*		•
Pride			←			•*			•		•*		•*		
Indignation/anger		•			→		•*	•*				•		•	•
Contempt/disgust		•						•						•*	•*
Pity/compassion	•							•						•	
Awe/elevation	•				←					•*				•	
Gratitude	•				←				•			•			

Note: Black dots (•) indicate a key role of the cognitive variable in the genesis of the corresponding moral emotion. Arrows indicate increased (↑) or decreased (↓) attribution of dominance or social status, according to the self and other perspectives (e.g., decreased "self by another" means that one believes that his or her own social status is judged to be reduced from the point of view of another person). Asterisks indicate that the role of the component for a given moral emotion can be either variable or only modulatory (but not essential).

medial PFC and the STS region (Daprati, Nico, Franck, & Sirigu, 2003; Jiang, Saxe, & Kanwisher, 2004; Pridham, Saxe, & Limbo, 2004; Saxe, 2004; Saxe et al., 2004a; Saxe & Kanwisher, 2003; Saxe, Xiao, Kovacs, Perrett, & Kanwisher, 2004b; Sirigu, Daprati, Ciancia, Giraux, Nighoghossian et al., 2004; Sirigu, Daprati, Pradat-Diehl, Franck, & Jeannerod, 1999). Because both agency and intentionality can independently provide sharp discriminations among certain moral emotions, they were included as separate subcomponents in table 1.2, although they probably partially share neural representations. For example, feeling guilt generally requires recognition of oneself as the agent of an action that leads to a bad outcome to another person; intentionality here is not as critical as agency. If the same outcome is contemplated but one does not perceive oneself as the agent, pity may be experienced instead. Intentionality plays a more central role than agency for other moral emotions; indignation, for example, tends to be more pervasive when there is a voluntary violation of social norms.

Norm Violation
Norms are abstract concepts that are firmly encoded in the human mind. They differ from most kinds of abstractions because they code for behavioral standards and expectations and are often associated with emotional reactions when violated (Nichols, 2002b). Despite the large variation in the content of norms and in how contextual elements are bound to them, virtually all human societies rely on normative systems for setting common grounds and limits for interpersonal transactions. A violation of a norm signals the violation of expectations and preferences of other people in the social milieu. Norm violations are salient and conspicuous events that draw upon the cultural specifics of a social group and their context. A violation of social norms is a critical element in the elicitation of certain moral emotions, although it is not sufficient for specifying which moral emotion will be elicited. For example, in the oddball task, there is a predictable chain of events (e.g., arbitrary sensory stimuli of a given category) that is suddenly broken by a nonmatch, unexpected event, or stimulus. This oddball effect, which marks a violation of an arbitrary norm, has been demonstrated to elicit brain responses in regions linked to conflict monitoring, behavioral flexibility, and social response reversals, such as the anterior cingulate cortex, anterior insula, and the lateral OFC (Blair & Cipolotti, 2000; Hornak, Bramham, Rolls, Morris, O'Doherty, et al., 2003). If arbitrary events were replaced by ones associated with social attitudes, however, violation of expectancies would be encoded as violations of social norms. Indeed, these brain regions were shown to be activated by written

stimuli describing moral violations that evoke anger and disgust (Moll et al., 2005a).

Knowing if and who violated a social norm requires both detecting the violation and attributing agency. These ingredients are necessary for eliciting and discriminating between self-critical (guilt, shame, and embarrassment) and other-critical (contempt, disgust, and indignation or anger) moral emotions. Guilt and shame are associated with self-violations of a social norm, while contempt, disgust, and anger or indignation result from the recognition that another person carried out the transgression. One still controversial issue is whether shame and embarrassment can be differentiated on the basis of the severity of the social violation, or on a categorical distinction between moral violations and violations of social conventions (Eisenberg, 2000; Harris, 2003; Tangney, 2000b).

Predicting Moral Emotions on the Basis of Cognitive-Emotional Components

According to our framework, the elicitation of moral emotions is implemented by dynamic PFC-temporolimbic network representations, which arise from coactivation of the components described earlier. Table 1.2 illustrates how these components might combine to give rise to specific moral emotions. Here we briefly describe the "recipe" of each moral emotion according to the postulated neurobiological ingredients and cite the brain regions putatively involved in each. It should be emphasized, however, that at least in some cases the evidence is still preliminary and should be considered provisional.

Guilt

Guilt emerges prototypically from (1) recognizing or envisioning a bad outcome to another person, (2) attributing the agency of such an outcome to oneself, and (3) being attached to the damaged person (or abstract value). Depending on the circumstance, the recognition that (4) a social norm was violated may lead to increased guilt. Guilt is associated with reduced self-esteem, which is not necessarily dependent on being observed by another person (Eisenberg, 2000; Harris, 2003; Tangney, 2000a, 2002; Tangney & Dearing, 2002). Recent neuroimaging data showed the involvement of the anterior PFC, the anterior temporal cortex, the insula, the anterior cingulate cortex, and the STS region in guilt experience (Shin, Dougherty, Orr, Pitman, Lasko et al., 2000; Takahashi et al., 2004).

Shame

This emotion follows (1) an action attributed to self-agency that is associated with (2) a violation of a social norm, leading to (3) a bad outcome to oneself (at least indirectly, such as damage to one's reputation), and (4) reduced self-esteem (and social dominance) as judged by oneself and others, which is often reliant on (5) the other's awareness of one's actions (Eisenberg, 2000; Harris, 2003; Tangney, 2000b), although this aspect is questioned by other authors (Baumeister, Stillwell, & Heatherton, 1994). While there are no available brain imaging studies on shame, brain regions similar to those demonstrated for embarrassment should be involved. The ventral part of the anterior cingulate cortex, also known as the subgenual area, has been associated with depressive symptoms, which are linked to decreased self-esteem (Fu, Williams, Cleare, Brammer, Walsh et al., 2004). Therefore, this brain region might also play a more specific role in the neural representation of shame.

Embarrassment

Embarrassment has traditionally been viewed as a variant of shame (Lewis & Steiben, 2004). In egalitarian cultures that have an independent construal of the self, embarrassment splits off from shame (Eisenberg, 2000; Haidt, 2003b; Tangney, 2002). Embarrassment follows (1) being the agent, (2) violating less severe social norms or conventions compared with shame, leading to recognition of (3) a bad outcome to oneself, and (4) a nonpervasive reduction of one's social dominance, which is dependent on (5) others' awareness (being observed). In contrast to guilt and shame, however, embarrassment is not thought to be associated with a significant reduction of self-esteem or a sustained decrease in self-attributed social dominance. The neural correlates of embarrassment have recently been addressed (Berthoz, Armony, Blair, & Dolan, 2002; Takahashi et al., 2004) and include the medial PFC, the anterior temporal cortex, the STS region, and the lateral division of the OFC.

Pride

The polar opposite of shame and embarrassment is pride. It is associated with (1) being the agent of an action leading to (2) good outcomes for oneself, in which there is an (3) increased attribution of social dominance and self-esteem. Perhaps not mandatory for the experience of pride is (4) the observation of one's socially desirable actions by others (being observed) and (5) performing an intentional action. So far, there is no clear evidence for the neural representation of pride, although it has been shown that patients with OFC lesions may experience this emotion inappropriately (Beer et al., 2003). We hypothesize that brain regions involved with mapping the intentions of other persons (e.g., the medial PFC and the STS region), and regions involved in reward responses (OFC, hypothalamus, septal nuclei, ventral striatum) may play a role in this emotion.

Indignation and Anger

Indignation and anger are elicited by (1) observing a norm violation in which (2) another person is the agent, especially if (3) the agent acted intentionally. Indignation relies on (4) engagement of aggressiveness, following an observation of (5) bad outcomes to the self or to a third party. We and others have shown that indignation evokes activation of the OFC (especially its lateral division), the anterior PFC, anterior insula, and anterior cingulate cortex (Blair, Morris, Frith, Perrett, & Dolan, 1999; Moll et al., 2005a).

Contempt

Contempt has been considered a blend of anger and disgust, and has sometimes been considered as a more subtle form of interpersonal disgust (Haidt, 2003b; Plutchik, 1980). For this reason it will be considered here together with disgust. Contempt and disgust mark distinctions of rank and prestige, especially in hierarchical societies. They are evoked by (1) devaluation of another's social status by oneself, i.e., attribution of decreased social dominance to another person (although upward contempt also exists), and (2) recruitment of aggressiveness to some degree. Contempt and disgust can be enhanced by (3) minor social norm violations in which (4) another person is the agent. Severe social violations, especially when intentional, will generally trigger indignation instead. While contempt has not been nominally addressed in experimental neuroanatomical studies, the neural representations of disgust have been shown to include the anterior insula, the anterior cingulate and temporal cortices, the basal ganglia, the amygdala, and the OFC (Buchanan, Tranel, & Adolphs, 2004; Calder, Keane, Manes, Antoun, & Young, 2000; Fitzgerald, Posse, Moore, Tancer, Nathan, & Phan, 2004; Moll et al., 2005a).

Pity and Compassion

These feelings are described as "being moved by another's suffering" (Haidt, 2003b; Harris, 2003). They require (1) the recognition of bad outcomes to another person (or social group) and (2) a sense of attachment. Preliminary functional imaging results in normal subjects point to the involvement of the anterior PFC, the dorsolateral PFC, the OFC, the anterior insula, and the anterior temporal cortex in pity or compassion (Moll et al., 2003). Further studies with more refined imaging techniques may be able to test our prediction that certain limbic regions, such as the hypothalamus, septal nuclei, and ventral striatum, would also be involved.

Awe and Elevation

Awe and elevation are poorly understood emotions that have received more attention recently (Haidt, 2003a). While these emotions can be experienced in nonmoral situations (e.g., when admiring a beautiful landscape or artwork), in social contexts they are likely to be elicited when one (1) observes the action of another agent and (2) experiences a positive feeling of attachment to this agent or to its accomplishment. Often this will be linked to (3) good outcomes to a third party (i.e., an altruistic action), although in other instances it can derive from observing other kinds of highly praised acts (e.g., an act of courage or an act that springs from other outstanding skills). Finally, awe is associated with the attribution of (4) increased social status to another agent. While the neuroanatomy of awe is still obscure, we predict that it will involve limbic regions associated with reward mechanisms, including the hypothalamus, ventral striatum, and medial OFC (Rolls, Kringelbach, & de Araujo, 2003; Tanaka et al., 2004), as well as cortical regions linked to perspective taking and perceiving social cues, such as the anterior PFC and the STS region (Moll et al., 2003).

Gratitude

This emotion is elicited by (1) detecting a good outcome to oneself, attributed to (2) the agency of another person, (3) who acted in an intentional manner to achieve the outcome. (4) Gratitude is associated with a feeling of attachment to the other agent and often promotes the reciprocation of favors. Recent studies using game-theoretic methods have started to address the brain regions involved with positive reciprocity (retribution of favors), with obvious implications for the neural underpinnings of gratitude. Activated brain regions included the ventral striatum, the OFC, and the anterior cingulate cortex (Rilling, Gutman, Zeh, Pagnoni, Berns, & Kilts, 2002; Singer, Kiebel, Winston, Dolan, & Frith, 2004).

Final Remarks and Future Directions

We have presented a novel approach to explain the shared and distinctive phenomenological characteristics of moral emotions on the basis of a set of social cognitive and emotional component representations. The basic cognitive components postulated can be linked to distinct neural systems based on evidence from neuroanatomical, neurochemical, lesion, or functional imaging studies. Owing to the complexity of this endeavor, this initial approach cannot be interpreted as a complete or inclusive model. Especially with respect to the representation of human social dominance and attitudes, and their relationships to self-esteem, the neuroscientific evidence is preliminary.

Future functional imaging studies and clinical investigations in patients with focal brain lesions aiming at the neural representation of moral emotions should be able to independently manipulate the components outlined here to test predictions inspired by this framework. Also, it would be of great interest to explore if and how these components interact during development in the path to moral maturity. It was not within the scope of this work to comprehensively describe the more general implications of moral emotions for human social cognition. However, we believe that a more detailed neuroscientific theory of moral emotions and attitudes is urgently needed to explain a variety of uniquely human aspects of social cognition, such as the culturally and individually shaped context dependence of human social behavior.

Moral emotions might prove to be a key venue for understanding how phylogenetically old neural systems, such as the limbic system, were integrated with brain regions more recently shaped by evolution, such as the anterior PFC, to produce moral judgment, reasoning, and behavior. The pace of development of the new field of moral neuroscience will critically depend on the free exchange of ideas, open and unbiased scientific discussions, and the design of experiments and models that link the humanities and biological sciences.

1.1   Processes and Moral Emotions

William D. Casebeer

In their ambitious chapter, Moll and colleagues articulate a theory of moral cognition designed to capture the neurobiological substrates responsible for the representation of moral emotions. This important foundational work is a critical part of a larger naturalistic project of making sense of the function and structure of moral judgment given the background assumptions (both ontological and methodological) of the various natural sciences. I applaud Moll and his team for their nascent naturalistic theory; however, I think it could be improved in some respects. The approach needs to (1) acknowledge the inevitability of bringing to bear a background normative moral theory in order to delimit the field of study, (2) make better sense of how basic neural reward-processing mechanisms either constitute or integrate with the six combinatorial elements of the moral emotions they discuss, and (3) leave room for an approach that weaves together the process view with the representational view of the moral emotions. Here I discuss each of these concerns in turn in the hope of encouraging Moll and colleagues to develop their theory yet further.

First, some commonplace observations about the philosophy of science. Theory development in a given domain requires delimiting the field of study in a manner that befits further progress. This is (perversely) an art as well as a science, requiring multiple judgment calls, especially at the beginning of scientific inquiry. For example, if I decided that the domain of electromagnetic wavelengths visible to the human eye under standard conditions included 4 nanometers up to about 400 nanometers, and then spent several years testing this youthful hypothesis that human beings can indeed see ultraviolet light, I would be sorely disappointed. My theory of "the nature of visible light" would have to be truncated, eliminating ultra-violet wavelengths from the domain of what is actually visible (usually wavelengths from about 400 to 700 nanometers). Refining a background theory of visible wavelengths is tantamount then to "fixing an ontology."

The nature of my scientific investigation is tutored by a theory about the nature of the domain, but the results then feed back into the background theory to modify that theory in the light of experimental evidence and vice versa. I may discover that experiments which initially did not seem to address my domain of study at all actually do, and I may pursue a new experimental regimen as a result. (Someone studying honeybee vision using a background theory of the nature of visible light informed only by human experiments would experience this because honeybees can indeed respond to ultraviolet wavelengths. In much the same way, someone concerned about moral judgment and valuation ought to pay attention to structures in the macaque brain originally thought to be implicated only in visual processing but which may actually constitute a proto-valuation function.)[1]

For a more complex example from the cognitive sciences, consider face recognition. Conducting an experiment in face recognition requires a background theory of what a face is; later, as our experiments push the risible boundaries of "facedom"—two black blobs and a smear are a *face?*— we may substantially modify both our theory of what a face is *and* our understanding of what experiments are actually pertinent to understanding face processing in the brain.[2] There isn't any good reason to think that the naturalistic study of moral cognition will be any different. Making progress, then, will require that we explicitly specify our theory of what the moral domain consists in. Otherwise, hidden assumptions will remain undiscussed, and those assumptions could hinder good experimental progress. As an ethicist and as a scientist, then, I would like to see less agnosticism about "nature's joints" for morality and more forthright discussion of what background normative moral theory is informing our theorizing. Here, tools from traditional moral inquiry—the moral psychologies and assumptions about the nature of morality captured by utilitarianism, deontology, and virtue theory—are useful at least initially, although they may require substantial modification by the end of inquiry.

Considering the domain of moral judgment and emotion to be restricted to "the laws of proper behavior and customs in daily life" (as Moll et al. offer at the beginning of their chapter) risks something on this count. For one, the word "law" is loaded. What if the proper domain of moral judgment consists, not in the divination of laws and rules, but instead in the learning of skills of moral coping? For another, the word "proper" smuggles in a lot of normative content that needs to be made explicit—proper as in "enhancing aggregate utility," or proper as in "conforming with the demands of pure reason"?[3] Even the word "custom" is tendentious, as normative moral philosophers would be at pains to tell us that judgments about what is customary may have no bearing on what morality actually demands of us and hence may not really be moral cognitive acts. These concerns are not so much objections as they are invitations to consider how assumptions about the domain of inquiry may mislead us with regard to the neural mechanisms most responsible for cognition and emotion in moral neuroscience.

This first concern informs my second: Moll and colleagues admirably summarize and extend a large body of cognitive neuroscience work, much of it accomplished by them. However, there are some noticeable absences of core neural processes that may be pertinent to emotion in the moral domain. Consider the neural mechanisms of reward processing;[4] these include swaths of neural acreage such as the midbrain dopamine-driven systems, limbic structures, and cortical regions. Medial prefrontal areas, orbitofrontal cortex, the amygdala, and the ventral striatum are all probably included in this circuit. A rich body of work, some based on neuroeconomic assumptions, has explored the role of this machinery for computing expected award in multiple domains of human behavior. If reward-processing machinery truly is a neural natural kind (my first concern looms large here), then a discussion of how it either links to or constitutes one of the six basic kinds of moral emotions would be useful. The most obvious move would be to collapse all of reward processing into the "outcome assessment" category, but this is to undervalue the role that reward processing may play in all kinds of cognitive acts, ranging from reasoning about justice to understanding one's own character.[5] For example, recent work has indicated that reward-related mechanisms, such as the caudate nucleus, may be involved in satisfying a desire to punish defectors who are trampling on social norms.[6] It is not clear how this translates into "outcome assessment"-style considerations. While psychological egoism of the simplistic "Ayn Rand is awesome" sort fails as both an empirical psychology and a normative moral theory, it may very well be that reward-processing considerations (perhaps only imperfectly captured with the label "egoism") may be part of a neural moral natural kind.

My final concern is also related to these two considerations. Moll argues that his theory is not just about the representational aspects of moral cognition but that—as a representational theory—it does a *better* job of explaining the neuroscientific data than a process-oriented approach (such as that proposed by Josh Greene, Patricia and Paul Churchland, or myself). This is a strong claim, and it is not borne out by his chapter. One reason why it is strong is that whether or not emotions have a representational function is a live debate in philosophy of mind. While I think emotions do have a representational function in appropriately tutored cognitive systems, to argue that moral emotions across the board are representations is inconsistent with the evolutionary naturalism that undergirds the chapter.

Rather than viewing representational and process-related views of neural structure and function as competitors, we should seek theories that are complementary and illuminate the ways in which the process of making moral judgments can result in representations that then coevolve with the judgmental processes that produced them. At the end of the day, rather than making representations primary, it is probably a better idea to make *processes of coping* primary because a lot of critters cope with their environments, whereas the view that representation is a necessary precursor to successful coping is more problematic. This nicely brings us full circle because normative moral theories that emphasize the skill-like aspects of moral cognition, such as an Aristotelian virtue theory, are not really discussed in the chapter by Moll and his colleagues. This (entirely understandable) shortcoming has caused us to deemphasize in the present study of moral cognition those aspects of moral emotion and reasoning most amenable to a virtue-theoretic understanding. Perhaps moral cognition is more like a game of real-life ethical ping pong ("I hit this and then that") than a game of imaginary ethical three-dimensional chess ("I represent this and then that").[7]

I look forward to seeing Moll and colleagues press their theory as far as the experimental evidence will take it, and I applaud their big-picture work. By highlighting connections to traditional normative moral theories and their psychologies, double checking the cognitive natural kinds that are used to build higher-level concepts, and dealing as much with capacity and skill as representation, I believe their research program will yield a fruitful bounty indeed.

Notes

1. See Platt and Glimcher (1999). This work has informed a flourishing field that is examining monkey saccades—eye movements—to plumb the neural mechanisms of valuation in hominid precursors.

2. To see this process in action, look at articles that attempt to operationalize concepts like "face" or "body," especially in studies of infant cognition, e.g., Slaughter, Stone, and Reed (2004).

3. For first attempts to integrate normative moral theory, moral psychology, and the moral neurosciences, see Casebeer (2003a) and Casebeer and Churchland (2003).

4. See McClure, York, and Montague (2004) for an introduction to fMRI work in this area.

5. Consider Elizabeth Phelps's remarks on "Learning, Trust, Morality and the Neural Circuitry of Reward" at a recent (October 26, 2005) New York Academy of Sciences public program on "Getting the Goods: The Neural Basis of Decision Making."

6. De Quervain, Fischbacher, Treyer, Schellhammer, Schnyder, Buck, & Fehr (2004).

7. This difference in emphasis has testable consequences; for one, it would have us spend more time examining neural mechanisms responsible for moral *action* than it would for moral judgment.

Catherine A. Hynes

In their chapter Moll and colleagues present a framework in which to define the neural basis of what they call moral emotions. According to this account, moral emotions are part of the representation of a moral situation and are present regardless of whether the processing is conscious or unconscious. Moral emotions are defined as the coactivation of neural representations of social cues, event knowledge, and emotion. They are proposed to arise from six subcomponents: attachment, aggressiveness, dominance, outcome assessment, agency and intentionality, and norm violation. The authors suggest that this representational approach is an improvement upon the process accounts proposed by other researchers.

This approach to empirical research on moral reasoning is laudable in its emphasis on the construction of models. The current body of cognitive neuroscience research on morality lacks the identification and definition of the basic components of moral reasoning, as well as the means by which they are assembled into larger and more complex constructs that ultimately result in the higher-order phenomenon of morality. The dearth of such models in the field makes it difficult to conduct empirical research, particularly when it concerns the brain, whose functional anatomy is as yet only partially defined. For these reasons, research on higher-order cognition risks being underspecified at both ends in the absence of a cognitive model. While the framework presented in Moll and colleagues' chapter has a great deal of merit, more specificity is required on a few particulars for it to drive forward the cognitive neuroscience of moral reasoning.

Most troubling is the absence of a definition of what constitutes "moral," which occupies a central conceptual position in the framework. Defining morality will reveal an important omission among the components of moral-emotional behavior: that of inhibition. In addition, the role of the basic emotions is overlooked in this framework, even though their relevance to moral-emotional behavior is demonstrable. The descriptions of the components of moral emotions are interesting and at times illuminating, but careful consideration shows that some of them are beset by complexities that are not accounted for in the model. Finally, although the role of propositional content is mentioned, it is not really addressed by the framework, and while most current cognitive neuroscience accounts of moral behavior are guilty of the same omission, a complete model of moral reasoning will necessitate the elucidation of this complex and thorny issue.

What Is Morality?

The main purpose of Moll and colleagues' chapter is to define the components of moral emotions that have known and describable neurophysiological correlates. Moral emotions, the authors assert, are distinguished from the six basic emotions (fear, sadness, anger, happiness, disgust, and surprise) by virtue of being "linked to the interest or welfare either of society as a whole or at least of persons other than the agent" (this volume, p. 2). Basic emotions, by contrast, could exist in a social vacuum and do not require the presence of a conspecific for their elicitation. The emotions listed by the authors under the rubric of "moral" include guilt, embarrassment, shame, and so on, all of which have traditionally been called social emotions in the psychological literature (e.g., Barrett & Nelson-Goens, 1997). Given that the definition proposed here for moral emotions is essentially that the emotions are social, one wonders how or if moral emotions are different from social emotions. One would assume that the distinction lies in the fact that social emotions pertain to social situations in general, whereas moral emotions are involved in a subset of social situations that involve morality. That what is moral necessarily concerns the social is not likely to be disputed; it is difficult to imagine a moral transgression in the absence of other people or sentient beings. But without a definition of what constitutes morality, there is some theoretical underspecificity in this framework.

As an example of the inability of the model to hone in on the moral subclass of social emotions, consider the feeling of shame. According to the framework, shame is generated at least in part by one's dominance status and one's self-esteem. Imagine a soccer star, famous for his accurate aim, who misses the penalty kick in a final on television. His self-esteem may indeed plummet and he may suffer from a decrease in his dominance status, particularly among soccer fans; moreover, he might truly feel ashamed of his performance, but the matter is not a moral one. It is certainly social; the publicness of his failure as well as the consequences of his behavior for his teammates are, agreed, contributors to his shame, but it does not seem right to describe his failure as a moral one. This emphasizes the need for a definition of morality to contextualize this framework; how are moral emotions different from social emotions?

Venturing onto the icy precipice of defining the moral, it is reasonable, if not complete, to suggest that morality refers to a set of behavioral imperatives that protect a society from the tendency of individuals to wantonly advance their own aims at the expense of the well-being of those around them. Moral imperatives serve to curtail these individual behaviors, as well as encouraging prosocial behaviors, and one of the mechanisms by which moral behavior is fostered may well be through moral emotions.

What about Inhibition and Basic Emotions?

The outline of a definition of morality just presented makes it clear that any model of the relationship between morality and emotion requires a treatment of inhibitory processes. Often, moral behavior will require that an individual inhibit his or her own gratification to improve the group situation, or at least prevent the detriment of the group situation. In fact, this definition of moral behavior is part of a time-honored tradition. The better you are at resisting selfish urges when the fulfillment of those urges will weaken or threaten the group, the more moral your behavior will be considered.

By positing a role for self-regulatory processes in morality-relevant emotional behavior, another gap in the framework of Moll and colleagues becomes apparent. Emotions can be viewed as a progress report on one's behavior; positively valenced emotions signal to the organism that it can carry on with whatever it has been doing, and they achieve this through motivational states. Through our reward system we are motivated to engage in behaviors that feel good. Negatively valenced emotions, on the other hand, signal to the organism that it should alter its behavior, or avoid the behavior or situation that engendered the negative emotional state. Thus, basic emotions are inherently regulatory with respect to the organism's behavior. It has been reported that others' displays of social emotions affect our judgments of them; Semin and Manstead (1982) report that people feel more kindly toward people who exhibit embarrassment when they commit social transgressions, as opposed to those who show no embarrassment. This phenomenon is not restricted to social emotions; others' display of basic emotions can allow us to make inferences about the morality of their character. Imagine a politician who is informed that a decision she has made has resulted in the death of two hundred foreign citizens. If she displays sadness and dismay, which suggests a desire to avoid a repeat situation, we would consider her more moral than if she displayed happiness or indifference. Thus, basic emotions and regulatory or inhibitory processes should be included in the framework of moral emotions.

Problematic Components

The discussion of aggressiveness as a component of moral behavior is unanticipated and intriguing. Moll and colleagues argue that without aggression one would be unlikely to experience moral disgust, contempt, and indignation, all of which contribute to moral behavior. Indeed, a lack of courage to express aggression toward authority figures or a social group may contribute to the well-known phenomenon of passive cooperation with behavior one knows to be immoral, perhaps most famously examined in Milgram's experiments (Milgram, 1963). On the other side of the coin, however, too much aggressiveness can be problematic for moral behavior and indeed for the appropriate expression of moral emotion. This again underscores the importance of self-regulation in moral conduct; too much aggression toward, say, a small child for behaving immorally, would itself be considered immoral in many societies.

Moll et al. propose attachment as a component of morality, which is problematic on further examination. While it is plausible that without any attachment relationships it would be difficult if not impossible to develop moral reasoning, an appreciation of the needs of others is required for one's own behavioral guidance. This is perhaps what is lacking in psychopaths, whose hallmark characteristic is arguably a lack of morality that is due to deficient emotional responding and poor attachment relationships (e.g., Frodi, Dernevik, Sepa, Philipson, & Bragesjo, 2001). Attachment relationships are known to aid in the development of a theory of mind (Peterson & Siegal, 2002), which may be the crucial thought process that enables the internalizing of morally appropriate behavior, rather than having it be driven by a fear of punishment. The authors propose that attachment is a component of gratitude, which is argued to induce a tendency to repay favors. It can, however, be demonstrated that gratitude can exist in the absence of attachment.

Imagine a moral code in which one is bound to protect the life of somebody who saves your life, and then imagine that your archnemesis saves your life. You might be grateful for having your life saved, even though you despise your savior. Alternatively, you might be resentful of having your life saved by your archnemesis or, humanly, you might feel a blend of the two emotions. In any event, the moral thing to do is to protect that person's life, regardless of your lack of attachment to that person. On the other side of the coin, there are situations in which attachment relationships promote immoral behavior. Imagine that your lover has committed murder; you are interrogated by the police and you lie to protect this person to whom you are attached. More subtle examples of this phenomenon may be involved in nepotism, cronyism, and even racism and sexism, when an individual promotes the group to which he or she is attached, rather than acting in an impartial manner.

The Role of Propositional Content

The small but growing body of cognitive neuroscientific investigation into moral reasoning has so far focused on what is similar about moral reasoning across individuals. This is a logical perspective to adopt when considering the brain; it is reasonable to assume that no major structural differences exist across cultures. Nonetheless, when morality is considered in its totality, the most striking feature of the human moral sphere is how two moral systems can have mutually inconsistent moral imperatives at the level of their propositional content (one code says people should not kill other people, another code says it's forgivable to kill in self-defense). It is perhaps the centrality of propositional content to moral systems that has kept morality within the domain of philosophical (as opposed to scientific) investigation until relatively recently. Any attempt at designing a framework within which to study moral behavior will have to describe how propositional content or semantic knowledge is able to generate different emotional reactions, depending on how that information is organized. If having different moral axioms, which are essentially different propositional contents, can lead to radically different emotions and therefore behaviors, this must be accounted for. Moll and colleagues do posit a role for propositional content in their chapter, but they are sparse on the details of and the empirical support for how this might function. More detail and evidence about how the structured event complex organizes emotional behavior would be particularly illuminating.

Conclusion

The chapter by Moll and colleagues makes the important argument that emotion is central to moral behavior and is not an extraneous process that interferes with moral reasoning. On the contrary, emotion sculpts both our behavior and that of others in order to give it a moral hue. The components that they posit are plausible and well situated in neurobiological theory and thus provide a good beginning for a foundation from which to build a cognitive neuroscience model of moral behavior. There remain some conceptual gaps in their framework that require attention before moving forward, but the general approach of this chapter is encouraging and useful. Nonetheless, until the theoretical specificity is improved, we should be extremely cautious about doing more experimental work in this area.

Response to Casebeer and Hynes

Jorge Moll, Mirella L. M. F. Paiva, Roland Zahn, and Jordan Grafman

First, we would like to express our gratitude to William Casebeer, Catherine Hynes, and Walter Sinnott-Armstrong and his colleagues for their constructive comments about our chapter.

In his commentary, Casebeer suggested that classical tools of inquiry provided by psychological and philosophical theories (including deontology, utilitarianism, and virtue theory) should be used, at least initially, to delimit the field of study of morality. In addition, he pointed out that our definition of morality as the laws of proper behavior and customs in daily life does not describe morality properly, since the terms "laws and customs" included in that definition need to be made explicit. We agree that our theoretical basis of morality was not spelled out explicitly enough in the chapter. We also did not discuss the similarities, differences, and advantages of our framework with respect to other models. Instead of adopting a traditional view of morality, we chose to use a broader definition that is explicitly articulated in our recent review paper (Moll, Zahn, de Oliveira-Souza, Krueger, & Grafman, 2005). Essentially, we defined morality based on empirically acquired cognitive neuroscience knowledge. Whether virtue theory, for example, better accommodates neuroscientific and psychological evidence of human moral behavior should only be a matter of experimental investigation.

From a cognitive neuroscience perspective, morality emerges from the integration of cognitive-affective neural mechanisms and social knowledge (learned during human development), influenced by the variability of genetic components and other neurobiological factors (e.g., changes in brain development induced by environmental influences). We contend that norms and customs always need to be understood within the cultural context of a social group. Although moral phenomena are intimately related to sociocultural context, morality is not merely the product of learning. While some philosophical theories are intended to identify the universal principles that should guide moral behavior, our perspective does not assume the existence of absolute moral values (although it does not exclude this possibility).

Hynes suggested that the definition proposed for moral emotions does not show how or if moral emotions are different from social emotions. In fact, our broad definition of morality does not make the distinction between moral and social emotions. So far, no distinguishing neural mechanisms have been demonstrated that would support a separation between moral and social emotions. Whether this distinction will still be theoretically useful in certain fields (e.g., social psychology or moral philosophy) is another issue. Regarding the distinction of moral and basic emotions, it is possible that virtually all emotions could become moral, depending on the context. For example, while fear has traditionally been recognized as a basic emotion, it assumes moral connotations when a speaker faces an audience for a controversial talk and fears failure, or when a wife fears losing a husband to illness before resolving a long-standing disagreement about the value of religion. Thus, fear or any other emotion can be associated with moral values and beliefs.

Casebeer also questioned the adoption of a representational-only view of moral emotions, suggesting that we should integrate processes into this scheme. According to our view, emotions are not dissociable from cognition, and neither compete with nor are controlled by rational cognitive processes. Instead, they are integrated into cognitive-affective neural assemblies, or representations. A process can be defined as the dynamic engagement of neural representations in a given behavioral context. We would agree with this view of a process, as long as one recognizes that behind the engagement of any process there lies a representation, encoded in neuronal assemblies. In addition, since even perception of the most elementary visual inputs is highly dependent on stored visual representations (Adolphs, 2006), it is reasonable to assume that interpreting highly complex social situations as morally relevant depends on the existence of complex cognitive-affective associations stored in distributed, large-scale neuronal assemblies (Moll, Zahn, de Oliveira-Souza, Krueger, & Grafman, 2005b).

With respect to the basic components of moral emotions as discussed in our chapter, we argue that attachment is a component required for certain moral emotions, such as compassion or gratitude. However, Hynes points out possible problems with this view and gives an example in which an individual could demonstrate gratitude to an enemy who saved his or her life, but suggests that in this case, attachment would not be present. This is an interesting question that in our view needs to be experimentally addressed in the future. Would attachment really be absent (e.g., hostage taking occasionally results in a "spared" hostage forming an attachment to a specific captor)? Perhaps if attachment was not evoked, real gratitude would not be manifest (although one could judge that a person "should" feel gratitude, and even manifest external signs of gratitude based on other motives—reputation, for example). Recent research in animal models and in humans supports the existence of specific neural systems for attachment and social bonding (Zak, Kurzban, & Matzner, 2005; Young & Wang, 2004) and these same systems are engaged in moral decision making, such as when making decisions to donate to altruistic causes (Moll, Krueger, Zahn, Pardini, de Oliveira-Souza, & Grafman, 2006).

We would like to thank again Catherine Hynes and Bill Casebeer for encouraging us to clarify what distinguishes our framework for studying moral emotions and cognition from a traditional philosophical one. The questions they raised and the ensuing debate will certainly help sharpen the neuroscientific perspective of moral emotions.

2   The Secret Joke of Kant's Soul

Joshua D. Greene

Two things fill the mind with ever new and increasing wonder and awe, the oftener and more steadily we reflect on them: the starry heavens above me and the moral law within me.

—Immanuel Kant

That such an unnatural use (and so misuse) of one's sexual attributes is a violation of one's duty to himself and is certainly in the highest degree opposed to morality strikes everyone upon his thinking of it. . . . However, it is not so easy to produce a rational demonstration of the inadmissibility of that unnatural use, and even the mere unpurposive use, of one's sexual attributes as being a violation of one's duty to himself (and indeed in the highest degree where the unnatural use is concerned). The ground of proof surely lies in the fact that a man gives up his personality (throws it away) when he uses himself merely as a means for the gratification of an animal drive.

—Immanuel Kant, "Concerning Wanton Self-Abuse"

Kant's Joke—Kant wanted to prove, in a way that would dumbfound the common man, that the common man was right: that was the secret joke of this soul. He wrote against the scholars in support of popular prejudice, but for scholars and not for the people.

—Friedrich Nietzsche

There is a substantial and growing body of evidence suggesting that much of what we do, we do unconsciously, and for reasons that are inaccessible to us (Wilson, 2002). In one experiment, for example, people were asked to choose one of several pairs of pantyhose displayed in a row. When asked to explain their preferences, people gave sensible enough answers, referring to the relevant features of the items chosen—superior knit, sheerness, elasticity, etc. However, their choices had nothing to do with such features because the items on display were in fact identical. People simply had a preference for items on the right-hand side of the display (Nisbett & Wilson, 1977). What this experiment illustrates—and there are many, many such illustrations—is that people make choices for reasons unknown to them, and they make up reasonable-sounding justifications for their choices, all the while remaining unaware of their actual motives and subsequent rationalizations.

Jonathan Haidt applies these psychological lessons to the study of moral judgment in his influential paper, "The Emotional Dog and Its Rational Tail: A Social Intuitionist Approach to Moral Judgment" (Haidt, 2001). He argues that for the most part moral reasoning is a post hoc affair: We decide what's right or wrong on the basis of emotionally driven intuitions, and then, if necessary, we make up reasons to explain and justify our judgments. Haidt concedes that some people, some of the time, may actually reason their way to moral conclusions, but he insists that this is not the norm. More important for the purposes of this essay, Haidt does not distinguish among the various approaches to ethics familiar to moral philosophers: consequentialism, deontology, virtue ethics, etc. Rather, his radical thesis is intended, if only implicitly, to apply equally to the adherents of all moral philosophies, though not necessarily well to moral philosophers as a group (Kuhn, 1991).

Jonathan Baron (1994), in contrast, draws a psychological distinction between consequentialist and nonconsequentialist judgments, arguing that the latter are especially likely to be made on the basis of heuristics, simple rules of thumb for decision making. Baron, however, does not regard emotion as essential to these heuristic judgments.

In this chapter, I draw on Haidt's and Baron's respective insights in the service of a bit of philosophical psychoanalysis. I will argue that deontological judgments tend to be driven by emotional responses and that deontological philosophy, rather than being grounded in moral *reasoning*, is to a large extent an exercise in moral *rationalization*. This is in contrast to consequentialism, which, I will argue, arises from rather different psychological processes, ones that are more "cognitive," and more likely to involve genuine moral reasoning. These claims are strictly empirical, and I will defend them on the basis of the available evidence. Needless to say, my argument will be speculative and will not be conclusive. Beyond this, I will argue that if these empirical claims are true, they may have normative implications, casting doubt on deontology as a school of normative moral thought.

Preliminaries

Defining Deontology and Consequentialism

Deontology is defined by its emphasis on moral rules, most often articulated in terms of *rights* and *duties*. Consequentialism, in contrast, is the view that the moral value of an action is in one way or another a function of its consequences alone. Consequentialists maintain that moral decision makers should always aim to produce the best overall consequences for all concerned, if not directly then indirectly. Both consequentialists and deontologists think that consequences are important, but consequentialists believe that consequences are the *only* things that ultimately matter, while deontologists believe that morality both requires and allows us to do things that do not produce the best possible consequences. For example, a deontologist might say that killing one person in order to save several others is wrong, even if doing so would maximize good consequences (S. Kagan, 1997).

This is a standard explanation of what deontology and consequentialism are and how they differ. In light of this explanation, it might seem that my thesis is false *by definition*. Deontology is rule-based morality, usually focused on rights and duties. A deontological judgment, then, is a judgment made out of respect for certain types of moral rules. From this it follows that a moral judgment that is made on the basis of an emotional response simply cannot be a deontological judgment, although it may appear to be one from the outside. Kant himself was adamant about this, at least with respect to his own brand of deontology. He notoriously claimed that an action performed merely out of sympathy and not out of an appreciation of one's duty lacks moral worth (Kant, 1785/1959, chap. 1; Korsgaard, 1996a, chap. 2).

The assumption behind this objection—and as far as I know it has never been questioned previously—is that consequentialism and deontology are, first and foremost, moral philosophies. It is assumed that philosophers know exactly what deontology and consequentialism are because these terms and concepts were defined by philosophers. Despite this, I believe it is possible that philosophers do not necessarily know what consequentialism and deontology really are.

How could this be? The answer, I propose, is that the terms "deontology" and "consequentialism" refer to *psychological natural kinds*. I believe that consequentialist and deontological views of philosophy are not so much philosophical inventions as they are philosophical manifestations of two dissociable psychological patterns, two different ways of moral thinking, that have been part of the human repertoire for thousands of years. According to this view, the moral philosophies of Kant, Mill, and others are just the explicit tips of large, mostly implicit, psychological icebergs. If that is correct, then philosophers may not really know what they're dealing with when they trade in consequentialist and deontological moral theories, and we may have to do some science to find out.

An analogy, drawing on a familiar philosophical theme: Suppose that in a certain tropical land the inhabitants refer to water by this symbol: ♦. And in their *Holy Dictionary* it clearly states that ♦ is a clear and drinkable liquid. (That is, the dictionary defines ♦ in terms of its "primary intension" (Chalmers, 1996).) One day an enterprising youngster journeys to the top of a nearby mountain and is the first of her people to encounter ice. Through a bit of experimentation, she discovers that ice is a form of water and excitedly tells the tribal Elders of her discovery. The next day she drags one of the Elders to the mountaintop, hands him some ice, and says, "Behold! ♦!" At which point the exasperated Elder explains that ♦ is a liquid, that the hard stuff in his hand is clearly not a liquid, and that he doesn't appreciate having his time wasted.

In a narrow sense the Elder is correct. The *Holy Dictionary* is the authority on what the local symbols mean, and it states clearly that ♦ refers to a clear, drinkable, liquid. But the Elder is missing the big picture. What he is forgetting, or perhaps never understood, is that many things in the world have underlying structures—"essences," if you prefer—that are responsible for making things appear and behave as they do, for giving them their functional properties. And because things have underlying structures, it is possible to refer to something, even make up a definition for it, without really understanding what it is (Kripke, 1980; Putnam, 1975). Of course, a linguistic community can insist that their definition is correct. No one's to stop them from using their symbols as they please. However, in doing this, they run the risk of missing the big picture, of denying themselves a deeper understanding of what's going on around them, or even within them.

Because I am interested in exploring the possibility that deontology and consequentialism are psychological natural kinds, I will put aside their conventional philosophical definitions and focus instead on their relevant functional roles. As noted earlier, consequentialists and deontologists have some characteristic practical disagreements. For example, consequentialists typically say that killing one person in order to save several others may be the right thing to do, depending on the situation. Deontologists, in contrast, typically say that it's wrong to kill one person for the benefit of others, that the "ends don't justify the means." Because consequentialists and deontologists have these sorts of practical disagreements, we can use these disagreements to define consequentialist and deontological judgments functionally. For the purposes of this discussion, we'll say that consequentialist judgments are judgments in favor of characteristically consequentialist conclusions (e.g., "Better to save more lives") and that deontological judgments are judgments in favor of characteristically deontological conclusions (e.g., "It's wrong despite the benefits"). My use of "characteristically" is obviously loose here, but I trust that those familiar with contemporary ethical debates will know what I mean. Note that the kind of judgment made is largely independent of who is making it. A card-carrying deontologist can make a "characteristically consequentialist" judgment, as when Judith Jarvis Thomson says that it's okay to turn a runaway trolley that threatens to kill five people onto a side track so that it will kill only one person instead (Thomson, 1986). This is a "characteristically consequentialist" judgment because it is easily justified in terms of the most basic consequentialist principles, while deontologists need to do a lot of fancy philosophizing in order to defend this position. Likewise, consider the judgment that it's wrong to save five people who need organ transplants by removing the organs from an unwilling donor (Thomson, 1986). This judgment is "characteristically deontological," not because many card-carrying consequentialists don't agree, but because they have to do a lot of extra explaining to justify their agreement.

By defining "consequentialism" and "deontology" in terms of their characteristic judgments, we give our empirical hypothesis a chance. If it turns out that characteristically deontological judgments are driven by emotion (an empirical possibility), then that raises the possibility that deontological *philosophy* is also driven by emotion (a further empirical possibility). In other words, what we find when we explore the psychological causes of characteristically deontological judgments might suggest that what deontological moral philosophy really is, what it is *essentially*, is an attempt to produce rational justifications for emotionally driven moral judgments, and not an attempt to reach moral conclusions on the basis of moral reasoning.

The point for now, however, is simply to flag the terminological issue. When I refer to something as a "deontological judgment," I am saying that it is a characteristically deontological judgment and am not insisting that the judgment in question necessarily meets the criteria that philosophers would impose for counting that judgment as deontological. In the end, however, I will argue that such judgments are best understood as genuinely deontological because they are produced by an underlying psychology that is the hidden essence of deontological philosophy.

Defining "Cognition" and "Emotion"

In what follows I will argue that deontological judgment tends to be driven by emotion, while consequentialist judgment tends to be driven by "cognitive" processes. What do we mean by "emotion" and "cognition," and how do these things differ?

Sometimes "cognition" refers to information processing in general, as in "cognitive science," but often "cognition" is used in a narrower sense that contrasts with "emotion," despite the fact that emotions involve information processing. I know of no good off-the-shelf definition of "cognition" in this more restrictive sense, despite its widespread use. Elsewhere, my collaborators and I offered a tentative definition of our own (Greene, Nystrom, Engell, Darley, & Cohen, 2004), one that is based on the differences between the information-processing requirements of stereotyped versus flexible behavior.

The rough idea is that "cognitive" representations are inherently neutral representations, ones that do not automatically trigger particular behavioral responses or dispositions, while "emotional" representations do have such automatic effects, and are therefore behaviorally valenced. (To make things clear, I will use quotation marks to indicate the more restrictive sense of "cognitive" defined here, and I will drop the quotation marks when using this term to refer to information processing in general.) Highly flexible behavior requires "cognitive" representations that can be easily mixed around and recombined as situational demands vary, and without pulling the agent in sixteen different behavioral directions at once. For example, sometimes you need to avoid cars, and other times you need to approach them. It is useful, then, if you can represent CAR in a behaviorally neutral or "cognitive" way, one that doesn't automatically presuppose a particular behavioral response. Stereotyped behavior, in contrast, doesn't require this sort of flexibility and therefore doesn't require "cognitive" representations, at least not to the same extent.

While the whole brain is devoted to cognition, "cognitive" processes are especially important for reasoning, planning, manipulating information in working memory, controlling impulses, and "higher executive functions" more generally. Moreover, these functions tend to be associated with certain parts of the brain, primarily the dorsolateral surfaces of the prefrontal cortex and parietal lobes (Koechlin, Ody, & Kouneiher, 2003; Miller & Cohen, 2001; Ramnani & Owen, 2004). Emotion, in contrast, tends to be associated with other parts of the brain, such as the amygdala and the medial surfaces of the frontal and parietal lobes (Adolphs, 2002; Maddock, 1999; Phan, Wager, Taylor, & Liberzon, 2002). And while the term "emotion" can refer to stable states such as moods, here we will primarily be concerned with emotions subserved by processes that in addition to being valenced, are quick and automatic, though not necessarily conscious.

Here we are concerned with two different kinds of moral judgment (deontological and consequentialist) and two different kinds of psychological process ("cognitive" and emotional). Crossing these, we get four basic empirical possibilities. First, it could be that both kinds of moral judgment are generally "cognitive," as Kohlberg's theories suggest (Kohlberg, 1971).[1] At the other extreme, it could be that both kinds of moral judgment are primarily emotional, as Haidt's view suggests (Haidt, 2001). Then there is the historical stereotype, according to which consequentialism is more emotional (emerging from the "sentimentalist" tradition of David Hume [1740/1978] and Adam Smith [1759/1976]) while deontology is more "cognitive" (encompassing the Kantian "rationalist" tradition [Kant, 1959]). Finally, there is the view for which I will argue, that deontology is more emotionally driven while consequentialism is more "cognitive." I hasten to add, however, that I don't believe that either approach is strictly emotional or "cognitive" (or even that there is a sharp distinction between "cognition" and emotion). More specifically, I am sympathetic to Hume's claim that all moral judgment (including consequentialist judgment) must have some emotional component (Hume, 1978). But I suspect that the kind of emotion that is essential to consequentialism is fundamentally different from the kind that is essential to deontology, the former functioning more like a currency and the latter functioning more like an alarm. We will return to this issue later.

Scientific Evidence

Evidence from Neuroimaging
In recent decades, philosophers have devised a range of hypothetical moral dilemmas that capture the tension between the consequentialist and deontological viewpoints. A well-known handful of these dilemmas gives rise to what is known as the "trolley problem" (Foot, 1967; Thomson, 1986), which begins with the *trolley* dilemma.

A runaway trolley is headed for five people who will be killed if it proceeds on its present course. The only way to save these people is to hit a switch that will turn the trolley onto a side track, where it will run over and kill one person instead of five. Is it okay to turn the trolley in order to save five people at the expense of one? The consensus among philosophers (Fischer & Ravizza, 1992), as well as people who have been tested experimentally (Petrinovich & O'Neill, 1996; Petrinovich, O'Neill, & Jorgensen, 1993), is that it is morally acceptable to save five lives at the expense of one in this case.

Next consider the *footbridge* dilemma (Thomson, 1986): As before, a runaway trolley threatens to kill five people, but this time you are standing next to a large stranger on a footbridge spanning the tracks, in between the oncoming trolley and the five people. The only way to save the five people is to push this stranger off the bridge and onto the tracks below. He will die as a result, but his body will stop the trolley from reaching the others. Is it okay to save the five people by pushing this stranger to his death? Here the consensus is that it is not okay to save five lives at the expense of one (Fischer & Ravizza, 1992; Greene et al., 2004; Greene, Sommerville, Nystrom, Darley, & Cohen, 2001; Petrinovich & O'Neill, 1996; Petrinovich et al., 1993).

People exhibit a characteristically consequentialist response to the *trolley* case and a characteristically deontological response to the *footbridge* case. Why? Philosophers have generally offered a variety of *normative* explanations. That is, they have assumed that our responses to these cases are correct, or at least reasonable, and have sought principles that *justify* treating these two cases differently (Fischer & Ravizza, 1992). For example, one might suppose, following Kant (1785/1959) and Aquinas (1265–1272/1988), that it is wrong to harm someone as a means to helping someone else. In the *footbridge* case, the proposed action involves literally using the person on the footbridge as a trolley stopper, whereas in the *trolley* case the victim is to be harmed merely as a side effect. (Were the single person on the alternative track to magically disappear, we would be very pleased.) In response to this proposal, Thomson devised the *loop* case (Thomson, 1986). Here the situation is similar to that of the *trolley* dilemma, but this time the single person is on a piece of track that branches off of the main track and then rejoins it at a point before the five people. In this case, if the person were not on the side track, the trolley would return to the main track and run over the five people. The consensus here is that it is morally acceptable to turn the trolley in this case, despite the fact that here, as in the *footbridge* case, a person will be used as a means.

There have been many such normative attempts to solve the trolley problem, but none of them has been terribly successful (Fischer & Ravizza,

1992). My collaborators and I have proposed a partial and purely descriptive solution to this problem and have collected some scientific evidence in favor of it. We hypothesized that the thought of pushing someone to his death in an "up close and personal" manner (as in the *footbridge* dilemma) is more emotionally salient than the thought of bringing about similar consequences in a more impersonal way (e.g., by hitting a switch, as in the *trolley* dilemma). We proposed that this difference in emotional response explains why people respond so differently to these two cases. That is, people tend toward consequentialism in the case in which the emotional response is low and tend toward deontology in the case in which the emotional response is high.

The rationale for distinguishing between *personal* and *impersonal* forms of harm is largely evolutionary. "Up close and personal" violence has been around for a very long time, reaching far back into our primate lineage (Wrangham & Peterson, 1996). Given that personal violence is evolutionarily ancient, predating our recently evolved human capacities for complex abstract reasoning, it should come as no surprise if we have innate responses to personal violence that are powerful but rather primitive. That is, we might expect humans to have negative emotional responses to certain basic forms of interpersonal violence, where these responses evolved as a means of regulating the behavior of creatures who are capable of intentionally harming one another, but whose survival depends on cooperation and individual restraint (Sober & Wilson, 1998; Trivers, 1971). In contrast, when a harm is *impersonal*, it should fail to trigger this alarmlike emotional response, allowing people to respond in a more "cognitive" way, perhaps employing a cost-benefit analysis. As Josef Stalin once said, "A single death is a tragedy; a million deaths is a statistic." His remarks suggest that when harmful actions are sufficiently impersonal, they fail to push our emotional buttons, despite their seriousness, and as a result we think about them in a more detached, actuarial fashion.

This hypothesis makes some strong predictions regarding what we should see going on in people's brains while they are responding to dilemmas involving personal versus impersonal harm (henceforth called "personal" and "impersonal" moral dilemmas). The contemplation of personal moral dilemmas like the *footbridge* case should produce increased neural activity in brain regions associated with emotional response and social cognition, while the contemplation of impersonal moral dilemmas like the *trolley* case should produce relatively greater activity in brain regions associated with "higher cognition."[2] This is exactly what was observed (Greene et al., 2004; Greene et al., 2001). Contemplation of personal moral dilemmas produced

relatively greater activity in three emotion-related areas: the posterior cingulate cortex, the medial prefrontal cortex, and the amygdala. This effect
was also observed in the superior temporal sulcus, a region associated with
various kinds of social cognition in humans and other primates (Allison,
Puce, & McCarthy, 2000; Saxe, Carey, & Kanwisher, 2004a). At the same
time, contemplation of impersonal moral dilemmas produced relatively
greater neural activity in two classically "cognitive" brain areas, the dorsolateral prefrontal cortex and inferior parietal lobe.

This hypothesis also makes a prediction regarding people's reaction
times. According to the view I have sketched, people tend to have emotional responses to personal moral violations, responses that incline them
to judge against performing those actions. That means that someone who
judges a personal moral violation to be *appropriate* (e.g., someone who says
it's okay to push the man off the bridge in the *footbridge* case) will most
likely have to override an emotional response in order to do it. This overriding process will take time, and thus we would expect that "yes" answers
will take longer than "no" answers in response to personal moral dilemmas
like the *footbridge* case. At the same time, we have no reason to predict a
difference in reaction time between "yes" and "no" answers in response to
impersonal moral dilemmas like the *trolley* case because there is, according
to this model, no emotional response (or much less of one) to override in
such cases. Here, too, the prediction has held. Trials in which the subject
judged in favor of personal moral violations took significantly longer than
trials in which the subject judged against them, but there was no comparable reaction time effect observed in response to impersonal moral violations (Greene et al., 2004; Greene et al., 2001).

Further results support this model as well. Next we subdivided the personal moral dilemmas into two categories on the basis of difficulty (i.e.,
based on reaction time). Consider the following moral dilemma (the *crying
baby* dilemma): It is wartime, and you and some of your fellow villagers
are hiding from enemy soldiers in a basement. Your baby starts to cry, and
you cover your baby's mouth to block the sound. If you remove your hand,
your baby will cry loudly, the soldiers will hear, and they will find you and
the others and kill everyone they find, including you and your baby. If
you do not remove your hand, your baby will smother to death. Is it okay
to smother your baby to death in order to save yourself and the other
villagers?

This is a very difficult question. Different people give different answers,
and nearly everyone takes a relatively long time. This is in contrast to other
personal moral dilemmas, such as the *infanticide* dilemma, in which a

teenage girl must decide whether to kill her unwanted newborn. In response to this case, people (at least the ones we tested) quickly and unanimously say that this action is wrong.

What's going on in these two cases? My colleagues and I hypothesized as follows. In both cases there is a prepotent, negative emotional response to the personal violation in question, killing one's own baby. In the *crying baby* case, however, a cost-benefit analysis strongly favors smothering the baby. After all, the baby is going to die no matter what, and so you have nothing to lose (in consequentialist terms) and much to gain by smothering it, awful as it is. In some people the emotional response dominates, and those people say "no." In other people, this "cognitive," cost-benefit analysis wins out, and these people say "yes."

What does this model predict that we will see going on in people's brains when we compare cases like *crying baby* and *infanticide*? First, this model supposes that cases like *crying baby* involve an increased level of "response conflict," that is, conflict between competing representations for behavioral response. Thus, we should expect that difficult moral dilemmas like *crying baby* will produce increased activity in a brain region that is associated with response conflict, the anterior cingulate cortex (Botvinick, Braver, Barch, Carter, & Cohen, 2001). Second, according to our model, the crucial difference between cases like *crying baby* and those like *infanticide* is that the former evoke strong "cognitive" responses that can effectively compete with a prepotent, emotional response. Thus, we should expect to see increased activity in classically "cognitive" brain areas when we compare cases like *crying baby* with cases like *infanticide*, despite the fact that difficult dilemmas like *crying baby* are personal moral dilemmas, which were previously associated with emotional response (Greene et al., 2001).

These two predictions have held (Greene et al., 2004). Comparing high-reaction-time personal moral dilemmas like *crying baby* with low-reaction-time personal moral dilemmas like *infanticide* revealed increased activity in the anterior cingulate cortex (conflict) as well as the anterior dorsolateral prefrontal cortex and the inferior parietal lobes, both classically "cognitive" brain regions.

Cases like *crying baby* are especially interesting because they allow us to directly compare the neural activity associated with characteristically consequentialist and deontological responses. According to our model, when people say "yes" to such cases (the consequentialist answer), it is because the "cognitive" cost-benefit analysis has successfully dominated the prepotent emotional response that drives people to say "no" (the deontological answer). If that is correct, then we should expect to see increased activity in the previously identified "cognitive" brain regions (the dorso-lateral prefrontal cortex and inferior parietal cortex) for the trials in which people say "yes" in response to cases like *crying baby*. This is exactly what we found. In other words, people exhibit more "cognitive" activity when they give the consequentialist answer.[3]

To summarize, people's moral judgments appear to be products of at least two different kinds of psychological processes. First, both brain imaging and reaction-time data suggest that there are prepotent negative emotional responses that drive people to disapprove of the personally harmful actions proposed in cases like the *footbridge* and *crying baby* dilemmas. These responses are characteristic of deontology, but not of consequentialism. Second, further brain imaging results suggest that "cognitive" psychological processes can compete with the aforementioned emotional processes, driving people to approve of personally harmful moral violations, primarily when there is a strong consequentialist rationale for doing so, as in the *crying baby* case. The parts of the brain that exhibit increased activity when people make characteristically consequentialist judgments are those that are most closely associated with higher cognitive functions such as executive control (Koechlin et al., 2003; Miller and Cohen, 2001), complex planning (Koechlin, Basso, Pietrini, Panzer, & Grafman, 1999), deductive and inductive reasoning (Goel & Dolan, 2004), taking the long view in economic decision making (McClure, Laibson, Loewenstein, & Cohen, 2004), and so on. Moreover, these brain regions are among those most dramatically expanded in humans compared with other primates (Allman, Hakeem, & Watson, 2002).

Emotion and the Sense of Moral Obligation

In his classic article, "Famine, Affluence, and Morality," Peter Singer (1972) argues that we in the affluent world have an obligation to do much more than we do to improve the lives of needy people. He argues that if we can prevent something very bad from happening without incurring a comparable moral cost, then we ought to do it. For example, if one notices a small child drowning in a shallow pond, one is morally obliged to wade in and save that child, even if it means muddying one's clothes. As Singer points out, this seemingly innocuous principle has radical implications, implying that all of us who spend money on unnecessary luxuries should give up those luxuries in order to spend the money on saving and/or improving the lives of impoverished peoples. Why, Singer asks, do we have a strict obligation to save a nearby drowning child but no comparable obligation to save faraway sick and starving children through charitable donations to organizations like Oxfam?

Many normative explanations come to mind, but none is terribly compelling. Are we allowed to ignore the plight of faraway children because they are citizens of foreign nations? If so, then would it be acceptable to let the child drown, provided that the child was encountered while traveling abroad? Or in international waters? And what about the domestic poor? This argument does not relieve us of our obligations to them. Is it because of diffused responsibility—because many are in a position to help a starving child abroad, but only you are in a position to help this hypothetical drowning child? What if there were many people standing around the pond doing nothing? Would that make it okay for you to do nothing as well? Is it because international aid is ultimately ineffective, only serving to enrich corrupt politicians or create more poor people? In that case, our obligation would simply shift to more sophisticated relief efforts incorporating political reform, economic development, family planning education, and so on. Are all relief efforts doomed to ineffectiveness? That is a bold empirical claim that no one can honestly make with great confidence.

Here we find ourselves in a position similar to the one we faced with the trolley problem. We have a strong intuition that two moral dilemmas are importantly different, and yet we have a hard time explaining what that important difference is (S. Kagan, 1989; Unger, 1996). It turns out that the same psychological theory that makes sense of the trolley problem can make sense of Singer's problem. Note that the interaction in the case of the drowning child is "up close and personal," the sort of situation that might have been encountered by our human and primate ancestors. Likewise, note that the donation case is not "up close and personal," and is not the sort of situation that our ancestors could have encountered. At no point were our ancestors able to save the lives of anonymous strangers through modest material sacrifices. In light of this, the psychological theory presented here suggests that we are likely to find the obligation to save the drowning child more pressing simply because that "up close and personal" case pushes our emotional buttons in a way that the more impersonal donation case does not (Greene, 2003). As it happens, these two cases were among those tested in the brain imaging study described earlier, with a variation on the drowning child case included in the *personal* condition and the donation case included in the *impersonal* condition (Greene et al., 2004; Greene et al., 2001).

Few people accept Singer's consequentialist conclusion. Rather, people tend to believe, in a characteristically deontological way, that they are within their moral rights in spending their money on luxuries for themselves, despite the fact that their money could be used to dramatically improve the lives of other people. This is exactly what one would expect if (1) the deontological sense of obligation is driven primarily by emotion, and (2) when it comes to obligations to aid, emotions are only sufficiently engaged when those to whom we might owe something are encountered (or conceived of) in a personal way.

Emotion and the Pull of Identifiable Victims

One aspect of someone's being "up close and personal" is that such a person is always, in some sense, an identifiable, determinate individual and not a mere statistical someone (Greene and Haidt, 2002; Greene et al., 2001). The drowning child, for example, is presented as a particular person, while the children you might help through donations to Oxfam are anonymous and, as far as you know, indeterminate.[4] Many researchers have observed a tendency to respond with greater urgency to identifiable victims, compared with indeterminate, "statistical" victims (Schelling, 1968). This is known as the "identifiable victim effect."

You may recall, for example, the case of Jessica McClure, a.k.a. "Baby Jessica," who in 1987 was trapped in a well in Texas. More than $700,000 was sent to her family to support the rescue effort (Small & Loewenstein, 2003; Variety, 1989). As Small and Loewenstein point out, that amount of money, if it had been spent on preventive healthcare, could have been used to save the lives of many children. This observation raises a normative question that is essentially the same as Singer's. Do we have a greater obligation to help people like Baby Jessica than we do to help large numbers of others who could be saved for less? If all else is equal, a consequentialist would say "no," while most people apparently would say "yes." Furthermore, most people, if pressed to explain their position, would probably do so in deontological terms. That is, they would probably say that we have a *duty* to aid someone like Baby Jessica, even if doing so involves great effort and expense, while we have no comparable duty to the countless others who might be helped using the same resources.

The same "up close and personal" theory of emotional engagement can explain this pattern of judgment. Others have proposed what amounts to the same hypothesis, and others still have gathered independent evidence to support it. In Thomas Schelling's seminal article on this topic, he observes that the death of a particular person invokes "anxiety and sentiment, guilt and awe, responsibility and religion, [but] . . . most of this awesomeness disappears when we deal with statistical death" (Schelling, 1968; Small & Loewenstein, 2003). Inspired by Schelling's observation, Small and Loewenstein conducted two experiments aimed at testing the hypothesis that "identifiable victims stimulate a more powerful emotional response than do statistical victims."

Their crucial move was to design their experiments in such a way that their results could count against all normative explanations of the identifiable victim effect, i.e., explanations that credit decision makers with normatively respectable reasons for favoring identifiable victims. This is difficult because the process of identifying a victim inevitably provides information about that victim (name, age, gender, appearance, etc.) that could serve as a rational basis for favoring that person. To avoid this, they sought to document a weaker form of the identifiable victim effect, which one might call the "determinate victim effect." They examined people's willingness to benefit determined versus undetermined individuals under conditions in which all meaningful information about the victims was held constant.

Their first experiment worked as follows. Ten laboratory subjects were each given an "endowment" of $10. Some subjects randomly drew cards that said "KEEP" and were allowed to retain their endowments, while other subjects drew cards that said "LOSE" and subsequently had their endowments taken away, thus rendering them "victims." Each of the nonvictim subjects was anonymously paired with one of the victims as a result of drawing that victim's number. The nonvictim subjects were allowed to give a portion of their endowments to their respective victims, and each could choose how much to give. However—the crucial manipulation—some nonvictim subjects drew the victim's number *before* deciding how much to give, while others drew the victim's number *after* deciding, knowing in advance that they would do so later. In other words, some subjects had to answer the question, "How much do I want to give to person #4?" (determined victim), whereas other subjects had to answer the question, "How much do I want to give to the person whose number I will draw?" (undetermined victim). At no point did the nonvictim subjects ever know who would receive their money. The results: The mean donation for the group who gave to determined victims was 60 percent higher than that of the group giving to undetermined victims. The median donation for the determined victim group was more than twice as high.

It is worth emphasizing the absurdity of this pattern of behavior. There is no rational basis for giving more money to "randomly determined person #4" than to "person #? to be randomly determined," and yet that is what these people did.[5] (Note that the experiment was designed so that none of the participants would ever know who chose what.) Why would people do this? Here, too, the answer implicates emotion. In a follow-up study replicating this effect, the subjects reported on the levels of sympathy and pity they felt for the determined and undetermined victims with whom they were paired. As expected, their reported levels of sympathy and pity tracked their donation levels (Small, personal communication 2/12/05).

One might wonder whether this pattern holds up outside the lab. To find out, Small and Loewenstein conducted a subsequent study in which people could donate money to Habitat for Humanity to provide a home for a needy family, where the family was either determined or to be determined. As predicted, the mean donation was 25 percent higher in the determined family condition, and the median donation in the determined family condition was double that of the undetermined family condition.

And then there is Baby Jessica. We can't say for sure that resources were directed to her instead of to causes that could use the money more effectively because of people's emotional responses (and not because of people's deontological reasoning about rights and duties), but what evidence there is suggests that that is the case. As Stalin might have said, "A determinate individual's death is a tragedy; a million indeterminate deaths is a statistic."

Anger and Deontological Approaches to Punishment

While consequentialists and deontologists agree that punishment of wrongdoing is necessary and important, they disagree sharply over the proper justification for punishment. Consequentialists such as Jeremy Bentham (1789/1982) argue that punishment is justified solely by its future beneficial effects, primarily through deterrence and (in the case of criminal law) the containment of dangerous individuals. While few would deny that the prevention of future harm provides *a* legitimate justification for punishment, many believe that such pragmatic considerations are not the *only* legitimate reasons to punish, or even the main ones. Deontologists such as Kant (1796–97/2002), for example, argue that the primary justification for punishment is *retribution*, to give wrongdoers what they deserve based on what they have done, regardless of whether such retribution will prevent future wrongdoing.

One might wonder, then, about the psychology of the typical punisher. Do people punish, or endorse punishment, because of its beneficial effects, or do people punish because they are motivated to give people what they deserve, in proportion to their "internal wickedness," to use Kant's phrase (Carlsmith, Darley, & Robinson, 2002; Kant, 1796–97/2002). Several studies speak to this question, and the results are consistent. People endorse both consequentialist and retributivist justifications for punishment in the abstract, but in practice, or when faced with more concrete hypothetical choices, people's motives appear to be predominantly retributivist. Moreover, these retributivist inclinations appear to be emotionally driven. People punish in proportion to the extent that transgressions make them angry.

First, let us consider whether punitive judgments are predominantly consequentialist or deontological and retributivist.[6] Jonathan Baron and colleagues have conducted a series of experiments demonstrating that people's punitive judgments are, for the most part, retributivist rather than consequentialist. In one study, Baron and Ritov (1993) presented people with hypothetical corporate liability cases in which corporations could be required to pay fines. In one set of cases, a corporation that manufactures vaccines is being sued because a child died as a result of taking one of its flu vaccines. Subjects were given multiple versions of this case. In one version, it was stipulated that a fine would have a positive deterrent effect. That is, a fine would make the company produce a safer vaccine. In a different version, it was stipulated that a fine would have a "perverse" effect. Instead of causing the firm to make a safer vaccine available, a fine would cause the company to stop making this kind of vaccine altogether, a bad result given that the vaccine in question does more good than harm and that no other firm is capable of making such a vaccine. Subjects indicated whether they thought a punitive fine was appropriate in either of these cases and whether the fine should differ between these two cases. A majority of subjects said that the fine should not differ at all. Baron and Ritov achieved similar results using a complementary manipulation concerning deterrent effects on the decisions of other firms. In a different set of studies, Baron and colleagues found a similar indifference to consequentialist factors in response to questions about the management of hazardous waste (Baron, Gowda, & Kunreuther, 1993).

The results of these studies are surprising in light of the fact that many people regard the deterrence of future harmful decisions as a major reason, if not the primary reason, for imposing such fines in the real world. The strength of these results is also worth emphasizing. The finding here is not simply that people's punitive judgments fail to accord with consequentialism, the view that consequences are ultimately the *only* things that should matter to decision makers. Much more than that, it seems that a majority of people give *no weight whatsoever* to factors that are of clear consequentialist importance, at least in the contexts under consideration.

If people do not punish for consequentialist reasons, what motivates them? In a study by Kahneman and colleagues (Kahneman, Schkade, & Sunstein, 1998), subjects responded to a number of similar hypothetical scenarios (e.g., a case of anemia due to benzene exposure at work). For each scenario subjects rated the extent to which the defendant's action was "outrageous." They also rated the extent to which the defendant in each case should be punished. The correlation between the mean outrage ratings for these scenarios and their mean punishment ratings were nearly perfect, with a Pearson's correlation coefficient (r) of 0.98. (A value of 1 indicates a perfect correlation.) Kahneman and colleagues conclude that the extent to which people desire to see a corporation punished for its behavior is almost entirely a function of the extent to which they are emotionally outraged by that corporation's behavior.

Carlsmith and colleagues (Carlsmith et al., 2002) conducted a similar set of studies aimed explicitly at determining whether people punish for consequentialist or deontological reasons. Here, as earlier, subjects were presented with scenarios involving morally and legally culpable behavior, in this case perpetrated by individuals rather than corporations. As before, subjects were asked to indicate how severe each person's punishment should be, first in abstract terms ("not at all severe" to "extremely severe") and then in more concrete terms ("not guilty/no punishment" to "life sentence"). The experimenters varied the scenarios in ways that warranted different levels of punishment, depending on the rationale for punishment. For example, a consequentialist theory of punishment considers the detection rate associated with a given kind of crime and the publicity associated with a given kind of conviction to be relevant factors in assigning punishments. According to consequentialists, if a crime is difficult to detect, then the punishment for that crime ought to be made more severe in order to counterbalance the temptation created by the low risk of getting caught. Likewise, if a conviction is likely to get a lot of publicity, then a law enforcement system interested in deterrence should take advantage of this circumstance by "making an example" of the convict with a particularly severe punishment, thus getting a maximum of deterrence "bang" for its punishment "buck."

The results were clear. For the experimental group as a whole, there was no significant change in punishment recommendations when the detection rates and levels of publicity were manipulated. In other words, people were generally indifferent to factors that according to consequentialists should matter, at least to some extent. This is in spite of the fact that Carlsmith et al., as well as others (Weiner, Graham, & Reyna, 1997), found that subjects readily expressed a general kind of support for deterrence-oriented penal systems and corporate policies.

In a follow-up study, subjects were explicitly instructed to adopt a consequentialist approach, with the consequentialist rationale explicitly laid out and with extra manipulation checks included to ensure that the subjects understood the relevant facts. Here, too, the results were striking. Subjects did modify their judgments when they were told to think like consequentialists, but not in a genuinely consequentialist way. Instead of becoming selectively sensitive to the factors that increase the consequentialist benefits of punishment, subjects indiscriminately ratcheted up the level of punishment in all cases, giving perpetrators the punishment that they thought the perpetrators deserved based on their actions, plus a bit more for the sake of deterrence.

What motivated these subjects' punitive judgments? Here, too, an important part of the answer appears to be "outrage." Subjects indicated the extent to which they were "morally outraged" by the offenses in question, and the extent of moral outrage in response to a given offense was a pretty good predictor of the severity of punishment assigned to the perpetrator, although the effect here was weaker than that observed in Kahneman et al.'s study.[7] Moreover, a structural equation model of these data suggests that the factors that had the greatest effect on people's judgments about punishment (severity of the crime, presence of mitigating circumstances) worked their effects through "moral outrage."

You will recall Small and Loewenstein's research on the "identifiable victim effect" discussed in the previous section. More recently they have documented a parallel effect in the domain of punishment. Subjects played an "investment game" in which individuals were given money that they could choose to put into a collective investment pool. The game allows individuals to choose the extent to which they will play cooperatively, benefiting the group at the chooser's expense. After the game, cooperators were given the opportunity to punish selfish players by causing them to lose money, but the punishing cooperators had to pay for the pleasure. As before, the crucial manipulation was between determined and undetermined individuals, in this case the selfish players. Some subjects were asked, "How much would you like to punish uncooperative subject #4?" while others were asked, "How much would you like to punish the uncooperative subject whose number you will draw?" Consistent with previous results, the average punishment was almost twice as high for the determined group, and once again the subjects' reports of their emotional responses (in this case a composite measure of anger and blame) tracked their behavior (Small & Loewenstein, 2005).

Recent neuroimaging studies also suggest that the desire to punish is emotionally driven. Alan Sanfey, Jim Rilling, and colleagues (Sanfey, Rilling, Aronson, Nystrom, & Cohen, 2003) conducted a brain imaging study of the ultimatum game to study the neural bases of people's sense of fairness. The ultimatum game works as follows. There is a sum of money, say $10, and the first player (the proposer) makes a proposal on how to divide it up between her or himself and the other player. The second player, the responder, can either accept the offer, in which case the money is divided as proposed, or reject the offer, in which case no one gets anything. Proposers usually make offers that are fair (i.e., a fifty-fifty split) or close to fair, and responders tend to reject offers that are more than a little unfair. In other words, responders will typically pay for the privilege of punishing unfair proposers, even when the game is played only once. Why do people do this?

The answer, once again, implicates emotion. The experimenters found that unfair offers, compared with fair offers, produced increased activity in the anterior insula, a brain region associated with anger, disgust, and autonomic arousal. Moreover, individuals' average levels of insula activity correlated positively with the percentage of offers they rejected and was weaker for trials in which the subject believed that the unfair offer was made by a computer program rather than a real person. Of course, it is conceivable that people were punishing in an attempt to deter unfair proposers from being unfair to others in the future, but that seems unlikely given the consistent finding that people are insensitive to manipulations that modulate the deterrent effects of punishment. Instead, it seems much more likely that people inflicted punishment for its own sake. And once again, it seems that this retributivist tendency is emotionally driven. A more recent neuroimaging study of punishment in response to violations of trust yields a similar conclusion (de Quervain, Fischbacher, Treyer, Schellhammer, Schnyder, et al., 2004). In this study, the extent of punishment was correlated with the level of activity in the caudate nucleus, a brain region associated with emotion and related more specifically to motivation and reward.

When people are asked in a general and abstract way about why it makes sense to punish, consequentialist arguments are prominent (Carlsmith et al., 2002; Weiner et al., 1997). However, when people are presented with more concrete cases involving specific individuals carrying out specific offenses, people's judgments are largely, and in many cases completely, insensitive to factors affecting the consequences of punishment. This is so even when the consequentialist rationale for responding to these factors is highlighted and when people are explicitly instructed to think like consequentialists. It seems, then, that consequentialist thinking plays a negligible role in commonsense punitive judgment and that commonsense punitive judgment is almost entirely retributivist and deontological, as long as the matter is sufficiently concrete. Moreover, the available evidence, both from self-reports and neuroimaging data, suggests that people's deontological and retributivist punitive judgments are predominantly emotional, driven by feelings of anger or "outrage."

Emotion and the Moral Condemnation of Harmless Actions

According to consequentialists, actions are wrong because of their harmful consequences. In contrast, deontologists, along with many commonsense moralists, will condemn actions that do not cause harm in any ordinary sense. For example, a deontologist would likely say that it is wrong to break promises, regardless of whether doing so would have harmful consequences. Jonathan Haidt (Haidt, Koller, & Dias, 1993) has conducted a series of studies of moral judgments made in response to harmless actions. Two themes relevant to the present discussion emerge from this work. First, the moral condemnation of harmless action appears to be driven by emotion. Second, experience that encourages a more "cognitive" approach to moral decision making tends to make people less willing to condemn harmless actions.

Haidt and two Brazilian colleagues conducted a cross-cultural study of moral judgment using a large set of subjects varying in socioeconomic status (SES), nationality (Brazilian versus American), and age (children versus adults). The subjects were presented with a number of scenarios involving morally questionable, harmless actions:

1. A son promises his dying mother that he will visit her grave every week after she has died, but then doesn't because he is busy.
2. A woman uses an old American or Brazilian flag to clean the bathroom.
3. A family eats its dog after it has been killed accidentally by a car.
4. A brother and sister kiss on the lips.
5. A man masturbates using a dead chicken before cooking and eating it.

Subjects answered questions about each case: Is this action wrong? If so, why? Does this action hurt anyone? If you saw someone do this, would it bother you? Should someone who does this be stopped or punished? If doing this is the custom in some foreign country, is that custom wrong?

When people say that such actions are wrong, why do they say so? One hypothesis is that these actions are perceived as harmful, whether or not they really are (Turiel, Killen, & Helwig, 1987). Kissing siblings could cause themselves psychological damage. Masturbating with a chicken could spread disease, etc. If this hypothesis is correct, then we would expect people's answers to the question "Does this action hurt anyone?" to correlate with their degree of moral condemnation, as indexed by affirmative answers to the questions: "Is this wrong?" "Should this person be stopped or punished?" "Is it wrong if it's the local custom?" Alternatively, if emotions drive moral condemnation in these cases, then we would expect people's answers to the question "If you saw this, would it bother you?" to better predict their answers to the moral questions posed. As expected, Haidt and colleagues found that an affirmative answer to the "Would it bother you?" question was a better predictor of moral condemnation than an affirmative answer to the harm question.[8]

Equally interesting were the between-group differences. First, the high-SES subjects in Philadelphia and Brazil were far less condemning than their low-SES counterparts, so much so that the high-SES groups in Philadelphia and Brazil resembled each other more than they resembled their low-SES neighbors. Second, people from less "westernized"[9] cities tended to be more condemning. Third, children in both places tended to be more condemning than adults. In other words, education (SES), westernization, and growing up were associated with more consequentialist judgments in response to the scenarios used here. These three findings make sense in light of the model of moral judgment we have been developing, according to which intuitive emotional responses drive prepotent moral intuitions while "cognitive" control processes sometimes rein them in. Education is to a large extent the development of one's "cognitive" capacities, learning to think in ways that are abstract, effortful, and often either nonintuitive or counterintuitive. The westernization factor is closely related. While westerners may not be any more "cognitively" developed than members of other cultures, the western tradition takes what is, from an anthropological perspective, a peculiarly "cognitive" approach to morality. Westerners are more likely than members of other cultures to argue for and justify their moral beliefs and values in abstract terms (P. Rozin, personal communication, 2/23/05). Moreover, western culture tends to be more pluralistic than other cultures, explicitly valuing multiple perspectives and an intellectual awareness that alternative perspectives exist. Finally, the capacity for "cognitive control" continues to develop through adolescence (V. A. Anderson, Anderson, Northam, Jacobs, & Catroppa, 2001; Paus, Zijdenbos, Worsley, Collins, Blumenthal, et al., 1999). Children, like adults, are very good at feeling emotions such as anger, sympathy, and disgust, but unlike adults they are not very good at controlling their behavior when experiencing such feelings (Steinburg & Scott, 2003). Thus, as before, there seems to be a link between "cognition" and consequentialist judgment.

In this study, the connection between a reluctance to condemn and consequentialism is fairly straightforward. Consequentialists do not condemn harmless actions.[10] The connection between the tendency to condemn harmless actions and deontology is, however, less straightforward and more questionable. It is not obvious, for example, that deontologists are any more likely than consequentialists to condemn flag desecration or eating the family dog. Similar doubts apply to the case of kissing siblings and the man who masturbates with a dead chicken, although it's worth noting that Kant argued that incest, masturbation, bestiality, and pretty much every other form of sexual experimentation are against the moral law (Kant, 1930; Kant, 1785/1994). The broken promise case, however, is "downtown deontology." Of course, not all deontologists would condemn someone for harmlessly breaking a promise to one's deceased mother, but anyone who would condemn such behavior (without appealing in some way to consequences) is exhibiting characteristically deontological behavior.[11] In light of this, it is worth examining this case more closely, and it turns out that this case fits the pattern for the intergroup differences quite well. Among high SES adults, the percentage of subjects in each city who said that this action should be stopped or punished ranged from 3% to 7%, while the percentage of low SES adults who said the same ranged from 20% (Philadelphia) to 57% (Recife, Brazil). Likewise, among high SES adults, the percentage who said that this behavior would be wrong even if it were the local custom ranged from 20% to 28%, while the corresponding percentages for low SES subjects ranged from 40% to 87%. The tendency to condemn this behavior also decreased with westernization, and within every group children were more willing to condemn it than adults. (If you want someone to visit your grave when you're dead, you can't beat poor children from Recife, Brazil. Ninety-seven percent endorsed punishing or stopping people who renege on grave-visiting promises, and 100% condemn cultures in which doing so is the custom.) Thus, the argument made earlier connecting "cognition" and consequentialism applies specifically to the case in which moral condemnation is most characteristically deontological. Haidt et al. did not provide data regarding the "Would it bother you?" question for this case specifically, but the fact that this case was not an exception to the general "cognitive" pattern (less condemnation in the presence of "cognition"-boosting factors) suggests that it is unlikely to be an exception to the general emotion-related pattern (condemnation correlated with negative emotions).

More powerful and direct evidence for the role of emotion in condemning harmless moral violations comes from two more recent studies. In the first of these, Thalia Wheatley and Jonathan Haidt (2005) gave hypnotizable individuals a posthypnotic suggestion to feel a pang of disgust upon reading the word "often" (and to forget that they received this suggestion). The other subjects (also hypnotizable individuals) were given the same treatment, except that they were sensitized to the word "take." The subjects were then presented with scenarios, some of which involved no harm. In one scenario, for example, second cousins have a sexual relationship in which they "_take/often_ go on _weekend trips to romantic hotels in the mountains." The subjects who received the matching posthypnotic suggestion (i.e., read the word to which they were hypnotically sensitized) judged this couple's actions to be more morally wrong than did the other subjects.

In a second experiment, Wheatley and Haidt used a scenario in which the person described did nothing wrong at all. It was the case of a student council representative who "_often_ picks" (or "tries to _take_ up") topics of broad interest for discussion. Many subjects who received matching posthypnotic suggestions indicated that his behavior was somewhat wrong, and two subjects gave it high wrongness ratings. Subjects said things like: "It just seems like he's up to something," "It just seems so weird and disgusting," and, "I don't know [why it's wrong], it just is." Again, we see emotions driving people to nonconsequentialist conclusions.

In a more recent study, Simone Schnall, Jonathan Haidt, and Gerald Clore (2004) manipulated feelings of disgust, not with hypnosis, but by seating subjects at a disgusting desk while they filled out their questionnaires. (The desk was stained and sticky, located near an overflowing trashcan containing used pizza boxes and dirty-looking tissues, etc.) These subjects responded to a number of moral judgment scenarios, including variations on the dog-eating and masturbation scenarios mentioned earlier. Here, as before, the disgust manipulation made people more likely to condemn these actions, though only for subjects who were rated as highly sensitive to their own bodily states.

Two Patterns of Moral Judgment

The experiments conducted by Greene et al., Small and Loewenstein, Baron et al., Kahneman et al., Carlsmith et al., Sanfey et al., de Quervain et al., and Haidt et al. together provide multiple pieces of independent evidence that deontological patterns of moral judgment are driven by emotional responses while consequentialist judgments are driven by "cognitive" processes. Any one of the results and interpretations described here may be questioned, but the convergent evidence assembled here makes a decent case for the association between deontology and emotion, especially since there is, to my knowledge, no empirical evidence to the contrary. Of course, deontologists may regard themselves and their minds as exceptions to the statistically significant and multiply convergent psychological patterns identified in these studies, but in my opinion the burden is on them to demonstrate that they are psychologically exceptional in a way that preserves their self-conceptions.

Why should deontology and emotion go together? I believe the answer comes in two parts. First, moral emotion provides a natural solution to certain problems created by social life. Second, deontological philosophy provides a natural "cognitive" interpretation of moral emotion. Let us consider each of these claims in turn.

First, why moral emotions? In recent decades many plausible and complementary explanations have been put forth, and a general consensus seems to be emerging. The emotions most relevant to morality exist because they motivate behaviors that help individuals spread their genes *within a social context*. The theory of kin selection explains why individuals have a tendency to care about the welfare of those individuals to whom they are closely related (Hamilton, 1964). Because close relatives share a high proportion of their genes, one can spread one's own genes by helping close relatives spread theirs. The theory of reciprocal altruism explains the existence of a wider form of altruism: Genetically unrelated individuals can benefit from being nice to each other as long as they are capable of keeping track of who is willing to repay their kindness (Trivers, 1971). More recent evolutionary theories of altruism attempt to explain the evolution of "strong reciprocity," a broader tendency to reward cooperative behavior and punish uncooperative behavior, even in contexts in which the necessary conditions for kin selection (detectable genetic relationships) and reciprocal altruism (detectable cooperative dispositions) are not met (Bowles & Gintis, 2004; Fehr & Rockenbach, 2004; Gintis, 2000). These theories explain the widespread human tendency to engage in cooperative behaviors (e.g., helping others and speaking honestly) and to avoid uncooperative behaviors (e.g., hurting others and lying), even when relatives and close associates are not involved. Moreover, these theories explain "altruistic punishment," people's willingness to punish antisocial behavior even when they cannot expect to benefit from doing so (Boyd, Gintis, Bowles, & Richerson, 2003; Fehr & Gachter, 2002; Fehr & Rockenbach, 2004). Other evolutionary theories make sense of other aspects of morality. For example, the incest taboo can be explained as a mechanism for avoiding birth defects, which are more likely to result from matings between close relatives (Lieberman, Tooby, & Cosmides, 2003). Finally, the emerging field of cultural evolution promises to explain how moral norms (and cultural practices more broadly) develop and spread (Richerson & Boyd, 2005).

Such evolutionary accounts of moral phenomena have received a great deal of attention in recent years (Pinker, 2002; Sober & Wilson, 1998; Wright, 1994), and therefore I will not elaborate upon them here. I will simply assume that the general thrust of these theories is correct: that our most basic moral dispositions are evolutionary adaptations that arose in response to the demands and opportunities created by social life. The pertinent question here concerns the psychological implementation of these dispositions. Why should our adaptive moral behavior be driven by moral emotions as opposed to something else, such as moral reasoning? The answer, I believe, is that emotions are very reliable, quick, and efficient responses to recurring situations, whereas reasoning is unreliable, slow, and inefficient in such contexts. (See Sober & Wilson (1998, chap. 10) on altruistic emotions versus hedonistic reasoning.)

Nature doesn't leave it to our powers of reasoning to figure out that ingesting fat, sugar, and protein is conducive to our survival. Rather, it makes us hungry and gives us an intuitive sense that things like meat and fruit will satisfy our hunger. Nature doesn't leave it to us to figure out that fellow humans are more suitable mates than baboons. Instead, it endows us with a psychology that makes certain humans strike us as appealing sexual partners, and makes baboons seem frightfully unappealing in this regard. And, finally, Nature doesn't leave it to us to figure out that saving a drowning child is a good thing to do. Instead, it endows us with a powerful "moral sense" that compels us to engage in this sort of behavior (under the right circumstances). In short, when Nature needs to get a behavioral job done, it does it with intuition and emotion wherever it can. Thus, from an evolutionary point of view, it is no surprise that moral dispositions evolved, and it is no surprise that these dispositions are implemented emotionally.

Now, onto the second part of the explanation. Why should the existence of moral emotions give rise to the existence of deontological philosophy?

To answer this question, we must appeal to the well-documented fact that humans are, in general, irrepressible explainers and justifiers of their own behavior. Psychologists have repeatedly found that when people don't know why they're doing what they're doing, they just make up a plausible-sounding story (Haidt, 2001; Wilson, 2002).

Recall, for example, the pantyhose experiment described earlier. The subjects didn't know that they were drawn to items on the right side of the display, but when they were asked to explain themselves, they made up perfectly rational, alternative explanations for their preferences (Nisbett & Wilson, 1977). In a similar experiment, Nisbett and Wilson (1977) induced subjects to prefer the laundry detergent Tide by priming them with word pairs like "ocean-moon" in a preceding memory test. When subjects explained their preferences, they said things like "Tide is the best-known detergent," or "My mother uses Tide," or "I like the Tide box." In an early experiment by Maier (Maier, 1931; Nisbett & Wilson, 1977), subjects had to figure out a way to tie together two cords hanging from the ceiling, a challenging task since the cords were too far apart to be reached simultaneously. The solution was to tie a heavy object to one of the cords so that it could swing like a pendulum. The subject could then hold onto one cord while waiting for the other one to swing into reach. Maier was able to help his subjects solve this problem by giving them a subtle clue. As he was walking around the room he would casually put one of the cords in motion. The subjects who were aided by this clue, however, were unaware of its influence. Instead, they readily attributed their insights to a different, more conspicuous cue (Maier's twirling a weight on a cord), despite the fact that this cue was demonstrated to be useless in other versions of the experiment.

In a similar experiment, Dutton and Aron (Dutton & Aron, 1974; Wilson, 2002) had male subjects cross a scary footbridge spanning a deep gorge, after which they were met by an attractive female experimenter. Control subjects rested on a bench before encountering the attractive experimenter. The subjects who had just braved the scary bridge, with their sweaty palms and hearts a'pounding, were more than twice as likely as the control subjects to call the experimenter later and ask her for a date. These individuals (many of them, at any rate) interpreted their increased physiological arousal as increased attraction to the woman they had met.

The tendency toward post hoc rationalization is often revealed in studies of people with unusual mental conditions. Patients with Korsakoff's amnesia and related memory disorders are prone to "confabulation." That is, they attempt to paper over their memory deficits by constructing elaborate stories about their personal histories, typically delivered with great confidence and with no apparent awareness that they are making stuff up. For example, a confabulating patient seated near an air conditioner was asked if he knew where he was. He replied that he was in an air-conditioning plant. When it was pointed out that he was wearing pajamas, he said. "I keep them in my car and will soon change into my work clothes" (Stuss, Alexander, Lieberman, & Levine, 1978). Likewise, individuals acting under posthypnotic suggestion will sometimes explain away their behaviors in elaborately rational terms. In one case, a hypnotized subject was instructed to place a lampshade on another person's head upon perceiving an arbitrary cue. He did as instructed, but when he was asked to explain why he did what he did, he made no reference to the posthypnotic suggestion or the cue: "Well, I'll tell you. It sounds queer but it's just a little experiment in psychology. I've been reading on the psychology of humor and I thought I'd see how you folks reacted to a joke that was in very bad taste" (Estabrooks, 1943; Wilson, 2002).

Perhaps the most striking example of this kind of post hoc rationalization comes from studies of split-brain patients, people in whom there is no direct neuronal communication between the cerebral hemispheres. In one study, a patient's right hemisphere was shown a snow scene and instructed to select a matching picture. Using his left hand, the hand controlled by the right hemisphere, he selected a picture of a shovel. At the same time, the patient's left hemisphere, the hemisphere that is dominant for language, was shown a picture of a chicken claw. The patient was asked verbally why he chose the shovel with his left hand. He answered, "I saw a claw and picked a chicken, and you have to clean out the chicken shed with a shovel" (Gazzaniga & Le Doux, 1978; Wilson, 2002). Gazzaniga and LeDoux argue that these sorts of confabulations are not peculiar to spilt-brain patients, that this tendency was not created when these patients' intercerebral communication lines were cut. Rather, they argue, we are all confabulators of a sort. We respond to the conscious deliverances of our unconscious perceptual, mnemonic, and emotional processes by fashioning them into a rationally sensible narrative, and without any awareness that we are doing so. This widespread tendency for rationalization is only revealed in carefully controlled experiments in which the psychological inputs and behavioral outputs can be carefully monitored, or in studies of abnormal individuals who are forced to construct a plausible narrative out of meager raw material.

We are now ready to put two and two together. What should we expect from creatures who exhibit social and moral behavior that is driven largely by intuitive emotional responses and who are prone to rationalization of their behaviors? The answer, I believe, is deontological moral philosophy. What happens when we contemplate pushing the large man off the footbridge? If I'm right, we have an intuitive emotional response that says "no!" This nay-saying voice can be overridden, of course, but as far as the voice itself is concerned, there is no room for negotiation. Whether or not we can ultimately justify pushing the man off the footbridge, it will always *feel* wrong. And what better way to express that feeling of non-negotiable absolute wrongness than via the most central of deontological concepts, the concept of a *right*: You can't push him to his death because that would be a violation of his *rights*. Likewise, you can't let that baby drown because you have a *duty* to save it.

Deontology, then, is a kind of moral confabulation. We have strong feelings that tell us in clear and uncertain terms that some things *simply cannot be done* and that other things *simply must be done*. But it is not obvious how to make sense of these feelings, and so we, with the help of some especially creative philosophers, make up a rationally appealing story: There are these things called "rights" which people have, and when someone has a right you can't do anything that would take it away. It doesn't matter if the guy on the footbridge is toward the end of his natural life, or if there are seven people on the tracks below instead of five. If the man has a right, then *the man has a right*. As John Rawls (1971, pp. 3–4) famously said, "Each person possesses an inviolability founded on justice that even the welfare of society as a whole cannot override" and, "In a just society the rights secured by justice are not subject to political bargaining or to the calculus of social interests." These are applause lines because they make emotional sense. Deontology, I believe, is a natural "cognitive" expression of our deepest moral emotions.

This hypothesis raises a further question. Why just deontology? Why not suppose that all moral philosophy, even all moral reasoning, is a rationalization of moral emotion? (This is the strong form of the view defended by Jonathan Haidt, 2001, whose argument is the model for the argument made here.)[12] The answer, I think, is that consequentialist moral judgment is not driven by emotion, or at least it is not driven by the sort of "alarm bell" emotion that drives deontological judgment. The evidence presented earlier supports this hypothesis, suggesting that consequentialist judgment is less emotional and more "cognitive," but it doesn't explain why this should be so. I argued earlier that there is a natural mapping between the content of deontological philosophy and the functional properties of alarmlike emotions. Likewise, I believe that there is a natural mapping between the content of consequentialist philosophy and the functional properties of "cognitive" processes. Indeed, I believe that consequentialism is inherently "cognitive," that it couldn't be implemented any other way.

Consequentialism is, by its very nature, systematic and aggregative. It aims to take nearly everything into account, and grants that nearly everything is negotiable. All consequentialist decision making is a matter of balancing competing concerns, taking into account as much information as is practically feasible. Only in hypothetical examples in which "all else is equal" does consequentialism give clear answers. For real-life consequentialism, everything is a complex guessing game, and all judgments are revisable in light of additional details. There is no moral clarity in consequentialist moral thought, with its approximations and simplifying assumptions. It is fundamentally actuarial.

Recall the definition of "cognitive" proposed earlier: "Cognitive" representations are inherently neutral representations, ones that, unlike emotional representations, do not automatically trigger particular behavioral responses or dispositions. Once again, the advantage of having such neutral representations is that they can be mixed and matched in a situation-specific way without pulling the agent in multiple behavioral directions at once, thus enabling highly flexible behavior. These are precisely the sorts of representations that a consequentialist needs in order to make a judgment based on aggregation, one that takes all of the relevant factors into account: "Is it okay to push the guy off the bridge if he's about to cure cancer?" "Is it okay to go out for sushi when the extra money could be used to promote health education in Africa?" And so on. Deontologists can dismiss these sorts of complicated, situation-specific questions, but consequentialists cannot, which is why, I argue, that consequentialism is inescapably "cognitive."

Some clarifications: First, I am not claiming that consequentialist judgment is emotionless. On the contrary, I am inclined to agree with Hume (1740/1978) that all moral judgment must have some affective component, and suspect that the consequentialist weighing of harms and benefits is an emotional process. But, if I am right, two things distinguish this sort of process from those associated with deontology. First, this is, as I have said, a weighing process and not an "alarm" process. The sorts of emotions hypothesized to be involved here say, "Such-and-such matters this much. Factor it in." In contrast, the emotions hypothesized to drive deontological judgment are far less subtle. They are, as I have said, alarm signals that issue simple commands: "Don't do it!" or "Must do it!" While such commands can be overridden, they are designed to dominate the decision rather than merely influence it.

Second, I am not claiming that deontological judgment cannot be "cognitive." Indeed, I believe that sometimes it is. (See below.) Rather, my hypothesis is that deontological judgment is affective at its core, while consequentialist judgment is inescapably "cognitive." One could, in principle, make a characteristically deontological judgment by thinking explicitly about the categorical imperative and whether the action in question is based on a maxim that could serve as a universal law. And if one were to do that, then the psychological process would be "cognitive." What I am proposing, however, is that this is not how characteristically deontological conclusions tend to be reached and that, instead, they tend to be reached on the basis of emotional responses. This contrasts with consequentialist judgments which, according to my hypothesis, cannot be implemented in an intuitive, emotional way. The only way to reach a distinctively consequentialist judgment (i.e., one that doesn't coincide with a deontological judgment) is to actually go through the consequentialist, cost-benefit reasoning using one's "cognitive" faculties, the ones based in the dorsolateral prefrontal cortex (Greene et al., 2004).

This psychological account of consequentialism and deontology makes sense of certain aspects of their associated phenomenologies. I have often observed that consequentialism strikes students as appealing, even as tautologically true, when presented in the abstract, but that its appeal is easily undermined by specific counterexamples. (See the earlier discussion contrasting people's real-world motives and abstract justifications for punishment.) When a first-year ethics student asks, "But isn't it obvious that one should do whatever will produce the most good?" all you have to do is whip out the *footbridge* case and you have made your point. Whatever initial "cognitive" appeal consequentialist principles may have is quickly neutralized by a jolt of emotion, and the student is a newly converted deontologist: "Why is it wrong to push the man off the footbridge? Because he has a *right,* an inviolability founded on justice that even the welfare of society as a whole cannot override!" Then it's time for a new counterexample: "What if the trolley is headed for a detonator that will set off a nuclear bomb that will kill half a million people?" Suddenly the welfare of society as a whole starts to sound important again. "Cognition" strikes back with a more compelling utilitarian rationale, and the student is appropriately puzzled. As this familiar dialectic illustrates, the hypothesis that deontology is emotionally based explains the *"NEVER!—except* sometimes" character of rights-based, deontological ethics. An alarmlike emotional response presents itself as unyielding and absolute, until an even more compelling emotional or "cognitive" rationale comes along to override it.

This hypothesis also makes sense of certain deontological anomalies, which I suspect will turn out to be the "exceptions that prove the rule." I have argued that deontology is driven by emotion, but I suspect this is not always the case. Consider, for example, Kant's infamous claim that it would be wrong to lie to a would-be murderer in order to protect a friend who has taken refuge in one's home (Kant, 1785/1983). Here, in a dramatic display of true intellectual integrity, Kant sticks to his theory and rejects the intuitive response. (He "bites the bullet," as philosophers say.) But what is interesting about this bit of Kantian ethics is that it's something of an embarrassment to contemporary Kantians, who are very keen to explain how Kant somehow misapplied his own theory in this case (Korsgaard, 1996a). Presumably the same goes for Kant's views of sexual morality (Kant, 1930, pp. 169–171; Kant, 1994). Modern academics are no longer so squeamish about lust, masturbation, and homosexuality, and so Kant's old-fashioned views on these topics have to be explained away, which is not difficult, since his arguments were never terribly compelling to begin with (see the epigraph). If you want to know which bits of Kant contemporary Kantians will reject, follow the emotions.

Normative Implications

Psychological "Is" and Moral "Ought"

The hypotheses advanced here concerning the respective psychological bases of consequentialism and deontology could certainly be wrong, but whether they are right or wrong cannot be determined from the armchair. Rather, it is an empirical matter. And although these hypotheses remain open to empirical challenge, I am from here on going to assume that they are correct in order to explore their broader philosophical implications. Since most moral philosophers do not regard their views as contingent upon the outcomes of particular debates in experimental psychology, this assumption should not be regarded as unduly restrictive.

Indeed, moral philosophers tend to steer clear of scientific controversies whenever possible on the grounds that scientific details are largely irrelevant to their enterprise: Science is about what is, while morality is about what ought to be, and never the twain shall meet (Hume, 1740/1978; Moore, 1903). Contrary to this received moral wisdom, I believe that science does matter for ethics, not because one can derive moral truths from scientific truths, but because scientific information can challenge factual assumptions on which moral thinking implicitly depends. The key point of contact between moral philosophy and scientific moral psychology is moral intuition. Moral philosophers from Plato (1987) on down have relied on their intuitive sense of right and wrong to guide them in their attempts to make sense of morality. The relevance of science then is that it can tell us how our moral intuitions work and where they come from. Once we understand our intuitions a bit better we may view them rather differently. This goes not only for moralists who rely explicitly on moral intuitions (Ross, 1930), but also for moralists who are unaware of the extent to which their moral judgments are shaped by intuition.

In recent years, several philosophers and scientists have questioned the reliability of moral intuitions and argued that understanding the psychology of moral intuition has normative implications (Baron, 1994; Greene, 2003; Horowitz, 1998; Sinnott-Armstrong, 2006; Unger, 1996). I will do the same, but in the following more specific way. I will argue that our understanding of moral psychology, as described here, casts doubt on deontology as a school of normative moral thought.

Rationalism, Rationalization, and Deontological Judgment

Your friend Alice goes on many dates, and after each one she reports back to you. When she extols the people she likes and complains about the ones she dislikes, she cites a great many factors. This one is brilliant. That one is self-absorbed. This one has a great sense of humor. That one is a dud. And so on. But then you notice something: All the people she likes are exceptionally tall. Closer inspection reveals that after scores of dates over several years, she has not given the thumb's up to anyone who is less than six-foot-four, and has not turned down anyone over this height. (You plug Alice's dating data into your statistics software and confirm that height is a near perfect predictor of Alice's preferences.) Suddenly it seems that Alice's judgment is not what you had believed, and certainly not what she believes. Alice, of course, believes that her romantic judgments are based on a variety of complicated factors. But, if the numbers are to be believed, she basically has a height fetish, and all of her talk about wit and charm and kindness is mere rationalization.

What this example illustrates is that it's possible to spot a rationalizer without picking apart the rationalizer's reasoning. Instead you need do only two things: First, you have to find a factor that predicts the rationalizer's judgments. Second, you have to show that the factor that predicts the rationalizer's judgments is not plausibly related to the factors that according to the rationalizer are the bases for his or her judgments. Using this strategy, I believe that one can make a pretty good case against rationalist versions of deontology such as Kant's; i.e., the ones according to which characteristically deontological moral judgments are justified in terms of abstract theories of rights, duties, etc. The case against such theories is already implicit in the empirical material presented earlier, but it is worth spelling it out.

The bulk of this chapter has been devoted to satisfying the first of the two requirements I listed, i.e., to identifying a factor, namely emotional response, that predicts deontological judgment. Next, we must consider the nature of the relationship between this predictive factor and the factors that according to rationalist deontologists are the bases for their judgments. By definition, a rationalist cannot say that that some action is right or wrong *because* of the emotions we feel in response to it. Nevertheless, as an empirical matter of fact (we are assuming), there is a remarkable correspondence between what rationalist deontological theories tell us to do and what our emotions tell us to do. Thus, in light of these data, there are a series of coincidences for which various rationalist deontologists must account. For example, according to Judith Jarvis Thomson (1986, 1990) and Frances Kamm (1993, 1996) (both of whom count as rationalists for our purposes), there is a complicated, highly abstract theory of rights that explains why it is okay to sacrifice one life for five in the *trolley* case but not in the *footbridge* case, and it *just so happens* that we have a strong negative emotional response to the latter case but not to the former. Likewise, according to Colin McGinn (1999) and Frances Kamm (1999), there is a theory of duty that explains why we have an obligation to help Singer's drowning child but no comparable obligation to save starving children on the other side of the world, and it *just so happens* that we have strong emotional responses to the former individuals but not to the latter. According to Kant (2002) and many other legal theorists (Lacey, 1988; Ten, 1987), there is a complicated abstract theory of punishment that explains why we ought to punish people regardless of whether there are social benefits to be gained in doing so, and it *just so happens* that we have emotional responses that incline us to do exactly that. The categorical imperative prohibits masturbation because it involves using oneself as a means (Kant, 1994), and it *just so happens* that the categorical imperative's chief proponent finds masturbation really, really disgusting (see epigraph). And so on.

Kant, as a citizen of eighteenth-century Europe, has a ready explanation for these sorts of coincidences: God, in his infinite wisdom, endowed people with emotional dispositions designed to encourage them to behave in accordance with the moral law. Kant famously avoided invoking God in his philosophical arguments, but it's plausible to think that his faith prevented him, along with nearly everyone else of his day, from being puzzled by the order and harmony of the natural world, including its harmony with the moral law. Moreover, in light of his background assumptions, you can't really blame Kant for trying to rationalize his moral intuitions. His intuitions derive from his human nature ("the moral law within"; Kant, 1788/1993), and ultimately from God. God's a smart guy, Kant must have thought. He wouldn't give people moral intuitions *willy nilly*. Instead, we must have the intuitions we have for *good reasons*. And so Kant set out to discover those reasons, if not by force of reason, then by feat of imagination.

Present-day rationalist deontologists, as citizens of the twenty-first century, cannot depend on the notion that God gave us our moral emotions to encourage us to behave in accordance with the rationally discoverable deontological moral truth. Instead, they need some sort of naturalistically respectable explanation for the fact that the conclusions reached by rationalist deontologists, as opposed to those reached by consequentialists, appear to be driven by alarmlike emotional responses. And their explanation needs to compete with the alternative proposed here, namely that rationalist deontological theories are rationalizations for these emotional responses—an explanation that already has an advantage, given that so much human behavior appears to be intuitive (Bargh & Chartrand, 1999) and there is a well-documented tendency for people to rationalize their intuitive behavior (Haidt, 2001; Wilson, 2002).

What sort of explanation can rationalist deontologists give? They will have to say, first, that the correspondence between deontological judgment and emotional engagement is not a coincidence and, second, that our moral emotions somehow track the rationally discoverable deontological moral truth. They can't say that our emotional responses are the *basis* for the moral truth, however, because they are *rationalists*. So they are going to have to explain how some combination of biological and cultural evolution managed to give us emotional dispositions that correspond to an independent, rationally discoverable moral truth that is not based on emotion.

Those charged with this task immediately face another disadvantage, which is the chief point I wish to make here. There are good reasons to think that our distinctively deontological moral intuitions (here, the ones that conflict with consequentialism) reflect the influence of morally irrelevant factors and are therefore unlikely to track the moral truth.

Take, for example, the *trolley* and *footbridge* cases. I have argued that we draw an intuitive moral distinction between these two cases because the moral violation in the *footbridge* case is "up close and personal" while the moral violation in the *trolley* case is not. Moreover, I have argued that we respond more emotionally to moral violations that are "up close and personal" because those are the sorts of moral violations that existed in the environment in which we evolved. In other words, I have argued that we have a characteristically deontological intuition regarding the *footbridge* case because of a contingent, nonmoral feature of our evolutionary history. Moreover, I have argued that the same "up close and personal" hypothesis makes sense of the puzzling intuitions surrounding Peter Singer's aid cases and the identifiable-victim effect, thus adding to its explanatory power.

The key point is that this hypothesis is at odds with any hypothesis according to which our moral intuitions in response to these cases reflect deep, rationally discoverable moral truths. Of course, the hypothesis I have advanced could be wrong. But do rationalist deontologists want to count on it? And do they have any more plausible positive explanations to offer in its place?

A similar hypothesis can explain our inclinations toward retributive punishment. Consequentialists say that punishments should only be inflicted insofar as they are likely to produce good consequences (Bentham, 1789/1982). Deontologists such as Kant (Kant, 2002), along with most people (Baron et al., 1993; Baron & Ritov, 1993), are retributivists. They judge in favor of punishing wrongdoers as an end in itself, even when doing so is unlikely to promote good consequences in the future. Is this a moral insight on their part or just a by-product of our evolved psychology? The available evidence suggests the latter.

As discussed earlier, it appears that the emotions that drive us to punish wrongdoers evolved as an efficient mechanism for stabilizing cooperation, both between individuals (Trivers, 1971) and within larger groups (Bowles & Gintis, 2004; Boyd et al., 2003; Fehr & Gachter, 2002). In other words, according to these models, we are disposed to punish because of this disposition's biological consequences. Moreover, natural selection, in furnishing us with this disposition, had a "choice," so to speak. On the one hand, Nature could have given us a disposition to punish by giving us, first, an innate desire to secure the benefits of future cooperation and, second, some means by which to recognize that punishing noncooperators is often a good way to achieve this end. In other words, Nature could have made us punishment consequentialists. Nature's other option was to give us a direct desire to punish noncooperators as an end in itself, even if in some cases punishing does no (biological) good. As noted earlier, Nature faces this sort of choice every time it generates a behavioral adaptation, and in pretty much every case, Nature takes the more direct approach. Psychologically speaking, we desire things like food, sex, and a comfortable place to rest because they are pleasant (and because their absence is unpleasant) and not because we believe they will enhance our biological fitness. The disposition toward punishment appears to be no exception to this general pattern. Psychologically speaking, we punish primarily because we find punishment satisfying (de Quervain et al., 2004) and find unpunished transgressions distinctly unsatisfying (Carlsmith et al., 2002; Kahneman et al., 1998; Sanfey et al., 2003).

In other words, the emotions that drive us to punish are *blunt biological instruments*. They evolved because they drive us to punish in ways that lead to (biologically) good consequences. But, *as a by-product of their simple and efficient design*, they also lead us to punish in situations in which no (biologically) good consequences can be expected. Thus, it seems that as an evolutionary matter of fact, we have a taste for retribution, not because wrongdoers truly deserve to be punished regardless of the costs and benefits, but because retributive dispositions are an efficient way of inducing behavior that allows individuals living in social groups to more effectively spread their genes.

Of course it's possible that there is a coincidence here. It could be that it's part of the rationally discoverable moral truth that people really do deserve to be punished as an end in itself. At the same time, it could *just so happen* that natural selection, in devising an efficient means for promoting biologically advantageous consequences, furnished us with emotionally based dispositions that lead us to this conclusion; but this seems unlikely. Rather, it seems that retributivist theories of punishment are just rationalizations for our retributivist feelings, and that these feelings only exist because of the morally irrelevant constraints placed on natural selection in designing creatures that behave in fitness-enhancing ways. In other words, the natural history of our retributivist dispositions makes it unlikely that they reflect any sort of deep moral truth.

I should emphasize that I am not claiming that consequentialist theories of punishment are correct because the tendency to punish evolved in order to produce good consequences. These "good consequences" need only be good from a biological point of view, and to assume that our ends must coincide with the ends of natural selection would be to commit the naturalistic fallacy in its original form (Moore, 1903). At the same time, I wish to make it clear that I am not asserting that any tendency that we have as an evolutionary by-product is automatically wrong or misguided. I wouldn't claim, for example, that it is wrong to love one's adopted children (who do not share one's genes) or to use birth control simply because these behaviors thwart nature's "intentions." My claim at this point is simply that it is unlikely that inclinations that evolved as evolutionary by-products correspond to some independent, rationally discoverable moral truth. Instead, it is more parsimonious to suppose that when we feel the pull of retributivist theories of punishment, we are merely gravitating toward our evolved emotional inclinations and not toward some independent moral truth.[13]

What turn-of-the-millennium science is telling us is that human moral judgment is not a pristine rational enterprise—that our moral judgments are driven by a hodgepodge of emotional dispositions, which themselves were shaped by a hodgepodge of evolutionary forces, both biological and cultural. Because of this, it is exceedingly unlikely that there is any rationally coherent normative moral theory that can accommodate our moral intuitions. Moreover, anyone who claims to have such a theory, or even part of one, almost certainly does not. Instead, what that person probably has is a moral rationalization.

It seems then that we have somehow crossed the infamous "is"/"ought" divide.[14] How did this happen? Didn't Hume (1978) and Moore (1903) warn us against trying to derive an "ought" from an "is?" How did we go from descriptive scientific theories concerning moral psychology to skepticism about a whole class of normative moral theories? The answer is that we did not, as Hume and Moore anticipated, attempt to *derive* an "ought" from an "is." That is, our method has been *inductive* rather than *deductive*. We have inferred on the basis of the available evidence that the phenomenon of rationalist deontological philosophy is best explained as a rationalization of evolved emotional intuition (Harman, 1977).

Missing the Deontological Point
I suspect that rationalist deontologists will remain unmoved by the arguments presented here. Instead, I suspect, they will insist that I have simply misunderstood what Kant and like-minded deontologists are all about. Deontology, they will say, isn't about this intuition or that intuition. It's not defined by its normative differences with consequentialism. Rather, deontology is about taking humanity seriously. Above all else, it's about

respect for persons. It's about treating others as fellow rational creatures rather than as mere objects, about acting for reasons that rational beings can share; and so on (Korsgaard, 1996a, 1996b).

This is, no doubt, how many deontologists see deontology. However, this insider's view, as I have suggested, may be misleading. The problem, more specifically, is that it defines deontology in terms of values that are not distinctively deontological, though they may appear to be from the inside. Consider the following analogy with religion. When one asks a religious person to explain the essence of his religion, one often gets an answer like this: "It's about love, really. It's about looking out for other people, looking beyond oneself. It's about community, being part of something larger than oneself." This sort of answer accurately captures the phenomenology of many people's religion, but it is nevertheless inadequate for distinguishing religion from other things. This is because many, if not most, nonreligious people aspire to love deeply, look out for other people, avoid self-absorption, have a sense of a community, and be connected to things larger than themselves. In other words, secular humanists and atheists can assent to most of what many religious people think religion is all about. From a secular humanist's point of view, in contrast, what is distinctive about religion is its commitment to the existence of supernatural entities as well as formal religious institutions and doctrines. And they are right. These things really do distinguish religious from nonreligious practices, although they may appear to be secondary to many people operating from within a religious point of view.

In the same way, I believe that most of the standard deontological/Kantian self-characterizations fail to distinguish deontology from other approaches to ethics. (See also Kagan, 1997, pp. 70–78, on the difficulty of defining deontology.) It seems to me that consequentialists, as much as anyone else, have respect for persons, are against treating people as mere objects, wish to act for reasons that rational creatures can share, etc. A consequentialist respects other persons and refrains from treating them as mere objects by counting every person's well-being in the decision-making process. Likewise, a consequentialist attempts to act according to reasons that rational creatures can share by acting according to principles that give equal weight to everyone's interests, i.e., that are impartial. This is not to say that consequentialists and deontologists do not differ. They do. It's just that the real differences may not be what deontologists often take them to be.

What, then, distinguishes deontology from other kinds of moral thought? A good strategy for answering this question is to start with concrete disagreements between deontologists and others (such as consequential-ists) and then work backward in search of deeper principles. This is what I have attempted to do with the *trolley* and *footbridge* cases and other instances in which deontologists and consequentialists disagree. If you ask a deontologically minded person why it is wrong to push someone in front of a speeding trolley in order to save five others, you will get characteristi-cally deontological answers. Some will be tautological: "Because it's murder!" Others will be more sophisticated: "The ends don't justify the means." "You have to respect people's rights." As we know, these answers don't really explain anything, because if you give the same people (on different occasions) the *trolley* case or the *loop* case (see earlier discussion), they will make the opposite judgment, even though their initial explana-tion concerning the *footbridge* case applies equally well to one or both of these cases. Talk about rights, respect for persons, and reasons we can share are natural attempts to explain, in "cognitive" terms, what we feel when we find ourselves having emotionally driven intuitions that are at odds with the cold calculus of consequentialism. Although these explanations are inevitably incomplete, there seems to be "something deeply right" about them because they give voice to powerful moral emotions. However, as with many religious people's accounts of what is essential to religion, they don't really explain what is distinctive about the philosophy in question.

In sum, if it seems that I have simply misunderstood what Kant and deontology are all about, it's because I am advancing an alternative hypoth-esis to the standard Kantian/deontological understanding of what Kant and deontology are all about. I am putting forth an empirical hypothesis about the hidden psychological essence of deontology, and it cannot be dismissed *a priori* for the same reason that tropical islanders cannot know *a priori* whether ice is a form of water.

Evolutionary Moral Psychology and Anthropocentric Morality

Earlier I made a case against rationalist deontology—the idea that our deontological moral intuitions can be justified by abstract theories of rights, duties, etc. There are, however, more modest forms of deontology. Rather than standing by our moral intuitions on the assumption that they can be justified by a rational theory, we might stand by them just because they are *ours*. That is, one might take an *anthropocentric* approach to moral-ity (see Haidt & Bjorklund, volume 2), giving up on the Enlightenment dream of deriving moral truths from first principles and settling instead for a morality that is contingently human.

This is the direction in which moral philosophy has moved in recent decades. Virtue ethics defines moral goodness in terms of human character (Crisp and Slote, 1997; Hursthouse, 1999). Like-minded "sensibility theorists" regard being moral as a matter of having the right sort of distinctively human sensibility (McDowell, 1985; Wiggins, 1987). Ethicists with a more metaphysical bent speak of moral properties that are "response dependent" (Johnston, 1995), moral sentiments that correspond to "quasi-real" moral properties (Blackburn, 1993), and moral properties that are "homeostatic clusters" of natural properties (Boyd, 1988). Even within the Kantian tradition, many emphasize the "construction" of moral principles that, rather than being true, are "reasonable for us" (Rawls, 1995), or, alternatively, the normative demands that follow from our distinctively human "practical identities" (Korsgaard, 1996b).

In short, moral philosophy these days is decidedly anthropocentric in the sense that very few philosophers are actively challenging anyone's moral intuitions. They acknowledge that our moral virtues, sensibilities, and identities may change over time, but they are not for the most part actively trying to change them.

The argument presented here makes trouble for people in search of rationalist theories that can explain and justify their emotionally driven deontological moral intuitions. But rationalist deontologists may not be the only ones who should think twice. The arguments presented here cast doubt on the moral intuitions in question regardless of whether one wishes to justify them in abstract theoretical terms. This is, once again, because these intuitions appear to have been shaped by morally irrelevant factors having to do with the constraints and circumstances of our evolutionary history. This is a problem for anyone who is inclined to stand by these intuitions, and that "anyone" includes nearly everyone.

I have referred to these intuitions and the judgments they underpin as "deontological," but perhaps it would be more accurate to call them non-consequentialist (Baron, 1994). After all, you don't have to be a card-carrying deontologist to think that it's okay to eat in restaurants when people in the world are starving, that it's inherently good that criminals suffer for their crimes, and that it would be wrong to push the guy off the *footbridge*. These judgments are perfectly commonsensical, and it seems that the only people who are inclined to question them are card-carrying consequentialists.

Does that mean that all nonconsequentialists need to rethink at least some of their moral commitments? I humbly suggest that the answer is "yes." Let us consider, once more, Peter Singer's argument concerning the moral obligations that come with affluence. Suppose, once again, that the evolutionary and psychological facts are exactly as I've said. That is, suppose that the *only* reason we say that it's wrong to abandon the drowning child but okay to ignore the needs of starving children overseas is that the former pushes our emotional buttons while the latter do not. And let us suppose further that the *only* reason that faraway children fail to push our emotional buttons is that we evolved in an environment in which it was impossible to interact with faraway individuals. Could we then stand by our commonsense intuitions? Can we, in good conscience, say, "I live a life of luxury while ignoring the desperate needs of people far away because I, through an accident of human evolution, am emotionally insensitive to their plight. Nevertheless, my failure to relieve their suffering, when I could easily do otherwise, is perfectly justified." I don't know about you, but I find this combination of assertions uncomfortable. This is not to say, of course, that I am comfortable with the idea of giving up most of my worldly possessions and privileges in order to help strangers. After all, I'm only human. But, for me at least, understanding the source of my moral intuitions shifts the balance, in this case as well as in other cases, in a more Singerian, consequentialist direction. As a result of understanding the psychological facts, I am less complacent about my all-too-human tendency to ignore distant suffering. Likewise, when I understand the roots of my retributive impulses, I am less likely to afford them moral authority. The same is true for whatever hang-ups I may have about deviant but harmless sexual behavior.

Taking these arguments seriously, however, threatens to put us on a second slippery slope (in addition to the one leading to altruistic destitution): How far can the empirical debunking of human moral nature go? If science tells me that I love my children more than other children only because they share my genes (Hamilton, 1964), should I feel uneasy about loving them extra? If science tells me that I am nice to other people only because a disposition to be nice ultimately helped my ancestors spread their genes (Trivers, 1971), should I stop being nice to people? If I care about myself only because I am biologically programmed to carry my genes into the future, should I stop caring about myself? It seems that one who is unwilling to act on human tendencies that have amoral evolutionary causes is ultimately unwilling to be human. Where does one draw the line between correcting the nearsightedness of human moral nature and obliterating it completely?

This, I believe, is among the most fundamental moral questions we face in an age of growing scientific self-knowledge, and I will not attempt to address it here. Elsewhere I argue that consequentialist principles, while not true, provide the best available standard for public decision making and for determining which aspects of human nature it is reasonable to try to change and which ones we would be wise to leave alone (Greene, 2002; Greene & Cohen, 2004).

Notes

Many thanks to Walter Sinnott-Armstrong, Jonathan Haidt, Shaun Nichols, and Andrea Heberlein for very helpful comments on this chapter.

1. Kohlberg was certainly partial to deontology and would likely say that it is more "cognitive" than consequentialism.

2. It turns out that determining what makes a moral dilemma "personal" and "like the footbridge case" versus "impersonal" and "like the trolley case" is no simple matter, and in many ways reintroduces the complexities associated with traditional attempts to solve the trolley problem. For the purposes of this discussion, however, I am happy to leave the personal-impersonal distinction as an intuitive one, in keeping with the evolutionary account given earlier. For the purposes of designing the brain imaging experiment discussed later, however, my collaborators and I developed a more rigid set of criteria for distinguishing personal from impersonal moral violations (Greene et al., 2001). I no longer believe that these criteria are adequate. Improving these is a goal of ongoing research.

3. It is worth noting that no brain regions, including those implicated in emotion, exhibited the opposite effect. First, it's not clear that one would expect to see such a result since the hypothesis is that everyone experiences the intuitive emotional response, while only some individuals override it. Second, it is difficult to draw conclusions from negative neuroimaging results because current neuroimaging techniques, which track changes in blood flow, are relatively crude instruments for detecting patterns in neural function.

4. Of course, some aid organizations deliberately pair individual donors with individual recipients to make the experience more personal.

5. First, when I say that this behavior cannot be rationally defended, I do not mean that it is logically or metaphysically impossible for a rational person to behave this way. Someone could, for example, have a basic preference for helping determined victims and only determined victims. I am assuming, however, that none of the subjects in this experiment have such bizarre preferences and that therefore their behavior is irrational. Second, I am not claiming that the general psychological tendency that produces this behavior has no "rationale" or that it is not adaptive. Rather, I am simply claiming that this particular behavior is irrational in this case. Few, if any, of the participants in this study would knowingly choose to respond to

the experimental manipulation (determined versus undetermined victim) by giving more to the determined victim. In other words, this experimental effect would have been greatly diminished, if not completely eliminated, had this experiment employed a within-subject design instead of a between-subject design.

6. I am assuming that within the domain of punishment, "deontological" and "retributivist" are effectively interchangeable, even though they are conceptually distinct. (For example, one could favor punishment as an end in itself, but in unpredictable ways that defy all normative rules.) So far as I know, all well-developed alternatives to consequentialist theories of punishment are, in one way or another, retributivist. Moreover, retributivism is explicitly endorsed by many noteworthy deontologists, including Kant (2002).

7. Some complications arise in interpreting the results of these two studies of "outrage" and punishment. It is not clear whether the "outrage" scale used by Kahneman et al. elicits a subjective report of the subject's emotional state or a normative judgment concerning the defendant's behavior. A skeptic might say that the so-called "outrage" rating is really just a rating of the overall moral severity of the crime, which, not surprisingly, correlates with the extent to which people think it warrants punishment.

The Carlsmith et al. study addresses this worry (though not intentionally), and suggests that it may have some validity. The outrage measure used in the Carlsmith et al. study asks explicitly for a subjective report: "How morally outraged were you by this offense?" And, perhaps as a result of this change in tactic, the connection between "outrage" and punitive judgment is weakened from near perfect to fairly strong. Note also that in choosing a strong word like "outrage" in a study of fairly mild, hypothetical crimes, the experimenters may have set the bar too high for subjective reports, thus weakening their results.

8. This result, however, only held for the subgroups that did the majority of the condemning. The subjects who were most reluctant to condemn harmless violations (chiefly high-SES, educated westerners) found harm where others did not and cited that as a reason for condemnation, an effect that Haidt has documented elsewhere and which he has dubbed "moral dumbfounding" (Haidt, Bjorklund, & Murphy, 2000).

9. "Westernization" refers to "the degree to which each of three cities [Philadelphia and two Brazilian cities, Porto Alegre and Recife] has a cultural and symbolic life based on European traditions, including a democratic political structure and an industrialized economy" (Haidt, Koller, & Dias, 1993, 615). Philadelphia is more westernized than Porto Alegre, which is more westernized than Recife.

10. A consequentialist might favor a prohibition against a class of actions, some of which are not harmful, if the prohibition produces the best available consequences. Likewise, a consequentialist might *pretend* to condemn (or publicly condemn, while

privately refraining from condemning) an action if this public condemnation were deemed beneficial.

11. Subjects were asked to justify their answers, and typical justifications for condemning this action did not appeal to consequences, but rather simply stated that it's wrong to break a promise.

12. Haidt (2001), however, believes that philosophers may be exceptional in that they actually do reason their way to moral conclusions (Kuhn, 1991).

13. That is, a truth independent of the details of human moral psychology and natural events that shaped it.

14. Most agree that the "is"-"ought" divide can be crossed when the "is" amounts to a constraint on what can be done, and is *a fortiori* a constraint on what "ought" to be done. For example, if it *is* the case that you are dead, then it is not the case that you *ought* to vote. The move from "is" to "ought" discussed later, however, is more substantive and correspondingly more controversial.

2.1　Moral Cognition and Computational Theory

John Mikhail

I

In his path-breaking work on the foundations of visual perception, David Marr distinguished three levels at which any information-processing task can be understood and emphasized the first of these:

Although algorithms and mechanisms are empirically more accessible, it is the top level, the level of computational theory, which is critically important from an information-processing point of view. The reason for this is that the nature of the computations that underlie perception depends more upon the nature of the computational problems that have to be solved than upon the particular hardware in which their solutions are implemented. (Marr, 1982, p. 27)

I begin with Marr to call attention to a notable weakness of Joshua Greene's wonderfully ambitious and provocative essay: its neglect of computational theory. A central problem moral cognition must solve is to recognize (i.e., compute representations of) the deontic status of human acts and omissions. How do people actually do this? What is the theory that explains their practice?

Greene claims that "emotional response . . . predicts deontological judgment" (this volume, p. 68), but his own explanation of a subset of the simplest and most extensively studied of these judgments—intuitions about trolley problems—in terms of a personal-impersonal distinction is neither complete nor descriptively adequate (Mikhail, 2002), as Greene now acknowledges in a revealing footnote. As I suggest below, a more plausible explanation of these intuitions implies that the human brain contains a computationally complex "moral grammar" (e.g., Dwyer, 1999; Harman, 2000; Mikhail, 2000; Mikhail, Sorrentino, & Spelke, 1998) that is analogous in certain respects to the mental grammars operative in other domains, such as language, vision, music, and face recognition (Jackendoff,

1994). If this is correct, then Greene's emphasis on emotion may be misplaced, and at least some of his arguments may need to be reformulated.

II

Consider the following variations on the trolley problem, which I designed to study the computations underlying moral judgments (Mikhail, 2000).

Bystander
Hank is taking his daily walk near the train tracks when he notices that the train that is approaching is out of control. Hank sees what has happened: the driver of the train saw five men walking across the tracks and slammed on the brakes, but the brakes failed and the driver fainted. The train is now rushing toward the five men. It is moving so fast that they will not be able to get off the track in time. Fortunately, Hank is standing next to a switch, which he can throw, that will turn the train onto a side track, thereby preventing it from killing the men. Unfortunately, there is a man standing on the side track with his back turned. Hank can throw the switch, killing him; or he can refrain from doing this, letting the five die. Is it morally permissible for Hank to throw the switch?

Footbridge
Ian is taking his daily walk near the train tracks when he notices that the train that is approaching is out of control. Ian sees what has happened: the driver of the train saw five men walking across the tracks and slammed on the brakes, but the brakes failed and the driver fainted. The train is now rushing toward the five men. It is moving so fast that they will not be able to get off the track in time. Fortunately, Ian is standing next to a *heavy object*, which he can throw *onto the track in the path of the train*, thereby preventing it from killing the men. Unfortunately, *the heavy object* is a man, standing *next to Ian* with his back turned. Ian can throw the *man*, killing him; or he can refrain from doing this, letting the five die. Is it morally permissible for Ian to throw the *man*?

Consensual Contact
Luke is taking his daily walk near the train tracks when he notices that the train that is approaching is out of control. Luke sees what has happened: the driver of the train saw *a man* walking across the tracks and slammed on the brakes, but the brakes failed and the driver fainted. The train is now rushing toward the *man*. It is moving so fast that *he* will not be able to get off the track in time. Fortunately, Luke is standing next to *the man, whom* he can throw *off the track out of the path of the train*, thereby preventing it from killing the *man*. Unfortunately, *the man* is *frail and* standing with his back turned. Luke can throw the man, *injuring* him; or he can refrain from doing this, letting the *man* die. Is it morally permissible for Luke to throw the *man*?

Disproportional Death

Steve is taking his daily walk near the train tracks when he notices that the train that is approaching is out of control. Steve sees what has happened: the driver of the train saw a man walking across the tracks and slammed on the brakes, but the brakes failed and the driver fainted. The train is now rushing toward the man. It is moving so fast that he will not be able to get off the track in time. Fortunately, Steve is standing next to *a switch*, which he can throw, that will turn the train onto a side track, thereby preventing it from killing the *man*. Unfortunately, there are *five men* standing on the side track with their backs turned. Steve can throw the switch, killing the *five men*; or he can refrain from doing this, letting the *one man* die. Is it morally permissible for Steve to throw the *switch*?

As is well known, problems like these can be shown to trigger widely shared deontic intuitions among demographically diverse populations, including young children (Gazzaniga, 2005; Greene, Sommerville, Nystrom, Darley, & Cohen, 2001; Hauser, Cushman, Young, Jin, & Mikhail, 2007; Mikhail, 2002; Mikhail et al., 1998; Petrinovich & O'Neill, 1996; Petrinovich, O'Neill, & Jorgensen, 1993; Waldmann & Dieterich, 2007). Here I wish to draw attention to some of their theoretical implications.

III

It is clear that it is difficult, if not impossible, to construct a descriptively adequate theory of these intuitions—and others like them in a potentially infinite series—based exclusively on the information given (Mikhail, 2000). Although each of these intuitions is triggered by an identifiable stimulus, how the mind goes about interpreting these hypothetical fact patterns and assigning a deontic status to the acts they depict is not something revealed in any obvious way by the scenarios themselves. Instead, an intervening step must be postulated: a pattern of organization of some sort that is imposed on the stimulus by the mind itself. Hence a simple perceptual model, such as the one implicit in Haidt's (2001) influential account of moral judgment, seems inadequate for explaining these intuitions.[1] Instead, as is the case with language perception (Chomsky, 1964), an adequate perceptual model must be more complex (figure 2.1.1).

The expanded perceptual model in figure 2.1.1 implies that, like grammaticality judgments, permissibility judgments do not necessarily depend only on the superficial properties of an action description, but also on how that action is mentally represented. In addition, it suggests that the problem of descriptive adequacy in the theory of moral cognition may be divided

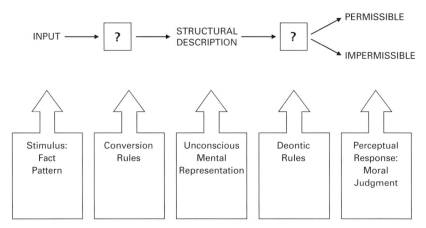

Figure 2.1.1
Expanded perceptual model for moral judgment (Mikhail, 2000).

into at least three parts: (1) the problem of describing the computational principles (deontic rules) operative in the exercise of moral judgment, (2) the problem of describing the unconscious mental representations (structural descriptions) over which those computational operations are defined, and (3) the problem of describing the chain of inferences (conversion rules) by which the stimulus is converted into an appropriate structural description.

IV

It seems equally clear that Greene's own explanation of these intuitions is neither complete nor descriptively adequate. In a series of papers, Greene argues that people rely on three features to distinguish the bystander and footbridge problems: "whether the action in question (a) could reasonably be expected to lead to serious bodily harm, (b) to a particular person or a member or members of a particular group of people (c) where this harm is not the result of deflecting an existing threat onto a different party" (Greene et al., 2001, p. 2107; see also Greene, 2005; Greene, Nystrom, Engell, Darley, & Cohen, 2004; Greene & Haidt, 2002). Greene claims to predict trolley intuitions and patterns of brain activity on this basis. However, this explanation is incomplete because we are not told how people manage to interpret the stimulus in terms of these features; surprisingly, Greene leaves this crucial first step in the perceptual process (the step involving conversion rules) unanalyzed. In addition, Greene's account is descriptively inadequate because it cannot explain even simple counter-examples like the consensual contact and disproportional death problems,[2]—let alone countless real-life examples that can be found in any casebook of torts or criminal law (Mikhail, 2002; Nichols & Mallon, 2006). Hence Greene has not shown that emotional response predicts these moral intuitions in any significant sense. Rather, his studies suggest that some perceived deontological violations are associated with strong emotional responses, something few would doubt or deny.

V

A better explanation of these intuitions is ready to hand, one that grows out of the computational approach Greene implicitly rejects. We need only assume that people are "intuitive lawyers" (Haidt, 2001) and have a "natural readiness" (Rawls, 1971) to compute mental representations of human acts in legally cognizable terms. The footbridge and bystander problems, for example, can be explained by assuming that these problems trigger distinct mental representations whose relevant temporal, causal, moral, and intentional properties can be described in the form of a two-dimensional tree diagram, successive nodes of which bear a generation relation to one another that is asymmetric, irreflexive, and transitive (Goldman, 1970; Mikhail, 2000). As these diagrams reveal, the key structural difference between these problems is that the agent commits multiple counts of battery prior to and as a means of achieving his good end in the footbridge condition (figure 2.1.2), whereas in the bystander condition, these violations are subsequent and foreseen side effects (figure 2.1.3).

The computational or moral grammar hypothesis holds that when people encounter the footbridge and bystander problems, they spontaneously generate unconscious representations like those in figures 2.1.2 and 2.1.3. Note that in addition to explaining the relevant intuitions, this hypothesis has further testable implications. For example, we can investigate the structural properties of these representations by asking subjects to evaluate probative descriptions of the relevant actions. Descriptions using the word "by" to connect individual nodes of the tree in the downward direction (e.g., "D turned the train by throwing the switch," "D killed the man by turning the train") will be deemed acceptable; by contrast, causal reversals using "by" to connect nodes in the upward direction ("D threw the switch by turning the train," "D turned the train by killing the man") will be deemed unacceptable. Likewise, descriptions using the phrase "in order to" to connect nodes in the upward direction along the vertical chain

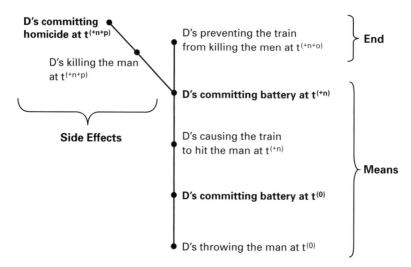

Figure 2.1.2
Mental representation of footbridge problem (Mikhail, in press).

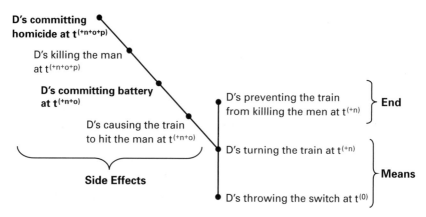

Figure 2.1.3
Mental representation of bystander problem (Mikhail, in press).

of means and ends ("D threw the switch in order to turn the train") will be deemed acceptable. By contrast, descriptions linking means with side effects ("D threw the switch in order to kill the man") will be deemed unacceptable. In short, there is an implicit geometry to these representations, which Greene and others (e.g., Sunstein, 2005) neglect, but which an adequate theory must account for (Mikhail, 2005).[3]

VI

The main theoretical problem raised by the computational hypothesis is how people manage to compute a full structural description of the relevant action that incorporates certain properties, such as ends, means, side effects, and *prima facie* wrongs like battery, when the stimulus contains no direct evidence for these properties. This is a poverty of the stimulus problem (see my contribution to volume 1 of this collection), similar in principle to determining how people manage to extract a three-dimensional representation from a two-dimensional stimulus in the theory of vision (e.g., Marr, 1982), or to determining how people recognize word boundaries in an undifferentiated auditory stimulus in the theory of language (e.g., Chomsky & Halle, 1968). Elsewhere I describe how these properties can be recovered from the stimulus by a sequence of operations that are largely mechanical (Mikhail, in press). These operations include (1) identifying the various action descriptions in the stimulus and placing them in an appropriate temporal and causal order, (2) applying certain moral and logical principles to their underlying semantic structures to generate representations of good and bad effects, (3) computing the intentional structure of the relevant acts and omissions by inferring (in the absence of conflicting evidence) that agents intend good effects and avoid bad ones, and (4) deriving representations of morally salient acts like battery and situating them in the correct location of one's act tree (Mikhail, 2000, 2002).[4] While each of these operations is relatively simple, the length, complexity, and abstract character of the process as a whole belies Greene's claim that deontological intuitions do not depend on "genuine" (this volume, p. 36), "complex" (this volume, p. 43), or "sophisticated abstract" (Greene & Haidt, 2002, p. 519) moral reasoning. In light of this, and of Greene's failure to provide an adequate description of the computations that must be attributed to individuals to explain their moral intuitions, his reliance on characterizations like these seems unwarranted.

VII

Greene rejects the computational hypothesis largely on the strength of a single counterexample, namely, Thomson's (1986) ingenious loop case. "The consensus here," he says, "is that it is morally acceptable to turn the trolley . . . despite the fact that here, as in the footbridge case, a person will be used as a means" (Greene, this volume, p. 42; see also Greene et al., 2001, p. 2106). To test this assumption, I devised the following two scenarios (Mikhail, 2000) and discovered that no such consensus exists.

Loop 1 (Ned)
Ned is taking his daily walk near the train tracks when he notices that the train that is approaching is out of control. Ned sees what has happened: the driver of the train saw five men walking across the tracks and slammed on the brakes, but the brakes failed and the driver fainted. The train is now rushing toward the five men. It is moving so fast that they will not be able to get off the track in time. Fortunately, Ned is standing next to a switch, which he can throw, that will temporarily turn the train onto a side track. There is a heavy object on the side track. If the train hits the object, the object will slow the train down, giving the men time to escape. Unfortunately, the heavy object is a man, standing on the side track with his back turned. Ned can throw the switch, preventing the train from killing the men, but killing the man. Or he can refrain from doing this, letting the five die. Is it morally permissible for Ned to throw the switch?

Loop 2 (Oscar)
Oscar is taking his daily walk near the train tracks when he notices that the train that is approaching is out of control. Oscar sees what has happened: the driver of the train saw five men walking across the tracks and slammed on the brakes, but the brakes failed and the driver fainted. The train is now rushing toward the five men. It is moving so fast that they will not be able to get off the track in time. Fortunately, Oscar is standing next to a switch, which he can throw, that will temporarily turn the train onto a side track. There is a heavy object on the side track. If the train hits the object, the object will slow the train down, giving the men time to escape. Unfortunately, *there* is a man standing on the side track *in front of the heavy object* with his back turned. Oscar can throw the switch, preventing the train from killing the men, but killing the man; or he can refrain from doing this, letting the five die. Is it morally permissible for Oscar to throw the switch?

Unlike other trolley problems, on which roughly 85–95 percent of individuals agree, there is substantial disagreement over the permissibility of intervening in the two loop cases. For example, in the initial study utilizing these problems, only 48 percent of individuals judged Ned's throwing the switch to be permissible, whereas 62 percent judged Oscar's throwing the switch to be permissible (Mikhail, 2002; see also Mikhail, 2000; Mikhail, Sorrentino, & Spelke, 1998). However, as these figures suggest, individuals did distinguish "Ned" and "Oscar" at statistically significant levels. These findings have since been replicated in a web-based experiment with several thousand subjects drawn from over 100 countries (Hauser, Cushman, Young, Jin, & Mikhail, 2007; see also Gazzaniga, 2005). Greene's account has difficulty explaining these findings, just as it has difficulty explaining the consensual contact and disproportionate death problems. All of these results, however, can be readily explained within a moral grammar framework (Mikhail, 2002).

VIII

In many respects, Greene's positive argument for an emotion-based approach to moral cognition seems quite plausible. Nevertheless, some of the evidence he adduces in its favor appears to be weaker than he assumes. His reaction-time data, for instance, are inconclusive, because the moral grammar framework makes the same predictions regarding people's reaction times and arguably provides a better explanation of them. One who permits throwing the man in the footbridge case must in effect overcome the prior recognition that this action constitutes an immediate and purposeful battery, and this process takes time; but one who prohibits throwing the switch in the bystander case need not override any such representation. Furthermore, while both the doing and forbearing of an action can be permissible without contradiction, the same is not true of the other two primary deontic operators (Mikhail, 2004). Hence Greene's reaction-time data can be explained by appealing to the cognitive dissonance resulting from the presence of a genuinely contradictory intuition in footbridge that is not present in bystander. By contrast, labeling the conflicting intuition a "prepotent negative emotional response" (Greene, this volume, p. 46) does not seem explanatory, for reasons already discussed.

Some features of Greene's experimental design also may be questioned. For example, the fact that it takes longer to approve killing one's *own* child (crying baby case) than it does to condemn "a teenage girl" for killing *hers* (infanticide case) (Greene, this volume, pp. 44–45) may not be entirely probative. Greene appears to covary multiple parameters here (cost versus benefit and first person versus third person), undermining confidence in his results. More significantly, Greene's experiments do not appear designed to investigate considered judgments in Rawls' sense, that is, judgments "in which our moral capacities are most likely to be displayed without distortion" (Rawls, 1971, p. 47), in part because most of his dilemmas are presented in the second person (e.g., "*You* are standing on a footbridge. . . . Is it appropriate for *you* to push the man?"). This presumably raises the emotional index of his scenarios and risks magnifying the role of exogenous factors.[5]

In addition, Greene does not appear to investigate deontic knowledge as such because he asks whether actions are appropriate instead of whether they are morally permissible.[6] That this question appears inapposite can be seen by considering the analogous inquiry in linguistics: asking whether an expression is "appropriate" rather than "grammatical." Chomsky (1957, p. 15) emphasized the importance of distinguishing grammatical from closely related but distinct notions like significant or meaningful, and the same logic applies here. Finally, whether one ought to perform a given action is distinct from whether the action is morally permissible, and Greene occasionally conflates this crucial distinction (see, e.g., Greene, Sommerville, Nystrom, Darley, & Cohen, 2001, p. 2105).

IX

These brief remarks are not meant to imply that Greene's project is without merit. On the contrary, I think his ideas are interesting, powerful, and at times even brilliant. His insight and creativity, clearly on display here, have helped give the field of moral psychology a much-needed boost. I would encourage him, however, to devote more effort to understanding the computational properties of moral cognition, in addition to its underlying mechanisms. Marr warned that "one has to exercise extreme caution in making inferences from neurophysiological findings about the algorithms and representations being used, particularly until one has a clear idea about what information needs to be represented and what processes need to be implemented" (Marr, 1982, p. 26). Without a better understanding of the rules and representations needed to explain widely shared moral intuitions, more caution would seem to be in order.

Notes

I wish to thank Josh Greene for writing such a thought-provoking essay and Walter Sinnott-Armstrong for his many helpful comments and suggestions on an earlier version of this commentary.

1. A notable feature of Haidt's social intuitionist model is that it provides no sustained analysis of the link between an eliciting situation and the intuitive response it generates (see Haidt, 2001, p. 814, figure 2).

2. Throwing the man in consensual contact is an action that "could reasonably be expected to lead to serious bodily harm to a particular person . . . where this harm is not the result of deflecting an existing threat onto a different party" (Greene et al., 2001, p. 2107). In Greene's account, therefore, if I understand it correctly, this case should be assigned to his moral-personal category and judged impermissible. Yet in one experimental study, 93 percent of the participants found this action to be permissible (Mikhail, 2002). Conversely, while throwing the switch in the disproportional death problem is an action that "could reasonably be expected to lead to serious bodily harm to . . . a particular group of people," it is also "the result of deflecting an existing threat onto a different party" (Greene et al., 2001, p. 2107). In Greene's account, therefore, it should be assigned to his moral-impersonal category and judged permissible. Yet in the same study, 85 percent of the participants found this action to be impermissible. How do individuals manage to come to these conclusions? The answer cannot be the one proposed by Greene et al. (2001). However, it may be that I am misinterpreting the intended scope of Greene's personal-impersonal distinction, in which case clarification would be welcome.

3. Figures 2.1.2 and 2.1.3 also raise the possibility, which Greene does not consider, that deontic intuitions can be explained on broadly deontological (i.e. rule-based) grounds without reference to rights or duties. Put differently, they suggest that these concepts (and statements incorporating them, e.g., "Hank has a right to throw the switch," "Ian has a duty not to throw the man," "The man has a right not to be thrown by Ian"), while playing an important perspectival role in deontological systems, are conceptually derivative in a manner similar to that maintained by Bentham and other utilitarian theorists (Mikhail, 2000, 2004; Tuck, 1979).

4. In the footbridge problem, for example, one must infer that the agent must *touch* and *move* the man in order to throw him onto the track in the path of the train, and the man would not *consent* to being touched and moved in this manner because of his interest in self-preservation (and because no contrary evidence is given). By contrast, in the consensual contact problem, one naturally assumes that the man *would* consent to being thrown out of the way of the train, even though doing so will injure him. The computational hypothesis holds that when people respond intuitively to these problems, they do in effect make these inferences, albeit unconsciously.

5. Of course, if one wishes to study performance errors as such, then it may make sense to manipulate and enhance the influence of exogenous factors. This seems to be the approach adopted by Haidt and his colleagues (e.g., Wheatley & Haidt, 2005; Schnall, Haidt, & Clore, 2004) in the studies of theirs that Greene relies upon.

6. See Greene et al. (2001) 2105 Data Supplement—Supplemental Data at http://www.sciencemag.org/cgi/content/full/293/5537/2105/DC1 (last visited 9/25/2001).

Mark Timmons

Doubting Deontology: Greene's Challenge

In his splendid chapter, Joshua Greene launches an all-out assault on deontological philosophy (moral theory) from the vantage point of recent empirical work in psychology and brain science. As I see it, there are at least three main options for the deontologist, ordered by how strongly they resist Greene's antideontology case. (1) Bold denial: deny that empirical work of the sort cited by Greene bears relevantly on normative moral theory generally and thus deontology in particular.[1] (2) Challenge: admit the philosophical relevance of empirical work, but challenge the empirical data brought forth by Greene by showing that there are flaws in the methodology, or that the results cannot be replicated, or something of this sort. (3) Acknowledgment: cautiously acknowledge the empirical data Greene presents, particularly his claim that commonsense deontological thinking is emotion laden, but explain how someone interested in developing a deontological moral theory can plausibly acknowledge the data in question.

I reject the first option on methodological grounds—I am sympathetic to Greene's claim that certain empirical findings are relevant to views in moral philosophy. As someone not trained in empirical science, I am not in a position to take up the challenge option and, anyway, I rather doubt that this option would pan out. So that leaves acknowledgment—the option I favor and which I will explore here. The main point I wish to make is that while Greene's arguments may work against some forms of deontology, they do not apply to other moral theories that are properly classified as deontological. Part of my strategy will be to refer to the work of some recent deontologists whose views do not seem to be affected by Greene's arguments, or at least whose views have the materials with which to mount a defense. I will proceed by considering what I take to be the four main antideontology arguments Greene employs, which I will call the misunderstanding argument, the coincidence argument, the no normative explanation argument, and the sentimentalist argument.

Defining Deontology

Deontology covers a large and rather diverse range of normative moral theories and so there is no simple way of defining it.[2] Because a very common philosophical understanding of deontology is being challenged by Greene, I need to explain how I propose to understand this view. There are four elements that seem to capture the views of such deontologists as Kant, Prichard, and Ross, who ought to count as deontologists if anyone does.

Deontology is a normative theory about the relationship between right action and value (the good) according to which (1) some actions are wrong (contrary to one's duty) owing directly to such features of the action as that it is an instance of breaking a promise, killing an innocent person, lying, injustice, and so on.[3] Such features have a reason-providing authority that may explain the action's status as being morally required (a duty), morally wrong, or morally optional. (2) Humanity has a kind of value, the proper response to which is respect rather than "promotion"; respect for humanity will permit and sometimes require that in some circumstances we not promote the best consequences as gauged from the consequentialist perspective. So characterized, deontology is supposed to contrast with its main competitors, consequentialism and virtue ethics. To make the relevant contrasts clear, we may add two corollaries as part of our characterization. (3) The rightness of an action (its being a duty) is not in general constituted by facts about how much overall intrinsic value would (actually or probably) be brought about by the action. This distinguishes it from consequentialism. (4) Deontology also denies that the rightness of an action is always constituted by facts about the characters or motives of actual or ideal agents, as is characteristic of virtue ethics.

I am not sure that this characterization is broad enough in its positive claims to capture all deontological normative theories, but it will serve present purposes well enough.[4] Let us now turn to Greene's misunderstanding argument, which would challenge this standard characterization.

The Misunderstanding Argument
Throughout much of his chapter, Greene argues that characteristic deontological responses to a range of cases are emotion-laden, intuitive "gut

reactions" rather than the result of applying rules to cases or some other rational method of moral evaluation. By dwelling on these characteristic deontological intuitions, Greene attempts to build a case for the dual claim that (1) deontology is a philosophical attempt to rationalize a range of intuitive moral reactions—characteristically deontological reactions—and (2) the true essence of deontology is a certain pattern of psychological, intuitive (nonconsequentialist) responses to real and imagined cases calling for moral judgment. Thus, deontologists have misunderstood the real essence of deontology.

Now one way to respond to Greene's appeal to intuitions is to point out that deontology need not attempt to capture all varieties of intuitive responses that he (Greene) is characterizing as deontological (a point which I'll develop in the next section) and that one can understand deontological views (at least in their Kantian versions) as having to do with respect for persons or what Kant called "humanity." This would be one way of characterizing the essence of deontology in terms of its distinctive content that would avoid Greene's deflationist psychological characterization of the view.[5] Greene anticipates this sort of move when, toward the end of his chapter, he writes:

Deontology, they [Kantians, especially of recent vintage] will say, isn't about this or that intuition. It's not defined by its normative differences with consequentialism. Rather, deontology is about taking humanity seriously. Above all else, it's about respect for persons. It's about treating others as fellow rational creatures rather than as mere objects, about acting for reasons that rational beings can share. (this volume, pp. 72–73)

According to Greene, this response won't do because attempting to characterize deontology in terms of such values as humanity and the equal respect that is a fitting response to this value will fail to distinguish deontology from other moral theories, including consequentialism. Greene says:

It seems to me that consequentialists, as much as anyone else, have respect for persons, are against treating people as mere objects, wish to act for reasons that rational creatures can share, etc. A consequentialist respects other persons and refrains from treating them as mere objects by counting every person's well-being in the decision-making process. Likewise, a consequentialist attempts to act according to reasons that rational creatures can share by acting according to principles that give equal weight to everyone's interests, i.e., that are impartial. (this volume, p. 73)

These remarks are supposed to block the attempt by philosophers to understand deontology in terms of a notion like respect for persons and thus

bolster the original two claims: (1) philosophers have not properly characterized a real difference between deontology and consequentialism and
furthermore (2) if we dwell on the differences in commonsense moral reactions that differentiate deontological responses from consequentialist
responses, we are led to real differences in the distinctive psychologies
of these responses. Deontologists thus mischaracterize their view and so
fail to understand its true nature. This is Greene's misunderstanding
argument.

In response, a Kantian deontologist is going to insist that even if consequentialists can talk about the importance of equal respect for all persons
and the value of humanity, there is still a nonconsequentialist, distinctively deontological conception of humanity that can serve as a basis (or
at least a partial basis) for systematizing deontological moral principles
of right conduct.[6] If this is right, then deontologists (at least those of a
Kantian bent) can, after all, characterize their moral theory by appeal to
the concept of humanity (properly interpreted). This point is, I think, well
illustrated in the work of two recent deontologists, Robert Audi (2004) and
T. M. Scanlon (1998). For brevity's sake, I'll make the point using Audi's
view; later I make use of some ideas from Scanlon.

Audi's "Kantian intuitionism" involves an attempt to (1) systematize a
Rossian theory of moral obligation (featuring a plurality of principles of
prima facie duty) by deriving them from the humanity formulation of the
categorical imperative and then (2) grounding the systematized set of
principles in a theory of intrinsic value.[7] The overall result is a value-based
deontology (Audi, 2004, p. 145). A value broad enough to serve as a ground
is what, following Kant, Audi calls dignity, together with the attitude of
respect that this status demands. So in the end, moral obligation is grounded
in considerations of respect for persons[8]—a Kantian, nonconsequentialist
notion of what constitutes respecting persons. Audi grants that the notions
of human dignity and respect are, as he says "open-ended": "Their application is limited, however, in that they operate together and (so far as we
are working within broadly Kantian constraints) both are fruitfully understood in reflective equilibrium with the categorical imperative, which in
turn must be understood in reflective equilibrium with Rossian duties"
(Audi 2004, p. 144; see also pp. 157–158).[9]

Thus, Greene is right to claim that deontologists will likely insist that
their theory is not about "this or that intuition." Rather, it is a distinctive
normative theory that can be understood (at least for Kantians) as trying
to capture in its theory of right conduct the appropriate way—a nonconsequentialist way—of respecting humanity. And isn't this sufficient for

properly characterizing deontology or at least Kantian strains of the view? So I don't think the deontologist—at least of a Kantian bent—is properly accused of not understanding the true essence of her theory. We can help strengthen this verdict by seeing how a deontologist can respond to some of Greene's other arguments.

Defending Deontology

In response to Greene's arguments against deontology, I think it is important to stress the importance of reflection in going from the raw materials of intuitive moral response to a moral theory. As Greene notes (in his remark about deontology not being about this or that intuition), the deontologist need not embrace unreflective moral reactions. Rather, the deontologist will claim that proper reflection on our various moral reactions of all sorts will yield a set of moral principles that we have reason to endorse, and that their overall structure will be deontological. Those principles in turn will help us discriminate "correct" or justified moral judgments from "incorrect" or unjustified moral judgments.

One clear example of the centrality of reflection in developing a version of deontology with a decidedly Kantian flavor is Scanlon's (1998) contractualist moral theory. The heart and soul of Scanlon's view is an account of proper moral thinking that is supposed to yield a set of moral principles (concerning our obligations to others) guided by the idea that a correct moral principle is one that we can justify to others. I won't elaborate the details of Scanlon's complex account of moral thinking here; I don't think they matter for present purposes. What does matter is that Scanlon proposes a roughly Kantian account of moral thinking that presumably has the power to move us beyond our unreflective moral judgments toward a deontological moral theory. Scanlon provides many examples of how his proposed methodology can take us beyond unreflective intuitions to a refined set of moral principles. I refer the reader in particular to what Scanlon says about the morality of taking human life (1998, pp. 199–200) and promising (1998, chap. 7). The centrality of reflection is also an important element of Audi's Kantian intuitionism.[10] Let us now turn to what are perhaps Greene's two strongest arguments against deontology.

The Coincidence Argument

Greene's critique is aimed at deontology per se, but in the latter part of his essay he begins referring to "rationalist deontology." Greene doesn't tell us what he means here by "rationalist," but I gather from what he says in the section entitled, "Rationalism, Rationalization, and Deontological Judgment," that talk of rationalist deontology involves at least these two claims: (1) Moral judgments are beliefs and not emotions and (2) there is an independent realm of moral facts that serve as truth-makers for true moral beliefs. The gist of Greene's case against rationalist deontology seems to be the following. In light of the evidence for the claim that characteristically deontological judgments are highly emotion-charged, together with the fact that there is a good evolutionary explanation for why we would have dispositions to make such judgments, the rationalist deontologist is going to have to explain how it is that there is this coincidence between our intuitive emotional reactions and an independent moral truth. Greene claims (this volume, p. 69) that Kant appeals to God in attempting to explain the coincidence and that any nontheological or metaphysical explanation is not likely to be forthcoming. For example, in connection with retributivist-deontological theories of punishment, Greene writes:

[I]t seems that retributivist theories of punishment are just rationalizations for our retributivist feelings, and that these feelings only exist because of the morally irrelevant constraints placed on natural selection in designing creatures that behave in fitness-enhancing ways. In other words, the natural history of our retributivist dispositions makes it unlikely that they reflect any sort of deep moral truth. (this volume, p. 71)

More generally about commonsense deontological thinking, he writes:

My claim at this point is simply that it is unlikely that inclinations that evolved as evolutionary by-products correspond to some independent, rationally discoverable moral truth. (this volume, p. 72)

So what I am calling the coincidence challenge to the deontologist comes to this: explain why we should think that our intuitive moral responses with this sort of evolutionary history are tracking independent moral facts?

Here Greene stacks the deck against the deontologist by assuming that moral realism is essential to deontology. It isn't. Scanlon's constructivist version of deontology accepts an essentially cognitivist account of moral judgment but claims that moral truth is constituted by some set of idealized attitudes or responses.[11] In Scanlon's view in particular, and constructivist views in general, there are no independent moral facts to which true moral judgments must correspond. Rather, the constructivist takes moral truth to be a matter of ideally justified moral judgments and principles. If a Kantian deontologist can provide a plausible account of moral thinking that takes us from unreflective intuitive judgments to a set of moral judgments which, ideally at least, constitute moral truth, then there would not seem to be some unexplained coincidence between the principles and judgments that a deontological theory yields and moral truth, so conceived. Thus, I don't see how the coincidence argument, as least as I understand it, is a challenge to deontology per se. (Maybe a realist-deontologist can mount a plausible defense against this objection, but I will leave that to others.)

Of course, Greene might say that there are more and less robust forms of independence and that his basic complaint applies mutatis mutandis to metaethical views that embrace the kind of modest independence featured in certain versions of moral constructivism like Scanlon's, according to which moral truth is independent of those moral principles we happen to accept. How would this version of the objection go? The idea would be that a constructivist deontologist owes us an explanation of why we have good normative reason to endorse deontological principles when the various commonsense deontological judgments seem to be the result of factors that are either morally irrelevant or at least not compatible with deontological reasons.

Again, I think this is a challenge that the deontologist can plausibly meet. For instance, Scanlon argues that we (non-amoralists) have reason to want our actions to be justifiable to others and that this reason provides a normative basis for explaining why moral reasons have the status and special importance they do seem to have.[12] So, in Scanlon's view, there is a good normative reason to endorse and care about the various moral reasons featured in a deontological theory.

The No Normative Explanation Argument

Another argument that Greene employs when he reviews the various bits of empirical evidence regarding commonsense deontological reactions is that attempts by deontologist philosophers to provide a normative characterization of the difference between deontological responses and consequentialist responses fail. In the trolley footbridge examples, for instance, one might propose (as a normative explanation of people's different reactions between these cases) the principle that one should not use another, innocent person merely as a means to some good end. Against this proposal, Greene cites Thomson's trolley loop example to show that this principle can't make the intuitively appropriate distinctions. Greene makes similar claims about other cases he discusses.

What does this apparent failure to come up with normative principles show about deontology? One might suppose that it only shows that philosophers have not discovered the correct normative principles that would explain the different reactions in question. Perhaps they involve significant complexity and are difficult to formulate properly. The underlying principles that explain grammatical competence display a certain level of complexity that requires linguistic theory to uncover. Why not think that a similar thing is true regarding competent moral judgment and moral theory? Or, even if one is skeptical of there being such principles, why suppose that the deontologist is committed to holding that there must be principles of this sort? To sharpen these two points, let us consider some examples.

One might think of Scanlon's deontological view as compatible with the idea that there are underlying moral principles that have sufficient explanatory force of the sort Greene seems to demand. For Scanlon, moral principles "are general conclusions about the status of various kinds of reasons for action" (1998, p. 199), and arriving at justified moral principles is often a complex task requiring interpretation and judgment. In Scanlon's view, moral thinking about cases often involves refining overly simple moral generalizations such as "don't kill" and "don't lie" in which we appeal to a complex of relevant considerations bearing on a particular case under consideration in arriving at a more refined complex principle that we can see can be justified to others. Such principles may again be refined in light of the details of some further case. The process is thus one of refinement. This model of moral principles would presumably have us begin with fairly crude generalizations that prohibit intentional killing of innocent persons and refine them in light of the various morally relevant considerations featured in the trolley loop case, attempting to arrive at a refined moral principle that no one could reasonably reject. Again, Scanlon's view can arguably yield principles that explain the rightness or wrongness of an action by mentioning those morally relevant considerations that bear on the case at hand.

Audi's normative moral theory perhaps represents the most direct response to Greene's remarks about the limits of the Kantian requirement that we not treat others as mere means. According to Audi's Kantian intuitionism that I mentioned earlier, we are able to derive a plurality of Rossian duties from Kant's humanity formulation of the categorical imperative, and we can use the requirement that we not treat others as mere means as a guide for our deliberations in cases where these duties conflict. Now Greene might think that Audi's view is a sitting duck for cases like the trolley loop case, where it looks as if one ought (or is at least morally permitted) to use the lone innocent worker as a means for saving a greater number of innocent people. Why suppose that the principle that we are to avoid treating people as mere means (the negative part of Kant's principle) states an exceptionless generalization? If one wants to claim that the lone innocent person is being used as a mere means (which is not entirely clear to me), then why not suppose that there can be difficult cases in which the all-things-considered morally correct thing to do is to treat the person as a mere means? In allowing for this possibility, we still have a very general moral principle that provides an important ceteris paribus constraint on morally permissible action and which can fulfill the unifying role envisioned by Audi.

Again, a deontologist might reject the idea that there are unrestricted moral principles that can be used to adjudicate conflicts among more particular principles of prima facie duty. This was Ross's view. He denied that there is a super principle that has relatively determinate implications and that can plausibly be used to adjudicate conflicts between prima facie duties. However, Ross's set of basic prima facie duties provides us with a moral framework within which we can reason about particular cases. In response to the trolley loop case, Ross would have us consider the details of the case in which the duties of beneficence and nonmaleficence seem most relevant and use practical judgment to adjudicate this particular conflict of prima facie duties.

Finally, it is worth mentioning that there are particularist versions of deontology of the sort we find in Prichard (1912/2002) that would deny that there are moral principles—of either the hard, exceptionless variety or of soft, ceteris paribus variety. So if Greene's objection here rests on the assumption that for the deontologist there must be moral principles that have the kind of determinacy sufficient to clearly and cleanly resolve hard moral cases, a particularist deontologist can simply deny the assumption.

The bottom line here is that Greene seems to suppose that the deontologist, in developing his or her theory, needs to come up with moral generalizations that (1) will distinguish deontological judgments (at least the ones a deontologist wants to endorse) from consequentialist judgments and (2) will articulate the normative basis for the judgments it implies. I think there are various ways in which this challenge can be met by deontologists who go in for moral principles, as illustrated by the views of Scanlon, Audi, and Ross. Also, a deontologist following Prichard need not embrace moral principles.

Developing Deontology

So far, I have been explaining how I think a rationalist-deontologist is likely to respond to Greene's arguments. In doing so, I have stressed (1) the importance of a decidedly deontological conception of humanity as a normative basis for deontological principles of right conduct, (2) the role of reflection in going from intuitive moral responses to a normative moral theory, (3) constructivism about moral truth, and (4) the role that principles might (or might not) play in a deontological moral theory. I suppose that Greene might think that all of this maneuvering is not really going to help the deontologist at the end of the day because the entire basis of deontological thinking is emotion-laden intuitive responses. One remaining objection that is largely implicit in Greene's chapter but worth bringing out is the sentimentalist argument.

The Sentimentalist Argument

Deontology is committed to the idea that moral judgments are beliefs or are more cognitive than the evidence shows us; in short, deontology is committed to moral rationalism. However, in light of empirical evidence about people's intuitive moral judgments, a nonrationalist, sentimentalist account of them is more plausible than rationalist accounts. Thus, deontology is mistaken.

I am generally sympathetic to sentimentalism—as long as one doesn't overplay the role of sentiment in moral judgment (as I believe many sentimentalists are inclined to do),[13] and as long as one does not give up on the idea that moral judgments are a species of belief.[14] Although all of the versions of deontology that I know of have been embedded in a rationalist metaethic, I don't see why one cannot embrace sentimentalism (or expressivism) and go on to defend a deontological moral theory. Sentimentalism is a metaethical account about the nature of moral judgment; deontology is a normative theory about the right, the good, and their relation to one another. Although sentimentalism may seem to fit most comfortably with consequentialism, accepting the former metaethical view does not commit one to the latter normative moral theory.[15] So again, I don't see how (without further elaboration) the empirical facts about emotion-laden, intuitive moral reactions pose a threat to deontology. Indeed, I would suggest that the way to develop a deontological moral theory is to do so within the framework of a broadly sentimentalist metaethic.

Conclusion

There are other important and pressing challenges that Greene raises that I cannot take up here, including doubts about the evidential credentials of moral intuitions generally.[16] As far as I can tell, deontology per se is not threatened by the empirical work cited by Greene; there are versions of deontology that can avoid Greene's arguments. The deontologist can appeal to a Kantian notion of respect for persons to systematize a set of soft ceteris paribus moral principles that are arrived at by an appropriate deontological method of moral deliberation that (if one accepts moral constructivism) constitute moral truth. Indeed, I suggest that empirical science can help the deontologist develop a sentimentalist metaethical framework to complement deontology. My colleague Michael Gill and I think the direction to go is toward a sentimentalist deontology, a view we plan to articulate and defend in the near future.

Notes

I wish to thank Robert Audi, Michael Gill, and especially Walter Sinnott-Armstrong for their many helpful comments on a previous version of this commentary.

1. Bold denial represents a denial of a "naturalizing" approach to philosophical problems.

2. See Freeman (2001) for a characterization of deontology that properly reflects this point.

3. With regard to metaphysical issues about the nature of right- and wrong-making properties or facts, one could distinguish among monist (Kant on some readings), pluralist (Ross 1930), and particularist (Prichard 2002) versions of deontology, but these intratheoretical differences will not be relevant for present purposes.

4. Points 1 and 2 may be too restrictive to count as requirements for a deontological theory, but all I am trying to do here is specify some common characteristics that we find in representatives of this kind of view, particularly those in the Kantian tradition who are the main target of Greene's criticisms.

5. Here I am taking Greene's misunderstanding argument as a challenge leveled against typical understandings of deontological moral theories in terms of their content. However, as Walter Sinnott-Armstrong pointed out to me, one might take Greene's challenge to be focused on the basis of deontological theories. I respond briefly to this latter form of challenge in a later section.

6. That the notion of equal respect is open ended and can be variously interpreted to fit with a variety of moral theories is a point nicely made by James Griffin (1986, p. 208; see also pp. 231, 239).

7. The kind of grounding in question is what Audi calls "ontic," which he contrasts with epistemic and inferential grounding (see Audi, 2004, p. 141).

8. Audi (2004, chap. 4, esp. pp. 141–145) holds that although moral obligations can be grounded in considerations of value, they do not need such ontic grounding to be known.

9. Audi (2004, p. 144) goes on to say that the relevant notion of dignity can be partially anchored in nonmoral notions of our rational capacities and sentience. Thus, there are some nonmoral constraints on the interpretation of this concept.

10. Audi appeals to reflection in defending a conception of epistemological intuitionism in ethics (2004, pp. 45–48) and in explaining how Kant's humanity formulation can be used to derive principles of prima facie duty (2004, pp. 90–105).

11. Other Kantian constructivists include John Rawls (1971, 1980), Christine Korsgaard (1996b), and Onora O'Neill (1996).

12. See Scanlon (1998, chap. 3, esp. pp. 153–168).

13. For instance, I think it is a mistake for a sentimentalist to understand the content of ordinary moral judgments as being about certain sentiments as Gibbard does. See Nichols (2004b, chap. 4) for a critique of Gibbard's view and Gibbard's (2006) reply to Nichols.

14. According to the metaethical view that Terry Horgan and I favor (which we are calling "cognitivist expressivism"), moral judgments are genuine beliefs (hence we are cognitivists), but they are not descriptive beliefs (which puts us into the expressivist-sentimentalist camp). Our view is meant to challenge any kind of sharp reason versus sentiment dichotomy. See Horgan and Timmons (2006) and a forerunner of this view in Timmons (1999).

15. Blackburn (1993, p. 164) makes this point. I thank Michael Gill for this reference.

16. See Sinnott-Armstrong (2006) for objections to moral intuitionism based on findings in empirical psychology.

Joshua D. Greene

Many thanks to John Mikhail and Mark Timmons for their thoughtful and challenging comments. Each of these authors teaches valuable lessons. The lessons they teach, however, are rather different, and so I will reply to them separately.

Reply to Mikhail

The first thing to note about John Mikhail's commentary on my chapter is that it is bold and incisive. Mikhail makes a number of strong claims about the limitations of my arguments, and many of these constitute serious challenges. The second thing to note about Mikhail's commentary on my chapter is that it is not really a commentary on my chapter. Rather, it is more or less a critique of my first neuroimaging paper (Greene, Sommerville, Nystrom, Darley, & Cohen, 2001), with some reference to subsequent interpretation (Greene & Haidt, 2002).

In my discussion here I advance a general empirical thesis: that deontological philosophy is largely a rationalization of emotional moral intuitions. While the results of my first neuroimaging study feature prominently in support of this thesis, my case is deliberately based on convergent evidence from many different experiments that bear directly on this issue (Baron, Gowda, & Kunreuther, 1993; Baron & Ritov, 1993; Carlsmith, Darley, & Robinson, 2002; de Quervain, Fischbacher, Treyer, Schellhammer, Schnyder, et al., 2004; Greene, Nystrom, Engell, Darley, & Cohen, 2004; Haidt, Koller, & Dias, 1993; Kahneman, Schkade, & Sunstein, 1998; Sanfey, Rilling, Aronson, Nystrom, & Cohen, 2003; Schnall, Haidt, & Clor, 2004; Small & Loewenstein, 2003, 2005; Wheatley & Haidt, 2005) as well as a number of experiments and theories that provide background support. In light of this, it is surprising that Mikhail focuses his attention exclusively on a single study. Despite this narrow focus, he raises a number of important issues, and I will address them here. I will argue that our disagreements are real, but not as deep they may appear to be. I will make some concessions, stand my ground in other instances, and attempt to show the way forward.

According to Mikhail, a "notable weakness" of my research program is my "neglect of computational theory," which I "implicitly reject." I do not reject computational theories, implicitly or otherwise. (On the contrary, some of my *best friends* are computational theories, although I sometimes forget to call them on their birthdays.) It is true, however, that I have no computational theory to call my own. At least not yet. Mikhail, in contrast, does have a computational theory of moral judgment, which he briefly summarizes in his commentary. While my theory is "incomplete" and "descriptively inadequate," the relevant data can, according to Mikhail, be "readily explained within a moral grammar framework."

In my 2001 paper, my co-authors and I put forth a specific account of the standard trolley intuitions (that it's morally acceptable to trade one life for five in the *trolley* (bystander) case, but not in the *footbridge* case). In his present commentary and elsewhere (Mikhail, 2000, forthcoming), Mikhail offers a competing account of this phenomenon. My current opinion is that both of these accounts are "incomplete" and "descriptively inadequate." Despite this, I think that both accounts reflect genuine insights. In the following pages I will attempt to explain what is right and not-so-right about our respective efforts to solve this problem.

The primary purpose of my first neuroimaging study was to find preliminary evidence for a set of related and fairly general ideas: Some moral decision making, I proposed, is driven by emotional intuitions, while other moral decision making is a product of abstract reasoning or is at least more "cognitive" (see my chapter here). I proposed further that this duality in moral thought is reflected in the standard trolley intuitions. When a moral violation is "personal" (as in the *footbridge* case), it triggers a strong, negative emotional response that inclines people to judge against it. When a moral violation is "impersonal" (as in the *trolley* case), there is no comparable emotional response, and the judgment is made in a "cooler," more "cognitive" way. This general idea has an evolutionary rationale. I propose that we are disposed to respond emotionally to the kinds of personal moral violations that featured prominently in the course of human evolution, compared with moral violations that are peculiarly modern in ways that make them more "impersonal." I believe that these general ideas are correct and that they are supported by a substantial and growing body of data, including more recent data not covered in my chapter.

In designing our study, my collaborators and I were not committed to a specific hypothesis concerning what, exactly, triggers the hypothesized emotional responses to cases like the *footbridge* case. Nevertheless, our experimental design required that we take a stab at answering this question. (fMRI data are noisy, requiring repeated stimuli within each experimental condition. This meant that we had to define one class of dilemmas that are like the *footbridge* case and a distinct class of dilemmas that are like the *trolley* case. That meant that we had to say, if only provisionally, what the crucial difference between the *trolley* and *footbridge* cases is.) This is what we came up with: A moral violation is categorized as "personal" (as in the *footbridge* case) if it (1) could reasonably be expected to lead to serious bodily harm, (2) to a particular person or a member or members of a particular group of people (3) where this harm is not the result of deflecting an existing threat onto a different party. Moral violations that fail to meet these three criteria (as in the *trolley* case) are categorized as "impersonal." My co-authors and I suspected that this way of drawing the personal versus impersonal distinction would not fare well in the long run, and said so, describing it as a "first cut" and as "by no means definitive." It is now clear that this way of drawing this distinction does not work, but not necessarily for the reasons that Mikhail and others (Nichols & Mallon, 2006) have suggested, as I will explain.

First, this provisional hypothesis does not predict that all personal moral violations (as in the *footbridge* case) will be deemed inappropriate, or even deemed inappropriate by a majority of people. Rather, we claimed that personal moral violations trigger emotional responses that *incline* people to judge against them, but that these emotional responses can be overridden, particularly by utilitarian considerations. Thus, cases in which people judge "personal" moral violations to be appropriate, as in Mikhail's "consensual contact" case (pushing someone out of the way of an oncoming trolley) and Nichols and Mallon's "catastrophe" case (killing one person to save billions of others) (Nichols & Mallon, 2006), pose no problem for our hypothesis. On the contrary, cases like these (i.e., cases in which there is an exceptionally strong utilitarian rationale for committing a personal moral violation) have provided essential reaction-time and neuroimaging data (Greene et al., 2004; Greene et al., 2001). Second, our provisional hypothesis does not predict that all impersonal moral violations will be deemed appropriate. Thus, for similar reasons, Mikhail's "disproportional death" case (turning a trolley onto five persons in order to save one) makes no trouble. According to our view, the absence of a personal moral violation means that there is little emotional response, which leads to a default, utilitarian decision-making process. The judgment produced by this utilitarian process depends, of course, on the balance of costs and benefits and is not determined simply by the fact that the dilemma in question is "impersonal."

That said, there are several cases that *do* make trouble for our provisional hypothesis. The most damaging of these was, unbeknownst to us, already in the philosophical literature. This is Frances Kamm's "Lazy Susan" case (Kamm, 1996), which I will not discuss here. (I have since tested a version of this case and confirmed that it is indeed a counterexample.) Another case that makes trouble for our provisional hypothesis is Nichols and Mallon's teacups case (Nichols & Mallon, 2006). They presented subjects with modified versions of the *trolley* and *footbridge* cases in which teacups were substituted for people. Subjects took the action in the teacuppified *footbridge* case to be a more serious rule infraction than the action in the teacuppified *trolley* case, despite the fact that both of these cases are "impersonal" (because there is no bodily harm involved in either case). These results strongly suggest that there is at least some aspect of the *trolley-footbridge* effect that has nothing to do with personal violence. Finally, there are Mikhail's cases of *Ned* and *Oscar*. As Mikhail points out, the differences in people's responses to these two cases cannot be explained by appeal to any version of the personal/impersonal distinction.

Despite all this, the *general theory* presented in my 2001 paper (and elaborated upon in my chapter here) is well supported by published data, with more on the way. This general theory encompasses several claims:

1. Intuitive responses play an important role in moral judgment.
2. More specifically, intuitive responses drive people to give nonutilitarian responses to moral dilemmas that have previously been categorized as "personal."
3. This includes the *footbridge* case.
4. These intuitive responses are emotional (i.e., constituted or driven by emotions).
5. Cases like the *footbridge* case elicit negative emotional responses because they involve a kind of harm that is in *some sense* more personal than other kinds of harm.
6. We respond more emotionally to these "personal" harms because such harms, unlike others, were prominent during the course of human evolution.

Claim (6) remains a matter of evolutionary speculation. There is a great deal of evidence in favor of (1) and for the general importance of emotion in moral judgment, much of it covered in my chapter here and elsewhere (Greene, 2005; Haidt, 2001). Regarding claims (2) and (4), there are the neuroimaging data from the 2001 paper itself. The "personal" cases produced increased activity in brain regions associated with emotion. These data have two principal limitations. First, these brain regions are not exclusively associated with emotion. Second, the activity observed in these brain regions could reflect incidental emotional activity that does not affect people's judgments. The reaction-time data presented alongside these neuroimaging data were collected in order to address this second concern.

The argument is as follows. If there is an emotional response that inclines people to say "no" to personal moral violations, then people should take longer when they end up saying "yes." If instead the emotional response is triggered later by the judgment itself, then it should have no effect on how long it takes people to make their judgments. And if the emotional response occurs in parallel with the judgment, then it could slow down people's judgments in a general way, but there is no reason to think that it would selectively interfere with one kind of answer. We found, as predicted, that "yes" answers are slower than "no" answers in response to personal moral dilemmas, with no comparable effect for impersonal dilemmas.

Mikhail claims that his theory can account for these data, but this is not so. According to my theory, people are slow to approve of personal moral violations because they must overcome a countervailing emotional response in order to do so. Mikhail suggests that they take longer because they "must overcome the prior recognition that this action constitutes an immediate and purposeful battery" (this volume, p. 89). While this could be true, it requires not only a major addition to Mikhail's theory, but an acknowledgment that there is real moral thinking (and not just noise and failures of "performance") outside of what Mikhail calls the "moral grammar." This is because Mikhail's theory makes no reference to any process that can overcome the initial deontic categorization produced by the moral grammar. Any such process is, from the point of view of Mikhail's theory, a *deus ex machina*. More specifically, Mikhail offers no positive explanation for why anyone would ever say that it's okay to push the guy off the footbridge. His theory, as stated, would be at its strongest if 100% of people said "no" to the *footbridge* case, which means that any "yes" answers given in response to this case are, as far as Mikhail's theory is concerned, just noise.

My view, in contrast, is that cases like the *footbridge* dilemma elicit competition between an intuitive emotional response and a more controlled and "cognitive" utilitarian response, supported by activity in the dorsolateral prefrontal cortex (Greene et al., 2004). If Mikhail thinks that the output of the moral grammar is often forced to compete with some other kind of response, then his view is much closer to my "dual-process" view than it otherwise appears to be. The same is true if these competing responses are taken to be *part of* the moral grammar. However, if these competing responses are taken to be part of a specifically *moral* grammar, then Mikhail needs to explain why these processes bear such a striking neural resemblance to functionally similar control processes at work in nonmoral contexts (Greene et al., 2004). In other words, the mechanism behind the utilitarian judgments appear to be *domain general*. In either case, Mikhail's response to the reaction-time data seems to turn his theory into a special case of the general theory outlined here (claims 1–5). We agree that something about the action in the *footbridge* case triggers an intuitive response that inclines people to say "no" (claims 1–3). The only question then is whether we should call this intuitive response "emotional" (claim 4). In my chapter, I explain what I mean by "emotion." For a representation to be "emotional," it must be quick, automatic, etc., and also *valenced*. It must "say" that something is good or bad. And isn't that a perfect description of what Mikhail's moral grammar is supposed to deliver? A little voice that pops out of nowhere and says "No! That would be wrong!"

Well, we could spend an academic eternity arguing about whether the outputs of Mikhail's moral grammar should be called "emotional" by definition. However, that's not necessary because there are now three (and possibly four) new and independent pieces of evidence supporting my claim that emotional processes are responsible for generating the sorts of nonutilitarian responses we typically see in the *footbridge* case. More generally, these results (which are discussed in the following paragraphs) provide further evidence that there is a qualitative difference between the competing psychological processes that drive utilitarian versus nonutilitarian responses, making it even more of a strain to describe these processes as part of a single "grammar." (Of course, any cognitive system can be described as implementing a grammar, depending on what one means by "grammar.")

Patients with frontotemporal dementia (FTD) are known for their "emotional blunting" and lack of empathy. Recently, Mario Mendez and others presented FTD patients, Alzheimer's patients, and normal control subjects with versions of the *trolley* and *footbridge* dilemmas (Mendez, Anderson, & Shapira, 2005). A strong majority in all three groups said that they would hit the switch in the *trolley* case, but, as predicted, the FTD patients diverged sharply in their responses to the *footbridge* case. While only 23 percent of the Alzheimer's patients and 19 percent of the normal control subjects said that they would push the guy off the *footbridge*, 57 percent of the FTD patients said they would do this, which is exactly what one would expect from patients who lack the emotional responses that drive ordinary people's responses to this case.

Michael Koenigs, Liane Young, and others have generated similar results in a recent study of patients with ventromedial prefrontal damage, another clinical population known for their emotional deficits (Damasio, 1994). They presented these patients with the set of "personal" moral dilemmas used in my 2001 study and found, as predicted, that these patients gave far more utilitarian answers than control patients and normal control subjects (Koenigs, Young, Cushman, Adolphs, Tranel, Damasio, & Hauser, 2007).

Valdesolo and DeSteno tested normal subjects with versions of the *trolley* and *footbridge* cases in conjunction with an emotion induction paradigm (Valdesolo & DeSteno, 2006). Subjects in the experimental condition watched a funny clip from *Saturday Night Live*. The control group watched a neutral film. Which film people watched had no significant effect on their responses to the *trolley* case, but the group that watched the SNL clip were about three times more likely to say that it's okay to push the man off the *footbridge*. Valdesolo and DeSteno predicted this for the following reason. If the negative response to the footbridge case is driven by a negative emotional response, then that response could be counteracted by a stimulus that produces a positive emotional response (i.e., a funny film clip).

Finally, my colleagues and I have conducted a cognitive load study (Greene, Morelli, Lowenberg, Nystrom, & Cohen, submitted) using difficult personal moral dilemmas (like the *crying baby* case). We have found that burdening subjects with a cognitive load slows down their utilitarian moral judgments while it has no effect on (and possibly even speeds up) their deontological judgments. This is to be expected if deontological judgments, but not utilitarian judgments, are driven by intuitive emotional responses. (Whether this study provides additional evidence for the involvement of intuitive *emotional* processes depends, however, on whether one accepts my definition of "emotion.")

The neuroimaging and reaction time data presented in my 2001 paper strongly suggest that intuitive emotional responses incline people toward deontological responses to "personal" moral dilemmas (including the *footbridge* case). Nevertheless, this first study left ample room for doubt. The studies just described, in contrast, leave little room for doubt. What, exactly, triggers these emotional responses, however, remains unknown. My original hypothesis is clearly wrong. Nevertheless, there is new evidence to suggest that the personal/impersonal distinction can be redrawn in a way that accounts for at least some of the data (claim 5). Fiery Cushman and colleagues have tested a version of the footbridge case in which the man on the footbridge, rather than getting pushed off the footbridge, can be dropped through a trapdoor operated by a nearby switch. They found that people judge saving the five to be more acceptable in the trapdoor version (Cushman, Young, & Hauser, 2006). (I independently ran the same experiment and got the same results.) These results strongly suggest that at least part of the *trolley-footbridge* effect has to do with "personalness," broadly construed.

What about Mikhail's alternative explanation of the *trolley-footbridge* effect? His theory can be understood on two levels. At the most general level, his theory is simply a descriptive restatement of the "doctrine of double effect," which turns crucially on the distinction between harming someone as a means and harming someone as a side effect. Mikhail's view goes further, however, in describing a plausible computational mechanism by which we might unconsciously distinguish means from side effect. (See also Michael Costa's similar theory [Costa, 1992]). Unfortunately, the means/side-effect distinction has severe limitations when it comes to explaining people's moral judgment behavior. And these limitations, of course, carry over to any more specific, computational account of how this distinction is applied. I will say, however, that Mikhail's theory is highly elegant and ingenious, and I suspect that there is something importantly right about it. Nevertheless, in its present form his theory doesn't work very well.

According to Mikhail's theory, subjects should say that any act of "intentional battery" (harming someone as a means) is wrong. However, as I have pointed out, people do not say this about the loop case (*Ned*), in which a person is used as a means to stop a trolley. In Mikhail's sample, about half of the subjects (48 percent) say that it is morally permissible for Ned to do this. While there may be no "consensus" in favor of running the guy over in this case, these data still make serious trouble for Mikhail's theory because approximately half the subjects *do the opposite of what his theory predicts*. To make matters worse, I have tested my own version of the *loop* case (using what I regard as less loaded language), and so far 73 percent of subjects say that it's morally acceptable to run the guy over. What's more, I have tested several other trolley variations that are structurally different from the *loop* case, but that still involve killing someone as a means. In response to one of these cases, 84% of subjects (so far) say that it's okay to sacrifice the one person. As Mikhail points out, the means/side-effect distinction accounts for the fact that 62% of his subjects say that it's okay for *Oscar* (side-effect loop) to kill the one person while only 48% of his subjects say that it's okay for *Ned* (means loop) to kill the one person. And that's something. As I've said, the personal/impersonal distinction does nothing to explain this effect, and based on the data from these two cases, I'm inclined to believe that there is something right about Mikhail's theory. Nevertheless, explaining the 14% gap in people's responses to these two cases, however impressive, is a far cry from explaining the 60% to 80% gap between the *trolley* and *footbridge* cases. There is a lot more going on here.

Before closing, let me respond to a handful of Mikhail's remaining criticisms. First, Mikhail raises a worry about confounds in the design of my 2001 study. The particular one that he cites (killing one's own child versus someone else's killing her child) is not a concern because no dilemmas that differed along this dimension were contrasted in this study. There is, however, a more general worry about confounds in this study because the dilemmas respectively designated as "personal" and "impersonal" may differ in any number of unforeseen ways. We acknowledged this possibility in our paper, calling our personal/impersonal distinction a "first cut" and emphasizing the need for further research aimed at figuring out exactly what differences between these two sets of stimuli elicit the differences we observed in the fMRI and reaction-time data. In our subsequent work we have designed our experiments (e.g., the second analysis in our second neuroimaging paper [Greene et al., 2004] and the cognitive load study described earlier) to avoid such confounds, examining differences in neural activity and reaction time that are based on subjects' *responses* rather than the stimuli to which the subjects are responding.

Second, Mikhail raises concerns about our use of moral dilemmas presented in the second person, which may be more emotional than dilemmas presented in the third person. That may be so, but that's not a reason to ignore them in one's attempts to understand moral psychology. Moreover, the behavioral results generated using the second-person versions of the *trolley* and *footbridge* cases are broadly comparable to those generated using the third-person versions. It would be strikingly unparsimonious to suppose that we need one psychological theory to account for the *trolley-footbridge* effect in third-person cases and a completely different theory to account for the same effect in second-person cases. Finally, Mikhail raises a concern about our asking subjects to judge whether actions are "appropriate" rather than "morally permissible." Because of this word choice, Mikhail claims, our study may not have been an investigation of "deontic knowledge as such." Our 2001 study used moral dilemmas that were identified as moral dilemmas by independent coders. Thus, whether or not our dilemmas required subjects to report their "deontic knowledge as such," we are confident that these dilemmas did require our subjects to make moral judgments, as ordinary people understand this activity.

Where to go from here? Based on data old and new, it is increasingly clear that intuitive emotional responses play a crucial role in the production of moral judgments, including those under consideration here. It is also increasingly clear that utilitarian considerations, supported by domain-general cognitive control mechanisms, can compete with, and in some cases override, these intuitive emotional responses. If these claims are correct, Mikhail's theory of "moral grammar" cannot serve as a general theory of moral judgment, or even as a general theory of trolley judgments. This is because his theory denies that emotions are anything other than sources of noise ("performance errors") and has no place for domain-general cognitive control mechanisms that can override intuitive responses.

Despite this, I believe that Mikhail's ideas are highly valuable. Within the framework of my "dual-process" model (Greene et al., 2004), there is an important unanswered question: What is the mechanism that triggers our intuitive emotional responses to cases like the *footbridge* case? My provisional hypothesis concerning the principles governing this mechanism is clearly wrong, although recent evidence suggests that the general idea behind this proposal ("personalness") has merit. It is equally clear that appeals to "personalness" will take us only so far. While the specific theory of "moral grammar" that Mikhail has offered has its limitations, I believe that the general ideas behind his theory have great merit and will prove useful in our attempts to understand the mechanisms behind our emotions.

Reply to Timmons

In his thoughtful and lucid commentary, Mark Timmons defends deontology with a twist. Why, he asks, can't we have an emotionally grounded deontology? This is an interesting proposal, worthy of serious consideration. Nevertheless, I remain skeptical.

Timmons identifies and evaluates four distinct arguments in my chapter, which he calls the *misunderstanding argument*, the *coincidence argument*, the *no normative explanation argument*, and the *sentimentalist argument*. He also identifies a number of deontological moves that in his opinion can strengthen an enterprising deontologist's position. In what follows I will clarify and/or defend these arguments (which I regard as parts of a single argument). In the process I will explain why I believe the philosophical moves Timmons recommends are unlikely to help the deontological cause.

The conclusion of the *misunderstanding argument* is that the hidden essence of deontology is a psychological disposition toward emotionally driven moral judgments. This, as I understand it, is an empirical claim. Since Timmons has generously agreed to grant me my empirical claims, the question then becomes: What follows from this? If we grant that, psychologically speaking, intuitive emotional responses motivate deontological philosophy, does that mean that deontological philosophy is mistaken? Couldn't deontological thinking be the right kind of thinking, regardless of our psychological motives for embracing it? It could. In principle. Deontologists may someday construct or discover an elegant, self-justifying moral system that explains exactly how we are to value humanity and what sorts of things are right and wrong as a result. And they could claim further, as Kant did, that people's real-life psychological motives for judging and behaving rightly are irrelevant to moral theory. The fundamental principles of morals, they might argue, stand alone like mathematical theorems, independent of the messy world of psychology. Well, that is the deontological dream. But, as I have argued, keeping that particular dream alive requires one to posit a strange set of coincidences, which brings us to . . .

The *coincidence argument:* In response to the *coincidence argument*, Timmons makes two closely related moves: (1) he emphasizes the role of reflection in deontology and (2) takes a constructivist approach to moral truth. The dialectic goes like this. I say, "What are the chances that all these emotional responses are tracking the moral truth? Wouldn't that be a helluva coincidence?" To which Timmons replies, "Not at all. You're assuming some sort of hard-core realist metaethic, with the Moral Truth hovering above us in the Platonic ether. If our emotions were to track *that* kind of truth, that would be a bizarre coincidence indeed. But moral truth doesn't have to be that way. In a *constructivist* account of moral truth, the moral truth is just whatever comes out of a process of *rational reflection*. So it's no surprise if the output of that process (the moral truth) reflects the input to that process (our emotional intuitions)."

While this response sounds promising, it leaves the deontologist caught between two horns of a dilemma. But before we talk horns, we need to distinguish between two types of deontology. "Ground-level" deontology, as I'll call it, is specifically committed to normative positions that are "characteristically deontological" and that are (ceteris paribus) at odds with consequentialism. Examples include Kant's infamous claim that it is wrong to lie to save someone's life (Kant, 1983) and the standard deontological view that it is wrong to push the guy off the *footbridge* in order to save five other people. It is this ground-level deontology that I had in mind in my chapter. There is, of course, a metaethical deontological tradition as well, which includes constructivist/contractualist philosophers like Rawls (1971) and Scanlon (1998). Their aim is to lay out a foundational theory of morality upon which a (nonutilitarian) ground-level theory can be "constructed." The construction process works as follows. We begin with our ordinary moral intuitions and commitments. Then we engage in some sort of rational reflection: "Are my current commitments consistent with rules that I would endorse if I were ignorant of my social position?" "Are my current commitments consistent with rules that no one could reasonably reject?" And through this reflective process our moral commitments are refined. At the ideal end of this reflective process, the moral principles to which we subscribe are the true ones.

So, here is the problem: judgments based on emotional intuitions go into this reflective process. Do they come out? If they do come out, then we have what computer scientists call the GIGO problem: "garbage in, garbage out." (That's horn 1.) If they don't come out, then the output isn't necessarily deontological in the sense that matters (horn 2). Let us work through this argument using the now-familiar case of Peter Singer's utilitarian challenge to the affluent world (Singer, 1972). Since we are granting all of my empirical claims, let's assume, once again, that I'm completely right about the relevant psychology and its natural history: The *only* reason we are motivated to make a moral distinction between nearby drowning children and faraway starving children is that the former push our emotional buttons and the latter do not. And the *only* reason we exhibit this pattern of emotional response is because we did not evolve in an environment, like our current environment, in which we could have meaningful interactions with faraway strangers. Now, we take our characteristically deontological, emotion-based moral responses to these two cases (drowning child versus international aid) and feed them into the rational reflection process. If they somehow make it through, we have a problem. The so-called "moral truth" now reflects arbitrary features of our evolutionary history. GIGO. If, instead, our characteristically deontological intuitions do not survive this process of rational reflection, then in what sense is the moral truth deontological? In the limiting case (which is consistent with the strong empirical assumptions I've been granted), all traces of our characteristically deontological intuitions are filtered out by the rational reflection process, and we are left with a ground-level utilitarian philosophy mounted upon a would-be deontological foundation. (This is more or less what John Harsanyi envisioned [Harsanyi, 1953, 1955].) My response to that is: Great! You can have your metaethical contractualism and constructivism as long as you are open to the possibility that the right ground-level theory is utilitarian and decidedly undeontological. As long as starving children get helped and people get shoved in front of speeding trolleys, that's all I care about.

Next we come to the *no normative explanation argument.* I point out that deontologists have a hard time justifying their judgments. Timmons points out that this does not mean that those judgments are necessarily wrong. It could be that deontologists just haven't yet worked out their arguments. Possible, sure. But I have also argued that these judgments can be explained in terms of patterns of emotional response and that these patterns reflect the influence of morally irrelevant factors. In light of this, wouldn't it be a strange coincidence if the correct moral theory just happened to map onto our moral emotions, which are sensitive to irrelevant factors? So this argument, too, brings us back to the *coincidence argument.*

Finally, we get to the *sentimentalist argument.* I have argued that deontologists who think they are rationalists are most likely rational*izers* of moral emotion. This is a problem for deontologists who insist on being genuine rationalists. But, Timmons asks, why can't deontologists embrace the emotive foundations of their judgments? The answer, once again, is GIGO. Kant was opposed to emotion-based morality because emotions are fickle and contingent in oh-so-many ways (Kant, 1959). About that, he was right.

3 | Without Morals: The Cognitive Neuroscience of Criminal Psychopaths

Kent A. Kiehl

Psychopathy is a personality disorder characterized by a profound lack of empathy and guilt or remorse, shallow affect, irresponsibility, and poor behavioral controls. The psychopath's behavioral repertoire has long led clinicians to suggest that they are "without conscience" (Hare, 1993). Indeed, Pinel (1801), who is credited with first identifying the condition, used the expression "madness without delirium" to denote the lack of morality and behavioral control in these individuals, which occurred despite the absence of any psychotic symptoms or defects in intellectual function. Thus, the psychopath presents clinically as a "walking oxymoron." On the one hand, the psychopath is capable of articulating socially constructive, even morally appropriate, responses to real-life situations. However, when left to his or her own devices, the psychopath's actions are frequently inconsistent with his or her verbal reports. It is as if the moment they leave the clinician's office, their moral compass goes awry and they fail seriously in most life situations. For example, I worked with a psychopath who developed an extensive plan to provide alimony and financial support for his children. He wrote and dispatched letters detailing this plan to his former wife and her lawyer. Sometime later during a follow-up interview I asked what he had been doing in the past few months. He provided elaborate details on his recent escapades in dining, entertainment, and travel. When I asked him if he had fulfilled any of his alimony plans, he just scoffed at me and said he hadn't given it a second thought.

In another case, I was working with a psychopath who had been convicted of killing his long-term girlfriend. During his narrative of the crime he indicated that the trigger that set him off was that she called him "fat, bald, and broke." After her insult registered, he went into the bathroom where she was drawing a bath and pushed her hard into the tile wall. She fell dazed into the half-full bathtub. He then held her under the water until she stopped moving. He wrapped her up in a blanket, put her in the car, drove to a deserted bridge, and threw her off. Her body was recovered under the bridge several days later by some railroad workers. When asked if what he had done was wrong, he said that he knew it was a bad idea to throw her off the bridge. When I probed further, he said that he realized that it was bad to actually kill her. This inmate was subsequently released from prison and then convicted of killing his next girlfriend. When I met up with him in the prison some years later, he indicated that his second girlfriend had "found new buttons to push." He was able to admit that he knew it was wrong to kill them.

In contrast, I had another patient who suffered from a different disorder, schizophrenia, and who had killed someone he believed had implanted a monitoring device in his head. Despite all evidence to the contrary, this latter patient could not be convinced that sacrificing his victim had been a bad thing. He was unable to articulate that it was wrong to kill this person. These cases illustrate that some psychiatric conditions are associated with impairments in understanding moral behavior, while psychopaths are unencumbered by moral imperatives. Indeed, I have yet to meet a psychopath who is incapable of telling right from wrong—at least verbally.

This characteristic of psychopaths—the absence of moral behavior in the presence of an otherwise intact intellect—has fascinated clinicians and researchers alike. We have come a long way in defining the essential characteristics and clinical symptomology of psychopathy. However, we are only beginning to unravel the relevant neural systems that appear to be implicated in the disorder. The purpose of this chapter is to review the literature on the neural systems that are associated with psychopathy. The first part of the review will draw upon studies of how cerebral insults or damage to regions of the brain may lead to symptoms and cognitive abnormalities consistent with those observed in psychopathy. The second line of evidence will draw upon cognitive and affective neuroscience studies of psychopathy. However, before we begin to review the neural systems implicated in this disorder, we must more precisely define what we mean by the term "psychopath."

Defining Psychopathy

For over 200 years clinicians have described a personality type characterized by a host of interpersonal and affective characteristics, including glibness, superficial charm, low empathy, lack of guilt or remorse, and shallow emotions. The condition also often included such behavioral traits as impulsivity, proneness to boredom, hot-headedness, and poor planning and decision making. Over the years the condition has been through an evolution in terminology, but many of the defining characteristics have remained constant. The modern concept of psychopathy was most clearly delineated by the observations and writings of the psychiatrist Hervey Cleckley (1941). Cleckley came to narrow the syndrome he called psychopathy to sixteen characteristics. Cleckley's characteristics were subsequently operationalized and transformed by Hare and colleagues into items on the Hare Psychopathy Checklist (Hare, 1980) and its successor, the Hare Psychopathy Checklist-Revised (PCL-R; Hare, 1991, 2003). The PCL-R is the most widely accepted diagnostic instrument for psychopathy (see table 3.1). The PCL-R assessment is performed by reviewing the participant's institutional records, including intake assessments and social worker assessments; psychological testing results; transcripts of patient interviews with psychologists, psychiatrists, and staff; and reports of institutional adjustment and transgressions. A semistructured interview covering school adjustment, employment, intimate relationships, family, friends, and criminal activity is conducted. The interview is particularly useful for eliciting information helpful for scoring the interpersonal and affective characteristics of psychopathy. Explicit criteria detailing each item are reviewed from the PCL-R manual and each item is scored on a three-point scale: 0 doesn't apply, 1 applies somewhat, and 2 definitely applies to the individual. The resulting scores range from 0 to 40 and the recommended diagnostic cutoff for psychopathy is 30 (Hare, 1991). Interviews are typically videotaped so that an independent rating can be obtained. The total assessment time typically ranges from 2 to 5 hours, is rigorous, and extensive training is required.

There is a substantial literature attesting to the reliability and validity of the PCL-R as a measure of psychopathy in incarcerated offenders, forensic patients, psychiatric patients, and substance abuse patients (Alterman, Cacciola, & Rutherford, 1993; Fulero, 1996; Hare, 1980, 1996a; Hare & Hart, 1993; Hare, Hart, & Harpur, 1991; Harpur, Hakstian, & Hare, 1988; Harpur, Hare, & Hakstian, 1989; Hart & Hare, 1989, 1996; McDermott, Alterman, Cacciola, Rutherford, Newman, & Mulholland, 2000; Rutherford, Alterman, & Cacciola, 1995, 2000; Rutherford, Alterman, Cacciola, & McKay, 1997). Using the PCL-R, it has been shown that psychopaths constitute 15–25 percent of the male and female prison population (Hare, 1991, 2003) and 10–15 percent of substance abuse populations (Alterman & Cacciola, 1991; Alterman, Cacciola, & Rutherford, 1993; Alterman, McDermott, Cacciola, Rutherford, Boardman, McKay, & Cook,

Table 3.1
The Hare Psychopathy Checklist-Revised

	Item	Two-factor model
1	Glibness/superficial charm	1
2	Grandiose sense of self worth	1
3	Need for stimulation	2
4	Pathological lying	1
5	Cunning/manipulative	1
6	Lack of remorse or guilt	1
7	Shallow affect	1
8	Callous/lack of empathy	1
9	Parasitic lifestyle	2
10	Poor behavioral controls	2
11	Promiscuous sexual behavior	—
12	Early behavioral problems	2
13	Lack of realistic, long-term goals	2
14	Impulsivity	2
15	Irresponsibility	2
16	Failure to accept responsibility	1
17	Many marital relationships	—
18	Juvenile delinquency	2
19	Revocation of conditional release	2
20	Criminal versatility	—

Source: Hare (1991, 2003).
Note: The items corresponding to the early two-factor conceptualization of psychopathy are listed (Harpur et al., 1988, 1989). Factor one is typically labeled the interpersonal and affective factor, while factor two is known as the social deviance factor. Items with "—" did not load on any factor.

1998). Using these assessment procedures we have learned that, relative to nonpsychopathic criminals, psychopathic criminals are responsible for a disproportionate amount of repetitive crime and violence in society (Hare, 1998). The average incarcerated psychopath has been convicted of five serious crimes by age 40 (Hemphill, Hare, & Wong, 1998). Considering the cost of policing, prosecuting, and incarcerating, the typical criminal psychopath is likely to cost society millions of dollars and untold emotional hardship throughout their lifetime.

Early factor analyses of the PCL-R items revealed two correlated dimensions or factors (see table 3.1; Harpur et al., 1988; Harpur et al., 1989). Factor 1 included items related to emotional and interpersonal relationships. Factor 2 items reflected impulsive and antisocial behaviors. This latter factor is most closely related to the *Diagnostic and Statistical Manual of Mental Illness* (*DSM IV*) classification of antisocial personality disorder (ASPD; American Psychiatric Association, 1994). It is important to note that although ASPD was intended to capture the essential components of psychopathy, it has been criticized for overly relying on antisocial behaviors while excluding many of the affective and interpersonal characteristics considered to be central to the construct of psychopathy (Alterman et al., 1998; Hare, 1996a; Hare et al., 1991; Hart & Hare, 1996; Widiger, Cadoret, Hare, Robins, Rutherford, et al. 1996). ASPD also has been questioned on grounds of specificity in prison populations (Hart & Hare, 1996). Nearly 80–90 percent of inmates in a maximum-security institution fulfill the criteria for ASPD, while only 15–25 percent score above the diagnostic criteria for psychopathy. In addition, the diagnostic confusion of psychopathy as putatively measured by ASPD has led to considerable confusion and hampered research efforts (see reviews by Alterman, McDermott, Cacciola, Rutherford, Boardman, McKay, & Cook, 1998; Hare et al., 1991; Robins, 1998). It is important to note that proper psychometric assessment of a condition is crucial, particularly when trying to relate it to psychophysiological or cognitive neuroscience data. The review that follows will be limited to studies that employed psychometric measures that are consistent with the classic conceptualization of psychopathy. That is, the preferred conceptualization of psychopathy is a disorder that includes both interpersonal and affective characteristics and deviant behavior.

In summary, researchers have made great strides in characterizing the psychometric assessment and classification of psychopathy over the past 20 years. The classic conceptualization of psychopathy is a disorder that includes both interpersonal and affective characteristics and behavioral traits.

Psychopathy and Neurology

One way to examine the possible neural regions implicated in psychopathy is to draw from studies of behavioral changes and cognitive impairments associated with damage to specific brain circuits. The most notable neurological case study in this regard is that of the railroad worker Phineas Gage (Harlow, 1848). Gage suffered a penetrating trauma to the prefrontal cortex (Damasio, Grabowski, Frank, Galaburda, & Damasio, 1994). He was transformed by this accident from a responsible railroad manager and husband to an impulsive, irresponsible, promiscuous, apathetic individual (Harlow,

1848). Many of Gage's symptoms are consistent with those classically associated with psychopathy.

Subsequent studies of patients with prefrontal lobe damage suggest that the orbital frontal cortex mediates many of the behaviors related to psychopathy (Blumer & Benson, 1975; Damasio, 1994). Damage to the orbital frontal cortex leads to a condition termed "pseudopsychopathy" (Blumer & Benson, 1975) or "acquired sociopathic personality" (Damasio, 1994). These conditions are characterized by problems with reactive aggression, motivation, empathy, planning and organization, impulsivity, irresponsibility, insight, and behavioral inhibition (Malloy, Bihrle, Duffy, & Cimino, 1993; Stuss, Benson, & Kaplan, 1983). In some cases patients may become prone to grandiosity (Blumer & Benson, 1975) and confabulation (Malloy et al., 1993; Schnider, 2001). Recent studies suggest that bilateral damage to the orbital frontal cortex is necessary to elicit changes in social behavior (Hornak, Bramham, Rolls, Morris, O'Doherty, et al., 2003). Moreover, patients with gross, extensive damage that is due to stroke or closed head injury are more likely to exhibit acquired sociopathic symptomology than patients with focal, circumscribed surgical lesions to the orbital frontal cortex (Hornak et al., 2003). These data suggest that some aspects of psychopathic symptomology may map onto the (dys)function of the orbital frontal cortex and adjacent regions.

However, the pseudopsychopathy or acquired sociopathy model does not appear to fully account for the constellation of symptoms observed in psychopathy. For example, patients with orbital frontal damage rarely show instrumental or goal-directed aggression—a cardinal feature of psychopathy (Hare, 1993). Orbital frontal patients also do not typically exhibit the callousness commonly observed in psychopathic individuals. Similarly, patients with acquired sociopathy, unlike psychopathic individuals, are characterized by lack of motivation, hoarding behavior, mood disturbances, incontinence, and failure or inability to make long-term plans (Blumer & Benson, 1975). Psychopathic individuals, on the other hand, often enjoy making grandiose life plans—they just fail to follow through with them. Recently, a case study of two patients who as infants suffered brain trauma to the prefrontal cortex (the frontal pole, orbital frontal, and anterior cingulate) found a higher incidence of callous behavior than is typically observed in patients who suffer similar lesions as adults (Anderson, Bechara, Damasio, Tranel, & Damasio, 1999). Unfortunately, psychopathy ratings were not performed, making it difficult to evaluate if these patients would meet the criteria for psychopathy. Nevertheless, these latter results suggest a neurodevelopmental facet to some psychopathic symptoms.

Patients with orbital frontal lesions show impairment on affective voice and face expression (Hornak et al., 2003; Hornak, Rolls, & Wade, 1996), response reversal or extinction (Blair & Cipolotti, 2000; Rolls, Hornak, Wade, & McGrath, 1994), and decision making (Bechara, Tranel, & Damasio, 2000). The animal literature shows that lesions to the orbital frontal cortex impair inhibitory performance on "no go" trials of "go/no go" paradigms (Iversen & Mishkin, 1970). Psychopaths have problems with processing certain aspects of affective speech and face stimuli (R.J.R. Blair, Jones, Clark, & Smith, 1997; Kosson, Suchy, Mayer, & Libby, 2002; Louth, Williamson, Alpert, Pouget, & Hare, 1998). Psychopaths, under certain contextual demands, also show poor response inhibition (Kiehl, Smith, Hare, & Liddle, 2000b; Lapierre, Braun, & Hodgins, 1995), response modulation (Newman & Kosson, 1986; Newman, Kosson, & Patterson, 1992; Newman, Patterson, & Kosson, 1987; Newman & Schmitt, 1998), and more recently, response reversal (Mitchell, Colledge, Leonard, & Blair, 2002). Boys with psychopathic tendencies and adult psychopaths tend to show impairments on the Bechara gambling test of decision making (R.J.R. Blair, Colledge, & Mitchell, 2001a; Mitchell et al., 2002), although not all studies have found this effect (Schmitt, Brinkley, & Newman, 1999).

In summary, damage to the orbital frontal cortex appears to be associated with some symptoms and cognitive impairments that may also be found in psychopaths. However, despite these apparent similarities, no studies have actually explicitly investigated how orbital frontal patients score on psychopathy measures. Similarly, many of the studies of cognitive function in psychopathy and orbital frontal patients have employed different cognitive tests, making inferences between studies problematic. It is only recently that identical tasks (i.e., response reversal) are being examined in both orbital frontal patients and in samples of psychopathic individuals (Mitchell et al., 2002). Thus, while the pseudopsychopathy or acquired sociopathy model appears to mimic some features of psychopathy, the two disorders differ in many respects. This raises the possibility that disturbances in brain regions other than the orbital frontal cortex may contribute to psychopathy.

Other brain regions that may be implicated in psychopathy include the anterior cingulate. Selective lesions to this area are rare, but when they do occur they tend to be related to emotional unconcern or apathy (Mesulam, 2000), hostility, irresponsibility, and disagreeableness (Swick, personal communication, 2003). Recently, Hornak and colleagues have shown that selective lesions to the bilateral anterior cingulate cortex produce disturbances in personality functioning similar to those observed in patients with orbital frontal lesions (Hornak et al., 2003). In humans, anterior cingulate lesions lead to perseveration (Mesulam, 2000), difficulties in affective face and voice identification (Hornak et al., 2003) and error monitoring (Swick & Jovanovic, 2002; Swick & Turken, 2002; Turken & Swick, 1999), and abnormalities in response inhibition (Degos, da Fonseca, Gray, & Cesaro, 1993; Tekin & Cummings, 2002). Psychopathy has long been associated with perseveration (see review by Newman, 1998), apathy (Cleckley, 1941; McCord & McCord, 1964), difficulties in identifying some affective face stimuli (R.J.R Blair et al., 1997; Kosson et al., 2002), and more recently, in error monitoring (Bates, Liddle, & Kiehl, 2003) and abnormalities as response inhibition (Kiehl et al., 2000b; Lapierre et al., 1995). Studies also have shown that the volume of the right anterior cingulate is positively correlated with harm avoidance (Pujol, Lopez, Deus, Cardoner, Vallejo, et al., 2002). Psychopaths are known to score low on harm avoidance measures (Hare, 1991). Thus it would appear that bilateral damage to the anterior cingulate and/or the orbital frontal cortex may lead to symptoms and cognitive impairments similar to those observed in psychopathy.

In addition to regions of the frontal cortex, regions in the temporal lobe may be linked to some symptoms of psychopathy. Damage to the medial temporal lobe in general (Kluever & Bucy, 1938, 1939) and the amygdala in particular (Aggleton, 1992) has long been associated with emotional and behavioral changes in monkeys. These changes include an unnatural propensity for approach behavior, or fearlessness and unusual tameness. Bilateral amygdala lesion monkeys also show excessive fascination with objects, often placing them in the mouth, and general hyperactivity and hypersexual activity. This collection of behaviors has been termed the Kluever-Bucy syndrome. Only a small minority of humans with bilateral amygdala lesions exhibited the full manifestation of the Kluever-Bucy syndrome, while the majority developed less severe emotional changes (Adolphs & Tranel, 2000). One case study reported that bilateral amygdala damage that was due to calcification associated with Urbach-Wiethe disease may be related to mild antisocial behavior, including rebelliousness, disregard for social convention, and lack of respect for authorities (Adolphs & Tranel, 2000).

Detailed psychological and personality assessments of patients with temporal lobe epilepsy suggest a high incidence of psychopathic-like behavior. Indeed, some studies have reported that preoperatively the prevalence of psychopathic-like behaviors is as high as 70 percent of patients with anterior temporal lobe epilepsy (Blumer, 1975; Hill, Pond, Mitchell, & Falconer, 1957). The structures that are commonly implicated in temporal lobe epilepsy include the amygdala, hippocampus, parahippocampal gyrus, and anterior superior temporal gyrus (temporal pole). It is interesting that removal of the anterior temporal lobe appears to alleviate these behavioral problems in the majority of cases. Hill and colleagues (1957) reported that improvements in personality functioning following temporal lobectomy included reduced hostility and violence, more appropriate sexual behavior (e.g., reduced use of prostitutes and sexual fetishes), increased warmth in social relationships, and increased empathy (see also Hood, Siegfried, & Wieser, 1983). It is also noteworthy that little or no intellectual deficits were observed in these patients after surgery for their epilepsy (Falconer & Serafetinides, 1963; Hill et al., 1957). Note that removal of the anterior temporal lobe reduced the psychopathic symptoms, implying that these behaviors might reflect pathological activity or disruption in the circuits that involve the anterior temporal lobes.

In a similar vein, elective amygdalotomies have been performed on patients with severe aggressive disorders. In general, the studies suggest that bilateral amygdalotomy reduces the severity and frequency of aggressive behavior and helps to restore emotional control (Bagshaw, Mackworth, & Pribram, 1972; Lee, Arena, Meador, & Smith, 1988; Lee, Bechara, Adolphs, Arena, Meador, Loring, et al., 1998). Amygdalectomized monkeys fail to show the heart rate and respiratory components of the orienting response, and their skin conductance responses are markedly depressed (Bagshaw et al., 1972).

Cognitive studies of patients with amygdala damage have revealed that these patients have difficulty with processing certain classes of affective stimuli. The right amygdala and adjacent medial temporal lobe regions appear to be involved with face processing difficulties, particularly those associated with affective states of withdrawal avoidance (A.K. Anderson, Spencer, Fulbright, & Phelps, 2000). Patients with bilateral amygdala damage judged unfamiliar individuals to be more approachable and trustworthy than control subjects, especially for faces rated as unapproachable and untrustworthy by control subjects (Adolphs, Tranel, & Damasio, 1998). Similarly, bilateral damage to the amygdala is associated with impairments in recognizing angry and fearful faces and affective intonations (Scott, Young, Calder, Hellawell, Aggleton, et al., 1997). The amygdala's role in processing fearful faces has been challenged by one study that found, after controlling for overall task difficulty, no selective disadvantage in amygdala lesion patients on fearful-face processing (Rapcsak, Galper, Comer, Reminger, Nielsen, et al., 2000).

The amygdala appears to be involved in extracting emotional salience from linguistic stimuli (Anderson & Phelps, 2001; Funayama, Grillon, Davis, & Phelps, 2001; Isenberg, Silbersweig, Engelien, Emmerich, Malavade, et al., 1999; Strange, Henson, Friston, & Dolan, 2000). Similarly, studies suggest that the fear-potentiated startle during processing of emotional pictures is dependent upon the medial temporal lobe (Angrilli, Mauri, Palomba, Flor, Birbaumer, et al., 1996), as is fear-potentiated startle during fear conditioning with verbal stimuli (Funayama et al., 2001). The amygdala, in particular the left region, appears to be implicated in aversive conditioning (Bechara, Damasio, Damasio, & Lee, 1995; Funayama et al., 2001; LaBar, LeDoux, Spencer, & Phelps, 1995). The orbital frontal cortex is also believed to be involved in aversive conditioning (Morris, Friston, & Dolan, 1998). In addition, as with patients who have orbital frontal damage, patients with amygdala damage are also impaired on the Bechara gambling test of decision making (Bechara, Damasio, Damasio, & Lee, 1999).

Psychopathy is associated with difficulties in processing some face stimuli, particularly disgust (Kosson et al., 2002) and distress cues (R.J.R. Blair et al., 1997). Distress cues are believed to be involved in aversive conditioning and are thought to rely upon the amygdala (R.J.R. Blair, 1995). The processing of disgust cues is not believed to rely upon the amygdala; rather, the relevant circuitry is thought to be the anterior insular cortex (Phillips, Young, Scott, Calder, Andrew, et al., 1998; Phillips, Young, Senior, Brammer, Andrew, et al., 1997). Adult psychopaths (Williamson, Harpur, & Hare, 1991) and children with psychopathic tendencies (Loney, Frick, Clements, Ellis, & Kerlin, 2003) show reduced facilitation for processing emotional words during affective lexical decision tasks. These latter results also suggest involvement of the amygdala in psychopathy. Psychopaths also do not show the same pattern of fear-potentiated startle during processing of emotional pictures, supporting the notion of amygdala (and orbital frontal) abnormality (Levenston, Patrick, Bradley, & Lang, 2000; Patrick, Bradley, & Lang, 1993; Sutton, Vitale, & Newman, 2002). This latter effect appears to be particularly related to the interpersonal and affective components of psychopathy (Patrick, Bradley, & Lang, 1993; Sutton et al., 2002).

It appears that damage to the amygdala and regions of the anterio-lateral temporal lobe are involved in certain symptoms of psychopathy, including aggression, impulsivity and poor behavioral control, and emotional unconcern and lack of empathy. It does not appear that medial temporal lobe insults result in pseudopsychopathic symptomology similar to that observed in patients with anterior cingulate and orbital frontal lesions.

It is worth mentioning that damage to other regions of the frontal cortex (i.e., superior frontal or dorsolateral prefrontal), parietal cortex, or occipital cortex, are not known to lead to behavioral symptoms or cognitive abnormalities consistent with psychopathy. Of note, damage to the dorsolateral frontal cortex classically leads to problems in the control, regulation, and integration of cognitive functions. Patients with dorsolateral prefrontal damage are often passive and display poor attention and working-memory function. These functions do not appear to be disrupted in psychopathy. In summary, studies of behavioral changes and cognitive impairments associated with focal brain damage suggest that the orbital frontal cortex, the anterior insula, the anterior cingulate of the frontal lobe and the amygdala, and adjacent regions of the anterior temporal lobe are implicated in psychopathic symptomology.

Psychopathy and Neurocognition

Utilizing the PCL-R (or its predecessors) for assessment, researchers have found that psychopathy is associated with performance abnormalities in several affective and cognitive domains. The purpose of this review is to examine the associated neural systems engaged in these cognitive and emotional processes. Reviews on behavioral correlates of psychopathy as they related to response modulation and attentional processes are available elsewhere (Harpur & Hare, 1990; Kosson & Harpur, 1997; Newman, 1998; Newman & Lorenz, 2002). The extant psychophysiological and cognitive neuroscience literature on psychopathy can be broadly classified into three general areas. These are (1) language, (2) attention and orienting processes, and (3) affect and emotion. Each of these areas will be reviewed, paying particular attention to studies that have used electrophysiology and brain imaging techniques. The findings from these areas will be synthesized and the common threads in each of the different cognitive domains will be linked to the same functional neural architecture. However, before reviewing the cognitive neuroscience of psychopathy, it might be helpful to review the relevant methods and terminology.

Event-Related Potentials

Event-related potentials (ERPs) are temporal segments of an ongoing electroencephalogram (EEG). These segments are time-locked to the onset of an event (e.g., abstract words) and averaged over many similar trial types to remove brain activity not relevant to the processing of the stimulus of interest. The resulting waveform is plotted as a function of time versus amplitude. The series of peaks and troughs, which are often labeled "components," are typically referred to by their polarity (e.g., negative wave, N; positive wave, P) and by their ordinal position after stimulus onset. ERP components can also be referred to by their polarity and latency in milliseconds from stimulus onset. A P1, for example, would be the first positive component following the stimulus. The N400, on the other hand, would be a negative component of the ERP peaking approximately 400 milliseconds after stimulus onset. Finally, some ERP components can be labeled according to their functional significance, as in the mismatch negativity or MMN.

ERPs provide precise characterization, on the order of milliseconds, of the temporal structure of information processing. However, characterizing the spatial distribution of the neural generators underlying these components is difficult because there is no unique solution to the inverse problem. The "inverse problem" refers to determining the unique dipole distribution believed to have generated the scalp potentials. In addition, if one was seeking to determine a description in terms of a sum of dipoles, one would also need to determine the relative strength of the dipoles. Thus, ERPs currently find their utility in providing precise temporal information. Precise spatial information (but limited temporal precision) about the relevant neural systems involved in processing certain stimuli is often studied with functional magnetic resonance imaging.

Functional Magnetic Resonance Imaging

Functional magnetic resonance imaging takes advantage of the fact that as neurons are engaged in a cognitive operation, a commensurate increase in local blood flow occurs. This enhanced blood flow supplies the metabolically active neurons with an increased supply of oxygenated blood. It is important that the increase in blood flow exceeds the amount needed to meet the additional demand for oxygen, leading to an increase in the concentration of oxygenated hemoglobin and a corresponding dilution of deoxyhemoglobin. The ratio of oxygenated to deoxygenated hemoglobin concentration produces a decrease in local magnetic field disturbance (i.e., spin dephasing), which results in a net increase in the magnetic resonance signal. This effect was termed the blood oxygen level-dependent (BOLD) contrast. The resulting signal from each region in the brain can then be plotted and analyzed as a function of intensity versus time. Currently, the temporal and spatial resolution of fMRI is on the order of seconds and millimeters, respectively. Functional MRI has been used in the past 12 years to characterize the neural correlates of many domains of cognitive function and is readily being applied to the study of psychopathology.

Psychopathy and Language Processes

Early research sought to identify impairments in cognitive functioning by examining the relationship between psychopathy and hemispheric lateralization for language function (Day & Wong, 1996; Hare, 1979; Hare & Jutai, 1988; Hare & McPherson, 1984; Jutai, Hare, & Connolly, 1987; Raine, O'Brien, Smiley, Scerbo, & Chan, 1990). These studies generally found that psychopathy appeared to be related to abnormalities in the cerebral lateralization for some language stimuli, particularly for language functions of the left hemisphere.

Subsequent research found that abnormalities in language processes were most prevalent when psychopathic individuals were required to perform tasks involving semantic processing (Gillstrom & Hare, 1988; Hare & Jutai, 1988; Hare & McPherson, 1984). For example, Hare and Jutai (1988) observed that psychopathic individuals made more errors than did nonpsychopathic control participants in an abstract semantic categorization task. However, psychopathic individuals performed no worse than control participants for a simple recognition task or categorical judgment task, suggesting that the observed cognitive abnormalities were present only when they were processing abstract semantic information (see also Hare, 1979).

More recently, Kiehl, Hare, McDonald, and Brink (1999a) examined psychopathic persons' ability to process abstract (e.g., justice) and concrete (e.g., table) words during a lexical decision task and during an abstract or concrete discrimination task. Previous studies have demonstrated that healthy subjects respond more quickly and accurately to concrete words than to abstract words in lexical decision and concrete-abstract discrimination tasks (Day, 1977; Holcomb, Kounios, Anderson, & West, 1999; James, 1975; Kounios & Holcomb, 1994; Kroll & Merves, 1986). These data led to the hypothesis that the cognitive operations, and by inference, the neural systems, involved in processing concrete and abstract words are normally dissociated (Holcomb et al., 1999; Kiehl, Liddle, Smith, Mendrek, Forster & Hare 1999c; Paivio, 1986, 1991; Schwanenflugel, Harnishfeger, & Stowe, 1988; Schwanenflugel & Stowe, 1989). Consistent with the hypothesis that psychopathic persons have difficulty processing abstract information, Kiehl et al. (1999a) found that criminal psychopaths, compared with non-psychopaths, made more errors trying to classify abstract words during a concrete-abstract discrimination task. These authors also recorded ERPs during this procedure and observed that psychopathic individuals failed to show the normal ERP differentiation between concrete and abstract words. In noncriminals and in criminal nonpsychopathic individuals, concrete words elicit greater ERP negativity in the 300–800 millisecond window than do abstract words (Kounios & Holcomb, 1994; Paller, Kutas, Shimamura, & Squire, 1987). This latter effect is strongest at frontotemporal electrode sites, suggesting that frontal-temporal generators are involved in the differentiation of concrete and abstract words.

Kiehl et al. (1999a) also found that psychopaths' ERP waveforms to all linguistic stimuli (all words and nonwords) were associated with a prominent late negativity maximal over frontal and central midline sites (see figure 3.1). The time window associated with this late negativity, 250–500 milliseconds (N350), was consistent with the epoch normally associated with the N400 component elicited during language tasks (Kutas & Hillyard, 1980, 1983, 1984). However, the canonical N400 component has a central-parietal distribution, while the N350 negativity observed in the psychopaths was clearly frontocentrally mediated. Thus, the functional significance of the N350 remained unclear.

Evidence from neuroimaging has shown that different brain regions are involved in processing abstract words and concrete words during lexical decision tasks. Studies using fMRI have shown that the hemodynamic response associated with processing abstract words during lexical decision tasks was associated with greater activity in the right anterior superior temporal gyrus and surrounding cortex than was processing of concrete words (Kiehl et al., 1999c; Kiehl, Smith, Mendrek, Forster, Hare, & Liddle, 2004). These data suggest that the behavioral and ERP abnormalities observed in psychopaths for processing abstract words during the context of lexical decision tasks may be related to the function of the right anterior temporal lobe. To directly examine this hypothesis, Kiehl et al. (2004) used fMRI to elucidate the abnormal functional neuroanatomy in a group of criminal psychopaths during performance of a concrete-abstract lexical decision task. Consistent with the hypotheses, the psychopaths failed to show the normal pattern of hemodynamic differentiation between abstract and concrete stimuli in the right anterior temporal lobe. Indeed, the right anterior superior temporal gyrus failed to activate during processing of abstract words relative to the baseline, suggesting that this brain region is functionally impaired in psychopaths—at least during the performance of lexical decision tasks (Kiehl, Smith, Mendrek, Forster, Hare, & Liddle, 2004).

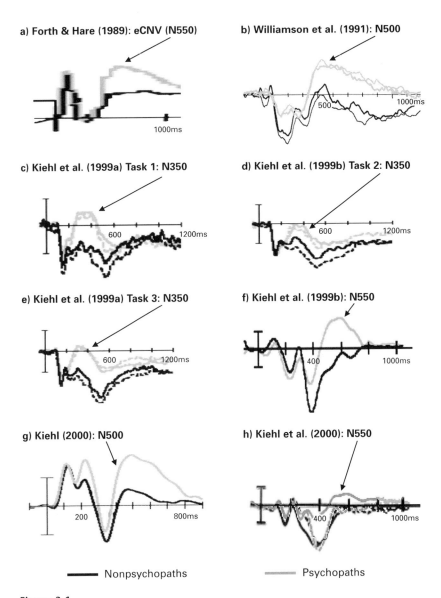

a) Forth & Hare (1989): eCNV (N550)

1000ms

b) Williamson et al. (1991): N500

500   1000ms

c) Kiehl et al. (1999a) Task 1: N350

600   1200ms

d) Kiehl et al. (1999b) Task 2: N350

600   1200ms

e) Kiehl et al. (1999a) Task 3: N350

600   1200ms

f) Kiehl et al. (1999b): N550

400   1000ms

g) Kiehl (2000): N500

200   800ms

h) Kiehl et al. (2000): N550

400   1000ms

——— Nonpsychopaths   ——— Psychopaths

Figure 3.1

Illustration of event-related potential (ERP) data from studies in criminal psychopaths depicting the late ERP negativities observed during (a) a motor preparation task (Forth & Hare, 1989), (b) an emotional lexical decision task (Williamson, Harpur, & Hare, 1991), (c) a concrete-abstract lexical decision task (Kiehl, Hare, McDonald, & Brink, 1999a), (d) a concrete-abstract discrimination task (Kiehl et al., 1999a), (e) an emotional polarity discrimination task (Kiehl et al., 1999a), (f) a visual oddball task (Kiehl, Hare, McDonald, & Liddle, 1999b), (g) an auditory oddball task (Kiehl, 2000), and (h) a go/no go response inhibition task (Kiehl et al., 2000). All figures are adapted to approximately the same time scale and amplitude (negative plotted up) and are from frontal or central electrode sites. eCNV = early contingent negative variation.

Abnormalities in language processing in response to emotional stimuli also have been observed in psychopathic individuals. Clinicians have long noted that psychopaths appear to "know the words but not the music" (Johns & Quay, 1962). That is, psychopaths appear to be able to describe the book meaning of emotional words, but the deeper, affective significance of these words is lost on them. For example, when asked to identify the emotion of a speaker on the basis of prosody, psychopaths appear to be impaired in the recognition of fearful vocal affect (R.J.R. Blair et al., 2002). Psychopaths also have difficulty categorizing emotional metaphors (Hervé, Hayes, & Hare, 2003). Evidence for abnormalities in language processing also comes from analyses of the speech of psychopathic individuals. Voice analyses show that such individuals do not express affective and neutral words differently (Louth et al., 1998).

Williamson, Harpur, and Hare (1991) studied psychopaths during the performance of an emotional lexical decision task. Studies have shown that healthy control participants respond faster and more accurately to letter strings that form emotional words (positive and negative in affect) than letter strings that form neutral words (Graves, Landis, & Goodglass, 1981). Williamson et al. found that psychopaths failed to show any difference in reaction time between emotional and neutral words. Psychopaths did, however, show better accuracy for emotional words than neutral words. Studies with healthy participants have shown that ERPs are sensitive to processing differences between emotional and neutral words as early as 200 milliseconds poststimulus (Begleiter, Gross, & Kissin, 1967). The general effect is that the ERPs are larger (more positive in this case) over central and parietal sites for emotional words than for neutral words. Psychopaths failed to show this ERP differentiation between emotional and neutral words, while criminal nonpsychopaths showed the expected ERP differentiation. Williamson et al. concluded that these data support the hypotheses that psychopaths have difficulty processing affective stimuli in the linguistic domain. Studies of patients with brain damage and functional brain imaging studies have linked the amygdala and the anterior and posterior cingulate with processing of affective words (Anderson & Phelps, 2001; Isenberg et al., 1999; Maddock & Buonocore, 1997).

Another interesting finding from the Williamson et al. (1991) ERP data was that psychopaths' ERPs to all linguistic stimuli (positive, negative, neutral words, and pseudowords) were characterized by a prominent late negativity at 500 milliseconds (N500) poststimulus at frontal and central electrode sites (see figure 3.1). Based on similarities in the morphology and topography of the psychopathic individuals' N350 (Kiehl et al., 1999a) and N500 (Williamson et al., 1991), Kiehl et al. (1999a) suggested a possible explanation for the functional significance of these components. The tasks employed by Williamson et al. and Kiehl et al. (1999a) involved lexicosemantic processing and required a concurrent behavioral response. Thus, in the 300–600 milliseconds after a word stimulus is presented, both semantic and decision-making processes are engaged and will elicit overlapping ERP components of opposite polarity. In general, presentation of a word stimulus in the absence of any on-line task demands will elicit a large ERP negativity in the 300–500 milliseconds time window (N4 or N400) rather than an ERP positivity. Thus, one interpretation of the psychopaths' frontocentral ERP negativities offered by Kiehl et al. (1999a) and Williamson et al. (1991) was that they may be related to an abnormally large N400. To the extent that the amplitude of the N400 reflects cognitive operations involved in processing the semantic meanings of words, these data are consistent with the hypothesis that psychopathy is associated with abnormal semantic processing. This latter interpretation is strengthened by the fact that abnormally large N400s have been reported in other psychopathological conditions with conceptual and empirical links to psychopathy (Niznikiewicz, O'Donnell, Nestor, Smith, Law, Karapelou, Shenton, & McCarley 1997).

Thus, at first glance there is considerable evidence that the late frontocentral ERP negativities observed in psychopaths during linguistic tasks may be related to abnormally large N400s. However, one study examining the N400 component in psychopaths during the performance of a classic sentence-processing task (Kutas & Hillyard, 1980) failed to find any evidence for abnormalities (Kiehl, Bates, Laurens, Hare, & Liddle, 2006). Thus, the N500 and N350 abnormalities observed in psychopaths do not appear to be related to the processes associated with the generation of the N400 component. This conclusion is tentative, however, pending further research.

In summary, studies of language processes suggest that psychopathy is associated with abnormalities in processing semantic and affective material. These abnormalities appear to be greatest when psychopaths are processing abstract stimuli and emotional stimuli. The processing of abstract word stimuli during lexical decision tasks is believed to rely upon the right anterior superior temporal gyrus. The processing of emotional word stimuli appears to rely upon the anterior and posterior cingulate and the amygdala. Thus, the extant language literature suggests that reduced activity is observed in psychopaths during language processing in the right anterior superior temporal gyrus, the amygdala, and the anterior and posterior cingulate.

Psychopathy: Conditioning, Attention, and Orienting Processes

Studies of attention and orienting can be traced back to the earliest days of psychophysiological research in psychopathy. In a classic study, Lykken (1957) found that psychopathic individuals (defined by ratings on Cleckley, 1941, criteria) failed to show conditioned autonomic increases in skin conductance in an aversive conditioning paradigm using electric shock (Lykken, 1957). Many studies examining the relationship between psychopathy and peripheral measures of autonomic nervous system functioning followed this study. These latter studies largely found that psychopathic individuals tend to show lower basal levels of skin conductance and exhibit smaller changes in skin conductance under a wide variety of experimental manipulations compared with nonpsychopathic inmates. In particular, psychopaths tend to show relatively small skin conductance changes to otherwise noxious stimuli, such as loud tones (Hare, Frazelle, & Cox, 1978), insertion of a hypodermic needle (Hare, 1972), and slides of mutilated faces (Mathis, 1970). Psychopaths also fail to show normal skin conductance increases in anticipation of receiving painful stimuli (Hare, 1965a; Hare & Quinn, 1971). Veit, Flor, Erb, Hermann et al. (2002) showed that psychopaths, relative to controls, show reduced hemodynamic activity in the orbital frontal cortex, the anterior cingulate, and the amygdala during an aversive conditioning study (Veit et al., 2002). It should be noted, however, that only four psychopathic individuals participated, and apparently only one or two met the criteria for psychopathy (i.e., PCL-R score greater than 30). Also, it appears that this latter study employed a within-subject or fixed-effects statistical analysis, which limits the inference that can be drawn to that of a case study.

The hippocampus is also believed to be involved in aversive conditioning. One study has reported a negative correlation between psychopathy scores and dorsal hippocampal volumes in violent offenders co-morbid with alcoholism (Laakso, Vaurio, Koivisto, Savolainen, Eronen, et al., 2001). Laakso et al. (2001) studied eighteen violent male offenders with a history of alcoholism and found that there was a strong negative correlation between dorsal hippocampal volume and PCL-R scores. This latter effect appeared to be strongest for factor 1 scores (interpersonal and affective) than for factor 2 scores (impulsive and behavioral). The data were interpreted as support for the model that the hippocampal dysfunction may be implicated in the poor aversive learning and acquisition of conditioned fear that characterizes psychopathy. Recently, Raine, Ishikawa, Arce, Lencz, Knuth, et al. (2004) found that unsuccessful psychopaths (individuals with a history of incarceration), compared with "successful" psychopaths (individuals without a history of incarceration) and healthy controls, had abnormal asymmetry in the anterior hippocampus. These data were interpreted as support for a neurodevelopmental perspective on psychopathy. This latter study was the first brain imaging work to compare "unsuccessful" with "successful" psychopaths. However, it appears that there were few individuals with PCL-R scores above the diagnostic cutoff (30 on the PCL-R) for psychopathy (Raine et al., 2004). Thus it remains to be determined if the results would generalize to individuals (successful or unsuccessful) with high scores on the psychopathy checklist.

This collection of abnormalities suggests that psychopaths have difficulty in fear conditioning, are relatively lacking in fear, and do not respond well in classical conditioning paradigms with punishment contingencies. An alternative interpretation, first proposed by Hare (1968), is that these results suggest abnormalities in orienting processes. That is, in all the psychophysiological studies listed here, an orienting response would be elicited by the salient cues or stimuli. The canonical orienting response is associated with a conjunction of peripheral and neuronal changes, including skin conductance increases, heart rate decreases, and blood pressure modulation. Sokolov (1963) is largely credited with describing the myriad experimental conditions under which orienting processes are engaged. In general, unpredictable, novel, or task-relevant salient stimuli, broadly defined, will lead to an orienting response (Sokolov, 1963). Indeed, Hare has suggested that deficient orienting processes or abnormalities in them might be a fundamental aspect of psychopathy (Hare, 1978).

ERP studies have been used to study aspects of the orienting response for many years in health and psychopathology. Processing of novel and salient (target) stimuli known to elicit an orienting response has been often been studied in the context of "oddball" paradigms. In a typical oddball paradigm, low-probability, task-irrelevant, novel stimuli (i.e., 10 percent of trials) and low-probability, task-relevant target stimuli (i.e., 10 percent of target trials or oddballs) are presented against a background of frequent or standard stimuli. Both novel and target stimuli are associated with a sequence of electrical components, the most prominent of which is a large, broadly distributed positive wave termed the P3 or P300. The P3s elicited by novel and target stimuli are believed to be related to processes involving attentional capture, allocation of cognitive resources, and contextual updating—all components linked to orienting processes.

There have been ten ERP studies on psychopathy defined according to PCL or PCL-R scores (Flor, Birbaumer, Hermann, Ziegler, & Patrick, 2002; Forth & Hare, 1989; Jutai & Hare, 1983; Jutai et al., 1987; Kiehl, 2000; Kiehl et al., 1999a; Kiehl, Hare, McDonald, & Liddle, 1999b; Kiehl et al., 2000b; Raine & Venables, 1988; Williamson et al., 1991). Nine studies have reported information concerning P3s in psychopathy, although only five studies employed paradigms in which the salience of stimuli was manipulated in a manner expected to elicit a canonical P3 response (Jutai et al., 1987; Kiehl, 2000; Kiehl, et al., 1999b; Kiehl et al., 2000b; Raine & Venables, 1988).

Jutai et al. (1987) found no significant difference between psychopaths and nonpsychopaths in the amplitude or latency of the P3. In contrast, Raine and Venables (1988) reported that the amplitude of parietal P3 to visual target stimuli elicited during a continuous performance task was greater in psychopaths than in nonpsychopaths. More recently, studies have shown that the P3 elicited during visual and auditory oddball tasks is slightly smaller over frontal, central, and parietal sites in psychopaths than in nonpsychopaths (Kiehl, 2000; Kiehl et al., 1999b). Similar effects were observed in psychopaths during performance of a response inhibition task (Kiehl et al., 2000b). In the remaining studies that reported information about P3, there was little evidence indicating that P3 amplitude was abnormal in psychopaths. However, these latter studies did not employ paradigms that manipulated the salience of the stimuli.

To summarize, in studies that have manipulated the salience of the stimuli in a manner expected to elicit a P3 response, one has reported a null finding (Jutai et al., 1987), one has reported enlarged P3s in psychopaths (Raine & Venables, 1988), and three studies, from independent samples, have reported reduced P3s in psychopaths (Kiehl, 2000; Kiehl et al., 1999b; Kiehl et al., 2000b). Thus, at present it is not clear whether the P3 is abnormal in psychopaths. However, perhaps more interesting and illuminating than the P3 in psychopathy is that a number of other ERP abnormalities were observed in psychopaths during processing of salient task-relevant target stimuli.

Recall that psychopaths' ERPs elicited by linguistic stimuli were characterized by an abnormal late negativity (N350, N500) that was maximal over frontal and central sites (Kiehl et al., 1999a; Williamson et al., 1991). In the studies that required on-line decision making but made no explicit demands on linguistic processing (and were recorded from frontal electrode sites), late ERP negativities also were observed in psychopaths (Kiehl, 2000; Kiehl et al., 1999b; Kiehl et al., 2000b). In two visual (nonlinguistic) target-detection tasks, psychopaths' waveforms were characterized by a late ERP negativity in the 300–500 millisecond time window (Kiehl et al., 1999b; Kiehl et al., 2000b). This ERP negativity was similar in morphology and topography to those observed in previous language tasks in psychopaths (see figure 3.1). In the auditory modality, Kiehl (2000) reported that 40 of 41 psychopaths showed an aberrantly large late frontocentral negativity for target stimuli in an oddball task. Psychopaths in this latter study also had a larger N2b and smaller P3 than did nonpsychopaths.

Similarly, Forth and Hare (1989) reported that the early contingent negative variation (CNV), which occurs at 300–800 milliseconds poststimulus, was abnormally large in psychopaths relative to nonpsychopaths at frontal sites (see figure 3.1). In the task used by Forth and Hare, the stimulus that elicited the early CNV was highly salient because the participants had to prepare to make a fast finger movement following the stimulus. It is therefore plausible that an alternative explanation for the presence of the large early CNV, during the same time window and a scalp topography typically associated with the late negativity in psychopaths, is that it is a late ERP negativity similar to that found in oddball and language tasks.

It is relevant to note that ERPs associated with oddball processing have been recorded in a wide range of psychiatric conditions with conceptual and empirical links to psychopathy. For example, Bauer and colleagues have shown that ASPD is reliably associated with reductions in the P3 component elicited during oddball tasks (Bauer, 2001a; Bauer & Hesselbrock, 1999; Bauer, O'Connor, & Hesselbrock, 1994). The P3 is also reduced in alcohol and substance abuse populations (Bauer, 1997, 2001b; Begleiter & Porjesz, 1995; Begleiter, Porjesz, Reich, Edenberg, Goate, et al., 1998; Iacono, 1998; Noronha, Eckard, & Warren, 1987; Pfefferbaum, Ford, White, & Mathalon, 1991). Psychopathy is known to be co-morbid with alcohol and substance abuse (Hemphill, Hart, & Hare, 1994; S.S. Smith & Newman, 1990). However, these ERP studies of ASPD, substance abuse, or alcoholism have not revealed any evidence of the late frontocentral ERP negativities seen in studies with psychopaths (Bauer, 2002).

In summary, studies have shown that psychopathy is associated with late frontocentral ERP negativities for a variety of stimuli. These abnormal ERP waveforms have been elicited by word stimuli (Kiehl et al., 1999a; Williamson et al., 1991), salient cues (Forth & Hare, 1989), simple visual stimuli (Kiehl et al., 1999b; Kiehl et al., 2000b), and task-relevant auditory stimuli (Kiehl, 2000). Indeed, every study that has reported ERPs from frontal electrode sites to salient task-relevant stimuli in a well-defined group of psychopaths has observed a late ERP negativity that was larger in psychopaths than in nonpsychopaths (Forth & Hare, 1989; Kiehl, 2000; Kiehl 1999a; Kiehl et al., 1999b; Kiehl et al., 2000b; Williamson et al., 1991). The consistency of these results is illustrated in figure 3.1. At least one common thread in these paradigms is that each is associated with orienting processes. Thus, a plausible interpretation for the functional significance of the frontocentral ERP negativities in psychopaths is that they are related to abnormal orienting processes. However, the neural systems implicated in these processes in psychopathy are still unclear.

The ERP data, from the oddball task in particular, have yielded precise information about the temporal stages of information processing in psychopaths. Studies have shown that ERP differences between psychopaths and nonpsychopaths emerge as early as 200 milliseconds poststimulus, with the psychopaths' enlarged N2b at frontal sites. The psychopaths' enlarged N2b is followed by a slightly smaller, broadly distributed P3 component and punctuated by the appearance of a late frontocentral negativity that is several times larger than that observed in nonpsychopaths. It is temping to infer from the ERP data that the neural generators associated with these abnormal components are located in frontal brain regions since the scalp-recorded ERPs are maximal over frontal electrode sites. However, locating ERP generators, particularly those occurring in later time windows, is problematic. Determining the neural generators underlying scalp-recorded ERPs is referred to as the "inverse problem," and there are an infinite number of combinations of electrical sources that could lead to the recordings observed at the scalp. This is particularly true for locating late components of an oddball task (Halgren & Marinkovic, 1996; Halgren, Marinkovic, & Chauvel, 1998). However, there are several additional avenues available to explore the neural systems underlying the processing of salient stimuli. A better understanding of which systems are engaged in processing oddball stimuli might lead to a better understanding of the neural circuits that are abnormal in psychopathy.

One of the first methods used to investigate the potential generators underlying the processing of salient or oddball stimuli was to record ERPs in patient populations with localized brain insults. The main tenet here is that if the circuits involved in processing salient stimuli are damaged, this should lead to observable abnormalities in the scalp-recorded ERPs. These studies found that frontal, temporal, parietal, and limbic structures are engaged during processing of oddball stimuli (see review by Soltani & Knight, 2000). It is interesting that in patients with temporal lobe damage, several studies found clear evidence for frontocentral ERP negativities during processing of salient target stimuli in oddball paradigms (R.J.

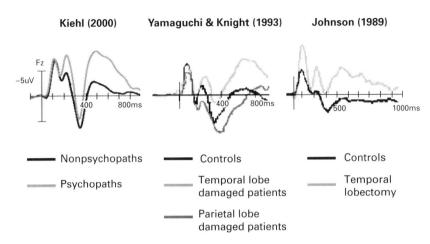

Figure 3.2

Comparison of the late ERP negativities elicited by auditory oddball stimuli in criminal psychopaths (Kiehl, 2000), patients with temporal lobe damage (Yamaguchi & Knight, 1993), and patients who had undergone temporal lobectomy for the treatment of intractable epilepsy (Johnson, 1989). All three groups are typified by an enhanced N2b, diminished frontal P3, and enlarged late negativity (N500) relative to control participants.

Johnson, 1993; Yamaguchi & Knight, 1993). Yamaguchi and Knight (1993) found that patients with temporal lobe damage, relative to controls or patients with parietal lobe damage, had enlarged N2bs, smaller P3s, and late frontocentral negativities (see figure 3.2). Similar effects were observed in epilepsy patients following resection of the anterior medial temporal lobe (the amygdala and anterior superior temporal gyrus) for the treatment of intractable epilepsy (R.J. Johnson, 1993). Paller and colleagues have also shown that frontocentral ERP negativities are elicited by auditory oddball stimuli in monkeys following temporal lobe lesions (Paller, McCarthy, Roessler, & Allison, 1992; Paller, Zola-Morgan, Squire, & Hillyard, 1988). These data suggest that an enlarged N2b, reduced P3, and late negativity at frontal sites elicited during processing of oddball stimuli appear to be characteristic of patients with temporal-limbic damage and criminal psychopaths (see figure 3.2 for comparison). Thus, it would appear that at present the most parsimonious interpretation for the late ERP negativities observed in psychopaths during processing of task-relevant salient stimuli is that they appear to be an electrophysiological signature of temporal-limbic brain abnormalities.

It is temping to conclude that these ERP components are linked to problems with orienting processes. Studies of patients with medial temporal lobe damage have shown that ERP abnormalities and autonomic responding elicited by orienting stimuli are impaired, despite the fact that these latter patients can reliably discriminate target and novel stimuli (Knight, 1996). These data suggest that the autonomic and neural components of the orienting response are impaired in patients with medial temporal lobe damage and in psychopathic individuals. It is also clear that diminished orienting processes (i.e., heart rate modulations, skin conductance changes, electrocortical responses) may not lead to impairment in task performance. That is, patients with medial temporal lobe damage and criminal psychopaths are not impaired in performing oddball tasks. Indeed, some data suggest that a lack of automatic orienting to salient stimuli may lead psychopaths to actually perform better than nonpsychopaths (Newman, Schmitt, & Voss, 1997). More studies are needed to examine the functional (and behavioral) significance of these orienting processes in psychopaths.

Another avenue available to examine the neural systems engaged during processing of salient stimuli is functional magnetic resonance imaging, event-related fMRI in particular. Studies using event-related fMRI have shown that in healthy individuals low-probability task-relevant target stimuli elicit a hemodynamic response in a diverse and widespread neuronal network, including sites in the amygdala and anterior superior temporal gyrus of the temporal lobe and the anterior and posterior cingulate of the limbic system (Ardekani, Choi, Hossein-Zadeh, Porjesz, Tanabe, et al., 2002; Casey, Forman, Franzen, Berkowitz, Braver, et al., 2001; Clark, Fannon, Lai, Benson, & Bauer, 2000; Desjardins, Kiehl, & Liddle, 2001; Horovitz, Skudlarski, & Gore, 2002; Kiehl, Laurens, Duty, Forster, & Liddle, 2001a; Kiehl & Liddle, 2003; Linden, Prvulovic, Formisand, Voellinger, Zamella, et al., 1999; Stevens, Skudlarski, Gatenby, & Gore, 2000). The results from these studies are closely parallel to the intracranial electrode data recorded from patients with brain pathology during similar tasks (Clarke, Halgren, & Chauvel, 1999a, 1999b; Halgren et al., 1998). To examine the hypothesis that psychopaths have hypofunctioning temporal-limbic circuits during processing of salient stimuli, Kiehl and colleagues (2000a) studied a group of criminal psychopaths using fMRI during performance of an auditory oddball task. Consistent with their hypothesis, psychopathy was associated with less hemodynamic activity in the bilateral amygdala, the anterior superior temporal gyrus, and the rostral and caudal anterior cingulate than was observed in control participants.

Psychopaths appeared to show normal hemodynamic activity to oddball stimuli in lateral frontal, parietal, posterior temporal, and occipital circuits.

A recent single photon-emission compared tomography (SPECT) study of violent offenders institutionalized in a psychiatric facility found that the interpersonal factor, but not the social deviance factor, of psychopathy was negatively correlated with perfusion in the temporal lobe and orbital frontal cortex (Soderstrom, Hultin, Tullberg, Wikkelso, Ekholm, et al., 2002). This was the first study to examine the factors of psychopathy and measures of hemodynamic activity. Unfortunately, the range of psychopathy scores was from 2 to 31, suggesting that few offenders were actually above the diagnostic cutoff of 30 for psychopathy (Hare, 1991, 2003). Nevertheless, as in other heterogeneous disorders (Liddle, 1995), these data suggest that the examination of the hemodynamic correlates of the factors of psychopathy may be fruitful.

To recap, studies of language, attention, and orienting processes suggest that the neural circuitry involved in psychopathy includes the amygdala; the anterior superior temporal gyrus; the orbital frontal cortex; and rostral, caudal, and posterior aspects of the cingulate gyrus.

Psychopathy and Affective Processing

A variety of different methods have been used to assess affective processes in psychopaths. The studies examining affective processes in psychopathy in the context of linguistic tasks were reviewed earlier. These studies largely found that psychopaths do not differentiate the subtleties between affective and neutral stimuli in the same way as criminal nonpsychopaths and healthy individuals (Intrator, Hare, Stritzke, Brichtswein, Dorfman, et al., 1997; Kiehl et al., 1999a; Williamson et al., 1991). It is particularly the case that these linguistic abnormalities appear to be manifest when psychopaths are processing negatively valenced stimuli (Day & Wong, 1996). Similarly, studies using the startle-reflex methodology have shown that psychopaths do not show the normal pattern of blink modulation when processing negatively valenced stimuli, as do nonpsychopaths and healthy individuals (Patrick et al., 1993). In healthy controls and in nonpsychopathic prisoners, startle probes presented during viewing of negative picture stimuli (e.g., mutilated faces) elicit a larger blink reflex response than during viewing of neutral or positive stimuli. However, this pattern of responding was not observed in psychopaths with high scores on the interpersonal and affective features of psychopathy. That is, the magnitude of the psychopaths' blink reflex was similar for processing of positive and negative stimuli, suggesting that negative stimuli did not elicit the same defensive response in psychopaths as it did in nonpsychopaths (see also Levenston et al., 2000). Indeed, one interpretation of the psychopaths' abnormal startle response is that they had an appetitive response to the negative stimuli. The neural circuitry of the startle response is relatively well understood and includes structures in the medial and lateral temporal lobe, in particular the amygdala. Similar abnormalities in startle processing have been observed in female psychopaths with elevated interpersonal and affective characteristics (Sutton et al., 2002).

Few other studies have directly examined the neural correlates of emotional processing in psychopaths. One study used fMRI to examine the neural systems associated with emotional processing in psychopaths during the context of an affective memory task (Kiehl et al., 2001c). In this study the participants were presented with a task that consisted of three phases: encoding, rehearsal, and recognition. In the encoding phase, a list of twelve words was presented serially. The participants were instructed to memorize the words and to mentally review them during the subsequent rehearsal phase. A recognition test followed in which the participants were presented with a list of twelve words, half of which had been presented during the encoding phase, and were asked to determine if the words were presented in the earlier list. They were not informed that half of the encoding-rehearsal-recognition phases contained all negative words and half contained neutral words. The experimental manipulation was therefore to examine the neural circuitry associated with differentiating emotional from neutral stimuli in psychopaths and controls. Consistent with previous research in healthy controls, in criminal nonpsychopaths and in noncriminal controls, the memory for affective stimuli was superior to that for neutral stimuli. Psychopaths showed a trend in this direction (see also Christianson, Forth, Hare, Strachan, Lindberg, & Thorell, 1996; Williamson et al., 1991). Importantly, there were no group differences in overall performance. This suggests that psychopaths were just as engaged in performance of the task as were the criminal nonpsychopaths and noncriminal controls.

The results of the imaging data indicated that psychopaths failed to show the normal pattern of differentiation between affective and neutral stimuli in the amygdala, ventral striatum, rostral and caudal anterior cingulate, and posterior cingulate. These latter limbic and paralimbic areas are normally associated with processing affective stimuli, and interestingly, are implicated in orienting processes (Cohen, Kaplan, Meadows, & Wilkinson, 1994). Recall, however, that psychopaths did show a trend toward better memory recall for negative than for neutral words. Thus, there should be some brain regions in which psychopaths show greater activity when processing negative than neutral stimuli than do controls. Psychopaths, but not controls, showed differences in brain activation for affective relative to neutral stimuli in the bilateral lateral frontal cortex. These latter areas are normally associated with semantic processing.

Thus, it appears that psychopathy is associated with hypofunctioning of temporolimbic circuits that are normally associated with affective processing and that perhaps lateral frontal brain regions are engaged in some compensatory manner. In other words, these findings are a nice recapitulation of the idea that psychopaths' brains "know the words, but not the music" (Johns & Quay, 1962). These data also provide support for the hypothesis that the excessive affect-related activity observed in psychopaths in the lateral frontotemporal cortex (Intrator et al., 1997) may compensate for reduced activity in limbic regions. However, this latter interpretation is still tentative pending further replication.

In summary, cognitive neuroscience studies of affective processing have found that the neural circuits embracing the temporolimbic system are either dysfunctional or hypofunctioning in psychopathy. In particular, the sites implicated include the amygdala, parahippocampal regions (Laakso et al., 2001; Raine et al., 2004), the anterior superior temporal gyrus, the rostral and caudal anterior cingulate, and the posterior cingulate. Similar abnormalities are observed in these neural circuits in psychopaths during performance of language, attention, and orienting tasks.

Psychopathy and the Paralimbic System

Studies of patients with brain damage suggest that regions of the frontal lobe, including the orbital frontal cortex and anterior cingulate, and regions of the temporal lobe, including the amygdala, parahippocampal gyrus, and anterior superior temporal gyrus are implicated in psychopathic symptomology. Psychophysiology studies employing event-related potentials have repeatedly shown that in psychopaths the brain potentials elicited by salient stimuli are associated with aberrant late negativities (see figure 3.1). These aberrant brain potentials are also observed in patients with temporal lobe damage in general and the amygdala and anterior superior temporal gyrus in particular (see figure 3.2). Cognitive neuroscience studies of psychopathy suggest that the anterior and posterior cingulate, insula, orbital frontal cortex, amygdala, and anterior superior temporal gyrus are dysfunctional or hypofunctioning in psychopathy during language, attention and orienting, and affective processing tasks. At first glance it might appear that these neural circuits implicated in psychopathy come from a heterogeneous and spatially remote collection of brain regions. However, neuroanatomists and cytoarchitectologists have grouped the anterior superior temporal gyrus (temporal pole), the rostral and caudal anterior cingulate, the posterior cingulate, the orbital frontal cortex, the insula, and the parahippocampal regions into the paralimbic cortex (Brodmann, 1909, 1994; Mesulam, 2000).

The paralimbic cortex, also referred to as the mesocortex, is interposed between the neocortex and allocortex (figure 3.3). It provides a gradual transition from primary limbic regions, including the septal region, substantia innominata, and the amygdaloid complex, to higher neocortical regions. It is important to note that there are dense connections between the paralimbic cortex and core limbic structures, in particular the amygdala. The amygdaloid complex is composed of both nuclear and cortical layers. These cortical features of the amygdala often extend into the paralimbic areas, blurring the boundaries between limbic and paralimbic regions (Mesulam, 2000). Thus, these regions may collectively be termed the paralimbic system.

These data suggest that the relevant functional neuroanatomy implicated in psychopathy is the paralimbic system. At present it is not known how or when in development these abnormalities in psychopathy arise. Clinical (Cleckley, 1976; Hare, 1993) and recent research data suggest that psychopathic symptoms are present at a very early age (Frick, 1995, 1998; Frick, Barry, & Bodin, 2000). Given that the brain structures implicated in psychopathy are linked by cytoarchitectural similarities, it is temping to argue that psychopathy may be neurodevelopmental in nature. However, at present there are little data to suggest structural brain alterations in psychopathy. Two structural MRI studies have shown that psychopathy is associated with hippocampal abnormalities (Laakso et al., 2001; Raine et al., 2004). Clearly, more research on functional and structural brain changes in psychopathy is needed.

It is important to recognize that the hypothesis that limbic and paralimbic structures are implicated in psychopathy is not new. Indeed, clinicians have speculated since the time of Phineas Gage (1800s) that frontal brain regions are implicated in the disorder (Harlow, 1848). Similarly, Fowles (1980) postulated that the basis of psychopathy was a deficiency in the behavioral inhibition system—a system that is believed to rely upon septohippocampal brain regions (see also Gorenstein & Newman, 1980). Raine (1993) has emphasized the role of the orbital frontal cortex in antisociality

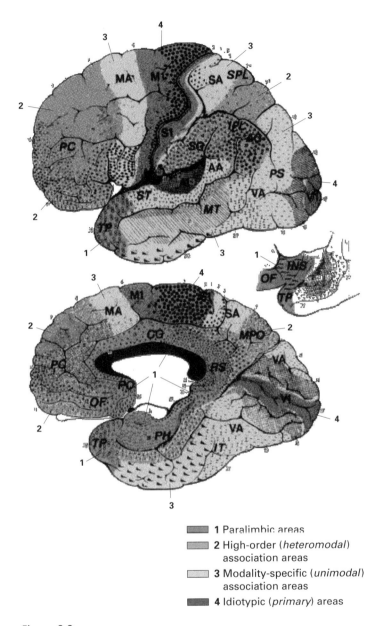

1 Paralimbic areas

2 High-order (*heteromodal*) association areas

3 Modality-specific (*unimodal*) association areas

4 Idiotypic (*primary*) areas

Figure 3.3

Illustration of the cytoarchitectural maps of Brodmann (1909) (adapted from Mesulam, 2000). The components of the paralimbic system include the orbital frontal cortex; the medial (amygdala and parahippocampal gyrus) and lateral (anterior superior temporal gyrus) temporal lobe; and the rostral, caudal, and posterior cingulate gyrus.

and psychopathy. Other researchers have argued that amygdala dysfunction is central to models of psychopathy (R.J.R. Blair, 2003, 2001, 2002). The argument that the paralimbic system is abnormal in psychopathy is consistent with these latter perspectives. However, the review offered here from the neurological literature suggests that selective lesions in the septal-hippocampal system, orbital frontal cortex, or amygdala do not lead to the complete manifestation of psychopathy. Moreover, the functional neuroimaging data suggest that in addition to these latter structures, the anterior and posterior cingulate are implicated in psychopathy. Thus, the argument presented here is that a broader view, encompassing all of the paralimbic system, is warranted.

It is also relevant to recognize that a potential limitation of this model is that most of the supporting evidence comes from studies examining brain function or from indirect evidence of behavioral changes in patients following brain damage or lesions. The definition of the paralimbic system is based on similarities in the cytoarchitecture or brain structure; however, there is a relative paucity of studies that have examined gray matter abnormalities in psychopathy. The few structural brain imaging studies in psychopathy suggest that hippocampal regions (i.e., paralimbic) are implicated in the disorder (Laakso et al., 2001; Raine et al., 2004). Future structural imaging studies may lead to a better understanding of whether the abnormalities in brain function observed in psychopaths may map onto structural brain pathology. Studies of brain metabolism (i.e., positron emission tomography, PET) may also provide insights into the relevant neuroanatomy implicated in psychopathy.

In summary, converging evidence suggests that psychopathy is associated with a dysfunction of the paralimbic system. This hypothesis is supported by indirect evidence from studies of behavioral changes following lesions or damage to this system. It is bolstered by findings from analogue studies and further supported by the extant cognitive neuroscience literature in psychopathy. The particular neural regions implicated include the orbital frontal cortex; the insula, the amygdala; the parahippocampal regions; the anterior superior temporal gyrus; and the rostral, caudal, and posterior cingulate. It is important to note that the studies reviewed employed the PCL-R or its derivatives to assess psychopathy (Hare, 2003). The PCL-R is widely considered to be the best metric for assessing psychopathy in forensic and clinical contexts. The replicability and consistency of the neurobiological findings are a further testament to the psychometric robustness of the PCL-R and the construct of psychopathy in general.

To conclude, this review has examined data from psychological, electrophysiological, and brain imaging studies in psychopathy during language, attention and orienting, and affective tasks. In addition, this review has considered indirect evidence from behavioral and cognitive changes associated with brain damage or insults. These converging results suggest that the relevant functional neural architecture implicated in psychopathy is the paralimbic system.

Note

The author would like to thank his mentors, Drs. Michael Levenson, Robert Hare, and Peter Liddle for their tutelage.

3.1 The Antisocials Amid Us

Ricardo de Oliveira-Souza, Fátima Azevedo Ignácio, and Jorge Moll

Kiehl has done an admirable job in describing the current state of the art on psychopathy, offering both a rich clinical view of the syndrome and a crisp summary of experimental work conducted with a range of psychological, electrophysiological, and imaging techniques. He also provides a comprehensive view on the putative links between brain regions involved in affective responses, semantic processing, and executive functions. We concur with his idea that the increased activity observed in psychopaths in the lateral frontal cortex might signal an increased reliance on certain cognitive mechanisms to compensate for a relative hypofunction of limbic subregions. We would emphasize that while such a vicarious compensatory function may help solve laboratory tasks, it does not translate automatically into real-life moral behavior. It would be interesting if Kiehl could comment on this aspect. He also speculates that psychopathy might arise from the dysfunction of a network of regions comprising the paralimbic system, a clear theoretical advance over commonly held views that tend to overestimate the role of specific brain regions, such as the ventromedial prefrontal cortex or the amygdala, in the genesis of psychopathy. Kiehl's framework agrees in essential ways with the model we recently proposed on how different brain networks engender normal and abnormal moral behavior (Moll, Zahn, de Oliveira-Souza, Krueger, & Grafman, 2005). In view of the richness of Kiehl's review of criminal psychopathy, we opted to provide some still unpublished evidence from our work on psychopathic behavior in community settings, i.e., in nonincarcerated individuals. Given the relative paucity of investigations using this population, we thought that bringing this topic to this forum would provide an opportunity to broaden the discussion to other faces of antisocial behavior disorders (ASBD).

As shown by Kiehl's account, most studies of psychopathy derive from work on incarcerated individuals (both psychopaths and nonpsychopaths)

and more recently on successful psychopaths who dwell in the community. ("Successful" in this context strictly refers to psychopaths whose crimes go undetected or who remain uncaught despite detection by law enforcement systems [Yang, Raine, Lencz, Bihrle, LaCasse, et al., 2005].) However, our attention has long been attracted to psychopathy from the perspective of the physician and the psychologist working outside forensic settings. We adopted a broad operational definition of ASBD as one that fulfills criterion A for antisocial personality disorder (American Psychiatric Association, 1994). In this commentary we argue that some individuals who meet the formal diagnostic criteria for ASBD or psychopathy primarily seen in nonforensic medical settings display certain characteristics that make them peculiar within the broader group of antisocials. Much of our desire to study these individuals was inspired by a practical need to improve our knowledge on the "prevalence of psychopathy in the general population, and its expression in ways that are personally, socially, or economically damaging, but that are not necessarily illegal or that do not result in criminal prosecution" (Hare, 1998). The phenomenology of community ASBD as it presents to us in real life is illustrated by two vignettes abstracted from our patient files. We argue that cases like these contrast in important ways with the criminal psychopath pictured by Kiehl.

Cases

Nonpsychopathic Antisocial

A 69-year-old housewife was brought to consultation by her daughter-in-law because of several months of despondency, lack of motivation, and nocturnal insomnia. She attributed her depression to the death of her husband 4 years earlier and to long-standing financial troubles. She tearfully stated that she loved her family and that they loved her too. Yet she could not understand how her two successful sons would leave her in constant need of money. She was treated with venlafaxine and her mood returned to normal in a few weeks. After a few appointments for dose adjustments, her granddaughter and daughter-in-law asked for a private conversation. They stated that she was a lovely grandmother whom they did care for, yet they had to take some "precautions" in their interactions with her. For example, she would lie for no reason and was pleased to create stories that caused serious conflicts among family members. In the past these stories seemed authentic to the point of threatening their marriages. Things did not get worse because their husbands soon advised their wives about the "difficult character" of their mother, which had been so ever since they were little children. Her impulsivity was most remarkable in her way of dealing with her finances. She never saved money and she spent whatever she got on small purchases or on clothes and shoes that she seldom wore. She often stole items from her daughters-in-law's houses, such as underwear and ashtrays. She would become verbally offensive if they refused to put more money in her bank account (which is what they eventually did in order to preserve her credit). When confronted with the incongruencies in her stories, she argued that she only did "the right thing": "after all, I raised my children all by myself without anybody's help."

Comments At first sight, this nice lady appears to be the antithesis of the proverbial psychopath. In fact, more than a year elapsed before we suspected she might have ASBD. A careful assessment of her behavior and attitudes based on several collateral sources of information, however, showed that she fit most criteria for ASBD. She scored 16/24 on the screening version of the Psychopathy Checklist (PCL:SV), thus she was below the threshold for psychopathy.[1]

Psychopathic Antisocial
The 32-year-old daughter of a prominent politician was brought by her mother for treatment for behavioral problems first noticed in late childhood. When she was 15, she dated a 19-year-old drug dealer who brought her marijuana and later cocaine. Her mother was alarmed when she attempted to sell musical instruments that had been stolen by her boyfriend, who had served a term in prison. By that time her academic performance had drastically deteriorated, and it took her 6 years to complete high school. She had an abortion when she was 16 and blamed her parents for that. She spent the night out and slept during the day. She engaged in voluntary community work in the *favelas* (slums) of Rio, where she became acquainted with swindlers and drug dealers. She was seen by several psychiatrists and psychologists, who did not see anything wrong with her, except "immaturity" and "a lack of limits from her parents." Given her characteristic behavioral impersistence, she would not remain in psychotherapy or any other treatment for more than a few weeks. Her boyfriends are often illiterate and physically abusive. She eventually gave birth to a child when she was 29. She believes that the infant's father is a former boyfriend who sold her drugs. Although she states that she loves her son, she often leaves him with strangers at home, caring little for feeding

schedules and clothing. When asked whether dealing or taking drugs is "right" or "wrong," she answers "wrong" without hesitation. However, when the question is rephrased in personal terms, she says that "drugs are the only way for socially sensitive people like myself to escape, at least momentarily, the oppression of capitalism." At present, she is attempting to persuade her father to support her plans to enter politics because "no one knows the problems of the poor as I do, based on my large experience while I worked with them." She is now certain that only by entering politics will she be able to accomplish the social projects that she has developed for years (but which no one has ever seen). Nevertheless, her relatives are fond of her and emphasize her compassionate and friendly nature, "as long as we comply with her wishes and needs."

Comments This woman was cognitively intact and scored 18/24 on the PCL:SV. Therefore, she met the criteria for ASBD as well as for psychopathy. She did not conform to the callous psychopath though, as she seemed capable of experiencing genuine prosocial feelings and never engaged in violent criminal behavior. This is a common situation worldwide; despite adequate parental support, some individuals may present an increasingly diversified host of antisocial behaviors and attitudes as they grow out of their adolescence.

Some Methodological Aspects Underlying the Concept of Community Antisocials and Psychopaths

Fifty-five individuals fulfilling a *DSM-IV* criterion A diagnosis for antisocial personality disorder were studied (American Psychiatric Association, 1994). They represent a subset of a larger group of patients referred by a colleague or relative for diagnostic evaluation, treatment, or counseling between 1989 and 2004. Psychopathy checklist scores were obtained in each of them. The PCL is a widely accepted measure of psychopathy originally developed for use in forensic settings. A screening version—the PCL:SV— was developed for use in civilian life as well. PCL:SV scores can range from 0 to 24, and scores higher than 17 are indicative of psychopathy (Forth, Brown, Hart, & Hare, 1996). Factor analyses revealed that PCL:SV scores load on two main factors: Factor 1 represents the emotional and personality characteristics of psychopathy, and Factor 2 reflects overall antisocial behavior and may be high even in nonpsychopathic antisocials.

Common presenting diagnoses included manic phase of bipolar disorder, attention deficit disorder, chemical dependence, "adolescence crisis," "parental neglect," "unjustified parental concerns," "lack of limits," "too much limits," "repressive parents," "unpredictable mood swings," "depression," "academic failure," "neurological immaturity," and "influence of bad peers." These expressions reflected parental concerns or the particular theoretical orientation of the referring professional. None of the individuals had previously received a diagnosis of personality disorder or psychopathy. They were independently classified as "parasites" or "predators" (Karpman, 1946); predators differed from parasites in their ability to plan and carry out the infliction of pain or physical harm to accomplish their goals. Whereas predators are typically involved in "cold blooded" violence (Woodworth & Porter, 2002), violent acts engaged in by parasites are typically of the reactive type. Formal evidence of violent criminal behavior was independently sought in all individuals.

Seventeen (31%) ASBDs had been involved with the criminal justice system for violent behavior (homicide and assault). A case-by-case analysis of their histories and behavioral styles indicated that they succeeded at avoiding imprisonment through financial help from relatives or breaches in the Brazilian penal system (Yang et al., 2005). By definition, these comprised the successful antisocials (SCAs). Seventeen antisocials were independently classified as predators. There was a significant overlap between being a violent criminal and being a predator ($\Phi = 0.71$, $p < 0.001$).[2] Cases such as these possibly set the grounds upon which the modern concept of psychopathy has been erected.

As stated earlier, our interest centered on the remaining 38 cases that we have called "true community antisocials" (TCAs). These were predominantly women, had more years of education, never perpetrated violent crimes, and led a parasitic lifestyle, with a roughly equal distribution of psychopaths and nonpsychopaths. Accordingly, TCAs had lower PCL:SV total and factor 1 and 2 scores and higher overall levels of sociooccupational functioning (table 3.1.1). This was reflected in an inverse relationship between the global assessment of functioning (GAF) scale and PCL:SV factor 2 ($r = -0.59$, $p < 0.001$) and factor 1 ($r = -0.28$, $p < 0.04$). The GAF is a measure of overall sociofunctional level that ranges from 1 (the lowest) to 100 (American Psychiatric Association, 1994). Another interesting finding was that of only a modest association between psychopathy and violent crime ($\Phi = 0.45$, $p < 0.001$). A few negative findings are also worthy of note: The age at first consultation, the global cognitive status (as assessed by the mini-mental state exam), and the frequency of alcohol and illicit drug abuse did not significantly differ between TCAs and SCAs.

Table 3.1.1

Contrasts between types of community antisocials

		Criminal (N = 17)	Noncriminal (N = 38)
Psychopathy	Yes	**15**	17
	No	2	21
Age at first interview (years)		34 ± 17	30 ± 15
Gender	Males	**13**	11
	Females	4	**27**
Education (years)		**8.6 ± 3.6**	**10.9 ± 2.9**
Alcohol and drug abuse	Yes	7	15
	No	10	23
Interpersonal callousness	Parasites	3	**34**
	Predators	**14**	3
Mini-mental state exam		27.7 ± 2.2	26.5 ± 3.5
GAF		**22 ± 4**	**36 ± 10**
PCL:SV	Factor 1	**10.9 ± 1.8**	**8.2 ± 2.5**
	Factor 2	**11.2 ± 1.1**	**8.2 ± 2.1**
	Total	**22.1 ± 2.5**	**16.5 ± 3.9**

Statistically significant differences ($p < 0.05$, two-tailed) appear in bold.

"True" Community Antisocials: A Distinctive Syndrome

In qualitative terms, TCAs showed a predictable pattern of feeling and acting that diverged in many ways from that of violent antisocials. This view was corroborated by a weak correlation between psychopathy and violent crime, indicating that although it is not casual, this association is far from necessary. The antisocial behaviors of TCAs consisted of recurrent and frequent violations of the rights of others for their own gain. For the most part, such violations consisted of minor infractions (truancy, lies, stealing small amounts of money) that would cause no serious harm if they were only sporadic. However, their recurrence ultimately resulted in substantial losses for those who supported the TCAs, usually a relative. They did not seem to care whether they were causing harm to their supporters, nor did they appear to be moved by the suffering they inflicted on others. Indeed, they seldom acknowledged their roles as agents of that suffering. When portrayed as perpetrators, they harshly disapproved their own conduct and even apologized for it. The knowledge of how to behave appropriately was expressed only rhetorically and had little, if any, impact on their behavioral guidance in real contexts. This bizarre dissociation of knowing from acting has led some authors to suggest that a new legal construct is needed to account for the "inability to guide one's behavior despite the availability of requisite knowledge" (Goldberg, 2001).

Interpersonal relational styles were individually fairly stable at an early age. Most were warm and outgoing, excelling in charm and wit in social encounters. They appeared genuinely concerned with the misfortunes of people unrelated to them, such as homeless children or victims of warfare and famine. This way of relating to others did not easily fit the picture of callousness and selfishness usually brought to mind by words like "antisocial" or "psychopath." This apparent paradox vanished in every case whenever they were caught in situations of conflict of interest, typically when they were expected to cooperate in hierarchical networks in which they had to obey dominant others. Then their behavior immediately reverted to a cluster of selfish actions and attitudes that eventually ended in verbal offenses and even physical aggression. Another important aspect of the TCA pattern refers to the low occupational capacity of these individuals, which sharply distinguished the TCAs from adjusted and productive individuals.

Closing Comments

Our results concur with those of Barry, Fleming, and Maxwell (1997), showing that community antisocials are often seen by health care professionals. They also emphasize the need to refine the typology of ASBD by analyzing different combinations of PCL subscores (Vitacco, Neumann, & Jackson, 2005). We have collected evidence in support of the hypothesis that such true community antisocials and the violent criminals who live in the community differ in critical ways.

If others confirm the typology of TCAs, it would be interesting to know in what ways TCAs differ from incarcerated antisocials and SCAs in terms of neurobehavioral profiles and cerebral mechanisms. From a practical point of view, antisocials probably come under medical and psychological attention more frequently than is usually realized. Unnecessary expenses with consultations, misguided psychotherapies, and ancillary exams could be avoided if ASBD were recognized earlier in the diagnostic process (Barry et al., 1997). Although chronic ASBD can hardly be remediated, an accurate diagnosis might improve the management of these individuals by those with whom they live. The study of TCA behavior as a distinct type of ASBD could as well illuminate specific features of the neural organization of human cooperation and altruism (Moll, Oliveira-Souza, & Eslinger, 2003; Moll et al., 2005).

Notes

1. Following Forth et al. (1996), psychopathy was defined by PCL:SV scores > 17.

2. The *phi* (Φ) coefficient is a measure of the strength of the association between categorical variables. It is interpreted as the Pearson's *r* or Spearman's *rho* (ρ), and can likewise vary from −1 to +1 (Welkowitz, Ewen, & Cohen, 1991).

Impaired Moral Reasoning in Psychopaths?
Response to Kent Kiehl

Jana Schaich Borg

Perhaps motivated by growing knowledge about the distinct functions of the ventromedial and dorsolateral prefrontal cortex, neuroscientists have become increasingly interested in traditional philosophical questions regarding the roles of emotion (often equated with affect) and reason (often equated with intellect or cognition) in sociomoral interaction and behavior. Psychopaths provide a particularly interesting opportunity to study this dissociation because their hypothesized impairments in the paralimbic system, credited as the emotional system of the brain, result in an "absence of moral behavior in the presence of an otherwise intact intellect" (this volume, p. 120). As the chapter by Kent Kiehl thoroughly outlines, cognitive neuroscience data have shown that psychopaths have deficits in emotional processing, yet they are still able to maintain a "mask of sanity" and rationalize what is morally right or appropriate (although they are not able to perform a related task of distinguishing between moral and conventional norms; Blair, 1995). It is not until psychopaths have to do what they define as morally correct that their performance obviously deviates from that of the normal population. Kiehl stated in a personal correspondence (October 5, 2005), "Psychopaths are not impaired in their ability to reason about what is right or wrong. They are only impaired in their ability to do or follow through with what they reason to be right or wrong." At first glance, then, it seems that psychopaths might provide evidence that emotion is not needed for moral reason or judgment. Emotion is only needed for moral action or practice.

Evidence from our group at Dartmouth College casts doubt on the view that emotion is unnecessary for successful moral reasoning. We completed an fMRI study exploring how dilemmas testing three moral doctrines—consequentialism, the doctrine of doing and allowing (DDA), and the doctrine of double effect (DDE)—are processed in the brain (Schaich Borg, Hynes, van Horn, Grafton, & Sinnott-Armstrong, 2006). Briefly, consequentialism claims that we morally ought to do whatever has the best overall consequences for ourselves and for others (Sinnott-Armstrong, 2003). The doctrine of doing and allowing states that it takes more to justify doing harm than to justify allowing harm (Howard-Snyder, 2002). The doctrine of double effect holds that it takes more to justify harms that were intended either as ends or as means than to justify harms that were known but unintended side effects (McIntyre, 2004). Thus, people who feel that it is wrong to pull the lever in the trolley dilemma (Foot, 1967; Thomson, 1976, discussed in Greene, Sommerville, Nystrom, Darley, & Cohen, 2001, in Greene, Nystrom, Engell, Darley, & Cohen, 2004, and in many of the contributions to this collection) are often sympathetic to the DDA, and people who feel it is wrong to push the stranger in the footbridge case are often sympathetic to the DDE. Most people have at least some intuitions consistent with these doctrines, as evidenced by the doctrines' significant roles in both law (in Good Samaritan laws and the concept of *mens rea*) and religion (such as when the Catholic Church cites a prohibition on intended harm to justify its official positions on abortion and euthanasia). Given their prevalence in moral intuition and practice, we thought the doctrines might also be useful tools to probe moral decision making in the brain. This indeed proved to be the case.

We asked subjects to respond to moral scenarios that were carefully controlled for immediate consequences (how many lives saved or lost), action (actively caused harm versus permitted or allowed harm), intention (intentionally caused harm versus only foreseen harm), and language (colorful language versus plain language) while being scanned in the fMRI scanner at Dartmouth. We found that activity in the orbitofrontal cortex and temporal pole was associated with the experimental factor of intention in moral scenarios, and activity in the dorsolateral prefrontal cortex was associated with the experimental factor of action in moral scenarios after all other factors were taken into account. Thus, our data suggest that intuitions associated with the doctrine of double effect are associated with emotional systems of the brain, while intuitions associated with the doctrine of doing and allowing are associated with activity in cognitive or reasoning systems in the brain.

If the paralimbic system—which includes the orbitofrontal cortex and temporal pole—is impaired in psychopaths as the evidence in Kent Kiehl's chapter suggests, and if our study accurately reports that moral decisions involving the DDE but not the DDA typically invoke activity in regions of the paralimbic system, then it is likely that psychopaths will not make moral distinctions consistent with the DDE, but will make moral decisions consistent with the DDA. In other words, psychopaths' paralimbic or *emotional* impairments may be responsible for impairments or at least consistent abnormalities in some types of moral *reasoning*. Evidence from patients with damage to the orbitofrontal cortex (often called "pseudopsychopaths" or patients with "acquired sociopathy") reported in Marc Hauser's chapter (volume 2) supports our prediction. Also of note, multiple studies have shown that psychopaths perform normally on tasks that require the identification and interpretation of others' intentions and mental states (Blair, Sellars, Strickland, Clark, Williams, Smith, & Jones, 1996; Richell, Mitchell, Newman, Leonard, Baron-Cohen, & Blair, 2003), so if psychopaths do not reliably make moral distinctions consistent with the DDE, their behavioral abnormalities will not be explained by deficits in a theory of mind.

Our research group speculates that a likely explanation for the patterns of brain activity observed in our fMRI study may be that intuitions associated with the DDA are mediated by conscious principles tied to well-taught rules like "Thou shall not kill," whereas intuitions associated with the DDE are mediated more by unconscious or inaccessible principles not tied to commonly articulated rules. These speculations are based on participants' comments about the experimental dilemmas and differences in activation observed in the right angular gyrus, a region involved in one's sense of agency. If activity in the paralimbic system represents use of unconscious moral principles, then we would hypothesize that psychopaths would also reason abnormally about other not yet identified unconscious moral principles. We would further predict that if such unconscious principles were explicitly taught and made conscious to psychopaths, their subsequent reasoning about the principles would quickly look and sound more like that of healthy individuals. However, in the latter case, psychopaths' judgments would be mediated by more cognitive or reasoning brain systems than the brain systems mediating the same judgments in nonpsychopaths. Further research is clearly needed to substantiate these particular predictions, but any research about psychopaths' specific rational or emotional deficits will provide unique insight into which neurological systems support reason and emotion. More fundamentally, such research may also help us understand what we really are trying to differentiate when we contrast these terms.

In closing, a brief comment should be made about the words "emotion" and "cognition" in cognitive neuroscience. While this classic distinction has been useful in initial efforts to sort out the neural underpinnings of sociomoral behavior, the terms "reason," "emotion," "intellect," or "cogni-tion" are commonly used in the scientific literature without defining what they are supposed to mean. For example, can psychopaths be said to have an "intact intellect," as proposed by Kiehl when they have the clear deficits in language processing and attention or orienting described in his chapter? Also recall that unlike control participants, a psychopath's ability to remember emotional words more than nonemotional words was nonsig-nificant at $p < 0.067$ in the study by Kiehl, Smith, Hare, Mendrek, Forster, Brink, and Liddle (2001c). Should psychopaths' "emotional" deficits never count as "cognitive" deficits, even if their "emotional" deficits result in an inability to enhance or facilitate memory with emotion, rendering their memory less effective than that of nonpsychopaths in many practical situ-ations? Not discussed by Kiehl here, it has been known since 1965 that psychopaths condition more slowly than nonpsychopaths during fear-conditioning paradigms and also show less generalization of the condi-tioned response to new stimuli (Hare, 1965b). Recent fMRI data suggest that these deficiencies are most likely due to psychopaths' lack of para-limbic activity during the conditioning phases of fear-conditioning para-digms (Birbaumer, Veit, Lotze, Erb, Hermann, et al., 2005). Is it accurate to say psychopaths have an "intact intellect" when they are impaired in their ability to learn to stay away from things that are bad for them? Finally, would it be fair to say psychopaths have an "intact intellect" if we find out in the future that they do in fact demonstrate abnormal moral reasoning?

These examples refer to psychopaths, but the language used in Kiehl's chapter is consistent with other scientific literature on morality. Perhaps the emerging field of moral neuroscience hasn't defined the terms "emotion," "reason," "cognition," "intellect," etc. because we aren't yet sure what they are. For many neuroscientists and for the purposes of this response, the terms "reason" and "emotion," respectively, are used as default labels for the distinction between bottom-up automatic processing (associated with affect) that is mediated primarily by a ventromedial neural system and top-down deliberative processing (associated with working memory) that is mediated primarily by a dorsolateral neural system. The ventromedial and dorsolateral systems do not typically act in isolation, however, and neither do whatever we instinctively mean by "reason" and "emotion"; they act in parallel and with constant interaction.

So what exactly do we, as philosophers or neuroscientists, want to dif-ferentiate in these terms? In my opinion, the vagueness of language used in moral neuroscience represents a lack of understanding that will remain as long as these linguistic terms are accepted as the best way to operationalize our inquiries. Researchers interested in the psychology and biology of morality should use their interdisciplinary insight to develop working definitions of what these terms are supposed to mean in a scientific context. Perhaps Kiehl can suggest how to apply the terms "emotion," "reason," and "cognition" to his theory of psychopaths with paralimbic, "emotional" dysfunction but "intact intellects."

3.3 | A Reply to de Oliveira-Souza, Ignácio, and Moll and Schaich Borg

Kent A. Kiehl

De Oliveira-Souza, Ignácio, and Moll, and Schaich Borg raise a number of interesting points in their commentaries that deserve consideration. The first issue raised by de Oliveira-Souza et al. concerns the interpretation of excessive activity in the lateral frontal cortex in psychopaths during the performance of affective tasks. In addition, the relevance of this effect to real-world moral decision-making behavior was questioned. With respect to the former issue, several studies have found that criminal psychopaths show larger (excessive) hemodynamic activity in the lateral frontal cortex during processing of emotional stimuli than do nonpsychopaths. This effect has been observed during an emotional memory task (Kiehl, Smith, Hare, Mendrek, Forster, Brink, & Liddle, 2001c), an emotional lexical decision task (Intrator, Hare, Stritzke, Brichtswein, Dorfman, et al., 1997), and an emotional picture processing task (Kiehl, Laurens, Celone, Pearlson, & Liddle, 2003). Psychopaths, relative to nonpsychopaths, also show reduced hemodynamic activity during emotional processing in multiple regions of the paralimbic system, including the amygdala and the anterior and posterior cingulate. Thus, one interpretation of the excessive brain activity in the lateral frontal cortex in psychopaths is that it represents compensatory process(es) for deficient paralimbic activity.

An alternative interpretation of the excessive lateral frontal cortex activity is that psychopaths engage in top-down cognitive control processes that suppress paralimbic activity during the processing of salient stimuli. Presumably top-down cognitive control processes utilize greater neural activity in psychopaths than in nonpsychopaths, and this activity is localized to the lateral frontal cortex. This latter interpretation would be favored by Newman and colleagues, who have put forth a top-down cognitive control theory of psychopathy (Newman, 1998; Newman & Lorenz, 2002). At present, both the top-down and compensatory interpretations of excessive hemodynamic activity in psychopaths are plausible. However, future research is needed to clarify these perspectives.

De Oliveira-Souza et al. also questioned whether the presence of excessive lateral frontal cortex activity in psychopaths during laboratory tasks might be related to real-world moral decision-making behavior. At present it is not possible to directly determine whether psychopaths (overly) rely on their lateral frontal lobes during real-world moral decision-making behavior. Perhaps the closest we can come to answering this question would be to study psychopaths during the performance of realistic moral decision-making paradigms using brain imaging.

Another important issue raised by de Oliveira-Souza et al. relates to the specificity of the construct of psychopathy to criminal populations. An interesting distinction between successful and unsuccessful psychopathy was raised. This classification of successful and unsuccessful psychopathy was coined by Ishikawa, Raine, Lencz, Bihrle, and Lacasse (2001; see also Widom, 1977). In their definition, the unsuccessful psychopath differs from the successful psychopath in that the former has been convicted for criminal offenses while the latter has not. This is not to say that the successful psychopath has not committed crimes. Indeed, successful psychopaths in the Ishikawa et al. study self-reported that they had committed similar numbers of thefts, drug offenses, and violent crimes as had the unsuccessful psychopaths (see table 2 in their study); they just reported no convictions for their crimes. Thus, serious criminal behavior appears to characterize successful as well as unsuccessful psychopaths.

The second case study provided by de Oliveira-Souza et al. is consistent with this characterization. The young woman they describe appears to have committed thefts, held and sold stolen property, and used and distributed drugs, despite never having been convicted of any crimes. This raises the issue of how the successful psychopath avoids criminal convictions and prison time. One might argue that mediating variables might be at work here, such as intelligence or socioeconomic status, both of which are powerful protective factors against incarceration. Ishikawa et al. found that the unsuccessful psychopaths came from lower socioeconomic strata than did the successful psychopaths. The successful psychopaths were also slightly younger than the unsuccessful ones.

It is also important to consider the impact that incarceration may have on brain function. While prison conditions vary widely, it is not unreasonable to think that spending years in prison might cause some deleterious effects on brain structure and function. Controlling for history of incarceration (and other environmental issues) is one of the reasons why it is standard practice in the psychopathy field to collect an incarcerated nonpsychopathic control group for comparison with the incarcerated psychopaths. This procedure isn't something that the "successful" psychopathy field has adopted. This raises the possibility that history of incarceration may mediate some of the reported group differences between successful and unsuccessful psychopaths.

It might be worth drawing parallel inferences from another clinical condition that occurs inside and outside of prison. Schizophrenia, like psychopathy, afflicts approximately one percent of the general population. Many patients with schizophrenia often serve time in prisons. However, it is difficult to imagine that there are significant differences between unsuccessful (i.e., incarcerated) and successful (i.e., nonincarcerated) patients with schizophrenia. That is, once you have a serious medical condition such as schizophrenia or psychopathy, it is more likely that mediating variables, such as family support and socioeconomic status, serve as protective factors against incarceration, than do neurobiological factors. Nevertheless, future research is needed to help clarify these issues.

De Oliveira-Souza et al. introduce the concept of antisocial behavioral disorder, which is defined using some of the diagnostic criteria from the *DSM-IV* category of antisocial personality disorder (ASPD). It should be noted that ASPD has long been criticized for its lack of specificity and poor construct validity, especially as it purports to measure psychopathy (Hare, Hart, & Harpur, 1991a; Hart & Hare, 1996; Rutherford, Cacciola, & Alterman, 1999; Widiger, Cadoret, Hare, Robins, Rutherford, et al., 1996). Thus, any new diagnostic category that seeks to utilize a subset of ASPD characteristics to define a new clinical condition or putatively assess psychopathy might be met with significant skepticism. De Oliveira-Souza et al. also introduce the concept of predatory versus parasitic criminal orientation (Karpman, 1946). In my experience, most individuals with psychopathy are capable of, and have committed, both predatory and parasitic behavior. Indeed, these latter types of behavior are central to scoring items on the Hare PCL-R. Thus, at present it is not clear whether these concepts will help to further refine the construct of psychopathy. It should be noted that much progress has been made in delineating psychometric properties of psychopathy using item response theory analyses (Bolt, Hare, Vitale, & Newman, 2004; Cooke & Michie, 1997, 2001; Cooke, Michie, Hart, & Clark, 2005; Hare & Neumann, 2005; Schrum & Salekin, 2006). This latter work has helped to more fully characterize the possible subtypes of psychopathy using state-of-the-art psychometric analyses.

The assessment issues described here highlight one of the most important aspects of conducting clinical research: proper psychometric assessment and sound theory guiding the development of assessment instruments.

As a case in point, even though the cognitive neuroscience literature on psychopathy is still in its infancy, it has already presented a number of clear candidate brain regions that appear to be implicated in the disorder. In my opinion, the consistency of this literature is based largely upon the careful assessment and characterization of psychopathy using the Hare Psychopathy Checklist-Revised (Hare, 1991). In this regard, it was pleasing to see de Oliveira-Souza et al.'s use of the Psychopathy Checklist-Screening Version (PCL-SV) to assess psychopathy in their studies of community samples. It will be exciting to compare the results of their studies with studies from incarcerated samples.

The comment by Schaich Borg brings to light a number of points that require clarification and a few additional ones that merit discussion. Two points that need clarification are the issue of intact intellectual function in psychopathy and the role (or lack thereof) emotion plays in the disorder. Additional discussion points include the interpretation of behavioral and fMRI findings in general and with respect to psychopathy in particular.

Schaich Borg's comment draws heavily upon my statements that psychopathy is associated with normal "intellectual" functioning and that the disorder is characterized by deficits in "emotional" functioning. These latter statements may appear at odds with one another. Estimates of intellectual functioning (i.e., IQ) play a prominent role in the etiology, management, and treatment of populations involved with the criminal-justice system. Estimates of IQ are one of the best predictors of externalizing psychopathology in youth (i.e., conduct disorder) and adulthood. However, youth with "callous and unemotional traits" and conduct problems have superior IQs compared with conduct-disordered youth without "callous and unemotional traits" (Christian, Frick, Hill, Tyler, & Frazer, 1997). This cohort of callous and unemotional youth (plus conduct problems) is believed to be the group most likely to develop adult psychopathy. Adults with psychopathy are also known to test average to above average on standard measures of IQ and neuropsychological functioning (Hare, 1984, 1991, 2003; Hart, Forth, & Hare, 1990). My statement that psychopathy is associated with normal intellectual functioning was meant to convey the fact that individuals with psychopathy have normal to above-normal estimates of IQ. That is, their psychopathology is not readily explained by deficits in intellectual functioning as estimated using standard IQ tests.

The finding of normal IQ in psychopathy is one of the interesting aspects of the disorder. Indeed, the observer is often struck, even mystified, by the psychopath's self-defeating behavior in the presence of a normal, or perhaps even keen, intellect (Cleckley, 1941, 1976). The finding of high

IQ in psychopathy may appear at odds with the literature demonstrating that estimates of IQ are one of the best predictors of externalizing behavioral disorders. This issue has led many researchers to suggest that there are most likely multiple pathways to serious criminal behavior. Thus, it is usually important in psychopathy research to ensure that the experimental group (i.e., psychopaths) does not differ from the control group (i.e., nonpsychopaths) in estimates of IQ, so that any group differences in the dependent variables of interest cannot be readily explained by deficits in IQ. Furthermore, it is important to clarify that my use of the phrase "normal intellectual functioning" did not mean to imply that psychopaths have normal cognition, reasoning, or any other aspect of mental processing. Rather, it simply means that low IQ does not appear to be pathognomonic of psychopathy.

Schaich Borg also suggests that psychopathy may be a good clinical condition to model moral decision making in the absence of emotion. That is, a clinical condition associated with behavioral deficits in emotion would potentially help dissociate the roles that emotion and cognition play in moral decision-making processes. Schaich Borg also wants to identify the neural systems underlying moral decision making. These points necessitate several assumptions and considerations of how behavioral data and brain imaging data are interpreted.

In order for a clinical condition to inform us whether emotion and cognition play different roles in moral decision making, one must have a condition that shows deficits in one domain and no deficits in the other. On the surface, psychopathy, with its apparent deficits in emotional processing and intact intellect (as estimated by IQ), may appear to suit Schaich Borg's needs. However, if we ignore the brain imaging data for a moment and simply consider whether psychopaths have deficits in performing emotion tasks, we might have a problem. A potential problem is that behavioral deficits in emotional processing in psychopathy are difficult to find. Schaich Borg cites the finding of Kiehl et al. (2001c) that psychopaths, unlike nonpsychopaths, failed to show significant enhanced recognition for emotional words relative to neutral words in a memory task (a t-test contrasting emotional versus neutral word recognition for the psychopathic group only reached trend levels of significance, $p < 0.067$). This effect, or rather, this lack of effect, was subsequently interpreted by Schaich Borg as evidence of psychopaths' "inability to enhance or facilitate memory with emotion, rendering their memory less effective than that of nonpsychopaths" (this volume, p. 162). However, the analyses cited do not support the conclusion that psychopaths and nonpsychopaths differed in their memory for emotional stimuli. Indeed, there were no group differences among criminal psychopaths, criminal nonpsychopaths, or noncriminal controls for emotional or neutral word memory in Kiehl et al.'s study. Rather, the most parsimonious interpretation of the behavioral data reported by these authors is that the psychopathic group did show better memory recognition for emotional words compared with neutral words; however, the effect only reached trend levels of significance because the study was underpowered ($n = 8$ per group).

Other studies have shown that psychopaths, like nonpsychopaths, correctly identify more emotional words than neutral words during lexical decision tasks (Williamson, Harpur, & Hare, 1991). Psychopaths are about 70 milliseconds slower to respond to emotional words than are nonpsychopaths during lexical decision tasks. However, this latter difference in reaction times for processing emotional words does not constitute a significant deficit per se, because psychopaths are completely capable of performing the task. Indeed, psychopaths do not differ from nonpsychopaths in self-reported ratings of the emotionality of words (Kiehl, Hare, McDonald, & Brink, 1999a; Kiehl et al., 2001c; Williamson, Harpur, & Hare, 1991). That is, psychopaths appear to have no deficits in rating or recognizing emotional stimuli. This is in contrast to patients with conditions that prohibit them from performing certain tasks. For example, patients with prosopagnosia who are completely unable to identify familiar faces are readily interpreted as having behavioral deficits. Thus, finding deficits in emotional processing remains elusive in psychopathy research, and this may hamper efforts to interpret any abnormalities in moral decision making in psychopaths as being related to deficits in emotional processes. Moreover, it is still not clear whether psychopathy is associated with impairments in cognition (Hiatt, Schmitt, & Newman, 2004; Newman, Schmitt, & Voss, 1997). Thus, while at first glance it may appear that psychopathy may provide unique insights into the role that emotion and cognition play in moral decision making, some careful interpretation and consideration of the issues raised here are warranted. This is not to say that understanding moral decision making in psychopathy is not worth pursuing. On the contrary, understanding the cognitive and emotional systems underlying moral decision making in psychopathy may help us to better understand and, it is hoped, effectively manage and treat the disorder.

With respect to the utility of using the construct of psychopathy to identify the neural systems underlying moral decision making, we are again presented with issues that may cloud the interpretation of any data. Psychopathy is believed to onset early in life, and the condition is very likely to be associated with abnormalities in neurodevelopmental processes. This may include altered migration of emotional (and cognitive) processes from paralimbic regions to other brain regions (i.e., neural plasticity). Recall that one interpretation of the excessive frontal activity observed in psychopaths during the performance of emotional tasks is that it represents compensatory activity for abnormalities in the paralimbic circuitry. It may be that the lateral frontal cortex is performing emotional computations that would normally be performed by the paralimbic cortex. After all, psychopaths do perform these tasks relatively normally. Again, it might be useful to draw parallel inferences from other disorders. Epilepsy, for example, a common cause of which is believed to be altered neurodevelopment, has been associated with reorganization of emotional and cognitive processes (Johnston, 2003). Thus, it is important to consider these issues when interpreting brain imaging data in clinical populations.

As a final aside, it should be noted that the presence of neural activity in functional brain imaging studies does not mean that the activated brain region was necessary for successfully performing a task (Halgren & Marinkovic, 1996; Kiehl, Stevens, Laurens, Pearlson, Calhoun & Liddle, 2005; Price & Friston, 1999; Price, Mummery, Moore, Frakowiak, & Friston, 1999). Distinguishing "necessary" brain regions from those that may be reflexively engaged (Kiehl et al., 2005) or those that are serving a supplemental function (Price et al., 1999) may require studying patients with focal brain damage. Schaich Borg does raise the issue that identifying the relevant moral decision-making circuits may be aided by examining patients with focal brain lesions. This approach may provide unique information for helping to delineate the "necessary" from the "sufficient" brain systems implicated in moral decision making. Moreover, studying patients with focal brain damage may help clarify the role that emotion and cognition play in moral decision making.

Internalism and the Evidence from Psychopaths and "Acquired Sociopaths"

Jeanette Kennett and Cordelia Fine

Morally good action requires both sincere moral judgment and moral motivation. Internalists claim in one way or another that these two things are internally connected. This may be because genuine moral judgments are, or are based in, conative states disposing us to act (sentimentalism), or because they are the products of our reason and so exert an influence on rational agents (rationalism), or because they are a special kind of belief that brings with it or generates desire.

Externalists, on the other hand, claim that the connection between moral judgment and action is forged by motives external to (that is, not necessarily implied by or required for) the judgment itself. They claim that moral judgments are beliefs like any others and that beliefs alone cannot motivate action. They can only do so in conjunction with some independently arising desire, say for truth, justice, or doing the right thing. These are desires that a rational agent, with full moral knowledge, might fail to have. Evidence from psychopathology has been recruited by philosophers on both sides of this debate and that is our focus in this chapter. First we will look at the evidence from psychopathy, then we will turn to cases of so-called acquired sociopathy.

Do Psychopaths Make Moral Judgments?

The psychopath is often thought to be the closest we can get to the amoralist of philosophical imagination.[1] The amoralist of course is the individual who supposedly makes moral judgments but is not at all motivated by them. He or she might agree that killing, promise breaking, and the like are wrong, but does not see this as having any practical relevance. The amoralist allegedly suffers no failing of moral knowledge or understanding; he just doesn't care about morality. The debate in moral philosophy has largely turned on whether the amoralist really makes moral judgments or only does so in an "inverted commas" sense: that is, a sense that "alludes to the value judgements of others without itself expressing such a judgement" (plato.stanford.edu/entries/moral-cognitivism). A genuine moral judgment is, minimally, one accepted and endorsed by the speaker.[2] If the amoralist really does make such judgments, then that would show that internalism, the view that moral judgment is ceteris paribus motivating, is false. Moral judgment would only contingently be connected to motivation. The amoralist's problem is that he simply fails to have desires (to help people, to be good) that most of us in fact have.

While we seem to be able to imagine amoralists, it is possible that our imaginations mislead us. Thought experiments may not be the best way to tackle the issue between internalists and externalists, since their different responses to the amoralist may just reflect their different initial conceptions of moral judgment. However, there are real psychopaths in the world who are totally unmoved by moral considerations and whose capacity for moral reasoning and moral judgment has received some attention. Do we have reasons independent of their manifest lack of moral concern to think that the psychopath's capacity for moral judgment and moral understanding is impaired? Or does the evidence support externalist claims by revealing unimpaired moral judgment and moral reasoning skills in the psychopath?

Several lines of evidence indicate relevant impairments in psychopaths. It appears that psychopaths do not possess the moral concepts of nonpsychopaths. Recent work by the cognitive neuroscientist James Blair has revealed significant differences between the psychological profiles of developmental psychopaths and normal individuals. Psychopathic adults and children with psychopathic tendencies are insensitive to the difference between actions deemed wrong for conventional reasons and those deemed wrong for moral reasons. Blair (1995; replicated in Blair, Jones, Clark, & Smith, 1995) assessed the sensitivity of incarcerated adult psychopathic offenders of normal intelligence to the moral-conventional distinction compared with nonpsychopathic offenders (all of whom were charged with murder or manslaughter).[3] He found that psychopathic offenders were insensitive to the distinction between moral and conventional transgressions. Unlike the nonpsychopathic offenders, the psychopathic group did not judge the acceptability of moral transgressions to be any less dependent upon authority jurisdiction than conventional transgressions. (In fact, incarcerated offenders continued to rate both moral and conventional transgressions as wrong after authority jurisdiction was removed. Blair suggested that they were "faking good.") He (1997) subsequently found that children with psychopathic tendencies made a significantly weaker moral-conventional distinction than nonpsychopathic children with emotional and behavioral difficulties. These are striking findings, since the moral-conventional distinction is made by normally developing children as young as 39 months of age (Smetana & Braeges, 1990).

The capacity to make the distinction between moral wrongs and conventional wrongs seems to be an essential step in moral development and basic to moral competence. However, while even normally developing preschool children are able to provide differentiated evaluations of the different kinds of violations (e.g., Smetana, Schlagman, & Adams, 1993), for psychopaths all rules seem to be of the same stuff. It is tempting to think that they see all rules as conventional, but this would be to overstate their grasp of conventional justifications. The evidence points rather to the idea that for the psychopath, both moral and conventional rules are annoying restrictions to be manipulated or ignored. None of these rules have normative force for them. On the other hand, normally developing children increasingly treat both moral and conventional considerations as normative—as directly providing (different kinds of) reasons for or against particular actions. As Jay Wallace (1999) points out, morality is widely taken to be a normative domain. Whether this is a conceptual truth or not, it seems clear that those who cannot grasp fundamental normative distinctions do not mean what the rest of us mean when using moral terms.

Studies on moral reasoning in psychopaths also tend to point toward inadequacies in their moral outlook, although the findings are mixed. Two early studies found that psychopathic delinquent groups performed at a lower stage of moral reasoning on Kohlbergian moral reasoning tasks compared with nonpsychopathic delinquent controls (Fodor, 1973; Jurkovic & Prentice, 1977).[4] In contrast, three other studies failed to find significant differences in the stage of Kohlbergian moral reasoning between psychopathic and nonpsychopathic delinquent groups (Chandler & Moran, 1990, Trevethan & Walker, 1989), or between psychopathic and nonpsychopathic adult criminals (O'Kane, Fawcett, & Blackburn, 1996), while Link, Scherer & Byrne (1977) found that adult psychopathic criminals reasoned at a higher level than controls. However, the O'Kane et al. (1996) study included only one patient who scored above criterion on the standard measure of psychopathy, the Psychopathy Checklist-Revised (Hare, 1991), a serious methodological weakness. Moreover, more fine-grained analyses of the two studies of delinquent youth revealed other interesting differences between the moral reasoning styles of delinquents with and without a diagnosis of psychopathy.

Chandler & Moran (1990), who gave their delinquent groups a number of questionnaires assessing moral and social attitudes, summarized their findings as suggesting that psychopathic delinquents are characterized by a dangerous combination of a strong sense of autonomy and the absence of any serious commitment to normal societal standards and sentiments. In other words, they appear to consider themselves above the rules to which most of society subscribes. Trevethan & Walker (1989) found that reasoning about real-life moral dilemmas (ones that the participants had personally encountered) differed between psychopathic and nonpsychopathic delinquent groups. Those in the psychopathic group were more likely to justify their moral reasoning in terms of the moral legitimacy of self-concerns. The authors suggest that "in more abstract situations, psychopaths are able to express more typical values and concerns, whereas in an actual situation, the practical considerations concerning self become more salient" (Trevethan & Walker, 1989, p. 100). In other words, this evidence also suggests that psychopaths make exceptions for themselves. Their hypothetical or third-personal moral judgments are inconsistent with their moral judgments about their own actual situations and actions, and indeed we question whether they ever spontaneously engage in moral assessments of their own projected actions.

Further evidence suggestive of inadequate understanding of moral concepts comes from studies of the speech of psychopaths. For example, the erratic, inconsistent, and contradictory nature of their pronouncements suggests that they do not possess the moral concepts of nonpsychopathic individuals. They are incompetent in the use of evaluative terms, as demonstrated by the examples in box 4.1.

Similarly, Eichler (1966) found that sociopathic delinquents made a greater number of "retractor" statements than controls (e.g., "John is an honest person. Of course, he has been involved in some shady deals!") Richard Joyce (2006a, pp. 55–56) suggests that statements like these are "Moore-paradoxical" because, although they contain no outright contradiction, "to state the whole is to void the speech act of the first part, leaving the listener confused as to what should be assumed about the speaker's attitude toward [it]" (p. 55). The whole does not make sense and one is tempted to say that the speaker doesn't really know what he is talking about. Psychopaths seem not to understand what is implied by the use of evaluative terms; they seem not to know how the different terms fit together. Glowing descriptions of one's mother's virtues are incompatible with calling her a bitch; vows to make her life easier are incompatible with stealing her money.

Box 4.1

Examples of psychopaths' incompetencies in use of evaluative terms (all examples from Hare, 1993)

> When asked if he had ever committed a violent offense, a man serving time for theft answered, "No, but I once had to kill someone." (p. 125)
>
> Asked how he had begun his career in crime, [a psychopath] said, "It had to do with my mother, the most beautiful person in the world. She was strong, worked hard to take care of four kids. A beautiful person. I started stealing her jewelry when I was in the fifth grade. You know, I never really knew the bitch—we went our separate ways." (p. 40)
>
> [Robert Hare] was once dumbfounded by the logic of an inmate who described his murder victim as having benefited from the crime by learning "a hard lesson about life." (p. 41)
>
> When asked if he experienced remorse over a murder he'd committed, one young inmate told us, "Yeah, sure, I feel remorse." Pressed further, he said that he didn't "feel bad inside about it." (p. 41)
>
> "My mother is a great person, but I worry about her. She works too hard. I really care for that woman, and I'm going to make it easier for her." When asked about the money he had stolen from her he replied, "I've still got some of it stashed away, and when I get out it's party time!" (p. 138)

The explanation for this incompetence seems at least in part to be that psychopaths suffer significant affective deficits; emotional words are devoid of their usual affective tags (see Hare, Williamson, & Harpur, 1988) and so get used by psychopaths in strange ways. For example, psychopaths have difficulty in grasping the positive or negative polarity of metaphors, even though they show normal semantic understanding of them (Hervé, Hayes, & Hare, 2003).

Also in line with their hypothesized insensitivity to the emotional meaning of affective words, psychopaths do not differentiate between neutral and emotionally charged words in their voice emphasis, unlike controls (Louth, Williamson, Alpert, Pouget, & Hare, 1998). Hare et al. (1988, p. 69) suggest that language does not have the same "richness of meaning" for the psychopath, nor the usual controlling influence over behavior.

It also seems relevant that according to Hare (1993, p. 136), psychopaths' thoughts and ideas are "organized into rather small mental packages and readily moved around." This is suggested by their unusual pattern of hand gestures during conversation. Psychopaths use significantly more "beats"—gestures thought to demark conceptual units within discourse—than do nonpsychopaths. Their attention shifts rapidly; they frequently change topics and go off track; and they have trouble maintaining a narrative thread (Gillstrom & Hare, 1988). We would suggest that the central notion of a normative requirement as one that persists in the absence of inclination is thus beyond a psychopath's grasp. Normative concepts involve a degree of unity of thought not to be obtained from these small disconnected mental packages.

Taken together, the evidence supports the claim that the supposed moral judgments of psychopaths are rightly understood in the inverted commas sense. The absence of moral motivation in psychopaths cannot therefore refute internalism. The recent debate among philosophers has focused rather on which internalist position is most favored by the evidence from psychopathy. Is it a version of sentimentalism (e.g., Nichols, 2002a) or of rationalism (e.g., Maibom, 2005)?

However, this debate may be premature. Adina Roskies (2003) has recently argued that unlike developmental psychopaths, patients with ventromedial frontal lobe (VM) damage possess unimpaired moral reasoning abilities yet are not motivated by moral judgments. If this is right, then these cases present a much more serious challenge to internalism.

A Better Case Against Internalism?

Roskies' (2003) argument can be briefly summarized as follows. First, she claims that VM patients are unimpaired with regard to their ethical beliefs and ethical judgments. However, VM patients, she argues, fail to be motivated by moral judgments. This failure is evidenced by their impaired ethical behavior and the absence of increased skin conductance responses (SCRs) in what she labels "ethically charged" situations. She therefore concludes that ethical judgments cannot be intrinsically motivational since this clinical group demonstrates a dissociation between ethical judgment and ethical motivation. We begin by making some preliminary comments on Roskies' metaethical project before examining her treatment and interpretation of the empirical literature.

Roskies' Target Version of Internalism

Roskies is concerned to evaluate only one brand of internalism, the brand that holds that "motivation is intrinsic to, or a necessary component of, moral belief or judgment." This motivation "must stem from the moral character of a belief or judgment itself" (Roskies, 2003, p. 52). Roskies limits herself to this brand of internalism since she thinks it is the only philosophically interesting brand available. She argues in particular that forms of internalism that tie internalism to practical rationality, such as that proposed by Michael Smith (1994), or which restrict the claim to "normal" agents, run the risk of being trivially true, or true by definition, and are thus too weak to be revealing about the nature of moral judgment. Roskies (2003) says that:

interesting forms of internalism attempt to set moral beliefs off from other varieties of belief: the motivational force of moral belief distinguishes them as special, since other types of belief are not intrinsically motivating. . . . Thus, the internalist will maintain that anyone who sincerely believes that morality dictates that he or she ought to give money to famine relief must thereby be motivated to give, although no such related motivation must attend the sincere belief that the law dictates he or she ought to pay his or her taxes. (p. 52)

The motivating character of such beliefs is left unelaborated by Roskies, but it is worth examining since it bears on her claim that motive internalism is more interesting and potentially revealing than other internalist positions.

We assume here that Roskies' target is a strict version of internalism. She speaks of the view that motivation is a *necessary component* of moral belief (our emphasis) so there is no ceteris paribus clause, and indeed she appears to think that Smith's employment of such a clause renders his position trivial and uninteresting. So any outright failure of moral motivation in cases where we have good reason to believe that the moral judgment is sincere will refute her target version of internalism. Victory for the externalist should be easy.

But who, exactly, is the foe? Strict-motive internalists who are also cognitivists,[5] but not rationalists, as specified by Roskies, are pretty hard to find but, unsurprisingly, they always take an absence of moral motivation to be evidence of some flaw or impairment at the level of cognition. For example, John McDowell (1979) suggests that the motivating power of the virtuous agent's judgment simply flows from his or her particular view of the facts and moreover that this view of the facts could not be shared by someone who was not so motivated. It is not clear in McDowell precisely how a view of the facts can by itself motivate agents in a particular way, but at one point he suggests that the world itself is not motivationally inert. It might be that here he is pointing to a distinctly Platonic understanding of moral belief and judgment. The special attribute of the virtuous person will be the capacity to apprehend certain non-natural facts or properties out in the world, facts or properties that are in themselves motivationally compelling. Less than virtuous people may pronounce the same words, but they haven't clearly apprehended these special facts. Their view of "the noble" is clouded or blurred by "a lively desire" (McDowell, 1979, p. 345). Philosophers such as John Mackie (1977) have attacked non-naturalist views by pointing to the implausibility of their epistemic and ontological commitments, rather than by producing empirical evidence against their internalist claims. Since non-naturalist views are not amenable to verification or falsification, it seems unlikely that they are Roskies' target.

A nonmagical reading of the claim that the world is not motivationally inert might perhaps be drawn from evolutionary psychology. The idea that certain features of our natural and social environment are such as to elicit the responses we identify as moral from creatures like us is not implausible. Note, however, that a brand of internalism arising from evolutionary accounts of morality will restrict its claim to normally functioning individuals, and Roskies has ruled this out of consideration also.

Perhaps the motive internalists that Roskies has in mind are those who hold that moral beliefs are thick rather than thin. McDowell in some interpretations falls into this category, as does David McNaughton (1988).[6] Since moral terms, properly understood, have emotive as well as descriptive meaning, the process of arriving at a moral judgment is also, for such internalists, the process of getting into the appropriate conative state. Certainly the case of psychopaths suggests that the capacity for moral judgment has affective inputs. Moral beliefs may thus be set off from ordinary beliefs. Although this version of motive internalism appears to be in line with the evidence from psychopathy, it could be vulnerable to counterexamples elsewhere, and that is what Roskies hopes to provide. Nevertheless, while one might think that such a view must be Roskies' target, it is not wholly clear that it is.

For one thing, the claims made about moral judgment by such motive internalists might not be sufficiently strict. We see no reason in principle why its proponents couldn't allow that certain conditions such as depression might block the motivation that normally flows from moral judgment without giving up on their central claim about the fundamental nature of moral judgment and moral belief. However, if the claim contains qualifying terms such as "normally," it is ruled out of consideration.[7] On the other hand, if the internalist claim is exceptionless (as McDowell wants to insist), then its proponents must be committed to the view that there are significantly fewer genuine moral judgments around than we might have thought, and so the view will be relatively invulnerable to counterexample. Roskies might want to pose a best-explanation style argument against this restricted account of moral judgment (as might other internalists), but even if she is successful, it is no more a victory for externalism than it is for other more plausible internalisms.

Second, the version of motive internalism outlined here might not be a sufficiently cognitivist account of moral judgment for Roskies. The view that ethical terms have emotive as well as descriptive meaning is fundamental to a number of noncognitivist accounts of moral judgment, but her comparison of moral and legal judgments suggests that she thinks these are cognitively on a par.[8] It sounds as if the judgments she is concerned with involve the bare cognition of some set of rules or directives. Her couching of the internalist claim she hopes to refute concerns sincere beliefs of the form: "morality dictates that I ought. . . ." The problem is that beliefs of this form are not the focus of any internalist claims since internalists do not think that beliefs of this form are necessarily moral judgments. There is a difference between reporting a moral norm, even one that includes you in its scope, as an anthropologist or sociologist might, and making a moral judgment. The internalist claim attaches only to the latter judgment. The former is a straw man.[9] Roskies needs to clarify what she means by the moral character of the belief or judgment from which moral motivation is supposed to stem to confirm that she is indeed arguing against a genuinely interesting and substantial version of internalism. In reviewing her empirical claims, however, we will simply focus on whether the evidence she cites does tend to undermine the broad thrust of internalist claims.

Five Dimensions of Moral Judgment

We propose that there are five possible dimensions of moral belief or judgment:

1. *Third personal*   what someone should do;
2. *Second personal*   what you should do (face-to-face advice);
3. *First personal*   what I should do;
4. *Armchair*   about hypothetical situations or about what kinds of principles we should adopt to govern our choices; and
5. *In situ*   what should be done in these actual circumstances.

Roskies specifies that the moral beliefs to be tested must be first-person "ought" beliefs; that is, they can't be beliefs about what someone else ought to do. However, we think it is necessary to be more precise about the first-personal beliefs that are relevant to the internalist claim since Roskies asserts that if she refutes belief internalism she will a fortiori refute judgment internalism on the grounds that "judgment plausibly entails belief" (2003, p. 53). Judgment may entail belief, in the sense that I can't judge I ought to do something without believing I ought to, but the reverse does not always hold. I can surely believe that I ought to keep my promise but fail to form the in situ judgment that I ought to keep my promise. Maybe my belief or my promise isn't foregrounded in my deliberations about what to do. Maybe I fail to notice that what I'm planning to do—go to the football game this afternoon, say—would be inconsistent with keeping the promise I made two weeks ago to meet you in the mall at 3:00 on Saturday the 22nd. If I forget my promise to you, or I don't notice that the time to keep it is now, then, although I believe I ought to keep my promises, including this one, I fail to form a judgment about what I ought to do right now, and so I fail to meet you. Of course I ought to form the judgment, but my failure to do so is not a failure of motivation. As we have described it, it can be a failure of attention or memory or inference. We take it that this kind of mismatch between moral belief and motivation to act wouldn't be enough to refute motive internalism. The relevant judgments are first person, in situ.

We now go on to discuss in more detail the empirical claims made by Roskies. We highlight that for her argument to be successful, she must be able to show two things. First she must show that VM patients make the relevant moral judgments, and second she must show that a deficit specifically in moral motivation in VM patients is the best explanation of their apparent failure to act in accordance with their allegedly unimpaired moral judgments.

Ethical Beliefs and Judgments in VM Patients

Roskies (2003, p. 57) states that "VM patients retain the declarative knowledge related to moral issues, and appear to be able to reason morally at a normal level. Significantly, their moral claims accord with those of normals." Roskies refers to VM patients; however, her evidence for this statement appears to come entirely from the single-case study of VM patient EVR. EVR certainly does seem to have normal declarative knowledge with regard to moral issues. He performed at an advanced level on a modified version of a dilemma from the Kohlberg moral reasoning battery

(Saver & Damasio, 1991). When queried informally on ethical dilemmas by Eslinger and Damasio (1985), he gave principled responses without hesitation. It would be hard to argue that his moral understanding is impaired or that he makes moral judgments only in the inverted commas sense. He thus seems to provide a much clearer test of internalist claims than do psychopaths.

Nevertheless, there are two problems for Roskies in her reliance on EVR. First, the moral judgment tests carried out on EVR all invited him to engage in third-personal armchair reasoning. This presents an immediate difficulty for Roskies' argument since responses to third-personal hypothetical dilemmas do not constitute the relevant "I ought" judgments needed to test the internalist claim. It is interesting that there is evidence that people demonstrate more mature moral reasoning about hypothetical than about personally experienced moral dilemmas, and that the latter are particularly affected by psychopathology in the form of psychopathy (Trevethan & Walker, 1989). It is therefore pertinent to ask whether EVR is also capable of first-personal moral reasoning.

Does EVR recognize when he is in a situation that falls under a third-personal hypothetical moral judgment? Can he translate the knowledge into the first person? Does he then make the relevant "I ought" judgment at the time of action? The following gives us a hint. Referring to tests of social cognition during which he had to come up with solutions to social problems, the authors report that "EVR noted with his customary insight that he came up with many options but '. . . I still would not know what to do'" (Saver & Damasio, 1991, p. 1246). A patient with focal frontal damage reported by Stuss (1991) appears to show a similar dissociation between third-personal knowledge and first-personal judgments. Taking on the role of a supervisor considering someone's (her own) significant problems at work, she offered a competent analysis of the situation and problem solving. Yet when asked for similar judgments from a first-personal perspective, her responses were unrealistic and failed to take her third-personal knowledge into account. A second point is that from the single case of EVR Roskies assumes normal declarative knowledge of moral issues in VM patients. However, moral reasoning has rarely been studied in VM patients. One other case reported in the literature is patient JS (Blair & Cipolotti, 2000). Blair and Cipolotti tested his performance on the moral-conventional distinction task. They found that JS, like psychopaths, failed to distinguish between moral and conventional transgressions. Perhaps the single case of EVR is enough to establish Roskies' claim that moral judgments are not intrinsically motivating, but we should be wary of moving to this conclusion before seeking alternative explanations of EVR's practical deficiencies.

Moral Motivation following VM Damage

Roskies' second premise to her thesis is that VM patients fail to show moral motivation, despite their intact moral knowledge. In support of this claim she cites evidence from their behavior in, and their affective responsiveness to, ethical situations.

Ethical Behavior

Roskies (2003, p. 57) states that "VM patients fail to reliably act as normals do in many ethically charged situations." Her evidence for this statement comes from two sources: descriptions of the change in behavior in Phineas Gage following his railway accident and the study of patient EVR. Yet although EVR has been described as an acquired sociopath (Eslinger & Damasio, 1985), the term is somewhat misleading in this context. In EVR's case, it was diagnosed on the basis of features such as an "inability to sustain consistent work behavior," "lack of ability to function as a responsible parent," and "defective planning." Roskies cites EVR's bankruptcy, divorce, unsuitable remarriages, inability to maintain employment, and defective future planning as evidence of moral ineffectiveness. It is not clear, however, that EVR's behaviors—however hapless—can be regarded as moral violations. For example, "[e]mployers complained about his tardiness and disorganization, although basic skills, manners, and temper were appropriate. Similar difficulties led to a deterioration of his marital life" (Eslinger & Damasio, 1985, p. 1731). This is not the description of a person careless of others' rights and welfare (as psychopaths are) or of behavior motivated by immoral intent.

Nor does it seem that EVR's behavioral difficulties are due to a specific impairment in moral motivation, the result of the loss, say, of a previously reliable enculturated desire to "do the right thing." That is the kind of desire that externalists typically posit as the source of moral motivation. Such a deficit doesn't seem apt to explain EVR's tardiness and disorganization. Rather, close examination of the clinical description of EVR suggests a very different cause, namely, that of impaired decision making in all domains of everyday life:

[EVR] needed about 2 hours to get ready for work in the morning, and some days were consumed entirely by shaving and hair-washing. Deciding where to dine might take hours, as he discussed each restaurant's seating plan, particulars of menu, atmosphere, and management. He would drive to each restaurant to see how busy it was, but even then he could not finally decide which to choose. Purchasing small items required in-depth consideration of brands, prices, and the best method of purchase. (Eslinger & Damasio, 1985, p. 1732)

Damasio and colleagues have characterized the impairment following VM damage as one of decision making, and this seems like a more accurate portrayal of EVR's deficit than a specific dysfunction in moral motivation. Similarly, it seems plausible that the loss of a sense of responsibility and an inability to honor commitments observed in Phineas Gage (Damasio, Grabowski, Frank, Galaburda, & Damasio, 1994), cited as evidence of moral dysfunction by Roskies, is attributable to a similar general decision-making deficit.

Roskies does address the alternative accounts that the dysfunction in VM patients is not moral, but is due to a more general difficulty in motivation or in acting in relation to evaluative judgments. However, her attempts to pinpoint the dysfunction to the moral domain are unconvincing. First, she argues against an impairment of general motivation by stating that patients retain appetitive motivations such as seeking food and eating. However, Eslinger & Damasio (1985) note that EVR was motivationally impaired with regard to everyday, morally neutral tasks:

EVR was not spontaneously motivated for action. He seemed not to have available, automatically, programs of action capable of driving him to motion. As he awoke, there was no evidence that an internal, automatic program was ready to propel him into the routine daily activities of self-care and feeding, let alone those of traveling to a job and discharging the assignments of a given day. It was as if he "forgot to remember" short- and intermediate-term goals. (p. 1738)

Roskies then argues against the possible argument that the deficit might be a general problem of "acting in relation to evaluative judgments" (2003, p. 58), citing apparently unaffected gustatory and aesthetic judgment. Yet Eslinger & Damasio (1985) describe how EVR refused to throw away old and useless possessions (e.g., three bags of empty orange juice concentrate cans, dead houseplants, six broken fans). As already noted, he had considerable difficulty making even small purchases and deciding where to eat. These observations again suggest a general problem in making decisions, in line with Damasio and colleagues' interpretation of the data.

Roskies finally attempts to address the concern raised earlier—that the behavior of VM patients (or rather, EVR) is not strikingly immoral. In defense of her thesis she argues that it is more reasonable to count as moral actions "a myriad of more subtle actions, such as keeping promises, discharging one's responsibilities and telling the truth" (2003, p. 58). However, a general deficit in decision making as described in EVR (e.g., the inability to decide where to eat) can easily account for a failure to keep a promise (e.g., to meet someone at a particular time) or to discharge responsibilities (e.g., as a parent, spouse, or employee), without suggesting an impairment specifically in moral motivation. There is no evidence that EVR harmed people for personal gain. There are also no reports of him telling lies. There is a second-hand report that Gage told stories "without any foundation except in his fancy" (Harlow, cited in Damasio, 1994, p. 11). However, there are no details, and this does not sound like intentionally deceptive lying motivated by the goal of personal gain. In other words, there is no evidence that EVR is guilty of even subtle acts of immorality.

Roskies also acknowledges that VM patients are rarely violent, as one might expect if this patient group is, as she claims, deficient in moral motivation. However, she argues that "to expect a person with a moral deficit to be an amoral monster may be unrealistic" (2003, p. 58). To explain why VM patients are rarely violent, she argues that prior to their brain injury they built up behavioral habits that prevent them from serious moral transgressions. In support of this argument she cites two patients who suffered early VM damage (Anderson, Bechara, Damasio, Tranel, & Damasio, 1999). These patients failed to acquire declarative moral knowledge and showed violent and remorseless behavior. Her argument is, we think, that unlike the patients who acquired their brain damage in adulthood, the early-onset patients have not had the opportunity to build up behavioral habits against aggression. This argument is highly speculative. Roskies offers no evidence to support her speculation that late-onset VM patients are protected by their behavioral habits against aggression, rather than by their retained moral judgments. Presumably prior to their injuries VM patients had also built up behavioral habits of performing the routine daily activities of self-care and feeding, for example, yet such habits clearly failed EVR postinjury. Roskies offers no explanation of why the habit against violence is spared while the habit of getting up and getting dressed is impaired. An alternative account is provided by Anderson et al.'s (1999) own interpretation of the data, which is that the ventromedial frontal cortex is necessary for the acquisition of moral knowledge. From this account it is tempting to suppose that a defect in moral understanding in early-onset patients might play a role in explaining their violent and remorseless behavior.

The Absence of Affective Responsiveness in Ethically Charged Situations
Roskies (2003, p. 57) asserts that "in ethically charged situations, VM patients seem to lack appropriate motivational and emotional responses, both at the level of their own subjective experience, and with regard to normal physiological correlates of emotion and motivation." It is particularly crucial for Roskies' argument that VM patients lack moral motivation since her thesis relies on the demonstration that this group displays moral belief in the absence of moral motivation. As she notes, "[f]ailure to act is suggestive of, but not proof of, lack of motivation" (p. 57). Roskies provides two main categories of evidence that moral motivation is absent in VM patients. First, she cites the work of Damasio and colleagues showing that VM patients fail to develop "somatic markers"—anticipatory SCRs during decision making—while performing the four-pack gambling task (e.g., Bechara, Damasio, Tranel, & Damasio, 1997). Second, she cites Damasio, Tranel, & Damasio's (1990) finding that VM patients do not show normal skin conductance responses to social stimuli. We have two objections to this part of Roskies' argument. First, we disagree with her assumption that the situations in which VM patients fail to show SCRs are in fact ethically charged. Moreover, we take issue with her claim that "the SCR is a reliable indicator of motivation for action" (p. 57).

Our first argument then is that neither the four-pack gambling task nor the social stimuli viewing task have a significant ethical dimension. The four-pack gambling task involves learning which of four packs of cards yields the best win-loss ratio. The participants play for money or pretend money. Roskies does not explain why she considers performing the task to be ethically charged, and we would argue that it contains no ethical component. The second task involves viewing social pictures (e.g., pictures of social disaster, mutilation, and nudity). For this to be considered to be an ethically charged task, Roskies must assume that participants are making ethical judgments about the pictures even though they are not asked to. While this is possible, although there is no reason to suppose that participants are doing this, there is a further problem. The task was administered under two conditions—passive and active viewing. In the passive condition, the participants simply viewed the slides. In the active condition, they were asked to comment on the slide and to say whether or not they liked it. The active condition would seem to be the one most likely to elicit ethical judgments. Yet under active viewing conditions, EVR and other VM patients showed normal SCRs to the pictures (Damasio et al., 1990).

Even if we are to accept that the two tasks described here are ethically charged, as Roskies requires for her argument, there is a further problem with her claim that the SCR represents moral motivation. In this assertion she departs from the interpretation of the SCR provided by Damasio and colleagues, who suggest that the SCR represents covertly or overtly held knowledge about the emotional value of the stimulus or option under consideration that guides decision making (e.g., Bechara, Damasio, & Damasio, 2000a):

> The somatic state is alerting you to the goodness or badness of a certain option-outcome pair.... Certain option-outcome pairs can be rapidly rejected or endorsed, and pertinent facts can be more effectively processed. The hypothesis thus suggests that somatic markers normally help constrain the decision making space by making that space manageable for logic-based, cost-benefit analyses. (p. 297)

Damasio's (1994) hypothesis regarding the impairment in EVR is not of a defect in motivation. He says that "the defect appeared to set in at the late stages of *reasoning*, close to or at the point at which choice making or response selection must occur" (p. 50, emphasis added). That is, the somatic marker functions to reduce the number of options and to "increase the accuracy and efficiency of the decision process" (p. 173). Thus, Roskies departs from the predominant account of the absence of the SCR in the two tasks we have described here by claiming that it is a manifestation of motivation for action.

Summary and Conclusion

Three main criticisms of Roskies' account have been raised. First, the moral judgments made by EVR are not of the kind needed to test her claim since they are third-personal hypothetical judgments. Second, there is the problem that EVR's behavior cannot be comfortably described as immoral or amoral. EVR in fact presents with unimpaired moral behavior, *within the constraints of his decision making deficit*. Third, there is inadequate support for the hypothesis that EVR and other VM patients are impaired in moral motivation. The interpretation currently accepted in the neuro-psychological literature is that their deficit is one of general decision making. Roskies has therefore not demonstrated the dissociation between moral judgment and moral motivation necessary to her argument. More-over, it is interesting to note that patient JS, whose moral understanding was found to be impaired, represents an acquired sociopathy patient with an immediately evident lack of moral regard in his behavior. During his stay in a long-term rehabilitation hospital:

[JS] assaulted and wounded a member of staff, frequently threw objects and furniture at people and was aggressive towards other patients. . . . On one occasion he continued to push around a wheelchair-bound patient despite her screams of terror. His "lack of remorse" was striking; he never expressed any regrets about the nurses he hit. He failed to accept responsibility for his actions, justifying his violent episodes in terms of the failures of others (e.g., they were too slow). Blair and Cipolotti (2000, p. 1124)

His pattern of behavior is therefore similar to that of Anderson et al.'s (1999) early-onset patients. In all three patients, a defect in moral understanding was associated with a significant deficiency in moral behavior. Similarly, as we have seen here, developmental psychopaths show an association between impaired moral understanding (e.g., Blair, 1995) and impaired moral behavior and antisocial acts (e.g., Cleckley, 1950; Hare & McPherson, 1984). In other words, thus far the clinical literature provides no support for externalist claims. It has not delivered up a single clear-cut example of the amoralist. Rather, it consistently supports an association between deficient moral behavior and deficient moral understanding. This cannot constitute proof of any internalist claim, but it does tend to support rather than undermine the general thrust of those claims. Among these patients EVR represents the externalist's best hope of a case of sincere moral judgment without moral motivation. We have argued that even here the evidence Roskies cites does not undermine any remotely plausible form of internalism. Perhaps better cases may be forthcoming. Until then, the central debate will be between internalists of different stripes.

Notes

1. Psychopathy is a developmental disorder in which callousness, manipulativeness, deceit, an indifference to the rights of others, and an absence of empathy and remorse form an important part of the clinical profile (Cleckley, 1950; Hare, 1991).

2. Philosophers such as Immanuel Kant and R. M Hare also insist that moral judgments must be universalizable.

3. The task assesses whether the individual believes that moral transgressions are less modifiable than conventional rules, using the "authority jurisdiction" question (e.g., "Would it be okay for Jim to pull another child's hair / [eat with his fingers] if the teacher says Jim can?").

4. In the Kohlberg moral reasoning tasks, subjects are given a series of moral dilemmas and their moral reasoning in response to the dilemmas and to questioning by the interviewer are scored according to which level of Kohlberg's six stages of morality they reflect.

5. Moral cognitivists hold that moral statements express beliefs and are thus capable of being true or false. Noncognitivists, on the other hand, think moral statements express conative states like desires or perform some other function, such as prescribing action.

6. McDowell (1985) offers a response-dependent or sensibility account in his article "Values and Secondary Properties." There he says that "to ascribe a value to something is to represent it as having a property which (although it is in the object) is . . . understood adequately only in terms of the appropriate modifications of human . . . sensibility" (p. 118). Sensibility theorists hold that moral judgments are representational states with both descriptive and directive aspects.

7. Roskies rules out qualifying terms that are not fully determinate because she thinks they will allow any exception to count as abnormal or irrational and effectively make the internalist claim unfalsifiable. We disagree. The problem arises only when the claim is definitional and offers no substantive account of rationality or normal functioning to ground debate over particular cases. We think Smith does offer a substantive account of practical rationality. Exception claims deserve to be dealt with on a case-by-case basis. It's a matter for debate whether, for example, depression or severe brain damage or intoxication constitute exceptions rather than counterexamples to internalist claims.

8. We assume Roskies thinks that the ordinary person's beliefs about the contents of the law constitute genuine legal judgments analogous to moral judgments. We don't think they are legal judgments, so the analogy doesn't hold. Judges and other legal practitioners make legal judgments in the required sense.

9. It is of course open to externalists to argue that this is all there is to moral judgment. Insofar as this is a purely conceptual claim, the debate between internalists and externalists cannot be settled by an appeal to the evidence.

Adina L. Roskies

An externalist about moral motivation holds that moral motivation is not necessarily implied by or required for moral judgment. Internalists, on the other hand, claim that moral judgment and moral motivation are in some way necessarily connected. There is a wide range of potential formulations for motive internalism, as wide as the range of potential necessary connections to be postulated and range of judgments that count as moral. Kennett and Fine argue for some version of internalism, both by criticizing my empirically motivated arguments against a version of internalism and by arguing that other evidence from neuroscience supports an internalist framework.

In the first part of this commentary I defend and clarify the rationale for my own arguments against a specific version of internalism. In the second part, I consider Kennett and Fine's objections to my counterexample to a strong internalist thesis. Finally, I briefly discuss Kennett and Fine's positive arguments to the effect that evidence from psychopathy actually points to the truth of internalism.

What Is Internalism?

In my 2003 paper I argue specifically against a strong internalist thesis: If an agent believes that it is right to φ in circumstances C, then he is motivated to φ in C. In that paper I explicate the reasons why I deny that this version of internalism properly characterizes the connection that holds between moral judgment and motivation. In their chapter here, Kennett and Fine argue against my view.

It may be helpful for me to begin by sketching a rough picture of the relation I believe does hold between moral judgment and motivation. In brief, we possess cognitive faculties that enable us to represent and reason about the world; among other things, these faculties enable us to make judgments and express them using language. We have other faculties that govern our affective states and provide input to systems that subserve action. The cognitive and affective faculties are subserved by different brain systems, as is evidenced by the fact that people can sustain damage to specific areas that results in specific cognitive or affective deficits. In humans the relevant brain areas are normally anatomically and functionally interconnected. Specifically, I hypothesize that those areas involved in moral judgments normally send their output to areas involved in affect, resulting in motives that in some instances cause us to act. In the paper of mine (Roskies, 2003) that is the target of Kennett and Fine's attack, I discuss patients with damage to the ventromedial cortex. I believe this is an area that forms a causal connection from the cognitive to the affective systems. If this link is severed, one would anticipate seeing judgment preserved but affect and motivation impaired, which is precisely the VM patients' clinical syndrome. Importantly, however, this link involves the output of systems subserving moral judgment. Moreover, the link is causal and thus contingent and not constitutive. This picture explains why I can accept the platitude that moral judgment often or usually leads to motivation, without accepting that it is necessarily or intrinsically motivating. If I am correct, internalism is false because the connection is not necessary.

Kennett and Fine criticize my focus on the claim of necessity. But necessity is part of the standard view of internalism. For instance, the *Cambridge Dictionary of Philosophy* defines motivational internalism as "the view that moral motivation is internal to moral duty . . . [T]he specific internal relation the view affirms is that of necessity"(p. 592).[1] The picture I sketched here should make it clear that one can accept the fact that moral judgments are often or even usually accompanied by moral motivation without accepting a necessity claim.

Kennett and Fine's preferred characterization of the internalist thesis, that "moral judgment is ceteris paribus motivating" (this volume, p. 174), is too permissive to count as an internalist thesis of the kind that has been at the center of metaethical disputes. First, given some unpackings of the ceteris paribus clause, it is a claim that I can accept while maintaining that moral judgment is not intrinsically or necessarily motivating (i.e., while being an externalist). Second, as I argued in my 2003 paper, such a claim is empty in the absence of a specification of ceteris paribus conditions. It could always be interpreted post hoc so that no evidence could serve to undermine it.

Insofar as Kennett and Fine's thesis is merely a defeasible descriptive claim about what human moral reasoning is usually like, I have no real quarrel with it—it is just not an internalist thesis. I take it that internalist philosophers have intended to offer something stronger than contingent claims about human wiring. Their theses have purported to be about the nature of morality and would thus have to hold true of any being capable of moral understanding, human or otherwise.

Only a view involving necessity or intrinsicality can distinguish moral beliefs and judgments from other types by their special content. Take, for example, Michael Smith's formulation of his practical rationality constraint as an objection to internalism. Smith's claim PI is the following: "If an agent believes that it is right to ϕ in circumstances C, then either he is motivated to ϕ in C or he is practically irrational" (Smith, 1993, p. 61). I take it that Smith means this to hold necessarily; there is no ceteris paribus clause here, nor does the claim contain a weakening term like "usually" or "normally." My objection is that Smith's position cannot stand as a defense against externalism without a substantive and independently motivated account identifying practical irrationality. In the absence of such an account (and one that does not rely heavily upon a ceteris paribus clause) the thesis is in danger of being vacuous as a characterization of internalism (see also Svavarsdottir, 1999).

In any case, Smith and I are really not opposed. I see Smith's view more as one that ties practical reasons and not specifically moral reasons to motivation, and thus not primarily as a view about the nature of moral judgment, but rather as a claim about our concept of moral judgment and how we think that judgment should link up to action. Notice, for instance, that Smith's practical rationality constraint can be applied to moral behavior regardless of whether the link between moral judgment and motivation is the intrinsic one of the internalist or an external one as the externalist holds. Even if I maintain an externalist view about the relation between moral judgment and motivation, I am at liberty to consider someone practically irrational if she fails to act as she judges she ought. Finally, I note that my exact claim about Smith's thesis is that "while we may ultimately want to accede to something like PI, on the face of it PI as an internalist thesis is too weak to be revealing about the nature of moral judgment . . . without a further account of what it is to be practically rational" (2003, pp. 53–54).

A second issue that arises in their criticisms of my 2003 paper is what types of judgments are relevant to an internalist thesis. The sorts of claims that the version(s) of internalism I target in my paper pick out are not, as Kennett and Fine claim, merely reports of moral norms, of the form "morality dictates I ought," but rather particular first-person hypothetical claims of the form "If C obtains, then I ought to ϕ." These are taken straight from the internalist literature upon which much of contemporary discussion of internalism is based (see note 1).

Kennett and Fine claim that the internalist thesis applies only to first-person judgments, but that VM patients have only been given third-person scenarios. Although this is true of the example scenarios reported in Eslinger and Damasio (1985), other experiments have given them first-person scenarios. In first-person hypothetical scenarios, their judgments also accord with those of normals (Adolphs, personal communication; see Roskies, 2005). Since these scenarios involve first-person moral judgments, and since the internalist holds that such first-person moral judgments (among others) entail motivation, one would expect to see some effect of motivation in these cases. The fact that when actually confronted with such scenarios VM patients fail to act as they judge provides prima facie evidence that they are not so motivated. This contrasts markedly with normal behavior.

In my 2003 paper I focused upon occurrent first-person moral judgments rather than standing beliefs in order to discount cases of absent motivation that Kennett and Fine describe as being consistent with internalism. These are cases in which one might hold a moral belief yet fail to be motivated because the belief is not occurrent and the relevant moral judgments are not formed, owing to failures of attention, memory, or inference.

It does not follow from these considerations about nonoccurrent beliefs that the only relevant judgments by which to test internalism are, as Kennett and Fine argue in their chapter, in situ judgments. One can surely make judgments about hypothetical situations. Kennett and Fine claim that the only internalist thesis that bears discussion is the following weak internalist thesis: If an agent makes the judgment that it is right to ϕ in situ, then he is motivated to ϕ. This is an exceedingly weak claim, and one that violates the spirit of most versions of internalism in the literature. It suggests that the action-guiding force thought to be characteristic of moral judgment is only necessarily connected to those judgments made in the particular circumstances in which the action is possible for that agent. The reason for this is unclear, for surely motivation is not restricted to in situ situations. If I believe or judge that killing is wrong, I am motivated not to kill at all times, not only when there is a knife in my hand and a person I dislike within my reach. One might think that it is because of my moral outlook that I am motivated not to steal, even in contexts where there is nothing to steal. Denying this seems to flout the idea that normative requirements are standing requirements, and thus they apply not only in in situ contexts, but in all contexts.

More important, the in situ claim seems orthogonal to the basic spirit of internalism, which holds that moral judgments are intrinsically motivating because of their moral content. The content of a judgment that it is right to ϕ does not vary according to whether the judger is in situ or not, just as the content of the judgment that it is raining does not alter if it is uttered in a context in which it is raining or in which it is not. Moral judgments about hypothetical situations are still moral judgments, and if they are supposed to be motivating because of their moral content, then one expects to see evidence of motivation in non-in situ cases as well. As far as I know, no other internalist has restricted the scope of sincere moral judgments to in situ cases.

In summary, internalist theses similar in spirit to the one I consider appear throughout the literature. These claims involve necessity because necessity is required to distinguish an internalist view from an externalist view that recognizes that moral judgment and motivation regularly co-occur. Nothing substantive differentiates Kennett and Fine's "more plausible internalisms" that do away with claims of necessity from the externalist account I offer. Moreover, internalist claims in the literature are not restricted to in situ situations. Kennett and Fine's in situ-restricted internalism with a ceteris paribus clause is such a weak thesis it is barely recognizable as a form of internalism.

The Evidence Against Internalism

The spirit of internalism is that it is (part of) the essence of moral beliefs that they be motivating. As such, a single counterexample is sufficient to refute it. So any example of a real moral judgment (of the right sort) not attended by moral motivation can serve as a falsifying instance of the strong philosophical thesis I target. In my 2003 paper, I argued that such a counterexample exists in the form of patients with damage to the ventromedial prefrontal cortex (VM patients).[2]

I should say at the outset that my 2003 paper was based upon inferences made from the literature available at the time, which was and still is scant. Moreover, the studies on VM patients were carried out by neurologists and neuroscientists who were not guided by the philosophical questions we are considering. Consequently, the evidence is far from ideal for determining whether indeed VM patients are counterexamples to internalism. A discussion of what precisely is needed to make this determination is the point of this exchange.

Kennett and Fine are mistaken in claiming that my evidence comes entirely from the case study of EVR. This is the most detailed case study available in the literature, but similar studies have been carried out with other VM patients, with a similar profile of results (Damasio, Tranel, & Damasio, 1990; Adolphs & Hauser, personal communication). A new study of seven VM patients (Young, Cushman, Adolphs, Tranel, & Hauser, 2006) also shows that these patients' judgments of moral culpability and intention mirror those of normals, in almost every way. Subtle differences (Koenigs et al., 2007) do not render the judgment nonmoral. For arguments to this effect, see Roskies 2005. Thus, there is a growing body of evidence attesting to the ability of VM patients to make moral judgments.

I now turn to Kennett and Fine's two other specific criticisms. First, they claim that the behavior of VM patients is not immoral or amoral. I disagree, although the details from EVR's case study are not definitive on this matter. The deficit from VM damage is quite broad, and is often characterized as a deficit that affects social decision making. However, insofar as moral failings are part of this social deficit, the deficit due to VM damage is also a moral deficit. At least, these patients perform acts they judge to be morally wrong. Thus, the internalist position that moral judgments entail motivation is still put under pressure by a nonspecific deficit insofar as it affects the moral. Although Kennett and Fine maintain that EVR's moral behavior is unimpaired "within the constraints of his decision-making deficit"(this volume, p. 188), it is precisely the character of this deficit that makes VM patients interesting test cases for internalism, for they appear to make moral judgments (at least within the constraints of the experimental situation), yet they fail to act accordingly in their real lives. Moreover, despite the fact that they exhibit generalized decreased initiative, they retain some capacity for motivation. In theory, then, VM patients are interesting test cases for internalism because they can both make moral judgments and exhibit motivation in some circumstances. What remains to be seen is whether their moral judgments result in motivation.

Kennett and Fine seem to think it important to show that a potential counterexample for internalism would be a person motivated by immoral intent. They argue that EVR is not a good test case for internalism, describing him as "not . . . a person careless of others' rights and welfare (as psychopaths are) or of behavior motivated by immoral intent" (this volume, p. 184). However, as I pointed out in my 2003 paper, lacking moral motivation is not the same as having immoral motivation. It is not of major consequence that VM damage does not lead to a specifically moral deficit, nor does it matter whether VM patients are moral monsters. Indeed, it would not matter if there were instances in which motivation co-occurred with moral judgment in these patients, as long as it wasn't always and necessarily the case. The possibility that the VM patients' lack of aggression is due to retained moral motivation rather than behavioral habit does not support the truth of internalism. As I have suggested, there is no reason to assume that an agent with a deficit in a contingent link between judgment and motivation would be overwhelmingly immoral, for that would require specific motivation to act against one's judgments, not lack of motivation to act. Only failure to be motivated to act according to one's moral judgments, not acting against them, is required to disprove internalism.

Moreover, Kennett and Fine think that a moral deficit must be specific. For instance, they write, "However, a general deficit in decision making as described in EVR . . . can easily account for a failure to keep a promise . . . or to discharge responsibilities . . . without suggesting an impairment specifically in moral motivation" (this volume, p. 186). Their call for evidence characterizing a specific impairment in moral motivation, as in the loss of "a previously reliable enculturated desire to 'do the right thing' " (this volume, p. 184) suggests a simplistic and unrealistic picture of externalism, not at all the sort of externalism I espouse. Nothing in the picture I prefer about what causes moral judgment to lead to motivation in most cases would suggest that frontal damage would lead to a specific or isolated deficit. Finally, Kennett and Fine claim that "Damasio and colleagues have characterized the impairment following VM damage as one of decision making, and this seems like a more accurate portrayal of EVR's deficit than a specific dysfunction in moral motivation" (this volume, p. 185). Contrary to Kennett and Fine's interpretation, my views are not in conflict with Damasio's claim that VM damage results in a decision-making deficit. Decision involves both judgment and action; EVR's moral deficits are just one aspect of his decision-making deficit. If internalism were correct, and moral judgments were intrinsically motivating, then the moral judgments of VM patients ought to be motivating even if they sustained deficits in linking deliberation and action in other realms. When speaking of VM patients' behavior in the gambling task, Bechara, Damasio, and Damasio (2000a) conclude that knowledge of correct action is not sufficient to drive behavior in VM patients: "Even without these biases, the knowledge of right and what is wrong may become available, as happened in 50% of the VM patients. However, by itself, such knowledge is not sufficient to ensure an advantageous behavior. Although the frontal patient may be fully aware of what is right and what is wrong, s/he still fails to act accordingly. These patients may 'say' the right thing, but 'do' the wrong thing" (p. 301). It is plausible, given the profile of the VM patient, that a similar deficit extends to the moral realm.

Kennett and Fine also bring up the cases of early VM damage and suggest that the differences between these and cases of later damage indicate that late-damage VM patients are not moral monsters because they are motivated by their retained moral judgments. While this is possible, it is also not crippling to an externalist, for what matters is not whether moral motivation is retained in some cases, but rather whether it ever fails to be present when moral judgment is. In my paper I am forthright about the implications early-damage patients have for our understanding of the acquisition of moral knowledge: "These patients with early damage fail to acquire the declarative knowledge of social and ethical norms which enable them to judge morally or act morally" (2003, p. 58). Evidence suggests that the VM cortex is important for the acquisition of moral knowledge, but not its retention or employment. That is why patients with late damage to the VM cortex prove so compelling as counterexamples to internalism.

Consider an analogy with another form of brain damage: VM patients are like amnestic patients with hippocampal damage; the hippocampus is necessary for the formation of novel long-term memories, but is not required for the retrieval of already established memories. No one is tempted to argue of them that they fail to have "real" memories of their pretrauma past. In addition, we don't believe that the content of a memory is dependent upon an intact hippocampus. The most common view is that it is part of the machinery required for the encoding of new memories. Similarly, VM patients with late damage have preserved moral knowledge (i.e., the content of their moral beliefs is unaltered) that they can access and use. Just as patients with hippocampal damage have real memories of their pretrauma past, VM patients are thus capable of making real moral judgments, not just moral judgments in the inverted commas sense. Then, if they lack moral motivation, internalism of the form I focus upon will be disproven.

Kennett and Fine's final criticism is that I have provided insufficient evidence that VM patients lack moral motivation in ethically charged situations. Specifically, they deny that the situations in which patients fail to show SCRs are ethically charged and that the SCR is a reliable indicator of motivation. While I do not characterize the Iowa gambling task as an ethically charged situation, I do take the picture-viewing task to be ethically charged. It involves presenting stimuli that have ethical valence: bodies mutilated by war, sexual stimuli, and so on. An ethically charged situation is merely a situation where moral reactions are normally likely to be elicited, and the differences between normals and VM patients in such situations are telling. Kennett and Fine are correct in pointing out that the studies in which the participants failed to show SCRs did not explicitly require the VM patients to make moral judgments. It remains to be seen whether in cases in which they do explicitly make moral judgments they have or lack SCRs.

However, the main issue here is whether SCRs are reliable indicators of motivation. This is a central issue that will require further empirical substantiation. Nevertheless, it is a plausible hypothesis and a testable one. Kennett and Fine seem to interpret my view as opposed to Damasio's, but I think Damasio and I are in agreement. While they say that Damasio's view is that the SCR represents knowledge of the emotional value of an option that guides decision making, it is clearly not knowledge in the classical, cognitive sense. It is, rather, a bodily indication of the emotional valence of an option, one that guides or affects decision making presumably through its motivational force (and can do so without conscious awareness of its operation). In fact, Damasio frequently refers to anticipatory SCRs as "unconscious biases." Damasio's interpretation of EVR's deficit is similarly not in conflict with mine, for he claims that EVR's defect "appeared to set in at the late stages of reasoning, close to or at the point at which choice-making or response selection must occur" (1994, p. 50; cited by Kennett & Fine in this volume, p. 188).

While Kennett and Fine choose to highlight the terms "knowledge" and "reasoning" in discussing Damasio's research, no such cognitive emphasis appears in Damasio's original text. Indeed, we are currently unable to determine which processes belong to reason and which to response selection or choice. Since the internalist thinks that motivation accompanies or issues from judgment, we would expect its manifestation to occur late in the reasoning-response loop. Motivation to make one choice or another, or to perform one action or another, would be expected to occur "close to or at the point at which choice-making or response selection must occur" (Damasio 1994, p. 50).

A further piece of anecdotal evidence supports my hypothesis: The SCR is absent in cases in which VM patients fail to act as they judge they ought to but is present in those cases in which they do act accordingly (Adolphs, personal communication). The evidence points to the fact that if an SCR is elicited, then motivation is present, and this provides some defeasible support for the converse: that if one is motivated, one produces an SCR. This is a clearly testable and falsifiable hypothesis for future research on the biological basis of motivation. If the SCR is indeed a reliable indicator of motivation, measuring SCRs would provide a direct assay of whether moral judgment leads to motivation, and one not dependent on inference from action. No doubt a deeper understanding of motivational structures and decision making will provide us with other finer-grained physiological measures of motivation.

Although the evidence I cite provides good reason to think that VM patients are examples of people who sometimes make moral judgments but are not motivated by them, the evidence is not conclusive. We might wonder whether stronger evidence could be garnered against internalism. A direct test of Kennett and Fine's very weak version of internalism would require experiments in which VM patients make moral judgments in situ. Presumably, if it could be shown that VM patients make moral judgments, lack SCRs, and fail to act as they judge they should in situations actually requiring moral judgment and action, many versions of internalism would be laid to rest. Unfortunately, even if such experiments would be the best test of the relevance of these patients to internalist claims, such tests are virtually impossible to perform given the constraints of ethical experimentation. Judgments about hypothetical situations, examination of behavior in experimental situations, measurement of SCRs, and inferences from the life histories of these patients are the only data available.

Nonetheless, Kennett and Fine do rightly point out that even given the strictures of ethical experimentation, the available data are inadequate to settle the question. Here their reservations echo my own: The sorts of tests that VM patients have been submitted to in order to characterize their deficits have been undertaken with a clinical and neuropsychological perspective, not a philosophical one, and consequently have not been ideally suited to determining the precise character of their moral deficits or to resolving questions of philosophical relevance. Most important, the experiments in the literature do not explicitly test the presence of SCRs at the very time when the subjects are making moral judgments. Such experiments would be significant for the advancement of this debate. In addition, in some experiments one can only infer that moral judgments were being made by VM patients. For example, it is unclear whether VM patients made moral judgments in the slide-viewing experiment (Damasio et al., 1990). The data do not allow us to distinguish between the possibilities that (1) they made moral judgments but did not exhibit SCRs in the passive viewing condition, and in the active condition describing what they saw enabled them to bypass the disconnection caused by their lesion, resulting in an SCR; or (2) they did not make moral judgments in the passive condition and only made them in the active condition, as Kennett and Fine claim.

On a related point, it is reasonable to ask whether when they are placed in actual situations requiring moral judgments, VM patients recognize them as moral situations. None of the available literature discusses this question, although it is postulated that VM patients reason more effectively about abstract than concrete cases (Trevethan & Walker 1989, 100, quoted by Kennett & Fine in this volume, p. 176). It remains a possibility that the data from Damasio et al. (1990) and the discrepancy between their real-life and abstract deliberations might be attributable to a quasi-perceptual deficit in recognizing a situation as moral.[3] The ideal experiments to resolve this question would (1) test the hypothesis that SCRs are a reliable indication of moral motivation in normals, and (2) measure SCRs in VM patients and normals simultanously as they make both first- and third-person moral judgments. These judgments will most likely have to be about hypothetical situations, but it is possible that experiments could be designed in which some actual moral deliberation requiring action, like promise keeping or honesty, could be directly tested.

Evidence from Psychopathy

In discussing whether psychopaths can stand as challenges to internalism, Kennett and Fine write, "Do we have reasons independent of their manifest lack of moral concern to think that the psychopath's capacity for moral judgment and moral understanding is impaired? Or does the evidence support externalist claims by revealing unimpaired moral judgment and moral reasoning skills in the psychopath?" (this volume, p. 174). They thus suggest that the only test of internalism can come from an agent with an unimpaired capacity for moral judgment and argue on that basis that psychopaths, who have evidence of impaired moral judgment, cannot challenge the internalist thesis.

I question whether only people with unimpaired judgment are potential counterexamples. It is worth considering what sorts of impairments might be relevant for ruling out cases as challenges to internalism. It cannot be that any departure from how normals judge or act can rule out a case, for there must be room at least for moral judgments that are impaired in their connection to motivation. While it seems that the strongest evidence against internalism might come from an agent who makes moral judgments that accord in all ways with those of normal people while being unmoved by those judgments, this is only because it is prima facie easier to argue that normal moral judgments are "really moral" or appropriately sincere, so that they speak to an internalist thesis. Conflicting moral judgments, at least in some respects, ought not to rule a case out as irrelevant, for we must allow room for moral disagreement. Thus, presumably what is relevant here is only that the judgments have the same type of content as do moral judgments made by people we consider normal; that is, that they have moral content.

It is not an accident that most internalist theses are theses about moral judgment, and not normal moral judgment (as in "the judgment normal people would make") or in situ moral judgment, so without some argument for why only unimpaired moral judgments could reveal the psychopath to be a counterexample to internalism, even abnormal moral judgments, as long as they are moral and sincere, should provide counterevidence for internalism. The evidence Kennett and Fine allude to regarding the abnormality of the moral concepts of psychopaths can rule them out as being counterexamples to internalism only if it is possible to convincingly argue that their "moral" judgments aren't really moral at all; that is, if they only make moral judgments in an inverted commas sense.

Kennett and Fine try to argue that psychopaths' moral judgments aren't moral in a few ways. First, they suggest that they lack the same moral concepts, for the psychopath does not make normal moral-conventional distinctions. However, the evidence Kennett and Fine cite about psychopaths is only sufficient for ruling them out as counterexamples if the ability to make the moral-conventional distinction is essential for making a moral judgment at all. (For a discussion of whether the moral-conventional distinction makes sense at all, see Kelly, Stich, Haley, Eng, & Fessler (2007), and Kelly and Stich (forthcoming).) It seems possible that one might lack the ability to properly make the moral-conventional distinction yet not lack all moral concepts or all moral competence. Psychopaths are still cognizant of what is morally right and wrong; they know that what they do is morally wrong and that they ought not to do it. Even if their concepts are impaired, it is plausible that they are nonetheless moral concepts.

Kennett and Fine's brief allusions to the emotional and attentional deficits suffered by psychopaths suggest that they believe that moral cognition requires affective normalcy. If it does, it would make psychopaths (and VM patients) an unlikely place to look for counterexamples to internalism. And if, as Kennett and Fine state, "normative concepts involve a degree of unity of thought" (this volume, p. 178) not to be achieved by persons with these attentional problems, it may therefore be that moral understanding is rendered beyond the psychopath's grasp.[4] However, this seems like an unsupported and debatable notion of the requirements for normative thought and one that needs to be supported by a justification for why moral judgments differ so much from judgments of other types.

At one point Kennett and Fine suggest that psychopaths have different meanings for their moral terms. One study they cite concluded that psychopaths have a "normal semantic understanding" of metaphors, yet they have an impaired understanding of their emotional valence (Hervé, Hayes, & Hare, 2003). Another study reported that psychopaths fail to use voice emphasis to differentiate between neutral and emotionally charged words (Louth et al., 1998). Although these studies do not specifically investigate moral terms, the implication is that psychopaths have impaired emotional processing of emotionally laden words. Thus, moral terms, along with other emotionally laden terms, have for them different "emotional meaning" (Kennett and Fine, p. 177). This suggests a two-factor approach to moral meaning, one component of which is damaged in the case of psychopaths (and presumably VM patients). The affective component of meaning would also presumably be damaged in cases of depression, listlessness, and the like. A direct consequence of this is that the meanings of a person's moral terms change with some changes in mood; the judgment "killing for profit is wrong" means different things in the mouth of my depressed, recently divorced friend and in mine, and in his again after he takes Prozac. This seems implausible. Without a justification for why semantic understanding isn't all you need for understanding semantics, this two-factor approach to meaning seems unmotivated.

Finally, at points (this volume, pp. 174–178) Kennett and Fine seem to think that the psychopaths' impaired moral judgments are due to differences in reasoning. They present a number of studies comparing moral reasoning in psychopaths and nonpsychopathic delinquents. The evidence they cite is mixed. Psychopaths in most recent studies seem to have abilities to reason that are equivalent to those of nonpsychopathic delinquents and criminals. However, one study (Trevethan & Walker, 1989) concludes that psychopaths are more likely to justify their judgments about real-life moral dilemmas in terms of the "moral legitimacy of self-concerns" (this volume, p. 176). Kennett and Fine fail to relate these findings to the question of internalism, but as I see it, they do not bear in their favor. If one thinks that nonpsychopathic delinquents, despite their evident failure to abide by legal codes, are able to reason normally about morality, then the reported similarities between reasoning in psychopaths and nonpsychopaths should lead one to conclude that the psychopaths' judgment is likewise normal in the relevant senses. Furthermore, the explication of the reported difference in reasoning in the one case cited suggests that while psychopathic and nonpsychopathic delinquents are distinguishable on the basis of the type of moral justification they offer for their judgments, psychopaths nonetheless are able to offer a moral justification. Differences in moral reasoning among psychopaths no more point to the absence of moral judgments than do differences in moral views among nonpsychopathic individuals. Thus, while the evidence might suggest that psychopaths have different moral views than do nonpsychopaths, it does not succeed in establishing that they lack moral concepts or an adequate understanding of them. Kennett and Fine's discussion of the psychopath's particular deficits does not support the view that a psychopath is rendered incapable of anything but moral judgments in an inverted commas sense.

Kennett and Fine conclude their discussion with the case of JS, a patient with impaired moral understanding and impaired moral behavior. JS looks very much like the cases of early damage discussed previously (although no indication is given by Kennett and Fine of the nature or extent or age of occurrence of his brain lesion). It is difficult to see why they think that this case and others that involve impaired understanding of moral concepts provide any support for internalism. It would be shocking and inexplicable if people who lacked moral understanding nonetheless consistently acted morally, just as it would be puzzling if a demonstrably colorblind person consistently used color terms correctly. These cases have no bearing upon the question of whether moral judgment entails moral motivation. Moreover, just pointing to the joint presence of moral belief and moral action, as in normals, and their joint absence, such as in JS, does not support an internalist position, for these correlations are equally consistent with my favored externalist view, that VM damage should be viewed as a disconnection syndrome in which the normal but contingent route from regions involved in moral deliberation and judgment to regions that mediate and motivate action is severed. Such disconnection makes it evident that in the real world moral judgment and moral motivation can come apart.

My argument against internalism is not meant to refute all the ways of conceiving of the connection between moral judgment and motivation; indeed, I believe there is a contingent connection. It was directed at a rather strong but common internalist thesis that moral judgment or belief is intrinsically motivating, a position I find implausible both on a priori and empirical grounds. That there are people who find such a thesis plausible and indeed worth defending is evidenced by the ferocity with which Kennett and Fine defend the internalist position against my proposed counterexample. The discussion has been beneficial in that they point out the areas in which the evidence is inconclusive because the best-designed tests of the cognition and behavior of VM patients have not yet been done. Perhaps this will inspire some researchers to undertake the appropriate experiments. Nevertheless, beyond these useful criticisms, Kennett and Fine's theoretical discussion of the issues fails to provide any reason to favor the thesis that moral beliefs or judgments are intrinsically motivating.

Notes

1. Kennett and Fine question whether anyone holds a thesis like the one I oppose. My opponents are, quite simply, those who think moral judgment necessarily entails moral motivation. Nagel, for instance, writes that "Internalism is the view that the presence of a motivation for acting morally is guaranteed by the truth of ethical propositions themselves" (Nagel, 1970, p. 7); and Harman echoes this, "To think you ought to do something is to be motivated to do it" (Harman, 1977, p. 33). Darwall characterizes judgment internalism as follows "Judgment internalism holds that if S judges (or believes, or sincerely asserts) that she ought to do A (or that she has reason to do A), then, necessarily, she has some motivation to do A" (Darwall, Gibbard, & Railton, 1997, p. 308). Smith also cites this version of internalism (1994, p. 61), though he finds the claim implausible and instead prefers a version connected to practical rationality. This view is found as early as 1787 in Price, "When we are conscious that an action is fit to be done, or ought to be done, it is not conceivable that we can remain uninfluenced, or want a motive to action" (1787/1969, p. 194). Other internalists also make claims of necessity, e.g., Blackburn (1984, p. 188): "It seems to be a conceptual truth that to regard something as good is to feel a pull toward promoting or choosing it."

2. Kennett and Fine surmise that I cannot be addressing non-naturalist internalists, since non-naturalists reject my naturalistic reliance on empirical evidence. Although their views may insulate non-naturalists from criticism from empirical data, it seems that ultimately it is the entire philosophical picture, construed as a whole, that must be evaluated with respect to others. An empirically well-founded and coherent externalist picture of moral judgment may well convince those deliberating between naturalist and non-naturalist views to adopt a naturalistic picture of morality, even if those with prior commitments to non-naturalism fail to be swayed.

3. There is a version of internalism (Tolhurst, 1998) that argues that what leads to motivation is the quasi-perceptual recognition that something "seems" wrong or right. If moral judgment requires this sort of nondeliberational perception of states of affairs as right or wrong, and if it can be shown that such perceiving is intrinsically connected to conative reactions, then perhaps a version of internalism would prevail in the face of VM evidence. Whether that would do the work traditionally supposed by internalists remains to be seen because it would link appearance rather than judgment to motivation.

4. Note that Kennett and Fine claim that "the central notion of a normative requirement [is] one that persists in the absence of inclination" (this volume, p. 178). If so, then grasping this normative requirement, or judging on the basis of it, ought to be possible in the absence of inclination. This is simply the externalist's claim.

4.2 | The Truth about Internalism

Michael Smith

In her 2003 paper on ethical judgments and acquired sociopathy, Adina Roskies argues against the following very strong version of motive internalism (strict motivational internalism, SMI):

It is conceptually necessary that if an agent judges that she morally ought to ϕ in circumstances C, then she is motivated to ϕ in C.

According to Roskies, SMI is implausible, given what we know about patients with ventromedial frontal lobe damage. These patients appear to make moral judgments with full understanding since their use of moral language is just as complex and competent after their VM damage as it was before. However, after their VM damage, and in contrast to the way they were before the damage, they lack moral motivation. It is thus not just logically possible for an agent to judge that he or she morally ought to act in a certain way and not be motivated, this is what we have come to expect when the agent in question has suffered VM damage. So herein lies the truth about internalism: If SMI is the only version of internalism worth discussing, then we have good empirical reasons to believe that internalism is false.

Jeanette Kennett and Cordelia Fine take Roskies to task in their chapter. Their complaints are multiple, but for present purposes I will focus on just one: Roskies' assumption that SMI is the only version of internalism worth discussing. SMI says that it is literally impossible for an agent to make a moral judgment and yet not be motivated, that any failure of motivation is indicative of a failure of understanding. Although this strong claim is accepted by some—Kennett and Fine cite John McDowell—they insist that it is far more common for internalists to make much weaker claims about the connection between moral judgment and motivation. They therefore spend some time formulating their own preferred weaker version of internalism, a version that they think is more worthy of critical attention by opponents and which Roskies' argument leaves intact.

Kennett and Fine are, I think, right that SMI posits a connection between moral judgment and motivation too strong to be credible. For one thing, SMI makes it hard to see how weakness of will—motivation contrary to better judgement—is so much as possible. Instead it seems to commit us to an implausible Socratic view of weakness of will as a defect, not of the will, but of the understanding. Like Kennett and Fine, I am, however, nonetheless attracted to internalism, so I applaud their attempt to formulate a weaker version, a version that is both immune to Roskies' criticisms and on which opponents of internalism might more profitably focus. However, the alternative version of internalism that they come up with is not the one that I would have proposed myself, so in this commentary I want to explain why and offer my own alternative (see also M. Smith, 1994, 1997). As it happens, the alternative I favor is one that Roskies herself considers briefly but dismisses in her 2003 paper. At the end I explain why I think that Roskies' rejection of this weaker version of internalism was too hasty.

The version of internalism that Kennett and Fine propose is weaker than SMI in two ways. First, it replaces the conceptually necessary connection posited by SMI with a ceteris paribus connection. Second, it restricts the circumstances in which this weaker ceteris paribus connection between moral judgment and motivation is supposed to apply to the circumstances in which the judgment itself pertains. Their preferred version of motive internalism can thus be stated as follows (K&FMI):

Other things being equal, if an agent makes the in situ judgment that she ought to ϕ in circumstances C—that is, if she judges that she ought to ϕ in circumstances C, believing herself to be in those circumstances—then she is motivated to ϕ.

However, I see two main problems with K&FMI. The first concerns the restriction to in situ judgments. The second concerns the weakening of the connection to one that holds only ceteris paribus.

Kennett and Fine provide the following argument for the restriction to in situ judgments.

I can surely believe that I ought to keep my promise but fail to form the in situ judgment that I ought to keep my promise. Maybe my belief or my promise isn't foregrounded in my deliberations about what to do. Maybe I fail to notice that what I'm planning to do—go to the football game this afternoon, say—would be inconsistent with keeping the promise I made two weeks ago to meet you in the mall at 3:00 on Saturday the 22nd. If I forget my promise to you, or I don't notice that the time to keep it is now, then, although I do believe I ought to keep my promises, including this one, I fail to form a judgment about what I ought to do right now, and so I fail to meet you. Of course I ought to form the judgment, but my failure to do so is not a failure of motivation. As we have described it, it can be a failure of attention or memory or inference. We take it that this kind of mismatch between moral belief and motivation to act wouldn't be enough to refute motive internalism. The relevant judgments are first person, in situ. (this volume, p. 182)

However, the conclusion of Kennett and Fine's argument, which is that we should restrict internalism to in situ judgments, does not follow from the premises they provide.

As stated, SMI requires that the content of people's motivations match the content of their moral judgments. When I believe that I ought to keep my promise to you now, SMI requires that I be motivated to keep my promise to you now. When I believe that I ought to keep my promise to meet you in the mall at 3:00 pm on Saturday the 22nd, SMI requires that I be motivated to meet you in the mall at 3:00 pm on Saturday the 22nd, and so on. Kennett and Fine point out, perfectly correctly, that if I believe that I ought to keep my promise to meet you in the mall at 3:00 pm on Saturday the 22nd but I don't believe that it is now that day and time, then I may not be motivated to meet you in the mall now. They also point out, again perfectly correctly, that this combination of moral belief and failure of motivation—believing that I ought to keep my promise to meet you in the mall at 3:00 pm on Saturday the 22nd, but not being motivated to meet you in the mall now—is not a counterexample to internalism. However, since it isn't a case in which there is a mismatch between the content of my moral belief and my motivation, it isn't a counterexample to SMI either. The argument they give thus provides us with no reason at all to think that SMI should be understood as making a claim about in situ judgements only.

What would motivate restricting SMI to in situ judgments? To motivate that restriction, Kennett and Fine would need to explain why we should suppose, on the one hand, that when I believe that I ought to meet you in the mall at 3:00 pm on Saturday the 22nd, I need not be motivated to meet you in the mall at 3:00 pm on Saturday the 22nd, even though when I believe that I ought to meet you in the mall now, I must be motivated to meet you in the mall now. It is tempting to think that no such explanation could be provided. The in situ moral belief would, after all, appear to be derived by putting the belief that I ought to meet you in the mall at 3:00 pm on Saturday the 22nd together with the belief that it is now 3:00 pm on Saturday the 22nd. However, if the in situ belief is derived from a non-in situ belief and a belief about what day and time it is now, then it is surely plausible to suppose that what explains the necessary connection between the in situ belief and the in situ motivation is the perfectly general claim that moral judgments and motivations must have matching contents, and that the in situ motivation is therefore also derived by putting together the non-in situ motivation—the motivation to meet you in the mall at 3:00 pm on Saturday the 22nd—together with that same belief about what day and time it is now. So not only do Kennett and Fine fail to provide a convincing argument for the restriction of internalism to in situ judgments, the restriction itself looks very difficult to motivate.

The second problem with K&FMI concerns the weakening of SMI so that the conceptually necessary connection is replaced by a ceteris paribus connection. The problem with this particular way of weakening SMI emerges if we look more closely at SMI itself. SMI is false if the connection between moral judgment and motivation is contingent, even if, as a matter of fact, the connection is nomically necessary. Suppose, for example, that there is a contingent psychological law connecting the psychological state that underlies moral judgment with motivation. In that case the connection between moral judgment and motivation would be contingent but, as a matter of fact, nomically necessary. SMI would be false even though, as it happens, we never find someone making a moral judgment without being correspondingly motivated.

Once we notice the possibility of such a contingent yet nomically necessary connection between moral judgment and motivation, the crucial question to ask is whether such a connection would vindicate the truth of some version or other of internalism. The answer, I take it, is that it would not. This is because the mark of internalism, whether the internalism in question is of the strong kind posited by SMI or of some weaker kind, must surely be that it posits some sort of conceptually necessary connection between moral judgment and motivation. Internalism is, after all, supposed to function as an a priori constraint on what is to count as a moral judgment. The connection between moral judgment and motivation must therefore hold in virtue of the content of the moral judgment itself. It cannot be a connection that we discover empirically by uncovering a contingent psychological law.

The problem with K&FMI should now be apparent. K&FMI posits a connection between moral judgment and motivation that holds other things being equal. What is it for other things to be equal? Suppose that there were a contingent psychological law connecting the state that underpins moral judgment with motivation. In that case, other things would be equal when the state that underpins moral judgment did its causal work. So if there were a contingent psychological law connecting the state that underpins moral judgment with motivation, then when other things are equal, someone who judges that they ought to act in a certain way would be motivated to act in that way. The existence of such a contingent psychological law would thus be sufficient to guarantee the truth of K&FMI. However, it would be insufficient to guarantee the truth of internalism, understood as a thesis that holds of conceptual necessity. So K&FMI doesn't state a version of internalism at all.

Of course, this leaves us with a problem. For if SMI states a version of internalism that is too strong to be credible, and if K&FMI doesn't state a version of internalism at all, then how exactly are we to formulate the weaker version of internalism on which opponents should focus? My own view is that the following weaker thesis (WMI) captures what's crucial:

It is conceptually necessary that if an agent judges that she morally ought to ϕ in circumstances C, then either she is motivated to ϕ in C or she is practically irrational.

WMI says that what is supposed to be a conceptual truth is not that agents are motivated to do what they judge themselves morally obliged to do— this is the claim SMI makes—but rather that a failure to be so motivated is a form of practical irrationality. Nor should it be surprising that SMI should need to be weakened in this way, for the earlier criticism of SMI was that it didn't allow for the possibility of weakness of will as a genuine defect of the will. The difference between SMI and WMI is precisely that it allows for this possibility. Weakness of the will is, after all, just the name we give to a kind of practical irrationality that explains why someone judges that they morally ought to act in a certain way without being motivated to act that way.

In her 2003 paper, Roskies in effect considers this formulation of internalism, but decides that it is not worth discussing. Her complaint is that without a substantive characterization of what it is to be practically rational, WMI is trivially true. Suppose, for example, that a defender of WMI refuses to provide such a substantive account and instead simply stipulates that an agent is practically irrational whenever she judges that she morally ought to ϕ in C but isn't motivated to ϕ in C. (It might be thought that I came close to doing that just now when I characterized weakness of the will.) Roskies' objection is that no one could object to WMI, so understood; it is trivially true, given the stipulation. So for WMI to be worth discussing, a defender of WMI must therefore provide a substantive account of what it is to be practically rational. Since no such account has been provided, Roskies concludes that WMI is best ignored.

I am not quite sure what Roskies thinks the defender of WMI needs to provide by way of a substantive account of practical rationality. On certain understandings, however, it seems to me that we should be skeptical about the truth of WMI given any such substantive account. Suppose, for example, that we substitute the kind of operational definition of what it is to be practically rational that a medical practitioner or a social worker might use in figuring out whether someone is capable of making autonomous choices: "able to describe the alternatives she faces, talk sensibly about their relative merits, and make a choice without getting flustered or overemotional." The trouble with WMI, given this operational definition of what it is to be practically rational, is obvious. Many people who aren't motivated to do what they judge they morally ought to do are nonetheless able to describe their alternatives, talk sensibly about their relative merits, and choose without getting flustered or overemotional. So, if we understand WMI in terms of such an operational definition of what it is to be practically rational, then WMI is no more credible than SMI.

It isn't clear why defenders of WMI should accept that their alternatives are either to stipulate a meaning for being practically rational (in which case WMI is trivially true) or to provide a substantive characterization of (say) the operational kind just mentioned (in which case WMI is obviously false). In other domains there is plainly a third kind of alternative. Consider, for example, the following claim about theoretical rationality (MORTAL):

If someone believes that Socrates is a man and she believes that all men are mortal, then either she believes that Socrates is mortal or she is theoretically irrational.

Again, under any plausible operational definition of what it is to be theoretically rational, MORTAL looks bound to turn out false. Suppose, for example, that we count people as theoretically rational if and only if they score higher than the average on the Scholastic Aptitude Tests (SATs; these are the standard assessment tests used to determine relative standing among high school students who compete for college entry in the United States). The trouble with MORTAL given this understanding of what it is to be theoretically rational is plain, for someone could easily score higher than the average on the SATs and yet fail to believe that Socrates is mortal when she believes that Socrates is a man and believes that all men are mortal. MORTAL, so understood, is thus plainly false. Moreover, any similar operational definition of what it is to be theoretically rational looks like it would make MORTAL turn out similarly false, for the simple reason that the respect in which someone who fails to believe that Socrates is mortal when she believes that Socrates is a man and that all men are mortal is irrational is precisely this very respect. This particular combination of belief and lack of belief—believing that Socrates is a man, believing that all men are mortal, but not believing that Socrates is mortal—constitutes an instance of theoretical irrationality. An operational definition, by contrast, at best identifies some feature that roughly correlates with such instances of theoretical irrationality.

Does this mean that the defender of MORTAL is reduced to stipulating what is to count as theoretically rational? That does not seem to be an accurate description of what is going on either. In order to see why, contrast the situation of someone trying to defend MORTAL with someone trying to defend the following claim (CAPITAL):

If someone believes that Canberra is the capital of Australia, then either she believes that Vienna is the capital of Austria or she is theoretically irrational.

If she is to succeed, then it seems that the defender of CAPITAL has no alternative but to stipulate that, as she uses the term "theoretically irrational," someone will count as theoretically irrational when she believes that Canberra is the capital of Australia but doesn't believe that Vienna is the capital of Austria. She has no alternative because she can provide no account of why this particular combination of belief and lack of belief constitutes an instance of theoretical irrationality in any ordinary sense. The defender of MORTAL, by contrast, can provide such an account. The explanation, very roughly, is that being theoretically irrational in the ordinary sense is a matter of a failure of sensitivity in the formation of your beliefs to what you take to be reasons for belief. The combination of belief and lack of belief that the defender of MORTAL thinks constitutes an instance of theoretical irrationality is an instance of just such an insensitivity, whereas the combination of belief and lack of belief that the defender of CAPITAL thinks is an instance of theoretical irrationality is not. That Socrates is a man and that all men are mortal are, by the lights of someone who believes these things, reasons for believing that Socrates is a man, as there is, by the lights of the person who has these beliefs, an inferential connection. But that Canberra is the capital of Australia is not, by the lights of someone who believes this to be so, a reason for believing that Vienna is the capital of Austria. There is not, by the lights of the person who has this belief, any such inferential connection.

The question for the defender of WMI is whether she can make a similar move. Can she explain why this particular combination of belief and lack of motivation—someone's believing that she morally ought to φ in C and yet lacking any motivation to φ in C—constitutes an instance of practical irrationality in an ordinary sense? If she can, then it isn't appropriate to describe her as merely stipulating what she means by "being practically irrational." My suggestion is that the defender of WMI can provide such an explanation. The explanation comes in three stages. Moreover, and importantly, at each stage the explanation remains faithful to the observation made earlier that according to internalists the connection between moral judgment and motivation must hold in virtue of the content of the moral judgment itself.

At the first stage the defender of WMI must argue that what it is that someone believes when she believes that an agent morally ought to φ in C is that φ-ing in C is that action in C, among the agent's alternatives, that uniquely maximizes value. At the second stage she must argue that what it is that someone believes when she believes that p has value is that p is something that she would want if she had a maximally informed and coherent and unified desire set. And at the third stage she must argue that the following combination of belief and lack of desire—someone's believing that she would want that p, if she had a maximally informed and coherent and unified desire set, but lacking any desire that p—constitutes an instance of practical irrationality in an ordinary sense. Although I fully admit that the claims made at all three stages of this explanation are controversial, it is, I think, important to note that the defender of WMI is in fact providing arguments at every stage and hence is not merely stipulating.

Consider, for example, what the defender of WMI might say in defense of the most controversial claim of all, the claim she makes at the third stage. What is especially striking about this claim is that it too trades on the idea that an agent's irrationality is a matter of her insensitivity to reasons. In this case, though, the reason the agent has, at least by her own lights, is a reason to desire that p: by her own lights, that she would want that p if she had a maximally informed and coherent and unified desire set provides her with a reason for wanting that p here and now, as she is actually. To be sure, the force of the putative reason is derivative. The putative reason-providing force of the complex fact derives entirely from the features of the agent's individual desires and their contents and the relationships among them and information that is supposed to make it the case that she would indeed want that p if she had a maximally informed and coherent and unified desire set. It provides the agent with a reason nonetheless (although contrast Scanlon, 1998, chap. 2).

Indeed, the practical irrationality in this case—the failure to be sensitive to the reasons for wanting—seems to be on the same level as the *theoretical* irrationality—the failure to be sensitive to one's reasons for believing— manifested by someone who believes that she would believe that p if she had a maximally (otherwise) informed and coherent and unified belief set, but who fails to believe that p. By her own lights, after all, the fact that she would believe that p if she had a maximally (otherwise) informed and coherent and unified belief set provides such an agent with a reason to believe that p. Again, the force of this putative reason is derivative. The putative reason-providing force of the complex fact derives entirely from the features of the agent's beliefs and their contents and the relationships among them that are supposed to make it the case that the agent would indeed believe that p if she had a maximally (otherwise) informed and coherent and unified belief set. It provides the agent with a reason nonetheless. The only difference between the two cases is that in the second one the agent manifests a failure to believe in accordance with what, by her own lights, are reasons for believing, whereas in the former case the reason is a reason for wanting.

The upshot is thus that Roskies was far too quick in her rejection of WMI. WMI states a weaker connection between moral judgment and motivation than that implied by SMI. Moreover, as we have seen, this weaker connection can be supported by arguments, not by a mere stipulation. Both defenders and opponents of internalism would therefore do best to confront these and similar arguments for WMI head-on; therein lies the truth about internalism.

Could There Be an Empirical Test for Internalism?

Jeanette Kennett and Cordelia Fine

In our chapter we argued that the empirical evidence cited by Roskies and other data we referred to do not in fact undermine internalism. In this brief rejoinder to the commentaries by Roskies and Smith, we want to further address the role of empirical evidence in this debate and in so doing clarify the project of our chapter.

Roskies and Smith agree that internalists claim that there is a necessary connection between moral judgment and motivation to act. Both argue that the claim we defend is too weak to be counted as an internalist claim since it says that the connection holds only ceteris paribus. We did not take ourselves to be offering or defending any particular formulation of weak motivational internalism and we will not attempt to do so here. Nevertheless, our use of the ceteris paribus clause was misleading and we welcome the chance to correct it. For the record, we do think that there is a conceptual connection between moral judgment and motivation, but we do not think that the connection is thereby empirically guaranteed. We agree with Smith that moral motivation must depend upon moral judgment in the right way. It cannot be a mere causal dependence, even one guaranteed by a psychological law. However, if the relevant dependence is rational dependence, then the connection, although conceptually necessary in rationalist accounts of moral judgment, is not empirically guaranteed since we are only contingently rational. It was partly this kind of contingency that we were seeking to cover with a ceteris paribus clause.[1] What we questioned therefore was the very strong claim that people must in fact be motivated by their moral judgments or internalism is undermined. We took Roskies to be holding all internalists to this strong claim, a claim that she takes to be amenable to empirical testing and disconfirmation. Since we disagree that internalists must be committed to the strong motivational claim, we wanted to consider whether some weaker and, in our view, more plausible motivational claims such as those defended by

Smith and other rationalists might also be challenged by the evidence cited by Roskies. We concluded that not even the strong claim was challenged by the case of EVR for the following reasons: We thought it questionable that his capacities for moral judgment were unimpaired, as Roskies argued; we thought that the evidence did not decisively show that he lacked moral motivation; and we argued moreover that there was evidence of broad practical irrationality on any ordinary conception of what it is to be rational. We will review some of the evidence in more detail shortly, but first we will address a more fundamental worry about the approach we and Roskies have taken.

Can Empirical Data Speak to the Philosophical Debate?

Smith's commentary invites the question of whether any empirical evidence could advance, decide, or even speak to the debate between internalists and externalists. He claims that internalism is a conceptual constraint on what is to count as a moral judgment, but clearly this is a conceptual constraint that externalists such as Roskies reject. We take it that the real debate between internalists and externalists is thus over what is to count as a moral judgment. Is moral judgment essentially practical? Is it, as Smith argues, "a conceptual truth that claims about what we are morally required to do are claims about our reasons" (M. Smith, 1994, p. 84)? Are moral judgments, as noncognitivists claim, expressions of sentiments of approval or disapproval toward some action or state of affairs and so intrinsically motivating? Or are claims about what is morally required rather to be thought of as judgments about the correct application of a set of moral standards to some situation, arrived at through the employment of "cognitive faculties that enable us to represent and reason about the world" (Roskies, this volume, p. 191) and which are conceptually independent of practical reason. The empirical evidence may be able to tell us which kind(s) of judgment EVR makes, but it cannot tell us whether they deserve to be called "moral judgments." That would appear to be the task of philosophers, not scientists.[2]

Any attempt to settle the debate between internalists and externalists by empirical examination of putative counterexamples to internalism cases appears doomed while each side uses the term "moral judgment" in a different sense. The psychopath might qualify as making moral judgments in the externalist story of what this involves but fail to satisfy one or more internalist criteria of what can count as a moral judgment. It should come as no surprise that the internalist claim turns out to be false when it is attached to an externalist account of moral judgment, and vice versa. Part of what we tried to do in our chapter to address this problem was to see if there was empirical support for the claim that the capacity for moral judgment is disturbed or impoverished in psychopathic and acquired sociopathy populations relative to the normal population. Let us now explain why we think this kind of data can be relevant, even if it is not decisive.

First, we think that philosophical accounts of moral judgment would be called into question if it turned out that they were highly esoteric. Rationalists like Smith take themselves to be providing an analysis of our folk concepts. The program of conceptual analysis is to refine and systematize the elements of our folk concept. While it thus to some degree idealizes and abstracts away from everyday practice, it simply can't be the case that those engaged in the practice do not for the most part have a mastery of the concepts. If it turned out that the folk do not, implicitly or explicitly, take themselves to be making any claims about anyone's reasons for action in making their everyday moral judgments, we would have reason to reject rationalist versions of internalism.[3] A similar point can be made for sentimentalist accounts of moral judgment. If it could be demonstrated that moral judgments are no more the product of affect than are mathematical judgments, then we would have reason to reject sentimentalism. With respect to these accounts, we think it would be significant if the folk do, but psychopaths do not, take moral judgments to generate requirements on action, or if the moral language of the folk, but not of psychopaths, is properly understood to have emotive as well as descriptive meaning. We claim that a growing body of evidence, some of which we reviewed, such as their poor performance on the moral-conventional distinction task and their incompetence in the use of evaluative language, suggests that psychopaths deviate so significantly from the folk that it is reasonable, on empirical grounds, to conclude that they do not have mastery of the relevant moral concepts. They therefore cannot constitute a counterexample to internalism.

Could There Be a Reliable Test for Moral Motivation?

Could empirical evidence play a more direct role in this debate? Roskies appears to think it can. Suppose EVR to be an unimpaired moral judge. Then clear evidence of outright failure of moral motivation would seem to rule out the strict motivational internalism, which Roskies asserts to be the only interesting version of internalism. (It would not rule out weak motivational internalism.) We challenged Roskies' evidence and her account of moral judgment, but we did not challenge her project. Here we will also address the feasibility of the project.

In our chapter we distinguished between third- and first-personal moral judgments and between hypothetical and situated judgments. We criticized Roskies' focus on third-personal hypothetical judgments in the case of EVR, suggesting that the relevant judgments for assessment of the internalist claim were first-personal in situ judgments. Both Roskies and Smith take us to task us on this score. Smith says:

> Kennett and Fine would need to explain why we should suppose, on the one hand, that when I believe that I ought to meet you in the mall at 3:00 pm on Saturday the 22nd, I need not be motivated to meet you in the mall at 3:00 pm on Saturday the 22nd, even though when I believe that I ought to meet you in the mall now, I must be motivated to meet you in the mall now. (this volume, p. 209)

Let us clarify our reasons for suggesting the restriction. We do not wish to deny that the internalist claim holds for hypothetical judgments of principle, such as "I ought to keep my promises," as well as for derived (or nonderived) in situ judgments such as "I ought to meet you in the mall now." In making our suggestion, we were responding to Roskies' project of providing empirical disconfirmation of internalist claims. We are increasingly doubtful about the prospects of characterizing the relationship between hypothetical moral judgments, motivation, and action in a way that would render motivation in accordance with a hypothetical judgment amenable to direct measurement. First, given plausible claims about how our hypothetical and third-personal moral judgments guide action, it is not clear that we can isolate *a* moral motive with, as Smith puts it "matching content" or that it would be a measurable event at all. Second, even if moral judgments and moral motivations must have matching contents, hypothetical and in situ moral judgments may often enough have varying contents. Anti-internalist conclusions drawn on the basis of evidence of a subject's third-personal hypothetical moral judgments and their in situ motivations are thus unsafe.

In rejecting our restriction of the claim to be tested to in situ judgments Roskies says:

> If I believe or judge that killing is wrong, I am motivated not to kill at all times, not only when there is a knife in my hand and a person I dislike within my reach. One might think that it is because of my moral outlook that I am motivated not to steal, even in contexts where there is nothing to steal. Denying this seems to flout the idea that normative requirements are standing requirements, and thus they apply not only in in situ contexts, but in all contexts. (this volume, pp. 194–195)

We agree that normative requirements are standing requirements; indeed we suggested in this volume that the psychopath's failure to understand this was evidence that he or she did not make moral judgments. Moreover, Roskies' account of how standing requirements guide action makes vivid the difficulty facing the empirical project of measuring moral motivation and thus for her interpretation of EVR.[4] Roskies (2003) suggests in her original piece that moral motivation is an event with measurable physiological correlates, e.g., skin conductance responses. But if it is correct to say, as she suggests in the passage cited here, that I am motivated not to kill, steal, cheat, and so forth, even when I am, say, curled up on the couch watching TV with my beloved with no thought of wrongful activity in mind, then it is hard to see how this could be the case.[5]

We think that this is not a problem for internalism, but clearly it is for efforts to settle the debate by resort to empirical evidence. Internalists might plausibly think of moral motives as functioning in the way suggested by Barbara Herman in her discussion of the Kantian motive of duty (1981). The motive of duty limits what may be done from other motives. Behavior such as not stealing when there is nothing to steal thus counts as being under the guidance of (hypothetical) moral judgment in virtue of the truth of a set of relevant counterfactuals. Even if there were desirable objects to steal and I could have gotten away with it, I would not have stolen them, and so on. If such counterfactuals are true of me, then it is appropriate to attribute the motive of duty, or more particularly the motive not to steal, etc. to me at all times and not just when I am placed in situations of opportunity and temptation. However, so conceived the motive of duty (or the motive not to steal, etc.) is not a positive motive to action and so is not itself something that could be isolated and measured. Indeed it may function by limiting what I take to be the options available to me. Stealing, murder, and the like aren't among my options.

A further problem arises for Roskies at this point on the assumption that EVR does make the relevant first-personal hypothetical moral judgments (as well as the third-personal judgments that were tested). As we have noted, EVR does not kill, steal, or cheat. Yet Roskies denies that EVR is motivated by his moral judgments. She appears to want to say that in the normal case agents are guided by motives not to commit moral wrongs at all times when they refrain from wrongdoing, whereas the correct explanation for EVR's conformity with standing moral prohibitions that he accepts is that he fortunately *lacks* a positive motivation to wrongdoing. This looks undesirably ad hoc. While both pictures could explain the absence of wrongdoing, we need a reason to suppose that Roskies is correct to distinguish the cases in the way that she does. We think the only evidence in her favor here is the evidence we cited of the difficulty EVR has in translating his judgments from the third to the first person—"I still would not know what to do"—but this calls into question her claim that EVR makes the relevant moral judgments in the first place.

Recall that Roskies interpreted the mismatch between EVR's superior third-personal hypothetical moral judgments and his hapless social behavior as evidence of a failure of moral motivation. We argued that the failure was not one of moral motivation, but one of judgment or decision making. EVR was unable to adequately translate his superior third-personal judgments into first-personal practical judgments.

The moral judgments we make in complex and ambiguous real-life situations may differ significantly from our armchair judgments—sometimes for the good reason that the context of action delivers relevant information that was unavailable to us in the armchair, and sometimes for not-so-good reasons. As a large body of research in social psychology shows, our judgments about, for example, the appropriateness of a person's behavior (e.g., Devine, 1989), a fitting punishment for a misdemeanor (e.g., Lerner, Goldberg, & Tetlock, 1998), responsibility and guilt (Forgas & Moylan, 1987), or the humor in a racist joke (Monteith & Voils, 1998) can vary significantly as a function of our current cognitive or emotional state. This suggests that in many cases our hypothetical moral judgments provide just one input into the situated judgment. In other words, for these sorts of ambiguous everyday moral judgments, there is no explicitly held moral norm that can be applied precisely from the abstract to the in situ situation; rather, our everyday moral judgments are on-line constructions that are highly sensitive to our emotional and cognitive state. Of course, there are presumably clear moral judgments for which these sorts of psychological effects will have insignificant influence, as in the sort of example Roskies provides (e.g., killing an innocent person whom you happen to dislike), which will translate clearly from abstract to real-life situations. However, as both we and Roskies have noted, there is no evidence that EVR fails to behave in line with such clear-cut and absolute moral rules. Roskies' case rests therefore on EVR's behavior in situations where the application of the hypothetical judgment is not so clear cut.

VM patients have particular difficulties with abilities that would seem essential for properly evaluating moral situations in complex real-world settings. For example, they lack appropriate emotional responses to social situations (e.g., Anderson, Barrash, Bechara, & Tranel, 2006), may have difficulty extracting or responding to subtle social cues from others (e.g.,

Mah, Arnold, & Grafman, 2005; Vecera & Rizzo, 2004), and are less likely to consider whether they are likely to regret their decisions (Camille, Coricelli, Sallet, Pradat-Diehl, Duhame, et al., 2004). So, to exemplify our point, EVR might fail to keep a promise to pick up his child from an event, say, not because he lacked either the general motivation to keep his promises or the motivation to keep this promise, but because he was cognitively incapable of deciding whether to travel by tram or subway (see Eslinger and Damasio's description of EVR's difficulty in choosing a restaurant, cited by us on pp. 184–185 [Eslinger & Damasio, 1985]). Similarly, he might invest and lose all of his money in a disastrous business venture, not because he lacked motivation to take good care of the family finances, but because he lacked the subtle social judgment skills necessary to discriminate between a business partner with sound credentials and one with dubious credentials and to make a sensible decision on those grounds.

Recent research lends support to our interpretation of EVR's behavior. Damage to the ventromedial frontal cortex impairs decision making in ways that appear to be unrelated to an absence of motivation. For example, in a task that involved choosing between different apartments, VM patients tended to focus on the pros and cons of a single apartment, rather than comparing information about categories such as rent and neighborhood across different apartments, as controls did (Fellows, 2006). Fellows and Farah (2005) also found that VM patients tend to look less far ahead when considering the future, compared with controls.

If the kinds of deficits suffered by EVR are consistent with the truth of even strong motivational internalism (as Smith and Roskies both appear to concede), then the mismatch between EVR's superior performance on third-personal hypothetical moral dilemmas and his actual behavior is not itself reason to doubt internalist claims. To reiterate, while we do not think that holders of strict motivational internalism or any other version of internalism are properly understood as making a claim restricted to in situ judgments, we do think that the only judgments for which a reliable empirical test of motivation might be available are first-person in situ judgments.[6]

This suggested focus on in situ judgments might still be disputed by Smith and Roskies for the following reason. In many cases where the agent's in situ judgment deviates from their hypothetical or armchair moral judgment, the in situ judgment will not count as a moral judgment at all. Judgments made under emotional pressures or cognitive load may be biased, self-serving, and so forth. They may give too much weight to nonmoral factors. Of course, not all in situ judgments that are at odds with the agent's hypothetical moral judgments will be flawed in these ways. However, the task of identifying those in situ judgments that do deserve to be called moral judgments from those that don't would considerably complicate the empirical project. For this reason, the focus should be on hypothetical moral judgments alone.

We think there may be a strong argument to be made along those lines, but it will be a philosophical argument, not an empirical one. And if that argument wins, then we think that the prospects of obtaining empirical disconfirmation of internalism are slim indeed.

Notes

1. Other kinds of contingencies include the kinds of inferential failures, innocent forgettings, etc. that we claimed could occur between hypothetical and in situ judgments and which could result in a failure to act in accordance with a hypothetical moral judgment. We do not commit ourselves to the view that all failures of motivation must be rational failures. Illness might sap one's motivation to act on a reason one accepts, but it is not clear that this would constitute an instance of irrationality.

2. Our point is that internalist claims cannot be refuted by evidence that might show that there is no intrinsic connection between the kind of judgments that Roskies counts as moral judgments and motivation, in advance of a substantive defense of the claim that such judgments do deserve the title of moral judgment. In our chapter in this volume we asked which internalists hold the view that Roskies is targeting in her article (2003). Roskies takes us to have been asking which, if any, internalists hold the view that moral judgments are in some way intrinsically or necessarily connected with motivation. In footnote 1 of her commentary she says, "My opponents are, quite simply, those who think moral judgment necessarily entails moral motivation." She then goes on to name contemporary philosophers who hold some version of this view, including Nagel, Harman, Darwall, and Blackburn. However, Roskies has misinterpreted our original question—we were not asking which internalists are internalists or which philosophers are internalists—and thus presents a misleading picture of what she is doing. For she was not in her 2003 article, and is not in her commentary, merely targeting an umbrella internalist claim that there is an intrinsic connection between moral judgment and motivation. She ties this claim to a particular and contested account of moral judgment. We wanted to know of any philosophers who both defend this account of moral judgment and claim a strict internal connection between such judgments and motivation. We do not think that the philosophers named by her fill the bill. Blackburn and Harman, for example, endorse versions of expressivism. Nagel is closest to holding the cognitivist account of moral judgment Roskies endorses, but nevertheless we think his focus on what is cognized, namely, reasons of a certain kind, sets his view

apart from hers and provides some inkling as to how such judgments could be motivating.

3. As one of us has argued elsewhere (Kennett, 2006), Smith's conceptual claim would be vindicated if the interpretation that makes the best sense of moral practice—widely observed patterns of justification, challenge, resentment, excuse, and so forth—is expressed in the platitude that moral requirements have the status of normative reasons.

4. We are not sure whether Roskies is here characterizing what she takes to be the strong motive internalist account of motivation or whether this is her own claim about how moral motivation must work when it does.

5. We agree with Roskies that it is currently not clear what the nonspecific skin conductance response represents in different experimental paradigms, and whether it is a reliable physiological correlate of motivation. (Anticipatory SCRs in the Iowa Gambling Task may, for example, correlate with the cumulative emotional associations of the option under consideration, rather than the motivation to select or avoid that option, as suggested by Tomb, Hauser, Deldin, and Caramazza [2002]. This experiment and the response to it made by Damasio, Bechara, and Damasio [2002a], highlight the difficulties in interpreting the functional significance of a skin conductance reponse, even within the context of a relatively simple experimental paradigm.) In any case, SCRs have never been measured in VM patients while they were asked to make moral judgments, so, as we argued previously, at this point no psychophysiological data definitively speak to the question of whether VM patients possess moral motivation.

6. Smith correctly points out that restriction of the internalist claim to in situ judgments does not weaken strong motivational internalism. Any outright failure to be motivated in accordance with an in situ moral judgment would for Roskies show internalism to be false. But of course Smith thinks we might well fail to be motivated in accordance with our in situ judgments. We might be weak willed or profoundly depressed. Such failures of motivation would not undermine Smith's weak motivational internalism. Smith does not argue that we will in fact be motivated by our moral judgments; his claim is that:

It is conceptually necessary that if an agent judges that she morally ought to ϕ in circumstances C, then either she is motivated to ϕ in C or she is practically irrational. (this volume p. 211)

Smith's weak motivational internalism does not seem susceptible to direct empirical disconfirmation and this seems in part to be Roskies' reason for setting it aside in her 2003 paper. Since Smith's commentary addresses Roskies' rejection of his weaker internalist claim more effectively than we could hope to do, we will set this issue aside.

5 | Varieties of Moral Agency: Lessons from Autism (and Psychopathy)

Victoria McGeer

The Roots of Moral Agency

What makes us moral creatures? What are our moral concerns? How do we come to make moral judgments and act from specifically moral motivations? These fundamental yet perplexing questions, once solely the province of philosophers and theologians, have been pursued with increasing interest by psychologists, anthropologists, evolutionary theorists, ethologists, and lately, cognitive neuroscientists, yielding new and often challenging insights into this critical aspect of our human condition.

We are unquestionably unique in the shape and quality of our moral experience and behavior—the "paragon of animals," as Shakespeare has Hamlet say, "in action how like an angel! in apprehension how like a god!" And yet because of these qualities—i.e., specifically moral experiences, projects, and concerns—we are likewise capable of immense and ingenious evil. Here, then, is a first and familiar paradox of our moral existence: We could not be as ungenerous in our condemnations, as cruel in our fanaticisms, as self- or other-destructive in our pursuits, if our lives were not animated through and through with moral purpose and concern. Moral agency is a double-edged sword and seems inevitably so, no matter how much we trumpet the glories of our moral sensibility. Why should this be the case? Is it because our moral capacities are fundamentally rooted in our sentimental natures—as Hume or Smith would maintain—so that we depend on various affective states to move us to care appropriately for, and sometimes inappropriately about, one another? Or are our moral capacities fundamentally reason-based or "cognitive," as Lawrence Kohlberg would say, where reason is given the dual job of arriving at appropriate moral conclusions and of channelling our "affective forces" to ensure that we act in accord with our moral judgments (1971)?[1] In this case, iniquitous behavior might stem from a failure of reason either to arrive at appropriate moral judgments or to control our affect in a morally accept-able way.

The relation between reason, emotion, moral judgment, and behavior is an old and contested one, with paradigm and opposing positions associated with Hume on one side and Kant on the other. Central to this theoretical division is the role of what is now often called "empathy"[2] in generating the kind of concern for others that motivates and regulates paradigmatic instances of our moral behavior. Hume, in keeping with his view that "the ultimate ends of human actions can never . . . be accounted for by reason, but recommend themselves entirely to the sentiments and affections of mankind" (Hume, 1777/1975, p. 293), argued that the capacity to feel with and like another—to enter sympathetically into their cares and concerns—was critical for developing and maintaining an other-regarding moral agency. Kant, by contrast, was deeply disdainful of the moral importance of empathy and/or sympathy, favoring a moral psychology motivated in its purest form by a rational concern for doing one's duty:

If nature had implanted little sympathy in this or that man's heart; if (being in other respects an honest fellow) he would be cold in temperament and indifferent to the sufferings of others—if such a man (who in truth would not be the worst product of nature) were not exactly fashioned by her to be a philanthropist, would he not still find in himself a source from which he might draw a worth far higher than any a good-natured temperament can have? . . . For love out of inclination cannot be commanded; but kindness done from duty—although no inclination impels us—is *practical* not *pathological* love, residing in the will and not in the propensions of feeling, in principles of action and not of melting compassion; and it is this practical love alone which can be the object of command. (Kant, 1785/1948: 398–389, as cited in Kennett, 2002, pp. 352–353; emphasis in original)

One fruitful way to pursue this debate in a contemporary context is by looking at the moral capacities of individuals in various clinical popula-tions. There we may expect to discern how particular abnormalities in cognitive and/or affective capacities compromise moral agency. Two popu-lations of particular interest in this regard are autistic individuals and psychopathic individuals. Both these populations seem to lack empathy in some sense of that word, and yet psychopathic individuals are well known for their lack of moral concern whereas individuals with autism can have strongly felt moral convictions despite the fact that their moral judgments are often impaired by the difficulties they have in understand-ing other points of view. What accounts for this difference?

In trying to resolve this puzzle, I begin by reviewing how the debate on empathy has unfolded in light of lessons that theorists have taken from the study of psychopaths. I then turn to the problem of autistic moral concern, basing my discussion on an insightful and challenging paper by Jeanette Kennett. Here I will agree with Kennett that even though a focus on empathy has yielded important insights into our moral nature, such an approach is also restricted in how much it can explain. However, pace Kennett, I resist the Kantian conclusion that "reverence for reason is the core moral motive" (Kennett, 2002, 355). Rather, I will conclude that the concern with affect has been too narrowly focused on empathy, and that this has stemmed in part from a persistent tendency in philosophy and other academic inquiries to try to locate the essence of our moral nature in a single cognitive capacity or affective disposition. This tendency is not as strong as it once was, but nevertheless it continues to shape contemporary debate.

Still, while old habits die hard, the evidence from development, psychopathology, cross-cultural studies, and even primate studies has been pushing us in a different direction for some time (Haidt, 2001; Shweder & Haidt, 1993; Shweder, Much, Mahapatra, & Park, 1997). And I think the evidence from autism supports this trend, for here I think we find some persuasive indication that our moral nature is shaped by (at least) three different tributaries of affectively laden concern which I tentatively label as follows: (1) concern or compassion for others, growing out of the attachment system and fostered mainly by a capacity for emotional attunement between self and other, although later also supported by perspective-taking skills; (2) concern with social position and social structure, growing out of the need to operate within a hierarchically organized communal world and fostered by our highly developed perspective-taking skills; and finally, (3) concern with "cosmic" structure and position, growing out of the need to bring order and meaning to our lives and fostered by our capacity to view ourselves in intertemporal terms. Although I won't be able to elaborate on these three spheres of affective concern in any great detail, my view is that they are responsible for producing the cross-cutting systems of value that give shape to our moral being, a shape that can be differentially influenced by affective and/or cognitive impairments that target any or all of these spheres of concern. This is what we see in both individuals with autism and individuals with psychopathy, even though the nature of their impairments gives rise to very different moral psychological outcomes.

The Importance of Empathy: Lessons from Psychopathy

Psychopaths have long been known for their apparent amoralism, specifically for their deep indifference to the cares and sufferings of others, leading them to act in cruel and often criminal ways.[3] Theorists have posed the following question: Is this primarily an emotional deficit that prevents psychopaths from empathizing or affectively experiencing the world from other points of view and so from taking account of how their activities may negatively affect others? Or is it some kind of cognitive deficit that makes psychopaths unable to see why the cares or concerns of others should matter to them, even though they are perfectly well aware of these cares and concerns?[4]

One noteworthy feature of psychopathic individuals is their apparent facility with mental state attribution. In sharp contrast to individuals with autism, for instance, they seem remarkably adept at reading the minds of others, if only to manipulate them. They are glib and frequent liars, passing themselves off with an easy charm that speaks to a ready, though perhaps superficial, understanding of social norms and expectations (Cleckley, 1955; Hare, 1993). This clinical impression is borne out by their normal performance on standard and advanced theory of mind tests (R.J.R. Blair, Sellars, Strickland, Clark, Williams, Smith, & Jones, 1996). Consequently, they appear to have no cognitive deficit in understanding others' states of mind, including their beliefs and desires, motives and intentions, cares and concerns. In one straightforward sense of this term, they have no difficulty with perspective taking (Nichols, 2002a).

In contrast with this cognitive capacity, psychopathic individuals have been found to be notably abnormal in their affective profile. Clinical reports indicate that they show "a general poverty of major affective reactions, particularly those that would be triggered by the suffering of others (remorse, sympathy), condemnation by others (shame, embarrassment), or attachment to others (love, grief)" (Haidt, 2001, p. 824; cf. Cleckley, 1955; Elliott, 1992; Hare, 1993). They have trouble recognizing some facial expressions of emotion, especially fear and sadness (R.J.R. Blair, Colledge, Murray, & Mitchell, 2001b; Stevens, Charman, & R.J.R. Blair, 2001). They also show an abnormal autonomic reaction to these emotions, responding to the distress cues of others (facial and vocal expressions) as if they were affectively neutral (R.J.R. Blair, Jones, Clark, & Smith, 1997). What impact might this lack of affective responsiveness, especially to distress, have on their moral capacities?

James Blair has argued that it likely has a significant impact, explaining, for instance, why psychopaths fail to distinguish between moral and conventional transgressions (R.J.R. Blair, 1995). Making such a distinction is now viewed as a critical indicator of moral capacity—of being able to regard activities in a specifically moral light and to make judgments about those activities that have a specifically moral character (Nucci, 2001;

Smetana, 1993; Turiel, 1979, 1983; Turiel, Killen, & Helwig, 1987; but for criticism, see Kelly, Stich, Haley, Eng, & Fessler, 2007). It is a distinction that is made cross-culturally (Hollos, Leis, & Turiel, 1986; Nucci, Turiel, & Encarnacion-Gawrych, 1983; Song, Smetana, & Kim, 1987) and begins to emerge in normally developing children from around the age of 39 months (Smetana, 1981). In normal populations, moral transgressions are characteristically regarded as rule or authority independent, i.e., they are viewed as wrong whether or not there is a rule proscribing them, whether or not someone in authority licenses them. Conventional transgressions, by contrast, are normally regarded as wrong only because the acts are proscribed by rules of acceptable social behavior; if the rules were changed or suspended, the proscribed acts would no longer count as wrong (Turiel, 1983).[5] One explanation for this is that moral transgressions are normally regarded as wrong—and more seriously wrong (less permissible) than other sorts of transgressions—because they provoke a strong affective response in us (Haidt, Koller, & Dias, 1993; Nichols, 2002b, 2004b). Thus, for instance, we code those transgressions that result in victims, individuals who suffer either physically or psychologically, as paradigm moral transgressions because of our affective response to the victims' imagined distress, something to which the psychopath is apparently blind. Hence, they fail to distinguish these sorts of moral transgressions from those that merely break the accepted rules of social life.[6]

In sum, this work on psychopaths seems to support the view that the capacity for moral thought and action is strongly dependent on our affective natures and in particular the capacity to respond empathetically to others' affective states, to experience a vicarious emotional response to how they affectively experience the world, and especially to feel some distress at their distress and suffering (see also Nichols, 2004b). This seems to speak to a Humean rather than a Kantian view of the roots of moral understanding and moral motivation. We develop a special concern for others and for their well-being because, as Hume says, "the minds of all men are similar in their feelings and operations. . . . As in strings equally wound up, the motion of one communicates itself to the rest; so all the affections readily pass from one person to another" (Hume, 1740/1978, pp. xix, 743). Or, in the words of contemporary psychologists Andrew Meltzoff and Keith Moore, "We 'do unto others' in a special way because there is a deeply felt equivalence between self and other. Without a sense of like-me-ness, we do not think our folk psychology and moral judgments would take the form that they do" (Meltzoff & Moore, 1999, p. 11).

The Limits of Empathy in Explaining Moral Agency: Lessons from Autism

Many people with autism are fans of the television show *Star Trek*. I have been a fan since the show started. When I was in college, it greatly influenced my thinking, as each episode of the original series had a moral point. The characters had a set of firm moral principles to follow, which came from the United Federation of Planets. I strongly identified with the logical Mr. Spock, since I completely related to his way of thinking.

I vividly remember one old episode because it portrayed a conflict between logic and emotion in a manner I could understand. A monster was attempting to smash the shuttle craft with rocks. A crew member had been killed. Logical Mr. Spock wanted to take off and escape before the monster wrecked the craft. The other crew members refused to leave until they had retrieved the body of the dead crew member. To Spock, it made no sense to rescue a dead body when the shuttle was being battered to pieces. But the feeling of attachment drove the others to retrieve the body so their fellow crew member could have a proper funeral. It may sound simplistic, but this episode helped me finally understand how I was different. I agreed with Spock, but I learned that emotions will often overpower logical decisions, even if these decisions prove hazardous. (Grandin, 1995, pp. 131–132)

This passage, written by Temple Grandin, a remarkably able individual with autism, articulates a puzzle for the view of moral agency that has been emerging thus far. For here and in other writings she combines her sensitivity and attraction to the existence of a moral order with her acknowledgment that she lacks the normal emotional profile of other human beings, specifically "the feeling of attachment" that drives others, for instance, to endanger themselves for the sake of a comrade, dead though he may be. Could it be that individuals with autism are lacking the basic kind of empathetic connection with others so far identified as being critical to the development of an other regarding moral concern? If so, why are they not like psychopaths in their callous disregard of others or, at the very least, in their insensitivity to the moral domain? Yet, on the contrary, as far as they are cognitively able, individuals with autism seem remarkably prone to view their own and others' behavior in moral terms; i.e., in terms of duties or obligations that ought to be binding on all people, even if their sense of the nature of these duties and obligations can seem naïve or bizarre from our point of view.

Consider, for example, the case of a young man with perfect pitch and a passion for pianos who could not fathom how anyone could be happy without a well-tuned piano. Upon discovering that there were people who in fact didn't have pianos, or who kept them out of tune, he thought there should be a constitutional amendment requiring every home to have a well-tuned piano (M.A. Dewey, 1992, discussed in Kennett, 2002). His aim was clearly not to benefit himself, but rather to improve the lives of those around him and thereby make the world a better place. Of course, his moral priorities are dramatically affected by his autism. Nevertheless, from this and many other such examples, it seems clear that individuals with autism can and often do have a strongly developed moral sensibility or, as Kant would say, a concept of duty deriving from "consciousness of a moral law" (Kant, 1797/1991, p. 400). Where does this moral consciousness come from?

In her groundbreaking paper, Jeanette Kennett (2002) argues that the fact that individuals with autism are often deeply motivated to do the right thing should make us rethink how critical the capacity for empathy is to the development of moral agency. For, as she says, they seem in many ways even worse off than individuals with psychopathy regarding their ability to connect with other people. Psychopaths at least have relatively intact perspective-taking skills, readily surpassing even the most able autistic individuals in detecting others' states of mind. And although psychopaths may have trouble seeing other people as fully real (Elliott, 1992, p. 210), perhaps because they lack any deep understanding of the range of emotions that animate them, the outsider status they experience in consequence seems less dramatic than what autistic individuals have reported about themselves, often saying that they feel like aliens beamed in from another planet, or, in the words of Temple Grandin, like "an anthropologist on Mars."

Of course, there are large individual differences among people with autism. Characterized as a spectrum disorder, autism can be diagnosed in individuals who are relatively low functioning (their autism is combined with other mental handicaps) all the way through to those who are relatively high functioning (with normal to high IQ, often good, although characteristically abnormal language skills, and often compensating cognitive strategies for coping with their autistic disabilities). However, despite this wide range of ability, individuals with autism show a characteristic triad of impairments, according to which a diagnosis is made. This includes: (1) a qualitative impairment in reciprocal social interactions, including a marked lack of awareness of others' feelings, abnormal comfort-seeking behavior at times of distress, impaired imitation, aversion to or abnormal physical contact, and lack of social play and peer friendships; (2) a qualitative impairment in nonverbal and verbal communication, including lack of eye gaze and facial expressions to initiate or modulate social interactions, abnormal prosody, echolalia, extreme literal-mindedness, and general difficulties with conversational pragmatics; and (3) impairments in imaginative abilities, including lack of pretend (especially role-taking) play in childhood, highly restricted and repetitive interests, and an obsessive insistence on routine and environmental stability.

Although autism is not usually diagnosed until around 18 months, what makes it particularly noticeable is the relative absence of all those behaviors by which typically developing children normally register their sense of the vast difference between people—i.e., subjectively animated creatures "like me"—and other things in their environment. Such behaviors include joint attention; reciprocal imitation games; social referencing behavior, where toddlers use the affective expressions on others' faces to guide their interactions with unknown objects, and so on (for a general discussion and review, see Baron-Cohen, Tager-Flusberg, & Cohen, 2000; Frith, 1989; Happé, 1994b). Indeed, this missing recognition of others "like me" can be so deep that one high-functioning adult would later remark: "I really didn't know there were other people until I was seven years old. I then suddenly realized that there were other people. But not like you do. I still have to remind myself that there are other people. I could never have a friend. I really don't know what to do with other people, really" (Hobson, 1992, p. 165, cited in Kennett, 2002).

What, then, is the source of autistic moral concern, since empathy in the sense of affective attunement with other people seems clearly beyond the scope of their experience?[7] Kennett suggests that the answer can be found in focusing on autistic rationality, specifically autistic individuals' susceptibility to and deep interest in the sense-making pull of reason. Indeed, she proposes that their "moral feelings are of a Kantian, rather than a Humean, cast" (2002, p. 352) since they seem to derive from a deeply felt practical concern to do the right thing, whatever that should turn out to be. We saw evidence of this Kantian sensibility in the Grandin passage quoted earlier, in which she explains that her liking for *Star Trek* is based on two things: first, that the characters in the show had "a set of firm moral principles to follow"; and, second, that she could identify with one of the characters in particular, the logical Mr. Spock, whose recommendations and behavior are guided by reason, not emotion. Grandin and other high-functioning individuals with autism seem particularly committed to the Kantian idea that their behavior (and everyone else's) should conform to a principle of reason that includes them in its scope. Thus, they are prepared to see other people's interests as reason giving in the same way as their own, even though, as Kennett says, their problems with perspective taking give them "great difficulty in discerning what those interests are" (2002, p. 354). Still, their apparent need to figure out the "right" thing to do based on taking the concerns and interests of others into account leads them to make quite extraordinary efforts to understand those concerns and interests. For instance, Temple Grandin writes of having built up a "tremendous library of memories of experiences, TV, movies, and newspapers" that she consults in order to understand what others might be up to and so guide her social behavior appropriately (Grandin, 1995, p. 137). Another very able individual, Jim Sinclair, writes of his need to develop a "separate translation code for every person I meet" (Sinclair, 1992, p. 300).

From such examples we seem to have clear evidence that even though a lack of empathy makes it extremely challenging for individuals with autism to act in morally appropriate ways, it does nothing to undermine their interest in so acting; it does nothing to undermine their moral concern. Yet if we turn our attention to psychopathic individuals once again, it now seems puzzling that their apparently less dramatic lack of empathy should so gravely undermine their capacity for moral concern. This puzzlement can be dispersed, Kennett suggests, once we recognize that contemporary theorists have become overly focused on the affective dimension of moral life, thanks no doubt to the tremendous importance of empathy in guiding normal human relations. For just as the pull of reason can explain the autistic individual's moralism, it seems likely that the psychopathic individual's amoralism might well be explained in terms of a failure of reason to operate in him with its normal motivational force (for a similar approach, see Maibom, 2005). Thus, Kennett proposes: "It is not the psychopath's lack of empathy, which (on its own, at any rate) explains his moral indifference. It is more specifically his lack of concern, or more likely lack of capacity to understand what he is doing, to consider the reasons available to him and to act in accordance with them" (2002, p. 354).

This failure of reason may seem surprising. After all, our image of the psychopath is of a person who is rather good at serving his own interests without care or concern for the damage he does to others; hence of someone who is rather good at thinking and acting in instrumentally rational ways. However, as Kennett argues, this image is misleading, ignoring the dramatic ways in which psychopaths are also compromised in their ability to make sound prudential judgments. As Carl Elliott observes: "[W]hile the psychopath seems pathologically egocentric, he is nothing like an enlightened egoist. His life is frequently distinguished by failed opportunities, wasted chances and behavior which is astonishingly self-destructive. This poor judgment seems to stem not so much from the psychopath's inadequate conception of how to reach his ends, but from an inadequate conception of what his ends are" (Elliott, 1992, p. 210, cited in Kennett, 2002). Thus, in Kennett's view, the psychopath is not able to regard others' interests as reason giving for him because he is not able to sustain a sense of why any interests should be reason giving, apart from the very short-term impulses that drive him from one action to the next. Perhaps it might be better to say that while the psychopath may have action-guiding impulses, he has no impulse-controlling interests since he has no "extended and coherent conception of his own or others' ends" from which such interests could be rationally derived (Kennett, 2002, p. 355). In this respect, high-functioning individuals with autism seem far better off. Their disabilities may make it difficult for them to form a clear or sophisticated conception of their own or others' ends, but they show a clear drive to give rational shape and meaning to their lives and to their interactions with other people. Hence, Kennett suggests, insofar as individuals with autism have "a basic conception of justification and of interests as reason-giving," (2002, p. 355) we can find in their psychological makeup a sufficient basis for moral agency, even if their lack of affective attunement leaves them rather unskilled in the moral domain.

Here, then, is the general conclusion to which Kennett thinks we are driven. On the one hand, if we focus on the moral limitations of individuals with autism, then it seems quite right to insist with the Humeans that affective attunement is hugely important for the development and operation of "autonomous, responsive, moral agency in human beings" (p. 357). Without any real sensitivity to the wide variety of pains, pleasures, and other emotions individuals experience under the myriad circumstances constituting normal social life, individuals with autism are seriously disadvantaged in developing a sophisticated understanding of the moral domain, either of the kinds of rules that ought to govern one's moral behavior (witness the young man with the passion for pianos) or indeed of the way rules ought to be applied, sometimes even set aside, to serve deeper moral ends. On the other hand, if we look at the moral capacities of individuals with autism, then it seems we must conclude that affective attunement is not necessary for the development of a genuine moral sensibility. Thus, Kennett suggests, "the story of how we normally *get* to be moral agents and the story of what is *required* for moral agency is not the same" (2002, p. 357). The social-cognitive abnormalities that distinguish autism from other developmental disabilities ensure a developmental trajectory that is not just delayed but deeply eccentric compared with a typical developmental trajectory. Nevertheless, at least among high-functioning individuals with autism, their relatively intact reasoning abilities, coupled with a drive for order and a need to make sense of their own and others' behavior, seems to support the emergence of a sense of duty or conscience that is, by contrast, entirely lacking in the psychopathic population. Thus, a comparison between these two atypical groups of individuals suggests to Kennett that it is Kant, not Hume, who has put his finger on "the essence of moral agency, the concern to act in accordance with reason which animates agency and which we cannot do without" (2002, p. 355). To be empathetically insensitive to others is to be seriously disadvantaged in the moral domain, but to be insensitive to reason—that is, insensitive to reason as generated and sustained by various self-organizing ends—is to fall out of the moral domain altogether. Hence Kennett concludes in keeping with Kant that "reverence for reason is the core moral motive, the motive of duty" (p. 355).

Reply to Kennett: Does Autistic Moral Agency Show Us that Reverence for Reason Is the "Core" Moral Motive?

There is no doubt that Kennett raises an important issue for a broadly Humean account of the roots of moral agency. In particular, she makes clear to us that any account of moral agency must attend to what I will call the "agential" side of these capacities as much as to their moral side. That is to say, for anyone to be a moral agent, they must at least be a certain kind of rational agent—an agent who is capable of controlling their immediate impulses in the service of some larger end; hence an agent to whom reason speaks. However, in Kennett's view, such an agent is the kind of agent in which reason has its own motivational force: "[O]nly individuals who are capable of being moved directly by the thought that some consideration constitutes a reason for action can be conscientious moral agents" (2002, p. 357). This is a strong conclusion, perhaps stronger than it needs to be in order to preserve Kennett's critical insight about the agential side of moral agency. So, in this section, my aim is to review some further evidence from autism to bolster a certain aspect of Kennett's insight (that responsiveness to reason may be necessary for moral agency), while at the same time questioning the Kantian spin she puts on it (that responsiveness to reason is sufficient for moral agency). At the very least, I will argue that Hume's emphasis on various kinds of affect must not be abandoned too quickly if we are to understand how certain ends become salient enough to compel our reason, thereby giving it some long-range appetitive control.

I begin with a word of caution. I have suggested that Kennett's conclusion may be overly strong in the modality of its claim about reason. There is another way in which it may be overly strong; namely, in its generality. Consider the form of Kennett's argument: (high-functioning) individuals with autism are unlike psychopaths in manifesting some degree of moral concern; therefore, despite the difficulties they have with moral judgment and moral behavior, individuals with autism must have some quality or capacity psychopaths lack that is "essential to the nature of [moral] agency" (2002, p. 357). The more general interpretation of this argument, intended by Kennett, is that a consideration of autistic moral capacities shows us something about the basic structure of moral agency *simpliciter*. Specifically, as she says, it shows us that a "reverence for reason is the core moral motive, the motive of duty" (p. 355). That is to say, anyone who is lacking in this reverence for reason will fail to be a moral agent. However, there is a less general interpretation of this argument that merits attention; namely, that a consideration of autistic moral capacities shows us something about the special structure of autistic moral agency. Specifically, it shows us that a certain reverence for reason can go some way toward compensating for the lack of empathetic attunement that is essential for the development of a typically structured moral agency. That is to say, anyone who is lacking in empathetic attunement and who lacks this reverence for reason will fail to be a moral agent. The more general interpretation says that reverence for reason is the core moral motive for all individuals. The less general interpretation says it plays a particular kind of compensating role in individuals with autism.

Why favor the less general interpretation? Consider a close analogy. As we have already noted, autistic individuals are greatly handicapped in the social domain. One way of characterizing their primary deficit is in terms of an inability to represent others' and possibly even their own mental states. They lack what is often termed a natural theory of mind; i.e., a disposition, fine-tuned through development, for simply reading off from others' expressions and (contextually situated) behavior the mental states that motivate and direct them. One classic way in which this deficit is manifested is in the so-called false-belief task, where subjects are required to attribute a false belief to a character in a story in order to predict what she will do next. Normally developing children begin to pass this test by the time they are 4 years old and developmentally delayed children by the time they have reached a corresponding mental age. This is not true of children with autism. They continue to experience difficulty with this task even at a much greater mental age. For instance, from a large sample of seventy autistic children compared with seventy normally developing children, Francesca Happé has shown that normally developing children have a 50 percent chance of passing false-belief tasks by the verbal mental age of 4, whereas autistic children have a 50 percent chance of passing only by the verbal mental age of 9.2 years (Happé, 1994b, pp. 71–73). Still, even though children with autism take more than twice as long to reach the same probability of success on this task as typically developing children, a "talented minority" will eventually pass, signaling that they have some capacity to represent others' mental states.

How can these results be explained? One possibility is that these talented children with autism have developed, after much delay, a relatively normal capacity for reading other minds. However, as many theorists have noted, the autistic capacity does not generalize easily to naturalistic settings. Furthermore, it is hard to say the capacity is still simply immature, since the kind of mistakes in mental state attribution that these individuals continue to make are very unlike the mistakes made by typically developing children at a much earlier age (Happé, 1994a). Hence, the more likely explanation of autistic "mindreading" is that some intellectually gifted individuals are able to use their advanced reasoning skills to "hack out" a solution to the puzzle of other minds, even while they continue to have no immediate or natural perception of others' mental states. As Temple Grandin says, "I have had to learn by trial and error what certain gestures and facial expressions mean" (Grandin, 1995, p. 135). In sum, the social cognition of individuals with autism remains extremely limited, with frequent and bizarre errors demonstrating a far from normal (albeit delayed) developmental trajectory. Thus, learning about the mechanisms of autistic social cognition tells us more about what the mechanisms of normal social cognition are *not* than about what they actually are. Perhaps the same will be true for the mechanisms underlying autistic moral concern.

Now let us look more closely at the abilities and disabilities of individuals with autism. What evidence might suggest that their moral sensibility is structured quite differently than the moral sensibility of typically developing individuals? To begin on a slightly downbeat note, recall that one feature of the autistic profile is an inflexibility of behavior that stems from an obsessive regard for rules and routines. Individuals with autism seem to have a great need to impose order on the world, no doubt because of neurological abnormalities that give rise to a disorienting, highly complicated, anxiety-inducing range of experiences. Clinical observations coupled with persistent subjective reports testify to an array of sensory abnormalities (auditory, tactile, olfactory, visual, nocioceptive) in many individuals with autism that make interacting with their environment extremely challenging. Indeed, they often find the mere physicality of other people's presence and/or social demands oppressive, such as being required to meet another's gaze or putting up with a "terrifying" embrace. On top of that, their difficulties in processing social and expressive cues make other people's behavior unpredictable and often overwhelming. Unsurprisingly, then, high-functioning individuals who can talk about what their autistic experience is like commonly report that fear and anxiety are their dominant emotions (Grandin, 1995, pp. 87–89). In eloquent testimony of this, Therese Jolliffe writes,

Normal people, finding themselves on a planet with alien creatures on it, would probably feel frightened, would not know how to fit in and would certainly have difficulty in understanding what the aliens were thinking, feeling and wanting, and how to respond correctly to these things. That's what autism is like. If anything were suddenly to change on this planet, a normal person would be worried about it if they did not understand what this change meant. That's what autistic people feel like when things change. Trying to keep everything the same reduces some of the terrible fear. (Jolliffe, Lansdown, & Robinson, 1992, p. 16)

Rules and routines help keep things the same, making the world emotionally and cognitively more approachable. To this end, autistic individuals are highly motivated to follow rules and are very concerned that others do so too. My downbeat suggestion, then, is that a good part of the behavior we identify as manifesting moral sensibility among individuals with autism may stem from a need to abide by whatever rules they have been taught without sharing our understanding of the ends those rules are meant to serve. In other words, for many such individuals, it may well be an open question as to how deeply their "moral" judgments and behavior are genuinely guided by moral concerns.

This issue is nicely illustrated by the following anecdote reported in one of the few studies of moral reasoning among autistic adults: "A young man with autism was participating in a board game called 'Scruples' which involves listening to stories and telling what you would do in each situation. He was given a scenario in which a store owner saw a woman stealing a small amount of food from his store. The store owner knew that this particular woman had no job, no one to support her, and several young children. The young man with autism was asked what he would do in the situation. He replied, 'Everyone has to go through the checkout line. It is illegal not to go through the checkout line. She should be arrested'" (Keel 1993, p. 49). Was this autistic man simply unable to comprehend the woman's need-driven motivation and hence incapable of seeing that a milder response was called for? Keel, who reports the case, favors this interpretation. She writes,

This reply certainly seems cold and uncaring. However, it reflects this young man's social cognitive deficits in perceiving the intent behind another's actions. Certainly, he had never been in a situation where he could not afford his groceries. He goes to the grocery store weekly and always goes through the checkout line. Additionally, he has always been taught not to steal. Without the ability to appreciate the perspective of another or to consider intent as well as consequence, he appeared unable to give any other answer. (1993, p. 49)

It is surely true that this young man lacked sufficient perspective-taking skills to understand the woman's probable state of mind. Yet the interesting question remains: How deep is his understanding of the prohibition against stealing? Does it rise to the level of a genuinely moral understanding, where rules are followed not just because they are rules, but rather because they serve some deeper moral end? There may be reasons to doubt this. For instance, it seems relatively clear from the anecdote that, even without perspective-taking skills, the young man knew that the woman had children to feed and no money to buy food. From a general knowledge of social norms, he might also have inferred that, as a mother, she had a moral obligation to feed them. Thus, he might also have inferred that this is a situation in which two moral imperatives are brought into conflict. However, he seems to have shown no awareness of this at all, concluding simply that the woman should be arrested because "it is illegal not to go through the checkout line." Thus, his judgment might have stemmed from nothing more than a constrained and routinized concern with situational rule following.

Of course, more would need to be established to come to any firm conclusion in this case. For instance, if the conflict between these two moral imperatives were explicitly laid out for the young man, would he show more hesitancy in his judgment about what should be done? Still, the general lesson remains that just as knowing intent can matter for making appropriate first-order moral judgments (was the woman malicious or desperate?), so it matters for determining whether first-order moral judgments genuinely reflect any moral understanding on the part of the person making the judgments. The rule-following judgments and behavior of some individuals with autism may be too unreflective for that.

I have emphasized this aspect of autistic disorder—obsessive desire for sameness, hence a need for rules and routines—for two different reasons.

First, as I have already indicated, I do think some caution needs to be exercised in interpreting the "moral" behavior of individuals with autism. It may well be that their particular abnormalities give rise to a simulacrum of naïve or innocent moral sensibility when in fact this sensibility can hardly be attributed at all. However, I don't wish to be entirely downbeat. It is certainly true, as Kennett points out, that the passion for rules and routines—hence for order in the world—already sets autistic individuals dramatically apart from psychopaths. They are prepared, as psychopaths are not, to discipline their own behavior and to judge others' behavior according to rules that they regard as universally binding. Moreover, it is difficult to say at what point having the mere simulacrum of moral sensibility shades into having a naïve or innocent moral sensibility where this involves having some understanding of the point of the rules one follows (for instance, to avoid harming others). Equally, it is difficult to say at what point having a naïve or innocent moral sensibility shades into the beginnings of a more sophisticated and genuinely autonomous moral sensibility where this would involve understanding such rules as answering to a principled moral sense of how things ought to be (for instance, as with the Amish teenagers (see note 5), that harming others is wrong in itself and hence to be avoided). Finally, since we know that autism is a spectrum disorder, with individuals varying widely in their abilities and disabilities, it should be no surprise to discover that individuals with autism vary significantly in the degree to which they are able to develop a genuine moral sensibility. So, despite the cautionary note I have sounded by emphasizing autistic rule-boundedness, I agree with Kennett that many high-functioning individuals do become autonomous moral agents; i.e., they become able and willing to govern their own behavior and to judge the behavior of others by reference to a deeper, more reflective consideration of the ends such behavior might be thought to serve.

Nevertheless, my second and larger point in emphasizing the predilection for rules and routines among individuals with autism is this: The need to impose order as a way of managing their environment predisposes high-functioning individuals with autism toward using their reason in a particular way. Specifically, it predisposes them toward discovering easy-to-follow principles behind whatever system of rules they find in place, even if those principles may be rather idiosyncratic from a nonautistic point of view. This point I think is nicely illustrated by Temple Grandin's reflections on her own rule-following behavior, which she sees as characteristically autistic:

For people with autism, rules are very important, because we concentrate intensely on how things are done. . . . Since I don't have any social intuition, I rely on pure logic, like an expert computer program, to guide my behavior. I categorize rules according to their logical importance. It is a complex algorithmic decision-making tree. There is a process of using my intellect and logical decision-making for every social decision. Emotion does not guide my decision; it is pure computing.

Learning a complex decision-making process is difficult. I had a strict moral upbringing, and I learned as a child that stealing, lying, and hurting other people were wrong. As I grew older I observed that it was all right to break certain rules but not others. I constructed a decision-making program for whether rules could be broken by classifying wrongdoing into three categories: "really bad," "sins of the system," and "illegal but not bad." Rules classified as really bad must never be broken. Stealing, destroying property, and injuring other people are in this category, and they were easy to understand. The "illegal but not bad" rules can often be broken with little consequence. Examples would be slight speeding on the freeway and illegal parking. The "sins of the system" category covers rules that have very stiff penalties for seemingly illogical reasons. Using my system has helped me negotiate every new situation I enter. (Grandin, 1995, pp. 103–104)

Grandin's "sins of the system" is a particularly interesting category, both for the kinds of norms or rules she classifies as such and for her attitude toward such rules. They tend to be rules having to do with social propriety or maintaining social order, and her attitude toward them is that these rules should be carefully observed even though she doesn't see the logic behind them. So why does she think they should be kept? The answer is probably mixed. At some level, she seems to manifest some concern for the social order as such, even though, as she often reports, it is also an order that she finds strangely alien. I discuss this possible motivation more in a later section. However, at another level, her motivation seems rather more expedient. For instance, she claims that in high school she regarded sex and smoking as the two greatest "sins of the system" and soon worked out "through careful observation and logic" that the teachers would give her considerable free rein as long as they were convinced that she would never engage in these prohibited activities (1995, pp. 102–103). In later life, her attitude toward sex and the social norms surrounding it has remained instrumentally cautious: "I still consider sex to be the biggest, most important 'sin of the system'. . . . It has caused the downfall of many reputations and careers. . . . I've remained celibate because doing so helps me to avoid the many complicated social situations that are too difficult for me to handle" (p. 133). Thus, we see in much of Grandin's rule-following behavior a rationally driven response to her persisting need to simplify, to order, to maintain clarity and control, even at the cost—if it is a cost—of avoiding what others consider to be morally loaded terrain ("carrying stiff penalties for seemingly illogical reasons"). Moreover, even in cases where she may evince a deeper understanding of why certain prohibitions exist, the need for clarity and control seems to play an important role in motivating her to toe a relatively "pure" moral line. For instance, with respect to lying she writes:

> Autistic people tend to have difficulty lying because of the complex emotions involved in deception. I become extremely anxious when I have to tell a little white lie on the spur of the moment. To be able to tell the smallest fib, I have to rehearse it many times in my mind. I run video simulations of all the different things that the other person might ask. If the other person comes up with an unexpected question, I panic. Being deceptive while interacting with someone is extremely difficult unless I have fully rehearsed all the possible responses. Lying is very anxiety-provoking because it requires rapid interpretations of social cues to determine whether the other person is really being deceived. (Grandin, 1995, p. 135)

It may be premature to base any strong conclusions about the basic structure of autistic moral agency on these observations about their rule-following behavior and the motivation behind it. Still, they do suggest that we must be cautious in assuming too much commonality, or at least commonality at the wrong level, between individuals with autism and typically developed individuals. However, it still seems fair to ask with respect to autistic individuals if reverence for reason might not be the core moral motive in them?

For reasons I will come to in the next (and concluding) section, I hesitate to speak of a core moral motive, even in individuals with autism. Still, I do agree with Kennett that in comparison with the moral agency of typically developed individuals, autistic moral agency seems far less permeated by affect and more deeply governed by reason. As Grandin says repeatedly of herself, navigating in the social world is a "strictly logical process." Now we might ask, why does reason speak with such force in autistic individuals? Why are they so prone to organize and judge their own and others' behavior in terms of rules they are willing to treat as universally binding, even if they have no direct affective insight into the rationale for at least some of these rules? The answer I am suggesting is that individuals with autism have an unusual (*arational*) passion for order, and it is this passion for order that both motivates their rule-oriented behavior and encourages them to such virtuoso displays of reason in trying to enlarge their understanding of the kind of order that exists in the social world so that they might participate in it.[8]

If the passion for order is as dominant in individuals with autism as this proposal suggests, then we might expect to see it manifested in all sorts of ways over and above their rule-following behavior. Indeed, there is good evidence for this. For instance, there are many reports of unusual play behavior in very early childhood. Specifically, children with autism are noted for lining their toys up in rows, or treating all the objects they encounter in a particular way (e.g., trying to make them spin). As they grow older they often develop unusual interests that may be quite idiosyncratic but which nevertheless have a certain taxonomic or ordering quality in common. For instance, there are reports of individuals with autism becoming obsessed with timetables, bus routes, birth dates, door colors, and even types of vegetables. Happé gives the example of one young man who learned the name of every type of carrot, of which there are more than fifty, just to be able to name them; he had no other interest in carrots (Happé, 1994b, p. 37). Grandin herself manifests her own passion for order in a number of remarkable ways. For instance, when she was a high school student learning about entropy, she claims to have "hated the second law of thermodynamics because I believed that the universe *should* be orderly" (1995, p. 193). This led in turn to a "totally logical and scientific" belief in God as "an ordering force that was in everything" (p. 193). Moreover, she has made a hobby over many years of collecting "many articles about spontaneous order and pattern formation in nature" because "I want scientific proof that the universe is orderly" (p. 192). In sum, we see this passion for order manifested in many different ways among individuals with autism and at all cognitive levels. Furthermore, among those who are relatively high functioning, it should be no surprise to see a peculiar reverence for reason in them, since reason is a tool par excellence for discovering or imposing order in the world, especially in the social world, which we know they find especially challenging.

Let me now return to the questions I raised at the beginning of this section and draw some provisional conclusions. First, I do agree with Kennett that being a moral agent requires one to have certain agential capacities, in particular the capacity to control one's impulses in the service of some larger ends (i.e., ends that trump one's parochial and immediate interests), the capacity to find value in these larger ends, and the capacity to put one's reason to work in the service of attaining such ends (minimally, through impulse control and more substantially through means-end reflection as well as reflection on the relative value of potentially competing ends). In my view, this makes reason, and the capacity to respond to the reasons one has, a prerequisite for moral agency. However, something must explain what motivates one to respond to the reasons one has, and indeed to use reason to reflect on the relative values of one's ends. Here I think affect does play a critical role along the lines that Hume proposed; that is, certain ends become particularly salient for us because of our (possibly idiosyncratic) affective investment in them. Hence they become ends that compel our rational attention, giving reason a platform from which to speak.

My second conclusion, then, speaks against Kennett's Kantianism, as far as I understand it. Reverence for reason is not the core moral motive; indeed, I doubt it is much of a motive at all, at least on its own, as something pursued for its own sake. Rather, in my view, respect for reason (which in some individuals may rise to reverence) derives from the practical (so not necessarily consciously endorsed) recognition that it is one of the most useful tools we have for prioritizing and accomplishing whatever ends we find affectively salient or compelling, whether they be finding and imposing order in the world, promoting our own or others' interests, or whatever. Thus, affect must play a critical role in moral agency, i.e., affect that is something apart from mere reverence for reason.[9] Moreover, *pace* Kennett, I take this rather Humean conclusion to be supported by a consideration of autistic moral agency. While autistic individuals may be lacking in the kind of empathetic attunement that provides the backbone of a typically developed moral agency, they do have a strong affective interest in living in the kind of world that is orderly, predictable, and, indeed, respectful of individual space. They like clear boundaries and prefer social transactions that are aboveboard and explicit. Thus, it is no surprise that we find in them an interesting and substantial variety of (genuine) moral agency.

My third and final conclusion of this section is therefore a pluralist one. I say that it is thanks to the predominating affective concerns of autistic individuals that many of them are able to develop a genuine kind of moral agency. It is genuine so far as it goes beyond a mere predilection toward rule-following for rule-following's sake. However, it is a distinctive kind of moral agency as far as the affective profile that underpins autistic valuing of certain ends and that consequently ensures a respect for others and their modes of life is substantially different in many ways from the affective profile that characterizes a more typical form of moral agency. Here I agree with Kennett, this time against Hume, that sympathy is not the only possible source of moral concern. However, Kennett is wrong, I think, to suggest that Humean sympathy must be replaced by some single fundamental source of moral concern that autistic individuals and normally developed individuals share in common. Yes, they do share a certain agential capacity for responding to reason, a capacity that high-functioning individuals are particularly prone to cultivate. And Kennett may be quite right to suggest that psychopaths are seriously impaired in this regard. However, the agential capacity for responding to reason is rooted in the capacity for valuing certain ends, and valuing certain ends is fundamentally rooted in the depth and quality of one's affective life. Since the affective lives of autistic individuals are substantially different from the lives of normally developed individuals, we should expect to see differences in the sort of ends that are valued and in the priorities assigned to these ends.

This accounts, I think, for the difficulties sometimes evinced in giving a consistent assessment of autistic moral behavior relative to the norm. On the one hand, it is sometimes claimed that individuals with autism display a kind of moral purity or innocence in their interactions with others that approximates a sort of moral ideal; but, on the other hand, they can also display rigidity, insensitivity, and even callousness toward others that makes their behavior fall rather short of any ideal. In my view, this inconsistency is to be expected. The truth is that autistic moral behavior must always be a mixed bag relative to the norm since it is driven by affective concerns that are rather different from the norm. This is not to say there is no common ground in these different varieties of moral agency, as I will next try to show. Rather, it is to say that a family resemblance in surface behavior need not imply the existence of identical or even substantially similar cognitive and/or affective profiles. We have already learned this lesson in the social cognitive domain as a consequence of trying to explain how high-functioning individuals with autism are sometimes able to reason about others' mental states despite impairments in their so-called theory of mind abilities. Perhaps it is time to learn this same lesson and explore its implications in the domain of moral psychology.

Varieties of Moral Agency: Speculative Reflections

I began this chapter by asking what makes us moral creatures. How do we come to make moral judgments and act from specifically moral motivations? What are our moral concerns? As the foregoing discussion ought to make plain, I think some general answers can be given to these questions, answers that acknowledge the importance of reason in our moral lives but which nevertheless give special attention to the central role of affect. Specifically, I claim in a broadly Humean way that we human beings are moral beings—and indeed the kind of moral beings we are—because of our affective natures. Our moral intuitions are generally grounded in a range of emotions that are part of the way we experience the world. Moreover, we develop our capacity for heeding the dictates of reason just because the ends for which our reason speaks are affectively charged; hence they become the ends we are able to value over our immediate or parochial interests. I will not say more in defense of this general position, for now my interest is in exploring, in a purely speculative way, the proposal I have made with respect to autistic moral agency: that the range of emotions in which their moral intuitions are grounded departs substantially from what might be considered the typical or normal range, producing in them a genuinely distinctive variety of moral agency. As I see it, this proposal faces a conceptual challenge that I would like to address briefly in this conclud-ing section: namely, in what sense could the affective profile of autistic individuals be that different from that of typically developing individuals while still supporting what is recognizably a genuine, albeit distinctive, variety of moral agency? In other words, how can there be enough com-monalities among the differences, and enough differences among the commonalities, to give rise to this possibility?

To sketch an answer to this question, I begin by noting that a preoccupa-tion with empathy in the domain of moral psychology can narrow our focus unduly when it comes to identifying the range of affective states that normally underlie our moral lives. Even when we understand empathy to be not an emotion in itself, but rather a disposition to be affectively attuned to, and even appropriately responsive to, another's affective states, it often carries a connotation of being compassionate, caring, or concerned for the well-being of another. However, as Jonathan Haidt has argued, not all morally relevant emotions can be understood in these terms. As he says, "there is more to morality than altruism and niceness. Emotions that motivate helping behavior are easy to label as moral emotions, but emo-tions that lead to ostracism, shaming and murderous vengeance are no less a part of our moral nature" (Haidt 2003b, p. 855). To arrive at this more inclusive understanding of the moral emotions, Haidt recommends that we take a functional approach to their identification. That is, even though we normally classify emotions such as anger, fear, sadness, joy, and so on according to their distinctive facial expressions, physiological changes, and phenomenological tone, we count certain manifestations of these as moral just in case they have particular kinds of eliciting conditions and give rise to particular kinds of action tendencies.

The rationale for this approach can be made evident once we follow Haidt in regarding all emotions as action-priming "responses to perceived changes, threats or opportunities in the world" (Haidt 2003b, p. 853). Of course, as he points out, many of these responses are concerned with our own self-interests narrowly conceived. However, we are perhaps unique among other species in expending a remarkable portion of our emotional energy reacting to events that have no direct impact on such interests, but are rather seen to affect the overall shape and structure of our (social) world and the other creatures (especially other people) in it. The philosopher P. F. Strawson is well known for making a similar point, observing that many of our "reactive attitudes"—a subset of emotions provoked by the activities of responsible agents—are felt precisely on behalf of others; i.e., they are felt in consequence of our perceiving someone else to be harmed or benefited by another person, even if we are not directly harmed or benefited ourselves. Strawson calls such reactive attitudes "impersonal," "generalized," or "vicarious," noting that there are particular emotions, such as indignation, that are particularly apt for being provoked in this way (Strawson, 1974). More interestingly still, we have many "self-reactive" attitudes by which we approve or disapprove of our own behavior as far as we regard that behavior as producing benefits and harms to others. Here pride, shame, and guilt are prime examples. In line with these observations, Haidt proposes a general scheme in which we classify our emotional reactions as moral to the degree that (1) they have "disinterested elicitors"; i.e., they are provoked by events touching concerns that reach beyond our narrow self-interest and (2) they have disinterested "action tendencies" (Haidt calls these "prosocial"); i.e., they prime us (motivationally and cognitively) to act in ways that benefit others or that uphold or benefit structures that we value, such as the "social order."

There is much to be said in defense of Haidt's functional characterization of the moral emotions. It is intuitively plausible, theoretically well motivated, and conceptually attractive in its simplicity and generativity. My only complaint, if it is a complaint, concerns Haidt's (understandable) tendency to focus exclusively on our more socially oriented interests. Thus, by way of a preliminary definition, he suggests that moral emotions are "those emotions that are linked to the interests or welfare of society as a whole or at least of persons other than the judge or agent" (Haidt, 2003b, p. 853). This is fine as far it goes. I agree with Haidt that in general we find in human beings two primary—and I would say distinct—spheres of disinterested concern.[10] These are a concern with others' well-being and a concern with the structure and maintenance of the social order, giving particular attention to how individuals find and occupy appropriate social roles. I call these distinct spheres of disinterested concern because I would argue they are rooted in quite distinct affective-cognitive systems, the first being the attachment system and the second being a system devoted to the production and distribution of social goods.

This first system has been much discussed in the developmental literature, and it makes sense from an evolutionary point of view if only because human neonates need to be strongly attached to particular significant others to ensure their own survival and development. As for the second system, it too makes sense from an evolutionary perspective since, like other social mammals, we are highly dependent on structured cooperative relations for acquiring and distributing resources. Thus, we are programmed to care about how those relations are maintained; we are programmed to care about how we and others fulfill our social roles, as well as what our particular social roles with their own rights and responsibilities should be. Still, important and predominating as these two spheres of concern are, I think there is yet a third sphere of disinterested concern that is also most likely rooted in a distinct cognitive-affective system. I tentatively label it (3) a concern with "cosmic" structure and position.

Why think there is such a distinct sphere of disinterested concern? To begin at the purely behavioral level, it seems clear that human beings are uniquely preoccupied with questions about the meaning of life, about the origin and fate of the universe, about our place in the great scheme of things, and about whether or not there is any great scheme of things at all. Moreover, these are not simply intellectual preoccupations. We care passionately about there being order in the universe, about there being some entity or entities—for instance, the Judeo-Christian God—that gives meaning and shape to it all, indeed, finding in such passions remarkable reservoirs of faith for systems of belief that otherwise have very little evidential support. Even among that small minority of individuals whose intellectual predilections and/or training prohibit any comfortable acceptance of belief on faith, many profess feelings of awe or wonder at the beauty science reveals in the ordering laws and patterns at all levels of nature, and even of deep contentment in the recognition that we human beings have our own place in all of that.

Why should the existence of such cosmic order matter to us so deeply? Why do we find it cognitively and aesthetically so appealing? Why does it inspire such reverence? And why do we feel a deepseated need to secure our own place in it? My answer to these questions must be incomplete and provisional. However, I suggest that these affectively laden concerns are at least partially rooted in pattern-seeking cognitive machinery that is uniquely well developed in *Homo sapiens* and which is dedicated to imposing order and meaning on our interactions with the physical world across time, making it seem a more stable place to us and locating for us a stable place within it. Once these points of reference are in place, we are motivationally primed to engage in long-term planning that leads to better success in navigating our environment. If this extremely sketchy account is on the right track, then at least there is an obvious evolutionary explanation for why a disinterested and deeply felt concern for cosmic structure and position is present in our species. Even if it isn't, the fact that we have such cosmically oriented affective concerns cannot be denied; and it becomes an interesting open question as to why we should have them, given that they seem unrelated to either our concern for the well-being of others or our concern for the social order.

Here, then, in a nutshell is my speculative proposal about the different varieties of (human) moral agency. I begin by summarizing what I think they share in common. To wit: all forms of human moral agency are rooted in affect. We are the kind of moral beings we are because we have powerful emotional reactions to certain kinds of events or situations; namely, events or situations that touch upon various disinterested concerns. Furthermore, in all human beings there are three distinct varieties of disinterested concern, rooted, I suggest, in distinct cognitive-affective systems: (1) a concern for the well-being of others, (2) a concern with social structure and social position, and (3) a concern with cosmic structure and cosmic position. Given these concerns, various events or situations will provoke different kinds of emotional responses, priming us to take different kinds of action. Sometimes, of course, our concerns will lead to emotional responses that are mutually reinforcing. For instance, I may feel indignant about someone causing another person harm both because it is socially disruptive and because it compromises the other's well-being. However, this won't always be the case. For instance, given my concern for the well-being of others, I may be inhibited in causing someone else distress. Yet, given my concern for social structure and position, I may feel angry with that person for offending against a social norm, provoking a desire to punish them and so cause them distress. In other words, these different spheres of concern can lead to emotional responses that pull in different, sometimes even conflicting directions. How we resolve such conflicts may well depend on which kind of concern is most dominant in us.

So here is my first suggestion: Moderately different varieties of moral agency can emerge as a consequence of how these three spheres of disinterested concern develop and interact in a given person, varying according to individual differences as well as under the sway of different cultural influences. Still, in typically developing individuals, we can expect to see a close family resemblance among these varieties of moral agency, for it seems to be a near-universal feature of the human affective profile that we are very much dominated by our concern for maintaining social order, hence for policing the ways individuals succeed or fail in playing their appropriate social roles. I say this because we have developed specialized skills for operating in the social world—our much-vaunted mindreading abilities—and we have a well-developed range of emotional responses that are very much adapted to the intricate patterns of our social interactions. Thus, we have other-condemning emotions such as anger, contempt, and disgust; self-condemning emotions such as shame, embarrassment, and guilt; other-praising emotions such as admiration, humility, and respect; and finally self-praising emotions such as pride and self-respect. Of course these emotional responses may be moderated in various ways by our compassion or sympathy for others, since we must, by many accounts, have rather well-developed empathetic capacities if we are to develop the advanced social-cognitive skills that support our intricate social interactions. Thus, we should expect to find in typically developing individuals a fairly well-entrenched concern for others' well-being, particularly for those with whom they are personally connected. Of course, the concern for cosmic order may be rather well developed too, although this seems to be the sphere of concern most deeply affected in typically developing individuals by cultural (including educational) influences. In any case, I think it is the dominance of our concern for social place and the extensive range of emotional responses we have developed as a consequence that explain the familiar paradox with which I began this chapter: that our capacity for cruelty as much as our capacity for kindness is rooted in our moral being.

I turn now to the question of autistic moral agency. How can it be such a distinctive variety of moral agency while still being distinctively human? My proposal is that what makes autistic moral agency distinctively human is that, just as with typically developing individuals, these three spheres of disinterested concern are operative in individuals with autism: concern with others' well-being, concern with social order, and concern with cosmic order.

This claim may seem surprising. After all, with regard to the first concern, a marked lack of empathy has traditionally been cited as a diagnostic feature in autistic spectrum disorder. Children with autism do not seem to tune into other people at all, seemingly even from the earliest stages of postnatal development. And yet, despite this fact, various studies show that a significant portion of children with autism do manifest some (maybe unusual) form of attachment behavior (Capps, Sigman, & Mundy, 1994; Dissanayake & Crossley, 1996, 1997; Rogers, Ozonoff, & Maslin-Cole, 1991; Shapiro, Sherman, Calamari, & Koch, 1987; Sigman & Mundy, 1989; Sigman & Ungerer, 1984). Furthermore, although their reactions are typically muted compared with those of normally developing children, there are children with autism who are able to recognize that others are in distress, and some even offer gestures of comfort (Bacon, Fein, Morris, Waterhouse, & Allen, 1998; Dissanayake, Sigman, & Kasari, 1996; Sigman, Kasari, Kwon, & Yirmiya, 1992; Haviland, Walker-Andrews, Huffman, Toci, & Alton, 1996). Based on his data, Blair has argued that children with autism do make the moral-conventional distinction, and this is because they are sensitive—unlike psychopaths—to the distress of others (R.J.R. Blair, 1996). For instance, they appear to show heightened autonomic response to pictures of distressed faces compared with pictures of neutral faces (R.J.R. Blair, 1999). Thus, some basic concern for the well-being of others is independent, Blair suggests, of advanced mindreading skills (R.J.R. Blair, 1996). However, given their very deep impairments in tuning into others and so developing advanced mindreading skills, it is no surprise that this basic concern with the well-being of others should remain fairly basic.

It is even less surprising that autistic individuals have a very unelaborated emotional repertoire relating to the most dominant of our concerns; that is, a concern for the social order and one's place within it. Nevertheless, I suggest that this concern is operative, at least at a basic level, in individuals with autism. Thus, we see many high-functioning individuals express a desire to fit in despite their rather heartbreaking awareness of their own inability to do so. "Passing for normal" and so observing the forms of social life is something with which they are greatly preoccupied.

Finally, we come to the concern for cosmic order. Here I think we find a sphere of concern that is underpinned by a relatively intact cognitive-affective system. Thus, it is this sphere of concern that dominates in autistic moral agency, and dramatically so. In consequence of this, we see the emergence of an entirely distinctive style of human moral agency, where the usual order of dominance among spheres of disinterested concern is completely inverted. Indeed, it is more than inverted; concern for social place and, to a much lesser extent, concern for the well-being of others have only the crudest of roles to play in shaping the emotional responses of autistic individuals to the kinds of situations that elicit such responses.

Because these are speculative proposals, I will not elaborate in any more detail. However, I want to close with a word about psychopathy. As mentioned in note 3, *DSM-III* replaced the term "psychopathy" with "antisocial personality disorder," a term that is still used in *DSM-IV* and *DSM-IV-TR* to refer to this disorder. Researchers and clinicians have questioned the validity of the diagnostic criteria associated with this change of label, claiming that too much emphasis has been placed on behavioral traits over far more indicative personality traits (R.J.R. Blair, Blair, Mitchell, & Peschardt, 2005; Hare, 1996b). In addition to this complaint, I find the new label somewhat ironic. On the one hand, I agree with Kennett that individuals with psychopathy are most likely seriously impaired in their capacity to use reason at all. However, in my view, this is because they have limited capacities for making any affective investment in ends that transcend their immediate and parochial interests. In other words, the three spheres of disinterested concern that are normally operative in human beings do not seem to be operative in them, owing to an overall flattening in the affective tone of their cognitive operations.

Now for a wild speculation: If concern for social place is strongly dominant in us and is supported by specialized skills in mindreading, then one might expect to see some faint semblance of at least this concern operating in individuals with psychopathy, especially given the fact that they seem to be relatively good at mindreading. Indeed, I think this may be the case. Individuals with psychopathy do show some concern with the social world, at least as far as that extends to getting the better of others whom they imagine to be trying to get the better of them. It is of course a seriously distorted concern with social position and social order, not tempered in the least by other sorts of disinterested concerns (for others' well-being, for cosmic structure and position) or even by a well-elaborated social emotional repertoire. Nevertheless, there is something characteristically human—indeed, something not unrelated to normal moral agency—that explains the psychopath's quest for dominance in the social world. Perhaps this also explains why they often do a much better job than autistic individuals at passing for normal (Babiak, 1995; Hare, 1996b).

Notes

1. In Kohlberg's own words: "We are claiming . . . that the moral force in personality is cognitive. Affective forces are involved in moral decisions, but affect is neither moral nor immoral. When the affective arousal is channelled into moral directions, it is moral; when it is not so channelled, it is not. The moral channelling mechanisms themselves are cognitive" (Kohlberg, 1971, pp. 230–231).

2. A word of caution: The term "empathy" is used in a wide variety of ways in the philosophical and psychological literature, so its meaning cannot be assumed. Often it is used to identify a particular other-regarding or other-directed emotion. Candidates are (1) concern for another's well-being, although I prefer the term "compassion" for this, and (2) distress at another's distress, more clearly designated by the acronym DAAD. However, the term has been better used, I think, not for a single emotion, but rather for an other-regarding disposition toward feeling or being affectively moved by the emotional state of another, whether that state be distress, joy, anger, or whatever (Eisenberg, 1991). This other-regarding disposition may be closer to what Hume meant by "sympathy," although certain passages suggest he might have thought sympathy in the sense of a particular emotion—i.e., compassion or concern—is necessary for having the dispositional capacity to respond in an affectively appropriate way to the feelings of another: "No quality of human nature is more remarkable, both in itself and in its consequences, than that propensity we have to sympathise with others, *and* to receive by communication their inclinations and sentiments, however different from and even contrary to our own" (Hume, 1740/1978, p. 743).

3. Psychopaths are now subsumed under what many researchers consider to be a more general (and less valid) diagnostic category: "antisocial personality disorder" or ASPD (see, for instance, *DSM-IV*-TR, 2000, p. 702). In the words of Robert Hare, "most psychopaths (with the exception of those who somehow manage to plow their way through life without coming into formal or prolonged contact with the criminal justice system) meet the criteria for ASPD, *but most individuals with ASPD are not psychopaths*" (Hare, 1996b). ASPD is diagnosed primarily on the basis of behavioral criteria, e.g. criminal behavior, so it is no surprise that ASPD is common in criminal populations. Psychopathy, on the other hand, has been more narrowly defined in terms of measurable interpersonal and affective characteristics, i.e., sustained personality traits, that will often produce criminal behavior. Such characteristics include "egocentricity, deceit, shallow affect, manipulativeness, selfishness, and lack of empathy, guilt or remorse" (Hare, 1996b). While it is no surprise to see such traits in the criminal population, Hare cautions that not all psychopaths will engage in obviously criminal behavior: "[P]sychopaths have little difficulty infiltrating the domains of business, politics, law enforcement, government, academia and other social structures" (Hare, 1996b, p. 40). Since my aim is to focus on this population, I will continue to use the term "psychopath" in this chapter, rather than "individuals with ASPD."

4. See the chapters by Kiehl and Kennett and Fine in this volume.

5. A particularly nice example of the authority dependence versus authority independence of different sorts of transgressions can be found in Nucci's study of Amish teenagers: 100 percent of those tested claimed that if God made no rule against working on Sunday, it would not be wrong to work on Sunday. By contrast, more than 80 percent claimed that if God had made no rule against hitting someone, it

would still be wrong to hit (Nucci, 1986). This brings to mind Socrates' Euthyphro question: Is an act just because the gods love it, or do the gods love it because it is just? Apparently for Amish teenagers, the answer depends on the nature of the act.

6. It is interesting that Blair's work on psychopaths shows that while they fail to make a significant moral-conventional distinction, they tend to process all transgressions as moral, at least as far as the criterion of authority jurisdiction is used. That is, the psychopaths tested tended to claim that both moral and conventional transgressions would be wrong independently of whether or not the acts in question were prohibited by someone in authority. However, when they were asked to explain why the acts would be wrong, the test subjects made significantly less reference to others' welfare or the existence of potential victims even in cases (typically identified as moral transgressions) where harm to the victim was clear. Hence Blair concludes that the assimilation of conventional to moral transgressions on the criterion of authority jurisdiction might well be an artifact of the population tested. That is, all the test subjects were "incarcerated and presumably motivated to be released. All wished to demonstrate that the treatments that they were receiving were effective. They would therefore be motivated to show that they had learned the rules of society" (R.J.R. Blair, 1995, p. 23) and presumably they would give assurances that they were prepared to abide by the rules, come what may. In any case, as Blair rightly points out, these test subjects were not able to make the distinction normally, in marked contrast to the control group (nonpsychopathic fellow inmates).

7. Actually, there is evidence that some autistic children do experience "empathy" in the less complicated sense of feeling distress at another's distress. I return to this issue later.

8. Kennett also takes note of the passion for order found in many autistic individuals (Kennett 2002, pp. 350–351), but seems to tie this to their reverence for reason. However, even if one places reverence for reason on the appetitive side of human psychology (see note 9), it seems to me that the passion for order is something quite distinct. Rationality may involve a preoccupation with certain kinds of order (e.g., consistency in one's beliefs), but there may be many kinds of order (e.g., lining up ducks in a row or ensuring that one takes a walk at precisely the same time every day) that serve no rational purpose at all. There is ample empirical evidence that autistic individuals care about order in this larger extrarational sense.

9. One complicating feature in my disagreement with Kennett is this: Contrary to the standard, and perhaps caricatured, contrast between Kant and Hume, Kennett maintains that moral feeling plays an important role in Kant's account of moral psychology. To wit, that we would not be moral creatures were we not affectively moved to respond to the dictates of reason. Hence, it seems that, according to Kennett's Kant, what motivates us to respond to the reasons there are is the sui

generis desire to think and act rationally. If this is an accurate representation of Kennett's (and/or Kant's) view of how human beings are psychologically structured, I am happy to be somewhat concessive. Indeed, Kennett cites some interesting empirical evidence on cognitive dissonance to support the claim that we are naturally and normally endowed to like acting in accord with reason and to dislike acting against it (2002, p. 354). (Rationalization, as Kennett points out, is a handy way to overcome our affective distaste for contravening the dictates of reason.) Still, my claim is that while the desire to think and act rationally may be deeply rooted in our (normal) human nature, I do not think it is sufficient on its own to account for moral thought and action, even in individuals with autism.

This is not to say I am taking a stand on the conceptual issue of whether it is possible for there to be creatures endowed simply with the desire to think and act rationally that are ipso facto moral creatures. Philosophically, I think this is a difficult thesis to defend, but my claim here is more modest. If you like, it is to deny a certain sort of existence proof: that autistic individuals exemplify such a type. It may be that autistic individuals do evince a stronger desire to think and act rationally than is normally found among typically developing human beings; there is some evidence of this. It may be that in autistic individuals the desire to be rational is experienced less as a means to other goals and more as an end in itself than in typically developing individuals; I think there is less evidence for this. Still, the question remains: What kind of affectively loaded interests do autistic individuals have—apart from being rational—that play a significant, indeed critical, role in the development of their moral sensibility? I have identified their passion for order as one such interest, but in fact I think this is only part of the story. I say more about the affectively laden interests of autistic individuals in the concluding section.

10. I follow Haidt and indeed many others in the literature in using the term "disinterested concern" to talk about interests that are not narrowly concerned with the self, either in terms of their focus or in terms of their playing into a calculus of costs and benefits accruing exclusively to oneself. Here the term is not meant to imply what it often does, namely, an emotionally neutral preoccupation, perhaps supported by reason alone.

5.1 Reasons, Reverence, and Value

Jeanette Kennett

In her chapter Victoria McGeer argues compellingly that the story of what makes us moral creatures is a more complex one than either Hume or Kant or their respective philosophical descendants have acknowledged. I think she is right that the terms of the debate between rationalists and sentimentalists must be modified. Recent evidence on moral development from the social and cognitive sciences and from psychopathology does not endorse the philosophers' traditional distinction between the affective and the cognitive, or their attempts to locate morality wholly in one or other domain. Indeed, I would argue that such evidence helps us to see that Humeans and Kantians have for the most part been talking past each other. Hume's account of morality is a descriptive, psychological account. Kant's is largely conceptual and normative. Once we acknowledge this, the possibility of reconciliation opens up. I take McGeer to be offering a contribution to such a conciliatory project.

The question of what, developmentally or in situ, makes us human beings sensitive to morally charged situations, such as another's suffering, is not the same question as the one Kant was centrally concerned with; namely, what it means to take those situations as generating normative reasons for action, as we must if our actions are to count as moral. In Kant, "reverence for reason" is not just another contingent motive that moral agents might do without. It is better described as the disposition that constitutes us as full agents, the disposition to act in accordance with our reasons as we understand them. In my 2002 paper, I argued in effect that it is the capacity to take some considerations as normative, as providing reasons that are independent of our desires of the moment, that psychopaths lack and that at least some autistic people possess. Perhaps this capacity is causally dependent in humans on affective responsiveness to others' distress, which again psychopaths lack and autistics possess to some degree (e.g., R.J.R. Blair, Colledge, Murray, & Mitchell, 2001b; R.J.R. Blair,

Jones, Clark, & Smith, 1997; R.J.R. Blair, 1999; Corona, Dissanayake, Arbelle, Wellington, & Sigman, 1998). However, I do not take this to undermine Kant's central claims, for his point is that one must move beyond simple emotional responsiveness to others in order to count as a moral agent.

McGeer acknowledges that reason has an essential role in constituting us as moral agents. However, her description of the role of reason is along the lines of Bernard Williams's sub-Humean account. She doubts that reason could itself be motivating. The main purpose of her chapter is thus to trace the tributaries of affectively laden concern that feed into moral agency and which might explain the differences we find between the moral profile or personality of autistic agents and other moral agents. She claims that we are moral beings, and indeed the kind of moral beings we are, because of our affective natures. Autistic individuals with deficiencies in empathy have a markedly different affective profile than normals. McGeer agrees that they share with other moral agents an agential capacity for responding to reason but argues that this capacity is rooted in their capacity to value certain ends and that valuing certain ends is fundamentally rooted in the depth and quality of one's affective life. Where Hume and his followers have gone wrong is in focusing exclusively on the role of empathy. Empathy may be the route to morality that most of us take, but it is not the only one. McGeer rightly reminds us that not all valuing is social in nature and that morality may be based in other concerns, including a concern for what she terms "cosmic order and meaning."

I will return to this last point later. First I want to clarify what I take to be the role of the motive of duty or reverence for reason and relate this to the capacity to value certain ends, because this may help to close the distance between McGeer's account and my own. Her ultimate rejection of Kantian accounts is based upon doubts that reason could be motivating and a justified concern that an adequate account of morality must take proper account of our affective natures. I think an adequate account of rationality must do the same. However, just as McGeer characterizes empathy as a disposition to respond to other's feelings, and not as a particular emotion such as compassion, so I think it is more accurate to characterize Kantian reverence for reason, not as a single motive, but as a disposition to seek and respond to normative considerations—which in normal circumstances will involve the disposition to feel and act accordingly. Once we have allowed that there are broad dispositions of this kind, I think there is no particular problem in talking of reason as motivating or seeing how it can incorporate our affective concerns.

Barbara Herman (1981) argues that for Kant duty is not a first-order motive; it is for the most part a regulating or limiting motive, acting to limit what we may do in pursuit of the ends that our desires, passions, principles, or practical interests may suggest to us. The question is whether these various incentives to the will provide genuine reasons for action. What, if anything, does my anger or pity or love of nature or interest in sport give me reason to do? In David Velleman's account of agency, our rational dispositions play a deep role in setting our ends. If we are to satisfy our agential motives—for self-understanding, self-knowledge, and so forth—deliberation needs to have a broad focus. It cannot just be about means. For intelligible ends can imbue our lives with a rationale and meaning and make us more intelligible to ourselves and others (Velleman, 1989, chap. 10).

What I am leading to is the suggestion that an affectively laden concern for cosmic order and meaning may be a manifestation of, or perhaps a further development of, the basic rational disposition to understand what we do, and to do what we can understand ourselves doing. Disorder, either in ourselves or in the world, may block the fulfillment of these concerns. It seems to me that empathy and concern for hierarchy or social structure are evolutionarily prior to any recognizably moral concern because they are prior to agency. We see them in animals. However, this third affective-cognitive system, named by McGeer as the one to focus upon in the case of autism, seems inextricably bound up with our capacity to be moral agents, not because it is specifically concerned with what most of us would take to be the content of human morality, but because it depends upon the capacity to see ourselves and others and the world in which we find ourselves diachronically, and this is fundamental to agency and to the valuing peculiar to agents.

It is plausible that we can value in simple ways without engaging in normative thought. Any animal with an attachment system can be thought of as a simple valuer. Normative valuing is more complex. Nonagents may in some sense value food, warmth, play, dominance, and routine, but they cannot value a happy marriage, a career, the composing of a symphony, the making of a garden, or the rule of law.

Normative values are only available to agents and indeed help constitute us as agents. The process of becoming an agent is the process of both cognitively and behaviorally transcending the present moment, of grasping and acting upon reasons that extend over time.

The recent surge of philosophical interest in the moral-conventional distinction has focused on the emergence of moral judgment in young children and has tended to overlook its cooccurrence with social and conventional judgment and prudential judgment. I think that what studies of the moral-conventional distinction most significantly and fundamentally track is the emergence of normative thought and normative concepts in children. I argue that the capacity for moral judgment is not separable from this general capacity for normative thought, which one can characterize in Kantian terms as a concern with, and responsiveness to, reasons. This is what (at least some) high-functioning autistic individuals possess and what psychopaths largely lack.

McGeer doubts that the passion for cosmic order and meaning is the same as a Kantian concern for reason. In the case of autism she convincingly argues that sensory and social confusion lead to a prominent concern for order, and this can explain autistic behavior across domains. Strict rules and routines make for a more predictable and manageable environment, even if the routine or activity is otherwise pointless.[1] Autistic individuals may thus become concerned that rules governing behavior be universally adhered to. However, as she says, this is not of itself moral concern and may never rise to it if the individuals concerned do not see the real point of moral practice. Nevertheless, an emerging concern and capacity to make sense of oneself and the world is plausibly, I think, the transition point between the simple valuing that arises directly from various affective responses and agential or normative valuing, and this at least some autistic people engage in. The same sense-making concern in a person who is at home in the social world, for whom the social world is easily explicable, will not find expression in the development of the explicit and firm rules that autistic individuals such as Temple Grandin use to guide their social behavior. So I agree with McGeer that our affective natures shape our moral profile and that the unusual pattern of affective concern seen in autism explains autistic moral distinctness.

Where we might still disagree is in whether there is some one fundamental concern that moral agents must possess and whether this concern can be characterized in any way that does not rely upon our agential capacities. I have argued here that a concern for reasons or, in Kantian terms, "reverence for reason" functions as a disposition to be motivated in the same way that empathy does. Is it "a" or "the" core moral motive? Here I readily concede that this concern is not peculiar to morality nor do we perform particular moral actions for the sake of acting in accordance with reason. Rather, it is a core or grounding motive of agents as such. However, I think that once we are, as agents, in the business of finding and responding to reasons, we cannot help but find that some of those reasons are moral reasons.

This last claim might be doubted and I do not have space to defend it here. I will return instead to the question of whether and how the other-regarding content of morality might be arrived at through routes other than empathy. What enables autistic individuals to see the point of much of moral practice in the absence or the significant muting of that empathic transference of concern between persons without which, Hume argued, morality could not get off the ground? How can they come to see other people's interests as reason giving? Interestingly, I think Blair's own work (R.J.R. Blair, 1996) suggests that moral judgment may be often enough arrived at through routes other than empathic identification.

One of the moral scenarios Blair used to test for the moral-conventional distinction, a child smashing a piano, does not have a direct victim. Autistic children with deficits in pretend play are unlikely to see the piano in the role of victim, as something that could experience harm, and they are equally unlikely to perform the imaginative feat of seeing others who might have enjoyed the piano as secondary victims and view the wrongness of the action as deriving from this harm. Indeed, it seems unlikely that normal children view the wrongness of smashing a piano in this way either. So something other than the perception of a victim must mediate the moral conventional distinction in cases such as these. The judgment that smashing a piano is wrong, even in the absence of a rule forbidding it, may arise directly from the perception of the piano as intrinsically valuable. Such ascriptions of value are common enough and include those based on aesthetic responses to music, art, and the natural world, all of which may underpin moral judgments related to their treatment. People often feel that these things matter, independently of them and of their connection to either welfare or convention. For autistic people, the judgment that other persons matter and the consequent taking of their interests as reason giving may thus arise independently of empathic identification with them. It may arise from a more disinterested contemplation of the complexities and capacities of the "piece of work" (to quote Hamlet) that is man.

This is speculation of course. The data may bear other interpretations, but they fit quite nicely with McGeer's speculation about the nature of the concern that most prominently shapes the autistic moral profile while leaving open the question of what account of morality is best supported by it.

Note

1. I doubt that McGeer believes that some of the repetitive behaviors and rote learning seen in autism qualify as being generated from an affectively laden concern for cosmic order and meaning. Therefore, the examples she gives do not count against my interpretation of this concern, insofar as it could underpin morality as being a part of, or generated by, a more general sense-making drive that agents must possess.

Heidi Maibom

The morality of people with mental disorders has received much attention recently, the hope being that it will help resolve the recently revived debate between sentimentalism and rationalism. We have relatively good knowledge of what psychological capacities are affected in different mental illnesses; thus, it is easier to determine the relative contribution of reason and emotion to morality. For instance, sentimentalists have argued that psychopathy favors their case since psychopaths are highly immoral, have profound emotional deficits, but have no rational impairments to speak of (Haidt, 2001; Nichols, 2002a). Rationalist sympathizers have retorted that psychopaths do have impaired practical reason, sufficient to undermine their moral capacities (Duff, 1977; Kennett, 2002; Maibom, 2005).

People with autism have poor social understanding and ability and impaired empathy, yet appear to have no moral deficits to speak of. This would not be puzzling if it were not for the fact that the most commonly quoted cause of psychopaths' immorality is that they have no empathic ability. The fact that people can have relatively intact morality while having impaired empathy raises important questions about traditional sentimentalism. Jeanette Kennett has argued that what is intact in people with autism is their capacity to be "moved directly by the thought that some consideration constitutes a reason for action" (Kennett, 2002, p. 357). Psychopaths, on the other hand, lack a proper conception of their own and others' ends.[1] McGeer's chapter is a reaction to this defense of rationalism. She agrees that empathy is not *the* source of morality, but she thinks it is a mistake to think of autistic morality as springing from a proper appreciation of reason-giving interests. Instead, she suggests that there are at least three different sources of morality: (1) concern for the well-being of others, (2) a concern with social structure and social position, and (3) concern with cosmic structure and cosmic position (this volume, pp. 229 and 251).

Although people with autism seem to have a largely intact capacity to regulate their behavior in accordance with moral norms and make appropriate moral judgments, their morality is somewhat peculiar. They cleave to rules in an unusual way. Taking exception to one—even when it seems justified—is something they are loath to do. It is tempting to conclude that they lack a deeper understanding of the reasons behind moral norms. McGeer is right to point out that this might be true of some autistic individuals, even though it is not true of all. In contrast to psychopaths, autistic individuals appreciate the moral significance of hurting others (R. J. R. Blair, 1996). Nevertheless, following rules takes on a life of its own in people with autism. Their knowledge of and concern with rules is not well connected to an appreciation of the original reasons behind them, with the result that they are not flexibly applied. McGeer calls this fixation "passion for order." Passion for order is an extreme manifestation of her third source of morality: concern with cosmic structure and position (henceforth, cosmic concern), which she claims is the most spared source of morality in people with autism. The overreliance on it gives rise to the peculiarities that are characteristic of autistic morality.

What is concern for cosmic structure and position? McGeer claims that both an admiration of ordered laws in the sciences and the need for religion to bring meaning and shape to the world are manifestations of this concern. The two certainly seem connected in the writings of Temple Grandin, an extraordinarily gifted person with autism:

My favorite of Einstein's words on religion is: "Science without religion is lame. Religion without science is blind." I like this because both science and religion are needed to answer life's great questions. . . . I am deeply interested in the new chaos theory, because it means that order can arise out of disorder and randomness. I've read many popular articles about it, because I want scientific proof that the world is orderly. . . . I hated the second law of thermodynamics because I believed that the universe *should* be orderly. (Grandin, 1995, pp. 191–192)

The idea that humans seek a greater meaning behind things is familiar. The degree to which that amounts to seeking order is, I think, an open question. For life or the world to make sense does not seem to require the sort of order that people with autism are concerned with. Seeking order is, of course, very different from creating order. Even if we grant McGeer that people seek not just meaning, but cosmic order, she must still explain how seeking such order is action guiding in the way that morality is. It is certainly true that the urge to find meaning in life has behavioral effects; if we are to believe Albert Camus, the failure to find it can cause one to commit suicide (Camus, 1955). However, cosmic concern seems more abstract and intellectual than practical concerns generally. It is not clear what moral actions this concern would motivate. Seeking enlightenment or salvation is often a very ego-centered enterprise that is only tenuously connected with the sort of concern for others that we traditionally connect with morality.[2] It may be that cosmic concern culminates in moral motivation through respect for a deity—the ordering force of the universe—whose desires must be obeyed. Now the question becomes, is some action morally good because God wants us to perform it, or does God want us to perform it because it is morally good? Even the intuitions of strict religious people speak in favor of the latter. When there is an overlap between what God commands and moral norms, the overwhelming majority judges that morally prohibited actions would still be morally wrong if God had not issued a prohibition against them. Indeed, the majority judges that God cannot change what is morally right or wrong (Nucci & Turiel, 1993). The moral realm appears to be relatively autonomous.

Even if what is right or wrong is independent of God's commands, there is still a distinctive motivation connected with religion, namely, the concern to obey the commands of God generally. If this concern is preeminent in people with autism, it is hardly surprising that their morality differs from ordinary morality. Autistic individuals should regard all moral transgressions as religious people regard the transgressions of God's commands. They are rules that must be followed, but not rules that have some ulterior justification (other than God wanting it so). However, this is the sort of downbeat interpretation that McGeer claims is not true of all autistic morality.

There is an additional reason for thinking that cosmic concern won't guide action in the way that moral concerns usually do. If McGeer is right about the role of cosmic concern in autistic morality, it must be that cosmic concern gives rise to the passion for order. Nevertheless, it is not clear why cosmic concern would manifest itself in a concern that the little things be done in the right way, e.g., that shoelaces are always tied in the same way and in the same order. Grandin's concern that the second law of thermodynamics not unsettle the order of the cosmos makes her *study* chaos theory, etc. She does not think that she can affect the order of the universe by changing her own or other people's behavior. This should lead us to look for a different origin of the passion for order. McGeer says one of the reasons that people with autism give for their obsession with order, routines, and rules is that it helps them understand what happens around them better and reduces their anxiety in social situations.

It is not hard to see that having to function in a society whose workings one does not comprehend can be anxiety inducing. Insisting that one's close social sphere be ordered in such a way that it is comprehensible and predictable is a way of managing those anxieties. In this case, however, a passion for order is an extreme manifestation of a more pedestrian human need: the need to understand others in order to be able to function socially. This looks much more like social concern, McGeer's second source of morality, than cosmic concern. Cosmic concern explains nothing about passion for order that social concern does not already explain. I do not see that cosmic concern, if indeed there is such a distinct motive, will serve as a source of morality. If social concern is what gives rise to passion for order, and passion for order is what characterizes autistic morality vis-à-vis ordinary morality, then social concern must be a source of moral value.

Social concern initially seems like a bad candidate for moral value, since moral norms are usually assumed to be authority-independent. However, McGeer follows Jonathan Haidt in thinking that what characterizes morality is its disinterestedness, not its independence of authority. As a sentimentalist, McGeer takes the source of morality to be in the emotions, and what makes an emotion moral is that it has disinterested elicitors and disinterested action tendencies (Haidt, 2003b). There are virtues to allowing a closer link between authority and moral motivation, even if they are not linked through the emotions. Obeying authority and conforming to perceived social demands are powerful motives for most people. I am thinking about the Milgram and the Stanford prison experiments (Milgram, 1963; Haney, Banks, & Zimbardo, 1973).

In Stanley Milgram's experiment, experimental subjects were paired with other subjects who, unbeknownst to them, were confederates of the experimenter. The former took the role of teachers and the latter that of students, and they were placed in different rooms. The students were given a test, and the teachers' role was to administer shocks increasing in intensity from mild to extremely severe for each wrong answer that the student produced. At the instigation of the experimenter, who instructed them to continue when they were hesitating, 26 out of 40 people went on to administer the highest possible shock to the students. All but 5 subjects continued to do so even after screaming, moaning, and kicking were heard from the room where the student was located and the student had ceased responding altogether. Of the subjects who refused to administer further shocks before reaching the maximum, not a single one ran to the aid of the student, nor did they insist that the experimenter do so (Zimbardo, Maslach, & Haney,

2000). Milgram took the experiment to demonstrate the extraordinary lengths ordinary people will go to, to obey an authority figure. Obedience, in the Milgram experiment, trumps competing moral considerations. The subjects had every reason to think that they were causing great pain and harm to another person. Nevertheless, they could be induced to do so relatively easily.

The Stanford prison experiment was an attempt to study prison behavior. A number of students, who had been screened for any psychological abnormalities or peculiarities, were chosen to play either prisoners or prison guards. Neither group was given instructions about how to behave, with the exception that the prison guards were told not to physically harm the prisoners. As situations started arising in the prison, the guards were merely instructed to handle the situation on their own. The experimenter, Philip Zimbardo, played the role of the prison superintendent and only intervened in the grossest moral violations. Within only 36 hours, the first student-prisoner had to be released owing to extreme psychological distress. He was crying, swearing, screaming, and his speech was incoherent and irrational (Zimbardo et al., 2000, p. 201). After 6 days the experiment was cut short because the moral viability of completing it was in serious doubt.

The prison guards had quickly become extremely abusive toward the prisoners. The abuse seemed to have begun as a response to a revolt by the prisoners, who were upset at their dehumanizing imprisonment experience. As a result the guards stripped the prisoners naked; put some of them in solitary confinement; deprived them of meals, pillows, or blankets; and forced them to do jumping jacks, pushups, and other meaningless activities. The most sadistic guards made the prisoners get up several times each night in order to count them. The ostensible purpose of the exercise was for the prisoners to learn their identification number, but the guards would also taunt, punish, and toy with the prisoners (Zimbardo et al., 2000, p. 201). The guards' abuses continued unabated after the revolt was crushed. Prisoners were made to clean dirty toilets with their bare hands, were refused access to toilet facilities, were forced to relieve themselves in a bucket that sometimes was not emptied, and so on. According to Zimbardo, it took all of one day for the student prison guards to settle into their roles. As in the Milgram experiments, the guards that were not abusive did nothing to prevent or stop the abuses of the other guards. Here it is not so much obedience to authority as conformity to perceived social roles that outcompetes concerns for human decency. The guards perceived themselves as being in a social role with the responsibility of managing rebellious prisoners, which to them justified countless transgressions of ordinary human decency and competing moral norms.

What can we learn about sources of morality from the Milgram and Stanford prison experiments? At a minimum, the experiments help us see how motives to obey authority and conform to social roles or expectations are extremely powerful. They also meet the criteria for being sources of morality for McGeer, since their elicitors are disinterested, as are their action tendencies. It is irrelevant that they conflict with moral motives in the two experiments since it is certainly possible for moral motives to conflict, and it is not hard to see how obedience and social conformity can serve moral ends. If obedience and the desire to conform are manifestations of social concern, and this capacity is relatively spared in people with autism by comparison with their empathic ability, it is easy to see why autistic morality would be peculiar by comparison with ordinary morality. The motive to conform to social rules and regulations would tend to blind people with autism to other morally significant factors that empathy is more likely to highlight: the effects of such rules on the well-being of particular individuals. As a consequence, the young man McGeer talks about judges that the unemployed single mother should be arrested for shoplifting. By contrast, psychopaths tend to regard social regulations as arbitrary and have no compunction about flouting them should the regulations conflict with what they want. Psychopaths tend to be highly antisocial. They also have a low tolerance for routine tasks and activities (Hare 1991, 1993).

Finding that they are largely absent in a group of people that is thought to be amoral provides good support for the idea that there are several sources of morality. With the added evidence of the strong motive to obey authority and to conform to perceived social demands found in ordinary people, McGeer has a strong case for social concern as a source of morality. Of course, being obedient or conforming to social norms does not itself appear to be morally praiseworthy. McGeer thinks that what characterizes moral agency is that one has "the capacity to control one's impulses in the service of some larger ends (i.e., ends that trump one's parochial and immediate interests), the capacity to find value in these larger ends, and the capacity to put one's reason to work in the service of attaining such ends" (this volume, p. 245). It therefore seems that it is the ability to put one's own interests aside that is fundamental to morality. To that extent, social concern as I have described it, in terms of obedience to authority and social conformity, is moral because it is an expression of us being willing to subordinate our will to interests other than narrowly selfish ones.

The proposal so far does not seem to go far enough in imbuing the sources of morality with the right kinds of concerns. Having dismissed cosmic concern as a bona fide source of morality, we are left with empathy and social concern. Leaving empathy to the side, McGeer's view implies that the behavior exhibited by the subjects in both the Milgram and the Stanford prison experiments stems from a moral source. The subjects subordinate their will to immoral but nonselfish ends. Here a source of good is also a source of evil. Perhaps it is impossible to find a source of morality that does not have this problem—a story could no doubt be told of how empathic concern for others might lead to evil or immoral acts—but should we not search further? Kant might have located the moral law in pure practical reason, but he fleshed it out in terms of universalizability and concern for others as ends in themselves (Kant 1785/1993). This brings us closer to something that looks like a source of morality. Might something like this be derived from social concern? I think it might. When I characterized social concern in terms of obedience to authority and social conformity, I did not do full justice to McGeer. Social concern includes, for her, concern with others' intentions. Where this sounds more morally relevant, it also sounds more Kantian, for what makes concern with others' intentions morally good cannot simply be that we are concerned to figure out what they intend. Even psychopaths are concerned with others in this sense. What makes this kind of concern relevant to morality is presumably that it consists of a recognition that others' ends generate reasons, reasons for me to act. This is, as far as I can see, Kantian rationalism in sentimentalist clothes. It is arrived at by adding affect to the reverence for reason that Kennett (2002) talks about. What reason does McGeer give that social concern is a superior way of thinking about these matters compared to respect for the moral law?

McGeer complains that "reverence for reason is not the core moral motive; indeed, I doubt it is much of a motive at all, at least on its own. . . . [R]espect for reason . . . derives from the practical . . . recognition that it is one of the most useful tools we have for prioritizing and accomplishing whatever ends we find affectively salient or compelling" (this volume, p. 246). However, McGeer's social concern looks like a simple transformation of the content(s) of the categorical imperative into affective ends. We are now concerned with others' intentions as reason giving in the right way. Without knowing how she can help herself to this form of motivation, it is unclear how this is much of an improvement on the sentimentalism versus rationalism debate. What is an improvement, I think, is that McGeer brings out the social character of morality. The way that we are constituted as social creatures cannot be underestimated when trying to understand the psychology of morality. Much of what we do we do because authorities or social structures and regulations make certain demands on us. It seems churlish to insist that our actions or intentions can never be morally praiseworthy in these cases. I doubt that even the most extreme Kantian would insist that a motive must be derived directly from a categorical imperative for it to be moral. If that were true, hardly any of us would be moral hardly any of the time. In principle, however, the motives that have moral worth can be derived in this way. An agent who acts out of obedience or social conformity can be morally praiseworthy as long as she or he is responsive to the moral law. She or he must have a general conception of the content and force of the categorical imperative and regard her moral judgments and motives as being related to them in the right way. Were she to realize that her motives to obey or conform conflicted with what the moral law required of her, her motivations would shift. If all this is true of the agent, it seems fair to say that her propensity to obey authority and conform to social roles, structures, and rules plays an important role in her morality.

Focusing on the social aspect of morality is necessary for understanding it correctly, and McGeer's chapter helps us see that more clearly. I think additional considerations can be added: lessons from the Milgram and Stanford prison experiments. Whereas it does not seem to be right to locate a source of morality directly in obedience and social conformity, recognizing what role these play when they are appropriately related to other sources of morality is of great importance.

Notes

1. Kennett overstates the extent to which people with autism are incapable of empathizing. Autistic people are capable of some form of empathy, thus they present a poor case against sentimentalism (R.J.R. Blair, 1996; Sigman, Kasari, Kwon, & Yirmiya, 1992; Yirmiya, Sigman, Kasari, & Mundy, 1992). To my mind, people with frontal lobe damage are a better example of people who are by and large moral, but who are incapable of experiencing empathy (Damasio, 1994; Kaszniak, Reminger, Rapcsak, & Glisky, 1999). They show that moral motivation does not require the ability to feel empathy.

2. See William James (1902/1972) for an excellent exposition of the egocentricity of sainthood.

5.3 Autism, Morality, and Empathy

Frédérique de Vignemont and Uta Frith

"Do unto others as you would have them do unto you" (Matthew 7:12). The golden rule of most religions assumes that the cognitive abilities of perspective taking and empathy are the basis of morality. According to Goldman (1995), you simulate what you would like to happen if you were in the situation of another and act accordingly. One would therefore predict that people who display difficulties in those abilities, such as people with psychopathy and autism, are impaired in morality. This seems to be confirmed by studies on psychopaths, who show deficits in both empathy and morality (R.J.R. Blair, Mitchell, & Blair, 2005). However, Kennett (2002) and McGeer in her chapter here suggest that in autism, the deficit of empathy does not lead to a deficit of morality. McGeer attempts to solve this paradox by investigating the roots of moral agency. She distinguishes a Kantian rational view of morality and a Humean emotional view of morality. She concludes that even if reason plays a key role in morality, this role is merely instrumental. Only emotions can constitute the motivation for moral behaviors. However, according to her, one should not reduce emotional motivation for morality solely to empathy. Other kinds of emotions may also play a role—emotions that would be available to people with autism.

This interesting chapter raises a major question that is challenging both for moral philosophy and cognitive neuropsychiatry. Why do autistics have a sense of morality while psychopaths do not, given that they both display a deficit of empathy? We would like here to refine some of the views on autism and morality. In order to do so, we will investigate whether autism really challenges a Humean view of morality. We will then provide a new conceptual framework based on the distinction between egocentric and allocentric stances, which may help us to make some predictions about the autistic sense of morality.

Autism: A Challenge for a Humean View of Morality?

Autism raises the following paradox:

(a) Humean view: Empathy is the only source of morality.
(b) People who have no empathy should have no morality.
(c) People with autism show a lack of empathy.
(d) People with autism show a sense of morality.

To solve this paradox, McGeer refutes premise (a) and its consequence (b). She concludes that empathy is not a necessary condition for morality. However, there may be other possible ways to solve the paradox, by refuting either (c) or (d). We will review these possibilities based on experimental work. However, we should keep in mind that both psychopathy and autism are heterogeneous, and impairments can range from severe to hardly perceptible. In addition, it is necessary to make allowances for comorbidity between the two disorders. For our present purposes we will consider here individuals with autism spectrum disorder (ASD) who have normal or superior intellectual ability and who show the following features: difficulty in reciprocal social interaction, communication impairments, a lack of flexibility with obsessive tendencies, and a single-minded pursuit of narrow interests.

A Lack of Empathy?

According to McGeer, the common factor between autism and psychopathy is the lack of emotional empathy (premise c). One possibility is that the empathy disorder results from abnormalities in emotion recognition and emotion matching in ASD (P. Hobson, 1986). However, in studies where the verbal mental age was matched, children with autism have not been shown to be impaired in emotion recognition (Adolphs, Sears, & Piven, 2001; Ozonoff, Pennington, & Rogers, 1990; Prior, Dahlstrom, & Squires, 1990; Castelli, 2005). They have intact autonomic responses when viewing pictures of people who are sad or afraid. Furthermore, most of the tasks used to evaluate empathy in ASD require both cognitive and affective skills (e.g., empathy quotient, Baron-Cohen & Wheelwright, 2004). Consequently, the tasks are unable to test emotional empathy per se. Emotion-processing abnormalities in autistic disorders cannot be properly understood in terms of a lack of emotions, but rather in terms of less complex emotions, less regulation of emotions, and less ability to reflect on one's own emotions (E. Hill, Berthoz, & Frith, 2004). Individuals with ASD have difficulties in integrating the cognitive and affective facets of another person's mental states (Shamay-Tsoory, Tomer, Yaniv, & Aharon-Peretz, 2002). None of these limitations rules out automatic emotional empathy. We assume that at least a subgroup of individuals with ASD may have emotional empathy, at least to some degree, even if they may not be able to reflect on their emotions.

The parallel drawn between psychopathy and autism based on a common lack of empathy does not seem to be fully justified. While psychopathy indeed is defined as severe disturbances in emotional empathy, it is less clear that individuals with ASD are unable to empathize (Blair, 2005). If we distinguish here between cognitive and emotional components of empathetic behaviors, we would claim that only the former is impaired in ASD, but not necessarily the latter. We attribute the lack of empathetic behavior claimed by a number of authors (Gillberg, 1992; Yirmiya, Sigman, Kasari, & Mundy, 1992) to mentalizing deficits (Batson, Fultz, & Schoenrade, 1987). One may suggest that the partial integrity of the emotional component in people with ASD might explain why they show apparently preserved moral behaviors, in contrast to people with psychopathy. However, do they really display a moral sense?

A Sense of Morality?

According to McGeer, if psychopathy and autism share the same lack of empathy, they differ at the level of morality. Based on several quotations from Temple Grandin, McGeer argues that moral sensibility would be partially preserved in ASD (premise d). How can we go beyond introspective reports and test morality experimentally? Moral rules can be used both to guide our own actions and to judge other people's actions. It is difficult to evaluate moral behaviors in ASD because several irrelevant factors can interfere with individuals' actions, preventing them from acting according to moral rules (e.g., executive disorder, for review see E.L. Hill, 2004). Here we will limit ourselves to moral judgments, which are more amenable to experimental investigations. Two distinctions are particularly useful: moral-conventional and wrong-bad.

The distinction between conventional and moral has been a major breakthrough in the study of morality (Turiel, 1983; Smetana, 1985). Having a moral sense means being able to distinguish between a moral violation (e.g., pulling someone's hair) and a conventional violation (e.g., chewing gum at school). The distinction is made from the age of 39 months and is cross-cultural (Smetana & Braeges, 1990; Song, Smetana, & Kim, 1987). In folk psychology, a moral violation is considered as universal and objective (Nichols & Folds-Bennett, 2003). A conventional violation is merely a question of context and authority. A moral violation is less permissible than a conventional violation. When asked why this is so, children's replies reflect the belief that a conventional violation depends on social order while a moral violation involves someone being hurt. According to Blair, the sense of morality ultimately derives from a violence inhibition mechanism (VIM) that is activated by distress cues. However, the story may not be so simple.

Not all the phenomena that lead to someone being hurt can be considered a consequence of a moral violation. Indeed, it is necessary to make the distinction between judging that something is wrong and judging that something is bad (Nichols, 2002b). An earthquake that kills thousands of people can cause severe distress and pain and as such is bad, but it is not wrong. Furthermore, if by hurting someone you help her, then the act cannot be considered a moral violation. One should temper the temporary pain or distress with the global happiness or good for the person. The act cannot be evaluated in itself without its background and its consequences, which may or may not justify it. Punishment is thought to be appropriate only for moral and conventional transgressions, but not for nontransgressions (see Davidson, Turiel, & Black, 1983; Zelazo, Helwig, & Lau, 1996).

There are thus at least three components in a moral violation: (1) it is a transgression of a normative rule, (2) this rule is not conventional or contextual, and (3) the transgression involves someone suffering without further moral justification. The question now is whether people with ASD can detect a moral violation.

Blair (1996) tested the capacity to draw a distinction between moral and conventional violations in children with ASD. The subjects were asked about the permissibility, the seriousness, and the authority jurisdiction of the violation. Individuals with ASD were not significantly different from controls on any of these questions. They were able to distinguish between moral and conventional violations despite their impairment in theory of mind. Blair concluded that individuals with ASD were able to detect distress in others. However, there are at least two problems here.

First, another study about recognition of faux pas seems to refine the previous results. A faux pas occurs when someone says something that he should not say because it may disturb or hurt someone else's feelings. Shamay-Tsoory et al. (2002) showed that two Asperger individuals were able to detect the faux pas, but not to understand them. It is interesting that they were not able to provide an appropriate explanation of why it was a faux pas. They referred to violations of rules (e.g., you are not supposed to do that) rather than to the fact that the victim of the faux pas was hurt. This result is consistent with another study in which the subjects had to judge culpability in different stories (Grant, Boucher, Riggs, & Grayson, 2005). Children with ASD were able to judge the culpability of children in the stories but were not able to justify why by appealing to the pain caused. We would like to suggest that people with ASD are able to detect someone's distress but are more interested in normative rules than in emotions.

A second problem comes from the classical task used by Blair. The critical question in distinguishing between moral and conventional violations concerns the authority jurisdiction: Would it be okay for a child to do X if the teacher says that the child can? The rule is moral if the child should not do X even if the teacher says that the child can do X. However, to understand that does not mean that one understands that it is a moral violation. Indeed, it merely means that it does not depend on the teacher's authority; it is beyond his or her jurisdiction. It could depend on someone else's authority, like one's parents. If so, it would still be a conventional violation.

In conclusion, we are not convinced that there is as yet sufficient evidence to rule out the possibility that individuals with mentalizing impairments have an intact moral sensitivity. It rather seems that they are able to detect a transgression of a normative rule and detect someone else's distress, but not necessarily to relate them to each other. Furthermore, there is no convincing evidence that they can understand that some rules are not conventional. Indeed, the introspective self-reports provided by McGeer can all be interpreted as the consequence of an acute sense of normative rules, but they do not provide any clue about the sense of morality. McGeer reports that Temple Grandin has no social intuition. The question is, does she have moral intuitions? Or is she merely an "expert computer program" as she claimed to be? We would like now to provide a new conceptual framework that may help to interpret the sense of morality in ASD patients.

Egocentrism and Allocentrism in Social and Moral Cognition

We suggest that it is misleading to characterize ASD as a lack of empathy associated with a preserved sense of morality. The limitations in social and moral cognition in ASD individuals require a more subtle conceptual framework that takes into account the difference between two kinds of attitudes. We would like here to introduce a distinction between egocentrism and allocentrism in social cognition, based on the distinction that is made in visuospatial perception (Frith & de Vignemont, 2005). We propose that it makes a difference whether the other person can be understood using an egocentric stance ("you") or an allocentric stance ("he/she/they").

The distinction between egocentric and allocentric representations was first made in spatial cognition (for a review, see Jacob & Jeannerod, 2003). The spatial location of the same object can be encoded either in its perceptual relation to the agent (egocentric representation) or in its relation to other objects independently of the agent (allocentric representation). Each of these representations plays a specific role. The egocentric representation is directly linked to the actions that the agent can perform toward the object. The allocentric representation relates objects together and allows comparing them with each other. Similarly, one can have two different attitudes toward the same person. When we adopt an egocentric stance, the other person is understood in her relationship with the self. This relationship can be based on more or less direct interactions (e.g., the person I am talking to), but also on social status (e.g., a member of my family or a colleague). What the other feels, thinks, or does is relevant for the self. It is necessary to know the other according to an egocentric stance if one wants to interact with the other and to locate oneself in the social world. When we adopt an allocentric stance, the other person is understood in her relationship with other people independently of the self. The allocentric stance allows you to understand that people exist outside their interactions with you. It is necessary for understanding the mutual relationships among people. The allocentric stance is detached from interactions with people, while the egocentric stance is immersed in social interactions and directly connected to them.

Egocentric and allocentric representations are normally in permanent interaction. Allocentric social knowledge is based on inferences drawn from memories of past egocentric interactions. Conversely, the egocentric stance is influenced by a wider allocentric knowledge of people. We suggest that this interaction is broken in Asperger syndrome.

Consequently, individuals with Asperger syndrome display extreme egocentrism, disconnected from allocentrism. Their social world is self-focused. They may forget, for instance, that people have their own life, outside their interaction with them. They often report being the victim and seem to be less sensitive to other people's suffering. One example of the ambivalence of morality in ASD individuals comes from the study of the sense of fairness using social economic games in simple one-to-one situations in autism (Sally & Hill, 2006). These games included the ultimatum and dictator games, where one partner can either offer or refuse a share of a given amount of points. High-functioning individuals with autism were using the same "irrational" principles as controls; that is, they refused to accept amounts given to them that were lower than about a third of the total and likewise offered amounts that were somewhat less than half the given amount. People with ASD are sensitive to whether they are being treated fairly or not. This is consistent with egocentrism. It is interesting that in the dictator game, the distribution of the offers differed for ASD individuals. Normal adults shaded their offers so that they could get one or two extra points for themselves. In contrast, adults with autism seemed to obey one of the two following rules: make a perfectly equal offer or keep everything. In this situation, there is no flexibility or degrees of fairness in ASD individuals, unlike normal adults. The rule used in the dictator game is mathematical and rigid. This is the consequence of an abstract allocentrism disconnected from egocentrism. People with ASD do not provide any description of how people do behave, but rather how people should behave. They live in a normative social world. We suggest that the so-called moral behaviors in ASD result from abstract allocentrism. These individuals thrive on the idea of rules, as noticed by McGeer. This is shown whenever autism spectrum individuals talk about rules that other people might follow in their social interactions that they feel they have worked out by logical analysis.

Baron-Cohen, Richler, Bisarya, Gurunathan, and Wheelwright (2003) showed that individuals with ASD had a higher score in systemizing quotient. Systemizing is defined as the drive to analyze, identify underlying rules, and build systems. People with ASD do not necessarily appeal to emotions or other mental states to understand the social world; they merely predict other people's behaviors on the basis of regularities among inputs, operations, and outputs:

There is a process of using my intellect and logical decision making for every social decision. Emotion doesn't guide my decision; it is pure computing. (Grandin, 1995, p. 103)

People with ASD have social knowledge and are able to see social structures and relationships in a detached way that can give rise to a reputation of being cold and distanced. However, their personal logic for how the social and the moral world should work may be formal and far from reality. It is even more difficult for them that ordinary people do not always follow the rules in their daily practice or can create their own rules (M. Dewey, 1991):

There are days when just trying to make sense of the rules for social interaction is too difficult. It is especially so when we take into account that individuals often write their own rules! For example, it's fine to take your clothes off to have a bath, but only a model takes her clothes off for the photographer; or you can laugh at that story, even though it's about a fat lady, because it's a joke. (Lawson, 2001, p. 98)

The human saga is just not reliable enough for me to predict. (Willey, 1999, p. 85)

It is not surprising that individuals with ASD are sensitive to normative rules, given that these rules are only way they have to cope with their lack of social intuitions. Still, it does not mean the rules they obey are nothing more than conventional for them.

We tentatively suggest that most individuals with ASD are not insensitive to the distress of other people. However, their emotional empathy may not go far enough and does not necessarily explain why they are able to make normative judgments and indeed genuinely act in a law-abiding way. We suggest that they are more interested in normative rules than in emotions because of an abstract allocentrism disconnected from egocentric interactions with others. It is difficult to understand whether the normative rules they obey are merely conventional, extracted from their abstract analysis of their surrounding, or properly moral. Only in the latter case would they believe that moral rules (as opposed to conventional rules) are objective and universal beyond anybody's jurisdiction. Only then can we decide whether autism really does challenge a Humean view of morality.

The Makings of a Moral Sensibility: Replies to Commentaries

Victoria McGeer

I am grateful to my commentators for their thoughtful responses to the speculative ideas explored in my chapter. These ideas are largely speculative because, despite a recent surge of interest in atypical moral psychology, it remains a largely uncharted area of interdisciplinary research. Hence, there are very few studies on which to base solid conclusions and very many questions—both empirical and conceptual—still left to answer. Nevertheless, what makes even the modest body of research in this area so tantalizing is the difficult issues it raises on two separate but related fronts. The first is more general, relating to long-standing philosophical debates about the nature of moral judgment and moral motivation. The second is more particular, relating to the specific difficulties involved in investigating atypical cognitive-affective profiles such as those found in autism and psychopathy. I say these two sets of issues are interrelated because our sense of what it is to have a moral sensibility is very much shaped by our understanding of the so-called normal case, sometimes making unusual departures from this norm quite difficult to characterize. In consequence, certain disagreements—for instance, about whether autistic individuals have a genuine but "impaired" moral sensibility—may not in the end turn on facts about specific cognitive and/or affective capacities, but on whether such capacities, and the behavior they motivate, constitute a genuine variety of moral agency. This brings us back to more general philosophical debates about the nature of moral judgment and moral motivation.

In this context, it seems fitting to ask about what we really gain philosophically by studying atypical moral psychology. After all, if we could simply take the presence or absence of a moral sensibility as (detectably) given, then it would make sense to investigate what cognitive and/or affective capacities are "spared" or "impaired" in particular disorders so as to determine what grounds this sensibility. Maybe this would even go some way toward settling the philosophical debate between sentimentalists and rationalists. Such has been the presumption, at any rate, on the basis of which many of the discussions about psychopathy and autism—including my own—have proceeded. However, in working on my own contribution to this volume, I came to realize that the issues raised by these populations are much more interesting and complex than this straightforward argumentative strategy suggests. Thus, I was led by degrees into a more complicated exploration of what in particular could be going on in autism, and also a more general exploration of what it takes to have any variety of moral sensibility at all.

My suggestions have no doubt raised more questions than they have answered, but I hope one of the virtues to be found in my chapter is at least a satisfying response to the question of what we gain philosophically by studying atypical moral psychologies. The answer is quite simple. Real cases—especially difficult real cases—often force increasing conceptual sophistication where no amount of thought experiments will do the same. Hence, we may not gain so much an answer to long-standing philosophical debates as a realization that more traditional accounts are misconceived in important ways. If we are lucky, we also begin to see the direction in which, conceptually speaking, we need to move in order to amend these accounts; and with these amendments we likewise gain a better understanding of the kinds of empirical questions we have yet to pose.

With this apologia in place, I turn now to more specific replies to the three commentaries on my chapter. Although I can't address all the issues raised, I will do my best to respond to at least a substantial few so far as these fall into the two categories already mentioned: (1) those concerned with more general philosophical questions (chiefly from Kennett and Maibom), which are discussed first; and (2) those concerned more specifically with autism (chiefly from de Vignemont and Frith), discussed in the second section.

What Makes Us Moral Agents: Philosophical Considerations

I am particularly grateful to Kennett for succinctly stating and thus emphasizing the bottom-line philosophical position toward which the arguments of my chapter have tended. To wit: "[T]he terms of the debate between rationalists and sentimentalists must be modified. Recent evidence on moral development from the social and cognitive sciences and from psychopathy does not endorse the philosophers' traditional distinction between the affective and the cognitive, or their attempts to locate morality wholly in one or other domain" (this volume, p. 259). Indeed, let me say again in my own voice that what matters for our being moral agents—that is, for being the sort of moral agents we are—is that we are reasoning creatures with a certain range of affectively determined concerns. Take away either the affective component or the reasoning component and you take away our capacity for moral agency. However, this statement, which is true in its way, is also somewhat misleading. It continues to suggest that these components are related in such a way that it might be possible to subtract one or the other of them; that it might be possible to find one "spared" and the other "impaired," say, in autism or psychopathy. This certainly has been one popular way of characterizing these disorders. Empirical investigation, however, shows that each of these disorders involves impairments of both reasoning and affect, albeit impairments of different sorts. This suggests that we should shift our theoretical focus away from making too much of the divide between reasoning and affect and toward understanding why particular impairments of reasoning are bound up with particular impairments of affect—and, beyond that, why particular cognitive-affective profiles seem particularly detrimental to moral agency (e.g., as in psychopathy), whereas others seem to be less so (e.g., as in autism).

That said, I see nothing wrong with the conceptual project of trying to clarify analytically what each of these components contributes to the making of a moral sensibility. Here again I am grateful to Kennett for stressing the difference between (1) the empirical project of understanding how human beings are psychologically structured to be aware of and responsive to morally charged situations (Kennett suggests this was Hume's primary concern) and (2) the conceptual-normative project of understanding what it means for an agent to take a situation as morally charged, as generating normative reasons for action, reasons of the form "I ought (morally) to φ" (Kennett suggests this was Kant's primary concern). Of course these projects are not unrelated, since the former must surely act as a kind of negative constraint on the latter. Whatever we think is conceptually necessary, psychologically speaking, for taking situations as morally charged had better be instantiated by those human beings we count as moral agents. However, it may be that those human beings we count as moral agents are only a subset of the possible psychological types. So one consequence of pursuing the conceptual-normative project is that we gain a better understanding of the range of moral-psychological possibilities, and with that a better understanding of the kinds of individuals we should count as genuine moral agents.

What, then, are the psychological requirements for seeing situations as morally charged? Here again I am sympathetic to Kennett's claim that it is not enough to have immediate desires or feelings (as animals might) that simply push and pull us about. That sort of psychology would make situations seem attractive or unattractive. Yet it would not allow for the kind of reflective and behavioral regulation that makes possible either (1) layering "I ought to φ" judgments (or cognates) over more immediate "I want to Ω" judgments (or cognates), which is required for moral evaluation; or (2) having "I ought to φ" judgments triumph over "I want to φ" judgments in producing action, which is required for moral behavior. By contrast, the kind of psychology that would allow for such feats of reflective regulation is one that according to Kennett incorporates a Kantian reverence for reason, which she takes to mean a regulating or limiting disposition to "seek and respond to normative considerations" (this volume, p. 260) or, alternatively, to "act in accordance with our reasons as we understand them" (this volume, p. 259). This kind of psychology would take situations in a normatively thick way, as generating reasons—what we might call regulative second thoughts—for thinking and acting in one way, even though our immediate desires, impulses, or feelings may sometimes pull us in a different direction altogether.

So far, so good. Now what precisely is involved in taking situations as generating reasons (regulative second thoughts) for us to act one way or another? One obvious point is that we must have certain look-ahead capacities, we must be able to calculate the consequences of doing (or not doing) different things. Yet that obviously is not enough. Even if we excelled at mapping out sets of consequences, we must be invested in certain particular outcomes for these calculations to eventuate in reasons to do (or not to do) the various things we contemplate. In a word, we must have future-directed ends—ends to which we are committed, ends that have the psychological power, therefore, of dictating what we ought to be doing, even sometimes against some current contrary impulses. Of course it stands to reason (hence, to the reason of reasoning agents) that the more coherent our ends, the stronger our reasons will be for or against doing any particular thing in the present. This is because the strength of our reasons will partly depend on their not speaking against one another—on their pulling as one in the same (or compatible) direction(s). Thus, so far as we are reasoning agents dispositionally structured to "seek and respond to normative considerations," it would not be surprising to find in us, in addition to the particular ends in which we invest, an interest in, or even a drive toward, making those ends as coherent as possible.

We now come to the nub of the issue: how to explain the fact of human beings coming to invest in particular future-directed ends, and especially in those ends that are relevant to moral agency. Kantians have traditionally emphasized reason as a critical component; Humeans (and other sentimentalists) have traditionally emphasized affect. In the spirit of rapprochement, I agree with Kennett that both are necessary. Investment in particular ends, whether short or long term, whether involving the self or involving others, is for us an affective phenomenon, and the degree of our investment indicates the strength of our feeling, our care, for those particular ends. However, I certainly agree that such feelings are not just the crude affective buzzes we may sometimes get in our moment-by-moment interactions with the world. Rather, they constitute a new level of feeling, shaped and reshaped by reflection, in light of experience and anticipation, and continually subject to the pressures of becoming part of a coherent profile. We could call such feelings "reflective feelings" in order to acknowledge the shaping role of reason. However, this is not to suggest that, phenomenologically speaking, such "reflective" feelings need be experienced as any less "hot," any less immediate, any less strong than their more basic counterparts. If anything, given their etiology, such feelings will have more staying power; they are not mere whims of the moment. More important, they will have a regulative authority that stems from the way they survive in us reflectively, as part of the process of reasoning about the ends toward which we are affectively drawn.

Our next question is, what are the ends relevant to moral agency? What sort of cares and concerns must we have in order to regulate our short- and long-term behavior according to "oughts" that have a recognizably moral flavor?

Obviously, as Maibom insists, concern or compassion for others must be of central importance. This striking feature of human psychology has been well researched under the omnibus rubric of "empathy." I think this term is unfortunate since there are a variety of cognitive-affective phenomena ambiguously designated by it. For instance, what is sometimes called "empathy" is not care or compassion for others at all, but rather perspective-taking skills, which, to my way of thinking, can support and enhance our concern for others but are not fundamental to the existence of such a concern. Research on psychopathy and autism has been particularly useful in emphasizing the need for some disentanglement, since both disorders have been characterized as involving impairments of empathy, although obviously these impairments are of very different types. In fact, I think theorists might be well advised to abandon the notion of empathy altogether as a well-defined (or definable) construct in cognitive research. Failing that, we need to exercise considerable caution in treating it as a unitary phenomenon usefully characterized as "spared" or "impaired." In any case, I have tried in my chapter to replace the notion of empathy with terminology that is no doubt still too crude, but which aims to be more precise in targeting the variety of concerns relevant to moral agency. So let me return now to a list of those concerns.

I begin, as I said, with care or compassion for others. I have speculated that this concern has its source in a distinct cognitive-affective system that develops naturally out of mechanisms responsible for early attachment and for the early recognition and attunement of emotions, but I agree that it is significantly enhanced by our more advanced perspective-taking skills. However, apart from this concern or compassion for particular others, I think there is another kind of concern for others that can sometimes look rather similar, namely, the concern that they be treated with the respect they deserve, given their place—or what ought to be their place—in the social order. Following Jonathan Haidt and other like-minded psychologists, I embrace the observation that many of our moral emotional responses are provoked by seeing individuals (including ourselves) undermining or supporting what we take to be the appropriate social order (guilt, shame, outrage, indignation, resentment, embarrassment, pride, complacency, and so on). Such emotional responses count as moral in this way of thinking because, as Haidt puts it, they have disinterested elicitors and disinterested action tendencies. In these cases, we react as we do, not because of our care or concern for particular others per se, but rather because we care about how individuals operate as social beings in a well-defined social structure. In a word, we care about the social structure in and of itself. We care that it is supported and maintained, and we are willing to punish and accept punishment when that social order is endangered or undermined. This strikes me as a different kind of concern from our care or compassion for particular others, and I speculate that it originates in quite a distinct affective-cognitive system, with its own particular phylogenetic and ontogenetic developmental history. Furthermore, although this concern is also supported and dramatically enhanced by our perspective-taking skills, I don't think such skills account for its existence any more than they do for the existence of our concern for particular others.

Does this exhaust the range of concerns that motivate specifically moral judgments and behavior? I have suggested not. Once we accept the idea that moral emotions should be functionally defined as emotional responses that have disinterested elicitors and disinterested action tendencies, then it seems clear that there is a range of such responses that manifest a concern for something even beyond the social order—a concern with maintaining something like what I have called cosmic structure and position. This is the concern that my commentators (both official and unofficial) have found most puzzling. This is not surprising because it's the one most underspecified in my chapter and so most in need of further elaboration and defense. This is a future project, but let me just mention a few considerations that favor the idea.

Many moral codes, perhaps more prominently in ancient and nonwestern cultures, have a number of prohibitions or exhortations about how to live in harmony with a universal order. The concept of such an order is of something impersonal and transcendent, a lawful way of being that governs the whole of the cosmos, including the workings of the natural world and all of the entities (gods, humans, or otherwise) that might exist within it. A nice example comes from the writings of Pythagoras: "*Themis* in the world of Zeus, and *Dike* in the world below, hold the same place and rank as *Nomos* in the cities of men; so that he who does not justly perform his appointed duty may appear as a violator of the whole order of the universe" (Cornford, 1957, p. 12). This idea of there being a morally relevant order in the universe is not unique to ancient Greece. It is also contained, for instance, in the ancient Egyptian concept of *Maat*, the Persian concept of *Asha*, the Chinese concept of the *Tao*, the Vedic Indian concept of *Rita*, as well as the Hindu concept of *Dharma*. In all of these traditions there is a moral imperative laid upon human beings to understand and follow the precepts of the universal way as these pertain to the peculiarities of human existence. Thus, there are specific prescriptions about how to organize one's daily routines and rituals, including how and what to eat, what to wear, how to bathe, how to treat others, and so on and so forth—all supposedly derived from a proper understanding of this universal order. Hence, I disagree with both Maibom and Kennett that the human preoccupation with cosmic structure and position is not especially conducive to adopting precepts with specifically moral content. If anything, many actions that are taken to fall outside the moral domain in some cultures (e.g., our own) are moralized by others precisely because of the way they prioritize this sort of concern (e.g., cleansing rituals, vegetarianism, or treating the environment in a certain way).

How, more specifically, should we characterize the affective-cognitive system in which our concern with cosmic structure and position is rooted? Why should we have such a concern in the first place? In my chapter I suggested that it stems from the need to locate ourselves in a spatiotemporal order of things. In my conception, this need parallels the need to locate ourselves in the social order of things and grows out of our uniquely human capacity to see the world (including ourselves) as extended in time. Now, it is interesting that even though Kennett doubts that the capacity for intertemporal perception is "specifically concerned with what most of us would take to be the content of human morality" (this volume, p. 261), she suggests that it may actually be fundamental to moral agency, since this is the capacity that allows us to conceptualize ends in the first place—ends in which we become affectively invested. I like this suggestion, but still I'm inclined to push it a bit further in order to explain why this inter-temporal capacity can lead to a substantively moral worldview. In my conception, while this capacity gives us certain abilities, it also creates in us a particular need; namely, the need to make sense of ourselves in the larger scheme of things and hence to "discover" (i.e., impose) a cosmic order on things, just as we "discover" (i.e., impose) a social order on our immediate interpersonal environment. Moreover, as in the social case, the "discovery" (i.e., imposition) of cosmic order will encourage the formation of many rituals and routines geared toward supporting and maintaining that order. Thus, we see throughout human history the birth of many substantive cosmic moral orders.

Now here's an interesting possibility: If this account is on the right track, then it may help clear up a phenomenon that is otherwise quite mysterious. Prima facie, our concern with particular others and our concern with social order have the most immediate moral content; but then doesn't it seem odd that such concerns are frequently and blatantly sacrificed for the sake of some greater good? What greater good could there be? My answer is: maintaining the cosmic order. Following Kennett's suggestion, I propose that the reason we are so committed to serving such an end has much to do with the fact that the affective-cognitive system in which this concern is rooted is fundamental, in evolutionary and developmental terms, to our very existence as moral agents. As a result, it has a kind of priority that cannot be easily overruled.

Before leaving the topic of the variety of affective concerns that I say go into the makings of a (typically human) moral sensibility, let me clear up one important source of confusion. Maibom, in her comments, worries that my proposal is too inclusive in the following sense: Many thoughts and actions that would count as morally motivated in my view are in fact deeply immoral by most intuitive measures. For instance, citing the evidence of the Milgram and Stanford prison experiments, she points out that our powerful drive to conform to social roles, perhaps out of an abiding concern for the social order, can lead us into "countless transgressions of ordinary human decency and competing moral norms" (this volume, p. 270).[1] Thus, Maibom questions whether it is really appropriate to count, for instance, our concern with social order as a genuine source of morality.

My response is that there seems to be an elision here between two different projects, and I'm grateful to Maibom for giving me the opportunity to disentangle the two. One project, which I take to be my own, is to explore what it takes to be any kind of moral agent at all, whether good or bad, i.e., the kind of agent that is an appropriate target for moral praise or blame. Such an agent, I claim, is one who must have certain capacities, both ratiocinative and affective, in order to be regulable by considerations that trump immediate and narrow self-interests. Such an agent must be capable of reasoning about ends toward which her activities tend, and she must be affectively invested in ends that make something other than her own well-being the focus of concern. A second project, reflected in Maibom's objection, is to consider what it takes for an agent to arrive at objectively correct moral judgments. What are the concerns an agent ought to have, or what should be the order among these concerns, for that agent to think and act in morally justified or praiseworthy ways? The latter project is concerned with delivering a substantive moral theory, whereas the former project is merely concerned with identifying the sorts of agents to whom such a moral theory could be appropriately addressed.

Now one might argue that unless an agent is moved to think and operate in accord with the correct substantive moral theory, she shouldn't count as a moral agent at all. This extreme view, which simply collapses the distinction between the immoral and the amoral, seems no more justified than an analogous view in the case of reasoning that would collapse the distinction between reasoning badly and not being in the game of reasoning at all. Of course, in the reasoning case, we can easily see that reasoning badly is an important phenomenon to investigate, especially from the perspective of understanding how the capacity for reasoning exposes less-than-ideal reasoners to certain kinds of liabilities that are entirely lacking in nonreasoning creatures. As George Eliot (echoing Hobbes) compellingly reminds us, it is "the power of generalising that gives men so much the superiority in mistake over the dumb animals" (Eliot, 1874/1996, p. 556). Likewise in the moral case, as I emphasize in my chapter, it is important to understand why our specifically moral interests and motives often drive us to acts of cruelty and destructiveness that have no place among the dumb animals.

Autism and Moral Agency: Conceptual and Empirical Considerations

Although my chapter in this volume was sparked by considering the problem of autistic moral agency, I will not say much on that topic here. In part this is because I agree so strongly with some of the points my commentators make, and in part because responding to certain other points would take me too far afield. For instance, in regard to the latter, de Vignemont and Frith make some fascinating remarks introducing a distinction between allocentric and egocentric representations of an agent's relationships with others, suggesting that both are involved in normal moral agency, but that the interaction between them has been "broken" in Asperger's syndrome. Consequently, individuals with this syndrome may display extreme egocentrism in their dealings with others, or extreme allocentrism (which I guess explains an apparently inflexible and disinterested commitment to rules, no matter what the consequences), but no shades of gray in between. That is to say, autistic individuals show little sign of motivating and modulating their rule following with the kind of egocentrically represented other-caring feelings that can be generated in particular situations because of how the plight of other affects the autistic person. In de Vignemont and Frith's account, it seems to be this sort of motivation and modulation that is necessary for genuinely moral behavior. As I said, I find this an interesting suggestion, but hesitate to comment in depth about how this proposal connects with my own without seeing a more detailed version. More mundane, I think, are the points on which I agree with de Vignemont and Frith, and I begin with these if only to bring the differences between our views into sharper focus.

As a way of introducing their own proposals, de Vignemont and Frith make the following summary claim: "it is misleading to characterize ASD as a lack of empathy associated with a preserved sense of morality" and, thus, explaining "the limitations in social and moral cognition in ASD patients require[s] a more subtle conceptual framework" (this volume, p. 277). Since this is precisely how I would summarize my own position, I take us to be engaged in similar kinds of exploratory conceptual projects, driven by the realization that received ways of characterizing autistic abnormalities are inadequate to what researchers are beginning to discover. Of course, we may have different views about the nature of the sophistications required: de Vignemont and Frith seem to favor a more purely cognitive approach to advancing our understanding of autistic motivation and behavior (i.e., by appealing to the need for a distinction between different types of representation), whereas I have suggested a need to develop our views in both affective and cognitive dimensions (i.e., by broadening our understanding of the range of concerns relevant to moral life and by seeing how these may be differently affected through an unusual profile of cognitive assets and deficits). Still, we agree on both these aspects of their negative claim: that autism should not be characterized as involving an "impaired" capacity for empathy, and/or a "spared" capacity for moral agency. Nevertheless, are the reasons for our agreement the same?

I have already voiced my own objection to any continued and unqualified use of the omnibus and ambiguous notion of empathy, so here just let me reiterate that it's precisely the kind of data that de Vignemont and Frith cite in connection with autism (and also psychopathy) that forces theorists to develop more precise theoretical constructs adequate to the task of distinguishing among the kinds of abnormalities manifested by these different populations; e.g., cognitive impairments in perspective-taking skills (as found in autism) versus impairments in at least some aspects of base-level affective responsiveness (as found in psychopathy). Perhaps it would be acceptable to retain the notion of empathy as long as theorists distinguish carefully enough between what de Vignemont and Frith refer to as the "cognitive and affective components of empathetic behaviors." This seems to be the preferred strategy adopted so far in the literature (for a review, see Hansman-Wijnands & Hummelen, 2006). However, I don't favor it myself because I think it encourages a tendency to characterize each of these components now as straightforwardly "spared" or "impaired." My bet is that this will also prove to be an unhelpful over-simplification insofar as normal empathetic development depends on the normal development of perspective-taking skills, and vice versa. Consequently, in my own positive account I have preferred simply to acknowledge that autistic individuals are, at some basic level, responsive to others' emotions, and then try to use this fact to account in part for the regulative concerns discernible in their reflection and in their activities.

Now what about the claim that autistic individuals show a "preserved sense of morality"? Once again, I agree with de Vignemont and Frith that this claim is misleading, and for many of the reasons they cite. As I point out in my chapter, autism is a spectrum disorder with individuals varying widely in terms of abilities and disabilities, even without factoring in issues of comorbidity; and for the very disabled end of the spectrum, it seems clear that no question of moral agency sensibly arises. What about those individuals who are relatively high functioning, i.e., where their autism is not associated with widespread and generally debilitating cognitive impairments? Here, too, I have argued in agreement with de Vignemont and Frith

that we need to be careful in attributing this to a "spared" moral sensibility, since behaviors that appear to be characteristic of moral judgment and
moral motivation may be underpinned by rather different kinds of cognitive and/or affective processes. (This indeed was my point in observing
that merely "passing" contrived theory-of-mind tests is no indication of a
"spared" theory-of-mind capacity, since very able individuals may use
compensating cognitive strategies for "hacking out" a correct solution to
these sorts of problems—strategies which, by the way, do not fare so well
in more naturalistic settings.) Thus, I agree that even though we see in
many autistic individuals a drive to discover and follow various sorts of
rules operative in our society, it remains an open question as to whether
this drive indicates any deep understanding of why we have such rules,
especially in those cases where typically developing individuals would
understand the rules to have a specifically moral character. For many
autistic individuals, I anticipate the answer would be "no," but surely not
for all, as indicated by the anecdotal evidence of autistic self-report.

Is the evidence sufficient for reaching this sort of conclusion? Of course
I agree with de Vignemont and Frith that speculations are not the same as
conclusions based on broad-ranging and systematic studies. There are
certain things we cannot say without having a great deal more data; for
example, we cannot say much in a general way about autistic rule following. Still, general conclusions are not the only ones worth making. If my
arguments are persuasive about what constitutes a moral sensibility, then
as long as the reported self-reflections of someone like Temple Grandin are
indeed her own reflections (and not, for instance, ghost written by someone
else), it seems we have all the evidence we need to conclude that at least
some high-functioning individuals with autism have a variety of moral
sensibility. Would I call this sense of morality "intact" or "preserved"?
Once again, my preference is not to use terms like these simply because,
to my ear anyway, they imply something like normal functioning, and, as
far as we can judge from the anecdotal evidence, autistic moral sensibility
(where it exists at all) is quite unlike the moral sensibility found in typically developing individuals.

In sum, my views are perhaps not so distant from de Vignemont and
Frith's as their commentary suggests. However, there are some critical
points on which we do substantively disagree, and I would like to conclude
by mentioning three of these. The first two, which involve only quick
observations, bear on de Vignemont and Frith's conception of what constitutes a moral sensibility. The third point requires somewhat fuller elaboration because it involves their interpretation of certain data. All in all,

however, these remarks tend in the same direction, namely, toward more optimism than de Vignemont and Frith yet evince about the possibility of autistic moral agency.

What does it mean to be possessed of a moral sensibility, according to de Vignemont and Frith? One thing they explicitly mention is the ability to recognize, and of course respond to, violations of moral, as distinct from conventional, norms. But what are moral violations? They identify such violations with acts that lead to others' suffering, but immediately qualify that equation by saying that the suffering so caused must not be morally justified. My first point of criticism is that this account of moral violations is circular. It doesn't tell us how to recognize moral violations unless we already have a sense of what it is for certain acts to be morally justified. The second criticism is related. If some acts that cause suffering in others are morally justified, then this means that there are concerns other than concerns about others' suffering that are morally relevant, concerns by reference to which these acts are presumably justified. Thus, de Vignemont and Frith owe us a fuller account, even on their own terms, of the range of concerns properly involved in the manifestation of a genuine moral sensibility. Once these have been articulated, de Vignemont and Frith may actually find that the normative preoccupations observed in autistic individuals are to some degree manifestations of such concerns, arguing in favor of these individuals possessing a genuine variety of moral sensibility despite their somewhat attenuated understanding of others' suffering.

The third criticism that I want to make bears on de Vignemont and Frith's interpretation of some data relevant to the question of why autistic individuals comply with certain norms. As background to this point, let me be clear that we all agree that some moral offenses are offenses because they cause (morally unjustified) suffering in others, and equally we all agree that autistic individuals can be quite reliable in complying with norms that prohibit such harms. However, de Vignemont and Frith suggest that when autistic individuals comply with those norms, they most likely comply for the wrong reasons: not because of a true sense of suffering that those affected undergo, but rather because of a sort of unreflective norm worship—rule following for rule following's sake. As I have said, I don't rule out this possibility, but I worry that de Vignemont and Frith may be embracing this conclusion a little too quickly given their interpretation of some recent studies.

Consider their reaction to Blair's 1996 study indicating that autistic individuals (unlike psychopaths) are able to make the moral-conventional distinction much like normal controls, thereby seeming to demonstrate an understanding of the moral import of certain norms (R.J.R. Blair, 1996). De Vignemont and Frith worry that because the subjects were only asked about the permissibility, the seriousness, and the authority jurisdiction of norm violations, the study is limited in what it can show. Specifically, it fails to rule out the possibility that autistic individuals have simply cottoned on to the fact that some transgressions are worse than others without truly understanding why. Other studies support such a possibility. For instance, Shamay-Tsoory and colleagues have shown that autistic individuals can be quite good at detecting when someone makes a faux pas, but they evince no understanding of why a faux pas is bad; i.e., according to de Vignemont and Frith, they evince no understanding that faux pas cause others distress (Shamay-Tsoory, Tomer, Yaniv, & Aharon-Peretz, 2002).[2] This concern may be further supported by reference to Temple Grandin's own case, where, in good anthropological style, she explicitly notes that some norm violations (which all involve social taboos) are treated more seriously than others, and despite the fact that she fails to understand the "logic" behind these prohibitions, she is committed to avoiding such "sins of the system."

Now I agree that these sorts of examples provide evidence for claiming that autistic individuals have (1) an interest in detecting and following different kinds of rules no matter what the rationale, and (2) an incapacity to understand why (typical) human beings should care about making or following at least some of these rules. However, I don't see that they support the stronger claim that autistic individuals are not capable of understanding the moral significance of some norms as far as this relates to harming others. Certainly Grandin herself is sensitive to the special quality of certain norms—for instance, against stealing, destroying property, and injuring other people. Even from a very young age she put these into a separate category from her so-called sins of the system.

Likewise, the faux pas study does not really support the idea of global autistic insensitivity to the wrongness of harming others. After all, even though others may suffer as a consequence of faux pas, there are really two counts on which one would not expect any deep understanding of this on the part of autistic individuals. The first is that faux pas usually involve norm violations having to do with respect for privacy, for social standing, or for some other aspect of social life to which autistic individuals are quite oblivious (cf. Grandin's failure to understand the rationale for certain social taboos, her "sins of the system"). The second count is that insofar as faux pas cause suffering, the sort of suffering in question is usually more psychological than straightforwardly physical, consisting in a range of highly developed social emotions—guilt, shame, embarrassment, and the like—that autistic individuals have little experience of themselves and difficulty detecting in others. Thus, autistic individuals may well be insensitive to the specific phenomena of harms caused in certain situations, but this, to echo Jeanette Kennett's earlier claims, says more about their incompetence as moral agents than it does about their being out of the game of moral reflection and regulation altogether.

Notes

1. Maibom also raises some interesting questions about the morally questionable phenomenon of obedience. I agree with her that the evidence shows that typically human beings are psychologically geared to defer to authority and that such deference is a mixed blessing. Clearly it makes us capable of living together in social groups, conforming to expectations without the need for a lot of heavy-duty threats or other mechanisms of compliance. However, such deference also has a downside, as the Milgram and Stanford prison experiments make clear. Yet how is all this connected with moral agency? I think there is no simple answer to this question because following rules, or deferring to authority, can clearly be done in different ways (as I indicated in my discussion of autistic rule following). For instance, one might defer to a rule or to some authority "mindlessly," as we might say; that is, one just automatically defers, no matter what (some autistic rule following may fall into this category). In my view, this is not the stuff of morally agential behavior, and perhaps what these experiments show is that even typically developed human beings are all too ready to abjure any semblance of such behavior.

However, when it comes to obedience, there are also other possibilities. Perhaps one defers on a particular occasion because one thinks it's the "right" thing to do. Now we are getting into the area of morally agential behavior, but this too comes in degrees. For instance, one might think something is the right thing to do because someone in authority said so, and the right thing to do is to defer unquestioningly to authority. This is clearly less agential than thinking one ought to defer to authority on some occasion because that authority has better access to determining what is independently the right thing to do. Alternatively, also more agentially, one might defer to authority on some occasion because that authority happens to dictate what one independently thinks is the right thing to do. Or one might defer to authority on some occasion because one independently values the sort of social structure in which authority is paid a certain amount of deference (within limits). I mention all these possibilities simply to emphasize the point that the relationship between obedience and moral agency is not straightforward, raising a host of interesting issues that are somewhat orthogonal to the main themes of my chapter and deserve far greater attention than I can give them here.

2. Are faux pas appropriately seen as wrong because they cause distress? I myself am sceptical of this analysis. I suspect that what makes such acts wrong is that they transgress socially accepted norms, and that whatever pain they cause is not primarily a function of the acts in and of themselves but instead a function of the fact that these acts are seen to be socially transgressive. In other words, faux pas are instrumentally rather than constitutively distressing insofar as their distress-causing properties are contingent upon an individual's understanding and acceptance of the social norms they transgress.

6 | Morality and Its Development

Jerome Kagan

One of the most significant features of our species is the ability to acquire symbolic representations that treat physically distinctive events as components of the same concept. The most precocious chimpanzee would not regard the skin of a banana and the bark of a tree as members of a common category. Because all concepts are constructions of a mind, rather than events in the world, there is usually debate regarding the meanings of these representations. The ancient Greeks brooded on the meaning of *paideia*; medieval Christians debated the meaning of papal authority; eighteenth-century naturalists debated the validity of the phlogiston theory. The controversies surrounding these concepts were either settled or ceased to be relevant as history moved on to new questions. However, the meanings of the paired concepts "good" and "bad," which are the semantic foundation of the more abstract term "morality," have always been, and continue to be, nodes of disagreement. This statement does not mean that these semantic terms define morality, only that they are its semantic components.

Humans cannot ignore these concepts because all individuals want to regard the self as "good." This salient motive presses continually for gratification. After each person satisfies the urgent biological states created by hunger, thirst, and pain, and the psychological desires for safety, sensory delight, and the acknowledgment of their existence by select others, the wish to regard the self as good, and to avoid compromise in that judgment, controls a great deal of behavior during most days. Frustration of this motive generates strong emotions that disturb the quality of consciousness required for the day's tasks and the serenity to which each person is entitled when those responsibilities have been met.

To What Does the Term "Moral" Refer?

Humans act in order to experience two distinctly different psychological states. One is a feeling that originates in changes in one or more of the sensory modalities, including an increase in pleasant excitation, as in sweet tastes, or a decrease in excitation, as occurs with the relief of pain. This motive for varied sensory states is present in all animals.

The second desired state, which is unique to humans and has its origin in thought rather than in sensation, involves the relation between a person's representations of his moral standards and his actions, feelings, or thoughts. The term "representation" refers to all of the mind's knowledge; moral standards are one type of representation. On the one hand, humans wish to avoid situations in which there is an inconsistency between their standards and their actions or intentions because those inconsistencies create an unpleasant state of uncertainty, shame, guilt, or anxiety. On the other hand, individuals also try to act in ways that create consonance between their representations of ideal, desirable states and their behaviors, thoughts, or feelings. When consonance occurs, the person momentarily experiences a feeling one might call "enhanced virtue." Economists ignore the distinction between the states of sensory pleasure and a state of consonance with a standard because these phenomena resist quantification at present. Thus, economists simply declare that all economic decisions are based on the desire to maximize satisfaction and leave to their readers the difficult task of detecting the meaning of satisfaction.

It is easier to compose sense definitions of "moral" than to stipulate the referents for a person's representations of the concepts good and bad. (The definitions of "good" and "bad" are reserved for a later discussion.) The adjective "moral" can be applied to different concepts: actions, intentions, judgments, feelings, consequences for others, and the self.

This chapter assumes that persons apply the adjective "moral" to a holistic representation of self, which includes the person's features, feelings, actions, and intentions. Unlike eye color or gender, application of the adjective "moral" to the self varies from hour to hour, day to day, and year to year. This judgment always depends on the relation between the agent's acts, thoughts, and feelings, on the one hand, and the standards linked to these representations, where "standard" refers to the ideal form of the actions, thoughts, and feelings the self believes he or she ought to express or command.

The Development of Morality

As children grow, they follow a universal sequence of stages in the development of morality (Kagan & Lamb, 1987). The first stage, seen during the first year, does not fit the definition of moral given here because infants are not consciously aware of the self and have no symbolic categories for this concept. Infants learn through conditioning mechanisms that certain behaviors are followed by some form of punishment. This first phase of moral development resembles the state of a puppy trained to lie down in response to a command.

The later stages do fit our definition. The next phase, usually seen by the second birthday, is characterized by a display of facial expressions or postures that suggest a state of uncertainty in situations that present temptations to violate a standard of action, even though the child may have never been punished for that act. For example, some 2-year-olds and almost all 3-year-olds will hesitate if a parent asks them in a gentle voice to pour prune juice on a clean tablecloth, an act that violates the family standard. Even though the child had never shown this behavior and could not have been punished for it, and the parent is requesting the child to conform, the child refuses. This refusal implies that the child possesses a concept of prohibited actions. A second example is seen when 2-year-olds are in a room of toys, some of which have had their integrity flawed (for example, a shirt with a missing button or a toy car with a missing wheel). Most children are attracted to the flawed objects and indicate through speech or posture that something is wrong by saying "yukky" or "boo-boo." Recognition of the flaw in the object's integrity indicates that the child has acquired an initial representation of the proper, or good, form for that object. A child who says "yukky" to a flawed truck that he did not break must have inferred that another person, or force, violated its integrity (Kagan, 1981). Parents from diverse cultures recognize that before the third birthday children become aware of standards for behavior. The Utku Eskimo who live in Hudson Bay call this awareness "ihuma"; those living on atolls in the Fiji chain call it "vakayalo" (Kagan, 1981, 1984).

The ability to infer causes is correlated with the ability to infer the thoughts and feelings of another person and contributes to a feeling of empathy. Laboratory experiments reveal that 2-year-olds are capable of making inferences. If an examiner places a trio of toys in front of a child, two of which have familiar names (for example, a doll and ball), but the third is unfamiliar, and the examiner says, "Give me the zoob," the child picks up the unfamiliar object. This response means that the child inferred that the unfamiliar word spoken by the examiner must refer to the unfamiliar object. Because all 2-year-olds have experienced the unpleasant feeling that follows being hurt, chastised, or teased, they are able to infer those psychological states in others. Hence, children are biologically prepared to restrain actions that might harm another. I believe that this restraint is acquired by every child, even if no aggressive action had ever been punished. A lowering of the head and a flushing of the face can also follow violation of a standard. This feeling, called "shame," requires the inference that another person might be entertaining a critical evaluation of oneself (Lewis, 1992).

The next phase, which usually occurs by the end of the third year, involves understanding the semantic concepts good and bad and applying these terms to objects, events, other people, and the self. It is now time to consider the meanings of "good" and "bad." The philosopher G. E. Moore (1903) argued that these meanings are given intuitively and cannot be defined objectively. Most citizens, and a majority of philosophers, are unhappy with this permissiveness and have tried to construct rational definitions with fixed referents. The varied solutions agree that the term "good" can apply to four distinct classes of events: the receipt of praise or affection; the avoidance of pain and punishment as well as feelings of anxiety, shame, or guilt; semantic consistency between one's actions and standards; and finally, sensory delight. The word "bad," by contrast, refers to criticism, anticipation of pain or punishment, semantic inconsistency between actions and standards, and sensory displeasure. It is unlikely that the different events called good or bad share any common biological state. The primary feature shared by these diverse events is their semantic label. Wittgenstein used the concept "game" to make the same point.

Once children have acquired the concepts good and bad, they apply them to their selves and oscillate with respect to their judgment, depending upon their behavior and experience during the past hours or days. One mother who found her 3-year-old boy pinching himself asked why he was doing it. He replied, "I don't like myself." This boy happened to be a bully in the neighborhood and was aware that his peers and their parents disapproved of him. Chronic sexual abuse can persuade a child that he or she is unredeemably bad. A very small proportion of these children can become excessively aggressive. One 11-year-old British girl who murdered two preschool boys she did not know had been sexually abused by her mother's male clients and was aware that her father was a criminal (Sereny, 1998). Because the girl had categorized herself as bad, she could murder without the passion of anger or the desire for material gain because she was being loyal to her category for her self.

The next stage, seen between 3 and 6 years of age, is characterized by a feeling of guilt following violation of a standard. Guilt cannot occur earlier because younger children are not cognitively able to relate a past event to the present and to appreciate that an action that harmed a person or object could have been suppressed. The integration of past with present, and the recognition that the self could have behaved otherwise, requires the maturation of brain circuits that permit these cognitive advances. The ability to relate the present moment to what happened in the past motivates children to wonder about causal relations between events. Hence, when a child harms a person or damages property, she relates that event to a prior intention or impulsive behavior and becomes vulnerable to a feeling of remorse. If the child appreciates that she could have suppressed the act that violated a standard, she is likely to feel guilty.

Most psychologists distinguish between the standards that are called conventional and those regarded as morally binding. Violation of a conventional standard is less often accompanied by guilt because children recognize that the standard is arbitrary and its violation would not be regarded as bad if adults had not decided to disapprove of its display. Three obvious examples are wearing a hat at the dinner table, eating with one's fingers, and failing to say "thank you" for a gift. By contrast, most children believe that unprovoked aggression toward another, deceiving a close friend, and indifference to the distressed state of a relative who needs help violate an absolute standard, and their violation often creates guilt. Even if adults in authority proclaimed that these behaviors were permissible, children would still regard them as bad. However, membership in the categories of conventional and moral is not timeless and has validity only during a particular historical era. History can change a conventional standard to a moral one or produce the reverse sequence. For example, at the turn of the twentieth century many American college students regarded avoiding the use of insulting racial or ethnic comments as a conventional standard. Most contemporary college students regard this avoidance as morally binding. Many nineteenth-century Americans regarded a wife's adulterous affair as a violation of a moral standard; today an extramarital affair is viewed by many Americans as violating a conventional standard. The Athenians of 400 B.C. regarded loyalty to the city as morally binding; contemporary Greeks treat this attitude as conventional.

The next stage in a child's development, observed between 5 and 10 years of age, is characterized by an understanding of the abstract concepts of fairness and the ideal. The profound maturational changes in the brain between 5 and 7 years of age are accompanied by the ability to relate an event to the larger context in which it appears and to sort events on more than one characteristic (Kagan & Hershkowitz, 2005). These advances are part of Piaget's stage of "concrete operations" (Piaget, 1952). School-age children believe that the severity of a punishment should match the seriousness of the crime and that task assignments should be adjusted to match the abilities of the individual. The emergence of a concern with fairness may have a partial origin in the more basic notion of "appropriate for the situation," which could originate in the many occasions children must adjust their behaviors to fit a situation. Children learn that they should speak louder in a noisy environment; exert greater force in picking up a heavy, compared with a light, object; and adjust their concentration to fit the difficulty of the task.

Children older than 6 years also imagine ideal, or perfect, forms. It is easy to explain how a child might learn that lying, stealing, and destruction of property are bad and will be punished. It is harder to explain how children construct the ideal form of a performance or act of courage because most children do not witness or attain the ideal and therefore cannot be praised for its display. At least two independent processes contribute to the construction of ideals. First, children note which characteristics are praised by their community and infer the more perfect forms of those characteristics, as well as the perfect forms of features that are the opposite of those criticized. A second contribution to the construction of an ideal relies on appreciating the difficulty of attaining a particular state. Mathematicians claim that the difficulty of apprehending a new solution is a critical feature of proofs that are deemed beautiful. The 10-year-old has learned that receiving a grade of 100 on every school quiz is praiseworthy but difficult. The adolescent knows that continued poise with strangers, refusing a temptation, and performing an unpleasant obligation are admired but difficult. Thus, individuals who possess, or who are believed to possess, desirable qualities that are difficult to acquire are idealized.

There is probably a biological contribution to a small number of idealized qualities. Infants prefer sweet tastes to sour ones; consonant chords to dissonant ones; circular patterns to linear designs; symmetry to asymmetry; and the color red to the color blue. The attraction to particular physical features in humans can be traced partly to a biological preference for relatively symmetrical, unblemished faces and particular body proportions. Local mores are always relevant; the seventeenth-century Dutch liked chubbier women than the twentieth-century Dutch. Thus, biology and experience are interlaced in the creation of representations of perfection. These representations lie waiting for encounters with those who possess the ideal features. Sadly, when an ideal state is attained, some individuals are likely to abandon it and select another. The enemy of every ideal is its attainment.

The construction of ideals shares features with the acquisition of grammar. Parents criticize children for statements that are factually incorrect but rarely criticize a grammatically incorrect sentence. Children acquire the grammar of their language by inferring the correct form from the speech they hear. The child's ability to imagine the perfect parent, soccer player, or friend, despite the lack of direct encounters with such individuals, requires a more mature prefrontal cortex able to generate thoughts of what is possible and semantic networks containing nodes for ideal forms.

Social Categories

School-age children also acquire the social categories to which the self belongs. Some of these categories are nominal. Nominal categories have fixed features. The ethical obligations attached to them apply to all members of the category. Gender and developmental stage are nominal categories for all children; religion and ethnicity can become nominal categories for some. Adults add nominal categories for their social class, vocation, and nationality. In the case of the latter, some obligations, like serving in the armed forces, do not apply to all members. A category is psychologically distinctive if it is selective and many in the community are not members of the category. The more distinctive the category, the more salient its psychological power.

Relational categories, by contrast, are defined by a particular relationship between the person and others. These include the categories of friend, son, daughter, sibling, wife, husband, parent, lover, employee, and teammate. The ethical obligations are to a specific person or persons and usually call for loyalty, affection, honesty, and nurture.

The distinction between nominal and relational categories is an instance of a more general principle in cognitive development. The child's first categorizations—dogs, cups, and eat—are based on a fixed set of features and/or functions shared by groups of objects, animals, people, or actions. Children must be cognitively more mature to understand that the meanings of relational categories, like left-right or big-small, are not fixed and can vary with the setting. A dog is bigger than a mouse but smaller than a lion. The refrigerator is to the right of the sink but to the left of the oven. Similarly, the category of friend applies to a specific other person, and the ethical obligations to one friend may be different from those that apply to a different peer.

Each nominal and relational category is linked to a set of obligatory actions and intentions. Boys have learned that they should not display excessive fear in times of danger. Some boys who have never done so are loyal to that obligation. If a child believes a category is appropriate for its self, and in addition experiences a vicarious emotion appropriate to someone in the category who has an experience with emotional implications, psychologists say the child is identified with that person or category. A Hispanic child who feels proud when a Hispanic is elected governor is identified with his ethnic category.

Children cannot avoid attempts to maintain semantic consistency among the features of the categories to which they belong and the evaluation of actions appropriate to the category. Uncertainty occurs if the child interprets a behavior as inconsistent with his category. The human brain reacts to semantic inconsistency. Every English-speaking adult shows a special waveform in the event-related potential of the EEG if he hears the sentence, "The woman is a banana," because the last word is inconsistent with the first four (Kagan, 2002). The behaviors we call "moral" are maintained, not only by anxiety over criticism or punishment and the anticipation of shame or guilt, but also by this form of uncertainty.

Egalitarian societies, like the United States, attach greater significance to moral standards linked to the relational categories because nominal categories imply differential status and privilege. Egalitarian societies do not want individuals to feel proud simply because they are members of a nominal category. In order to extract virtue from a relational category, the person must carry out the obligatory actions. Egalitarian societies want their citizens to feel more virtuous because of how they behave with others, and not because they are members of a particular ethnic, religious, or vocational group. A priest, physician, and teacher are allowed to feel good at the end of the day because of their benevolent ministrations to others, and not because of their achieved status.

The Bases for Ethical Obligations

Two factors contribute to the power of nominal and relational categories to contribute to a conception of the self as moral. The child's first words apply to objects and events with relatively fixed features, like milk, food, and eat. All objects called dogs should bark, have fur, and be playful. If they do not, they are less than ideal dogs. Thus, when children learn the names for nominal categories, like boy, adolescent, or Catholic, they are prepared to believe that these words, too, name a set of psychological characteristics that apply to members of the category. Children believe they ought to be loyal to the characteristics of the categories to which they belong and experience as much dissonance if they stray from these obligations as they would if they saw a four-footed animal without fur who never barked but nonetheless was called a dog.

A second basis for the moral power of social categories is that membership can enhance a person's feeling of virtue. Many residents of Boston in the late 1830s were proud of their municipal category because they knew that other Americans regarded their city as the hub of the young nation. Far fewer current Boston residents feel virtuous simply because they live in this urban setting, rather than in New York or Chicago, despite the recent championships of the Boston Red Sox and the New England Patriots. Thus, two different processes motivate children to be loyal to the moral requirements linked to their social categories: the conviction that the category is a real thing whose properties should be preserved and the sense of enhanced virtue that can accompany membership in the category.

Some social categories that were awarded virtue in the past have lost some of their moral potency because the virtue gained from membership in the past has been diluted. The amount of variation in the features displayed by those within a category modulates the strength of the imperatives linked to the category's obligations. The less varied the members of the category, the stronger the motive to be loyal to its ethical obligations. Contemporary Americans are informed by the media that some mothers abandon their children; fathers desert their families; teachers and doctors go on strike; scientists make up evidence; workers call in sick when they aren't; corporate executives lie and steal; priests abuse young boys; and 60-year-old men wearing sneakers and blue jeans divorce their wives of 30 years to consort with 25-year-old single women. The broad advertisement of these violations dilutes the coherence of the category and the power to create guilt in those who violate the standards linked to their category. A serious change in the understanding of the category "bird" would occur if there were an increase in the number of birds that neither sang nor flew.

Social categories can also lose their ethical potency if membership no longer awards virtue to its members. Many white Americans feel morally bound to acknowledge the dignity of citizens of color; Christians must acknowledge the sacredness and spirituality of those belonging to other religions. Hence, the categories of white and Christian have become less potent sources of virtue than they were before the Civil War. America's desire to be egalitarian, which I and a majority of Americans celebrate, requires denying a feeling of privilege to categories that two centuries earlier were sources of virtue. Nineteenth-century, white Christian males whose parents and grandparents were born in America could reassure their selves of their virtue simply by recognizing they were members of this category. The rebellion against this basis for smug satisfaction with the self, which accelerated in the late 1960s, denies this prize to any social category. Every American must attain his or her supply of virtue through behavior and accomplishment.

Because most persons believe the accumulation of wealth requires effort and talent, this prize seems to be a possibility for most citizens. By contrast, gaining admission to an elite college or studying the cello with a master seems easier for particular class groups. Thus, Americans have made material wealth a primary index of virtue. No goal as glittering as equality of dignity can be had without a price.

Critics of American society note its excessive concern with money. Although this motive was also present in colonial times, it has become an obsession. The preoccupation with the material is understandable if we acknowledge the community's commitment to awarding more dignity to members of economically disadvantaged, ethnic minorities. When Americans realized that public schools were failing the children of the poor, the earlier, optimistic premise that attainment of an education and, later, upward mobility were possible for all with talent and motivation lost some validity. Furthermore, many citizens were reluctant to use academic failure in children as a sign of an ethical flaw in their parents. If outstanding academic achievement was more likely for children born to parents living in clean, quiet, middle-class suburbs, it was not fair to blame poor children for events that were beyond their control. The replacement of the traditional symbols of virtue by the acquisition of wealth has allowed many, but not all, to harbor the belief, some might say the illusion, that this concrete sign of personal worth is attainable. This change in the evaluation of money has had some benevolent consequences. America has become more tolerant of its ethnic minorities, and urban disturbances motivated by ethnic tensions occur less often. Perhaps a celebration of wealth is the price America must pay to enjoy a reduction in social tension. There are no free lunches.

One consequence of the loss of the moral power of social categories has been an increased reliance on a person's feelings of pleasure and satisfaction, rather than the feelings of others, as a criterion for selecting behaviors or goals that might enhance virtue. Our culture cooperates by reminding everyone of Jefferson's declaration that happiness is a right. I suggest that many infer that trying to be happy is a moral obligation. "To be happy" is the answer most American adolescents give to the question, "What do you want from life?" This imperative requires a weakening of the ethical constraints linked to relational categories. Although most persons feel freer when relational categories lose their power, many remain vulnerable to uncertainty over the ethical goals they should pursue. It took only five centuries for western Europeans to replace enhanced spirituality as the ethical goal one should pursue, first with rationality and later with sensory delight. Although Adam Smith urged self-interest 250 years ago, a careful reading of his writings reveals that he expected everyone to want the approval of friends and neighbors. That motivation guaranteed civility and conformity to social norms. Smith could not have anticipated that so many in this century would be indifferent to the attitudes of neighbors and treat the opinions of others as imposing no constraints on what the self does.

The ethical obligations attached to relational categories have also been weakened by dissemination of biological research, provoked by Darwin's ideas, telling the public that humans are close relatives of apes. Many contemporary adults have been persuaded that they share important psychological features with other primates. This movement, called sociobiology, claims that the facts of evolution imply that humans are prepared by their genes to be self-interested and motivated to maximize their own status, pleasure, and reproductive potential. Scientific evidence has become the arbiter of many moral issues: Is an embryo living? Is violence on television bad for children? Does affirmative action have a benevolent effect on the education of minority students? However, it is an error to assume that any human ethic is an obvious derivative of any class of animal behavior. A concern with right and wrong, guilt, and the desire to feel virtuous are unique human properties that are discontinuous with any animal property.

Some sociobiologists assume that animals are capable of altruism and defend an evolutionary basis for these behaviors. However, "altruistic," as a descriptor for a human behavior, emphasizes the fact that the agent is aware of the need of another and has a conscious intention to be of assistance. When "altruism" is applied to animals, it refers only to behaviors that might benefit another. Biologists cannot theorize about the intentions of mice or monkeys; hence they categorize as altruistic any act that benefits another. This strategy awards a special meaning to the term "altruistic." If someone puts an old television set in the trash and a poor passerby takes the television set home for personal use, the former has not committed an altruistic act, even though the latter benefited. Even if a person's action did not help another, it could be regarded as altruistic. An adult who jumps in a cold lake to save a child but because of incompetence drowns both of them has committed an altruistic act because the adult's intention was benevolent. Many parents with altruistic motives toward their children behave in ways that do not benefit the child. The central semantic feature of the network for human altruism is not the outcome of an action, but a behavior preceded by an intention to help someone perceived to be in need.

Each person holds a number of moral standards that permit him or her to decide without delay what action to implement when there is a choice. However, most individuals are silent if they are asked to provide a foundation for the decision. The inability to justify one's moral intuitions with more than the phrase, "It feels right," generates unease. As a result, persons or groups that raise their hand to announce they can supply an answer to the question, "Why do I believe this is right?" are celebrated. The church was an effective source of justification for Europeans for over 1,500 years until the public placed science in the position of the judge of what is right or wrong, for many Americans believe that the facts of nature should provide the rationale for resolving some human moral dilemmas. The problem, however, is that humans are selfish and generous, aloof and empathic, hateful and loving, dishonest and honest, disloyal and loyal, cruel and kind, arrogant and humble. Most persons feel a little guilt over an excessive display of the first member of each of those seven pairs. The resulting emotion is uncomfortable, and humans are eager to have it ameliorated. Confession to a priest or psychotherapy is effective for some if the priest or therapist is respected. I suspect that some people feel a little better when they learn from television and the newspapers that their less social motives are natural consequences of their relationship to apes. The current high status of the biological sciences has made it possible for evolutionary biologists to serve as therapists to these individuals.

Temperament and Morality

Although this chapter is concerned primarily with universals in the development of morality, there is variation in the degree to which individuals experience anxiety, shame, guilt, or dissonance following violations of a standard. Kochanska and her colleagues have found that fearful toddlers show stronger signs of conscience at age 5 than do fearless ones (Kochanska, 1997; Kochanska, Tjebkes, & Forman, 1998; Kochanska, Coy, & Murray, 2001; Kochanska, Gross, Lin, & Nichols, 2002).

My work on temperamental biases in young children is relevant to this issue. Although all children are capable of feeling uncertainty, anxiety, fear, shame, empathy, and guilt, they vary in the frequency and intensity of those emotions. Some of this variation, but not all, is the result of a child's temperament. The term "temperament" refers to heritable variation in profiles of behavior and mood that emerge early in development (Kagan, 1994). I suspect that many, but not all, temperaments are the result of heritable variation in the concentration of the more than 150 molecules that affect brain function, together with the density and location of their receptors. Because there is a large number of possible neurochemical profiles, there will be many temperaments.

Two temperamental categories that have been studied extensively refer to a young child's typical reactions to unfamiliar events, objects, or situations. Some children become emotionally restrained, cautious, and avoidant; others are spontaneous and usually approach the unfamiliar. Children who are consistently shy, timid, or avoidant with unfamiliar people, objects, or situations because of an inherited temperamental bias are called "inhibited." Children who are sociable and approach the unfamiliar because of their temperament are called "uninhibited." Variation in the excitability of the amygdala, owing to a neurochemical profile, contributes to these two temperaments because one important function of the amygdala is to respond to unexpected or discrepant events (Kagan, 1994; Kagan & Snidman, 2004).

My colleagues and I have been studying the infant characteristics that predict inhibited or uninhibited behavior in the second year. Infants born with a neurochemistry that renders their amygdala excitable to unfamiliarity should show high levels of motor activity and more frequent crying when they are presented with unfamiliar events. Infants born with a different neurochemistry that raises the threshold of the amygdala's response to unfamiliarity should show minimal motor activity and little distress in response to the same stimuli.

We have studied more than 500 healthy, Caucasian children born at term to middle-class families. Each 4-month-old was classified as high or low reactive, depending upon whether they showed frequent and vigorous motor activity and crying, or the opposite profile of infrequent motoricity and minimal crying. We measured four biological variables at age 11 that are indirect indexes of amygdalar excitability. The 11-year-old children who had been high-reactive infants showed greater EEG activation in the right, compared with the left, hemisphere to states of uncertainty. This asymmetry of activation could be due to greater feedback from the cardio-vascular and other bodily systems to brain sites on the right side. This asymmetry should be accompanied by greater activity in the right amyg-dala and greater right than left hemisphere activation (Cahill, 2000; Cameron, 2001).

The most convincing support for the assumption that high reactives have a more excitable amygdala is found in an unexpected location. There is a fixed sequence of steps that occurs when a person hears a sound. Ini-tially, a strip of receptors in the inner ear is excited and these receptors send their neural reaction to five structures before the information arrives in the auditory cortex. The fourth structure in this series is called the infe-rior colliculus. Because the amygdala sends neural projections to the inferior colliculus, a more excitable amygdala will be accompanied by a more excited inferior colliculus. Scientists measure the excitability of the inferior colliculus by recording, from scalp electrodes, the size of the wave-form appearing at 6 milliseconds to a series of click sounds. Children with a larger than average waveform presumably have a more excitable amygdala.

High-reactive adolescents showed a larger waveform in response to the click sounds than did the low reactives. High reactives also showed greater sympathetic tone in the cardiovascular system, because the amygdala enhances sympathetic tone in the heart and circulatory vessels. Finally, high reactives showed a larger event-related potential with unfamiliar visual scenes, because the amygdala projects to the locus ceruleus and the ventral tegmentum. These structures send projections to the cortex that can enhance the synchronization of pyramidal neurons and produce a larger waveform in response to a discrepant event.

The 11-year-olds who had been high-reactive infants were more vulner-able than low reactives to the experience of guilt because of greater sym-pathetic activity and therefore more regular feedback from the body to the amygdala and the ventromedial prefrontal cortex. A person could report feeling guilt even though they did not experience any change in physiol-ogy. That is, some children might say they felt guilty over lying, but neither the act nor the confession was accompanied by any physiological reaction.

The 11-year-olds, who were visited at home, were asked to rank twenty printed statements descriptive of their personality from the most (a rank of 1) to the least characteristic of themselves (a rank of 20). One item was,

"I feel bad if one of my parents says that I did something wrong." There was no difference between high and low reactives in the mean rank given this item. However, the high reactives who said that this statement was very characteristic of themselves showed a larger number of the signs of amygdalar excitability than did the low reactives who ranked this item as equally characteristic of themselves, as well as the high reactives who did not admit to feeling guilty.

The fact that more high reactives who admitted to feelings of guilt showed biological signs of amgydalar arousal suggests that these children were more vulnerable to experiencing guilt than were the other children. Most children can be socialized to feel shame or guilt following violation of a standard, but a small proportion are especially vulnerable to this emotion because of their temperament.

The mothers of these children ranked twenty-eight statements describing their 11-year-old children from most to least characteristic. One item, which referred to how the child behaved when chastised, was: "Is sensitive to punishment." The high- and low-reactive girls differed in their rank on this item. Seventy-three percent of high-reactive, but only 58 percent of low-reactive, girls were given ranks suggesting they were extremely sensitive to punishment. Of equal interest is the fact that the high-reactive girls described as sensitive to punishment showed greater activation in the right parietal area than the high-reactive girls described as less sensitive. The high-reactive boys who were described as sensitive to punishment had larger brainstem-evoked potentials from the inferior colliculus than the high-reactive boys who were not sensitive. Thus, two biological variables that distinguished between high and low reactives also differentiated high reactives described by their mothers as sensitive to punishment from those who were less sensitive (Kagan & Snidman, 2004).

Summary

Kant believed that people acted morally because an acceptance of the categorical imperative required, as a rational conclusion, proper behavior. Reason was the guardian of morality and therefore of social harmony. The American philosophers Peirce (1905) and Dewey (1922), in contrast, argued that anticipation of anxiety, shame, and guilt were the more important reasons for loyalty to ethical standards. The conflict between these two bases for morality can be seen in modern industrialized societies. The balance between a feeling of virtue that follows enhancing another and the pleasure that follows the enhancing of one's self has shifted toward a preference for the latter. Each year more Americans ignore their gender, ethnicity, vocation, place of residence, friendship, or religion as guides to action and sources of virtue. As a result, they feel freed from the moral obligations attached to these categories and rely more on the anticipation of sensory delight and a feeling of self-enhancement through accomplishment as a guide for action and source of reassurance that they are managing their lives correctly.

It is likely that one day scientists will synthesize a drug that blocks feelings of guilt but does not affect the knowledge that a behavior is wrong. It is less certain that the widespread use of this drug will eliminate loyalty to the mutual obligations among citizens that make a society habitable. Nonetheless, we should be vigilant, for humans, unlike gorillas, can hold representations of envy, hostility, and anger, even toward those they do not know, for a long time. Therefore, feelings of empathy and the anticipation of anxiety, guilt, or shame may restrain rudeness, dishonesty, and aggression when Kant's reason fails.

The evolution of the human brain was accompanied by a preoccupation with good and bad, the ability to infer the feelings and thoughts of others, and a continual desire to enhance the self's virtue. The current concern with perfecting the self, and the increased tolerance for the ethical standards of all groups, have, I believe, weakened the power of altruism and love as ways to enhance a feeling of virtue. Some narcissism is probably necessary for the emotions of hope, joy, and love, but an excessive level, like too much steak, sun, and strawberry shortcake, is malevolent. Montaigne's warning, "Moderation, above all," is a useful maxim to rehearse.

Morality, Culture, and the Brain: What Changes and What Stays the Same

Nathan A. Fox and Melanie Killen

In his chapter, Jerome Kagan outlines the factors that he associates with the development of morality. He views the development of moral reasoning and behavior to be under the guidance of the emergence of cognition. Underlying these processes are critical maturational changes in brain circuitry. Kagan's interpretations of the empirical findings lead him to formulate the following developmental trajectory. Children's thinking about morality is first linked to the emergence of a sense of self, to states of uncertainty that are generated by violations of what are viewed as social standards. Later, the emergence of causal inference and empathic response drive moral behavior, as does the understanding that another person may be critically evaluating one's behavior. The next important stage in moral development, according to Kagan, involves the evocation of feelings of guilt following violation of a standard. This period is linked to a rudimentary understanding of good and bad. In the next stage, and owing to changes in their cognitive understanding of the world, children are able to relate one event to a larger context and sort events on more than one characteristic. Concepts of fairness and the ideal are linked to this period. Each of these periods or stages involves the emergence of new cognitive achievements and, according to Kagan, underlying these achievements are corresponding changes in brain circuitry.

Overall, Kagan's perspective fits well with current social neuroscience research that views moral reasoning as another set of cognitive processes that involve specific brain circuitry (Greene, Nystrom, Engell, Darley, & Cohen, 2004). These circuits are not unique to morality (e.g., there is no moral center in the brain). Rather, the circuits central to moral reasoning involve those underlying specific states of feeling (e.g., guilt) and cognitive processes (symbolic cognitive thought). These emerge and are interconnected over the course of human development. His general developmental outline draws on global cognitive developmental stages of moral development, with an inclusion of socialization constructs, such as guilt and empathy. While current moral developmental theory and research has extended beyond the traditional models that Kagan relies on most heavily (for example, social-domain theory contrasts with global stage approaches, and interactional socialization theory contrasts with traditional socialization models that underplay the role of cognition and peer relationships), there are many elements of Kagan's characterization of the developmental sequence of morality that reflect recent developments in the literature.

Kagan emphasizes three main points throughout his essay. The first is that in our current social context, moral obligations are no longer attached to relationships, that is, to one's family, ethnicity, religion, or friendships; instead, individuals rely on feelings of self-enhancement as a guide for what is right or wrong. The second is that human moral reasoning is unique and qualitatively different from that of other animals. This point is stressed throughout and is linked to the changes in symbolic cognitive thought that emerge in human development and that do not appear present in other species. The third point emphasized throughout is the role of historical context in the attribution of what is considered conventional versus absolute in moral standards.

Kagan's view about social relationships, that is, that morality has moved away from relying on social relationships, could be perceived as a positive trend. This detachment allows children to make judgments independent of their close social ties to others, who typically are like them and thus are not members of other social categories or outgroups. Yet, if this independence becomes too extreme, children are left without the social support and guidance to understand connections between acts and consequences and to understand how their behavior affects others.

Research in moral developmental psychology (see Killen, Margie, & Sinno, 2006), points to the complexities of social relationships and the diverse forms of influence that bear on the emergence and development of moral judgment. On the one hand, children develop morality from interactions with peers and adults (Damon, 1983; Turiel, 2002). Through reciprocal exchanges and experiences, children develop notions of how to treat others and what it means to be fair, just, and equal. On the other hand, children begin to form static categories of others, which often results in stereotyping and implicit biases (Killen et al., 2006). When stereotyping leads to prejudice and discrimination, there is a conflict with basic moral values of equality and fairness. This conflict reflects a struggle of values that children, adolescents, and adults have to confront, and even more so in a multicultural society.

It is interesting to note that most of Kagan's essay concentrates on human universals, rather than cultural specificity, for describing morality and its developmental trajectory. The issue of universality and cultural relativity has served as a source of heated and lively debate for many exchanges among moral theorists and researchers. Along with the discussion about emotions and rationality, cultural specificity and universality rank at the top of the list of contentious issues in the field of morality. Kagan appears comfortable with the human universal position, which is consistent with most researchers who investigate moral judgment and reasoning (see the recent *Handbook of Moral Development*, edited by Killen & Smetana, 2006).

Much research has documented how young children in a wide range of cultures construct theories of fairness, justice, and equality in a similar manner and as a function of reflections upon their own social experiences. This approach suggests that if morality exists, it has to do with the set of principles that individuals use to treat others in a just, fair, and caring manner (e.g., universality). Culture has an influence, no doubt. Culture has an influence not in the way that morality is defined but in the way that social relationships (parents, peers) communicate moral values, and the opportunities made available to children to act upon their moral decisions. There is clearly wide variability in cultural ideologies, but the way in which these ideologies are interpreted by children is quite complex. These ideologies are accepted, rejected, transformed, and translated by children, adolescents, and adults.

Kagan's view that morality is uniquely human is different from current perspectives by Frans de Waal (1996) and other primatologists who have observed nonhuman primates demonstrating caring and reciprocal behaviors within various social group encounters. These primatologists, for the most part, however, rarely use the term "morality" per se because it is clear that obtaining information about intentions and motives is quite difficult in nonhuman primate studies. Marina Cords (Cords & Aureli, 2000) reports observational data on peaceful conflict resolution strategies not so much to document morality in monkeys but to counter the "aggressive nature" argument that dominated primatology research for several decades. A goal of this work is to show that conflicts are not necessarily resolved through dominance hierarchies, but are sometimes resolved through reconciliation and nonaggressive means. Kagan, though, would not view these behaviors as signifying moral acts. Rather, he argues that that altruism is "a behavior preceded by an intention to help someone perceived to be in need" (this volume, p. 308).

Kagan's third main point involves an acknowledgment of the theoretical distinction put forward by many developmental psychologists—that moral principles are different from conventional rules and regulations. Much research (see Smetana, 2006) has shown that children, adolescents, and adults treat moral principles (e.g., justice, others' welfare, and rights) differently from conventional regulations that have been created by group consensus to ensure the smooth functioning of social groups (see Turiel, 2002). Conventions can vary from trivial matters of etiquette (eat spaghetti with a knife and fork) to important aspects of social organization (cultural traditions and rituals). Kagan proposes that what counts as moral or conventional has changed historically. This could mean one of two things. Either the content changes or what is moral changes. Most researchers would argue that while the content changes, what counts as morality does not (see Turiel, 2002). For example, Kagan describes the change that has come about regarding the use of ethnic slurs by college students (conventional in a previous generation and morally wrong in the current generation). The implication is that making an ethnic slur used to be considered okay from a moral viewpoint, and now it is considered wrong. Taking the view that the change has been one of content and not of morality, one could argue that what has changed is the understanding that using ethnic slurs causes others to suffer (the content) rather than the view that it used to be okay to harm people and now it's not okay (morality). And of course, recipients of such slurs, even a generation ago, recognized it as wrong, indicating that not everyone thought it was okay 50 years ago (and unfortunately not everyone views it as wrong today, as evidenced by college campus examples of racism and anti-Semitism).

Thought and action, emotion and cognition, universality and cultural specificity. These pairings were for a long time treated as dichotomized polarities of morality. We have made some progress in our theorizing to the extent that we recognize that morality includes all of these. As Kagan states, morality concerns intentions and motives as well as patterns of social interactions. Temperament and rationality are complementary aspects; while morality is about universals, culture clearly has an influence on the developmental emergence and trajectory of this process.

The Fabric of Our Moral Lives: A Comment on Kagan

Paul J. Whalen

In his chapter, Kagan offers a description of the fibers comprising the tapestry that is society, morality, and individual temperament. We learn of the author's impressive command of the field of childhood development, his distaste for sociobiology, and his disappointment with human society in its current form (plus we now know he's a Red Sox fan). I see all of this as a good thing; Kagan makes his biases plain for the reader to evaluate.

Human behavior is as complex as the neural substrates that necessarily support such complexity. For this reason, perhaps, neuroscientists often choose to focus their work on a single brain structure. Indeed, in Kagan's chapter we learn that the activity of a brain area called the amygdala, a bilateral structure buried beneath the cortex within the medial temporal lobe, can explain temperament, which in turn can explain moral development. Can morality be localized to a single structure occupying roughly 2000 cubic millimeters of space within the human brain? Is this a fair characterization of Kagan's position?

One of the more important points that Kagan offers is that there are individual differences in children's capability to feel social emotions such as shame or empathy. If variability in a given behavior can be correlated with variability in brain reactivity, we are one step closer to potentially identifying the neural generator of that behavior. It remains to be seen then whether the ability to point to a brain area associated with a behavior adds anything to our understanding of that behavior. So let us look at Kagan's specific example as it relates to morality.

Jerome Kagan has spent his life studying how children handle uncertainty. Through his work we know that if one records a child's behavior in response to something as simple as placing an unfamiliar object in front of her, we can predict all sorts of important social outcomes for that child. For example, children who are more inhibited on these tests will be more avoidant of other people and will be at an increased risk of developing social anxiety disorders later in life. In his chapter, we learn that society might indirectly derive some benefit from the existence of this behavioral profile in that inhibited children will be more moral.

The basis for this argument is that inhibited children are more physiologically reactive during the experience of social emotions like guilt. Thus they will work harder to avoid these feelings and will in turn behave in a more moral fashion. Since the amygdala is a brain area that is known to be directly involved in driving autonomic reactivity, it follows that the amygdala should be more reactive in inhibited children. Kagan provides information consistent with this proposal. First, inhibited children show greater cortical reactivity (measured as either EEG or ERPs), and the amygdala is known to directly drive the reactivity of cortical neurons. Second, inhibited children show greater reactivity in midbrain sensory areas (e.g., auditory), and the amygdala is known to modulate the responsivity of these systems. Third, inhibited children show greater cardiovascular reactivity, and the amygdala has a profound influence over the cardiovascular system. Finally, Kagan was part of a research team that offered more direct evidence for amygdala hyperreactivity in inhibited children. A functional brain imaging study showed that inhibited children showed greater amygdala reactivity to pictures of novel faces compared with uninhibited children.

These are promising observations that will serve us well in our quest to understand something as complex as moral behavior (or physiological reactivity for that matter). There is more to do. Kagan briefly mentions other brain regions that are sure to be involved. The ventromedial prefrontal cortex is an area of the brain that can exert inhibitory control over areas of the brain such as the amygdala. Since inhibited and uninhibited children differ in the degree of their impulsivity, this circuit will most likely prove to be a critical component of resistance to temptation. If one assumes that the prefrontal cortex has access to information concerning past experiences and their relation to present circumstances (something Kagan argues is critical to moral behavior), then there is much to be done to discern how exactly this circuit interacts with brains regions like the amygdala to produce the behavioral profile described as inhibited. To elaborate, are these children prisoner to a hyperreactive amygdala system whose very responsivity produces a change in one's internal visceral state that is in and of itself aversive (and thus avoided)? Or does this behavioral profile originate more as the result of a failure of the prefrontal cortical system to regulate the amygdala? That is, perhaps uninhibited children are able to utilize additional information from the environment about the moral abilities of others, see that they fit well within this range, and effectively regulate amygdala reactivity. I think the answer to this conundrum would help us to parse out whether greater physiological reactivity during guilt is evidence that one feels more guilty or is better thought of as greater distress given an equal amount of guilt.

Taken together, Kagan has woven a good deal of disparate information together from neuroscience, child development, and social psychology to create a promising patchwork from which to begin to think about the question of morality. The amygdala is clearly a player in physiological reactivity, and thus implicating this brain region in the greater degree of physiological reactivity observed in inhibited children is well founded. In addition, Kagan is one of the scientists who has highlighted the particular role of the amygdala in uncertainty, the hallmark of the behavioral indices of being an inhibited child. This contribution cannot be underestimated because many have assumed that the amygdala is involved solely in strong emotional reactivity, such as intense fear. However, large changes in state, like fear, as important as they are, remain relatively infrequent events. Kagan's model allows the amygdala to have a profound influence on development because in addition to strong changes in emotional state, amygdala reactivity is predicted by something as subtle and innocuous as noticing a change in the environment, a form of learning that occurs on a moment-to-moment basis. In the course of these constant and continuous calculations, the amygdala will most likely constitute a fluid component of a number of overlapping but distinct neural circuits, changing its role within a given circuit in an almost chameleonlike fashion. Identifying such intricate neural interactions will be a challenge for the future because as Kagan's chapter details, these calculations permeate experience (good versus bad; self versus other, etc.) comprising an essential strand within the fabric of moral behavior.

6.3 Reply to Fox and Killen and Whalen

Jerome Kagan

Happily, neither Fox and Killen nor Whalen found much to criticize in my chapter. The small number of disagreements center on the functions of moral emotions. Fox and Killen note that I view moral reasoning as a set of cognitive processes, but they do not add the important point that maturing cognitive abilities permit the progression from anxiety to shame to guilt over violating prohibitions on actions across the period from age 2 to 6 years.

Fox and Killen suggest that I deny the significance of social relationships. That claim is not quite correct. I suggest that the nominal categories of gender, religion, and ethnicity no longer supply the moral assurance they did a century earlier, and that the relational categories of friend, son or daughter, and parent have increased in importance. However, the moral obligations associated with relational categories vary with the nature of the relationship; that is, the obligations of a daughter are different from those attached to the category of friend. I do not imply that the secular weakening of the obligations of the relational categories is a positive trend in our society. Rather, this trend leaves a person with a primary obligation to enhance only one's own self. If that imperative is carried to an extreme, it has questionable consequences for society.

Whalen goes a little too far when he states that I believe the amygdala is responsible for all important temperamental biases and variations in morality. The temperamental bias my colleagues and I call a high-reactive infant appears to be influenced by the excitability of the amygdala, and adolescents who were high-reactive infants are more religious than others. Nevertheless, many religious adolescents were not high-reactive infants and have no special temperament. Furthermore, many temperamental biases are influenced by neurobiological profiles that have little to do with the amygdala. Whalen is correct to point out that a compromised prefrontal cortex could result in a more excitable amygdala and an inhibited child.

My assumptions can be summarized in six points.

1. All children are biologically prepared to infer the thoughts and feelings of others by the third birthday.

2. As a result, children can empathize with the distress of others and infer that adults are evaluating the actions they have learned are prohibited. Hence, they are motivated to suppress these acts and to feel the affect of shame for violations.

3. After they learn the semantic concepts of good and bad, by age 3, they apply them to acts and to the self and experience an emotion of uncertainty or guilt if they behave in ways that are classified as bad.

4. Cognitive advances permit children by age 5 or 6 to conclude that they are responsible for acts that violate a prohibition, and as a result they are vulnerable to feeling guilty.

5. By 5 to 8 years, children believe they belong to a number of symbolic categories and feel they have an obligation to be loyal to the ethical standards linked to each category they assume applies to them.

6. Cognitive advances at 12 to 15 years render adolescents vulnerable to a feeling of dissonance if they detect inconsistency in their set of moral beliefs.

7 Adolescent Moral Reasoning: The Integration of Emotion and Cognition

Abigail A. Baird

Prologue

They took Shanda to a crumbling, deserted castle where they taunted her, harassed her, and threatened to kill her. They tried to cut her throat with the knife; they hit her and tried to strangle her. After she lost consciousness, they thought she was dead, so they threw her in the trunk of the car. Whenever she screamed or cried, they would open the trunk and beat her with a tire tool. They continued this until the early hours of the morning. While deciding what to do with Shanda, Hope sprayed Windex on her wounds. They decided to burn Shanda. They drove out to the countryside, took her out of the trunk, threw gasoline on her and set her on fire. She was alive and conscious when this happened. She died from smoke inhalation. Then they went to McDonald's for breakfast. "Shanda looks like this," said one, pointing to the fried meat patty and laughing.

No drugs or alcohol were involved in this incident.

Shanda Renee Sharer was killed in 1992 by four girls, three of whom she had never met before that night. Laurie Tackett was 17 years old. Melinda Loveless was 16; Hope Rippey and Toni Laurence were both 15. Shanda was 12 years old.

The torture and murder of Shanda went on for nearly 10 hours, during which there were countless opportunities for any one of the girls to alert an authority, or help Shanda, or even suggest to the others that what they were doing was wrong. The behavior of the girls who murdered Shanda suggests an utter disregard for the most fundamental of moral standards: to not physically harm others. Individuals who commit this sort of transgression are often called "psychopaths." In the United States, current rates of psychopathy are estimated at less than 1 percent of the population. So how did four of them end up together on that fateful night in 1992? While it is arguable that one of the girls responsible for Shanda's death may have suffered from psychopathy, it is improbable that the other three did. What, then, precipitated their participation in this tragedy? This chapter will argue that their participation was, in their minds, not all that different from taunting a classmate for wearing "uncool" jeans, or passing a note about someone whom the group determined needed a lesson taught to them. It will be proposed that while the specifics of the case above are truly exceptional, the underlying reasoning is surprisingly consistent with normal adolescent development.

There is a stark difference between knowing something is wrong and feeling that something is wrong. I will argue that in the case of moral development, knowing precedes feeling and that "gut" feelings about wrongdoing are explicitly taught and over time become rapid automatic responses to moral dilemmas. A developmentally ordered progression exists in moral development, in which conditioned behavior precedes explicit thought. Through the social learning that takes place in adolescence, thoughts and behaviors become associated with emotions that in their most evolved and mature state produce socially appropriate behavior with relatively little cognitive influence. Autonomous moral behavior is undoubtedly the integration of many developmental processes. This chapter discusses the roles of cognition, self-conscious emotion, and the transition from a parent-centered to a peer-centered social world with regard to the emergence of a social morality in adolescence. I will also argue that the development that takes place in adolescence, namely, the integration of intense visceral emotion with social cognition, is essential for a fully developed moral reasoning that functions preemptively, with minimal cognitive effort.

Foundations

Humans are not born with a moral sense. We are, however, given an innate capacity to develop one, much in the way we have now come to view acquisition of language (see Hauser, volume 2). Unlike language, the most basic indications of this capacity can be seen within the first few months of life. There are two fundamental building blocks that set the stage for the emergence of moral reasoning. The first relies on conditioning. Conditioning is based on the fact that we learn to associate specific stimuli with specific responses. As early as 4 months of age, children are able to retain a stimulus-response pairing (see Rovee-Collier & Hayne 1987 for a review). In the case of desired behavior, parents are able to impart an aversive sensory response to certain infant behaviors that will decrease the likelihood of the behavior reoccurring. For example, if an infant bites the mother's nipple while nursing, the mother is likely to respond by abruptly removing the nipple from the infant's mouth, displaying an angry face, and perhaps delivering a sharp "no!"; all three of these events are aversive to an infant. In this example, the infant is not able to reflect on past experience or potential outcomes of biting and therefore has no reason to not bite. Once an infant is able to associate its actions with concomitant outcomes (i.e., punishment), it becomes possible to shape its behavior. This basic interaction—that others may impose an undesirable, sensory-based consequence in response to your behavior—forms the foundation of social learning.

As a result of the development described here, children's first behaviors are based on the avoidance of punishment and the seeking of reward (such as a smile or comforting embrace). Parents (or caretakers) exclusively supply the rules of the world, and there is no questioning of these rules. At this point in development, children obey because adults tell them to obey. Kohlberg termed this type of reasoning preconventional thinking. The next important gain toward moral reasoning takes place following the emergence of the child's ability to reflect on the past and to integrate past and present. These important cognitive advances enable a new type of moral thought, whereby children strive to behave in consonance with internalized standards of appropriate behavior. They are able to regulate many aspects of their behavior and are increasingly aware that they may be responsible for an act that causes harm to another. Generally around 5 years of age children become aware that their prior actions could have been modified, and this realization forms the foundation of the emotional experience of guilt (see Kagan's chapter in this volume for a more detailed description). Guilt at this stage, however, is fundamentally different from that experienced by most adults. The "guilt" of transgressions at this age is a cognitive awareness, following a violation of internalized standards that triggers the previously acquired conditioned fear response.

The establishment of both these advances requires that the child be capable of modifying his or her present behavior based on either past experience or environmental response (most often that of the parent or caretaker). The next significant advance in development takes place during adolescence, when abstract thought enables an individual to envision and anticipate situations that they have not directly experienced. This is also a time when social cognition takes center stage and the role of moral dictator shifts from primarily the parents to primarily peers (Walker & Taylor, 1991).

Cognitive and Emotional Development in Adolescence

Adolescence is the period of life between puberty and adulthood. Adolescence begins at the onset of puberty, which technically refers to the time at which an individual becomes capable of reproduction. While estimates vary, pubertal onset generally occurs between the ages of 10 and 12 for girls and between 13 and 15 for boys. Once a child is of reproductive age, he or she has entered adolescence but is still far from adulthood. Adolescence describes this transitional time, when the individual undergoes major changes in physiological, social, emotional, and cognitive functioning that over a period of years enable him or her to become an adult member of society. The hallmark of adolescent cognition is the qualitative change that adolescent thinking undergoes. Their thought becomes more abstract, logical, and idealistic. Adolescents are more capable of examining their own thoughts, others' thoughts, and what others are thinking about them, and are more likely to interpret and monitor the world around them. What this suggests is that the primary change in adolescent cognition is a dramatic improvement in the ability to think and reason in the abstract. Piaget (1954) believed that adolescents are no longer limited to actual, concrete experiences as anchors for thought. They can cognitively generate make-believe situations, events that are entirely hypothetical possibilities, or strictly abstract propositions. The primary gain in adolescent cognition is that in addition to being able to generate abstract thought, they are able to reason about the products of their cognition. This "thinking about thinking" forms the foundation for both metacognition and introspection.

Adolescent thought emerges in phases. In the first phase, the increased ability to think hypothetically produces unconstrained thoughts with unlimited possibilities. In fact, early adolescent thought often disregards the constraints of reality (Broughton, 1978). During the later phases, adolescents learn to better regulate their thoughts, measuring the products of their reasoning against experience and imposing monitoring or inhibitory cognitions when appropriate. By late adolescence, many individuals are able to reason in ways that resemble adults. However, it is clear that the emergence of this ability depends in great part on experience and therefore does not appear across all situational domains simultaneously. Adultlike thought is more likely to be used in areas where adolescents have the most experience and knowledge (Carey, 1988). During development, adolescents acquire elaborate knowledge through extensive experience and practice in multiple settings (e.g., home, school, sports). The development of expertise in different domains of life bolsters high-level, developmentally mature-looking thought. Experience and the ability to generalize about their experiences give older adolescents two important improvements in reasoning ability. Greater experience and an improved system for organizing and retrieving the memories of experience enable the adolescent to recall and apply a greater number of previous experiences to new situations. In addition, an increased ability to abstract and generalize may allow adolescents to reason about a situation that they have not directly experienced. Improvements in cognition largely result from synergistic maturation in working memory capacity, selective attention, error detection, and inhibition, all of which have been shown to improve with maturational changes in brain structure and function.

Perhaps the most consistently reported finding associated with adolescent brain development is the decrease of gray matter and the increase of white matter throughout the cortex, but most significantly within the frontal cortex (see Giedd, Blumenthal, Jeffries, Castellanos, Liu, et al., 1999; Sowell, Thompson, Holmes, Batth, Jernigan, et al., 1999 for reviews). The prefrontal cortex is of paramount interest in human development largely because of its well-understood function with regard to cognitive, social, and emotional processes in adulthood. The converging evidence of prolonged development and organization of the prefrontal cortex throughout childhood and adolescence (Huttenlocher, 1979; Chugani, Phelps, & Mazziotta, 1987; Diamond, 1988, 1996) may suggest an important parallel between brain development and cognitive development.

As the brain matures, starting with a newborn, its neurons will develop synapses, which link neurons to neurons and transmit information through one another. At first this growth is uninhibited. However, as the infant reaches toddler age, the brain begins to eliminate some synapses between neurons in order to help the brain transmit information more efficiently. The synapses and neurons that were activated most during growth are the ones that will be preserved. Synaptic pruning is the elimination of synapses in the brain that are used less frequently, facilitating growth of a more efficient brain. One striking difference regarding the development of the prefrontal cortex relative to other cortical areas is the continuation of synaptic pruning into young adulthood. This decrease in synaptic density during adolescence coincides with the emergence of newly entwined cognitive and emotional phenomena. The secondary process that is taking place during this time is the fortification of synaptic connections that will remain into adulthood. There has been further speculation that this "use it or lose it" process may represent the behavioral and, ultimately, the physiological suppression of immature behaviors that have become obsolete owing to the new demands of adulthood (Casey, Giedd, & Thomas, 2000). One can imagine that a response to a particular event in the environment will be potentiated by repeated exposure and subsequent strengthening of the relation between that event and the generation of the appropriate response. The delayed maturation of this brain region allows an individual to adapt to the particular demands of his or her unique environment.

The decline of gray matter in the prefrontal cortex in adolescence has been taken to be a marker of neural maturation as a result of synaptic pruning (Bourgeois, Goldman-Rakic, & Rakic, 1994; Paus, Collins, Evans, Leonard, Pike, et al., 2001). The idea of decreasing gray matter as a result of synaptic death is borne out in the work of Casey and colleagues (see Casey et al., 2000 for a review), which consistently demonstrates an increased volume of cortical activity in younger adolescents, who perform less well on tasks of cognitive control and attentional modulation. This pattern of greater brain activity in children relative to adults is suggestive of a gradual decrease in the brain tissue required to perform the task. This decrease may parallel the loss rather than the formation of new synapses observed in postmortem studies.

Many researchers have documented that while there are age-related decreases in gray matter in the prefrontal cortex, the overall cortical volume does not change significantly. Not surprisingly, the cortical volume remains stable because of simultaneous increases in white matter volume that may be equally important for functionality. The greater volume of frontal white matter observed during adolescence is most likely the result of greater axonal myelination. Myelin is the fatty sheath that covers and insulates the neural wires (axons) of the brain. It has been well established that myelination has a direct impact on the speed and efficiency of neural processing. At the level of the neuron, increased myelination leads to increased propagation speed of the action potential and reduced signal attenuation. At a macroscopic level, this type of maturation facilitates synchrony and coordination, both regionally and across the whole brain.

One specific frontal region within which increases in myelination have been observed is the anterior cingulate cortex, an area known for its prominent role in the mediation and control of emotional, attentional, motivational, social, and cognitive behaviors (Vogt, Finch, & Olson, 1992). A significant positive relationship between age and total anterior cingulate volume (which has been attributed to increases in white matter) has been well documented (Casey, Trainor, Giedd, Vauss, Vaituzis, et al., 1997). It is thought that this relationship may reflect improved cortical-cortical and cortical-subcortical coordination. The projections from both cortical and subcortical regions to the cingulate observed in adult subjects are known to contribute to the coordination and regulation of cognitive and emotional processes. A critical question with regard to human development has been the exact developmental course of these projections. Activity of the dorsal portion of the anterior cingulate cortex has been shown to play a crucial role in autonomic control and the conscious interpretation of somatic state. Furthermore, maturation of the dorsal anterior cingulate cortex has been consistently related to self-control and behavioral inhibition (see Isomura & Takada, 2004 for a recent review). The dorsal anterior cingulate may be an important center for the creation of second-order representations of body state. Second-order representations are the product of integrating first-order sensory information from insular and somatosensory cortices with cognitive and contextual information available to the cingulate. Critchley, Mathias, and Dolan (2001) found that the right anterior cingulate and left posterior cingulate were key areas for the creation of second-order representations. The authors suggested that the right anterior cingulate plays a specific executive role in the integration of autonomic responses with behavioral effort. The notion that an individual's perception and subsequent interpretation of his body state determines his emotional experience is an idea that dates back to the work of William James.

Without the bodily states following on the perception, the latter would be purely cognitive in form, pale, colourless, destitute of emotional warmth. We might then see the bear, and judge it best to run, receive the insult and deem it right to strike, but we could not actually *feel* afraid or angry. (James, 1884, p. 190)

and later:

If we fancy some strong emotion, and then try to abstract from our consciousness of it all the feelings of its bodily symptoms, we find we have nothing left behind, no "mind-stuff" out of which the emotion can be constituted, and that a cold and neutral state of intellectual perception is all that remains. (James, 1884, p. 193)

More recent work has added to this idea by emphasizing the role that emotional experience may play in decision making. The somatic marker hypothesis (Damasio, 1994) suggests that external or internal stimuli initiate a body state that is associated with pleasurable or aversive somatic markers. These markers function to guide a person's behavior by biasing their selection toward actions that result in an increase in pleasurable somatic markers (while avoiding actions resulting in aversive somatic markers). This hypothesis further argues that emotional states associated with prior decision outcomes are used to guide future decisions based on the potential emotional (somatic) consequence. For example, when a choice is followed by a bad outcome, an affective reaction becomes associated with that choice. Once the affective reaction is sufficiently well established, the reaction occurs before a choice is made. Anticipation of a bad outcome before a bad choice is made prevents the bad choice and leads instead to a better choice. Thus, a somatic marker of good and bad options improves the probability of optimal decision making. According to this theory, optimal decision making is not simply the result of rational, cognitive calculation of gains and losses but rather is based on the good or bad emotional reactions to prior outcomes of choices. In essence, rational choice is guided by emotional reactions that bias decision making. Over time, somatic markers help to reduce the complexity of decision making by providing a "gut" feeling that does not require effortful cognition (Hinson, Jameson, & Whitney, 2002).

Within the context of the somatic marker hypothesis, the insula has been described as critical for the initial representation and the reenactment of somatic markers (Bechara, 2001). In this view, increased activation in the insula may signal the intensity of the somatic state. A number of studies have demonstrated a consistent relation between the human emotion of disgust and the subjective body state that accompanies insular activity. It is thought that activity in the insula signals distress in the central viscera and that the emotion of disgust has evolved to reside amidst the neural circuitry used to learn food aversions (i.e., the hardware that makes you avoid any food that has ever made you sick; see Adolphs, 2002, for a review). If the insula signal is associated with aversive somatic markers, a relatively large activation during a decision-making situation would signal a potentially aversive outcome and may guide the individual to avoid the selection of an undesirable alternative (Paulus, Rogalsky, Simmons, Feinstein, & Stein, 2003).

The synthesis of visceral and cognitive information is critical to successful adolescent development. Initially, evidence of this synthesis is reflected in the involvement of cognition in second-order representations. This involvement takes the form of reasoning about the connection between visceral states and their environmental (either internal or external) correlates. For example, the adolescent learns to associate the feeling of "butterflies" in his or her stomach with first interactions with their "crush" and later with thoughts about their "crush." Young children can describe the feeling of "butterflies" in their stomachs, but most would be unlikely to attribute the cause of this feeling to anything abstract like an encounter or a cognition. This awareness of one's visceral sense is the next important step toward adultlike moral reasoning. At this point in development, the somatic concern that was associated with punishment for violating a standard is replaced with a visceral sense of guilt. The emergence of somatic markers enables adolescents to avoid committing transgressions because they can anticipate how they might feel following such an event.

The child who hesitates before breaking one of their parent's rules would most likely possess the physiology of a fear-conditioned animal; that is, increased amygdala arousal, heightened vigilance, amplified heart rate and muscle tension—everything required for the "fight or flight" response. In contrast, an adolescent who hesitates before breaking one of their parent's rules would most likely possess the physiology of someone who is about to ingest something that previously gave them food poisoning or, more specifically, increased activity in the anterior cingulate and insula accompanied by some form of gastric distress. At this point "feeling bad" has taken on a new meaning, one ensconced in the cognitive and emotional processes of the individual. Guilt has now been transformed from "wait until your father gets home" to "I feel absolutely sick about what happened." The development of abstract reasoning also enables the adolescent to reflect on this most recent iteration of cognitive and emotional development and sets the stage for self-conscious emotions.

Self-Conscious Emotions

A thorough account of moral development is required to consider the influence of emotion. For many theorists (Eisenberg, 1986; Hoffman, 1991) the role of emotion in moral development has focused on empathy and other vicarious emotional responses. Empathy, for the purposes of the present discourse, is operationalized as experiencing the same feelings as another individual. This differs from sympathy, which is defined as feelings of concern, compassion, or sorrow for another individual. A number of researchers (as cited in Fabes et al., 1999) have noted that empathy is composed of both a cognitive and an affective dimension and that the development of empathy closely parallels the development of more general cognitive skills.

Developmental improvements in cognition lead to a new class of emotions called self-conscious emotions. Self-conscious emotions are a set of complex emotions that emerge relatively late in development and require certain cognitive abilities for their elicitation (Lewis, 2000). Whereas the primary emotions that appear early, such as joy, sadness, fear, and anger, have received considerable attention, the later-appearing self-conscious emotions have received relatively little attention. There are most likely many reasons for this. One reason may be that self-conscious emotions cannot be described solely by examining a particular set of facial movements; they require the observation of bodily action more than facial cues (Darwin, 1872). The elicitation of self-conscious emotions involves elaborate cognitive processes that have at their heart the notion of self. It is the way we think or what we think that becomes the elicitor of pride, shame, guilt, or embarrassment.

Darwin not only described the basic, primary, or early emotions, but also theorized about the self-conscious emotions. Darwin saw these later emotions as involving the self. For example, he believed that blushing was caused by how we appear to others, "the thinking about others thinking of us . . . excites a blush" (1872, p. 325). Darwin repeatedly emphasized the idea that these emotions were qualitatively unique in that they relied exclusively on the opinion of others, regardless of the valence of that opinion. This requirement also indicates something special about the cognitive processes that contribute to the formation of the self-conscious emotions because they require a cognitive awareness of not only the existence of the thoughts of others, but also the ability to speculate regarding the contents of these thoughts (Lewis, 2000). The reliance upon additional cognitive processes for the generation of self-conscious emotions also distinguishes them from primary emotions in terms of their neurophysiology.

Many researchers, including Darwin, have described the primary emotions as being hardwired or genetically determined, but the number of these primary emotions must remain relatively small. These are the universal emotions that are consistent across cultures and are believed to derive from basic human instincts or propensities (see Adolphs, 2002). In this way, primary emotions are a bit like primary colors in that by varying the combinations and intensities, the entire spectrum can be created. To have these more complex and subtle emotions cemented in our genetic code or neurophysiology would limit the capacity for learning and plasticity that makes us unique as humans. That is why their appearance, both behaviorally and in terms of the brain structures that enable them, is the work of development. The emergence of self-conscious emotion closely parallels the changes in neural physiology described in the previous section. Importantly, the emergence of this type of emotion, as well as the concomitant neural "hardware," may also represent essential scaffolding for more mature moral reasoning. At this point the adolescent is able to recognize the relation between his or her own body state and emotion and reflect upon their interaction. Owing to this advance, the adolescent is also able to experience and reflect upon self-conscious emotions. What remains to be developed is the ability to apply these newfound abilities to the experiences of others. This is enabled by the blending of one's self with that of one's peers.

Imagined Audience

The theory of adolescent egocentrism delineates two separate but related ideation patterns: the imaginary audience and the personal fable. The imaginary audience refers to adolescents' tendency to believe that others are always watching and evaluating them; the personal fable refers to the belief that the self is unique, invulnerable, and omnipotent (Elkind, 1967). The cognitions reflected by both constructs seem to parsimoniously describe the reasons for feelings and behaviors typically associated with early adolescence, such as self-consciousness, conformity to peer group norms, and risk taking (Vartanian, 2000).

The imaginary audience and personal fable are creations of the important improvements in adolescent cognition. They appear to be a by-product of the increases in abstract thought and self-awareness. Much in the way that a child learning a new rule of language commits errors of application (cars, dolls, apples, *sheeps*) adolescents make errors in applying their new reasoning skills. The adolescent errs in overapplying his or her new ability to recognize the thoughts and feelings of others, and in this instance cannot differentiate their own feelings from those of others (imagined audience). At the other extreme the adolescent fails to realize the commonality of his or her own thoughts and feelings and feels overly unique (personal fable). The imagined audience is thought to be constantly scrutinizing the adolescent, and the adolescent assumes that the evaluations of the imagined audience will match their own (Elkind, 1967). The personal fable reflects the mistaken belief that one's feelings and experiences are uniquely different from those of others (Elkind, 1967). The adolescent may therefore come to believe that "others cannot understand what I'm going through," "that won't happen to me," and "I can handle anything." The imaginary audience and personal fable seem to describe what have been viewed as typical facets of adolescent behavior. For example, self-consciousness and conformity to the peer group with regard to appearance can be understood as stemming from the belief that others are always watching and judging. Feelings of isolation and risk-taking behavior can be viewed as products of a personal fable (Vartanian, 2000).

At the core of the imagined audience is a significant improvement in perspective taking, which is fueled by the emergence of the ability to think increasingly abstractly that accompanies early adolescence. Perspective taking is the ultimate integration of emotion and cognition. It relies on the perception of the self and the other, as well as a cognitive appreciation of emotional states. Thus, perspective taking requires both cognitive and emotional perspective taking, as well as self-regulation. Perspective taking is believed to undergo a series of stagelike developmental progressions (Selman, 1980) that reflect the transition from egocentric to sociocentric functioning and an eventual understanding of the internal and external states of others and their social context. Depending on situational demands, an appropriate response could require emotional perspective taking (empathy), cognitive perspective taking (theory of mind), or the integration of both.

Selman's theory, which charts the developmental course by which children come to be aware of and coordinate the cognitive, social, and emotional perspectives of the self and others, provides a better background for understanding both the imagined audience and the personal fable. Lapsley and Murphy (1985) have proposed that Selman's theory of social perspective taking and interpersonal understanding provides an excellent explanation for the emergence, and eventual minimization, of the imagined audience and personal fable. It has been suggested that both the imaginary audience and personal fable might be products of what Selman described as level-three social perspective taking ability. Level three corresponds to the age period during which thoughts related to both the imaginary audience and the personal fable peak, most often between 10 and 15 years. This period is typified by the ability to consider the self and other perspectives simultaneously from a third-party or "observing ego" perspective. This differs substantially from the abilities of the level-two child, who is limited to sequentially considering one perspective at a time, so that the self and the other are never able to occupy the same cognitive space.

The new abilities related to the perspective of item observing ego also enable adolescents to view themselves as both the agent and an object in social interactions. A lack of coordination or skill with this new ability is believed to underlie the imaginary audience ideation, owing to the enhanced self-consciousness inherent in this cognitive development (Damon & Hart, 1982; Lapsley & Murphy, 1985). The acquisition of level-four social perspective-taking ability is believed to decrease imaginary audience and personal fable ideations. Upon reaching this final stage of development, the older adolescent is capable of considering and coordinating multiple third-party perspectives that form a generalized social perspective (Selman, 1980). This perspective alleviates self-consciousness because the adolescent can better see the self within the context of the "larger matrix of social perspectives" (Lapsley & Murphy, 1985, p. 214). This is fundamentally an issue of increasing capacity, and in this way this last stage is akin to metasocial cognition in that the level-four appreciation of unconscious mental processes helps to appropriately scale back the imaginary audience and personal fable ideation.

Hoffman (1991) has added to this, suggesting that by late childhood and early adolescence, coinciding with perspective taking and development of a concept of self, adolescents can empathize with a generalized group of others and their life situation. This newfound ability to empathize with a group of needy others might predict relatively sophisticated forms of moral behaviors—behaviors that involve groups of people. Thus, this transition may be important in the development of empathy and may help to explain relatively sophisticated moral behaviors in adolescence and adulthood. Somewhere between the influence of the imagined audience and empathy for one's social group exists the powerful import of the peer group.

The Importance of Peers

Part of leaning how to respond to environmental demands is knowing one's self and one's position in the world. The self-concept of adolescents changes as they realize that they are individuals. However, being an individual does not necessarily indicate much about your specific identity or how to fit into the different domains of your life. Teens desire validation and approval from various groups of people in their lives (e.g., parents, other family members, adults, friends, and classmates). All of these people contribute to an adolescent's perception of identity, but all have different values and expectations (Harter, Waters, & Whitesell, 1998). The juxtaposition of these different social pressures may explain why adolescents use different self-descriptions in different social contexts (Harter et al., 1998).

When children are young, parents serve as the local law. They create and enforce right behavior and act as the authority that oversees the development of an individual's morality. In many ways, parents can be conceptualized as external frontal lobes for their children, helping to interpret environmental demands, and to construct and execute appropriate responses. Given the behavioral consequences of having an immature frontal cortex, parents assume a number of frontal functions by instructing their children in the absence of their own abstract reasoning. Parents attempt to maintain control of where and with whom a child associates in order to minimize behavioral transgressions in the absence of the child's ability to make good decisions. Importantly, parents also provide feedback that allows a child to modify its behavior.

Adolescence changes forever the interaction between parents and their children. As children mature, they must learn new social skills in order to renegotiate their relationships with family members and peers. As discussed previously, the maturation of the frontal cortex produces significant improvements in behavioral and emotional control, decision making, and perhaps most important, abstract reasoning. If everything has gone according to plan, the adolescent is well on his or her way to being proficient at independent thought and autonomous morality. Despite the cognitive development that takes center stage during puberty, it is important to keep in mind that the primary purpose of puberty is to make individuals capable of reproduction. As teenagers develop a functionally reproductive adult body, they also develop increased interest in sex. So, while the body is preparing for this, the mind is trying to line up the combination of behaviors that will gain an individual access to potential mates. Teenagers focus more of their energy on peer groups. Within peer groups, teens learn how to talk, walk, and act around each other. In other words, you would no more call an electrician to fix your running toilet than you would ask your parents for help in navigating middle school (Walker, Hennig, & Krettenauer, 2000).

Research has suggested that it is not wholly accurate to refer to this time as a switch "from" parents "to" peers. It is more precise to describe this time as one when the parent's role changes and peers are more prominently added to the lives of adolescents. Theorists such as Piaget (1932) and Kohlberg (1969) have argued that parents have a minimal and non-specific role in their children's moral development primarily because of their position of unilateral authority. Both theorists have expanded on this to say that in adolescence the role of the parents and family, while not unimportant, pales in comparison with the critical contributions of peers to moral development. Developmental psychologists have asserted that owing to both their equal developmental status and the reciprocal nature of their relationships, peers are thought to provide the necessary scaffolding for moral development. More recently, however, research has demonstrated that the development of moral reasoning over a 4-year period was predicted by the nature of both parents' and peers' interactions in moral discussions, but what each type of relationship contributed was significantly different (Walker et al., 2000). Regardless of context, the key to moral development was the individual's use of their own cognitive skills to elicit and assimilate the knowledge of others. Conversely, situations where information was imparted in a unidirectional lecture style (often associated with parental advice) were associated with very slow rates of moral development (Walker et al., 2000).

What parental influence does offer the developing adolescent is a high disparity in moral stage. Because parents are most frequently operating at a higher stage of moral reasoning than their children, they are able to offer a consistent base from which their children can learn. Although the knowledge necessary to navigate specific moral dilemmas is most effectively supplied by peers, overarching moral concepts are best imparted by those with higher-level moral reasoning (Walker & Taylor, 1991). Much like the idea of language being best taught under the conditions of shared attention, so too is the case of moral development. When the adolescent initiates the interaction, it is an indicator to the parent or caretaker that there is an open window through which adult-level moral principles may be imparted.

There is also a way in which social conflict and the resolution of such conflict facilitates the development of moral reasoning. There is, however, great contextual distinction with regard to the efficacy of facilitation through social conflict. In effect, parents cannot do it, only peers can. The finding that interfering interactions in a peer context facilitates moral development seems at first glance counterintuitive but can be interpreted as consistent with the Piagetian view that egalitarian relationships among friends permit less constrained expressions of conflict than do asymmetrical child-parent relationships (as cited in Walker et al., 2000). Indeed, other empirical evidence indicates the facilitating effect of such interactions among peers. It makes adaptive sense, then, that adolescents spend an inordinate amount of time with friends. During a typical weekend, adolescents spend more than twice as much time with peers as they do with their parents (Condry, 1987). In a regular school day, teens have an average of 299 interactions with peers (Barker & Wright, 1951). During the limited time teens spend away from their friends, if they are not conversing on the phone or computer, they are most likely thinking about their peer groups. Based on the empirical and theoretical data on the importance of social self-perceptions during the teenage years (Jacobs, Vernon, & Eccles, 2004), it is perfectly reasonable for teenagers to place great importance on their friendships. Adolescents turn to peer groups for emotional support and perceive group approval as an indication of social acceptability (Brown, Mounts, Lamborn, & Steinberg, 1993).

Some theorists contend that friends have coercive power, that is, friends give reinforcement for socially approved behaviors and punishment for noncompliance with group standards (French & Raven, 1959, cited in Savin-Williams & Berndt, 1990). This power is wielded through discreet, subtle means of approval and reward, or disapproval, teasing, and rejection (Savin-Williams & Berndt, 1990). Within groups of friends, this type of social feedback is probably healthy and constructive because it helps adolescents develop mature social skills (e.g., empathy, perspective taking, good listening skills). If there is anything similar among kids who are perceived as socially potent or "popular," it is that they are good at controlling their coercive power. Coercive power is most likely achieved through a number of strategies, including the manipulation of both interpersonal relationships and portrayal of the imagined audience (e.g., "Don't wear that, *everyone* will hate you" or conversely "*Everyone* thought you were awesome in yesterday's game"). This could mean they inspire teammates to work harder in practice; they encourage other members of the orchestra to practice their instruments; or they challenge others to try out a new activity. Conversely, it could mean they pressure their friends into sneaking out, drinking alcohol, or other dangerous risk-taking behaviors.

Finally, it is not unreasonable for teens to accept the universal ethical constraints linked to peer group membership in return for the feeling of virtue and self-enhancement that membership in a peer group provides.

Summary

I have outlined here an important developmental progression that results in the construction of adult-level moral reasoning. Four basic stages are described. The first stage is based on classical conditioning through which behaviors come to be unconsciously paired with sensory outcomes and are consequently reduced or encouraged. In stage two the child has advanced to the point of being able to internalize mental schemas that represent behavioral standards and has the ability to integrate past and present; concurrently it has gained some ability in the area of self-regulation. During this stage, the conditioned aversions still exist but have changed from classical to operant in form. Specifically, at this stage there is a conscious understanding of the relation between behavior and outcome and the child begins to make deliberate choices about its behavior based on consideration of previously learned outcomes. The third stage in this development heralds the emergence of abstract thought and the recognition of internal visceral states in relation to thoughts and/or behaviors. This enables both self-awareness and the formation of self-conscious emotions. The fourth and final stage integrates self-perceptions with other perceptions, permitting empathy for other individuals, both known and unknown. What awakens during this last stage is the sense of belonging to a larger society, an important requirement for engaging in socially based moral reasoning. This sense of being a member of a society will eventually enable the individual to act in accordance with the society's prescribed moral code; for example, while it is considered immoral for parents to strike their children in the United States, this is not the case in many other societies in the world.

This developmental progression that eventually results in moral thought is subject to a great deal of individual variation, however. All of the stages described here must be achieved in order to avoid pathology. Waddington (1975) proposed that there are developmental pathways, or required epigenetic routes, which can be thought of as a number of valleys of varying height and width on a developmental landscape. Regulatory processes (including those grounded in the self and in others) ensure that the organism (conceptualized as a ball rolling down the slope of the landscape across time) returns to its channel (or valley) after small perturbations. Large perturbations, such as never acquiring a cognitive representation of one's visceral sense, can result in a significantly different developmental course. Thus, for the normal child, development will result in the same end point despite the small perturbations that arise from individual differences in things like basic temperament and life experience.

A deviation from the normal path early in development (high up on the hill) or at a decision point, or a major perturbation in later development may cause the child to take a different developmental path and reach a discrete set of possible alternative end states. For example, consider the case of psychopathy. There is a form of this disorder that is considered to arise from early (i.e., a relatively small deviation at the top of the hill) perturbations in amygdalar function (see Blair, 2001 for a review), so that the first stage of development (and therefore the subsequent stages) is not achieved. It is also possible to acquire psychopathy (see Tranel, 1994 for a review) from pervasive damage to the prefrontal cortex in adulthood; this would be considered a major perturbation at the bottom of the hill.

Characterization of the neurobehavioral development of moral reasoning in adolescence is necessary to identify perturbations associated with both neurophysiological and behavioral pathology. Without a clear delineation of normative changes during development, it would be impossible to determine whether anomalies in moral reasoning are associated with neuropathological variations or idiosyncrasies of normal maturation. When an adolescent rapidly gains 6 inches in height and 30 pounds in weight, as is typical in a year, the effects on coordination can be striking. References to the "gawky" teen, or the "awkward stage" abound in our culture; these same attributions should be applied to the growth of moral reasoning. Akin to the way that an adolescent gradually gains control over the changing entity that is his or her body, the building blocks of moral reasoning are assembled, toppled, and reassembled until a structure fitting the individual's needs is created. And it is through the ever-evolving architecture of this structure that we are able to exist as both an individual and a community.

Epilogue

During the first week of December 1992, Laurie Tackett gave an exclusive interview to Chris Yaw, a reporter from WKRC-TV in Cincinnati, Ohio.

"I didn't think she was going to go that far," Tackett said. "It wasn't really the fact that I can't believe I'm doing this. It was the fact that I can't believe this is happening. I told her [Melinda] it was stupid." She continued, "Shanda hugged me. She asked me not to let Melinda do it. She was crying . . . there wasn't anything I could do. (http://www.crimelibrary.com/notorious_murders/young/shanda_sharer)

What catastrophic events in moral development led those four young girls to torture and kill 12-year-old Shanda? There is nothing in the pages that precede this one that can satisfactorily explain the reasons behind the incidents that took place. Reading Laurie's comments, it is clear that at the very least she had absolutely no visceral aversion to the acts that she and the others committed. By way of information, Laurie Tackett was the one who in the end burned Shanda alive, after trying unsuccessfully to strangle her to death. Thankfully, we are not often in the position of having to explain tragedies of this nature. Perhaps that is part of why this case is so gut-wrenchingly inconceivable. However, as anyone who has been singled out and picked on in their teen years knows, there is a level on which the events are hauntingly familiar.

Note

I wish to express my sincere gratitude to Walter Sinnott-Armstrong and Jonathan Fugelsang for their time and effort spent providing feedback on the many versions of this manuscript. I would also like to thank Jane Viner, Catherine Fiscella, and Craig Bennet for their amazing effort in preparing this manuscript for publication.

Daniel K. Lapsley

In her far-ranging chapter Baird attempts to frame an integrative account of adolescent moral reasoning by drawing upon key insights from diverse theoretical literatures. Three claims about moral reasoning are prominent. One is that mature moral functioning is highly automatized and requires little cognitive effort. The second is that mature functioning requires the integration of social cognition with visceral emotion. The third is that this integration of cognition and emotion is effected during adolescence and is underpinned by the physical maturation of the prefrontal cortex. A number of other developmental processes are also invoked to explain autonomous moral behavior, including the emergence of self-conscious emotions, the construction of imagined audiences through enhanced per-spective-taking skills, and certain dynamics of adolescent friendship and peer group participation.

There is a fourth objective that was motivated by the prologue's chilling account of the murder of Shanda Renee Sharer by four teenaged girls. The insouciance of Shanda's killers shocks our moral sensibilities, but we are assured by Baird that heinous moral conduct is banal or, alternatively, that similar mechanisms underlie both ordinary and heinous moral failure. Torture and murder command the same developmental explanation as does taunting unpopular and "uncool" classmates, passing gossipy notes, and teaching "lessons." The epilogue does not quite redeem this promise of a consistent explanation, although the lack of "visceral aversion" dis-played by the killers perhaps underscores the chapter's main contention—that mature, autonomous moral behavior requires a tight connection between reasoning and emotion.

Baird's chapter does seem to orient moral psychology in a promising direction. For the past 30 years the study of moral functioning has been dominated by developmental studies of moral reasoning. It was Kohlberg's theory, in particular, that galvanized a generation of researchers to take up the study of moral reasoning, to chart its developmental trajectory, and to explore the implications of sociomoral development for education and clinical practice (Lapsley, 2006). Like most theories in the cognitive developmental tradition, emotions were treated as a nuisance or as an impediment to moral deliberation, although later clarifications did attempt to carve out a motivating role for moral emotions in the pursuit of justice (Kohlberg, Levine, & Hewer, 1983; Kohlberg, Boyd, & Levine, 1990).

Moreover, Kohlberg's paradigm was driven by one overriding concern, which was to show how the resources of a stage theory of moral development could be used to defeat ethical relativism. He used the language of ethics, not only to define the moral domain, but to hold out a model of deliberative competence that resolved tough moral dilemmas, generated consensus, and upheld the primacy of the moral point of view. There is much to admire about this remarkable research program. Nevertheless, moral stage theory, with its narrow focus and strong philosophical agenda, left unaddressed many topics of interest to moral psychology. Of course, no particular theory can explain everything. It can only be held accountable for the problem that it stakes out for itself. Still, there is a growing sense that we must open up the theoretical playbook in order to develop more comprehensive models of moral functioning.

Consequently, the preoccupations of the stage-and-structure paradigm are giving way to a diversity of theoretical perspectives that attempt to come to grips with a wide range of behavior in the moral domain (Killen & Smetana, 2006). One strategy is to explore integrative possibilities with other domains of psychological research (Lapsley & Narvaez, 2005). If Kohlberg can be said to have moralized the study of psychology by folding ethical theory into developmental explanation, the next generation of research seems ready to psychologize the study of moral functioning by appealing to theoretical and empirical psychological literatures that stray far from the cognitive developmental tradition, including the literatures on self and identity, motivation, personality research, and cognitive science. Baird's attempt to account for moral reasoning by appealing to various psychological literatures, including cognitive neuroscience, is a contribution to this emerging tradition.

I think she is on to something with her insight that mature moral functioning requires cognitive-affective integration. Of course, others have made this point too, most notably Hoffman (1983, 2000). But the novelty and importance of Baird's work is to show how this integration is grounded in neurobiological development. Her account of the maturation of the prefrontal cortex during adolescence and its possible role in underpinning

the development of decision making, self-control, and emotional regulation is part of a broad interest in developing a multilevel perspective that
attempts to explain complex social behavior by reference to brain-behavior
relationships (Cacioppo, 2002; Cacioppo, Bernston, Lorig, Norris, Rickett,
& Nussbaum, 2003; Spear, 2000). This perspective will require integrative
linkages between social science and neuroscience (Adolphs, 2003). Indeed,
given evidence of a neurological basis of moral behavior (Dolan, 1999),
and a greater interest in exploring the implication of cognitive neuroscience for social cognition (Adolphs, 1999, 2001) and ethical theory
(Casebeer, 2003b), the emergence of a social neuroscience (Cacioppo,
2002) of morality cannot be far behind.

Baird draws attention to one aspect of moral functioning that these new
perspectives will be required to explain, which is that everyday moral
behavior is highly automatized and takes place outside of consciousness
and intentional control (e.g., Epley & Caruso, 2004). The intersection of
the morality of everyday life and the automaticity of everyday life must
be large and extensive (Narvaez & Lapsley, 2005).

Baird's model specifies that in early moral development cognition
(knowing) precedes emotion (feeling), at least after infancy. In adolescence,
social learning serves to integrate cognition and emotion in such a way
that moral functioning is highly automatized and requires little conscious
awareness. In her view, the integration of emotion and social cognition
during adolescence is the foundation of a "fully developed moral reasoning" that requires little cognitive effort. As noted previously, fully developed and highly automatized moral reasoning that is tightly integrated
with emotions is supported by the physical maturation of the prefrontal
cortex during adolescence. Alternatively, Baird approvingly cites Damasio's
somatic marker hypothesis to provide an explanation of the source of our
visceral moral feelings and to make the case that optimal moral decision
making is as much driven by somatic markers as it is by rational calculation of costs and benefits (but see Turiel, 2006, for another view).

Baird takes on the daunting challenge of attempting to capture the main
elements of moral development from infancy to adulthood in just four
basic stages. The first stage involves the classical conditioning of the infant
"through which behaviors come to be unconsciously paired with sensory
outcomes and are consequently reduced or encouraged" (this volume,
p. 338). The second stage involves a movement from classical to operant
conditioning of aversions in early childhood. At this stage youngsters also
reflect upon past and present in light of internalized standards, engage in
self-regulation, and experience guilt. The third stage awaits the cognitive

development of adolescence, where thinking is more complex, abstract, and logical. Adolescents are better able to organize biographical memories, make generalizations, and draw valid inferences. They also have a better awareness than do children of their "visceral sense." "At this point in development," Baird writes, "the somatic concern that was associated with punishment for violating a standard is replaced with a visceral sense of guilt" (this volume, p. 331). Moreover, part of this visceral sense is the ability to make accurate attributions about the source of one's emotional response. For example, unlike children, adolescents are able to link visceral emotion (e.g., "butterflies" in the stomach) to abstract things (e.g., thoughts about a "crush"). In Baird's view, the ability to link emotion and thought in this way "enables both self-awareness and the formation of self-conscious emotions" (this volume, p. 339). Finally, the fourth stage describes a member-of-society perspective where one is able to reason from the point of view of the broad social polity and its "prescribed moral code" (this volume, p. 339). A stage like this is also the summit of perspective taking (Selman, 1980), self-understanding (Damon & Hart, 1982), and conventional moral reasoning (Kohlberg et al., 1983).

Baird acknowledges the inevitability of wide individual differences in a stage sequence of such broad strokes (which is sure to miss many details), yet suggests that every stage must be realized "in order to avoid pathology" (this volume, p. 339). This claim is hard to understand. Surely immature moral reasoning is not pathological, and no developmental stage theory holds out the prospect that everyone can perform at the highest level of competence described by the final stage of a sequence. The false move in this argument is the assumption that mature moral reasoning is isomorphic with neurological maturation. So, if one's thinking is immature, thought and emotion must be inadequately integrated, with disastrous, even pathological consequences, of which the Shanda story is the case example. The killers of Shanda Renee Sharer had deficient moral reasoning, in Baird's account, because the maturation of the prefrontal cortex in these teens had not yet welded the visceral sense with moral considerations. As a result they could blithely torture and murder Shanda because they lacked self-awareness and self-conscious emotions that such integration affords. We recognize in Shanda's killers a pathological indifference to suffering, to be sure, yet Baird implies that such pathology is not exceptional. It shows up in banal forms in individuals who have not yet reached the highest moral stage.

This thesis, if I understand it, is highly speculative. No one doubts that social cognition, emotion, and behavior involve the brain, but there is no consensus on the psychological or behavioral significance of prefrontal maturation for the moral domain, and certainly no linkages have been established between brain function and the sort of member-of-society abstractions that characterize deliberative moral competence. It is not known whether the cognitive-emotional integration that accompanies neuroanatomical maturation during adolescence is necessary, sufficient, or irrelevant for the display of a normal range of moral affect, judgment, and behavior. For all we know, the level of cognitive-emotional integration that is minimally necessary for the normal tolerance of moral behavior comes on-line much earlier in development, say, with the neurobiological integration of cognition and emotion that occurs during early childhood (e.g., Blair, 2002). Tracing the developmental trajectory of social cognitive-affective mechanisms, including the neurobiological evidence of such integration, from early childhood to early adulthood, would constitute an informative line of research and serve as a foundation for theoretical speculation about the role of prefrontal maturation in adolescent moral reasoning.

The four-stage model presents additional challenges. It describes infancy and early childhood as a behaviorist paradise of classical and operant conditioning, and social learning as the mechanism that unites cognition with emotions, but not until adolescence. Baird writes "A developmentally ordered progression exists in moral development, in which conditioned behavior precedes explicit thought. Through the social learning that takes place in adolescence, thoughts and behaviors become associated with emotions that . . . produce socially appropriate behavior with relatively little cognitive influence" (this volume, p. 324). However, this account will not command assent, given what is known about infant cognition (Haith & Benson, 1998), the early emergence of internalized conscience (Kochanska & Thompson, 1997), the motivational and organizational role of emotions (Izard & Ackerman, 2000), and regulation of emotion (Gross, 1998; Cole, Martin & Dennis, 2004), including the integration of cognition and emotion in the first years of life (Bell & Wolfe, 2004; Izard, 1978). Indeed, as Abe and Izard (1999, p. 534) point out, "young children's moral understanding develops gradually through socioemotional interactions that involve interplay of the emotions and cognitive systems" at the beginning of the second year of life. Hence the association of thoughts, behavior, and emotions has a much longer developmental history than Baird's account would lead us to believe, certainly long before adolescence (see, e.g., Rothbart, Derryberry, & Posner, 1994).

Some cognitive elements of the four-stage model also require more specification. For example, young children are said to move from the operant learning of the early toddler period to Kohlberg's first stage of moral reasoning around age 5, except that Kohlberg's theory has nothing to say about moral reasoning of children at this age. According to Baird, mature moral reasoning requires the emergence of self-conscious emotion, which in turn requires both sophisticated cognitive awareness and changes in neural physiology. However, the emergence of self-conscious emotion, including emotions of moral significance (e.g., empathy, guilt, shame, embarrassment), is more commonly thought to be an achievement of early childhood (Tangney & Fischer, 1995).

Perhaps it is not the emergence of self-conscious emotion that attends mature moral reasoning in adolescence but rather the ability to be self-reflective about one's emotional state, or the ability to put self-conscious emotion at the service of sophisticated perspective taking. Although there is evidence that empathy and perspective taking are related to prosocial moral judgment in adolescence (Eisenberg, Zhou, & Koller, 2001), and that some forms of moral judgment (e.g., cognitive empathy and forgiveness) show neuropsychological specificity in adults (Farrow, Zheng, Wilkinson, Spence, Deakin, Tarier, Griffiths, & Woodruff, 2001), there is currently an insufficient empirical basis for drawing developmental conclusions about the neural activation of empathic and other moral concerns (Hastings, Zahn-Waxler, & McShane, 2006).

The role that emotions play in this account also deserves comment. The basis for the claim that cognition precedes emotion is not defended by Baird, but it is contested in the literature (Abe & Izard, 1999). For example, according to differential-emotions theory, emotions are the primary motivational system in human behavior and serve to organize perception, cognition, and behavior (Izard & Ackerman, 2000). Emotions influence perceptual vigilance, guide memory retrieval, and constrain the attentional resources available for reflective appraisal and response selection (Bugental & Goodnow, 1998). Robinson and Acevedo (2001) showed, for example, how "emotional vitality" during infancy predicted cognitive and language skills in later childhood, a sequence precisely opposite the one suggested by Baird.

Of course, the primacy of cognition over emotion has a long history in moral psychology and ethical theory, but it seems odd to see it affirmed here in an account that also invokes the somatic marker hypothesis. Rather than a relationship of precedence or of primacy, emotion and cognition are better considered an "intricately bound developmental process" (Bell & Wolfe, 2004, p. 366). Indeed, as Bugental and Goodnow (1998, p. 416) put it, "emotional states influence what is perceived and how it is processed, and the interpretations made of ongoing events subsequently influence emotional reactions and perceptual biases." It is likely that cognitive-affective mechanisms interact in complex ways across the developmental terrain, with little cause for affirming precedence at one stage but wedded connection at another. Emotional processes play a fundamental role in social cognitive development at every developmental period (Abe & Izard, 1999).

Finally, Baird's willingness to fold automaticity into her account of adolescent moral reasoning will be resisted by many moral development researchers, largely because it offends the assumption of phenomenalism that Kohlberg laid down as a prerequisite for conceptualizing the moral domain (see, e.g., Kohlberg et al., 1983). However, on this score I stand with her. The assumption of phenomenalism asserts that the moral status of behavior depends upon the phenomenological perspective of the agent. It asserts that a behavior has no particular moral status unless it is motivated by an explicit moral judgment that is conscious, effortful, and deliberative. However, this assumption is problematic. For one thing, the principle of phenomenalism attaches a privilege to private mental states that is philosophically suspect (Wittgenstein, 1958). Moreover, it has the unintended consequence of rendering moral conduct something rare and occasional. If the morality of everyday life were to follow the requirements of the principle of phenomenalism, there would be very few instances of moral behavior to speak of, given the fact that most social cognition is not conscious, effortful, and deliberative but is instead automatic, implicit, and on the margin of conscious awareness (Bargh, 1997; Bargh & Ferguson, 2000; Bargh & Chartrand, 1999).

The unmistakable next wave in moral psychology, in my view, will attempt to account for the moral dimensions of human experience given the implicit quality of social information processing. Fortunately, there are ways to get to moral automaticity that do not require us to give up our assumptions about the rational or cognitive bases of moral reasoning, such as appeals to social-cognitive mechanisms (Lapsley & Narvaez, 2004) or the development of moral expertise (Narvaez & Lapsley, 2005). Baird suggests another mechanism that is rooted in neuroanatomical maturation. Whatever the truth of the matter, she is fundamentally correct in pointing out an important new trend in moral psychology, which is how to account for implicit moral cognition in the automaticity of everyday life.

Can Baird's View of Adolescent Morality Inform Adolescent Criminal Justice Policy?

Katrina L. Sifferd

Baird begins and ends her discussion of adolescent morality with a terrifying account of four teenaged girls torturing and murdering a 12-year-old girl named Shanda. Baird tells us in her prologue that it is "improbable" that three of the girls who participated in the murder suffered from psychopathy and that the underlying reasoning of the girls who participated in the crime was "surprisingly consistent with normal adolescent development" (this volume, p. 324). Baird's epilogue returns to Shanda's story and closes with the following claim: "As anyone who had been singled out and picked on in their teen years knows, there is a level on which the events [of Shanda's murder] are hauntingly familiar" (this volume, p. 340).

One might think that Baird is asserting that at least three of the teens who participated in Shanda's brutal torture and murder were, in a sense, ordinary adolescents. This thought is quite alarming. If the reasoning of these murderous girls is consistent with normal adolescent decision making—if ordinary teens are capable of torture and murder—it would seem that we might want to rethink our public policies concerning teens, e.g., our policy of allowing them to freely roam public streets and shopping malls. Indeed, after reading her prologue, one might feel that Baird's chapter should be used to support legislation requiring all teens to attend some sort of military boarding school, away from the vulnerable public.

This interpretation of Baird's view of adolescent morality can't be right. Baird herself notes that tragedies such as Shanda's murder are very rare; the vast majority of teens do not participate in severely amoral or vicious behavior. While adolescents are more likely than adults to engage in risky and even criminal behavior, this behavior rarely constitutes a violent crime. While some aspect of the decision making of Shanda's murderers might be normal for an adolescent, there must have been some additional contributing factor or circumstance that played a role in Shanda's death, something that pushed the three teens' actions outside the range of normal teen behavior.

To fully explore the culpability of Shanda's killers, it would be necessary to examine both their juvenile status as a factor mitigating that culpability and the possibility that one or more of Shanda's killers may be subject to some sort of psychological disorder or pathology, which could also lessen culpability. Baird's chapter, however, is only helpful for understanding the impact of juvenile status on culpability. The chapter focuses upon the development of moral decision making in the typical adolescent, and only hints at the way that this normal developmental process may go awry.

The question of the effect of juvenile status on culpability, particularly criminal culpability, is a topical one. The current trend in juvenile justice is often to ignore the psychological capacity of a juvenile offender, especially when he or she has committed a particularly violent crime. In response to the tragic details of high-profile murder cases, legislators and the public have pushed for adult-level legal responsibility and penalties for adolescent violent offenders, ignoring the traditional requirement that punishment of a criminal be proportional to the blameworthiness of the offender. In response, the U.S. Supreme Court has recently stepped in to limit states' powers to punish juvenile offenders by deeming them ineligible for the death penalty.[1]

Consideration of blameworthiness requires examination of an offender's psychology. Only offenders whose decision-making processes are sufficiently similar to that of a normal adult are generally deemed to be fully blameworthy for the consequences of their decisions. In accordance with the principle of proportionality, the U.S. criminal justice system tends to treat a person who is involuntarily intoxicated, severely mentally ill, or severely mentally retarded as less blameworthy than an adult whose decision-making capacity is operating normally. Similarly, it has been assumed that "[T]he vicissitudes of youth bear directly on the young offender's culpability and responsibility for the crime."[2]

The idea that juveniles are less blameworthy was institutionalized in the United States by the development of a separate juvenile court system. Just as juveniles were thought to be incapable of voting, drinking alcohol, and making contracts or medical decisions before the age of 18, in the early twentieth century they were similarly presumed to be incapable of fully forming criminal intent before their legal majority. Juvenile court proceedings emphasized rehabilitation of the juvenile offender, and their informality allowed judges to individualize sentences in an attempt to get offending juveniles back on track. This focus on rehabilitation and not retribution was justified by the juveniles' lesser culpability.

By the 1980s, however, there was widespread dissatisfaction with the juvenile courts. A rise in juvenile crime and the shocking facts of certain high-profile cases helped to propel frustration with the efficiency of the system into a tsunami of new legislation allowing juveniles to be transferred to adult court and allowing more severe penalties in the juvenile courts. Transfers and more severe penalties under the new legislation tend to be triggered by facts about the offense and not the offender, thereby constituting a rejection of the principle of proportionality, at least as applied to juveniles who commit serious crimes.[3]

Some psychologists and legal academics have worked hard to fight against the recent changes to our handling of juvenile offenders, precisely by attempting to draw policy makers' attention to data on juvenile psychology. For example, Elizabeth Scott and Laurence Steinberg have published articles arguing that because "developmental factors influence their criminal choices, young wrongdoers are less blameworthy than adults under conventional criminal law conceptions of mitigation" (E.S. Scott & Steinburg, 2003, p. 801).[4] They support this claim by noting that recent data on the psychological development of adolescents directly inform the determination of criminal responsibility in juveniles by providing information on both adolescent choice and adolescent character. According to Scott and Steinburg, although teens have capacities for reasoning and understanding fairly close to those of adults by midadolescence, these teens are still substantially less capable when it comes to using these skills to generate real-life decisions. This is largely due to teens' slow advancement in psychosocial development (E.S. Scott & Steinburg, 2003, p. 811).

Scott and Steinburg claim that the psychosocial factors most relevant to the differences in capacity for judgment between adolescents and adults are (1) peer orientation, (2) attitudes toward and perception of risk, (3) temporal perspective, and (4) capacity for self-management (E.S. Scott & Steinburg, 2003, p. 813). Susceptibility to peer pressure appears to peak around the age of 14 and decline slowly through the high school years (Steinberg & Silverberg, 1986). Adolescents seem to overvalue the opinions of their peers, even to the point of disregarding risk to their health or safety or risk to another's health or safety. (Note that unlike adults, adolescents usually commit crimes in the company of peers.) Overall, adolescents seem particularly risk friendly, especially when compared with adults (Furby & Beyth-Marom, 1992, p. 813). Adolescents also weigh short-term consequences of decisions—both risks and rewards—much more heavily in making choices than do adults (Scott & Steinburg, 2003, p. 814), and they appear to be less able to imagine events that have not yet occurred and of which they have no first-hand experience. Finally, Scott and Steinberg note that impulsivity and sensation seeking increases in middle adolescence and early adulthood and declines thereafter.[5]

Because of the differences between adolescent and adult decision making, Scott and Steinburg, and many others who do research on adolescent psychology, argue that juveniles are not as blameworthy as adults for their actions and thus their criminal responsibility is mitigated. Of course, not all adolescents exhibit the same capacity for decision making and judgment; generally, the influence of psychosocial factors fades in the process of maturing, leading to better decision making (by normal adult standards). Thus, older adolescents may be considered more blameworthy than younger adolescents, although it seems that there should be some opportunity to consider an older juvenile's individual level of culpability, at least at sentencing. From a public policy perspective, however, it is especially important to consider a younger juvenile's blameworthiness when assessing culpability.[6]

Baird's discussion of the stages of adolescent morality should be considered a significant contribution to the discussion of adolescent culpability. Her view largely confirms the conclusions of Scott and Steinburg and can be considered to bolster their claims with evidence from cutting-edge psychological research, such as that in the field of neuroscience. In addition, Baird's perspective on the development of adolescent morality provides a motive— separate from concerns of adolescent blameworthiness—to retain a separate juvenile justice system that focuses upon rehabilitative sanctions.

Baird argues that prior to adolescence most children learn what behaviors to perform via simple conditioning (Baird's stage one). Later, they gain the ability to reflect upon decisions made in the past and their consequences and internalize standards of appropriate behavior (Baird's stage two). At this point children become aware that their prior behaviors should have been modified, which forms the foundation for guilt.

As a result of these two stages, a child is capable of making present decisions based upon either lessons learned via past experience or current environmental response. Baird sees experience as primarily responsible for the emergence of adultlike reasoning. "Greater experience and an improved system for organizing and retrieving the memories of experience enable the adolescent to recall and apply a greater number of previous experiences to new situations" (this volume, p. 327).

Another important hallmark in adolescent decision making is the development of abstract thought, which enables the child to envision and anticipate situations they have not directly experienced (Baird's stage three). Baird supports her argument that adolescents become increasingly able to participate in abstract thought by noting that in adolescence gray matter is slowly replaced with white matter throughout the cortex (but most significantly in the frontal cortex). Increased white matter in the anterior cingulate cortex leads to increased ability in mediation and control of emotional, attentional, motivational, social, and cognitive behaviors. By the end of this process, a juvenile is more in control of his behavior and less impulsive.

Around the same time the adolescent is developing the ability to participate in abstract thought, Baird argues that social cognition takes center stage and "the role of moral dictator shifts from primarily the parents to primarily peers" (this volume, p. 325). This means that adolescents begin to focus upon feedback from others as an indication of whether an act was right or wrong. Much of this feedback takes the form of emotions felt by the adolescent, or somatic markers. Increasing levels of white matter in the dorsal anterior cingulate may lead adolescents to gain the ability to create second-order representations of body state. This in turn can lead to adolescents becoming more aware of their emotional states, including emotional states felt in response to the outcomes of an act or, later, emotions generated in response to mere thoughts about potential conduct. Acts that are known to generate bad emotional feedback are avoided because an adolescent can "anticipate how they might feel following such an event" (this volume, p. 331).

Baird argues that adolescents become aware of self-conscious emotions, such as pride, shame, guilt, or embarrassment last. Such emotions are directly related to thinking about the thoughts of others. For adolescents, the persons that most often cause feelings of pride or shame are peers. Baird notes that the ability of adolescents to speculate upon an audience for their actions tends to be overapplied when it first develops; teens may believe that people are watching and evaluating them even when this isn't the case. Adolescents also tend to make mistakes because they think that the new emotions they are feeling are unique to them. Thus Baird says they participate in a personal fable. Only later do they realize that such emotions are a part of the universal human experience.

In sum, Baird's stage three, the stage of moral decision making that appears to develop in the heart of adolescence, is "typified by the ability to consider the self and other perspectives simultaneously from a third-party or 'observing ego' perspective" (this volume, p. 324). Experience consisting of positive or negative feedback becomes internalized so that the complexity of moral decisions is diminished, because somatic markers provide "a 'gut' feeling that does not require effortful cognition" (this volume, p. 330).

Baird confirms Scott and Steinburg's claims that adolescents lack the control of emotional, attentional, motivational, social, and cognitive behaviors that adults exhibit. As a result, Baird notes that young adolescents are more impulsive in their decision making than adults. Baird also focuses upon the important role that experience plays in juvenile decision making. Scott and Steinburg claim that one difference between adolescent and adult decision making is the inability of adolescents to imagine the consequences of a new act or acts performed under new circumstances. Baird similarly argues that to some extent better decision making—better attitudes toward risk to oneself and others—is learned. Exposure to new experiences allows a teen to make better choices when similar experiences arise in the future.

In addition, Baird, like Scott and Steinburg, stresses the importance of peer relationships in adolescent decision making. However, Baird offers us a more sophisticated understanding of the interaction between adolescents and their peers. While the juvenile culpability literature has traditionally viewed peers as an impediment to good adolescent decision making (primarily because peer opinion is overvalued), Baird argues that peers play a vital role in the overall development of adolescent moral decision making. She claims that emotional feedback in response to the consequences of certain decisions provides important information regarding how the adolescent should act in the future. This feedback is most often provided by one's peer relationships.

This leads us to one troubling consequence of Baird's view. It seems she claims that the quality of one's moral decision making is going to depend upon the sort of experiences one has as an adolescent and the sort of peer relationships one has. If one earns positive feedback from one's peers (and thus feels positive emotions) from engaging in violence, and negative feedback (and thus negative emotions) from refraining from violence, an adolescent's sense of right and wrong will become skewed.

If this is true, the influence of peers on adolescent decision making has more implications for juvenile justice policy than just providing more evidence that adolescents may be less blameworthy than adults. It also prescribes applying penalties to juveniles that may interrupt a cycle of peer influence that results in a skewed moral compass. One of the justifications of the institution of a separate juvenile justice system was the aim of getting adolescents who appeared to be going astray back on track. In cases where the juvenile was a first-time offender, or where his crime was fairly minor, this was accomplished by increased supervision of the juvenile within his community. Judges or probation officers would attempt to expose juveniles to positive influences by making them participate in a mentoring program, or a drug rehabilitation program, or by making them get a job or stay in school. Repeat offenders or those who were considered a risk to public safety were sent to a juvenile detention center, not an adult prison, because it was thought that adult offenders could influence juveniles to continue their antisocial behavior.

If Baird is right, this was a reasonable response to juvenile crime. It is likely that a juvenile sent to an adult prison would see other inmates as his peers, a situation that is likely to lead to an increased likelihood of criminal behavior. Studies support this idea. Juveniles sent to adult prisons are not more likely to be deterred from future crime; instead, they are more likely to recidivate than juveniles who commit the same type of crime but are sent to juvenile prisons (Butts & Mitchell, 2000).

However, we should not be too quick to jump from a particular reading of Baird's view to concrete public policy. To understand the extent to which Baird's perspective provides support for rehabilitative programming for juvenile offenders, we need more details about the stage of adolescent moral development at which a juvenile develops a moral sense of right and wrong through emotional feedback. First, at what age range does this stage occur? Does it occur over a wide age range (e.g., across the ages of 12 to 17) or a fairly narrow one (e.g., during the ages of 14 to 16)? Second, once an adolescent's moral sense is developed, is it permanent? Or can new environments and experiences continue to affect the operation of one's moral sense well into adulthood? The answers to these questions would help to identify the phase of adolescence where rehabilitation programming would have the greatest effect. It would also help us locate the point at which adolescents can be transferred to adult court without concern that the transfer will have negative effects on the adolescent's moral reasoning.

It would also be helpful to know how Baird thinks the pathology of a moral sense or moral reasoning could emerge. If an adolescent develops a pathology of moral reasoning during one of the stages of its development, does this mean she or he is stuck in this stage? More important, is there any way to identify these adolescents and separate them from other juveniles undergoing the normal process of moral development? Such identification would be significant because it would seem that some pathologies of the development of moral reasoning (e.g., if an adolescent's personal fable became especially exaggerated, and they could not feel empathy) would make an adolescent immune to rehabilitative programming (but possibly eligible for mitigated culpability owing to a mental illness).

Conclusion

Faced with the terrible facts of juvenile crimes such as those committed against Shanda, legislatures have been turning away from proportionality in juvenile culpability and rehabilitation as a legitimate policy aim for a system handling juvenile offenders. Baird doesn't provide us with an explanation of what exactly went wrong with the decision making of Shanda's murderers. She doesn't discuss what extreme circumstances or pathology might have led those particular adolescents to commit a seriously violent crime. However, by providing us with additional support for proportionality of punishment for juveniles and for a juvenile justice system focused upon rehabilitation, her discussion of the typical development of adolescent morality gives us even more reason to believe that current juvenile justice policy is headed in the wrong direction.

Notes

1. *Roper v. Simmons*, 543 US 551 (2005).

2. *Eddings v. Oklahoma*, 455 US 104, 115–116 (1982).

3. In *Roper v. Simmons* the court stated, "Whether viewed as an attempt to express the community's moral outrage or as an attempt to right the balance of wrong to the victim, the case for retribution is not as strong with a minor as it is with an adult. Retribution is not proportional if the law's most severe penalty is imposed on one whose culpability or blameworthiness is diminished, to a substantial degree, by reason of youth and immaturity" [*Roper v. Simmons*, 543 US 551, 571 (2005)].

The court noted that crime control or public safety concerns similarly failed to support the application of the death penalty to juveniles because, generally, teens are less susceptible to deterrence and "the likelihood that the teenage offender has made the kind of cost-benefit analysis that attaches any weight to the possibility of execution is as remote as to be virtually nonexistent" (*Roper*, 572).

In his dissent, however, Justice Scalia appeared to support the view that when a crime is severe enough, one should focus upon the facts of the crime and not upon the blameworthiness of the offender, even when that offender is eligible for the death penalty. Scalia describes the brutal facts of the murder committed by the defendant Simmons and then notes that states supporting the juvenile death penalty had cited similarly tragic facts surrounding other crimes committed by juveniles. "Though these cases are assuredly the exception rather than the rule, the studies the Court cites in no way justify a constitutional imperative that prevents legislatures and juries from treating exceptional cases in an exceptional way—by determining that some murders are not just the acts of happy-go-lucky teenagers, but heinous crimes deserving of death" (Scalia Dissent, *Roper*, 619).

4. See also E.S. Scott (2001), Steinburg and Cauffman (1996), Steinburg and Scott (2003).

5. E.S. Scott & Steinburg (2003), citing Steinburg and Cauffman (1996, p. 260).

6. Again, we should consider the blameworthiness of young offenders even when they commit particularly serious crimes. Nevada and Colorado, for example, can transfer children as young as 10 years to adult court if there is reason to believe they have committed a murder. Twenty-three states have provisions allowing the transfer of juveniles who commit serious crimes to adult court, where no minimum age is specified.

Reply to Sifferd and Lapsley

Abigail A. Baird

I appreciate Lapsley and Sifferd's comments on my chapter. They make several excellent points, the range of which is too great to be completely addressed in this response. I will therefore focus this essay on the issue of psychopathology, an issue raised by both Lapsley and Sifferd. This response is organized into two sections: the first deals with pathological disruption in the proposed model of moral development, and the second addresses the idea that horrific moral transgressions often occur in the absence of any discernable psychological pathology.

Collectively, the scientific literature has described the function of human development as enabling the individual to pass their genetic material on to the next generation. Because of this predisposition, development is an extremely plastic process, enabling human infants to follow an infinite number of developmental paths. Ideally, the developmental path is constrained by environmental demands that not only complement the individual's biology but also forge behavioral outcomes that result in the individual's eventual reproductive success (see Waddington, 1975). Certain processes within human development build upon themselves. This recurrent recapitulation can be seen in both neural and behavioral development (see Gould, 1977). Other processes develop in such a way that each period constitutes a unique time, with individual environmental demands and idiosyncratic milestones (see Björklund, 1997 for a review). It is the complex interaction of these two developmental courses (and most likely others yet to be discovered) that gives rise to observable human development. The acknowledgment of both trajectories is critical to understanding how deficits at one stage are equally likely to ripple their way through what remains of development, or be compensated for (with varying degrees of success) by the developmental periods that follow.

Defining pathology within a developmental context is a tricky business. Behavior that is not in accord with social norms is fairly easy to detect but often quite difficult to explain. For the purposes of this discussion, an explanation of moral transgressions is divided into two general categories: knowing and not knowing. Transgressions resulting from not knowing describe behaviors that are the result of the individual's lack of knowledge, either of the expected social norm or of the full consequences of their behavior. These violations mostly likely involve problems with learning. It is further important to note that knowledge in this context can be either emotional, cognitive, or some combination of the two. There are also instances when individuals possess sufficient knowledge of social norms as well as the potential repercussions of their actions but are unable or unwilling to regulate their behavior. Violations of this nature are most likely related to problems with behavioral regulation. In addition, it is important to note that both types of transgressions can result from disruptions at the level of hardware (neurobiological) and/or the installed software (inappropriate information from the environment). The discussion that follows focuses largely on how we come to possess knowledge of what is moral.

Based on our current understanding, the human brain does not correspond with human behavior in a direct fashion. As a result, the complex relationships among brain structure, brain function, human behavior, and psychopathology require cautious speculation. The theoretical descriptions that follow, therefore, are given with the understanding that brain-based anomalies often result in little or no behavioral consequences. Implicit in this discussion is also the idea that the brain and behavior have a reciprocal relationship, meaning that experience is fully capable of rendering pathological brain structure and/or function (see Mazziotta, 2000 for a review). In order to understand how moral pathology might emerge, these qualifiers must be considered.

If human beings are not hardwired for moral behavior, then it is up to some developmental process to produce it. At the core of the proposed model of moral development is the coordination of emotion and cognition. This interaction changes form in response to individual social, emotional, and cognitive demands, and manifests in both continuous and discontinuous change during development. During the described stages, the relationship between cognition and emotion changes both quantitatively and qualitatively and reaches its apex during a sensitive period in early adolescence. Finally, the developmental synergy between emotion and cognition relies heavily on individual differences in visceral sense, sensitivity to that sense and individual differences in cognitive ability, insight, and emotionality.

While this may seem to be an inordinate number of variables, it most likely only begins to describe the immense complexity of this developmental process. It is precisely this complexity, however, that makes human behavior so malleable. This behavioral plasticity is undoubtedly one of the great accomplishments of human evolution. Developmental processes, however, work on an honor principle, meaning that most of them rely on the integrity of brain structure and function as well as the utility of the feedback they receive from the environment. There is little opportunity within development to properly test the universality of either of these. For example, in contemporary America, a man from the Middle East who holds another man's hand in a display of friendship might be perceived as making a sexual advance. More relevant to this discussion are children who grow up without the neural hardware or experiential feedback required to develop a moral sense that is consistent with what law and society deem appropriate. At the risk of being overly simplistic, the goal of most developmental processes is to keep one alive and in the best long-term position to pass on one's genetic material. Understandably, this goal takes on different forms and requires significantly different things at different points in development. For example, giggling and smiling goes a long way toward survival for infants and even young children, but does very little when it comes to paying for groceries as an adult.

Developmental Neuropathology

The first stage of moral development requires that infants acquire the ability to match their own actions with concomitant outcomes. These outcomes range from highly pleasurable to highly aversive, and it is through the conditioned association of the infant's behavior with sensory-based consequences that the earliest forms of learning are instantiated. Disruptions in this ability have been consistently associated with early amygdalar dysfunction and acquired psychopathy. LeDoux and colleagues (1994) have stressed the importance of the amygdala in fear detection and conditioning, describing it as a neural system that evolved to detect danger and produce rapid protective responses without conscious participation. The central nucleus of the amygdala has been described as essential for the expression of autonomic and somatic fear responses elicited by both learned and unlearned threats. These responses are controlled through efferent connections from the central amygdala to the brainstem nuclei (Rogan & LeDoux, 1996). The amygdala has also been characterized as a higher-order convergence zone for the social homeostatic and survival-related meanings of complex stimuli (Damasio, 1994). Taken together, these lines of evidence describe the amygdala as a structure that has evolved to help the human animal recognize and learn the emotional meanings of stimuli in their environment and produce appropriate behavioral responses.

More recently, Blair (2005) demonstrated that individuals with early amygdalar damage were not capable of learning a conditioned response based on the facial expressions of others, but showed no deficits in conditioned learning when the stimulus was a basic threat, such as bared teeth. Perhaps most striking about this type of primal deficit is that among individuals with average or above-average cognitive functioning, their inability to extract meaning from social and emotional cues in childhood often attracts little attention, and it is not noticed until the multifaceted pressures of adolescence stress the individual and precipitate maladaptive behavior. It is much more common, however, that disruptions of this early stage lead to pervasive difficulties in social and emotional processing (most prominently, social attachments), where moral transgressions appear alongside a multitude of maladaptive behaviors (Baird, Veague, & Rabbit, 2005; Blair, 2005).

Dysfunction of specific areas within the frontal cortex, specifically the orbital, ventromedial prefrontal and cingulate cortices have been consistently associated with psychopathy (Damasio, 1994; Raine, Buchsbaum, Stanley, Lottenberg, Abel, & Stoddard, 1994; Kiehl, chapter 3 in this volume). Historical as well as recent reports have suggested that some, but not all, of the characteristics associated with psychopathy may also be acquired following damage to these same regions (Harlow, 1848; Anderson, Bechara, Damasio, Tranel, & Damasio, 1999; Barrash, Tranel, & Anderson, 2000), implicating these regions in the manifestation of psychopathic behavior. Pathological lying, irresponsibility, promiscuous sexual behavior, labile affect, and lacking feelings of guilt or remorse are just a few of the behaviors that are seen in persons experiencing ventromedial (Anderson et al., 1999) and orbitofrontal damage (Damasio, 1994). While damage to these regions does not inevitably result in the development of psychopathic behavior, individuals with this type of damage are likely to demonstrate behaviors associated with psychopathy (i.e., impulsivity, remorselessness, problems with emotional processing).

Although there is little doubt that disruption of frontal cortical systems contributes significantly to the symptomatology of psychopathy, it is equally plausible that the neural systems underlying this personality disorder have both local and distributed components (Damasio, 1994). Blair has argued that a dysfunction of the amygdala may be primarily responsible for behavior associated with psychopathy. It has been well established that damage to the amygdala results in impairments in affect recognition (Adolphs, Baron-Cohen, & Tranel, 2002; Anderson & Phelps, 2001). Relevant to the establishment of reciprocal influence between the amygdala and the prefrontal cortex is the time course of this connectivity. Arguably, these prefrontal regions and subcortical limbic structures could be working together. It is conceivable that a dysfunction in one of these regions could lead to the manifestation of psychopathy within the normal range, while a dysfunction in both areas may result in the marked differences in behavior seen in criminal and clinical populations. That is, persons with a hyporesponsive amygdala might show the behavioral problems associated with psychopathy, but not the personality style differences (i.e., manipulativeness, callousness). Individuals with specific prefrontal deficits may manifest personality traits resembling those of primary psychopaths, but without the behavioral impulsivity consistently observed among psychopathic individuals. Only with the combined attenuated capabilities of both regions would individuals develop full-blown clinical psychopathy and most likely demonstrate criminal behavior.

More specific to developmental processes, medial temporal lobe structures are functionally mature very early in life, while the human frontal cortex does not reach full functional maturity until after puberty. Therefore, it is plausible that early in development many aspects of behavior may be regulated by medial temporal lobe structures. Furthermore, it is conceivable that during later development frontal regions begin to exert a more powerful influence, so that what were once largely survival-based unconscious behaviors become increasingly entwined with more conscious cognitive and social processes. To date, however, few studies have explored the developmental path of this functional connectivity. It has been established that during adolescence there is a substantial increase in the density and myelination of projections between medial temporal regions and frontal cortices (see Benes, Vincent, Molloy, & Khan, 1996; Cummings, 1995 for a review of the specific circuits). Investigations using nonhuman primates have suggested that selective aspects of normal frontal development may rely on medial temporal lobe integrity (Bertolino, Saunders, Mattay, Bachevalier, Frank, & Weinberger, 1997).

Additional studies of nonhuman primates suggest that early damage to the amygdala has a deleterious effect on later social and emotional learning and behavior, while lesions of the amygdala in adulthood do not produce the same types of behavioral impairments (Bachevalier, 1991). It is not entirely clear, though, how these findings extend to human development. It is possible that the functionality of early-developing brain regions (i.e., temporal lobe structures) may serve to guide, at least in part, later-developing regions (i.e., frontal cortices). Taken together, the studies mentioned here suggest a model of functional connectivity that in early life begins with the medial temporal influence on the frontal cortices and later is driven by frontal regulation of medial temporal lobe structures. This is a process that takes place over many years and is the product of both pre-programmed neural development and environmental influence. Implicit in this development sequence is the assumption that the information available from the environment is not only advantageous for the individual but also is in accord with the moral standards of that individual's society. Unfortunately, even when neural development and coordination are within normal limits, exceptional environmental circumstances can produce highly deviant behavior.

No Sicker than Your Average Nazi

Both Sifferd and Lapsley had very strong reactions to the chapter's opening vignette, which described the torture and murder of Shanda Sharer by four teenaged girls. Almost as troubling was my claim that not all the girls involved in Shanda's murder were psychiatrically compromised, and in fact acted consistently with the normal trajectory of moral development.

If the reasoning of these girls is consistent with "normal" adolescent decision making—if ordinary teens are capable of torture and murder—it would seem that we might want to rethink our public policies concerning teens; e.g., our policy of allowing them to freely roam public streets and shopping malls. (Sifferd, this volume, p. 351)

There is a fourth objective that was motivated by the prologue's chilling account of the murder of Shanda Renee Sharer by four teenaged girls. The insouciance of Shanda's killers shocks our moral sensibilities, but we are assured by Baird that heinous moral conduct is banal, or, alternatively, that similar mechanisms underlie both ordinary and heinous moral failure. Torture and murder command the same developmental explanation as does taunting unpopular and "uncool" classmates, passing gossipy notes, and teaching "lessons." (Lapsley, this volume, p. 343)

Statistically, given that less than 1% of the U.S. population can be diagnosed with antisocial personality disorder (3% of the population for men, 1% for women) or psychopathy (less than 1% for both men and women), it approaches statistical impossibility for all four girls involved in Shanda's murder to be diagnosable. (Note: At the time of its dissolution, the Nazi party had more than 8.5 million members.) Statistical frequency, however, hardly places either Shanda's murderers or the actions of the Third Reich in the "conventional" category. As noted by Sifferd in her commentary, the vast majority of people (including adolescents) do not commit violent acts. I am a bit surprised that the reviewers responded as strongly as they did to my suggestion that acting in accordance with your peers is normal behavior.

We are fundamentally social animals that rely on the fluid exchange of social, emotional, and cognitive knowledge for our survival. This fluidity enables highly dynamic and adaptive behavioral output. Improvements in abstract thinking during adolescence enable significant advances in not only the way that they are able to understand their own thoughts and feelings but also in their ability to understand other individuals' experiences. Knowledge of the thoughts, beliefs, and feelings of others is the well from which springs the capacity for both great compassion and great harm. The improvements in abstract thought also help individuals to think about how they might feel about something in the future, or to strategize about theoretical behavioral responses to situations that may occur in the future. The appropriate behavioral response to most situations requires a specific combination of thought and feeling. Poor decisions are often made when one relies on inappropriate amounts of either thought or feeling. For example, a parent who punches the 6-year-old bully who hit their own child has reacted without thinking it through; similarly, a parent who admonishes his or her child for wanting a popular brand of jeans has reacted without considering what it feels like to be made fun of at school. We come to understand the conventional levels of thought and feeling in most behaviors through social feedback.

Adolescence is a particularly sensitive period for the acquisition of social knowledge. Similar to the accelerated period of language acquisition observed between 18 and 24 months, adolescence heralds a time of unprecedented sensitivity to peers, who as a collective stipulate normative behavior. During this time there is also a new-found proficiency in the processing and assimilation of social knowledge. An adolescent is neither a child nor an adult, in the way that a caterpillar is neither larva nor butterfly. This stage in development has a unique set of features that are focused on acquiring access to mates in a way that does not exist prior to or following this period. This access to mates requires successful navigation of the peer-infested social waters. As a result of this thirst for social and relational knowledge (again reminiscent of the zeal with which the 2-year-old acquires new vocabulary) adolescence is the pinnacle of peer learning. "If so-and-so jumped off the Brooklyn Bridge would you"? This phrase is popular because we understand, at some level, the importance and absurdity of adolescents' reliance on peers. Adolescence, however, is not the only period during which social influence exists, and in fact the research on social influence is far more extensive. The well-known work of Milgram, Zimbardo, Watson, and Bandura, among others, has convincingly demonstrated that human behavior is both socially and situationally constrained in ways that are often hard to imagine.

In 1992 the world witnessed horrific acts of violence among Bosnians, as belief-driven genocide once again took center stage in a civil war that pitted countryman against countryman. When it was over it had claimed an estimated 100,000 lives and produced more than two million refugees. Perhaps most bewildering about the war in Bosnia was the fact that a previously peaceful people had, without any direct provocation, raped, tortured and killed neighbors, students, colleagues, and wives with whom they had lived happily for years. In his book *Love thy Neighbor* Peter Maass described how the Serbians' complete control of the media and constant barrage of propaganda managed to tip the balance of civilization and convince the most mild-mannered individuals that "the cruelties of the past awaited Serbs unless they were on the offensive and committed preemptive genocide. Twisted and sharp, the blade of history was lobotomizing them." Maass's imagery is incredibly useful in understanding how this sort of behavior comes to be. While it is well beyond the scope of this essay to delve into the deep and broad psychology of war and genocide, it is mechanistically relevant to the development of moral reasoning to understand how the thoughts and feelings of others can exert such a profound influence on our own behavior.

[my studies demonstrate] a propensity for people to accept definitions of action provided by legitimate authority. That is, although the subject performs the action, he allows authority to define its meaning. (Milgram, 1974 p. 145; bracketed portion added.)

Maass's use of "lobotomy" powerfully conjures an image of an individual who is devoid of all cognitive influence, who is ready to act in self-defense on emotion-fueled rage. If the right amount and type of propaganda from those in power has the potential to interfere with the cognition of adults who possess decades of actual experience with one another, then it is certainly conceivable that the emotional influence of peer pressure on an uncoordinated cognitive and emotional system, with little or no actual experience, could wreak similar havoc.

More recently, the torture and abuse of American prisoners of war at Abu Ghraib prison received national attention, not only from the mass media, but also from social psychologists who sought to understand and contextualize the soldiers' egregious behavior.

Given an environment conducive to aggression and prisoners deemed disgusting and subhuman, well established principles of conformity to peers and obedience to authority may account for the widespread nature of the abuse. In combat conformity to one's unit means survival, and ostracism is death. The social context apparently reflected the phenomenon of people trying to make sense of a complex, confusing, ambiguous situation by relying on their immediate social group. (Fiske, Harris, & Cuddy, 2004, p. 1483)

Taken out of context, rarely has a more accurate description of seventh grade been written. Most would also agree that few things are as complex, confusing, and ambiguous as the all-inclusive metamorphosis that accompanies adolescence. Without being glib, this analogy is meant to underscore that the situation in adolescence is one of heightened vulnerability to the influence of socially potent leadership. Furthermore, this type of influence abounds; it is just that (relative to antisocial behavior) it is not as newsworthy when a popular kid convinces his friends that Britney Spears is "cool." What is also hauntingly familiar about the account of the psychology underlying the soldiers' behavior is how closely it parallels the day-to-day adolescent existence. During combat, Fiske and colleagues remind us, ostracism is a death sentence.

A recent report examined 13,465 adolescents and determined that, "adolescent females who are isolated from the adolescent community or whose relationships are intransitive and likely dissonant are at greater risk for suicidal thoughts than are girls who are embedded in cohesive friendship groups" (Bearman & Moody, 2004, p. 94). Specifically, Bearman and Moody found that ostracism was the second most common cause of attempted suicide among adolescent girls. Staying with your "unit" and keeping the social homeostasis is critical to adolescent survival. The complex interaction of the need to belong and the need to learn both proximal and distal social norms may help us better understand why adolescents may be at once entirely insolent in response to their parents and readily comply with every whim and opinion of their clique's leader. Basically, both their short-term and long-term survival depends on it.

Torture is partly a crime of socialized obedience. Subordinates not only do what they are ordered to do, but what they think their superiors would order them to do, given their understanding of the authority's overall goals. (Fiske et al., 2004, p. 1482)

I didn't stop it, I couldn't stop it. I don't care what anyone else says. If I would've tried anything different, I would've been dead, lying there with her and they would never know. I was terrified of Melinda and Laurie. Melinda had a knife and was going to kill Shanda. I didn't get help because I was scared they would kill me too. (Toni Lawrence, following her sentencing for her involvement in the murder of Shanda Shearer.)

It is true that every person encounters infinite opportunities every day to harm others, but very rarely does so. It is critical to keep this in mind, and it is most likely the case because the evolution of human society has not favored occurrences with probabilities as low as Shanda's murder.

Richard Joyce

Suppose two people are having a moral disagreement about, say, abortion. They argue in a familiar way about whether fetuses have rights, whether a woman's right to autonomy over her body overrides the fetus's welfare, and so on. But then suppose one of the people says, "Oh, it's all just a matter of opinion; there's no objective fact about whether fetuses have rights. When we say that something is morally forbidden, all we're really doing is expressing our disapproval of it." The other person protests: "No!—that's totally wrong. Of course there are objective moral truths." And suppose their dispute now settles on this new matter of whether there are objective moral facts, and the debate continues. They have now stopped discussing abortion and are discussing the nature of any moral debate about abortion; they have stopped doing ethics and started doing metaethics. If wondering about what one morally ought to do is to engage in ethical thought, then wondering about what one is doing when one wonders about what one morally ought to do is to engage in metaethical thought.

When we make public moral judgments, are we stating facts or are we just expressing our opinions? And if there are moral facts, then what kind of facts are they? Can moral judgments be true or false? Can moral judgments be justified, and if so, how? These kinds of questions are the domain of metaethics. (I'm not saying that there is a crisp and principled line to be drawn between metaethics and regular ethical discourse, but it is, if nothing else, a pedagogically useful division of labor.)

Thus, the issue of whether a body of empirical data can have any metaethical implications is different from the issue of whether it can have ethical implications. We might be wary of the claim that purely descriptive information could have any ethical implications for the oft-cited reason that one cannot derive an "ought" from an "is." (As a matter of fact, the ban on deriving an "ought" from an "is" is a piece of philosophical dogma that I don't subscribe to, but let that pass for now.) Even if there were an a priori prohibition on deriving evaluative conclusions from factual premises, this need not stand in the way of *meta*ethical implications being drawn from factual premises, for a metaethical claim is not an ethical "ought" claim; it is more likely to be a claim about how we use the word "ought" in ethical discourse, which is a perfectly empirical matter.[1] Indeed, I think metaethicists tend to be open to the possibility of empirical work shedding light on their field. Recently there has appeared a wealth of data that a metaethicist might take an interest in: findings from neuroscience, developmental psychology, evolutionary psychology, social psychology, evolutionary biology, experimental economics, cross-cultural anthropology, and even primatology. However, although all this research is doubtlessly of interest to a metaethicist, does any of it actually contribute to the resolution of any of our perennial metaethical questions? This chapter confines itself to addressing just two points: Can neuroscience support moral emotivism and can neuroscience undermine moral rationalism? (Since one of my main intentions is to disambiguate the diverse ways in which the terms "emotivism" and "rationalism" are used, it would be pointless to attempt a generic definition of either here at the outset.)

The first point will not require much discussion to arrive at a negative answer. Perhaps this will be of no surprise to philosophical readers; indeed, many may be astonished that anyone would be tempted to answer the question positively. Yet there has crept into the literature a tendency to describe certain empirical data, both from neuroscience and from social psychology, as supporting "emotivism." Jonathan Haidt leaves us in little doubt that he takes his research to vindicate "Hume's emotivist approach to ethics" (Haidt, 2001, p. 816), and elsewhere he is described explicitly as an "emotivist" by Joshua Greene et al. (Greene, Nystrom, Engell, Darley, & Cohen, 2004, p. 397). Greene and colleagues also take their own neuroscientific research to confirm a view that steers "a middle course between the traditional rationalism and the more recent emotivism that have dominated moral psychology" (2001, p. 2107). Haidt (2003b, p. 865) describes Freud as an emotivist (or, at least, "a rare but ready ally" of emotivism) on the grounds that he took reasoning to be often just a rationalization of subconscious desires. This terminology is taken up by others who assert that "emotivist perspectives on moral reasoning hold that emotional reactions precede propositional reasoning" (Fessler, Arguello, Mekdara, & Macias 2003, p. 31). It should be fairly obvious to anyone familiar with the metaethical tradition that these empirical scientists are using the word "emotivism" differently from philosophers. It would be fruitless and churlish to make this the basis of criticism; psychologists may, of course, use the word how they wish. It is nevertheless important to forestall any possible misconception that the empirical data support what philosophers call "emotivism," and I am satisfied if the following comments achieve this modest aim.

The question of whether neuroscience can undermine moral rationalism suffers from the same cross-disciplinary terminological confusion, since for many psychologists, "emotivism" and "rationalism" are taken to denote two poles of a continuum, defined according to which faculty is in charge in the production of moral judgment. Again, Haidt explicitly takes himself to be providing evidence against rationalist models of moral judgment, while Greene et al. also talk of their findings challenging rationalism (2004, p. 397). For metaethicists, by contrast, although emotivism and rationalism are generally considered contraries, they are very different kinds of theory. One is a theory about the linguistic function of moral utterances; the other is usually taken to concern the justificatory basis of actions. To a certain degree this is just another case of two academic disciplines using the same words in a divergent manner, and to that extent there is little to get excited about. However, it is worrying that the empirical scientists in question often purport to connect their findings to the moral rationalism that is found in the philosophical tradition (e.g., they mention Kant, Rawls, etc.), and indeed there is some work that tries to use empirical findings to refute specific versions of rationalism that have been formulated and expounded by moral philosophers (e.g., Nichols, 2004b, to be discussed later). Most of this chapter will be devoted to teasing apart different claims that might pass under the rubric "moral rationalism," with an eye to gauging just what empirical research—especially that of a neuroscientific nature—might contribute. A subproject of this investigation will be a brief discussion of whether evidence from neuroscience—specifically, the phenomenon of acquired sociopathy—helps break an impasse within metaethics over whether moral judgment necessarily implicates motivation.

Can Neuroscience Support Moral Emotivism?

Emotivism is a metaethical theory that had its heyday in the 1930s and 1940s but continues to attract a fair share of attention. Emotivism is a theory about moral language, most clearly construed as concerning the function of public moral utterances. It states that when we make a moral judgment, we are not expressing a belief (i.e., are not making an assertion), but rather are expressing some kind of conative mental state, such as a desire, emotion, or preference. Often moral emotivism is attributed to David Hume in the eighteenth century, but I think this is quite mistaken. Hume certainly thinks that emotions ("passions") play an important and possibly essential role in moral judgment, but one struggles to find him saying anything that implies that moral language *functions to express* emotions (see Joyce forthcoming a).

One of the earliest clear statements of emotivism comes from A. J. Ayer in 1936, who claimed that the judgment "Stealing money is wrong" does not express a proposition that can be true or false, but rather it is as if one were to say *"Stealing money!!"* with the tone of voice indicating that a special feeling of disapproval is being expressed (Ayer, 1936/1971, p. 110). It was Ayer's logical positivism that led him to such a view. Convinced that all meaningful statements must be either analytic or empirically verifiable, and faced with a chunk of language that appeared to be neither, the only way to grant the meaningfulness of this language was to deny that it consisted of statements.

Emotivism can be presented either as a semantic or as a pragmatic theory. One might claim that the sentence "Stealing is wrong" *means* "Boo to stealing!" This is a semantic version since it makes a claim about what the sentence really means; it provides a translation scheme from something with a propositional structure ("Stealing is wrong") to something nonpropositional ("Boo to stealing!"). It claims that the moral predicates (". . . is wrong," etc.) are predicates only at the grammatical level, not at the logical level. Alternatively, moral emotivism can be presented as a pragmatic theory, holding that the meaning of moral judgments like "Stealing is wrong" is exactly what it appears to be (whatever that is), but that when we employ such sentences in moral discourse we are not asserting them; rather, we are by convention using them to express disapproval or some other conative state. What these two types of emotivism have in common is that they claim that when we make a public moral judgment we are, despite appearances to the contrary, not expressing a belief. Let's say, to make things simple, that they hold instead that we are expressing an emotion.

One might be tempted to think that a lot of recent research from psychology and neuroscience supports emotivism, since this research shows that emotions play a central role in moral deliberation. I leave it to others to present this evidence in detail (see Prinz in volume 1, Haidt and Nichols in volume 2, and Moll and Greene in volume 3). Looking no further than the abstracts of two central papers, we find Moll and colleagues writing that "emotion plays a pivotal role in moral experience" (Moll, de Oliveira-

Souza, Eslinger, Bramati, Murao-Miranda, Andreiuolo, & Pessoa, 2002b, p. 2730), while Greene and Haidt conclude that "recent evidence suggests that moral judgment is more a matter of emotion and affective intuition than deliberative reasoning" (2002, p. 517). Surely, one might think, if we find that when we hook up people's brains to a neuroimaging device, get them to think about moral matters, and observe the presence of emotional activity, emotivism is supported.

No, it isn't. We need to pay attention to what is meant by "express" when we talk about what kind of mental state a public utterance expresses. Sometimes "express" is used to denote a causal relation. If we say that by kicking over her brother's sand castle Emily expressed her anger, we may mean that anger caused her action or that it is an important element in an adequate explanation of the action. If it turns out that Emily in fact isn't angry at all, we will have to reject this explanation. However, often "express" is used differently. When Emily later apologizes for kicking over the sand castle, she expresses regret. Suppose, though, that Emily's apology is insincere, in the sense that she has not an ounce of regret for what she did. This doesn't change the fact that she apologized. An insincere apology still succeeds in being an apology (just as an insincere promise is still a promise, and an insincere assertion is still an assertion). Nor does insincerity change the fact that Emily thereby expressed regret, for an apology *is* an expression of regret. Here "express" does not denote an explanatory or causal relation holding between Emily's utterances and her mental states. Rather, it indicates a much more complex relation holding among Emily, her brother, and a range of linguistic conventions according to which when a person utters "I'm sorry" in the appropriate circumstances then she has (among other things) *expressed regret*.[2] Thus, it is perfectly possible that one can express regret over something when in fact one has no regret at all. This shows that the expression relation cannot be a causal or explanatory one, but is rather a matter of linguistic convention.

When the metaethical emotivist claims that moral judgments express emotions, he or she is using "express" in the same way as when we say that an apology expresses regret, or that an assertion expresses a belief. Once this is understood, it becomes apparent that the most that neuroscientific discoveries could establish is that public moral judgments are *accompanied* by emotions, and perhaps that they are *caused by* emotions, but further arguments would be needed to show that public moral judgments *express* those emotions. It is entirely possible that moral judgments are typically caused by emotional activity but nevertheless function linguistically as assertions (i.e., expressions of belief).

Hume, for example, favored a projectivist account of moral phenomenology; he spoke of the mind's "great propensity to spread itself on external objects" (Hume, 1740/1978, p. 167), and claimed that "taste" (as opposed to reason) "has a productive faculty, and gilding and staining all natural objects with the colours, borrowed from internal sentiment, raises in a manner a new creation" (Hume, 1751/1983, p. 88). The idea is that certain events or states of affairs cause us to feel emotions—such as anger, disgust, or approval—which we then "project" onto our experience, seeing the world as containing qualities that it does not in fact contain. It's not that our emotions cause us to experience external events as having emotions (which would just be bizarre), but rather our emotions cause us to experience external events as having normative properties like *demanding anger*, or *being wrong*. It is often assumed that moral projectivism and moral emotivism go hand in hand (indeed, the terms are sometimes used as if they are synonyms), but this is mistaken. From the fact that its seeming to someone as if a situation has the property of being wrong is to be explained by the situation having prompted in him the emotion of anger or disgust, it does not follow that the way he articulates things—uttering "That situation is wrong"—*functions to express* those emotions. It is, in fact, hard to see how projectivism and emotivism could go happily together. The crucial thing to notice is that projectivism implies an account of how the world *seems* to those who are doing the projecting, it seems to them as if it contains properties. Since we can assume that the language with which they discuss the matter will reflect their experience, then when they say things like "That act was wrong," it seems safe to assume, absent any reason to think otherwise, that they are expressing their belief that the external situation instantiates this property. However, if they are expressing their beliefs on the matter (that is, asserting that the act is wrong), then they cannot simply be expressing their emotions.

My point here is not to argue in favor of moral projectivism, but to use it to illustrate a possible scenario where emotions are centrally implicated in the production of moral judgments but nevertheless the public form of these judgments may be entirely assertoric. Nor am I claiming that projectivism entails the denial of emotivism, only that moral cognitivism is its more natural partner.[3] The only way to settle the matter is to investigate directly the nature of the linguistic conventions surrounding our moral discourse, not the nature of neurological etiology. Uncovering such linguistic conventions may be in substantial part an empirical inquiry; we might think of it as "sociolinguistics." To this extent I think that emotivism certainly could be supported by empirical evidence, but this evidence would concern how we use moral language. I take it that appealing to this kind of evidence—examining linguistic practices, uncovering shared intuitions about far-fetched thought experiments, etc.—is fairly pervasive in metaethics, and indeed in philosophy in general. As to other forms of empirical evidence (in particular the evidence from neuroscience and psychology) revealing what is going on in our brains when we make moral judgments, these findings I think should give no particular consolation to the moral emotivist.

Can Neuroscience Undermine Moral Rationalism?

We have just seen the dangers of thinking of emotivism simply as the view that morality necessarily has "something to do with" the emotions. By contrast, it is difficult to characterize moral rationalism more precisely than to say that it is the claim that morality necessarily has "something to do with" rationality. I say this because moral rationalists are a motley bunch. It is precisely because of this indeterminacy that one cannot be too confident in saying that one argument, or one body of empirical evidence, undermines rationalism. I think that there are certain types of rationalism that do look shaky as the result of empirical evidence, but there are other kinds that remain untouched. And I'm also inclined to think that the latter kind of rationalism—the kind apparently immune from empirical debunking—is the more metaethically interesting variety. I will proceed by disambiguating three versions of moral rationalism: psychological rationalism, conceptual rationalism, and justificatory rationalism.

Psychological Rationalism

Psychological rationalism is the view that moral decisions and moral deliberations causally flow from a rational faculty. The theory has a long and distinguished career in philosophy. Plato thought of moral judgments as the product of the rational faculty, which apprehends eternal moral truths. Aquinas thought that humans have an innate rational faculty called "synderesis" that informs us of our moral obligations. Hume's well-known dichotomizing of the issue was focused on whether morals are "the product of reason" or "the product of passion." To the extent that there is also a tradition of moral rationalism in psychology—represented by such figures as Piaget and Kohlberg—then psychological rationalism is its core thesis.[4]

We must begin by making some broad distinctions. First we should distinguish the claim that the activity of the rational faculty is necessary for moral judgment from the stronger claim that such activity is necessary and sufficient. According to strong psychological rationalism, moral judgments are the product of the rational faculty *alone*. We should also distinguish synchronic from diachronic versions of psychological rationalism. The former holds that every moral judgment flows from activity in the agent's rational faculty occurring at the time (or, fudging slightly, shortly before the time) of the moral judgment. A diachronic version allows that moral judgment may not be accompanied by such rational activity, but that such activity was necessary at some developmental point in the past. We could even understand the diachronic version in evolutionary terms, as the claim that the evolutionary emergence of the rational faculty was a necessary (and sufficient) prerequisite to the emergence of human moral judgment.

I want to stress that I am not taking it for granted that it is obvious what the terms "rational faculty" and "emotional faculty" mean. There is room for a great deal of discussion on this topic, but not in this chapter. Here I am willing to employ these terms in a rough-and-ready way because my intention is just to clarify the dialectic at a broad level. I concede that it is possible that empirical science (including neuroscience) will cast into doubt the very idea of there being a rational faculty and an emotional faculty. If so, then all versions of psychological rationalism will be shown to be founded on an empirical misconception. If, on the other hand, the rational-emotional faculty dichotomy turns out to be broadly scientifically respectable (as I assume in what follows), then it is an empirical issue, and in part a neuroscientific issue, whether a certain phenomenon (moral deliberation) causally involves one or the other, or both of these faculties.

However, we should be aware of how tricky it might be to undermine psychological rationalism. Merely observing an enormous amount of emotional activity when subjects engage in moral thinking is insufficient to invalidate any version of the theory, for I would be surprised if any of the historical supporters of rationalism—even supporters of strong synchronic psychological rationalism—would object to the claim that of course moral thinking engages our passions. I doubt that Plato or Aquinas or Kant (another conspicuous moral rationalist) would have been in the least surprised to learn that neuroimaging reveals a great deal of emotional arousal in subjects when they are asked to contemplate hiring someone to tie up and rape their wife, or selling their young daughter to a pornographer (two examples from the 2001 fMRI study done by Josh Greene and colleagues). A great deal of the moral realm concerns actions and persons who prompt anger, or indignation, or disgust, or sympathy; and no plausible version of moral rationalism denies this fact. The eighteenth-century moral rationalist Richard Price wrote: "Some impressions of pleasure and pain, satisfaction or disgust, generally attend our perceptions of virtue and vice. But these are merely their effects and concomitants, and not the perceptions themselves" (1758/1974, p. 44). The supporter of strong synchronic psychological rationalism can allow that activity of the rational faculty, although necessary and sufficient for moral judgment, nevertheless on many occasions (or as a matter of fact always) is accompanied by emotional excitement. In order to refute this theory it is not enough to observe that moral deliberation is reliably attended by emotional activity; one would have to show that moral deliberation is not also accompanied by rational activity. Neuroimaging could in principle yield this result, although as far as I know it hasn't yet. (One major challenge to such a project would be first to operationalize the occurrence of "activity in the rational faculty.")

Another conspicuous test procedure would be to investigate subjects who have various kinds of rational and/or emotional impairment and see how this affects their capacity to engage in moral deliberation. Suppose, first, that we were to locate subjects who are perfectly able to make moral judgments but who suffer impaired rational faculties. We might be tempted to conclude on this basis that rational activity is not necessary for moral judgment, and thus that both strong and weak synchronic psychological rationalism stand refuted. However, this strategy is undermined by the general reflection that a defective system may nevertheless continue to yield undamaged outputs of a certain sort, just as a faulty memory faculty may nevertheless recall certain events with great clarity or a faulty clock may nevertheless reliably convey the accurate date. It is quite possible that moral judgment is the product of the rational faculty, but that this faculty can suffer certain forms of impairment while still merrily turning out well-formed moral judgments. Strictly speaking, what we would need to observe in order to refute the claim that rational activity is necessary for moral judgment is a subject who continues to make moral judgments despite having *no* rational activity. It is unclear what criteria would need to be fulfilled before we were satisfied that we had such a subject. (Having no rational activity, I am sure it will be agreed, is a pretty severe affliction.) Furthermore, such evidence would still leave diachronic versions of psychological rationalism viable, for even if moral judgment is possible without rational activity occurring there and then, nevertheless it is possible that activity of a rational faculty was necessary at some earlier point in time.

We might, on the other hand, locate a second kind of subject: one who has intact rational faculties but who appears unable to engage properly in moral thinking. Such cases would seem to show that rational activity is not (synchronically) sufficient for moral judgment, thus refuting strong synchronic psychological rationalism. Apparently we do have at least this kind of evidence. Shaun Nichols (2002a, 2004b) argues that psychopaths represent a class of persons whose rational faculties are intact, whose emotional faculties are impaired, and whose capacity to engage in moral deliberation is defective (see also R.J.R. Blair, 1995; R.J.R. Blair, Jones, Clark, & Smith, 1997). Assuming that this is an accurate description of the phenomenon of psychopathy, these subjects pose a serious challenge for strong synchronic psychological rationalism. The weak synchronic psychological rationalist, however, need not be troubled by the phenomenon of psychopathy because it is consistent with this evidence that activity of the rational faculty remains necessary for moral judgment.

Conceptual Rationalism

Conceptual rationalism is the view that a reference to practical rationality will appear in any adequate explication of our moral concepts, that it is a conceptual truth that moral transgressions are transgressions of practical rationality. Though I should not like to exclude the possibility of neuroscience having an influence on what conclusions should be drawn about the content of concepts, it must be confessed that it is difficult to see how that contribution might transpire. Of course, the matter of how one should proceed to uncover the content of concepts is a good question about which philosophers argue. Insofar as uncovering concepts means figuring out what we mean by the words we use to express those concepts, and figuring out what we mean by the words we use is a matter of figuring out how we *use* those words, and figuring out how we use words is an empirical matter, then uncovering the content of concepts is an empirical matter. Nevertheless, it is difficult to see what neuroscience in particular could contribute to this empirical process.

Nichols (2002a, 2004b) has performed an empirical survey of people's intuitions which, he argues, casts conceptual rationalism into doubt. His argument has a two-part structure. First he suggests that conceptual rationalists are committed to the following thesis:

Simple motivation internalism[5]   Anyone who judges that she is morally required to φ will be motivated to comply.

Given this first step of arguing that conceptual rationalism implies simple motivation internalism, a natural way of attacking conceptual rationalism would be to argue that simple motivation internalism is false. However, this strategy (which I will come to in a moment) is not actually Nichols's line of attack. Rather, his second step is to argue that ordinary people readily admit the existence of persons who represent counterexamples to motivation internalism, and thus the status of motivation internalism as a conceptual truth is doubtful. Nichols conducted an experiment in which subjects were given a description of a psychopathic individual, John, who claims to know the difference between right and wrong while remaining utterly unmotivated to act accordingly. Then the subjects were asked whether John really made moral judgments. Most subjects maintained that he did. Nichols concludes that it appears to be a "folk platitude that psychopaths understand that it is morally wrong to hurt others but don't care." It is important to note that Nichols doesn't think that real psychopaths actually do represent a counterexample to motivation internalism. As I mentioned before, it would appear that their capacity to engage in moral deliberation is fairly defective. Nichols's argument is simply that most people naively and perhaps erroneously believe that psychopaths represent a counterexample to motivation internalism, and thus motivation internalism cannot be a conceptual truth.

What are we to make of this argument? First I should remind you that it is not my concern to defend conceptual rationalism; for all I care it may be false. My intention is just to identify what bears on it and what does not. Since Nichols's evidence against conceptual rationalism is in no sense neuroscientific but rather concerns what ordinary people are likely to say about psychopaths, it is not strictly within my purview. Nevertheless, I want to make a few brief comments, since they do bear directly on what follows.

The moral rationalist that Nichols has most clearly in his sights is Michael Smith (1994). Smith certainly is a conceptual rationalist and also endorses a form of moral internalism; he also thinks that the former supports the latter. However, we need to look carefully at the version of moral internalism that Smith endorses, for it isn't this simple variety. Smith doesn't think that moral judgment *guarantees* motivation; his version of motivation internalism is altogether more normative:

Smith's normative motivation internalism   Anyone who judges that she is morally required to φ will be motivated to comply, or she is irrational.

Elsewhere Smith says that a person making a moral judgment will be motivated to comply "absent the distorting influences of weakness of will and other similar forms of practical unreason" (1994, p. 61), and these other forms of practical unreason are listed elsewhere in his book as "psychological compulsions, physical addictions, emotional disturbances, depression, spiritual tiredness, accidie, illness and the like" (1994, p. 154). This clarification suggests the following thesis, which is best interpreted as an explication of (rather than an alternative to) the former:

Smith's substantive motivation internalism Anyone who judges that she is morally required to φ will be motivated to comply, absent the distorting influences of weakness of will, psychological compulsions, physical addictions, emotional disturbances, depression, spiritual tiredness, accidie, illness, and the like.

The main problem with Nichols's empirical test concerning people's views about psychopaths is that it apparently targets neither of Smith's versions of motivation internalism. The subjects were not asked whether John the imaginary psychopath might be suffering from weakness of will or spiritual tiredness, or whether he might be accused of irrationality for remaining unmoved by his moral judgments. All the test shows is that people readily countenance the falsity of *simple* motivation internalism, but Smith never denied that.

A second thing that can be said in Smith's defense is that he has a rather distinctive view of what a conceptual truth is. Conceptual truths, for Smith, can be exceedingly unobvious to ordinary speakers. To have competence with a concept is to know *how* to use the word that stands for the concept—and that know-how may be difficult to articulate, even for the people who have it. By analogy, it might be a bad way of figuring out how a champion swimmer swims by asking him to describe his swimming technique. Hence, Smith is not impressed with questionnaires designed to reveal people's intuitive responses to set questions. Such questionnaires may have *some* bearing on conceptual content, but they are a long way from settling the matter. If you want to know the content of a concept, then the best person to ask—Smith thinks—is an expert who has examined the patterns of use of moral language as it is employed in real life.

Thus, Smith is not forced to retreat from his conceptual rationalism in the face of Nichols's empirical evidence. Let me turn now to a different form of argument. I mentioned earlier the possibility of another kind of case that might be made against conceptual rationalism, this one also starting with the first step of showing that conceptual rationalism implies simple motivation internalism, and then making the second step of showing that simple motivation internalism is false. This argument is of interest to us because it has been claimed that neuroscientific evidence does indeed reveal simple motivation internalism to be false. Adina Roskies

(2003) offers the evidence of patients suffering from localized injury to the ventromedial cortex who appear to make normal moral judgments while remaining utterly disinclined to act accordingly. Antonio Damasio and colleagues (Damasio, Tranel, & Damasio, 1990) have referred to this phenomenon as "acquired sociopathy."

It must be emphasized that Roskies is not out to attack conceptual rationalism; her target is only simple motivation internalism. However, if the link from conceptual rationalism is in place, then one could use her results to mount such an attack. In what follows I will argue that both steps of this argument fail. The link from conceptual rationalism to simple motivation internalism can be severed (thus severing any *modus tollens* link running in the other direction), and in any event the empirical case against even simple motivation internalism is flawed.

Let's first look more carefully at this supposed implication from conceptual rationalism to motivation internalism. Nichols offers no discussion of this point, content to note that "the most prominent and influential versions of Conceptual Rationalism are tied to [Motivation Internalism], and I will simply assume in what follows that Conceptual Rationalism is committed to [Motivation Internalism]" (2004b, p. 72 n. 3). This implication is not to be assumed without comment, for it is obvious that in order to move from conceptual rationalism as a premise to motivation internalism as a conclusion, an additional bridging premise in needed—one that links rational requirements to motivation. I'll call the thesis "rational internalism."

Premise 1: Conceptual rationalism To judge that one is morally required to ϕ is to judge that one is rationally required to ϕ.
Premise 2: Simple rational internalism Anyone who judges that she is rationally required to ϕ will be motivated to comply.
Therefore: Simple motivation internalism Anyone who judges that she is morally required to ϕ will be motivated to comply.

Smith certainly endorses a version of rational internalism, which allows him to move from conceptual rationalism to motivation internalism. But, again, it isn't this simple form that he endorses; as before, it is a normative version that he argues for: that anyone who judges that she is rationally required to ϕ will be motivated to comply *or she is irrational*. He argues at some length for the view that what it is to judge that some action is rationally required of you is to believe that a fully rational version of yourself would desire that you do that thing. For someone—Fred—to judge that practical rationality is on the side of eating another slice of pizza is for Fred to judge that an idealized version of himself (that is, idealized in the respect of being granted full information and perfect powers of reflection) would advise the actual less-than-ideal Fred to have another slice of pizza. Suppose, then, that Fred does indeed believe this: that he would desire another slice of pizza if he were fully rational, but in fact doesn't desire another slice of pizza. Is he irrational? Smith answers: "Most certainly," for Fred has failed to have a desire that by his own lights it is rational for him to have.

Notice, though, that with a normative version of rational internalism the only version of motivation internalism that may be validly derived is also the normative variety, yielding this argument:

Premise 1: Conceptual rationalism   To judge that one is morally required to φ is to judge that one is rationally required to φ.

Premise 2: Normative rational internalism   Anyone who judges that she is rationally required to φ will be motivated to comply, or she is irrational.

Therefore: Normative motivation internalism   Anyone who judges that she is morally required to φ will be motivated to comply, or she is irrational.

However, this kind of normative motivation internalism is one that Roskies admits the empirical evidence does not refute. In fact, she disparages Smith's brand of motivation internalism as "too weak to be revealing about the nature of moral judgment" since, she thinks, it leaves entirely open what is to count as irrationality (2003, p. 53). We have already seen that this charge is a bit unfair to Smith, for he does provide an inventory of phenomena that are supposed to jointly constitute practical irrationality. It is true that his list ends with an unsatisfying ". . . and the like," but he doesn't leave matters entirely open. In any case, subjects suffering from acquired sociopathy are unlikely to represent counterexamples to Smith's motivation internalism since it is doubtful that we would describe them as free from "emotional disturbance" or "illness." I strongly suspect Smith would be willing to add "brain damaged" to his list.

If we want *simple* motivation internalism as our conclusion, then validity requires that we have a matching version of *simple* rational internalism as the bridging premise. (This argument was presented on p. 383.) The problem now is that such a version of rational internalism doesn't look like a good contender for an obvious truth at all; certainly there is nothing in Smith's work supporting such a standpoint. Moreover, it seems that many of the reasons that would lead one to doubt simple motivation internalism will also lead one to doubt the truth of simple rational internalism. If we are willing to acknowledge the existence of agents whose motivational structures are so impaired that we can imagine them sincerely saying "Yes, I know that I morally ought to φ, but I just lack any motivation in favor of φ-ing," then what is there to stand in the way of us also acknowledging motivational impairment that leaves an agent sincerely saying "Yes, I know that I *rationally* ought to φ, but I just lack any motivation in favor of φ-ing"?

In other words, motivation internalism and rational internalism look like they will stand or fall together. This is good news for the conceptual rationalist. Simple motivation internalism may be false, but if the matching rational internalism is also false, then the link to conceptual rationalism is severed. Or normative rational internalism may be true, but if the only version of motivation internalism that may thus be derived is also the true kind, then again the conceptual rationalist has nothing to worry about. At the very least, once we acknowledge that conceptual rationalism alone doesn't imply moral internalism, but requires another substantive bridging premise, then we must admit that the falsity of moral internalism is insufficient to sink conceptual rationalism, since this thesis can always be saved by dumping the bridging premise instead.

I noted that Roskies' target is not conceptual rationalism, but simple motivation internalism. Doubts may also be raised as to whether the empirical evidence she cites even has any impact on the well-entrenched metaethical dispute over motivation internalism. In order for those subjects suffering from acquired sociopathy to count as "walking counterexamples to this internalist thesis," as Roskies (2003, p. 51) claims they are, two things need be true of them: They must make moral judgments and they must have no motivation to comply. The second requirement is something that can, to a reasonable extent, be empirically operationalized. Roskies cites the subjects' flat skin-conductance responses when faced with emotionally charged or value-laden stimuli, which is supported by clinical histories indicating motivational impairments. The problem is that the criteria for having made a moral judgment are not similarly operationalized. The very notion of a moral judgment is sufficiently indeterminate that the conspicuous possibility is that there is a legitimate sense in which these subjects are making moral judgments and an equally legitimate sense in which they are not. My suspicion is that it is precisely this indeterminacy that explains why the cottage industry in metaethics regarding motivation internalism has been so long locked in this tedious impasse.

If we treat moral judgment primarily as a kind of linguistic performance—as a speech act—then it is indeed reasonable to assume that these patients are capable of making moral judgments (although see Kennett in chapter 4 of this volume). Of course, when we treat moral judgment this way, then we hardly need an appeal to modern neuroscience to refute the internalist thesis, for such moral judgments lacking motivation are no more exceptional than insincere apologies. Picture the situation of a person trying to curry favor with another by agreeing with all her evaluative assessments. Perhaps a young man decries the plight of farm animals in order to impress his new vegetarian sweetheart, despite the fact that he really couldn't care less. If moral judgments are considered just as speech acts, then our besotted pretender has surely made one (albeit insincerely) while lacking any motivation to comply. The existence of such a phenomenon is unremarkable.

If, on the other hand, we prefer to treat moral judgment as more of a psychological event, as a kind of internal "mental assent" to an evaluative proposition, then serious doubt arises as to whether the subjects suffering from acquired sociopathy really are making moral judgments in this more robust sense.

This dilemma may be clarified by again comparing the case of apologizing. Apologies considered as speech acts can of course be insincere; they can be successfully performed by persons lacking any regret. However, we might on occasion prefer to speak of apologies in a different sense. We may want to use the term to denote the type of mental event that occurs in a person's mind when she truly embraces her apology, when she genuinely has regret and acknowledges responsibility "in her own heart" (so to speak). Evidence that people can make apologies sans regret in the former sense clearly does not amount to evidence that people can make apologies sans regret in the latter sense. If there were a type of brain damage that left people incapable of feeling genuine regret, this wouldn't necessarily leave them lacking the concept of an apology. Such people may know what apologies are, and may even learn when to say "Sorry" in appropriate circumstances in order to avoid social exclusion, but we may well decide that there is an important sense in which they are unable to apologize *sincerely*.

It is not clear what sense of moral judgment Roskies has in mind. She emphasizes the subjects' linguistic skills—pointing out that they have "mastery of moral terms" and that "their language and declarative knowledge structures are intact" (2003, p. 60)—and this might be taken to suggest that she thinks of moral judgment as a linguistic performance, in which case motivation internalism surely stands refuted (but we hardly needed any fancy empirical evidence to demonstrate this). On the other hand, perhaps she is treating this linguistic competence merely as evidence of some kind of mentalistic moral judgment. But why should we accept that it does count as evidence? One might be tempted to say that linguistic competence is evidence of conceptual competence, and thus the subjects suffering from acquired sociopathy retain mastery of the moral concepts; when they say "Killing is morally wrong" they know what they are saying. And thus (one might be tempted to add) if such persons are able to apply the moral concepts to the appropriate kinds of items (e.g., not to pieces of furniture or days of the week), then despite their impairments they retain the capacity to make moral judgments in the psychological sense indicated.

However, these temptations will appeal only to those who already harbor cognitivist leanings; the moral noncognitivist, by contrast, will remain unimpressed and untempted. The traditional noncognitivist (one version of whom is the emotivist) denies that moral judgment consists of applying concepts, and, indeed, to the extent that he claims that the predicates ". . . is morally good," ". . . is morally prohibited," etc. are only grammatical predicates but are not logical predicates, then he may even deny that there exist such concepts as *moral wrongness, moral requirement*, etc. (in the same way as one might deny that *yum!* or *boo!* count properly as concepts). Suppose, for example, that there are well-entrenched linguistic conventions according to which when one makes a public moral judgment one thereby expresses subscription to the relevant normative framework (see Gibbard, 1990). If this is correct, then to make a moral judgment in the psychological sense will involve a sincere subscription to the norms indicated by the public judgment. Since such "subscription" is (*ex hypothesi*) a motivation-implicating state, it follows that moral judgment in this sense implies motivation. Such a noncognitivist, accordingly, treats those subjects suffering from acquired sociopathy, not as counterexamples to motivation internalism, but as counterexamples to the proposition that mastery of the moral language suffices for the occurrence of moral judgment.

Roskies, it would seem, has made herself immune to such complaints by putting to one side the possibility that moral judgments may function to do anything other than express beliefs. She writes: "For the purposes of this paper, I will assume moral cognitivism to be true" (2003, p. 53), and admits that "[t]he arguments presented here do not suffice to refute internalism in a non-cognitivist framework" (p. 64). This is curious given that the biggest fans of motivation internalism in metaethics have traditionally been the noncognitivists, and indeed much of the philosophical interest in the thesis lies in the supposition that its resolution promises to shed light on the cognitivist-noncognitivist dispute (although whether this is a reasonable expectation is moot—see Joyce 2002, forthcoming a). Most moral philosophers who embrace pure cognitivism—the view that the linguistic function of a moral judgment is exhausted by its belief-expressing quality—see motivation internalism as an unlikely and unnecessary thesis. This assessment arises not from any neuroscientific research, but generally from reflection on the Humean psychological thesis that beliefs and desires are but contingently linked entities.[6] In other words, once the conditionality of Roskies' argument is highlighted, much of the metaethical interest in it evaporates.

Over the past few paragraphs I have been casting doubt on the supposition that neuroscientific evidence sheds light on the entrenched metaethical debate over simple motivation internalism. I have argued neither that this internalist thesis is true nor that it is false. My point is rather that the notion of a moral judgment is sufficiently pliable to allow reasonable precisifications according to which internalism is pretty obviously false, and equally reasonable precisifications according to which it may be true. The latter depends on whether the sincere acceptance of a moral judgment implicates motivational structures, which in turn depends on whether there exist linguistic conventions according to which public moral judgments function to express (inter alia, perhaps) conative attitudes. To the extent that this is an empirical matter, it is a job for sociolinguistics; I see no obvious place for a significant contribution from neuroscience. This is a noteworthy conclusion in its own right, but my broader aim has been to undermine the claim that neuroscientific evidence establishes a premise (the falsity of simple motivation internalism) that might be used in an attack on conceptual rationalism.

Justificatory Rationalism

Let me turn finally to justificatory rationalism. According to this view, moral transgressions are rational transgressions; moral villains are irrational. This is distinct from the claim made by the conceptual rationalist since it doesn't assert a conceptual connection. This is important, for it makes it all the clearer that collating people's intuitions on the issue (in the manner of Nichols's aforementioned experiment) has little bearing on the matter.

In order to gain a rough idea of how this kind of moral rationalist thinks the justificatory process may proceed, let us briefly consider the views of Peter Singer. Singer argues that natural selection has granted humans an innate tendency to look favorably upon actions that benefit one's family and a tendency to dislike actions that harm them. However, Singer goes on to argue, we have also been granted by natural selection a rational faculty. Rationality allows a person to realize:

> I am just one being among others, with interests and desires like others. I have a personal perspective on the world, from which my interests are at the front and center of the stage, the interests of my family and friends are close behind, and the interests of strangers are pushed to the back and sides. But reason enables me to see that others have similarly subjective perspectives, and that from "the point of view of the universe" my perspective is no more privileged than theirs. (Singer, 1995, p. 229)

Reason, Singer seems to be saying here, demands that one recognize the welfare of others as being as objectively valuable as one's own welfare. It wouldn't follow from this that we all need to be totally impartial in our actions—showing no favor to friends and family—for that might lead to a very unhappy state of affairs. However, it is at least supposed to show that, for instance, it is unacceptable for me to go up to an innocent stranger and punch him for my amusement. Given that I would demand not to be punched, I am rationally required to acknowledge that there is an equal demand that the stranger not be punched. Regardless of how plausible we find this view (I certainly have few sympathies with such thoughts),[7] I think it fair to say that this is the core intuition motivating many moral rationalists: Michael Smith, Christine Korsgaard, Thomas Nagel, Alan Gewirth, and indeed Inmanuel Kant. I would go so far as to call it the dominant thread of western moral rationalism. Simon Blackburn has described the rationalist's goal of finding a "knock-down argument that people who are nasty and unpleasant . . . are above all *unreasonable*"—that such villains "aren't just selfish or thoughtless or malignant or imprudent, but are reasoning badly"—as the "holy grail of moral philosophy" (Blackburn, 1984, p. 222).

The main point I wish to stress is the distinction between justificatory rationalism and psychological rationalism, and the simplest way of achieving this is to point out that justificatory rationalism primarily concerns action, not judgment, whereas psychological rationalism concerns the sources of moral judgment.[8] Let us say that a certain person is morally required to give to a particular charity, and suppose that she does so. The justificatory rationalist's purview extends only to the claim that she would have been irrational had she refrained from giving to the charity. As to the question of what may have motivated her action, the justificatory rationalist is silent. Perhaps she didn't do it for a moral consideration at all. Or even if she did do it because she thought it morally obligatory, the justificatory rationalist is silent about the source of this moral judgment. Perhaps it springs from her rational faculty, or perhaps it flows from seething emotional activity, and emotional activity alone, or perhaps, as Haidt argues (volume 2), her judgment is a post hoc construction to some knee-jerk emotional response. The justificatory rationalist is not saying that moral judgments always, or even typically (or even, in principle, *ever*) causally flow from the proximate activity of a rational faculty, but rather that the principles of rationality favor a certain degree of impartiality in our dealings with each other, from which it follows that a person's rational faculty would, if properly exercised and unimpeded, recognize this fact. However, perhaps the properly exercised and unimpeded rational faculty is a rare thing.

It is possible that Singer does see a causal link between the rational faculty and moral judgment in evolutionary terms. Perhaps if our ancestors had never evolved the sophisticated rational abilities that humans at present enjoy, we would never have gotten beyond liking actions that help ourselves and our kin and disliking actions that harm them, in which case perhaps we would never have started making *moral* judgments at all. And in this light Singer might be interpreted as a kind of psychological rationalist (as, indeed, Nichols interprets him 2004b, p. 68), but it is vital to note that to the extent that this is a reasonable interpretation it is a historical diachronic version of psychological rationalism that Singer is pressing. He is not arguing that all (or even many) moral judgments are caused by the operations of the rational faculty of the person making the judgment. Even for those persons who do not properly exercise their rational faculty, who act selfishly and show extreme partiality toward their kith and kin (bearing in mind that this may be nearly all of us, nearly all the time), it nevertheless may be that a degree of impartial benevolence in their actions *is* rationally required, and thus such people are *being* irrational. To the extent that Singer endorses this claim (his views on this matter in fact have a complexity to which I am unable to do justice here), it is a justificatory rationalism that he advocates. And it is this consideration that also makes it obvious that the truth (or otherwise) of justificatory rationalism will not be affected by neuroscientific research concerning what is going on in people's brains when they make moral judgments, for the theory is compatible with just about any discovery concerning the springs of moral judgment and action. All that is required of human psychology in order for justificatory rationalism to be reasonable is that we at least fulfill the minimal requirements for being rational agents, for I take it that few persons would support the view that creatures constitutionally incapable of complying with rational considerations as such can still be subject to rational requirements. Lions, for instance, cannot be accused of irrationality (or immorality) for failing to adequately take into account the welfare of gazelles. However, this is a modest constraint and one that we can be fairly confident will not be affected by neuroscientific advances. Even if neuroscience were to scotch the idea that there is anything like a rational faculty in the brain, we could still claim to have the skills sufficient for being rational beings. Even if empirical data were to show that irrationality pervades our decisions, this would (ironically) presuppose that humans fulfill the prerequisites for being rational in some more broad sense of the term, for only beings with the capacity for rationality can be properly criticized as acting and thinking irrationally (which is why we don't accuse lions of being irrational).

Certain generic descriptions of moral rationalism may encourage one to overlook the fundamental difference between psychological and justificatory rationalism. Asserting that moral judgments "derive from" rationality is ambiguous (as is the phrase "have their source in"). It can be read etiologically as concerning the actual mechanisms that produce moral judgments, which Haidt does when he describes the rationalist as holding that "moral knowledge and moral judgment are reached primarily by a process of reasoning and reflection" (2001, p. 814). Or it can be read normatively, as concerning the principles that underwrite and justify the contents of moral judgments, regardless of the causal source of those judgments. Both kinds of rationalist can legitimately claim to be seeking "the foundations" of morality, but they are in fact engaged in different pursuits. The empirical evidence may refute psychological rationalism—and neuroscience may contribute to its downfall—without this in any way compromising the moral rationalist's project of finding a rational foundation for ethics.

A More Optimistic Conclusion?

I have undertaken here the modest task of sorting out a few potential cross-disciplinary confusions, some of which are purely terminological. Given that such confusions can lead to misunderstanding and wasted academic effort, this seems a worthy task to perform at a time when the empirical sciences have begun to enrich moral philosophy in ways that were not anticipated a generation ago, but which we can now expect will burgeon in coming years. Because the tone of this chapter has largely been negative about the contributions neuroscience may offer metaethics, I want to stress that there is no cause for general pessimism regarding the possibility that such contributions may be forthcoming in ways that have not been discussed. I am in fact confident that empirical data, including that of a neuroscientific nature, will contribute to a number of metaethical issues. My guess is that the greatest contribution will be to moral epistemology, although perhaps in ways that will be found unsettling (see Joyce 2006a, chap. 6; 2006b). Walter Sinnott-Armstrong (2006), for example, argues that empirical psychology reveals many moral judgments to have attributes that by ordinary epistemic standards render them in need of independent confirmation. Whatever privileged status we might have otherwise accorded a held belief (based on a principle of epistemic conservatism, say) is undercut if we discover that belief to be partial, controversial, clouded by emotion, subject to illusion, or explicable by unreliable or disreputable sources. Certainly neuroscience and social psychology have revealed moral deliberation to be frequently clouded by emotion (even in cases when we wouldn't ordinarily think so), so this is an instance of empirical data having a direct metaethical payoff.

Neuroscience may also have a role to play in establishing that the human moral faculty is innate (in some sense of the word). It is not unlikely that a picture of an innate moral faculty will emerge that will not assume moral thinking to have evolved in order to detect a realm of moral facts, but rather that such thinking enhanced our ancestors' reproductive fitness by soothing and reinforcing prosocial relations (see Joyce, 2006a, 2006c). Since such a hypothesis concerning the genealogy of human moral judgment would nowhere presuppose that any such judgment is true, one might very well claim that this would amount to an empirical confirmation that moral judgments satisfy Sinnott-Armstrong's final criterion, that of deriving from an unreliable source.[9]

I said that there is no need to be pessimistic concerning the possibility of the empirical sciences contributing to metaethics, although one may well find this particular kind of positive contribution pessimistic (in another sense) if one dislikes the direction in which the argument leads us. The general worry is that empirical discoveries about the genealogy of moral judgments may undermine their epistemic status and ultimately detract from their authoritative role in our practical deliberations. This is a possibility to be taken seriously and explored carefully.

Notes

Thanks to Adina Roskies, Peter Singer, Walter Sinnott-Armstrong, and Michael Smith for comments.

1. Insofar as some metaethicists offer prescriptions about how the word "ought" *ought* to be used, metaethics sometimes steps beyond the descriptive. Even in such cases, however, metaethicists are still not pushing *ethical* "ought" claims.

2. "Among other things" indicates that although one cannot apologize without expressing regret, one can admit to having regret without thereby apologizing; an apology also requires an admission of responsibility, for example (Kort, 1975; Joyce, 1999).

3. Moral cognitivism is the view that public moral judgments typically express beliefs, i.e., are assertions. If one defines cognitivism as the view that moral judgments express *only* beliefs, and emotivism as the view that they express *only* conative states, then the two are obviously incompatible. However, if these optional appearances of "only" are removed, then a mixed cognitivist and emotivist view becomes possible (and indeed I think there is much to be said in its favor). According to such a view, moral language is in this respect like certain pejorative terms. To call someone a "kraut," for example, is both to express a belief (that the person is German) and to express an attitude of contempt (see Copp, 2001; Joyce, 2006a, and forthcoming a). Given the complicating possibility of this mixed view, what the footnoted sentence should really say is that the natural partner of projectivism is a metaethical view that endorses a cognitivist element (a comment that would, without this accompanying explanation, be likely to confuse).

4. What I am calling "psychological rationalism" Shaun Nichols (2002a, 2004b) calls "empirical rationalism." I prefer my label since it emphasizes that this is the tradition of moral rationalism that one finds in the field of psychology. Were it not for the ugliness of the phrase, I think "facultative rationalism" would be a good label.

5. Following Michael Smith (1994), Nichols actually calls this thesis "the practicality requirement," although I will defer to metaethical tradition and call it "motivation internalism," qualifying it as "simple" to contrast it with variants to be discussed shortly.

6. Most moral cognitivists who embrace simple motivation internalism (such as John McDowell) adopt some fairly unorthodox views about beliefs and desires in order to square things. In fact, however, if one is treating moral judgments as speech acts, it is perfectly possible that they might be necessarily linked to motivation-implicating states without functioning to express such states. One need not deny Humean views on beliefs and desires in order to acknowledge this. Consider yet again the act of apologizing. The criteria for an apology to have occurred involve the need for both parties to be versed in a range of relevant linguistic conventions; for example, the addressee must hear and understand the words uttered and the speaker must take it that this is the case. The satisfaction of these criteria will require both speaker and addressee to have certain *beliefs*; for example, the speaker must believe that his addressee hears and understands. This connection is a necessary

(and a priori) one. It is not possible that any person could succeed in apologizing to another person without having such a belief. Yet we would hardly say that the act of apologizing—the utterance of "I'm sorry" in the appropriate circumstances—*functions to express the belief that one's audience hears and understands*. This suffices to show that the occurrence of a type of speech act may require that the speaker have a certain kind of mental state, although the speech act doesn't function to express that state. Thus, moral cognitivism and simple motivation internalism may be compatible without denying Humean psychology (see Joyce, 2002).

7. See Joyce (2001, chaps. 4 and 5).

8. There is, of course, a natural bridge from practice to judgment. If punching someone is rationally unjustified, then it follows that the decision or judgment to refrain from punching that person could be justified by an appeal to the principles of practical rationality. Nevertheless, this observation does not imply that justificatory rationalism has anything to say about *moral* judgment, for one can justify an action by appealing to practical rationality without making a moral judgment. Given my present desires, it may be practically rational for me to pause in writing this footnote to make a cup of tea, and I could justify this decision by an appeal to the principles of practical rationality, but no moral judgment would figure in my deliberations.

9. It is worth comparing this for clarity with a different psychological phenomenon for which an evolutionary hypothesis seems plausible: humans' simple arithmetic skills. Would the fact that we have such a genealogical explanation of our simple mathematical judgments serve to demonstrate that they are the product of an unreliable source? Surely not, for false mathematical judgments just aren't going to be very useful: Being chased by three lions, you observe two quit the chase and conclude that it's now safe to slow down. The truth of "1 + 1 = 2" is a background assumption to any reasonable hypothesis of how this belief might have enhanced reproductive fitness.

8.1 | Moral Rationalism and Empirical Immunity

Shaun Nichols

With the rapid recent growth of naturalized metaethics, Richard Joyce's chapter sounds an appropriate cautionary note. It is easy to be overwhelmed by sexy new data and to neglect the difficulties in using the data to draw major philosophical conclusions. One of the central views in the sights of naturalists has been moral rationalism. Jonathan Haidt (2001), Joshua Greene (chapter 2 in this volume), Jesse Prinz (2007), and I (2002a, 2004b) have all used recent empirical findings to challenge moral rationalist views. Although Joyce is not himself a moral rationalist (see Joyce, 2001), he deftly works to beat back our attacks on moral rationalism. Here my goal is to uphold the view that empirical work can challenge moral rationalism in response to Joyce's insightful chapter.

Joyce distinguishes three kinds of rationalist claims: psychological, conceptual, and justificatory rationalism.[1] According to psychological rationalism, "moral decisions and moral deliberations causally flow from a rational faculty" (this volume, p. 377).[2] Conceptual rationalism is the view that "it is a conceptual truth that moral transgressions are transgressions of practical rationality" (this volume, p. 380). And justificatory rationalism is the view that "moral transgressions are rational transgressions; moral villains are irrational" (this volume, p. 388). The key empirical charge against psychological rationalism is that there are rational agents (psychopaths) who nonetheless have serious impairments in their capacity for moral judgment (Nichols, 2004b; Prinz, 2007). Joyce doesn't take issue with this challenge against psychological rationalism, allowing that rational faculties might not be sufficient for moral judgment.[3] Rather, he argues that empirical data will leave conceptual and justificatory rationalism largely untouched. Thus, the focus here will be on whether empirical evidence bears on those two forms of rationalism. Where necessary, I will help myself to the assumption that psychological rationalism (construed as the view that rational faculties suffice for moral judgment) is false.

Conceptual Rationalism and Empirical Immunity

Conceptual rationalism is, of course, a claim about concepts. The central thesis is that it is a conceptual truth that moral requirements are rational requirements. The discussion here, as in Joyce's chapter, will focus on Michael Smith's treatment, since he has been one of the most articulate and clear advocates of conceptual rationalism in the recent literature. As Smith puts it, "our concept of a moral requirement is the concept of a reason for action; a requirement of rationality or reason" (1994, p. 64). Smith maintains that conceptual rationalism entails motivation internalism,[4] according to which "It is supposed to be a conceptual truth that agents who make moral judgments are motivated accordingly, at least absent weakness of the will and the like" (Smith, 1994, p. 66). Thus, conceptual rationalism is committed to the claim that it is a conceptual truth that people who make moral judgments are motivated by them.

In an earlier paper, I reported some preliminary evidence that lay people ("the folk") have intuitions that do not conform to the thesis of conceptual rationalism (Nichols, 2002a). In particular, people seem to allow the existence of a "rational amoralist," a person who makes moral judgments without being motivated by them. Undergraduate students were presented with the following case (among others):

John is a psychopathic criminal. He is an adult of normal intelligence, but he has no emotional reaction to hurting other people. John has hurt and indeed killed other people when he has wanted to steal their money. He says that he knows that hurting others is wrong, but that he just doesn't care if he does things that are wrong. Does John really understand that hurting others is morally wrong?

In the study, most of the participants said that John the psychopath did really understand that hurting others is morally wrong, even though he didn't care if he did things that are wrong. The empirical work is presented as a prima facie objection to conceptual rationalism of the sort Smith promotes. Let's call it the empirical challenge. Obviously the challenge isn't meant as a refutation, for several responses are available to the conceptual rationalist. Let's turn to some of those replies.

Joyce has two different replies to the evidence on behalf of the conceptual rationalist, but I want to begin by charting a third possible reply. The conceptual rationalist might deny that folk views are relevant at all. Rather, the conceptual rationalist might say that conceptual rationalism is not about folk concepts. "After all," the antagonist says, "why should we trust the folk on such an important matter as the nature of moral concepts?

And you don't need any experiments to convince me that the folk are generally ignorant. Not to mention foolish. No, the conceptual rationalist is making a claim about the concepts of G. E. Moore and the like."

This smacks of elitism, but the real problem with it is that conceptual analysis so construed sacrifices any relevance outside the confines of the ivory towers. To be sure, such conceptual analysis would be insulated from empirical evidence on folk intuitions, but at the cost of marginalizing the entire enterprise. In short, this view of conceptual analysis faces the problem of the audience. Why should the vast majority of the population who are not analytic philosophers care about the analysis of the concepts that are parochial to G. E. Moore and his cronies? And if the philosophers are just talking among themselves, with no promise of contact with the outside world, why should the outside world continue to fund their endeavors?

I begin with this anti-folk concept reply to get it out of the way. This is not a reply that Smith (or Joyce) would make, for it is not the way Smith construes his project. On the contrary, Smith follows the Lewisian tradition in which conceptual analysis is precisely the analysis of folk concepts. And in the Lewisian tradition, the method of analysis depends critically on charting the folk platitudes surrounding the concepts. Thus, Smith writes, "To say that we can analyse moral concepts, like the concept of being right, is to say that we can specify which property the property of being right is by reference to platitudes about rightness: that is, by reference to descriptions of the inferential and judgemental dispositions of those who have mastery of the term 'rightness' " (1994, p. 39). Smith is, then, in agreement with the idea that conceptual rationalism is a claim about folk concepts.

Joyce's first reply on behalf of the conceptual rationalist is to question the reach of the data. He suggests that by conducting different experiments we might find that folk responses do not really conflict with Smith's motivation internalism because Smith's account does not say that anyone who judges that something is morally required will be motivated to comply, *tout court*. Rather, Smith says that such a person will be motivated to comply "absent the distorting influences of weakness of will and other similar forms of practical unreason" (1994, p. 61). Smith goes on to say, "it is supposed to be a conceptual truth that agents who make moral judgements are motivated accordingly, at least absent weakness of the will and the like" (p. 66). As Joyce rightly notes, the experiments did not test for this: "The subjects were not asked whether John the imaginary psychopath might be suffering from weakness of the will or spiritual tiredness, nor whether he might be accused of irrationality for remaining unmoved by his moral judgments" (this volume, p. 382). That is, by getting better versions of the question, we might show that the empirical challenge is based on a misinterpretation of people's responses.

I find this kind of objection entirely welcome. That is the essence of the game. Indeed, I would hope that in future the matter will be investigated empirically. I must say though that I'd be surprised if the changes Joyce suggests would make much difference. To see why, consider a case that is much more entrenched: Satan. In the United States, a solid majority of the people believe in the devil,[5] and I would expect that most of them think that Satan understands perfectly well which things are morally wrong and that he doesn't care to avoid those things; indeed, he wants to bring those things about. Furthermore, part of what seems to make Satan so very evil is that he is not weak willed, spiritually tired, etc. Satan is the rational amoralist par excellence. Even those who think that Satan doesn't exist most likely think that Satan is possible, or at any rate, if Satan isn't possible, his possibility isn't precluded by the fact that Satan would have to be a rational amoralist. So I expect that the empirical challenge for conceptual rationalism would persist even in studies with additional controls. Nonetheless, I wholeheartedly welcome the claim that the experiments are limited and would need to be supplemented to sustain the challenge to conceptual rationalism.

The second response Joyce makes on behalf of the conceptual rationalist seems much more radical and defiantly not in the spirit of the game. Here, Joyce writes:

Conceptual truths, for Smith, can be exceedingly unobvious to ordinary speakers. To have competence with a concept is to know how to use the word that stands for the concept—and that know-how may be difficult to articulate, even for the people who have it. By analogy, it might be a bad way of figuring out how a champion swimmer swims by asking him to describe his swimming technique. Hence, Smith is not too impressed with questionnaires designed to reveal people's intuitive responses to set questions. Such questionnaires have some bearing on conceptual content, but they are a long way from settling the matter. If you want to know the content of a concept, then the best person to ask—Smith thinks—is an expert who has examined the patterns of use of moral language as it is employed in real life. (this volume, p. 382).

This kind of response is much more dismissive of the possibility of learning much about folk concepts by consulting the folk. Two clarifications about the empirical challenge are in order. First, the empirical challenge does not deny the existence of a platitude supporting motivation internalism. Rather, the challenge emerges because there is evidence of a platitude in the opposite direction. The challenge arises because the evidence suggests that either folk platitudes give no credence to motivation internalism or folk platitudes are inconsistent with respect to motivation internalism. The second clarification is that the empirical challenge does not assume that the folk can tell us everything about their concepts or that folk responses settle the matter. On the contrary, presumably folk conceptual analysis will also draw on other resources, including processes like reflective equilibrium. So even if it is a platitude that there can be a rational amoralist, we might want to discard this platitude under reflective equilibrium.

Now, with these caveats in mind, it would be rather surprising for the Lewisian analyst of folk concepts to take a generally dismissive attitude about folk responses, for the analysis is supposed to depend crucially on platitudes, and we do rather expect the folk to recognize their own platitudes. Here there is a striking and instructive disanalogy with Joyce's example of the champion swimmer. Smith maintains that the way to characterize the folk mastery of moral concepts is by reference to platitudes, but this is presumably not how one would characterize the champion swimmer's mastery of the backstroke. That is, we wouldn't expect folk platitudes to be the key source of information about the mechanics underlying a mastery of the backstroke. In addition, since Smith's approach to analyzing folk concepts proceeds by characterizing the folk's "inferential and judgmental dispositions," the experimental investigation of folk responses is a powerful resource for charting the contours of folk concepts (for discussion see e.g., Nichols, 2004a, 2006). If we really want to understand folk concepts, we will want to exploit these resources to their fullest. This need not mean that we exclude the expertise that philosophers have to offer. Nevertheless, when the philosopher-experts disagree on some central feature of folk concepts, it seems particularly useful to see what the folk have to say. That is exactly what gave rise to the preliminary study mentioned earlier. Philosophers who have examined the patterns of use of moral terms disagree about whether the folk concept of moral requirement is internalist or externalist. Thus, I looked to the folk to see whether their intuitions about a controversial case (the rational amoralist) conformed to internalist or externalist accounts.

Although I am happy to allow that reflective equilibrium might overturn the folk response, it would be rather disingenuous simply to dismiss folk responses when they are in concert with the analysis offered by your opponent. In the present case the folk responses fit the views of externalists like David Brink (1989). Of course, this doesn't mean that the challenge establishes that the externalist account of folk concepts is right. However, it does, I think, put a burden on the conceptual rationalist to explain why it is appropriate to ignore this particular folk intuition.[6]

Justificatory Rationalism and Empirical Immunity

One of the most interesting contributions of Joyce's chapter is his emphasis on justificatory rationalism, a view that has been largely neglected by those working in naturalistic metaethics. As Joyce notes, justificatory rationalism needs to be distinguished from psychological rationalism, and he goes on to argue that justificatory rationalism is insulated from the empirical facts. Much of this is quite convincing, but I want to argue that the empirical facts can pose a significant, if indirect, threat to justificatory rationalism.

According to Joyce, the justificatory rationalist is trying to find a rational foundation for ethics and show that moral transgressions are rational transgressions. In effect, justificatory rationalism is trying to show that there is a purely rational argument that justifies the contents of our moral judgments. Crucially, Joyce argues that the failure of psychological rationalism will not undermine justificatory rationalism:

[T]he truth (or otherwise) of justificatory rationalism will not be affected by neuroscientific research concerning what is going on in people's brains when they make moral judgments, for the theory is compatible with just about any discovery concerning the springs of moral judgment and action. All that is required of human psychology in order for justificatory rationalism to be reasonable is that we at least fulfill the minimal requirements for being rational agents. (this volume, p. 390)

Joyce is quite right that the failure of psychological rationalism would not deal a direct blow to justificatory rationalism. That is, the falsity of psychological rationalism can not show that there is no rational foundation for ethics. What it can do, I think, is undercut the force of various justificatory rationalist arguments. As a result, certain findings about the actual nature of moral judgment might provide a serious difficulty for the project of justificatory rationalism. I will consider here the justificatory rationalist arguments of the two philosophers discussed most by Joyce: Peter Singer and Michael Smith.

Joyce uses Singer as an exemplar of justificatory rationalism and says that the central idea that identifies Singer as such a rationalist is his view that "the principles of rationality favor a certain degree of impartiality in our dealings with each other, from which it follows that a person's rational faculty would, if properly exercised and unimpeded, recognize this fact" (this volume, p. 390). Joyce draws from the following passage from Singer for illustration:

Reason makes it possible to see ourselves in this way because, by thinking about my place in the world, I am able to see that I am just one being among others, with interests and desires like others. I have a personal perspective on the world, from which my interests are at the front and center of the stage. . . . But reason enables me to see that others have similarly subjective perspectives, and that from "the point of view of the universe" my perspective is no more privileged than theirs. Thus my ability to reason shows me the possibility of detaching myself from my own perspective and shows me what the universe might look like if I had no personal perspective. (Singer, 1995, p. 229)

Singer actually disavows justificatory rationalism (personal communication), but the preceding line of reasoning easily lends itself to justificatory rationalism, so I will follow Joyce in treating it as a justificatory rationalist argument. It is no doubt true that from the perspective of the universe, my perspective enjoys no advantage over another's perspective. Shortly following on the quoted passage, Singer goes on to point out that "the major ethical traditions all accept . . . a version of the golden rule," and the golden rule, of course, fits well with taking the perspective of the universe (p. 230). Somewhat later he writes, "the reduction of pain and suffering, wherever it is to be found . . . may not be the only rationally grounded value, but it is the most immediate, pressing, and universally agreed upon one. . . . If we take the point of view of the universe, we can recognize the urgency of doing something about the pain and suffering of others" (p. 232).

In reading these passages, I find myself nodding in agreement about how sensible the golden rule is and how it is indeed urgent that we try to reduce the pain and suffering of others. In short, I feel the pull of the justificatory rationalist argument. However, let's look at the argument more closely. The argument calls attention to the salient fact that from the perspective of the universe, there is no rational basis for privileging my own perspective. This leads the justificatory rationalist to the conclusion that we should reduce pain and suffering wherever we find it. But by what conveyance do we get to move from "from the perspective of the universe there is no rational basis for privileging my own perspective" to "rationality indicates that we should reduce pain and suffering, wherever it may be found"?[7] Why, that is, should I give priority (or indeed credence) to the perspective of the universe when it comes to deciding the rational thing for me to do?

From the perspective of the universe, it's not rational to privilege my own perspective, but how do I get from that fact to the conclusion that I should not privilege my own perspective? Of course, even justificatory rationalists would typically agree that the mere fact that a person's inclination is not rationally privileged from the perspective of the universe does not show that it's irrational for him to follow that inclination. From the perspective of the universe, my preference for vanilla over chocolate ice cream enjoys no advantage over another's preference for the opposite, but it would hardly be irrational of me to follow my preference when ordering ice cream; it would be bizarre to conclude that I shouldn't follow my preference. From the perspective of the universe, when it comes to pain and suffering, my perspective isn't privileged. How does the justificatory rationalist use this to draw the strong conclusion that it's irrational for me to privilege my perspective, that I shouldn't privilege my own perspective?

It seems likely that one key factor here is the intuition that favoring my own perspective seems unfair, unjust, wrong. That is, I find the following claim powerfully intuitive.

Justification principle Rationality reveals that from the perspective of the universe my interests are not privileged, so I should not privilege them to the exclusion of the interests of others.

I suspect that the force of the preceding argument derives largely from the support it gets from the intuitiveness of claims like the justification principle. Given that my perspective has no elevated status from the perspective of the universe, there is something intuitively repugnant about discounting the perspectives of others.[8]

Of course, relying on intuitions in philosophy isn't exactly disreputable, so there is no easy objection to make on those grounds alone. Intuition plays a central role in many venerable philosophical arguments. However, in the present case, I'll suggest that if psychological rationalism is false, this will call into question whether our intuitions in favor of claims like the justification principle can carry much weight in a justificatory rationalist argument. In some cases, the causal origin of an intuition can render the intuition inappropriate support for certain arguments. In the present case, if psychological rationalism is false, then intuitions in favor of claims like the justification principle might suffer from such a grounding problem with respect to the justificatory rationalist argument. A grounding problem arises when an argument depends on an intuition and the source of that intuition makes it an inappropriate basis of support for that argument.

Let us assume that psychological rationalism is false. Indeed, let us assume that our capacity for moral judgment depends crucially on certain emotions such that if we lacked those emotions (but retained our rational faculties) our capacity for moral judgment would be seriously defective.[9] For present purposes it is unobjectionable to assume such a sentimentalist moral psychology since the question is whether the empirical facts can undercut the plausibility of justificatory rationalism. The problem is that if such a sentimentalist moral psychology is right, then it is probably illicit for the justificatory rationalism to rely on lay intuitions in favor of claims like the justification principle. Those lay intuitions are most likely a product of nonrational affective mechanisms, and it is quite possible that we would not find these claims intuitive if we lacked the affective responses. That is, we can't rely on the intuitiveness of the claims if their intuitiveness is rooted in our nonrational, emotional faculties. This will drastically limit the argumentative resources available to the justificatory rationalism.

If psychological rationalism is false (and sentimentalism is true), then the justificatory rationalist needs to be wary of relying on normative intuitions regarding the pain and suffering of others. This is analogous to the wariness we would have about a person's judging the relative facial attractiveness of a group of children that included their own child. If asked to make such an assessment, provided one is interested in the truth, the rational thing to do is to recuse oneself. I can't trust myself to be a good judge in such a scenario, for I know that my feelings for my children can contribute to my perception of how beautiful they are. Just as I would recuse myself from judging the relative facial beauty of children in my daughter's first grade class, so too would I recuse myself from judging whether it's rational to follow the perspective of the universe when making decisions about the suffering of others. On the assumption that sentimentalism is right, I know that my own intuitions about such matters are influenced by the emotions that I have.

Whether a particular intuition has a problematic source will often vary by individual. So, while it might be illicit for one person to accept an argument based on his intuition that p, it might be appropriate for another person to accept that argument based on her intuition that p because their intuitions might have different sources, and those different sources might have differences in whether they deprive the intuition of warrant. Ironically if certain kinds of sentimentalist accounts are right (e.g., R.J.R. Blair, 1995; Nichols, 2004b; Prinz, 2007), the one population whose intuitions about the justification principle would not be compromised (with respect to justificatory rationalist arguments) is psychopathic. Imagine a pure psychopath, a person who has the psychopathic profile in full. Our psychopath has fully intact rational faculties. He recognizes that hitting people for fun is prohibited, but he doesn't think that it counts as importantly different from other prohibited actions, like jaywalking. Furthermore, let us suppose that his moral deficit is a consequence of an emotional deficit. For those of us who aren't psychopathic, our intuitions about the justification principle will be influenced by our emotions, but the psychopath doesn't have this problem. His intuitions will be grounded in his rational faculties. Thus, the psychopath's intuitions would not suffer the grounding problem that renders our intuitions about the justification principle ineligible for supporting justificatory rationalism.[10] Of course, if the justificatory rationalist has to rest his hopes on the moral intuitions of psychopaths, his hopes are likely to be dashed. There is little reason to expect that the pure psychopath will find the justification principle powerfully intuitive.

Notice that if psychological rationalism turns out to be true,[11] then the justificatory rationalist argument given here is relieved from the grounding problem that I have raised. If psychological rationalism is right, then our moral intuitions are not compromised by having an emotional underpinning. This serves to underscore my claim that the empirical issues really do have a bearing on arguments for justificatory rationalism. If psychological rationalism is wholly wrong, then we need to be wary about justificatory rationalist arguments that draw on folk intuitions. If, on the other hand, psychological rationalism is right, then such wariness is unnecessary. If the intuitiveness of the justification principle derives from a rational faculty, then there is nothing untoward about relying on this intuition to make the case that ethics has a rational foundation.

Let us turn now, more briefly, to an argument from Michael Smith. Smith points out that we might find that under idealized conditions of reflection there will be a convergence in views about what is right and wrong.

Why not think . . . that if such a convergence emerged in moral practice then that would itself suggest that these particular moral beliefs, and the corresponding desires, do enjoy a privileged rational status? After all, something like such a convergence in mathematical practice lies behind our conviction that mathematical claims enjoy a privileged rational status. So why not think that a like convergence in moral practice would show that moral judgements enjoy the same privileged rational status? . . . . It remains to be seen whether sustained moral argument can elicit the requisite convergence in our moral beliefs, and corresponding desires to make the idea of a moral fact look plausible. . . . Only time will tell. (Smith, 1993, pp. 408–409)

Smith can be interpreted here as making a justificatory rationalist argument and the argument, so construed, is not without merit. In essence, it is an inference to the best explanation. The convergence in mathematics gives us reason to think that there are some mind-independent facts that mathematicians are getting at. Math has a privileged rational status. Assume that we find the same convergence in the case of morality. Wouldn't this give us a close parallel, hence wouldn't this show that morality also has privileged rational status?

Here again, I think it depends on how the empirical facts turn out. Crucially, if psychological rationalism turns out to be false and some version of sentimentalist moral psychology is correct, then we might get a sentimentalist explanation of the convergence that displaces the justificatory rationalist explanation. Namely, we might explain convergence as a result of the fact that we have similar emotional repertoires that lead us to have similar kinds of moral judgments. In this case, we would lose the argument that ethics has a privileged rational status. The best explanation for convergence would not parallel the explanation given for mathematics. Rather, it would be deeply rooted in the nonrational character of our minds. If that is correct, then we can hardly show that ethics has a rational foundation by appealing to convergence.

Conclusion

Joyce's chapter rightly emphasizes that the empirical facts have marked limitations when it comes to evaluating conceptual and justificatory rationalism. Empirical facts about folk intuitions do not by themselves provide the analysis of a folk concept, and the empirical facts can never show that there is no rational foundation for ethics. However, I am more optimistic that the empirical facts can make important contributions to debates over conceptual and justificatory rationalism. While empirical facts about folk intuitions do not constitute an analysis of folk concepts, they do provide a vital source of information about folk concepts, a source that can't be dismissed lightly when the intuitions converge with the analysis of your opponent. As for justificatory rationalism, it's true that the empirical facts can't refute the existence of a rational foundation for the content of our moral judgments. However, the arguments meant to establish a rational foundation for ethics often are hostage to empirical facts. For instance, in some cases, justificatory rationalist arguments depend on intuitions that can't carry the requisite weight if a sentimentalist account of those intuitions is correct. So, although cognitive scientists should be cautious about drawing quick conclusions about metaethics from their empirical findings, metaethicists should recognize that their debates are not immune from those findings.

Notes

I am most grateful to Richard Joyce and Walter Sinnott-Armstrong for helpful suggestions on an earlier draft.

1. Joyce uses "psychological rationalism" for the view that I labeled "empirical rationalism" (Nichols, 2002a), but I am happy enough to adopt his terminology for present purposes.

2. Walter Sinnott-Armstrong notes that on one natural reading of this characterization, psychological rationalism is almost certainly true. Here is his example: Sometimes we have good reason to trust a given person's views concerning a wide range of issues. On the basis of a person's prior trustworthiness, we might reasonably accept her testimony that it is morally wrong to buy new furniture made from the wood of old-growth forests. I might thus use reason alone to arrive at the conclusion that I shouldn't buy such furniture. Thus, if the definition of psychological rationalism is simply that sometimes we make moral judgments that causally flow from rational faculties, then psychological rationalism seems safe from science. However, the point of psychological rationalism is that moral judgments are ultimately a product of rational faculties. Rational faculties are supposed to be the basic font of our moral judgment. Sentimentalists, on the other hand, maintain that the basic font of our moral judgment critically involves the emotions. However, both sentimentalists and psychological rationalists can agree that once judgments have been established, then those judgments can be used in subsequent episodes of pure reasoning. For instance, one can use reason to derive some new moral conclusion from one's standing moral judgments. Or, as in Sinnott-Armstrong's example, one can reason to moral conclusions from what one takes to be reliable testimony. The opponent of psychological rationalism maintains that these cases are derivative, and that if we trace back to the origins of moral judgment, we will find that its springs are not located exclusively in the rational faculty.

3. Joyce does maintain, rightly, that a weaker version of psychological rationalism, according to which rational faculties are necessary for moral judgment, remains unscathed by any empirical evidence.

4. Smith uses the term "practicality requirement," but I will follow Joyce's terminology here.

5. In a 2004 Gallup poll, 70 percent of the U.S. respondents said that they believed in the devil. http://www.pollingreport.com/religion.htm.

6. One interesting possibility available to the conceptual rationalist is to maintain that although the folk responses reveal a platitude that defies motivation internal-

ism, this platitude is in fact psychologically effete; it is just a bit of cognitive effluvium that doesn't affect moral cognition outside of such artificial settings. Notice, however, that this is yet another empirical question. We can't determine whether the anti-internalist platitude is cognitively impotent simply by doing an a priori analysis.

7. One might make a case that the golden rule is prudentially rational. For instance, perhaps adopting the golden rule is the best way to ensure that one will get the benefits of reciprocity. Justificatory rationalists strive to support the contents of our moral judgments without drawing on such crassly self-interested considerations.

8. Perhaps there is another way to construct the argument, but if it doesn't depend on some such intuition, then it is unclear to me how the argument is supposed to work.

9. That is, defective compared with the capacity for moral judgment exhibited in normal adults.

10. The presence of a grounding problem depends both on the source of the intuition and the argument to which it is supposed to contribute. The source of an intuition might render it inappropriate for some arguments but not others. If the intuitiveness of the justification principle derives from a sentimentalist source, one is ill-advised to use the intuitiveness of the justification principle as central support for justificatory rationalism. However, it might well be acceptable for a philosophical sentimentalist to use the intuitiveness of the justification principle as support in arguments about the right thing to do.

11. One important line of defense for psychological rationalism is that a distinctive rational defect underlies the moral defect in psychopathy (see e.g., Maibom, 2005).

8.2 Hedonic Reasons as Ultimately Justifying and the Relevance of Neuroscience

Leonard D. Katz

Richard Joyce, who believes that morality is globally mistaken in making normative claims on people that do not wholly derive from their own desires or institutional commitments (2001, 2006a), in his chapter defends ethics from more piecemeal undermining by neuroscience while suggesting that it will be undermined globally in other ways. My perspective is very different. I think that while some parts of natural human morality may rest on illusion, hedonically grounded practical reasons, and at least those parts of morality that rest on them, very likely have some objective normative standing. I will suggest that the hedonic good and bad in human life provide a grounding for this. Since harms and benefits are central to much, although not all, of natural human morality (including duties not to harm or deprive of goods), and suffering is often an unproblematic and important harm, just as pleasure, or happiness, is often an unproblematic and important good, the normative status of hedonic reasons bears importantly on central parts of natural human morality. Their standing is subject to undermining by any neuroscientific and other discoveries suggesting that they are based merely in recently evolved adaptations for shared confabulation that serves social cooperation. However, their standing is also open to similarly scientific confirmation that our intuitive hedonic judgments and reasons really respond to perceptions of psychologically and biologically deep affective realities that are plausibly a source of ultimate and objective normatively justifying reasons.

Hedonic Reasons, Evolutionary Debunking, and the Relevance of Neuroscience

Ethics is concerned not only with what we as individuals owe each other (as is central to morality narrowly conceived; e.g., Scanlon, 1998) but also with what is ultimately good and bad in human life and what makes it so.

Denying truth or objectivity to all of ethics (as in Joyce 2001, 2006a; cf. Nichols, 2004b) involves rejecting (in their unqualified and unrelativized form) all such questions, or at least all their possible answers except "Nothing at all." If not only all of morality but all of normative ethics is falsehood or fiction (Joyce 2001, 2006a), then that life is ever at all good, worthwhile, or bad, or any of these more at some times than at others, would be a falsehood or fiction, too. On the other hand, if life is really sometimes good or bad, or better or worse, and can sometimes be made better or less bad, there are ultimate considerations in favor of doing so, ultimately justifying normative reasons for action.

Pleasure (feeling good or happiness) seems to be really good and (affective) pain (suffering or feeling bad) really bad, so that our having either of them really matters. If so, we have reasons in favor of pleasure and against pain. Hedonically based reasons seem to apply not only to the person whose pleasure or suffering is immediately concerned who thereby has reason to seek or avoid it. Such reasons seem also to apply generally and most saliently to others who can prevent or end suffering (cf. Nagel, 1986, pp. 156–162). Such reasons thus seem to be objective, or perspective invariant. Further, it is hard to see how the seeming perception of one's own pleasure and of its goodness or of one's own suffering and of its badness could be discredited by being shown to be based in affective reactions in the way that, it has been claimed, undermines many moral judgments (see Greene, chapter 2 in this volume). Where then is there room for projective error here? It may even seem that the notion of projective error, to which projectivist nonrealists about value appeal, presupposes some real value that we erroneously project upon outward things. These sources, it has seemed to many persons seeking a rational basis for ethics, are just the real goodness of pleasure and badness of suffering.

Evolutionary debunking, such as Joyce envisages here and argues elsewhere (Joyce 2001, 2006a), apparently for all of ethics, seems a different strategy. All our beliefs about value, even those about hedonic value, may be argued to be illusory on the ground that they are most parsimoniously explained, not by their truth, but by natural selection for fitness-enhancing adaptations to which the truth of these beliefs is irrelevant. There is then no reason to believe that these adaptations track (as perception does) rather than distort any corresponding reality (Street, 2006). If this strategy works for all of morality, it seems we would have no reason to regard any of our moral beliefs as true rather than illusory, even, for example, that we have objective reasons to avoid causing others needless suffering by inflicting gratuitous bodily harm.

However, plausible alternative evolutionary stories may be told about the origins of some ethical beliefs that are less damaging to their epistemic standing and even supportive of it. For example, it is plausible that pleasure and suffering, by whatever mix of natural necessity and historical contingencies of the evolutionary acquisition of function, reliably track aspects of our physiological well- and ill-being. In the mammalian and perhaps also in the avian lineages, a strong selection for infantile and juvenile displays of affective states that can be readily understood and used by caregivers seems the rule. These displays seem crucial to the young receiving the nutrition, warmth, and emotional nurture needed for survival. Such states and their recognition may then come to provide a basis for affective communication among adults in social species. There seems to be considerable overlap between coevolved neural mechanisms for perceiving one's own emotional states and those of others (e.g., Preston and de Waal, 2002; Panksepp, 2005; Singer & Frith, 2005). That the representations involved are affective representations would not make them any less information giving. If experiencing pleasure really has objective value and suffering has objective disvalue, they could carry that information, too. However, if the neural states, affective experiences, and values are not distinct in nature, but only conceptually different, no additional information or complexity in the world would be involved. This, rather than simplicity or parsimony relative to conceptual frameworks that are more finely grained than the world (in separating physiology, experience, and value), seems to be what we should consider when we weigh the relative plausibility of competing views. Thus, considerations of parsimony need not favor views of nature as devoid of either experience or value.

The scientific details that may fill out such a story are being supplied by neuroscience. So is information that may support alternative, more debunking stories, in which pleasure's apparent value is only a misleading projection of our desires or pursuits. Perhaps neuroscience suggests *some* positive affect is like that, but it seems not all is (see Katz, 2006, 3.2, 3.3; references and links to scientists' websites supplied there). And even if the good of life, the ill of suffering, and the importance of which of these we experience are constructed, the result would be no merely anthropocentric construction, as Haidt and Björklund (chapter 4 in volume 2) and Greene (chapter 2 in this volume) seem to suggest for all of morality and presumably for all of value as well. Rather, any such construction would seem to be one in which at least many higher vertebrates share. In our search for practical reasons that can withstand the test of objectivity (Nagel 1970, 1986), this much invariance in perspective may seem no trifling achievement and to provide a basis from which we may seek more.

Substantive Normative Practical Reasons versus Structural Rationality

In value-realist versions of hedonistic utilitarianism and indeed in any view that contains a value-realist hedonic component, the value of pleasure and the disvalue of suffering are no illusions, but figure among the truths on which whatever of ethics survives the test of rational reflection is to be built. In such a view, to say there would be no such value in a universe without life is not to say that truths about it can be only "true for us" or are created by our collectively accepting them, as Haidt and Björklund seem to say (volume 2, chapter 4) about all morality. Rather, there being no such value without life would be an ordinary fact, on a par with (and perhaps identical to) there being no physiological activity of some kind in a world without life. Even if there were no actual life worth living or avoiding, there would still be facts about the value of the pleasure or suffering that would obtain if there were such life, facts that would still obtain without anyone creating or accepting them.

Modern rejection of such realism about all normative practical reasons is older than liberal distaste for browbeating moralizing (e.g., Bernard Williams 1981, 1995, on whose relevant views see, contrastingly, Scanlon, 1998, pp. 48–49, 363–373 and Joyce, 2001) but not as old as awareness of moral diversity (which different prioritizing of shared values, e.g., social peace and collective well-being versus justice and individual liberty, along with differences in circumstances, may go far to explain). Its essentials may be found in Thomas Hobbes (1651), whose views of reason as mere calculation (*Leviathan* part I, chap. v, chap. 1–6,) and of goodness as a projection of our survival-driven desires (Part I, chap. vi, par. 7 and Part I, chap. xv, par. 40) foreshadow the explicit means-end instrumentalism about all practical reason (supported by evolutionary debunking of any more absolute value claims) that writers such as Joyce now maintain (2001). In this view, all normative reasons for action (for Joyce, outside institutions) derive from agents' aims, wants, or desires and can have validity only relative to these. (I assume Joyce's use of "interests" is similarly relativized to these and thus does not extend substantially beyond them.)

On such views, someone miserably depressed and consequently so unmotivated as to have lost all desires that would be served by seeking treatment known to be efficacious would have no reason to accept such treatment. Similarly, drug addicts single-mindedly given over to their craving and living a miserable life as a result would have no reason to change (but only instrumental reasons not to), to the extent that addiction excludes all competing or potentially controlling desires (and, for Joyce, would continue to do so under conditions of full information and careful reflection). This would presumably hold even if the sufferers acknowledged in a merely cognitive way the (supposed) reasons we (mistakenly) urge upon them, while lacking any corresponding desire to change. The depressive and the addict, if they acknowledged any such objective and absolute reasons, independent of their wants or desires, would, like us, be making mistakes. This seems a high price to pay for the (dubious, as I have argued) parsimony of a value-free metaphysics, especially when, as post-Newtonians and contemporaries of first-generation string theorists, we know we inhabit a world far richer and stranger than any allowed by Hobbes's purely mechanistic materialism and the evolved intuitive physics on which it is based.

Views that similarly based practical reason in actual or hypothetical choice, preference, or desire, and value in the fulfillment of one or the other of these, were common in the twentieth century, not only in areas of the social sciences that aim only at descriptive or predictive adequacy (e.g., in those parts of economics concerned with prices in markets), but also in more prescriptive fields such as welfare economics, game theory, decision theory, and ethical theory. However, the past few decades have seen a revival among analytic philosophers of more classically realist views of practical reason, in which practical reasons are seen as normatively applicable to action, planning, wanting, and sometimes also to feeling in much the same way as normative reasons apply to theoretical thinking and reasoning (e.g., Thomas Nagel, more fully in his later work, e.g., 1986, chaps. VIII and IX, and 1997, chaps. 6 and 7, than in his seminal 1970 work; Joseph Raz, 1975 and 1999, chap. 2; T. M. Scanlon, 1998, chap. 1; Derek Parfit, 2001 and forthcoming, chap. 1).

This perspective need not involve saying that people who fail to respond to such reasons ideally are irrational or "reasoning badly," as Richard Joyce suggests here in discussing Peter Singer, who explicitly disavows similar claims (1995, pp. 232–233). Both expressions may be best reserved for narrower uses marked by inconsistency in acknowledged commitments or errors in inference. One may say this while maintaining that there are other failures to respond appropriately to normative reasons that are not irrational in these ways (Scanlon, 1998, pp. 25–30 and 2007; Kolodny, 2005; cf. Parfit, forthcoming). One may even maintain that there are substantive normative practical reasons that are supplied by the facts of a case, while denying that we have similarly noninstrumental reasons to comply with the structural rationality of consistency and reasoning (Kolodny, 2005; Scanlon, 2007).

From this perspective, just as there are failures to respond appropriately to reasons for belief that are not failures in consistency or reasoning (as when one unreasonably refuses to accept the evidence of one's senses or mechanically accepts the conclusion of a valid argument when it would be more reasonable to reconsider one's premises), similarly one may fail to respond appropriately to substantive normative practical reasons as one should. And one can do this without any logical inconsistency or "reasoning badly" that would implicate one in structural irrationality consisting in internal incoherence among one's attitudes of believing, desiring, intending, willing, and the like (which some in the older rationalist and continuing Kantian philosophical traditions have thought to be involved in any failure to respond appropriately to moral reasons).

Objective Experiential Values versus Projections of Present Desires

Writers in this value- or reason-realist tradition often regard cases of hedonic reasons or value as providing clear illustrative cases of justifying reasons given directly by the facts of the case, rather than deriving from the direction of our aims or desires. However, two recent opponents see the same cases as supporting their own desire-based views (Copp & Sobel, 2002, p. 272; Sobel, 2005). In Scanlon's example (1998, pp. 42–47; 2002, pp. 339–340), the fact that one's current appetite for coffee ice cream will make eating it enjoyable gives one reason to eat some now. However, that is very different from one's having an ultimate reason to fulfill this appetite, let alone any and all desire merely as such, as those holding desire-based views of reasons for action have supposed. Use of the language of wanting, preference, liking, and desiring in describing hedonic cases by some on the realist side of this controversy (e.g., Parfit, 1984, pp. 493–494; Katz 1986, pp. 47–48, on which see Katz 2006, n. 35; Parfit, 2001; Scanlon, 2002) has led their opponents to believe they thus concede, even as they deny, that desire plays an ultimate justifying role in the case of hedonic reasons, and even that their refusal to believe in desire-grounded reasons more generally is therefore unmotivated (Copp & Sobel, 2002; Sobel, 2005; cf. Kagan, 1992).

There are, however, different kinds of state that may be legitimately called "desires" and the like. Few if any of these provide ultimate sources of reasons to fulfill the desires by achieving their aims, which is what is at issue here. Some even involve an appearance that there are reasons grounding the desire on which its correctness depends (Nagel, 1970, pp. 29–30; Schueler, 1995; Scanlon, 1998, pp. 32–49 and 2002, pp. 337–342). "Liking" also has various relevant uses; one, like one use of "being pleased," involves nothing beyond pleasure itself. Since the experience of pleasure would not be separable from this liking, there is no room for the objection that, since any experience might not be liked, pleasure could not be a valuable experience grounding reasons, so that any hedonic value or reasons must ultimately derive from the contingent direction, upon an experience, of a desire.[1] Further, if good moods are to count as pleasure (as they should, at least for some purposes of value theory), pleasure, at least in the general case, seems neither to be nor to involve any intentional attitude (such as desire is), but at most a preintentional stance that may be objectless, although it may naturally extend to intentional attitudes if suitable psychological contexts arise (Katz, 2006, esp. 2.3.3).

Recent work in neuroscience suggests a dissociation between the neural dopamine systems often involved in motivation and the more properly hedonic systems (e.g., Berridge, 2004; Depue & Morrone-Strupinsky, 2005; Katz, 2005, 2006). What is relevantly at issue in this science is not whether Berridge's core neural process or processes of "liking" are purely affective and distinct from all processes that have some motivational function (which Berridge denies). Rather it is whether the natural view—that hedonic value or reasons fundamentally concern the quality of the subject's affective experience—coheres better with science than the opposed view, which makes any hedonic justificatory reasons instead derive from the direction of the subject's desires or aims—and presumably attributes all appearances to the contrary to confabulation. Whatever the exact relations of (the possibly diverse forms of) pleasure to motivational processes may be, and even if pleasure is one or more neural motivational processes that may broadly be considered forms of desire, it still seems plausible that what matters fundamentally is how it (affectively) feels. Pleasure, however it is biologically or psychologically caused or constituted, does not seem to be the same thing as desire's fulfillment conditions coming to pass. This may happen after the subject is dead or in the pleasureless craving of addiction, which may be simultaneously fulfilled without felt hedonic satisfaction. This is what we should anyway expect; the logical relation of fulfillment (analogous to satisfaction, in the logician's special sense) and felt experience seem radically different. While our naïve and natural concept of pleasure (which perhaps has its reference fixed by ties to behavioral and social affective displays, such as the genuine Duchenne smile) may prove too undiscriminating for many purposes of neuroscience, hedonic psychology, and hedonic ethics, it seems likely that at least some of its emerging neurally and experientially more refined successors would then serve in its place to show a coherence between science and a realist picture of hedonic value (cf. Katz, 2006).

Nature, by whatever mixture of chance and natural necessity, of natural selection and other less predictable evolutionary processes, has given us capacities for theoretical understanding in fundamental physics and higher mathematics that were of no conceivable use (as such) in the adaptive environments in which our hominid line evolved. For similarly unknown reasons it has made us phenomenally conscious experiencers of affective happiness and suffering. More comprehensibly, given this, it has made us social animals who use the same affectively qualified representations by which we think of our own affective experiences to attribute similar experiences to others, to react emotionally to these, and to construct human moralities in part on the basis of the responses that such experiences seem to demand. That, in part, is why Joyce's projected science of sociolinguistics, which presumably would look only at the communicative and strategic uses of ethical language, would not satisfactorily dispose of this part of morality. Language is here intimately bound up with thoughts and purposes with deeper roots, which reach below group-level and dyadic sociality to phenomenal experience itself, with which the experienced reality of hedonic value seems intertwined. We are acquainted with these before we distinguish ourselves from others.

Perhaps it was not for nothing that the radically empiricist Epicureans attributed epistemic priority to the infant's unqualified and unenculturated perception of the goodness of pleasure and badness of pain (Brunschwig, 1986). It may be not such perceptions (or the conceptually elaborated cognitions and ethical reasons to which they give rise), but rather our employment of our later-developing distinctions between oneself and others and between in-group and outsiders to justify special spheres of self-interest and particular loyalty, that should be regarded as epistemically discredited by their genealogies in natural selection and cultural evolution (cf. Katz 1986, sect. 5.4).

Perhaps pursuing this line of thought rather than following Joyce would be only exchanging one evolutionary just-so story and metamythology for another. In my favorite story, real hedonic value grounds substantive ultimate normative practical reasons, with any additional self-interested reasons illusory. In Joyce's account, merely instrumental reasons are grounded only in groundless desire, whose ends in themselves have no real value. In stark contrast, some of us think desire in itself, and taken as such, adds no new reasons at all, as cases of desire for worthless ends (that are also without good causal consequences, such as one's increased enjoyment in games one wants to win) seem to show. Unpacking elements of these two packages and reassembling them into others is of course possible. However, the contrast between these broad theoretical pictures may serve to illustrate, better than a bare appeal to impartial reason, what is at issue in the passage from Peter Singer (1995, pp. 225–233) quoted in part by Joyce in his chapter (p. 389), in which Singer seems to follow the fuller arguments of Henry Sidgwick (1874/1907, Bk. III, chap. xiii and Bk. IV, chap. ii) and Thomas Nagel (1970, 1986), without, however, the cognitivist and realist perspective they share. Which stories will provide the best guidance in working toward a unified understanding of all that our experience and its scientific understanding bring to the table remains to be seen. An informed decision on whether hedonic value provides a plausible stopping point in any debunking of ethics, as I have suggested, must await a more complete understanding of our intermeshed cognitive, motivational, and affective constitution and situation; in achieving this understanding, the neurosciences, along with other sciences, have roles to play. One might say that such questions matter greatly were it not that part of what is in question is whether anything really does. Matters, that is, not by being something people care about or desire, but in a way that gives such caring and desiring their correctness and point. This, affective experience (not through any motivational force or intentional direction upon objects which it may or may not have, but by how it feels) seems most clearly to do.

Note

1. This objection is posed in Sobel (2005) against Scanlon and also against Parfit (2001), using Scanlon's own example. See Scanlon's earlier response (2002, pp. 337–342) to Copp and Sobel (2002, pp. 269–272). Compare, with Sobel's objection, Trigg (1970, pp. 121–123); compare, with Scanlon's response, Sidgwick (1874/1907, pp. 46–47). For a discussion of the nature of pleasure that is relevant to Sobel's repeated claims that pleasure is not an experience, apparently following Ryle, see Katz (2006). See also Ruth Chang (2004), whose view of the controversy discussed here and of its upshot is in some ways similar to Scanlon's, Parfit's, and my own apparently slightly differing views, although it is not identical to any of them.

Richard Joyce

To reject a false theory on the basis of an unsound argument is, in my opinion, as much an intellectual sin as to embrace a false theory. Thus, although I am no fan of any particular form of moral rationalism (and, indeed, on occasion have gone out of my way to criticize it), when rationalism is assailed for faulty reasons, I find myself in the curious position of leaping to its defense (which goes to show that in philosophy it isn't the case that one's enemy's enemy is one's friend). This puts me at something of a dialectical disadvantage, since my "defense" of moral rationalism has strict limits. I will defend it against specific kinds of criticism, but I have no interest in defending it *simpliciter*. It is important to bear in mind that what is in dispute between Shaun Nichols and myself is not the truth or falsity of moral rationalism, but rather what kind of evidence bears on the matter.

Concerning psychological rationalism, Nichols and I have no argument. Concerning conceptual rationalism, there are two sources of disagreement. First, Nichols acknowledges that the experimental design that he originally employed was inadequate to refute Michael Smith's brand of conceptual rationalism, since the subjects were not asked whether the imaginary psychopath was irrational. Nevertheless, Nichols doubts that this would have made much difference to the outcome, pointing to the widespread view of Satan, who is popularly conceived of as "the rational amoralist par excellence." The problem with this response is that "rational" is, in the vernacular, a fairly amorphous and indeterminate term, concerning which (I'll wager, in advance of experimental evidence) ordinary people have vague, conflicting, pliable, and quite possibly downright confused opinions. There is certainly a sense in which Satan is considered rational. He is good at math, could get an A+ in Logic 101 without breaking a sweat, and is extremely effective at means-end reasoning. But surely we should acknowledge another sense in which ordinary people may hesitate about Satan's rationality: They may suspect that there is something irrational about Satan's *ends* (his desire to inflict endless suffering, etc.). They may be tempted by the thought that the way that Satan has failed to see things "correctly" (i.e., the way God sees them) counts as some kind of rational failure; indeed, they may simply think that Satan's evil character is evidence of his irrationality. Whether there is any philosophical sense to be made of the idea that practical ends can be assessed as rational or irrational is something that can, of course, be doubted; it is a long-standing problem in moral philosophy. However, that there exists a body of widespread firm (but possibly nebulous) opinions favoring this idea is something about which it seems to me there can be little doubt. After all, all those neo-Kantians who devote their energies to making sense of the idea must be picking up on *something* in the popular consciousness. I predict that when they are questioned about rationality (e.g., when asked to assess Satan in this manner), ordinary subjects will be easily manipulated either to assert or deny claims of the form "X is rational," depending on the framing of the query. (On framing effects in general, see Kahneman and Tversky, 1979.)

This brings us nicely to the second, more general, disagreement between Nichols and myself over conceptual rationalism: namely, the extent to which consulting the opinion of ordinary speakers (using questionnaires and the like) is likely to cast interesting light on conceptual content. Michael Smith is skeptical on the grounds that conceptual content is best conceived of as a systematization of the platitudes surrounding a term, where these platitudes are "descriptions of the inferential and judgmental dispositions of those who have mastery of the term," (1994, 89). Note Smith's reference to *dispositions*, which he understands as a kind of knowledge of *how* to use a term. In Smith's opinion, what we end up with when we systematize platitudes—that is, when we analyze a concept—is knowledge-that about knowledge-how (Smith, 1994, p. 38). The key characteristic of knowledge-how, of course, is that those who possess it, even those who are masters of it, may be quite unable to articulate it. (How many of us can describe with any precision what we do with our bodies when we descend a flight of stairs?) When platitudes concern knowledge-how, then, pace Nichols, one should not "rather expect the folk to recognize their own platitudes," any more than one should expect a concert pianist to be able to articulate how her eyes scan the musical notation. Of course, there's no harm in asking the folk for their opinion, and there's no reason to be dismissive of their reply (just as it may be interesting to see what the concert pianist has to say about her eye movements), but what really needs to be directly examined is how the folk use their terms in everyday interaction and decision making (just as what we really need to do in order to find out about a pianist's eye movements is to observe them in action).

My principal goal in my chapter was to emphasize how the traditional philosophical form of moral rationalism concerns practical justification. Such justification, I claimed, is unlikely to be tractable by a posteriori methods. This latter claim was something I put forward as more or less obvious, without submitting much by way of argument. Nichols responds by offering some interesting thoughts concerning how justification may in fact be affected by empirical discoveries. His argument is based on the general claim that empirical discoveries about the genealogy of certain beliefs can show those beliefs to be epistemically unjustified.[1] More specifically, he argues that justificatory rationalism depends for its plausibility on the acceptance of a certain intuitive premise which, when its psychological sources become known, will be epistemically undermined. Yet more specifically, he argues that justificatory rationalism depends on the acceptance of a justification principle, but that our acceptance of this intuitive principle in fact derives from "nonrational affective mechanisms" in such a way as to cast our acceptance of this principle into doubt.

The general point that beliefs can be epistemically undermined on the basis of their origins is one with which I have much sympathy; indeed, I have advocated the idea myself on several occasions (Joyce, 2001, 2006a, 2006b), including in the closing paragraphs of my chapter. I also agree that having their source in "nonrational affective mechanisms" may be one way that beliefs (or intuitions) may be debunked (see also Sinnott-Armstrong, 2006). However, I doubt very much that justificatory rationalists see their argument as turning on a premise that enjoys the backing of nothing more than its "seeming intuitive." Indeed, I would go so far as to say that the urge to avoid building their theory on so shaky a basis is one of the justificatory rationalists' guiding intellectual motives. The challenge for the justificatory rationalist, then, is to provide an argument (including a premise that, if not along the lines of Nichols's justification principle, then at least is playing the same role) that appeals to more than just powerful intuition—that does in fact command the assent of any rational observer. At this point in the debate, it must be stressed, I really must shift to speaking vicariously, outlining what I assume the rationalist's response will be rather than pressing an argument that I have any genuine faith in. It must also be confessed that I am a poor proxy for a real committed moral rationalist, because I have a long-standing puzzlement about this point in a justificatory rationalist's argument (in just the way Nichols has), and I too harbor grave doubts that the rationalist's argument will ultimately work. (See my later comments on Katz.) However, I at least recognize that the justificatory rationalist is *endeavoring* to base the argument on something firmer than intuition.

Many justificatory rationalist arguments, for example, ultimately boil down to some sort of "Treat like as like" principle: If two things are qualitatively the same in a certain respect, then it is incorrect to treat them as if they were not alike in that respect. This principle is supposed to extend to the guidance of our treatment, not just of persons, but of cats, books, and rocks. The justificatory rationalist thinks that denying such a principle is not merely counterintuitive, but palpably incoherent. Consider, by comparison, the logical rule of *modus ponens*. To what do such logical rules owe their central place in deductive reasoning? This very good question is not one for which I would hazard an answer here; it is enough for our purposes to make the negative observation that the status of *modus ponens* does not derive simply from its intuitive obviousness; or, at the very least, if the rule *is* based on intuition, it is in a manner that does not undermine our commitment to it. The justificatory rationalist hopes to invest "Treat like as like" with an analogous status: not derived simply from intuitive obviousness; or, at the very least, if based in intuition, then in a manner that does not undermine our commitment to it. The fact that "Treat like as like" is supposed to be a cool-headed basic truth of practical rationality—holding as much for our treatment of rocks as for persons—casts doubt on the plausibility of the conjecture that our acceptance of it is grounded, ultimately and problematically, in the activity of emotional mechanisms. The aspiration to prescribe fairness on the basis of rationally compelling premises, rather than relying on any sentimental appeal that fairness may happen to have, is precisely what distinguishes justificatory rationalism from its rivals.

Leonard Katz offers a very different set of critical comments, focused less on the arguments presented in my chapter and more on a broader philosophical program that I have advocated in other books and articles. That program, in essence, is to argue that the most justified position to take with respect to moral discourse and thought is analogous to the atheist's view of religious discourse and thought. This "error-theoretic" view holds that although our moral judgments aim at the truth, they systematically fail to secure it. Space does not permit me to attempt to mount a defense of this form of moral skepticism; I must be content with making a few brief comments and at least locating the crux of the disagreement between Katz and myself.

It should be noted that although one could in principle be a moral error theorist by implication—either because one endorses a radical global error theory (thus being skeptical of morality along with modality, colors, other minds, cats and dogs, etc.), or because one endorses an error theory about all normative phenomena—typically the moral error theorist thinks that there is something especially problematic about morality and does not harbor the same doubts about normativity in general. The moral error theorist usually allows that we can still deliberate about how to act; she thinks that we can still make sense of actions harming or advancing our own welfare (and others' welfare), and thus she thinks that we can continue to make sense of various kinds of nonmoral "ought"s, such as prudential ones.[2] Thus, the moral error theorist can without embarrassment assert a claim like "One ought not harm others," as long as it is clear that it is not a *moral* "ought" that is being employed. (In the same way, an atheist can assert that one ought not covet one's neighbor's wife, as long as it clear that this isn't an "according to God" proscription.) Holding a moral error theoretic position does not imply any degree of tolerance for those actions we generally abhor on moral grounds. Although the moral error theorist will deny (when pressed in all seriousness) that the Nazis' actions were morally wrong, she also denies that they were morally right or morally permissible; she denies that they were morally *anything*. This does not prevent her from despising and opposing the Nazis' actions as vehemently as anyone else.

It must also be remembered that there are many possible routes to a moral error theory, and one must not assume that the metaethical position is refuted if one argumentative strategy in its favor falters. Perhaps the error theorist thinks that for something to be morally bad (e.g.) would imply or presuppose that human actions enjoy a kind of unrestricted autonomy, while thinking that in fact the universe supplies no such autonomy (see Haji, 1998, 2003). Perhaps she thinks that for something to be morally bad would imply or presuppose a kind of inescapable, authoritative imperative against pursuing that thing, while thinking that in fact the universe supplies no such imperatives (Mackie, 1977; Joyce, 2001). Perhaps she thinks that for something to be morally bad would imply or presuppose that human moral attitudes manifest a kind of uniformity, while thinking that in fact attitudes do not converge (Burgess, 2007). Perhaps she thinks that there exists no phenomenon whose explanation requires that the property of moral badness be instantiated, while thinking that explanatory redundancy is good ground for disbelief (Hinckfuss, 1987). Perhaps she thinks that tracing the history of the concept *moral badness* back to its origins reveals a basis in supernatural and magical forces and bonds—a defective metaphysical framework outside which the concept makes no sense (Hägerström, 1953). Perhaps she thinks all these things and more besides. Perhaps she is impressed by a number of little or medium-sized considerations against morality, none of which by itself would ground an error theory, but all of which together constitute A Big Problem. (In what follows, however, for ease of reference I will speak as if the error theorist accuses morality of just one monolithic failure.)

Most straightforward objections to the moral error theoretic position fall into one of two categories. The opponent may acknowledge that the putatively problematic attribute that the error theorist assigns to morality really is problematic, but deny that this attribute is an essential component of morality; a normative framework stripped of the troublesome element will still count as a morality. Alternatively, the opponent may accept that the putatively problematic attribute is a non-negotiable component of anything deserving the name "morality," but deny that it really is problematic. So, for example, if the error theorist is claiming that moral properties require a kind of pure autonomy that the universe does not supply, then one type of opponent will insist that morality requires nothing of the sort, while another will insist that the universe does indeed contain such autonomy.

Katz's commentary includes elements of both kinds of objection. First, he admits that "some parts of natural human morality may rest on illusion," but thinks that there is plenty that remains unscathed after the error theorist's attack. In particular, he thinks that the types of objection that I have raised in favor of moral skepticism do not undermine the existence of objective hedonic values, and much of morality can be built upon these values. Second, Katz focuses on a specific "problematic attribute" of morality on which I have concentrated earlier efforts (especially in my 2001 book)—namely, that morality centrally depends on our having desire-transcendent practical reasons—and he argues that this attribute is in fact not problematic at all; objective hedonic values can ground desire-independent reasons.

Katz's second strategy is clearly his dominant one (the first is, in any case, hard to assess, since he leaves it unclear which bits of morality he is willing to concede are "illusory"), so it will be the focus of what little remains of this rejoinder. The general pattern of this dialectic is one that any error theorist will face over and over again: A contender property (or cluster of properties) is brought forward, for which it is claimed (A) that it is instantiated by the world and (B) that it satisfies the criteria sufficient to count as a morality. The error theorist's commitment involves denying either (A) or (B), usually (B). By comparison, think again of the atheist. Imagine him being assailed by opponents offering accounts of God designed to dispel his doubts: "Well, God is just *love*, and you believe in love, don't you?—so you believe in God." The atheist's answer, obviously, is that it is simply wrong to literally identify God with love, and were someone really to insist on doing so, then she would be using either the term "God" or the term "love" (or, I suppose, the word "is") in an eccentric and stipulative manner. To believe in the thing denoted by the vernacular English word "God" involves a range of unusual ontological commitments that believing in love does not.

Although Katz's opposition to moral skepticism is nowhere near as crass as the "God is love" example, the broad structure of my defense is the same: To believe in the things denoted by the English words "moral rightness," "evil," "moral badness," "moral duty," etc. involves a range of commitments that believing in pleasure and pain will not supply. The way that I have formulated the debate in the past (Joyce, 2001) has invited Katz to think that what is crucial to our dispute is whether pleasure and pain will supply reasons. I am now not so sure that this is a necessary, or the most perspicacious, way of proceeding, but in any case I won't change tack now. The questions that need to be put to this particular contender are the following: Does pain (say) ground values? Does pain ground reasons? Does pain ground objective reasons? Does pain ground moral normativity? It seems pretty clear that Katz conceives of these questions roughly as a building sequence, such that if any one of them receives a "no," this will upset the plausibility of the subsequent questions receiving a positive answer. My view is that the sequence might be reasonably interrupted at *any* point, although space doesn't allow the development of supporting arguments. I will instead close by cutting right to the heart of the problem.

Let me grant for the sake of argument that my pain is a (negative) value for me. Let me also grant that my pain supplies me with reasons for acting. And I'll also grant (again, purely *arguendo*) that these reasons are (in some sense of the term) objective. The trouble begins by wondering why my pain is a value for, and why it supplies reasons to, anyone other than me. There is a gaping chasm between "My pain gives me reason to act" and "My pain gives you reason to act." Without this chasm being bridged, the values and reasons that Katz manages to squeeze into the world will not ground a morality, for moral normativity centrally involves other persons being loci of value and imposers of duties. Although I do not wish to exclude the possibility of self-promoting moral values and duties, I would argue adamantly that a normative system consisting wholly of such values and duties—in which one's duties to others are entirely contingent on what effect the discharge of those duties has on one's own pleasure states, and in which the value of others depends completely on their bearing on one's own hedonic welfare—does not count as a *moral* system.

Katz would, I think, concur. He recognizes that if pleasure and pain are to undergird the whole moral system, it is vital that one individual's pleasure and pain episodes can ground *someone else's* values and reasons—someone, that is, who isn't the least bit sympathetic to the individual in question. However, on this absolutely vital step he is content to offer no more than "cf. Nagel 1986." The use of "cf." leaves us guessing the extent to which Katz endorses Thomas Nagel's views, but we are forced to assume that he has at least some sympathy, for Katz offers nothing else that promises to accomplish this crucial step in the argument. Although Nagel's views are subtle and influential, in my opinion his attempt to show that an episode of pain—irrespective of whose pain—provides *anybody* with reason to alleviate that pain, must count as a notable and noble failure (see Dancy, 1988; Mack, 1989; Carlson, 1990). To demonstrate this I would really need to go through the relevant passages of Nagel's works claim by claim, which I cannot do here. I must be satisfied to observe that on this point of contention hinges the whole of Katz's case against my brand of moral skepticism, and on this point we disagree.

Notes

1. Or *render* those (formerly justified) beliefs epistemically unjustified (depending on one's epistemological tastes).

2. For a detailed discussion of the moral error theorist's attitude toward prudential normativity, see Joyce (forthcoming b). Certain passages here are taken from this paper.

References

Abe, J. A. A., & Izard, C. E. (1999). The developmental functions of emotions: An analysis in terms of differential emotions theory. *Cognition and Emotion, 13,* 523–549.

Adolphs, R. (1999). Social cognition and the human brain. *Trends in Cognitive Science, 3,* 469–479.

Adolphs, R. (2001). The neurobiology of social cognition. *Current Opinion in Neurobiology, 11,* 231–239.

Adolphs, R. (2002). Neural systems for recognizing emotion. *Current Opinion in Neurobiology, 12*(2), 169–177.

Adolphs, R. (2003). Cognitive neuroscience of human social behavior. *Nature Reviews Neuroscience, 4,* 165–178.

Adolphs, R. (2006). How do we know the minds of others? Domain-specificity, simulation, and enactive social cognition. *Brain Research, 1079,* 25–35.

Adolphs, R., & Tranel, D. (2000). Emotion, recognition, and the human amygdala. In J. P. Aggleton (Ed.), *The amygdala: A functional analysis* (Vol. 2, pp. 587–630). New York: Oxford University Press.

Adolphs, R., Baron-Cohen, S., & Tranel, D. (2002). Impaired recognition of social emotion following amygdala damage. *Journal of Cognitive Neuroscience, 14,* 1264–1274.

Adolphs, R., Sears, L., & Piven, J. (2001). Abnormal processing of social information from faces in autism. *Journal of Cognitive Neuroscience, 13,* 232–240.

Adolphs, R., Tranel, D., & Damasio, A. R. (1998). The human amygdala in social judgment. *Nature, 393*(6684), 470–474.

Aggleton, J. P. (1992). The functional effects of amygdala lesions in humans: A comparison with findings in monkeys. In J. P. Aggleton (Ed.), *The amygdala:*

Neurobiological aspects of emotion, memory, and dysfunction (pp. 485–503). New York: Wiley-Liss.

Allison, T., Puce, A., & McCarthy, G. (2000). Social perception from visual cues: Role of the STS region. *Trends in Cognitive Sciences, 4*, 267–278.

Allman, J., Hakeem, A., & Watson, K. (2002). Two phylogenetic specializations in the human brain. *Neuroscientist, 8*, 335–346.

Alterman, A. I., & Cacciola, J. S. (1991). The antisocial personality disorder diagnosis in substance abusers: Problems and issues. *Journal of Nervous & Mental Disease, 179*(7), 401–409.

Alterman, A. I., Cacciola, J. S., & Rutherford, M. J. (1993). Reliability of the revised psychopathy checklist in substance abuse patients. *Psychological Assessment, 5*(4), 442–448.

Alterman, A. I., McDermott, P. A., Cacciola, J. S., Rutherford, M. J., Boardman, C. R., McKay, J. R., & Cook, T. G. (1998). A typology of antisociality in methadone patients. *Journal of Abnormal Psychology, 107*(3), 412–422.

American Psychiatric Association. (1994/2000). *Diagnostic and statistic manual of mental disorders* (4th edn.) (*DSM-IV*). Washington, DC: American Psychiatric Association.

Anderson, A. K., & Phelps, E. A. (2001). Lesions of the human amygdala impair enhanced perception of emotionally salient events. *Nature, 411*(6835), 305–309.

Anderson, A. K., Spencer, D. D., Fulbright, R. K., & Phelps, E. A. (2000). Contribution of the anteromedial temporal lobes to the evaluation of facial emotion. *Neuropsychology, 14*(4), 526–536.

Anderson, S. W., Barrash, J., Bechara, A., & Tranel, D. (2006). Impairments of emotion and real-world complex behavior following childhood- or adult-onset damage to ventromedial prefrontal cortex. *Journal of the International Neuropsychological Society, 12*, 224–235.

Anderson, S. W., Bechara, A., Damasio, H., Tranel, D., & Damasio, A. R. (1999). Impairment of social and moral behavior related to early damage in human prefrontal cortex. *Nature Neuroscience, 2*(11), 1032–1037.

Anderson, V. A., Anderson, P., Northam, E., Jacobs, R., & Catroppa, C. (2001). Development of executive functions through late childhood and adolescence in an Australian sample. *Developmental Neuropsychology, 20*, 385–406.

Angrilli, A., Mauri, A., Palomba, D., Flor, H., Birbaumer, N., Sartori, G., & di Paola, F. (1996). Startle reflex and emotion modulation impairment after a right amygdala lesion. *Brain, 119*(Pt. 6), 1991–2000.

Aquinas, T. (1988). Of killing. In W. P. Baumgarth & R. J. Regan (Eds.), *On law, morality, and politics* (pp. 226–227). Indianapolis, IN: Hackett. (Original work written 1265–1273)

Ardekani, B. A., Choi, S. J., Hossein-Zadeh, G. A., Porjesz, B., Tanabe, J. L., Lim, K. O., Bilder, R., Helpern, J. A., & Begleiter, H. (2002). Functional magnetic resonance imaging of brain activity in the visual oddball task. *Cognitive Brain Research, 14*(3), 347–356.

Arsenio, W. F., & Lemerise, E. A. (2004). Aggression and moral development: Integrating social information processing and moral domain models. *Child Development, 75,* 987–1002.

Audi, R. (2004). *The good in the right.* Princeton, NJ: Princeton University Press.

Ayer, A. J. (1971). *Language, truth and logic.* Harmondsworth, UK: Penguin Books. (Original work published 1936)

Babiak, P. (1995). When psychopaths go to work. *International Journal of Applied Psychology, 44,* 171–188.

Bachevalier, J. (1991). Memory loss and socioemotional disturbances following neonatal damage to the limbic system in monkeys. *Advances in Neuropsychology and Psychopharmocology, 1,* 129–140.

Bacon, A. L., Fein, D., Morris, R., Waterhouse, L., & Allen, D. (1998). The responses of autistic children to the distress of others. *Journal of Autism and Developmental Disorders 28*(2), 129–142.

Bagshaw, M. H., Mackworth, N. H., & Pribram, K. H. (1972). The effect of resections of the inferotemporal cortex or the amygdala on visual orienting and habituation. *Neuropsychologia, 10*(2), 153–162.

Baird, A. A., Veague, H. B., & Rabbitt, C. E. (2005). Developmental precipitants of borderline personality disorder. *Developmental Psychopathology, 17*(4), 1031–1049.

Bandura, A., Underwood, B., & Fromson, M. E. (1975). Disinhibition of aggression through diffusion of responsibility and dehumanization of victims. *Journal of Personality and Social Psychology, 9,* 253–269.

Bargh, J. A. (1997). The automaticity of everyday life. In R. S. Wyer, Jr. (Ed.), *The automaticity of everyday life: Advances in social cognition* (Vol. X, pp. 1–61). Mahwah, NJ: Lawrence Erlbaum Associates.

Bargh, J. A., & Chartrand, T. L. (1999). The unbearable automaticity of being. *American Psychologist, 54,* 462–479.

Bargh, J. A., & Ferguson, M. J. (2000). Beyond behaviorism: On the automaticity of higher mental processes. *Psychological Bulletin, 126,* 925–945.

Barker, R. G., & Wright, H. F. (1951). *One boy's day: A specimen record of behavior.* New York: Harper & Brothers.

Baron, J. (1994). Nonconsequentialist decisions. *Behavioral and Brain Sciences, 17,* 1–42.

Baron, J., & Ritov, I. (1993). Intuitions about penalties and compensation in the context of tort law. *Journal of Risk and Uncertainty, 7,* 17–33.

Baron, J., Gowda, R., & Kunreuther, H. (1993). Attitudes toward managing hazardous waste: What should be cleaned up and who should pay for it? *Risk Analysis, 13*(2), 183–192.

Baron-Cohen, S., & Wheelwright, S. (2004). The empathy quotient: An investigation of adults with Asperger syndrome or high-functioning autism, and normal sex differences. *Journal of Autism and Developmental Disorders, 34*(2), 163–175.

Baron-Cohen, S., Richler, J., Bisarya, D., Gurunathan, N., & Wheelwright, S. (2003). The systemizing quotient: An investigation of adults with Asperger syndrome or high-functioning autism, and normal sex differences. *Philosophical Transactions of the Royal Society of London* (Series B, *Biological Sciences), 358*(1430), 361–374.

Baron-Cohen, S., Tager-Flusberg, H., & Cohen, D. (Eds.). (2000). *Understanding other minds: Perspectives from developmental cognitive neuroscience.* Oxford: Oxford University Press.

Barrash, J., Tranel D., & Anderson, S. W. (2000). Acquired personality disturbances associated with bilateral damage to the ventromedial prefrontal region. *Developmental Neuropsychology, 18,* 355–381.

Barrett, K. C., & Nelson-Goens, G. C. (1997). Emotion communication and the development of the social emotions. In K. C. Barrett (Ed.), *The communication of emotion: Current research from diverse perspectives. New directions for child development* (No. 77, pp. 69–88). San Francisco: Jossey-Bass.

Barry, K. L., Fleming, M. F., & Maxwell, L. B. (1997). Conduct disorder and antisocial personality in adult primary care patients. *Journal of Family Practice, 45,* 151–158.

Bartels, A., & Zeki, S. (2004). The neural correlates of maternal and romantic love. *NeuroImage, 21,* 1155–1166.

Bates, A. T., Liddle, P. F., & Kiehl, K. A. (2003). Error monitoring abnormalities in criminal psychopaths. Unpublished data.

Batson, C. D., Fultz, J., & Schoenrade, P. A. (1987). Adults' emotional reactions to the distress of others. In N. Eisenberg & J. Strayer (Eds.), *Empathy and its development* (pp. 163–185). Cambridge: Cambridge University Press.

Bauer, L. O. (1997). Frontal P300 decrements, childhood conduct disorder, family history, and the prediction of relapse among abstinent cocaine abusers. *Drug and Alcohol Dependence, 44*(1), 1–10.

Bauer, L. O. (2001a). Antisocial personality disorder and cocaine dependence: Their effects on behavioral and electroencephalographic measures of time estimation. *Drug and Alcohol Dependence, 63*(1), 87–95.

Bauer, L. O. (2001b). CNS recovery from cocaine, cocaine and alcohol, or opioid dependence: A P300 study. *Clinical Neurophysiology, 112*(8), 1508–1515.

Bauer, L. O. (2002). Differential effects of alcohol, cocaine, and opioid abuse on event-related potentials recorded during a response competition task. *Drug Alcohol Depend, 66*(2), 137–145.

Bauer, L. O., & Hesselbrock, V. M. (1999). P300 decrements in teenagers with conduct problems: Implications for substance abuse risk and brain development. *Biological Psychiatry, 46*(2), 263–272.

Bauer, L. O., O'Connor, S., & Hesselbrock, V. M. (1994). Frontal P300 decrements in antisocial personality disorder. *Alcoholism, Clinical and Experimental Research, 18*(6), 1300–1305.

Baumeister, R. F., Stillwell, A. M., & Heatherton, T. F. (1994). Guilt: An interpersonal approach. *Psychology Bulletin, 115*, 243–267.

Bearman, P. S., & Moody, J. (2004). Suicide and friendships among American adolescents. *American Journal of Public Health, 94*(1), 89–95.

Bechara, A. (2001). Neurobiology of decision-making: Risk and reward. *Seminars in Clinical Neuropsychiatry, 6*(3), 205–216.

Bechara, A., Damasio, H., & Damasio, A. R. (2000a). Emotion, decision making and the orbitofrontal cortex. *Cerebral Cortex, 10*, 295–307.

Bechara, A., Damasio, H., Damasio, A. R., & Lee, G. P. (1999). Different contributions of the human amygdala and ventromedial prefrontal cortex to decision-making. *Journal of Neuroscience, 19*(13), 5473–5481.

Bechara, A., Damasio, H., Tranel, D., & Damasio, A. R. (1997). Deciding advantageously before knowing the advantageous strategy. *Science, 275*(5304), 1293–1295.

Bechara, A., Tranel, D., & Damasio, H. (2000b). Characterization of the decision-making deficit of patients with ventromedial prefrontal cortex lesions. *Brain, 123*(11), 2189–2202.

Bechara, A., Tranel, D., Damasio, H., Adolphs, R., Rockland, C., & Damasio, A. R. (1995). Double dissociation of conditioning and declarative knowledge relative to the amygdala and hippocampus in humans. *Science, 269*(5227), 1115–1118.

Beer, J. S., Heerey, E. A., Keltner, D., Scabini, D., & Knight, R. T. (2003). The regulatory function of self-conscious emotion: Insights from patients with orbitofrontal damage. *Journal of Personality and Social Psychology, 85*, 594–604.

Begleiter, H., & Porjesz, B. (1995). Neurophysiological phenotypic factors in the development of alcoholism. In H. Begleiter & B. Kissin (Eds.), *The genetics of alcoholism* (pp. 269–293). New York: Oxford University Press.

Begleiter, H., Gross, M. M., & Kissin, B. (1967). Evoked cortical responses to affective visual stimuli. *Psychophysiology, 3,* 336–344.

Begleiter, H., Porjesz, B., Reich, T., Edenberg, H. J., Goate, A., Blangero, J., Almasy, L., Foroud, T., Van Eerdewegh, P., Polich, J., Rohrbaugh, J., Kuperman, S., Bauer, L. O., O'Connor, S. J., Chorlian, D. B., Li, T. K., Conneally, P. M., Hesselbrock, V., Rice, J. P., Schuckit, M. A., Cloninger, R., Nurnberger, J., Jr., Crowe, R., & Bloom, F. E. (1998). Quantitative trait loci analysis of human event-related brain potentials: P3 voltage. *Electroencephalography and Clinical Neurophysiology, 108*(3), 244–250.

Bell, M. A., & Wolfe, C. D. (2004). Emotion and cognition: An intricately bound developmental process. *Child Development, 2,* 366–370.

Benes, F. M., Vincent, S. L., Molloy, R., & Khan, Y. (1996). Increased interaction of dopamine-immunoreactive varicosities with GABA neurons of rat medial prefrontal cortex occurs during the postweanling period. *Synapse, 23*(4), 237–245.

Bentham, J. (1982). *An introduction to the principles of morals and legislation.* London: Methuen. (Original work published 1789)

Berridge, K. C. (2004). Motivation concepts in behavioral neuroscience. *Physiology & Behavior, 81*(2), 179–209.

Berthoz, S., Armony, J. L., Blair, R. J., & Dolan, R. J. (2002). An fMRI study of intentional and unintentional (embarrassing) violations of social norms. *Brain, 125,* 1696–1708.

Bertolino, A., Saunders, R. C., Mattay, V. S., Bachevalier, J., Frank, J. A., & Weinberger, D. R. (1997). Altered development of prefrontal neurons in rhesus monkeys with neonatal mesial temporo-limbic lesions: A proton magnetic resonance spectroscopic imaging study. *Cerebral Cortex, 7*(8), 740–748.

Birbaumer, N., Veit, R., Lotze, M., Erb, M., Hermann, C., Grodd, W., & Flor, H. (2005). Deficient fear conditioning in psychopathy: A functional magnetic resonance imaging study. *Archives of General Psychiatry, 62*(7), 799–805.

Björklund, D. F. (1997). The role of immaturity in human development. *Psychological Review, 122*(2), 153–169.

Blackburn, S. (1984). *Spreading the word.* Oxford: Oxford University Press.

Blackburn, S. (1993). *Essays in quasi-realism.* New York: Oxford University Press.

Blair, C. (2002). School readiness: Integrating cognition and emotion in a neurobiological conceptualization of children's functioning at school entry. *American Psychologist, 57,* 111–127.

Blair, J., Blair, K., Mitchell, D., & Peschardt, K. (2005). *The psychopath: Emotion and the brain.* Oxford: Blackwell.

Blair, R. J. R. (1995). A cognitive developmental approach to morality: Investigating the psychopath. *Cognition, 57*(1), 1–29.

Blair, R. J. R. (1996). Brief report: Morality in the autistic child. *Journal of Autism and Developmental Disorders, 26*(5), 571–579.

Blair, R. J. R. (1997). Moral reasoning in the child with psychopathic tendencies. *Personality and Individual Differences, 22,* 731–739.

Blair, R. J. R. (1999). Psychophysiological responsiveness to the distress of others in children with autism. *Personality and Individual Differences, 26,* 477–485.

Blair, R. J. R. (2001). Neurocognitive models of aggression, the antisocial personality disorders, and psychopathy. *Journal of Neurology, Neurosurgery, and Psychiatry, 71*(6), 727–731.

Blair, R. J. R. (2002). Neuro-cognitive models of acquired sociopathy and developmental psychopathy. In J. Glicksohn (Ed.), *The neurobiology of criminal behavior: Neurobiological foundation of aberrant behaviors* (pp. 157–186). Dordrecht, Netherlands: Kluwer Academic.

Blair, R. J. R. (2003). Neurobiological basis of psychopathy. *British Journal of Psychiatry, 182,* 5–7.

Blair, R. J. R. (2005). Responding to the emotions of others: Dissociating forms of empathy through the study of typical and psychiatric populations. *Consciousness and Cognition, 14*(4), 698–718.

Blair, R. J. R., & Cipolotti, L. (2000). Impaired social response reversal: A case of "acquired sociopathy". *Brain, 123*(Pt. 6), 1122–1141.

Blair, R. J. R., Colledge, E., & Mitchell, D. G. (2001a). Somatic markers and response reversal: Is there orbitofrontal cortex dysfunction in boys with psychopathic tendencies? *Journal of Abnormal Child Psychology, 29*(6), 499–511.

Blair, R. J. R., Colledge, E., Murray, L., & Mitchell, D. G. (2001b). A selective impairment in the processing of sad and fearful expressions in children with psychopathic tendencies. *Journal of Abnormal Child Psychology, 29*(6), 491–498.

Blair, R. J. R., Jones, L., Clark, F., & Smith, M. (1995). Is the psychopath "morally insane"? *Personality and Individual Differences, 19*(5), 741–752.

Blair, R. J. R., Jones, L., Clark, F., & Smith, M. (1997). The psychopathic individual: A lack of responsiveness to distress cues? *Psychophysiology, 34*(2), 192–198.

Blair, R. J. R., Mitchell, D. G., Richell, R. A., Kelly, S., Leonard, A., Newman, C., & Scott, S. K. (2002). Turning a deaf ear to fear: Impaired recognition of vocal affect in psychopathic individuals. *Journal of Abnormal Psychology, 111*(4), 682–686.

Blair, R. J. R., Mitchell, D., & Blair, K. (2005). *The psychopath: Emotion and the brain.* Malden, MA: Blackwell.

Blair, R. J. R., Morris, J. S., Frith, C. D., Perrett, D. I., & Dolan, R. J. (1999). Dissociable neural responses to facial expressions of sadness and anger. *Brain, 122*(Pt. 5), 883–893.

Blair, R. J. R., Sellars, C., Strickland, I., Clark, F., Williams, A.,. Smith, M., & Jones, L. (1996). Theory of mind in the psychopath. *Journal of Forensic Psychiatry, 7*(1), 15–25.

Blumer, D. (1975). Temporal lobe epilepsy and its psychiatric significance. In D. F. Benson & D. Blumer (Eds.), *Psychiatric aspects of neurological disease* (pp. 171–198). New York: Grune & Stratton.

Blumer, D., & Benson, D. F. (1975). Personality changes with frontal lobe lesions. In D. F. Benson & D. Blumer (Eds.), *Psychiatric aspects of neurological disease* (pp. 151–170). New York: Grune & Stratton.

Bolt, D. M., Hare, R. D., Vitale, J. E., & Newman, J. P. (2004). A multigroup item response theory analysis of the psychopathy checklist—revised. *Psychological Assessment, 16*(2), 155–168.

Botvinick, M. M., Braver, T. S., Barch, D. M., Carter, C. S., & Cohen, J. D. (2001). Conflict monitoring and cognitive control. *Psychological Review, 108*, 624–652.

Bourgeois, J. P., Goldman-Rakic, P. S., & Rakic, P. (1994). Synaptogenesis in the prefrontal cortex of rhesus monkeys. *Cerebral Cortex, 4*(1), 78–96.

Bowles, S., & Gintis, H. (2004). The evolution of strong reciprocity: Cooperation in heterogeneous populations. *Theoretical Population Biology, 65*, 17–28.

Boyd, R. N. (1988). How to be a moral realist. In G. Sayre-McCord (Ed.), *Essays on moral realism* (pp. 181–228). Ithaca, NY: Cornell University Press.

Boyd, R., Gintis, H., Bowles, S., & Richerson, P. J. (2003). The evolution of altruistic punishment. *Proceedings of the National Academy of Sciences of the United States of America, 100*, 3531–3535.

Brink, D. (1989). *Moral realism and the foundation of ethics.* Cambridge: Cambridge University Press.

Brodmann, K. (1909). *Vergleichende lokalisationlehre der grosshirnrinde in ihren prinzipien dargestellt auf grund des zellenbaues.* Leipzig: U.A. Barth.

Brodmann, K. (1994). *Localisation in the cerebral cortex* (L. J. Garey, Trans.). London: Smith-Gordon. (Original work published 1909)

Brody, A. L., Saxena, S., Fairbanks, L. A., Alborzian, S., Demaree, H. A., Maidment, K. M., et al. (2000). Personality changes in adult subjects with major depressive disorder or obsessive-compulsive disorder treated with paroxetine. *Journal of Clinical Psychiatry*, *61*, 349–355.

Broughton, J. M. (1978). Criticism of the developmental approach to morality. *Catalog of Selected Documents in Psychology*, *8*, MS. 1756.

Brown, B. B., Mounts, N., Lamborn, S. D., & Steinberg, L. (1993). Parenting practices and peer group affiliation in adolescence. *Child Development*, *64*, 467–482.

Brunschwig, J. (1986). The cradle argument in Epicureanism and Stoicism. In M. Schofield & G. Striker (Eds.), *The norms of nature: Studies in Hellenistic ethics* (pp. 113–144). Cambridge: Cambridge University Press; Paris: Editions de la Maison des Sciences de l'Homme.

Buchanan, T. W., Tranel, D., & Adolphs, R. (2004). Anteromedial temporal lobe damage blocks startle modulation by fear and disgust. *Behavioral Neuroscience*, *118*, 429–437.

Buck, A., & Fehr, E. (2004). The neural basis of altruistic punishment. *Science*, *305*, 1254–1258.

Bugental, D. B., & Goodnow, J. J. (1998). Socialization processes. In W. Damon (Ed.), *The handbook of child psychology* (5th edn.). *Social, emotional and personality development* (N. Eisenberg, Vol. Ed., pp. 389–462). New York: Wiley.

Burgess, J. P. (2007). Against ethics. *Ethical Theory and Moral Practice*. (Originally written in 1978)

Bush, G., Luu, P., & Posner, M. I. (2000). Cognitive and emotional influences in anterior cingulated cortex. *Trends in Cognitive Science*, *4*, 111–127.

Butts, J. A., & Mitchell, O. (2000). Brick by brick: Dismantling the border between juvenile and adult justice. In C. M. Friel (Ed.), *Boundary changes in criminal justice organizations* (Vol. 2, pp. 167–213). Washington, DC: US Department of Justice, Office of Justice Programs.

Cacioppo, J. T. (2002). Social neuroscience: Understanding the pieces fosters understanding the whole and vice versa. *American Psychologist*, *57*, 819–831.

Cacioppo, J. T., Bernston, G. G., Lorig, T. S., Norris, C. J., Rickett, E., & Nusbaum, H. (2003). Just because you're imaging the brain doesn't mean you can stop using your head: A primer and set of first principles. *Journal of Personality and Social Psychology*, *85*, 650–661.

Cahill, L. (2000). Modulation of long-term memory storage in humans by emotional arousal. In J. P. Aggleton (Ed.), *The amygdala* (2nd edn., pp. 425–441). New York: Oxford.

Calder, A. J., Keane, J., Manes, F., Antoun, N., & Young, A. W. (2000). Impaired recognition and experience of disgust following brain injury. *Nature Neuroscience, 3,* 1077–1078.

Cameron, O. G. (2001). Interoception. *Psychosomatic Medicine, 63,* 697–710.

Camille, N., Coricelli, G., Sallet, J., Pradat-Diehl, P., Duhamel, J.-R., & Sirigu, A. (2004). The involvement of the orbitofrontal cortex in the experience of regret. *Science, 304,* 1167–1170.

Camus, A. (1955). *The myth of Sisyphus.* New York: Knopf.

Capps, L., Sigman, M., & Mundy, P. (1994). Attachment security in children with autism. *Development and Psychopathology, 6,* 249–261.

Carey, S. (1988). Are children fundamentally different kinds of thinkers and learners than adults? In K. Richardson & S. Sheldon (Eds.), *Cognitive development to adolescence.* Hillsdale, NJ: Lawrence Earlbaum Associates.

Carlsmith, K. M., Darley, J. M., & Robinson, P. H. (2002). Why do we punish? Deterrence and just deserts as motives for punishment. *Journal of Personality and Social Psychology, 83,* 284–299.

Carlson, G. (1990). Pain and the quantum leap to agent-neutral value. *Ethics, 100,* 363–367.

Casebeer, W. D. (2003a). Moral cognition and its neural constituents. *Nature Reviews Neuroscience, 4,* 840–846.

Casebeer, W. D. (2003b). *Natural ethical facts: Evolution, connectionism and moral cognition.* Cambridge, MA: MIT Press.

Casebeer, W. D., & Churchland, P. S. (2003). The neural mechanisms of moral cognition: A multiple-aspect approach to moral judgment and decision-making. *Biology and Philosophy, 18,* 169–194.

Casey, B. J., Forman, S. D., Franzen, P., Berkowitz, A., Braver, T. S., Nystrom, L. E., Thomas, K. M., & Noll, D. C. (2001). Sensitivity of prefrontal cortex to changes in target probability: A functional MRI study. *Human Brain Mapping, 13*(1), 26–33.

Casey, B. J., Giedd, J. N., & Thomas, K. M. (2000). Structural and functional brain development and its relation to cognitive development. *Biological Psychology, 54,* 241–257.

Casey, B. J., Trainor, R., Giedd, J. N., Vauss, Y., Vaituzis, C. K., Hamburger, S. D., Kozuch, P., & Rapoport, J. L. (1997). The role of the anterior cingulate in automatic and controlled processes: A developmental neuroanatomical study. *Developmental Psychobiology, 30*(1), 61–69.

Castelli, F. (2005). Understanding emotions from standardized facial expressions in autism and normal development. *Autism, 9*(4), 428–449.

Chalmers, D. J. (1996). *The conscious mind: In search of a fundamental theory.* New York: Oxford University Press.

Chandler, M., & Moran, T. (1990). Psychopathy and moral development: A comparative study of delinquent and nondelinquent youth. *Development and Psychopathology, 2,* 227–246.

Chang, R. (2004). Can desires provide reasons for action? In R. J. Wallace, P. Petit, S. Scheffler, & M. Smith (Eds.), *Reason and value: Themes from the moral philosophy of Joseph Raz* (pp. 56–90). Oxford: Oxford University Press.

Chomsky, N. (1957). *Syntactic structures.* The Hague: Mouton.

Chomsky, N. (1964). *Current issues in linguistic theory.* New York: Pantheon.

Chomsky, N., & Halle, M. (1968). *The sound pattern of English.* Cambridge, MA: MIT Press.

Christian, R. E., Frick, P. J., Hill, N. L., Tyler, L., & Frazer, D. R. (1997). Psychopathy and conduct problems in children: II. Implications for subtyping children with conduct problems. *Journal of the American Academy of Child & Adolescent Psychiatry, 36*(2), 233–241.

Christianson, S.-A., Forth, A. E., Hare, R. D., Strachan, C., Lindberg, L., & Thorell, L.-H. (1996). Remembering details of emotional events: A comparison between psychopathic and nonpsychopathic offenders. *Personality & Individual Differences, 20*(4), 437–443.

Chugani, H. T., Phelps, M. E., & Mazziotta, J. C. (1987). Positron emission tomography study of human brain functional development. *Annals of Neurology, 22*(4), 487–497.

Clark, V. P., Fannon, S., Lai, S., Benson, R., & Bauer, L. O. (2000). Responses to rare visual target and distractor stimuli using event-related fMRI. *Journal of Neurophysiology, 83*(5), 3133–3139.

Clarke, J. M., Halgren, E., & Chauvel, P. (1999a). Intracranial ERPs in humans during a lateralized visual oddball task: I. Occipital and peri-Rolandic recordings. *Clinical Neurophysiology, 110*(7), 1210–1225.

Clarke, J. M., Halgren, E., & Chauvel, P. (1999b). Intracranial ERPs in humans during a lateralized visual oddball task: II. Temporal, parietal, and frontal recordings. *Clinical Neurophysiology, 110*(7), 1226–1244.

Cleckley, H. (1941/1950/1955/1976). *The mask of sanity: An attempt to clarify some issues about the so-called psychopathic personality.* St. Louis, MO: C. V. Mosby.

Cohen, R. A., Kaplan, R. F., Meadows, M. E., & Wilkinson, H. (1994). Habituation and sensitization of the orienting response following bilateral anterior cingulotomy. *Neuropsychologia, 32*(5), 609–617.

Cole, P. M., Martin, S. E., & Dennis, T. A. (2004). Emotion regulation as a scientific construct: Methodological challenges and directions for child development research. *Child Development, 2*, 317–333.

Condry, J. (1987). Enhancing motivation: A social developmental perspective. In M. L. Maehr & D. A. Kleiber (Eds.), *Advances in motivation and achievement* (Vol. 5: Enhancing Motivation, pp. 23–49). Greenwich, CT: JAI Press.

Cooke, D. J., & Michie, C. (1997). An item response theory analysis of the Hare Psychopathy Checklist—Revised. *Psychological Assessment, 9*(1), 3–14.

Cooke, D. J., & Michie, C. (2001). Refining the construct of psychopath: Towards a hierarchical model. *Psychological Assessment, 13*(2), 171–188.

Cooke, D. J., Michie, C., Hart, S. D., & Clark, D. (2005). Assessing psychopathy in the UK: Concerns about cross-cultural generalisability. *British Journal of Psychiatry, 186*, 335–341.

Copp, D. (2001). Realist-Expressivism: A neglected option for moral realism. *Social Philosophy and Policy, 18*, 1–43.

Copp, D., & Sobel, D. (2002). Desires, motives, and reasons: Scanlon's rationalistic moral psychology. *Social Theory and Practice, 28*(2), 243–276.

Cords, M., & Aureli, F. (2000). Reconciliation and relationship quality. In F. Aureli & F. B. M. de Waal (Eds.), *Natural conflict resolution* (pp. 177–198). Berkeley: University of California Press.

Cornford, F. M. (1957). *From religion to philosophy*. New York: Harper.

Corona, R., Dissanayake, C., Arbelle, S., Wellington, P., & Sigman, M. (1998). Is affect aversive to young children with autism? Behavioral and cardiac responses to experimenter distress. *Child Development, 69*, 1494–1502.

Costa, M. (1992). The trolley problem revisited. In J. M. Fischer & M. Ravizza (Eds.), *Ethics: Problems and principles* (pp. 293–302). Orlando, FL: Harcourt, Brace, Jovanovich.

Crisp, R., & Slote, M. (Eds.). (1997). *Virtue ethics*. New York: Oxford University Press.

Critchley, H. D., Mathias, C. J., & Dolan R. J. (2001). Neuroanatomical basis for first- and second-order representations of bodily states. *Nature Neuroscience, 4*(2), 207–212.

Cummings, J. L. (1995). Anatomic and behavioral aspects of frontal-subcortical circuits. *Annals of the New York Academy of Sciences, 15*(769), 1–13.

Cunningham, W. A., Nezlek, J. B., & Banaji, M. R. (2004). Implicit and explicit ethnocentrism: Revisiting the ideologies of prejudice. *Personality and Social Psychology Bulletin, 30*, 1332–1346.

Cushman, F., Young, L., & Hauser, M. (2006). The role of conscious reasoning and intuitions in moral judgments: Testing three principles of harm. *Psychological Science, 17*(12), 1082–1089.

Damasio, A. R. (1994). *Descartes' error: Emotion, reason, and the human brain.* New York: Grosset/Putnam.

Damasio, A. R., Tranel, D., & Damasio, H. (1990). Individuals with sociopathic behavior caused by frontal damage fail to respond autonomically to social stimuli. *Behavioural Brain Research, 41*, 81–94.

Damasio, H., Bechara, A., & Damasio, A. R. (2002). Reply to Tomb et al. *Nature Neuroscience, 5*(11), 1104.

Damasio, H., Grabowski, T., Frank, R., Galaburda, A. M., & Damasio, A. R. (1994). The return of Phineas Gage: Clues about the brain from the skull of a famous patient. *Science, 264*(5162), 1102–1105.

Damon, W. (1983). *Social and personality development.* New York: Norton.

Damon, W., & Hart, D. (1982). The development of self-understanding from infancy through adolescence. *Child Development, 53*, 841–864.

Dancy, J. (1988). Contemplating one's Nagel. *Philosophical Books, 29*, 1–15.

Daprati, E., Nico, D., Franck, N., & Sirigu, A. (2003). Being the agent: Memory for action events. *Consciousness and Cognition, 12*, 670–683.

Darwall, S., Gibbard, A., & Railton, P. (Eds.). (1997). *Moral discourse and practice.* Oxford: Oxford University Press.

Darwin, C. (1872). *The expression of the emotions in man and animals.* New York: Greenwood Press.

Davidson, P., Turiel, E., & Black, A. (1983). The effect of stimulus familiarity on the use of criteria and justifications in children's social reasoning. *British Journal of Developmental Psychology, 1*, 49–65.

Day, J. (1977). Right-hemisphere language processing in normal right-handers. *Journal of Experimental Psychology: Human Perception & Performance, 3*(3), 518–528.

Day, R., & Wong, S. (1996). Anomalous perceptual asymmetries for negative emotional stimuli in the psychopath. *Journal of Abnormal Psychology, 105*(4), 648–652.

de Quervain, D. J.-F., Fischbacher, U., Treyer, V., Schellhammer, M., Schnyder, U., Buck, A., & Fehr, E. (2004). The neural basis of altruistic punishment. *Science, 305*, 1254–1258.

de Waal, F. B. M. (1996). *Good natured: The origins of right and wrong in humans and other animals*. Cambridge, MA: Harvard University Press.

Degos, J. D., da Fonseca, N., Gray, F., & Cesaro, P. (1993). Severe frontal syndrome associated with infarcts of the left anterior cingulate gyrus and the head of the right caudate nucleus. A clinico-pathological case. *Brain, 116*(Pt. 6), 1541–1548.

Depue, R. A., & Morrone-Strupinsky, J. (2005). A neurobehavioral model of affiliative bonding: Implications for conceptualizing a human trait of affiliation. *Behavioral and Brain Sciences, 28*(3), 313–395.

Desjardins, A. E., Kiehl, K. A., & Liddle, P. F. (2001). Removal of confounding effects of global signal in functional magnetic resonance imaging analyses. *NeuroImage, 13*, 751–758.

Devine, P. G. (1989). Stereotypes and prejudice: Their automatic and controlled components. *Journal of Personality & Social Psychology, 56*(1), 5–18.

Dewey, J. (1922). *Human nature and conduct*. New York: Holt.

Dewey, M. (1991). Living with Asperger's syndrome. In U. Frith (Ed.), *Autism and Asperger syndrome* (pp. 184–206). Cambridge: Cambridge University Press.

Dewey, M. A. (1992). Autistic eccentricity. In E. Schopler & G. B. Mesibov (Eds.), *High-functioning individuals with autism* (pp. 281–288). New York: Plenum.

Diamond, A. (1988). Abilities and neural mechanisms underlying AB performance. *Child Development, 59*(2), 523–527.

Diamond, A. (1996). Impaired sensitivity to visual contrast in children treated early and continuously for phenylketonuria. *Brain, 119*(Pt. 2), 523–538.

Dissanayake, C., & Crossley, S. A. (1996). Proximity and sociable behaviours in autism: Evidence for attachment. *Journal of Child Psychology and Psychiatry 37*, 149–156.

Dissanayake, C., & Crossley, S. A. (1997). Autistic children's responses to separation and reunion with their mothers. *Journal of Autism and Developmental Disorders 27*, 295–312.

Dissanayake, C., Sigman, M., & Kasari, C. (1996). Long-term stability of individual differences in the emotional responsiveness of children with autism. *Journal of Child Psychology & Psychiatry & Allied Disciplines, 37*, 461–467.

Dolan, R. J. (1999). On the neurology of morals. *Nature Neuroscience, 2*, 927–929.

Duff, A. (1977). Psychopathy and moral understanding. *American Philosophical Quarterly, 14*, 189–200.

Dutton, D. G., & Aron, A. P. (1974). Some evidence for heightened sexual attraction under conditions of high anxiety. *Journal of Personality and Social Psychology, 30*, 510–517.

Dwyer, S. (1999). Moral competence. In K. Murasugi & R. Stainton (Eds.), *Philosophy and linguistics* (pp. 169–190). Boulder, CO: Westview Press.

Edwards, D. H., & Kravitz, E. A. (1997). Serotonin, social status and aggression. *Current Opinion in Neurobiology, 7*, 812–819.

Ehrlich, P. R. (2000). *Human natures: Genes, cultures, and the human prospect.* Washington, DC: Island Press.

Eichler, M. (1965). The application of verbal behavior analysis to the study of psychological defense mechanisms: Speech patterns associated with sociopathic behavior. *Journal of Nervous and Mental Disease, 141*(6), 658–663.

Eisenberg, N. (1986). *Altruistic emotion, cognition and behavior.* Hillsdale, NJ: Lawrence Erlbaum Associates.

Eisenberg, N. (1991). Values, sympathy and individual differences: Towards a pluralism of factors influencing altruism and empathy. *Psychological Inquiry 2*(2), 128–131.

Eisenberg, N. (2000). Emotion, regulation, and moral development. *Annual Review of Psychology, 51*, 665–697.

Eisenberg, N., Zhou, Q., & Koller, S. (2001). Brazilian adolescents' prosocial moral judgment and behavior: Relations to sympathy, perspective taking, gender-role orientation and demographic characteristics. *Child Development, 72*, 518–534.

Eliot, G. (1996). *Middlemarch.* New York: Oxford University Press. (Original work published 1874)

Elkind, D. (1967). Egocentrism in adolescence. *Child Development, 38*, 1025–1034.

Elliott, C. (1992). Diagnosing blame: Responsibility and the psychopath. *Journal of Medicine and Philosophy, 17*, 200–214.

Epley, N., & Caruso, E. M. (2004). Egocentric ethics. *Social Justice Research, 17*, 171–187.

Eslinger, P. J., & Damasio, A. R. (1985). Severe disturbance of higher cognition after bilateral frontal lobe ablation: Patient EVR. *Neurology, 35*(12), 1731–1741.

Eslinger, P. J., Flaherty-Craig, C. V., Benton, A. L. (2004). Developmental outcomes after early prefrontal cortex damage. *Brain and Cognition, 55*, 84–103.

Estabrooks, G. H. (1943). *Hypnotism.* New York: E. P. Dutton.

Fabes, R. A., Carlo, G., Kupanoff, K., & Laible, D. (1999). Early adolescence and prosocial/moral behavior I: The role of individual processes. *Journal of Early Adolescence, 19*(1), 5–16.

Falconer, M. A., & Serafetinides, E. A. (1963). A follow-up study of surgery in temporal lobe epilepsy. *Journal of Neurology, Neurosurgery, & Psychiatry, 26*(2), 154–165.

Farrow, T. F. D., Zheng, Y., Wilkinson, I. D., Spence, S. A., Deakin, J. F. W., Tarrier, N., Griffiths, P. D., & Woodruff, P. W. R. (2001). Investigating the functional anatomy of empathy and forgiveness. *Neuroreport, 12*, 2433–2438.

Fehr, E., & Gachter, S. (2002). Altruistic punishment in humans. *Nature, 415*, 137–140.

Fehr, E., & Rockenbach, B. (2004). Human altruism: Economic, neural, and evolutionary perspectives. *Current Opinion in Neurobiology, 14*, 784–790.

Fellows, L. K. (2006). Deciding how to decide: Ventromedial frontal lobe damage affects information acquisition in multi-attribute decision making. *Brain, 129*(4), 944–952.

Fellows, L. K., & Farah, M. J. (2005). Dissociable elements of human foresight: A role for the ventromedial frontal lobes in framing the future, but not in discounting future rewards. *Neuropsychologia, 43*, 1214–1221.

Fessler, D. (1999). Toward an understanding of the universality of second-order emotions. In A. Hinton (Ed.), *Beyond nature or nurture: Biocultural approaches to the emotions* (pp. 75–116). New York: Cambridge University Press.

Fessler, D. M. T. (2001). Emotions and cost-benefit assessment: The role of shame and self-esteem in risk-taking. In G. Gigerenzer & R. Selten (Eds.), *Bounded rationality: The adaptive toolbox* (pp. 191–214). Cambridge, MA: MIT Press.

Fessler, D. M. T. (2004). Shame in two cultures: Implications for evolutionary approaches. *Journal of Cognition & Culture, 4*, 207–262.

Fessler, D. M. T., Arguello, A. P., Mekdara, J. M., & Macias, R. (2003). Disgust sensitivity and meat consumption: A test of an emotivist account of moral vegetarianism. *Appetite, 41*, 31–41.

Finger, S., (2001). *Origins of neuroscience: A history of explorations into brain function.* New York: Oxford University Press.

Fischer, J. M., & Ravizza, M. (Eds.). (1992). *Ethics: Problems and principles.* Fort Worth, TX: Harcourt Brace Jovanovich College Publishers.

Fiske, S. T., Harris, L. T., & Cuddy, A. J. (2004). Why ordinary people torture enemy prisoners. *Science, 306*(5701), 1482–1483.

Fitzgerald, D. A., Posse, S., Moore, G. J., Tancer, M. E., Nathan, P. J., & Phan, K. L. (2004). Neural correlates of internally generated disgust via autobiographical recall: A functional magnetic resonance imaging investigation. *Neuroscience Letters, 370*, 91–96.

Flor, H., Birbaumer, N., Hermann, C., Ziegler, S., & Patrick, C. J. (2002). Aversive Pavlovian conditioning in psychopaths: Peripheral and central correlates. *Psychophysiology, 39*(4), 505–518.

Fodor, E. M. (1973). Moral development and parent behavior antecedents in adolescent psychopaths. *Journal of Genetic Psychology, 122*, 37–43.

Foot, P. (1967). The problem of abortion and the doctrine of double effect. *Oxford Review, 5*, 5–15. [Reprinted in P. Foot, *Virtues and vices* (pp. 19–32). Oxford: Blackwell, 1978.]

Forgas, J. P., & Moylan, S. (1987). After the movies: Transient mood and social judgments. *Personality & Social Psychology Bulletin, 13*(4), 467–477.

Forth, A. E., & Hare, R. D. (1989). The contingent negative variation in psychopaths. *Psychophysiology, 26*(6), 676–682.

Forth, A. E., Brown, S. L., Hart, S. D., & Hare, R. D. (1996). The assessment of psychopathy in male and female noncriminals: Reliability and validity. *Personality and Individual Differences, 20*, 531–543.

Fowles, D. C. (1980). The three arousal model: Implications of Gray's two-factor learning theory for heart rate, electrodermal activity, and psychopathy. *Psychophysiology, 17*(2), 87–104.

Freeman, S. (2001). Deontology. In L. C. Becker & C. B. Becker (Eds.), *Encyclopedia of ethics* (2nd edn., Vol. 1, pp. 391–396). London and New York: Routledge.

Frick, P. J. (1995). Callous-unemotional traits and conduct problems: A two-factor model of psychopathy in children. *Issues in Criminological & Legal Psychology, 24*, 47–51.

Frick, P. J. (1998). Callous-unemotional traits and conduct problems: Applying the two-factor model of psychopathy to children. In D. J. Cooke, A. E. Forth, & R. D. Hare (Eds.), *Psychopathy: Theory, research, and implications for society* (pp. 161–188). Dordrecht, Netherlands: Kluwer Academic.

Frick, P. J., Barry, C. T., & Bodin, S. D. (2000). Applying the concept of psychopathy to children: Implications for the assessment of antisocial youth. In C. B. Gacono (Ed.), *The clinical and forensic assessment of psychopathy: A practitioner's guide* (pp. 3–24). Mahwah, NJ: Lawrence Erlbaum Associates.

Frith, U. (1989). *Autism: Explaining the enigma*. Oxford: Blackwell.

Frith, U., & de Vignemont, F. (2005), Egocentrism, allocentrism, and Asperger syndrome. *Consciousness and Cognition, 14*(4), 719–738.

Frodi, A., Dernevik, M., Sepa, A., Philipson, J., & Bragesjo, M. (2001). Current attachment representations of incarcerated offenders varying in degree of psychopathy. *Attachment and Human Development, 3*(3), 269–283.

Fu, C. H., Williams, S. C., Cleare, A. J., Brammer, M. J., Walsh, N. D., Kim, J., et al. (2004). Attenuation of the neural response to sad faces in major depression by antidepressant treatment: A prospective, event-related functional magnetic resonance imaging study. *Archives of General Psychiatry, 61,* 877–889.

Fulero, S. (1996). Review of the Hare psychopathy checklist—revised. In J. C. Conoley & J. C. Impara (Eds.), *12th mental measurements yearbook* (pp. 453–454). Lincoln, NE: Buros Institute.

Funayama, E. S., Grillon, C., Davis, M., & Phelps, E. A. (2001). A double dissociation in the affective modulation of startle in humans: Effects of unilateral temporal lobectomy. *Journal of Cognitive Neuroscience, 13*(6), 721–729.

Furby, L., & Beyth-Marom, R. (1992). Risk taking in adolescence: A decision-making perspective. *Developmental Review, 12*(1), 1–44.

Gazzaniga, M. S. (2005). *The ethical brain.* New York: Dana Press.

Gazzaniga, M. S., & Le Doux, J. E. (1978). *The integrated mind.* New York: Plenum.

Gibbard, A. (1990). *Wise choices, apt feelings.* Cambridge, MA: Harvard University Press.

Gibbard, A. (2006). Moral feelings and moral concepts. In R. Shafer-Landau (Ed.), *Oxford studies in metaethics* (pp. 195–215). Oxford & New York: Oxford University Press.

Giedd, J. N., Blumenthal, J., Jeffries, N. O., Castellanos, F. X., Liu, H., Zijedenbos, A., Paus, T., Evans, A. C., & Rapoport, J. L. (1999). Brain development during childhood and adolescence: A longitudinal MRI study. *Nature Neuroscience, 2*(10), 861–863.

Gillberg, C. L. (1992). The Emanuel Miller Memorial Lecture 1991. Autism and autistic-like conditions: Subclasses among disorders of empathy. *Journal of Child Psychology and Psychiatry, 33*(5), 813–842.

Gillstrom, B. J., & Hare, R. D. (1988). Language-related hand gestures in psychopaths. *Journal of Personality Disorders, 2*(1), 21–27.

Gintis, H. (2000). Strong reciprocity and human sociality. *Journal of Theoretical Biology, 206,* 169–179.

Glare, P. G. W. (1982). *Oxford Latin dictionary.* New York: Oxford University Press.

Goel, V., & Dolan, R. J. (2004). Differential involvement of left prefrontal cortex in inductive and deductive reasoning. *Cognition, 93,* B109–B121.

Goel, V., Grafman, J., Tajik, J., Gana, S., & Danto, D. (1997). A study of the performance of patients with frontal lobe lesions in a financial planning task. *Brain, 120*(Pt. 10), 1805–1822.

Goldberg, E. (2001). *The executive brain: Frontal lobes and the civilized mind*. New York: Oxford University Press.

Goldman, A. (1970). *A theory of human action*. Princeton, NJ: Princeton University Press.

Goldman, A. (1995). Empathy, mind and morals. In M. Davies & T. Stone (Eds.), *Mental simulation: Philosophical and psychological essays* (pp. 185–208). Oxford: Blackwell.

Gorenstein, E. E., & Newman, J. P. (1980). Disinhibitory psychopathology: A new perspective and a model for research. *Psychological Review, 87*(3), 301–315.

Gould, S. J. (1977). *Ontogeny and phylogeny*. Cambridge, MA: Harvard University Press.

Grandin, T. (1995). *Thinking in pictures: And other reports from my life with autism*. New York: Doubleday.

Grant, C. M., Boucher, J., Riggs, K. J., & Grayson, A. (2005). Moral understanding in children with autism. *Autism, 9*(3), 317–331.

Graves, R., Landis, T., & Goodglass, H. (1981). Laterality and sex differences for visual recognition of emotional and non-emotional words. *Neuropsychologia, 19*, 95–102.

Greene, J. (2002). The terrible, horrible, no good, very bad truth about morality and what to do about it. Doctoral dissertation, Princeton University, Princeton, NJ.

Greene, J. (2003). From neural "is" to moral "ought": What are the moral implications of neuroscientific moral psychology? *Nature Reviews Neuroscience, 4*, 846–849.

Greene, J. (2005). Cognitive neuroscience and the structure of the moral mind. In P. Carruthers, S. Laurence, & S. Stich (Eds.), *The innate mind: Structure and contents* (pp. 338–352). New York: Oxford University Press.

Greene, J., & Cohen, J. (2004). For the law, neuroscience changes nothing and everything. *Philosophical Transactions of the Royal Society of London* (Series B, *Biological Sciences*), *359*, 1775–1785.

Greene, J., & Haidt, J. (2002). How (and where) does moral judgment work? *Trends in Cognitive Sciences, 6*(12), 517–523.

Greene, J. D., Morelli, S. A., Lowenberg, K., Nystrom, L. E., & Cohen, J. D. (submitted). Cognitive load selectively interferes with utilitarian moral judgment.

Greene, J. D., Nystrom, L. E., Engell, A. D., Darley, J. M., & Cohen, J. D. (2004). The neural bases of cognitive conflict and control in moral judgment. *Neuron, 44,* 389–400.

Greene, J. D., Sommerville, R. B., Nystrom, L. E., Darley, J. M., & Cohen, J. D. (2001). An fMRI investigation of emotional engagement in moral judgment. *Science, 293*(5537), 2105–2108.

Greenwald, A. G., Banaji, M. R., Rudman, L. A., Farnham, S. D., Nosek, B. A., & Mellott, D. S. (2002). A unified theory of implicit attitudes, stereotypes, self-esteem, and self-concept. *Psychological Review, 109,* 3–25.

Griffin, J. (1986). *Well-being.* Oxford: Oxford University Press.

Gross, J. (1998). The emerging field of emotion regulation: An integrative review. *Review of General Psychology, 2,* 271–299.

Gusnard, D. A., Akbudak, E., Shulman, G. L., & Raichle, M. E. (2001). Medial prefrontal cortex and self-referential mental activity: Relation to a default mode of brain function. *Proceedings of the National Academy of Sciences of the United States of America, 98* (7), 4259–4264.

Hägerström, A. (1953). *Inquiries into the nature of law and morals.* Stockholm: Almqvist & Wiksell.

Haidt, J. (2001). The emotional dog and its rational tail: A social intuitionist approach to moral judgment. *Psychological Review 108*(4), 814–834.

Haidt, J. (2003a). Elevation and the positive psychology of morality. In C. L. M. Keyes & J. Haidt (Eds.), *Flourishing: Positive psychology and the life well-lived* (pp. 275–289). Washington, DC: American Psychological Association.

Haidt, J. (2003b). The moral emotions. In R. J. Davidson, K. R. Scherer, & H. H. Goldsmith (Eds.), *Handbook of affective sciences* (pp. 852–870). Oxford: Oxford University Press.

Haidt, J., Bjorklund, F., & Murphy, S. (2000). Moral dumbfounding: When intuition finds no reason. (Unpublished manuscript, University of Virginia, Charlottesville.)

Haidt, J., Koller, S. H., & Dias, M. G. (1993). Affect, culture and morality, or is it wrong to eat your dog? *Journal of Personality and Social Psychology 65*(4), 613–628.

Haith, M., & Benson, J. B. (1998). Infant cognition. In W. Damon (Ed.), *Handbook of child psychology* (5th edn.) Vol. 2: *Cognition, perception and language* (D. Kuhn & R. S. Sielger, Vol. Eds., pp. 199–254). New York: Wiley.

Haji, I. (1998). *Moral appraisability.* Oxford: Oxford University Press.

Haji, I. (2003). *Deontic morality and control.* Cambridge: Cambridge University Press.

Halgren, E., & Marinkovic, K. (1996). General principles for the physiology of cognition as suggested by intracranial ERPs. In C. Ogura, Y. Koga, & M. Shimokochi (Eds.), *Recent advances in event-related brain potential research* (pp. 1072–1084). Amsterdam: Elsevier.

Halgren, E., Marinkovic, K., & Chauvel, P. (1998). Generators of the late cognitive potentials in auditory and visual oddball tasks. *Electroencephalography & Clinical Neurophysiology, 106*(2), 156–164.

Hamilton, W. D. (1964). The genetical evolution of social behavior. *Journal of Theoretical Biology, 7*, 1–52.

Haney, C., Banks, C., & Zimbardo, P. (1973). Interpersonal dynamics in a simulated prison. *International Journal of Criminology and Penology, 1*, 67–97.

Hansman-Wijnands, M. A., & Hummelen, J. W. (2006). [Differential diagnosis of psychopathy and autism spectrum disorders in adults. Empathic deficit as a core symptom]. *Tijdschrift voor Psychiatrie 48*(8), 627–636.

Happé, F. (1994a). An advanced test of theory of mind: Understanding of story characters' thoughts and feelings by able autistic, mentally handicapped and normal children and adults. *Journal of Autism and Developmental Disorders, 24*, 129–154.

Happé, F. (1994b). *Autism: An introduction to psychological theory.* Cambridge, MA: Harvard University Press.

Happé, F. (2003). Theory of mind and the self. *Annals of the New York Academy of Sciences, 1001*, 134–144.

Hare, R. D. (1965a). Psychopathy, fear arousal and anticipated pain. *Psychological Reports, 16*(2), 499–502.

Hare, R. D. (1965b). Temporal gradient of fear arousal in psychopaths. *Journal of Abnormal Psychology, 70*(6), 442–445.

Hare, R. D. (1968). Psychopathy, autonomic functioning, and the orienting response. *Journal of Abnormal Psychology, 73*(3, Pt. 2), 1–24.

Hare, R. D. (1972). Psychopathy and physiological responses to adrenalin. *Journal of Abnormal Psychology, 79*(2), 138–147.

Hare, R. D. (1978). Electrodermal and cardiovascular correlates of psychopathy. In R. D. Hare & D. Schalling (Eds.), *Psychopathic behavior: Approaches to research* (pp. 107–143). Chichester, UK: Wiley.

Hare, R. D. (1979). Psychopathy and laterality of cerebral function. *Journal of Abnormal Psychology, 88*(6), 605–610.

Hare, R. D. (1980). A research scale for the assessment of psychopathy in criminal populations. *Personality & Individual Differences, 1*(2), 111–119.

Hare, R. D. (1984). Performance of psychopaths on cognitive tasks related to frontal lobe function. *Journal of Abnormal Psychology, 93*(2), 133–140.

Hare, R. D. (1991). *Manual for the Hare Psychopathy Checklist—revised.* Toronto: Multi-Health Systems.

Hare, R. D. (1993). *Without conscience: The disturbing world of the psychopaths among us.* New York: Pocket Books.

Hare, R. D. (1996a). Psychopathy—A clinical construct whose time has come. *Criminal Justice and Behavior, 23*(1), 25–54.

Hare, R. D. (1996b). Psychopathy and antisocial personality disorder: A case of diagnostic confusion. *Psychiatric Times, 13*(2), 39–40.

Hare, R. D. (1998). Psychopaths and their nature: Implications for the mental health and criminal justice systems. In E. Theodore Millon, E. Erik Simonsen, M. Birket-Smith, & R. D. Davis (Eds.), *Psychopathy: Antisocial, criminal, and violent behavior* (pp. 188–212). New York: Guilford.

Hare, R. D. (2003). *Manual for the Hare Psychopathy Checklist—revised* (2nd edn.). Toronto: Multi-Health Systems.

Hare, R. D., & Hart, S. D. (1993). Psychopathy, mental disorder, and crime. In H. Sheilagh (Ed.), *Mental disorder and crime* (pp. 104–115). Newbury Park, CA: Sage.

Hare, R. D., & Jutai, J. W. (1988). Psychopathy and cerebral asymmetry in semantic processing. *Personality & Individual Differences, 9*(2), 329–337.

Hare, R. D., & McPherson, L. M. (1984). Psychopathy and perceptual asymmetry during verbal dichotic listening. *Journal of Abnormal Psychology, 93*(2), 141–149.

Hare, R. D., & Neumann, C. S. (2005). Structural models of psychopathy. *Current Psychiatry Reports, 7*(1), 57–64.

Hare, R. D., & Quinn, M. J. (1971). Psychopathy and autonomic conditioning. *Journal of Abnormal Psychology, 77*(3), 223–235.

Hare, R. D., Frazelle, J., & Cox, D. N. (1978). Psychopathy and physiological responses to threat of an aversive stimulus. *Psychophysiology, 15*(2), 165–172.

Hare, R. D., Hart, S. D., & Harpur, T. J. (1991). Psychopathy and the DSM-IV criteria for antisocial personality disorder. Special issue: Diagnoses, dimensions, and DSM-IV: The science of classification. *Journal of Abnormal Psychology, 100*(3), 391–398.

Hare, R. D., Williamson, S. E., & Harpur, T. J. (1988). Psychopathy and language. In T. E. Moffitt & S. A. Mednick (Eds.), *Biological contributions to crime causation* (pp. 68–92). Dordrecht, Netherlands: Martinus Nijhoff.

Harlow, J. (1848). Passage of an iron rod through the head. *Boston Medical Surgical Journal, 34*, 389–393.

Harman, G. (1977). *The nature of morality: An introduction to ethics*. New York: Oxford University Press.

Harman, G. (2000). *Explaining value and other essays in moral philosophy*. New York: Oxford University Press.

Harpur, T. J., & Hare, R. D. (1990). Psychopathy and attention. In T. E. James (Ed.), *The development of attention: Research and theory. Advances in psychology*, (Vol. 69, pp. 429–444). Amsterdam: Elsevier.

Harpur, T. J., Hakstian, A. R., & Hare, R. D. (1988). Factor structure of the psychopathy checklist. *Journal of Consulting & Clinical Psychology, 56*(5), 741–747.

Harpur, T. J., Hare, R. D., & Hakstian, A. R. (1989). Two-factor conceptualization of psychopathy: Construct validity and assessment implications. *Psychological Assessment, 1*(1), 6–17.

Harris N. (2003). Reassessing the dimensionality of the moral emotions. *British Journal of Psychology, 94*, 457–473.

Harsanyi, J. (1953). Cardinal utility in welfare economics and in the theory of risk-taking. *Journal of Political Economy, 61*, 434–435.

Harsanyi, J. (1955). Cardinal welfare, individualistic ethics, and interpersonal comparisons of utility. *Journal of Political Economy, 63*, 309–321.

Hart, S. D. (1998). Psychopathy and risk for violence. In D. J. Cooke, A. E. Forth, & R. D. Hare (Eds.), *Psychopathy: Theory, research, and implications for society* (pp. 355–374). London: Kluwer Academic.

Hart, S. D., & Hare, R. D. (1989). Discriminant validity of the psychopathy checklist in a forensic psychiatric population. *Psychological Assessment, 1*(3), 211–218.

Hart, S. D., & Hare, R. D. (1996). Psychopathy and antisocial personality disorder. *Current Opinion in Psychiatry, 9*(2), 129–132.

Hart, S. D., Forth, A. E., & Hare, R. D. (1990). Performance of criminal psychopaths on selected neuropsychological tests. *Journal of Abnormal Psychology, 99*(4), 374–379.

Harter, S., Waters, P., & Whitesell, N. R. (1998). Relational self-worth: Differences in perceived worth as a person across interpersonal contexts among adolescents. *Child Development, 69*(3), 756–766.

Hastings, P. D., Zahn-Waxler, C., & McShane, K. (2006). We are, by nature, moral creatures: Biological bases of concern for others. In M. Killen & J. Smetana (Eds.),

Handbook of moral development (pp. 483–516). Mahwah, NJ: Lawrence Erlbaum Associates.

Hauser, M. O., Cushman, F. A., Young, L., Jin, R., & Mikhail, J. M. (2007). A dissociation between moral judgments and justifications. *Mind & Language, 22*(1), 1–21.

Haviland, J. M., Walker-Andrews, A. S., Huffman, L., Toci, L., & Alton, K. (1996). Intermodal perception of emotional expressions by children with autism. *Journal of Developmental and Physical Disabilities, 8,* 77–88.

Heekeren, H. R., Wartenburger, I., Schmidt, H., Schwintowski, H. P., & Villringer, A. (2003). An fMRI study of simple ethical decision-making. *Neuroreport, 14,* 1215–1219.

Hemphill, J. F., Hare, R. D., & Wong, S. (1998). Psychopathy and recidivism: A review. *Legal & Criminological Psychology, 3*(Pt. 1), 139–170.

Hemphill, J. F., Hart, S. D., & Hare, R. D. (1994). Psychopathy and substance use. *Journal of Personality Disorders, 8*(3), 169–180.

Herman, B. (1981). On the value of acting from the motive of duty. *Philosophical Review, 90*(3), 359–382.

Hervé, H. F., Hayes, P., & Hare, R. D. (2003). Psychopathy and sensitivity to the emotional polarity of metaphorical statements. *Personality & Individual Differences, 35*(7), 1497–1507.

Hiatt, K. D., Schmitt, W. A., & Newman, J. P. (2004). Stroop tasks reveal abnormal selective attention among psychopathic offenders. *Neuropsychology, 18*(1), 50–59.

Hill, D., Pond, D. A., Mitchell, W., & Falconer, M. A. (1957). Personality changes following temporal lobectomy for epilepsy. *Journal of Mental Science, 103,* 18–27.

Hill, E. L. (2004). Executive dysfunction in autism. *Trends in Cognitive Sciences, 8*(1), 26–32.

Hill, E., Berthoz, S., & Frith, U. (2004). Brief report: Cognitive processing of own emotions in individuals with autistic spectrum disorder and in their relatives. *Journal of Autism and Developmental Disorders, 34*(2), 229–235.

Hinckfuss, I. (1987). The moral society: Its structure and effects. *Discussion Papers in Environmental Philosophy, 16.* Canberra: Philosophy Program (RSSS), Australian National University.

Hinson, J. M., Jameson, T. L., & Whitney, P. (2002). Somatic markers, working memory, and decision making. *Cognitive, Affective and Behavioral Neuroscience, 2*(4), 341–353.

Hobbes, T. (1651). *Leviathan.* London: Printed for Andrew Crooke.

Hobson, P. (1986). The autistic child's appraisal of expressions of emotion. *Journal of Child Psychology and Psychiatry, 27*, 321–342.

Hobson, R. P. (1992). Social perception in high-level autism. In E. Schopler & G. Mesibov (Eds.), *High-functioning individuals with autism* (pp. 157–186). New York: Plenum.

Hoffman, M. L. (1983). Affective and cognitive processes in moral internalization: An information-processing approach. In R. M. Sorrentino & E. T. Higgins (Eds.), *Handbook of motivation and personality: Foundations of social behavior* (pp. 244–280). New York: Guilford.

Hoffman, M. L. (1991). Empathy, social cognition, and moral action. In W. M. Kurtines & J. L. Gewirtz (Eds.), *Handbook of moral behavior and development* (Vol. I: *Theory*). Hillsdale, NJ: Lawrence Erlbaum Associates.

Hoffman, M. L. (2000). *Empathy and moral development: Implications for caring and justice.* Cambridge: Cambridge University Press.

Holcomb, P. J., Kounios, J., Anderson, J. E., & West, W. C. (1999). Dual-coding, context-availability, and concreteness effects in sentence comprehension: An electrophysiological investigation. *Journal of Experimental Psychology: Learning, Memory, & Cognition, 25*(3), 721–742.

Hollos, M., Leis, P., & Turiel, E. (1986). Social reasoning in IJO children and adolescents in Nigerian communities. *Journal of Cross-Cultural Psychology, 17(3)*, 352–374.

Hood, T., Siegfried, J., & Wieser, H. (1983). The role of stereotactic amygdalotomy in the treatment of temporal lobe epilepsy associated with behavioral disorders. *Applied Neurophysiology, 46*(1–4), 19–25.

Horgan, T., & Timmons, M. (2006). Cognitivist expressivism. In T. Horgan & M. Timmons (Eds.), *Metaethics after Moore* (pp. 255–298). Oxford: Oxford University Press.

Hornak, J., Bramham, J., Rolls, E. T., Morris, R. G., O'Doherty, J., Bullock, P. R., & Polkey, C. E. (2003). Changes in emotion after circumscribed surgical lesions of the orbitofrontal and cingulate cortices. *Brain, 126*(Pt. 7), 1691–1712.

Hornak, J., Rolls, E. T., & Wade, D. (1996). Face and voice expression identification in patients with emotional and behavioral changes following ventral frontal lobe damage. *Neuropsychologia, 34*(4), 247–261.

Horovitz, S. G., Skudlarski, P., & Gore, J. C. (2002). Correlations and dissociations between BOLD signal and P300 amplitude in an auditory oddball task: A parametric approach to combining fMRI and ERP. *Magnetic Resonance Imaging, 20*(4), 319–325.

Horowitz, T. (1998). Philosophical intuitions and psychological theory. In M. DePaul & W. Ramsey (Eds.), *Rethinking intuition* (pp. 143–160). Lanham, MD: Rowman & Littlefield.

Howard-Snyder, F. (2002). Doing vs. allowing harm. In E. N. Zalta (Ed.), *The Stanford encyclopedia of philosophy*. Stanford, CA: The Metaphysics Research Lab, Center for the Study of Language and Information, Stanford University.

Hume, D. (1975). *Enquiries concerning human understanding and concerning the principles of morals*. Oxford: Clarendon Press. (Original work published 1777)

Hume, D. (1978). *A treatise of human nature* (L. A. Selby-Bigge & P. H. Nidditch, Eds.). Oxford: Oxford University Press. (Original work published 1740)

Hume, D. (1983). *An enquiry concerning the principles of morals*. Indianapolis: Hackett. (Original work published 1751)

Hursthouse, R. (1999). *On virtue ethics*. New York: Oxford University Press.

Huttenlocher, P. R. (1979). Synaptic density in human frontal cortex—developmental changes and effects of aging. *Brain Research, 163*, 195–205.

Iacono, W. G. (1998). Identifying psychophysiological risk for psychopathology: Examples from substance abuse and schizophrenia research. *Psychophysiology, 35*(6), 621–637.

Insel, T. R., & Fernald, R. D. (2004). How the brain processes social information: Searching for the social brain. *Annual Review of Neuroscience, 27*, 697–722.

Intrator, J., Hare, R. D., Stritzke, P., Brichtswein, K., Dorfman, D., Harpur, T., Bernstein, D., Handelsman, L., Schaefer, C., Keilp, J., Rosen, J., & Machac, J. (1997). A brain imaging (single photon emission computerized tomography) study of semantic and affective processing in psychopaths. *Biological Psychiatry, 42*(2), 96–103.

Isenberg, N., Silbersweig, D., Engelien, A., Emmerich, S., Malavade, K., Beattie, B., Leon, A. C., & Stern, E. (1999). Linguistic threat activates the human amygdala. *Proceedings of the National Academy of Sciences of the United States of America, 96*(18), 10456–10459.

Ishikawa, S. S., Raine, A., Lencz, T., Bihrle, S., & Lacasse, L. (2001). Autonomic stress reactivity and executive functions in successful and unsuccessful criminal psychopaths from the community. *Journal of Abnormal Psychology, 110*(3), 423–432.

Isomura, Y., & Takada, M. (2004). Neural mechanisms of versatile functions in primate anterior cingulate cortex. *Reviews in Neuroscience, 15*(4), 279–291.

Iversen, S. D., & Mishkin, M. (1970). Perseverative interference in monkey following selective lesions of the inferior prefrontal convexity. *Experimental Brain Research, 11*, 376–386.

Izard, C. E. (1978). On the ontogenesis of emotions and cognition-emotion relationships in infancy. In M. Lewis & L. A. Rosenblum (Eds.), *The development of affect* (pp. 389–413). New York: Plenum.

Izard, C. E., & Ackerman, B. P. (2000). Motivational, organizational and regulatory functions of discrete emotions. In M. Lewis & J. M. Haviland-Jones (Eds.), *Handbook of emotions* (pp. 253–264). New York: Guilford.

Jackendoff, R. (1994). *Patterns in the mind: Language and human nature.* New York: Basic Books.

Jacob, P., & Jeannerod, M. (2003). *Ways of seeing.* New York: Oxford University Press.

Jacobs, J. E., Vernon, M. K., & Eccles, J. S. (2004). Relations between social self-perceptions, time use, and prosocial or problem behaviors during adolescence. *Journal of Adolescent Research, 19*(1), 45–62.

James, C. (1975). The role of semantic information in lexical decisions. *Journal of Experimental Psychology: Human Perception and Performance, 14*, 130–136.

James, W. (1884).What is an emotion? *Mind, 9*, 188–205.

James, W. (1972). *The varieties of religious experience.* London: Fontana Press. (Original work published 1902)

Ji, L. J., Peng, K., & Nisbett, R. E. (2000). Culture, control, and perception of relationships in the environment. *Journal of Personality and Social Psychology, 78*, 943–955.

Jiang, Y., Saxe, R., & Kanwisher, N. (2004). Functional magnetic resonance imaging provides new constraints on theories of the psychological refractory period. *Psychological Science, 15*, 390–396.

Johns, J. H., & Quay, H. C. (1962). The effect of social reward on verbal conditioning in psychopathic and neurotic military officers. *Journal of Consulting & Clinical Psychology, 26*, 217–220.

Johnson, R. J. (1989). Auditory and visual P300s in temporal lobectomy patients: Evidence for modality-dependent generators. *Psychophysiology, 26*(6), 633–650.

Johnson, R. J. (1993). On the neural generators of the P300 component of the event-related potential. *Psychophysiology, 30*(1), 90–97.

Johnston, M. (1995). Dispositional theories of value. In M. Smith (Ed.), *Meta-ethics.* Aldershot, UK: Dartmouth.

Johnston, M. V. (2003). Brain plasticity in paediatric neurology. *European Journal of Paediatric Neurology, 7*(3), 105–113.

Jolliffe, T., Lansdown, R., & Robinson, C. (1992). Autism: A personal account. *Communication, 26*(3), 12–19.

Joyce, R. (1999). Apologizing. *Public Affairs Quarterly, 13*, 159–173.

Joyce, R. (2001). *The myth of morality.* Cambridge: Cambridge University Press.

Joyce, R. (2002). Expressivism and motivation internalism. *Analysis, 62*, 336–344.

Joyce, R. (2006a). *The evolution of morality.* Cambridge, MA: MIT Press.

Joyce, R. (2006b). Metaethics and the empirical sciences. *Philosophical explorations* (Vol. 9, pp. 133–148).

Joyce, R. (2006c). Is morality innate? In P. Carruthers, S. Lawrence, & S. Stich (Eds.), *The innate mind: Culture and cognition.* New York: Oxford University Press.

Joyce, R. (Forthcoming a). Expressivism, motivation internalism, and Hume. In C. Pigden (Ed.), *Reason, motivation, and virtue.* Palgrave Macmillan.

Joyce, R. (Forthcoming b). Morality, schmorality. In P. Bloomfield (Ed.), *Morality and self-interest.* Oxford: Oxford University Press.

Jurkovic, G. J., & Prentice, N. M. (1977). Relation of moral and cognitive development to dimensions of juvenile delinquency. *Journal of Abnormal Psychology, 86*(4), 414–420.

Jutai, J. W., & Hare, R. D. (1983). Psychopathy and selective attention during performance of a complex perceptual-motor task. *Psychophysiology, 20*(2), 146–151.

Jutai, J. W., Hare, R. D., & Connolly, J. F. (1987). Psychopathy and event-related brain potentials (ERPs) associated with attention to speech stimuli. *Personality & Individual Differences, 8*(2), 175–184.

Kagan, J. (1981). *The second year.* Cambridge, MA: Harvard University Press.

Kagan, J. (1984). *The nature of the child.* New York: Basic Books.

Kagan, J. (1994). *Galen's prophecy.* New York: Basic Books.

Kagan J. (1996). On attachment. *Harvard Review of Psychiatry, 3*(2), 104–106.

Kagan, J. (2002). *Surprise, uncertainty and mental structures.* Cambridge, MA: Harvard University Press.

Kagan, J., & Hershkowitz, N. (2005). *A young mind in a growing brain.* Mahwah, NJ: Lawrence Erlbaum Associates.

Kagan, J., & Lamb, S. (1987). *The emergence of morality in young children.* Chicago: University of Chicago Press.

Kagan, J., & Snidman, N. (2004). *The long shadow of temperament.* Cambridge, MA: Harvard University Press.

Kagan, S. (1989). *The limits of morality*. New York: Oxford University Press.

Kagan, S. (1992). The limits of well-being. *Social Philosophy and Policy, 9*, 169–189. [Reprinted in E. F. Paul, F. D. Miller, & J. Paul (Eds.), *The good life and the human good* (pp. 169–189). Cambridge: Cambridge University Press, 1992.]

Kagan, S. (1997). *Normative ethics*. Boulder, CO: Westview Press.

Kahneman, D., & Tversky, A. (1979). Prospect theory: An analysis of decision under risk. *Econometrica, 47*(2), 263–291.

Kahneman, D., Schkade, D., & Sunstein, C. R. (1998). Shared outrage and erratic rewards: The psychology of punitive damages. *Journal of Risk and Uncertainty, 16*, 49–86.

Kamm, F. M. (1993). *Morality, mortality*. Vol. I: *Death and whom to save from it*. New York: Oxford University Press.

Kamm, F. M. (1996). *Morality, mortality*. Vol. II: *Rights, duties, and status*. New York: Oxford University Press.

Kamm, F. M. (1999). Faminine ethics: The problem of distance in morality and Singer's ethical theory. In D. Jamieson (Ed.), *Singer and his critics* (pp. 162–208). Oxford: Blackwell.

Kant, I. (1930). *Lectures on ethics*. Indianapolis, IN: Hackett.

Kant, I. (1948). Groundwork of the metaphysic of morals. In Kant, *The Moral Law*. London: Hutchinson. (Original work published 1785)

Kant, I. (1959). *Foundations of the metaphysics of morals*. Indianapolis, IN: Bobbs-Merrill. (Original work published 1785)

Kant, I. (1983). *On a supposed right to lie because of philanthropic concerns*. In Kant, *Grounding for the Metaphysics of Morals* (J. W. Ellington, Trans., pp. 162–166). Indianapolis, IN: Hackett. (Original work published 1785)

Kant, I. (1991). The doctrine of virtue. In Kant, *The Metaphysics of Morals*. Cambridge: Cambridge University Press. (Original work published 1797)

Kant, I. (1993). *Critique of practical reason* (3rd edn.). Upper Saddle River, NJ: Prentice-Hall. (Original work published 1788)

Kant, I. (1993). *Grounding for the metaphysics of morals* (J. W. Ellington, Trans.). Indianapolis: Hackett. (Original work published 1785)

Kant, I. (1994). The metaphysics of morals. In Kant, *Ethical philosophy*. Indianapolis, IN: Hackett. (Original work published 1785)

Kant, I. (2002). *The philosophy of law: An exposition of the fundamental principles of jurisprudence as the science of right*. Union, NJ: Lawbook Exchange. (Original work published 1796–1797)

Karpman, B. (1946). Psychopathy in the scheme of human typology. *Journal of Nervous and Mental Disease, 103,* 276–288.

Kaszniak, A., Reminger, S., Rapcsak, S., & Glisky, E. (1999). Conscious experience and autonomic response to emotional stimuli following frontal lobe damage. In S. Hameroff, A. Kaszniak, & D. Chalmers (Eds.), *Toward a science of consciousness III* (pp. 201–213). Cambridge, MA: MIT Press.

Katz, L. D. (1986). Hedonism as metaphysics of mind and value. Doctoral dissertation, Department of Philosophy, Princeton University, Princeton, NJ.

Katz, L. D. (2005). Opioid bliss as the felt hedonic core of mammalian prosociality—and of consummatory pleasure more generally? *Behavioral and Brain Sciences, 28*(3), 356.

Katz, L. D. (2006). Pleasure. In E. N. Zalta (Ed.), *Stanford encyclopedia of philosophy.* Stanford, CA: The Metaphysics Research Lab, Center for the Study of Language and Information, Stanford University. Retrieved from http://plato.stanford.edu/archives/spr2006/entries/pleasure/.

Keel, J. H. (1993). A study of moral reasoning in adults with autism. In *School Psychology* (p. 63). Chapel Hill: University of North Carolina.

Kelly, D., & Stich, S. (forthcoming). Two theories about the cognitive architecture underlying morality. In P. Carruthers, S. Laurence, & S. Stich (Eds.), *The Innate Mind, Vol. III: Foundations and the Future.* New York: Oxford University Press.

Kelly, D., Stich, S., Haley, K. J., Eng, S., & Fessler, D. M. T. (2007). Harm, affect, and the moral /conventional distinction. *Mind and Language.*

Kennett, J. (2002). Autism, empathy and moral agency. *Philosophical Quarterly, 52*(208), 340–357.

Kennett, J. (2006). Do psychopaths really threaten moral rationalism? *Philosophical Explorations, 9,* 69–82.

Keverne, E. B., & Curley, J. P. (2004). Vasopressin, oxytocin and social behaviour. *Current Opinion in Neurobiology, 14,* 777–783.

Kiehl, K. A. (2000). A neuroimaging investigation of affective, cognitive, and language functions in psychopathy. Doctoral dissertation, University of British Columbia, Vancouver, B.C.

Kiehl, K. A., & Liddle, P. F. (2003). Reproducibility of the hemodynamic response to auditory oddball stimuli: A six-week test-retest study. *Human Brain Mapping, 18*(1), 42–52.

Kiehl, K. A., Bates, A. T., Laurens, K. R., Hare, R. D., Forster, B. B., & Liddle, P. F. (2000a). Electrophysiological and hemodynamic evidence for fronto-temporal abnormalities in psychopathic offenders. Paper presented at the annual meeting of the Society for Psychophysiological Research, San Diego, California.

Kiehl, K. A., Bates, A. T., Laurens, K. R., Hare, R. D., & Liddle, P. F. (2006). Brain potentials implicate temporal lobe abnormalities in criminal psychopaths. *Journal of Abnormal Psychology, 115*(3), 443–453.

Kiehl, K. A., Hare, R. D., McDonald, J. J., & Brink, J. (1999a). Semantic and affective processing in psychopaths: An event-related potential study. *Psychophysiology, 36*, 765–774.

Kiehl, K. A., Hare, R. D., McDonald, J. J., & Liddle, P. F. (1999b). Reduced P3 responses in criminal psychopaths during a visual oddball task. *Biological Psychiatry, 45*(11), 1498–1507.

Kiehl, K. A., Laurens, K. R., Celone, K., Pearlson, G. D., & Liddle, P. F. (2003). Abnormal affective picture processing in criminal psychopaths: Evidence supporting the paralimbic dysfunction hypothesis. Paper presented to the Society for Psychophysiological Research, Chicago, IL.

Kiehl, K. A., Laurens, K. R., Duty, T. L., Forster, B. B., & Liddle, P. F. (2001a). An event-related fMRI study of visual and auditory oddball tasks. *Journal of Psychophysiology, 21*, 221–240.

Kiehl, K. A., Liddle, P. F., Smith, A. S., Mendrek, A., Forster, B. B., & Hare, R. D. (1999c). Neural pathways involved in the processing of concrete and abstract words. *Human Brain Mapping, 7*(4), 225–233.

Kiehl, K. A., Smith, A. M., Hare, R. D., & Liddle, P. F. (2000b). An event-related potential investigation of response inhibition in schizophrenia and psychopathy. *Biological Psychiatry, 48*(3), 210–221.

Kiehl, K. A., Smith, A. M., Hare, R. D., Mendrek, A., Forster, B. B., Brink, J., & Liddle, P. F. (2001c). Limbic abnormalities in affective processing by criminal psychopaths as revealed by functional magnetic resonance imaging. *Biological Psychiatry, 50*(9): 677–684.

Kiehl, K. A., Smith, A. M., Mendrek, A., Forster, B. B., Hare, R. D., & Liddle, P. F. (2004). Temporal lobe abnormalities in semantic processing by criminal psychopaths as revealed by functional magnetic resonance imaging. *Psychiatry Research: Neuroimaging, 130*, 27–42.

Kiehl, K. A., Stevens, M. S., Laurens, K. R., Pearlson, G. D., Calhoun, V. D., & Liddle, P. F. (2005). An adaptive reflexive processing model of neurocognitive function: Supporting evidence from a large-scale (n = 100) fMRI study of an auditory oddball task. *NeuroImage, 25*, 899–915.

Killen, M., & Smetana, J. G. (Eds.). (2006). *Handbook of moral development*. Mahwah, NJ: Lawrence Erlbaum Associates.

Killen, M., Margie, N. G., & Sinno, S. (2006). Morality in the context of intergroup relationships. In M. Killen & J. Smetana (Eds.), *Handbook of moral development* (pp. 155–183). Mahwah, NJ: Lawrence Erlbaum Associates.

Kluever, H., & Bucy, P. C. (1938). An analysis of certain effects of bilateral temporal lobectomy in the rhesus monkey, with special reference to "psychic blindness." *Journal of Psychology, 5*, 33–54.

Kluever, H., & Bucy, P. C. (1939). Preliminary analysis of functions of the temporal lobes in monkeys. *Archives of Neurology & Psychiatry, 42*, 979–1000.

Knight, R. T. (1996). Contribution of human hippocampal region to novelty detection. *Nature, 383*(6597), 256–259.

Kochanska, G. (1997). Multiple pathways to conscience for children with different temperaments. *Developmental Psychology, 33*, 228–240.

Kochanska, G., & Thompson, R. (1997). The emergence and development of conscience in toddlerhood and early childhood. In J. E. Grusec & L. Kuczynski (Eds.), *Parenting and children's internalization of values* (pp. 53–77). New York: Wiley.

Kochanska, G., Coy, K. C., & Murray, K. T. (2001). The development of self-regulation in the first four years of life. *Child Development, 72*, 1091–1111.

Kochanska, G., Gross, J. N., Lin, M., & Nichols, K. E. (2002). Guilt in young children. *Child Development, 73*, 461–482.

Kochanska, G., Tjebkes, T. L., & Forman, D. R. (1998). Children's emerging regulation of conduct. *Child Development, 69*, 1378–1389.

Koechlin, E., Basso, G., Pietrini, P., Panzer, S., & Grafman, J. (1999). The role of the anterior prefrontal cortex in human cognition. *Nature, 399*, 148–151.

Koechlin, E., Ody, C., & Kouneiher, F. (2003). The architecture of cognitive control in the human prefrontal cortex. *Science, 302*, 1181–1185.

Koenigs, M., Young, L., Cushman, F., Adolphs, R., Tranel, D., Damasio, A., & Hauser, M. (2007). Damage to the prefrontal cortex increases utilitarian moral judgements, *Nature, 446*, 908–911.

Kohlberg L. (1969). Stage and sequence: The cognitive-developmental approach to socialization. In D. A. Goslin (Ed.), *Handbook of socialization theory and research* (pp. 347–480). Chicago: Rand McNally.

Kohlberg, L. (1971). From is to ought: How to commit the naturalistic fallacy and get away with it in the study of moral development. In T. Mischel (Ed.), *Cognitive development and epistemology* (pp. 151–235). New York: Academic Press.

Kohlberg, L., Boyd, D., & Levine, C. (1990). The return of Stage 6: Its principle and moral point of view. In T. Wren (Ed.), *The moral domain: Essays in the ongoing discussion between philosophy and the social sciences* (pp. 151–181). Cambridge, MA: MIT Press.

Kohlberg, L., Levine, C., & Hewer, A. (1983). Moral stages: A current formulation and a response to critics. In J. A. Meacham (Ed.), *Contributions to human development* (Vol. 10, pp. 1–174). Basel: Karger.

Kolodny, N. (2005). Why be rational? *Mind, 114,* 509–563.

Korsgaard, C. M. (1996a). *Creating the kingdom of ends.* New York: Cambridge University Press.

Korsgaard, C. M. (1996b). *The sources of normativity.* Cambridge & New York: Cambridge University Press.

Kort, L. F. (1975). What is an apology? *Philosophical Research Archives, 1,* 78–87.

Kosson, D. S., & Harpur, T. J. (1997). Attentional functioning of psychopathic individuals: Current evidence and developmental implications. In J. A. Burack & J. T. Enns (Eds.), *Attention, development, and psychopathology* (pp. 379–402). New York: Guilford.

Kosson, D. S., Suchy, Y., Mayer, A. R., & Libby, J. (2002). Facial affect recognition in criminal psychopaths. *Emotion, 2*(4), 398–411.

Kounios, J., & Holcomb, P. J. (1994). Concreteness effects in semantic priming: ERP evidence supporting dual-coding theory. *Journal of Experimental Psychology: Learning, Memory, & Cognition, 20,* 804–823.

Kripke, S. A. (1980). *Naming and necessity.* Cambridge, MA: Harvard University Press.

Kroll, J. F., & Merves, J. S. (1986). Lexical access for concrete and abstract words. *Journal of Experimental Psychology: Learning, Memory, & Cognition, 12*(1), 92–107.

Kuhn, D. (1991). *The skills of argument.* Cambridge: Cambridge University Press.

Kutas, M., & Hillyard, S. A. (1980). Reading senseless sentences: Brain potentials reflect semantic incongruity. *Science, 207*(4427), 203–205.

Kutas, M., & Hillyard, S. A. (1983). Event-related brain potentials to grammatical errors and semantic anomalies. *Memory and Cognition, 11*(5), 539–550.

Kutas, M., & Hillyard, S. A. (1984). Brain potentials during reading reflect word expectancy and semantic association. *Nature, 307*(5947), 161–163.

Laakso, M. P., Vaurio, O., Koivisto, E., Savolainen, L., Eronen, M., Aronen, H. J., Hakola, P., Repo, E., Soininen, H., & Tiihonen, J. (2001). Psychopathy and the posterior hippocampus. *Behavioural Brain Research, 118*(2), 187–193.

LaBar, K. S., LeDoux, J. E., Spencer, D. D., & Phelps, E. A. (1995). Impaired fear conditioning following unilateral temporal lobectomy in humans. *Journal of Neuroscience, 15*(10), 6846–6855.

Lacey, N. (1988). *State punishment: Political principles and community values.* London: Routledge & Kegan Paul.

Lapierre, D., Braun, C. M. J., & Hodgins, S. (1995). Ventral frontal deficits in psychopathy: Neuropsychological test findings. *Neuropsychologia, 33*(2), 139–151.

Lapsley, D. K. (1996). *Moral psychology.* Boulder, CO: Westview Press.

Lapsley, D. K. (2006). Moral stage theory. In M. Killen & J. Smetana (Eds.), *Handbook of moral development* (pp. 37–66). Mahwah, NJ: Lawrence Erlbaum Associates.

Lapsley, D. K., & Murphy, M. N. (1985). Another look at the theoretical assumptions of adolescent egocentrism. *Developmental Review, 5,* 201–217.

Lapsley, D. K., & Narvaez, D. (2004). A social cognitive view of moral character. In D. K. Lapsley & D. Narvaez (Eds.), *Moral development, self and identity* (pp. 189–212). Mahwah, NJ: Lawrence Erlbaum Associates.

Lapsley, D. K., & Narvaez, D. (2005). Moral psychology at the crossroads. In D. K. Lapsley & F. C. Power (Eds.), *Character psychology and character education* (pp. 18–35). Notre Dame, IN: University of Notre Dame Press.

Lawrence, A. D., Calder, A. J., McGowan, S. W., & Grasby, P. M. (2002). Selective disruption of the recognition of facial expressions of anger. *Neuroreport, 13,* 881–884.

Lawson, W. (2001). *Life behind glass: A personal account of autism spectrum disorder.* London: Jessica Kingsley.

LeDoux, J. E. (1994). Emotion, memory and the brain. *Scientific American, 270,* 32–39.

Lee, G. P., Arena, J. G., Meador, K. J., & Smith, J. R. (1988). Changes in autonomic responsiveness following bilateral amygdalotomy in humans. *Neuropsychiatry, Neuropsychology, & Behavioral Neurology, 1*(2), 119–129.

Lee, G. P., Bechara, A., Adolphs, R., Arena, J., Meador, K. J., Loring, D. W., & Smith, J. R. (1998). Clinical and physiological effects of stereotaxic bilateral amygdalotomy for intractable aggression. *Journal of Neuropsychiatry & Clinical Neurosciences, 10*(4), 413–420.

Lerner, J. S., Goldberg, J. H., & Tetlock, P. E. (1998). Sober second thought: The effects of accountability, anger and authoritarianism on attributions of responsibility. *Personality and Social Psychology Bulletin, 24,* 563–574.

Levenston, G. K., Patrick, C. J., Bradley, M. M., & Lang, P. J. (2000). The psychopath as observer: Emotion and attention in picture processing. *Journal of Abnormal Psychology*, *109*(3), 373–385.

Lewis, M. (1992). *Shame: The exposed self*. New York: Free Press.

Lewis, M. (2000). The emergence of human emotions. In M. Lewis & J. M. Haviland-Jones (Eds.)., *Handbook of emotions* (2nd edn., pp. 265–280). New York: Guilford.

Lewis, M. D., & Stieben, J. (2004). Emotion regulation in the brain: Conceptual issues and directions for developmental research. *Child Development*, *75*, 371–376.

Liddle, P. F. (1995). Regional cerebral blood flow and subsyndromes of schizophrenia. In J. A. den Boer, H. G. M. Westenberg, & H. M. van Praag (Eds.), *Advances in the neurobiology of schizophrenia* (Vol. I, pp. 189–204). Wiley series on clinical and neurobiological advances in psychiatry. Chichester, UK: Wiley.

Lieberman, D., Tooby, J., & Cosmides, L. (2003). Does morality have a biological basis? An empirical test of the factors governing moral sentiments relating to incest. *Proceedings of the Royal Society of London* (Series B, *Biological Sciences*), *270*, 819–826.

Linden, D. E., Prvulovic, D., Formisano, E., Voellinger, M., Zanella, F. E., Goebel, R., & Dierks, T. (1999). The functional neuroanatomy of target detection: An fMRI study of visual and auditory oddball tasks. *Cerebral Cortex*, *9*(8), 815–823.

Link, N. F., Scherer, S. E., & Byrne, P. N. (1977). Moral judgment and moral conduct in the psychopath. *Canadian Psychiatric Association Journal*, *22*, 341–346.

Loney, B. R., Frick, P. J., Clements, C. B., Ellis, M. L., & Kerlin, K. (2003). Callous-unemotional traits, impulsivity, and emotional processing in adolescents with antisocial behavior problems. *Journal of Clinical Child and Adolescent Psychology*, *32*(1), 66–80.

Louth, S. M., Williamson, S. E., Alpert, M., Pouget, E. R., & Hare, R. D. (1998). Acoustic distinctions in the speech of male psychopaths. *Journal of Psycholinguistic Research*, *27*(3), 375–384.

Lykken, D. T. (1957). A study of anxiety in the sociopathic personality. *Journal of Abnormal & Social Psychology*, *55*, 6–10.

Mack, E. (1989). Against agent-neutral value. *Reason Papers*, *14*, 76–85.

Mackie, J. L. (1977). *Ethics: Inventing right and wrong*. New York/London: Penguin Books.

Maddock, R. J. (1999). The retrosplenial cortex and emotion: New insights from functional neuroimaging of the human brain. *Trends in Neuroscience*, *22*, 310–316.

Maddock, R. J., & Buonocore, M. H. (1997). Activation of left posterior cingulate gyrus by the auditory presentation of threat-related words: An fMRI study. *Psychiatry Research*, *75*(1), 1–14.

Mah, L. W. Y., Arnold, M. C., & Grafman, J. (2005). Deficits in social knowledge following damage to ventromedial prefrontal cortex. *Journal of Neuropsychiatry and Clinical Neurosciences*, *17*(1), 66–74.

Maibom, H. (2005). Moral unreason: The case of psychopathy. *Mind & Language*, *20*(2), 237–257.

Maier, N. R. F. (1931). Reasoning in humans: II. The solution of a problem and its appearance in consciousness. *Journal of Comparative Psychology*, *12*, 181–194.

Malloy, P., Bihrle, A., Duffy, J., & Cimino, C. (1993). The orbitomedial frontal syndrome. *Archives of Clinical Neuropsychology*, *8*, 185–201.

Marr, D. (1982). *Vision: A computational investigation into the human representation and processing of visual information*. New York: W. H. Freeman.

Mathis, H. (1970). Emotional responsivity in the antisocial personality. Unpublished Doctoral Dissertation, The George Washington University, Ann Arbor, Michigan.

Mazziotta, J. C. (2000) Imaging: Window on the brain. *Archives of Neurology*, *57*(10), 1413–1421.

McClure, S. M., Laibson, D. I., Loewenstein, G., & Cohen, J. D. (2004). Separate neural systems value immediate and delayed monetary rewards. *Science*, *306*, 503–507.

McClure, S. M., York, M. K., & Montague, P. R. (2004). The neural substrates of reward processing in humans: The modern role of fMRI. *Neuroscientist*, *10*, 260–268.

McCord, W. M., & McCord, J. (1964). *The psychopath: An essay on the criminal mind*. Princeton, NJ: Van Nostrand.

McDermott, P. A., Alterman, A. I., Cacciola, J. S., Rutherford, M. J., Newman, J. P., & Mulholland, E. M. (2000). Generality of psychopathy checklist–revised factors over prisoners and substance-dependent patients. *Journal of Consulting & Clinical Psychology*, *68*(1), 181–186.

McDowell, J. (1979). Virtue and reason. *Monist*, *62*, 331–350.

McDowell, J. (1985). Values and secondary qualities. In T. Honderich (Ed.), *Morality and objectivity* (pp. 110–129). London: Routledge & Kegan Paul.

McGinn, C. (1999). Our duties to animals and the poor. In D. Jamieson (Ed.), *Singer and his critics* (pp. 150–161). Oxford: Blackwell.

McIntyre, A. (2004). Doctrine of double effect. In E. N. Zalta (Ed.), *The Stanford encyclopedia of philosophy*. Stanford, CA: The Metaphysics Research Lab, Center for the Study of Language and Information, Stanford University.

McNaughton, D. (1988). *Moral vision: An introduction to ethics*. New York: Basil Blackwell.

Mega, M., Cummings, J., Salloway, S., & Malloy, P. (1997). The limbic system: An anatomic, phylogenetic, and clinical perspective. *Journal of Neuropsychiatry and Clinical Neurosciences*, *9*, 315–330.

Meltzoff, A. N., & Moore, M. K. (1999). Persons and representation: Why infant imitation is important for theories of human development. In J. Nadel & G. Butterworth (Eds.), *Imitation in infancy* (pp. 9–35). Cambridge: Cambridge University Press.

Mendez, M. F., Anderson, E., & Shapira, J. S. (2005). An investigation of moral judgment in frontotemporal dementia. *Cognitive and Behavioral Neurology*, *18*, 193–197.

Mesulam, M. M. (Ed.). (2000). *Principles of behavioral and cognitive neurology* (2nd edn.). New York: Oxford University Press.

Mikhail, J. (2000). Rawls' linguistic analogy: A study of the "generative grammar" model of moral theory described by John Rawls in "A Theory of Justice." Doctoral dissertation, Cornell University, Ithaca, NY.

Mikhail, J. (2002). Aspects of the theory of moral cognition: Investigating intuitive knowledge of the prohibition of intentional battery and the principle of double effect. Georgetown University Law Center Public Law & Legal Theory Working Paper No. 762385. Retrieved from: http://ssrn.com/abstract=762385.

Mikhail, J. (2004). Islamic rationalism and the foundation of human rights. In A. Soeteman (Ed.), *Pluralism and the law: Proceedings of the 20th IVR World Congress* (Vol. 3: *Global Problems*, pp. 61–70). Stuttgart: Franz Steiner Verlag.

Mikhail, J. (2005). Moral heuristics or moral competence? Reflections on Sunstein. *Behavioral and Brain Sciences*, *28*, 557–558.

Mikhail, J. (In press). *Rawls' linguistic analogy*. New York: Cambridge University Press.

Mikhail, J., Sorrentino, C., & Spelke, E. (1998). Toward a universal moral grammar. In M. A. Gernsbacher & S. J. Derry (Eds.), *Proceedings, Twentieth Annual Conference of the Cognitive Science Society* (p. 1250). Mahwah, NJ: Lawrence Erlbaum Associates.

Milgram, S. (1963). Behavioral study of obedience. *Journal of Abnormal and Social Psychology*, *67*, 371–378.

Milgram, S. (1974). *Obedience to authority: An experimental view*. New York: Harper & Row.

Miller, E. K., & Cohen, J. D. (2001). An integrative theory of prefrontal cortex function. *Annual Review of Neuroscience, 24*, 167–202.

Milne, E., & Grafman, J. (2001). Ventromedial prefrontal cortex lesions in humans eliminate implicit gender stereotyping. *Journal of Neuroscience, 21*, RC150.

Mitchell, D., Colledge, E., Leonard, A., & Blair, R. J. R. (2002). Risky decisions and response reversal: Is there evidence of orbito-frontal cortex dysfunction in psychopathic individuals? *Neuropsychologia, 40*(12), 2013–2022.

Moll, J., de Oliveira-Souza, R., Bramati, I. E., & Grafman, J. (2002a). Functional networks in emotional moral and nonmoral social judgments. *NeuroImage, 16*, 696–703.

Moll, J., de Oliveira-Souza, R., & Eslinger, P. J. (2003). Morals and the human brain: A working model. *NeuroReport, 14*, 299–305.

Moll, J., de Oliveira-Souza, R., Eslinger, P. J., Bramati, I. E., Mourao-Miranda, J., Andreiuolo, P. A., & Pessoa, L. (2002b). The neural correlates of moral sensitivity: A functional magnetic resonance imaging investigation of basic and moral emotions. *Journal of Neuroscience, 22*, 2730–2736.

Moll, J., de Oliveira-Souza, R., Tovar-Moll, F., Ignacio, F. A., Bramati, I., Caparelli-Daquer, E. M., & Eslinger, P. J. (2005a). The moral affiliations of disgust: A functional MRI study. *Cognitive and Behavioral Neurology, 18*(1), 68–78.

Moll, J., Eslinger, P. J., & de Odeliveira-Souza, R. (2001). Frontopolar and anterior temporal cortex activation in a moral judgment task: Preliminary functional MRI results in normal subjects. *Arquivos de Neuro-Psiquiatria, 59*, 657–664.

Moll, J., Krueger, F., Zahn, R., Pardini, M., de Oliveira-Souza, R., & Grafman, J. (2006). Human fronto-mesolimbic networks guide decisions about charitable donations. *Proceedings of the National Academy of Sciences USA, 103*(42), 15623–15628.

Moll, J., Zahn, R., de Oliveira-Souza, R., Krueger, F., & Grafman, J. (2005b). The neural basis of human moral cognition. *Nature Reviews Neuroscience, 6*, 799–809.

Monteith, M. J., & Voils, C. I. (1998). Proneness to prejudiced responses: Toward understanding the authenticity of self-reported discrepancies. *Journal of Personality & Social Psychology, 75*, 901–916.

Moore, G. E. (1903). *Principia ethica*. Cambridge: Cambridge University Press.

Morgan, D., Grant, K. A., Gage, H. D., Mach, R. H., Kaplan, J. R., Prioleau, O., Nader, S. H., Buchheimer, N., Ehrenkaufer, R. L., & Nader, M. A. (2002). Social dominance in monkeys: Dopamine D2 receptors and cocaine self-administration. *Nature Neuroscience, 5*, 169–174.

Morris, J. S., Friston, K. J., & Dolan, R. J. (1998). Experience-dependent modulation of tonotopic neural responses in human auditory cortex. *Proceedings of the Royal Society of London* (Series B, *Biological Sciences*), *265*(1397), 649–657.

Nagel, T. (1970). *The possibility of altruism*. Oxford: Oxford University Press.

Nagel, T. (1986). *The view from nowhere*. New York: Oxford University Press.

Nagel, T. (1997). *The last word*. New York: Oxford University Press.

Narvaez, D., & Lapsley, D. K. (2005). The psychological foundations of everyday morality and moral expertise. In D. Lapsley & C. Power (Eds.), *Character psychology and character education* (pp. 140–165). Notre Dame, IN: University of Notre Dame Press.

Newman, J. P. (1998). Psychopathic behavior: An information-processing perspective. In D. J. Cooke, A. E. Forth, & R. D. Hare (Eds.), *Psychopathy: Theory, research, and implications for society* (pp. 81–104). Dordrecht, Netherlands: Kluwer Academic.

Newman, J. P., & Kosson, D. S. (1986). Passive avoidance learning in psychopathic and nonpsychopathic offenders. *Journal of Abnormal Psychology*, *95*(3), 257–263.

Newman, J. P., & Lorenz, A. R. (2002). Response modulation and emotion processing: Implications for psychopathy and other dysregulatory psychopathology. In R. J. Davidson, J. Scherer, & H. H. Goldsmith (Eds.), *Handbook of affective sciences* (pp. 1043–1067). New York: Oxford University Press.

Newman, J. P., & Schmitt, W. A. (1998). Passive avoidance in psychopathic offenders: A replication and extension. *Journal of Abnormal Psychology*, *107*(3), 527–532.

Newman, J. P., Kosson, D. S., & Patterson, C. M. (1992). Delay of gratification in psychopathic and nonpsychopathic offenders. *Journal of Abnormal Psychology*, *101*(4), 630–636.

Newman, J. P., Patterson, C. M., & Kosson, D. S. (1987). Response perseveration in psychopaths. *Journal of Abnormal Psychology*, *96*(2), 145–148.

Newman, J. P., Schmitt, W. A., & Voss, W. D. (1997). The impact of motivationally neutral cues on psychopathic individuals: Assessing the generality of the response modulation hypothesis. *Journal of Abnormal Psychology*, *106*(4), 563–575.

Nichols, S. (2002a). Is it irrational to be immoral? How psychopaths threaten moral rationalism. *Monist*, *85*(2), 285–304.

Nichols, S. (2002b). Norms with feeling: Towards a psychological account of moral judgment. *Cognition*, *84*(2), 221–236.

Nichols, S. (2004a). Folk concepts and intuitions: From philosophy to cognitive science. *Trends in Cognitive Sciences*, *8*(11), 514–518.

Nichols, S. (2004b). *Sentimental rules: On the natural foundations of moral judgment.* New York: Oxford University Press.

Nichols, S. (2006). Folk intuitions about free will. *Journal of Cognition and Culture,* 6(1/2), 57–86.

Nichols, S., & Folds-Bennett, T. (2003). Are children moral objectivists? Children's judgments about moral and response-dependent properties. *Cognition, 90*(2), B23–32.

Nichols, S., & Mallon, R. (2006). Moral dilemmas and moral rules. *Cognition, 100*(3), 530–542.

Nietzsche, F. (1974). *The gay science.* New York: Random House.

Nisbett, R. E., & Masuda, T. (2003). Culture and point of view. *Proceedings of the National Academy of Sciences of the United States of America, 100,* 11163–11170.

Nisbett, R. E., & Wilson, T. D. (1977). Telling more than we can know: Verbal reports on mental processes. *Psychological Review, 84,* 231–259.

Niznikiewicz, M. A., O'Donnell, B. F., Nestor, P. G., Smith, L., Law, S., Karapelou, M., Shenton, M. E., & McCarley, R. W. (1997). ERP assessment of visual and auditory language processing in schizophrenia. *Journal of Abnormal Psychology, 106*(1), 85–94.

Noronha, A., Eckard, M., & Warren, K. (1987). *In particular, the effect of chronic alcoholism is particularly pronounced on the P300 ERP.* Bethesda, MD: United States Public Health Service.

Nucci, L. (1986). Children's conceptions of morality, social conventions and religious prescription. In C. Harding (Ed.), *Moral dilemmas: Philosophical and psychological reconsiderations of the development of moral reasoning.* Chicago: Precedent Press.

Nucci, L. (2001). *Education in the moral domain.* Cambridge: Cambridge University Press.

Nucci, L., & Turiel, E. (1993). God's words, religious rules, and their relation to Jewish and Christian children's concept of morality. *Child Development, 64,* 1475–1491.

Nucci, L., Turiel, E., & Encarnacion-Gawrych, G. E. (1983). Social interactions and social concepts: Analysis of morality and convention in the Virgin Islands. *Journal of Cross-Cultural Psychology, 14,* 469–487.

O'Neill, O. (1996). *Towards justice and virtue.* Cambridge: Cambridge University Press.

O'Kane, A., Fawcett, D., & Blackburn, R. (1996). Psychopathy and moral reasoning: Comparison of two classifications. *Personality and Individual Differences, 20*(4), 505–514.

Okuda, J., Fujii, T., Ohtake, H., Tsukiura, T., Tanji, K., Suzuki, K., Kawashima, R., Fukuda, H., Itoh, M., & Yamadori, A. (2003). Thinking of the future and past: The roles of the frontal pole and the medial temporal lobes. *NeuroImage, 19,* 1369–1380.

Ozonoff, S., Pennington, B., & Rogers, S. (1990). Are there emotion perception deficits in young autistic children? *Journal of Child Psychology and Psychiatry, 31,* 343–363.

Paivio, A. (1986). *Mental representaions: A dual coding approach.* Oxford: Oxford University Press.

Paivio, A. (1991). Dual coding theory: Retrospect and current status. *Canadian Journal of Psychology, 45,* 255–287.

Paller, K. A., Kutas, M., Shimamura, A. P., & Squire, L. R. (1987). Brain responses to concrete and abstract words reflect processes that correlate with later performance on test of recall and stem-completion priming. In R. Johnson, J. Rohrbaugh, & R. Parasuraman (Eds.), *Current trends in brain potential research* (pp. 360–365). Amsterdam: Elsevier.

Paller, K. A., McCarthy, G., Roessler, E., & Allison, T. (1992). Potentials evoked in human and monkey medial temporal lobe during auditory and visual oddball paradigms. *Electroencephalography & Clinical Neurophysiology, 84*(3), 269–279.

Paller, K. A., Zola-Morgan, S., Squire, L. R., & Hillyard, S. A. (1988). P3-like brain waves in normal monkeys and in monkeys with medial temporal lesions. *Behavioral Neuroscience, 102*(5), 714–725.

Panksepp, J. (2005). On the neuro-evolutionary nature of social pain, support, and empathy. In Murat Aydede (Ed.), *Pain: New essays on its nature and the methodology of its study* (pp. 367–382). Cambridge, MA: MIT Press.

Parfit, D. (1984). *Reasons and persons.* Oxford: Oxford University Press.

Parfit, D. (2001). Rationality and reasons. In D. Egonsson, J. Josefsson, B. Petersson, & T. Rønnow-Rasmussen (Eds.), *Exploring practical philosophy: From actions to values* (pp. 17–39). Aldershot, UK: Ashgate.

Parfit, D. (Forthcoming). *Climbing the mountain.*

Patrick, C. J., Bradley, M. M., & Lang, P. J. (1993). Emotion in the criminal psychopath: Startle reflex modulation. *Journal of Abnormal Psychology, 102*(1), 82–92.

Paulus, M. P., Rogalsky, C., Simmons, A., Feinstein, J. S., & Stein, M. B. (2003). Increased activation in the right insula during risk-taking decision making is related to harm avoidance and neuroticism. *NeuroImage, 19*(4), 1439–1448.

Paus, T., Collins, D. L., Evans, A. C., Leonard, G., Pike, B., & Zijdenbos, A. (2001). Maturation of white matter in the human brain: A review of magnetic resonance studies. *Brain Research Bulletin, 54*(3), 255–266.

Paus, T., Zijdenbos, A., Worsley, K., Collins, D. L., Blumenthal, J., Giedd, J. N., Rapoport, J. L., & Evans, A. C. (1999). Structural maturation of neural pathways in children and adolescents: In vivo study. *Science, 283*, 1908–1911.

Peirce, C. S. (1905). What pragmaticism is. *Monist, 15*, 161–181.

Peterson, C. C., & Siegal, M. (2002). Mind reading and moral awareness in popular and rejected preschoolers. *British Journal of Developmental Psychology, 20*, 205–224.

Petrinovich, L., & O'Neill, P. (1996). Influence of wording and framing effects on moral intuitions. *Ethology and Sociobiology, 17*, 145–171.

Petrinovich, L., O'Neill, P., & Jorgensen, M. (1993). An empirical study of moral intuitions: Toward an evolutionary ethics. *Journal of Personality and Social Psychology, 64*(3), 467–478.

Pfefferbaum, A., Ford, J. M., White, P. M., & Mathalon, D. (1991). Event-related potentials in alcoholic men: P3 amplitude reflects family history but not alcohol consumption. *Alcoholism: Clinical and Experimental Research, 15*(5), 839–850.

Phan, K. L., Wager, T., Taylor, S. F., & Liberzon, I. (2002). Functional neuroanatomy of emotion: A meta-analysis of emotion activation studies in PET and fMRI. *NeuroImage, 16*, 331–348.

Phelps, E. (2005). Learning, trust, morality and the neural circuitry of reward. October 26, 2005 New York Academy of Sciences public program on "Getting the Goods: The Neural Basis of Decision Making."

Phillips, M. L., Young, A. W., Scott, S. K., Calder, A. J., Andrew, C., Giampietro, V., Williams, S. C., Bullmore, E. T., Brammer, M., & Gray, J. A. (1998). Neural responses to facial and vocal expressions of fear and disgust. *Proceedings of the Royal Society of London* (Series B, *Biological Sciences*), *265*(1408), 1809–1817.

Phillips, M. L., Young, A. W., Senior, C., Brammer, M., Andrew, C., Calder, A. J., Bullmore, E. T., Perrett, D. I., Rowland, D., Williams, S. C., Gray, J. A., & David, A. S. (1997). A specific neural substrate for perceiving facial expressions of disgust. *Nature, 389*(6650), 495–498.

Piaget, J. (1932). *The moral judgement of the child*. London: Routledge & Kegan Paul.

Piaget, J. (1952). *The origins of intelligence in children*. New York: International Universities Press.

Piaget, J. (1954). *The construction of reality in the child*. New York: Basic Books.

Pinel, P. (1801). *Abhand lung uber Geisteverirrunger oder Manie*. Wien, Austria: Carl Schanmberg.

Pinker, S. (2002). *The blank slate: The modern denial of human nature*. New York: Viking.

Plato (1987). *The republic*. New York: Penguin Classics. (Original work published approximately 360 B.C.E.)

Platt, M. L., & Glimcher, P. W. (1999). Neural correlates of decision variables in parietal cortex. *Nature, 400*, 233–238.

Plutchik, R. (1980). *Emotion: A psychoevolutionary synthesis*. New York: Harper & Row.

Preston, S. D., & de Waal, F. B. M. (2002). Empathy: Its ultimate and proximate bases. *Behavioral and Brain Sciences, 25*, 1–72.

Price, C. J., & Friston, K. J. (1999). Scanning patients with tasks they can perform. *Human Brain Mapping, 8*(2–3), 102–108.

Price, C. J., Mummery, C. J., Moore, C. J., Frakowiak, R. S., & Friston, K. J. (1999). Delineating necessary and sufficient neural systems with functional imaging studies of neuropsychological patients. *Journal of Cognitive Neuroscience, 11*(4), 371–382.

Price, R. (1969). A review of the principal questions in morals. In D. D. Raphael (Ed.), *The British moralists*. New York: Oxford University Press. (Original work published 1787)

Price, R. (1974). *Review of the principal questions in morals* (D. D. Raphael, Ed.). Oxford: Clarendon Press. (Original work published 1758)

Prichard, H. J. (2002). Does moral philosophy rest on a mistake? In J. McAdam (Ed.), *Moral writings*. Oxford: Oxford University Press. (Original work published 1912)

Pridham, K., Saxe, R., & Limbo, R. (2004). Feeding issues for mothers of very low-birth-weight, premature infants through the first year. *Journal of Perinatology & Neonatal Nursing, 18*, 161–169.

Prinz, J. (2007). *The emotional construction of morals*. Oxford: Oxford University Press.

Prior, M., Dahlstrom, B., & Squires, T. (1990). Autistic children's knowledge of thinking and feeling states in other people. *Journal of Autism and Developmental Disorders, 31*, 587–602.

Pujol, J., Lopez, A., Deus, J., Cardoner, N., Vallejo, J., Capdevila, A., & Paus, T. (2002). Anatomical variability of the anterior cingulate gyrus and basic dimensions of human personality. *NeuroImage, 15*(4), 847–855.

Putnam, H. (1975). The meaning of "meaning." In K. Gunderson (Ed.), *Language, mind, and knowledge* (pp. 131–193). Minneapolis: University of Minnesota Press.

Raine, A. (1993). *The psychopathology of crime.* San Diego: Academic Press.

Raine, A., & Venables, P. H. (1988). Enhanced P3 evoked potentials and longer P3 recovery times in psychopaths. *Psychophysiology, 25,* 30–38.

Raine, A., Buchsbaum, M. S., Stanley, J., Lottenberg, S., Abel, L., & Stoddard, J. (1994). Selective reductions in prefrontal glucose metabolism in murderers. *Biological Psychiatry, 36,* 365–373.

Raine, A., Ishikawa, S. S., Arce, E., Lencz, T., Knuth, K. H., Bihrle, S., LaCasse, L., & Colletti, P. (2004). Hippocampal structural asymmetry in unsuccessful psychopaths. *Biological Psychiatry, 55*(2), 185–191.

Raine, A., O'Brien, M., Smiley, N., Scerbo, A., & Chan, C. J. (1990). Reduced lateralization in verbal dichotic listening in adolescent psychopaths. *Journal of Abnormal Psychology, 99*(3), 272–277.

Ramnani, N., & Owen, A. M. (2004). Anterior prefrontal cortex: Insights into function from anatomy and neuroimaging. *Nature Reviews Neuroscience, 5,* 184–194.

Rapcsak, S. Z., Galper, S. R., Comer, J. F., Reminger, S. L., Nielsen, L., Kaszniak, A. W., Verfaellie, M., Laguna, J. F., Labiner, D. M., & Cohen, R. A. (2000). Fear recognition deficits after focal brain damage: A cautionary note. *Neurology, 54*(3), 575–581.

Rawls, J. (1971). *A theory of justice.* Cambridge, MA: Harvard University Press.

Rawls, J. (1980). Kantian constructivism in moral theory. *Journal of Philosophy, 77,* 515–572. [Reprinted in S. Freeman (Ed.), *John Rawls: Collected papers.* Cambridge, MA: Harvard University Press, 1999.]

Rawls, J. (1995). Construction and objectivity. In M. Smith (Ed.), *Metaethics.* Aldershot, UK: Dartmouth.

Raz, J. (1975). *Practical reason and practical norms.* London: Hutchinson.

Raz, J. (1999). *Engaging reason: On the theory of value and action.* Oxford: Oxford University Press.

Richell, R. A., Mitchell, D. G. V., Newman, C., Leonard, A., Baron-Cohen, S., & Blair, R. J. R. (2003). Theory of mind and psychopathy: Can psychopathic individuals read the "language of the eyes"? *Neuropsychologia, 41*(5), 523–526.

Richerson, P. J., & Boyd, R. (2005). *Not by genes alone: How culture transformed human evolution*. Chicago: University of Chicago Press.

Rilling, J., Gutman, D., Zeh, T., Pagnoni, G., Berns, G., & Kilts, C. (2002). A neural basis for social cooperation. *Neuron, 35*, 395–405.

Robins, L. N. (1998). The intimate connection between antisocial personality and substance abuse. *Social Psychiatry and Psychiatric Epidemiology, 33*(8), 393–399.

Robinson, J. L., & Acevedo, M. C. (2001). Infant reactivity and reliance on mother during emotion challenges: Prediction of cognition and language skills in a low-income sample. *Child Development, 72*, 402–415.

Rogan, M. T., & LeDoux, J. E. (1996). Emotion: Systems, cells, synaptic plasticity. *Cell, 85*, 469–475.

Rogers, S. J., Ozonoff, S., & Maslin-Cole, C. (1991). A comparative study of attachment behavior in young children with autism and other psychiatric disorders. *Journal of the American Academy of Child and Adolescent Psychiatry, 26*, 483–488.

Rolls, E. T., Hornak, J., Wade, D., & McGrath, J. (1994). Emotion-related learning in patients with social and emotional changes associated with frontal lobe damage. *Journal of Neurology, Neurosurgery & Psychiatry, 57*, 1518–1524.

Rolls, E. T., Kringelbach, M. L., & de Araujo, I. E. (2003). Different representations of pleasant and unpleasant odours in the human brain. *European Journal of Neuroscience, 18*, 695–703.

Roskies, A. (2003). Are ethical judgments intrinsically motivational? Lessons from "acquired sociopathy." *Philosophical Psychology, 16*(1), 51–66.

Roskies, A. (2005). A case study in neuroethics: The nature of moral judgment. In J. Illes (Ed.), *Neuroethics: Defining the issues in research, practice, and policy*. Oxford: Oxford University Press.

Ross, W. D. (1930). *The right and the good*. Oxford: Oxford University Press.

Rothbart, M. K., Derryberry, D., & Posner, M. I. (1994). A psychobiological approach to the development of temperament. In J. E. Bates & T. D. Wachs (Eds.), *Temperament: Individual differences at the interface of biology and behavior* (pp. 83–116). Washington, DC: American Psychological Association.

Rovee-Collier, C., & Hayne, H. (1987). Reactivation of infant memory: Implications for cognitive development. *Advances in Child Development and Behavior, 20*, 185–238.

Rozin, P., Lowery, L., Imada, S., & Haidt, J. (1999). The CAD triad hypothesis: A mapping between three moral emotions (contempt, anger, disgust) and three moral codes (community, autonomy, divinity). *Journal of Personality and Social Psychology, 76*, 574–586.

Rutherford, M. J., Alterman, A. I., & Cacciola, J. S. (1995). Reliability and validity of the revised psychopathy checklist in opiate- and cocaine-addicted women. *Issues in Criminological & Legal Psychology, 24*, 136–141.

Rutherford, M. J., Alterman, A. I., & Cacciola, J. S. (2000). Psychopathy and substance abuse: A bad mix. In C. G. Gacono (Ed.), *The clinical and forensic assessment of psychopathy: A practitioner's guide* (pp. 351–368). Mahwah, NJ: Lawrence Erlbaum Associates.

Rutherford, M. J., Alterman, A. I., Cacciola, J. S., & McKay, J. R. (1997). Validity of the psychopathy checklist-revised in male methadone patients. *Drug & Alcohol Dependence, 44*(2–3), 143–149.

Rutherford, M. J., Cacciola, J. S., & Alterman, A. I. (1999). Antisocial personality disorder and psychopathy in cocaine-dependent women. *American Journal of Psychiatry, 156*(6), 849–856.

Sally, D. & Hill, E. (2006). The development of interpersonal strategy: Autism, theory-of-mind, cooperation and fairness. *Journal of Economic Psychology, 27*(1), 73–97.

Sanfey, A. G., Rilling, J. K., Aronson, J. A., Nystrom, L. E., & Cohen, J. D. (2003). The neural basis of economic decision-making in the ultimatum game. *Science, 300*, 1755–1758.

Saver, J. L., & Damasio, A. R. (1991). Preserved access and processing of social knowledge in a patient with acquired sociopathy due to ventromedial frontal damage. *Neuropsychologia, 29*(12), 1241–1249.

Savin-Williams, R. C., & Berndt, T. J. (1990). Friendship and peer relations. In S. S. Feldman & G. R. Elliot (Eds.), *At the threshold: The developing adolescent* (pp. 277–307). Cambridge, MA: Harvard University Press.

Saxe, R. (2004). Light-curing times. *Journal of the American Dental Association, 135*, 18 (author reply, 20).

Saxe, R., & Kanwisher, N. (2003). People thinking about thinking people. The role of the temporo-parietal junction in "theory of mind." *NeuroImage, 19*, 1835–1842.

Saxe, R., Carey, S., & Kanwisher, N. (2004a). Understanding other minds: Linking developmental psychology and functional neuroimaging. *Annual Review of Psychology, 55*, 87–124.

Saxe, R., Xiao, D. K., Kovacs, G., Perrett, D. I., & Kanwisher, N. (2004b). A region of right posterior superior temporal sulcus responds to observed intentional actions. *Neuropsychologia, 42*, 1435–1446.

Scanlon, T. M. (1998). *What we owe each other.* Cambridge, MA: Harvard University Press.

Scanlon, T. M. (2002). Replies. *Social Theory and Practice, 28*(2), 337–358.

Scanlon, T. M. (2007). Structural irrationality. In M. Smith, F. Jackson, R. Goodin, & G. Brennan (Eds.), *Common minds.* New York: Oxford University Press.

Schaich Borg, J., Hynes, C., Van Horn, J., Grafton, S., & Sinnott-Armstrong, W. (2006). Consequences, action, and intention as factors in moral judgments: An fMRI investigation. *Journal of Cognitive Neuroscience, 18,* 803–817.

Schelling, T. C. (1968). The life you save may be your own. In S. B. Chase (Ed.), *Problems in public expenditure analysis* (pp. 127–176). Washington, DC: Brookings Institution.

Schmitt, W. A., Brinkley, C. A., & Newman, J. P. (1999). Testing Damasio's somatic marker hypothesis with psychopathic individuals: Risk takers or risk averse? *Journal of Abnormal Psychology, 108*(3), 538–543.

Schnall, S., Haidt, J., & Clore, G. (2004). Irrelevant disgust makes moral judgment more severe, for those who listen to their bodies. Unpublished manuscript.

Schnider, A. (2001). Spontaneous confabulation, reality monitoring, and the limbic system—a review. *Brain Research Reviews, 36*(2–3), 150–160.

Schrum, C. L., & Salekin, R. T. (2006). Psychopathy in adolescent female offenders: An item response theory analysis of the psychopathy checklist: Youth version. *Behavioral Sciences & the Law, 24*(1), 39–63.

Schueler, G. F. (1995). *Desire: Its role in practical reason and the explanation of action.* Cambridge, MA: MIT Press.

Schulkin, J. (2004). *Bodily sensibility: Intelligent action.* New York: Oxford University Press.

Schwanenflugel, P. J., & Stowe, R. W. (1989). Context availability and the processing of abstract and concrete words in sentences. *Reading Research Quarterly, 24*(1), 114–126.

Schwanenflugel, P. J., Harnishfeger, K. K., & Stowe, R. W. (1988). Context availability and lexical decisions for abstract and concrete words. *Journal of Memory & Language, 27*(5), 499–520.

Scott, E. S. (2001). Criminal responsibility in adolescence: Lessons from developmental psychology. In T. Grisso & R. Schwartz (Eds.), *Youth on trial: A developmental perspective on juvenile justice* (pp. 291–324). Chicago: University of Chicago Press.

Scott, E. S., & Steinburg, L. (2003). Blaming youth. *Texas Law Review, 81*(3), 799–841.

Scott, S. K., Young, A. W., Calder, A. J., Hellawell, D. J., Aggleton, J. P., & Johnson, M. (1997). Impaired auditory recognition of fear and anger following bilateral amygdala lesions. *Nature, 385*(6613), 254–257.

Seger, C. A., Stone, M., & Keenan, J. P. (2004). Cortical activations during judgments about the self and another person. *Neuropsychologia, 42,* 1168–1177.

Selman, R. L. (1980). *The growth of interpersonal understanding: Developmental and clinical analyses.* New York: Academic Press.

Semin, G. R., & Manstead, A. S. R. (1982). The social implications of embarrassment displays and restitution behaviour. *European Journal of Social Psychology, 12,* 367–377.

Sereny, G. (1998). *Cries unheard.* New York: Holt.

Shamay-Tsoory, S. G., Tomer, R., Yaniv, S., & Aharon-Peretz, J. (2002). Empathy deficits in Asperger syndrome: A cognitive profile. *Neurocase, 8*(3), 245–252.

Shapiro, T., Sherman, M., Calamari, G., & Koch, D. (1987). Attachment in autism and other developmental disorders. *Journal of the American Academy of Child and Adolescent Psychiatry, 26,* 606–616.

Shin, L. M., Dougherty, D. D., Orr, S. P., Pitman, R. K., Lasko, M., Macklin, M., Alpert, N. M., Fischman, A. J., & Rauch, S. L. (2000). Activation of anterior paralimbic structures during guilt-related script-driven imagery. *Biological Psychiatry, 48,* 43–50.

Shweder, R. A., & Haidt, J. (1993). The future of moral psychology: Truth, intuition and the pluralist way. *Psychological Science, 4,* 360–365.

Shweder, R. A., Much, N. C., Mahapatra, M., & Park, L. (1997). The "big three" of morality (autonomy, community and divinity), and the "big three" explanations of suffering. In A. Brandt & P. Rozin (Eds.), *Morality and health* (pp. 119–169). New York: Routledge.

Sidgwick, H. (1907). *Methods of ethics* (7th edn.). London: Macmillan. (Original work published 1874)

Sigman, M., & Mundy, P. (1989). Social attachments in autistic children. *Journal of the American Academy of Child and Adolescent Psychiatry, 28,* 74–81.

Sigman, M., & Ungerer, J. A. (1984). Attachment behaviors in autistic children. *Journal of Autism and Developmental Disorders, 14,* 231–244.

Sigman, M., Kasari, C., Kwon, J., & Yirmiya, N. (1992). Responses to the negative emotions of others by autistic, mentally retarded, and normal children. *Child Development, 63,* 796–807.

Sinclair, J. (1992). Bridging the gaps: An inside-out view of autism. In E. Schopler & G. B. Mesibov (Eds.), *High-functioning individuals with autism* (pp. 294–302). New York: Plenum.

Singer, P. (1972). Famine, affluence and morality. *Philosophy & Public Affairs, 1*, 229–243.

Singer, P. (1995). *How are we to live?: Ethics in an age of self-interest.* Amherst, NY: Prometheus Books.

Singer, T., & Frith, C. (2005). The painful side of empathy. *Nature Neuroscience, 8*(7), 845–846.

Singer, T., Kiebel, S. J., Winston, J. S., Dolan, R. J., & Frith, C. D. (2004). Brain responses to the acquired moral status of faces. *Neuron, 41*, 653–662.

Sinnott-Armstrong, W. (2003). Consequentialism. In E. N. Zalta (Ed.), *The Stanford encyclopedia of philosophy*. Stanford, CA: The Metaphysics Research Lab, Center for the Study of Language and Information, Stanford University.

Sinnott-Armstrong, W. (2006). Moral intuitionism meets empirical psychology. In T. Horgan & M. Timmons (Eds.), *Metaethics after Moore* (pp. 339–365). New York: Oxford University Press.

Sirigu, A., Daprati, E., Ciancia, S., Giraux, P., Nighoghossian, N., Posada, A., & Haggard, P. (2004). Altered awareness of voluntary action after damage to the parietal cortex. *Nature Neuroscience, 7*, 80–84.

Sirigu, A., Daprati, E., Pradat-Diehl, P., Franck, N., & Jeannerod, M. (1999). Perception of self-generated movement following left parietal lesion. *Brain, 122*(Pt. 10), 1867–1874.

Slaughter, V., Stone, V. E., & Reed, C. (2004). Perception of faces and bodies. *Current Directions in Psychological Science, 13*, 219–223.

Small, D. A., & Loewenstein, G. (2003). Helping a victim or helping the victim. *Journal of Risk and Uncertainty, 26*, 5–16.

Small, D. A., & Loewenstein, G. (2005). The devil you know: The effects of identifiability on punitiveness. *Journal of Behavioral Decision Making, 18*, 311–318.

Smetana, J. G. (1981). Preschool children's conceptions of moral and social rules. *Child Development, 52*, 1333–1336.

Smetana, J. G. (1985). Preschool children's conceptions of transgressions: Effects of varying moral and conventional domain-related attributes. *Developmental Psychology, 21*, 18–29.

Smetana, J. G. (1993). Understanding of social rules. In M. Bennett (Ed.), *Development of social cognition: The child as psychologist* (pp. 111–141). New York: Guilford.

Smetana, J. G. (2006). Social-cognitive domain theory. In M. Killen & J. Smetana (Eds.), *Handbook of moral development* (pp. 119–154). Mahwah, NJ: Lawrence Erlbaum Associates.

Smetana, J. G., & Braeges, J. L. (1990). The development of toddlers' moral and conventional judgments. *Merrill-Palmer Quarterly, 36,* 329–346.

Smetana, J. G., Schlagman, N., & Adams, P. W. (1993). Preschool children's judgments about hypothetical and actual transgressions. *Child Development, 64*(1), 202–214.

Smith, A. (1976). *The theory of moral sentiments.* Oxford: Oxford University Press. (Original work published 1759)

Smith, M. (1993). Realism. In P. Singer (Ed.), *A companion to ethics* (pp. 399–410). Cambridge, MA: Blackwell.

Smith, M. (1994). *The moral problem.* Oxford: Basil Blackwell.

Smith, M. (1997). In defence of *The moral problem*: A reply to Brink, Copp and Sayre-McCord. *Ethics, 108,* 84–119.

Smith, S. S., & Newman, J. P. (1990). Alcohol and drug abuse-dependence disorders in psychopathic and nonpsychopathic criminal offenders. *Journal of Abnormal Psychology, 99*(4), 430–439.

Sobel, D. (2005). Pain for objectivists: The case of matters of mere taste. *Ethical Theory and Moral Practice, 8,* 437–457.

Sober, E., & Wilson, D. S. (1998). *Unto others: The evolution and psychology of unselfish behavior.* Cambridge, MA: Harvard University Press.

Soderstrom, H., Hultin, L., Tullberg, M., Wikkelso, C., Ekholm, S., & Forsman, A. (2002). Reduced frontotemporal perfusion in psychopathic personality. *Psychiatry Research: Neuroimaging, 114*(2), 81–94.

Sokolov, E. N. (1963). *Perception and the conditioned reflex.* New York: Macmillan.

Soltani, M., & Knight, R. T. (2000). Neural origins of the P300. *Critical Reviews in Neurobiology, 14*(3–4), 199–224.

Song, M., Smetana, J. G., & Kim, S. Y. (1987). Korean children's conception of moral and conventional transgression. *Developmental Psychology, 23,* 577–582.

Sowell, E. R., Thompson, P. M., Holmes, C. J., Batth, R., Jernigan, T. L., & Toga, A. W. (1999). Localizing age-related changes in brain structure between childhood and adolescence using statistical parametric mapping. *NeuroImage, 9*(6, Pt. 1), 587–597.

Spear, L. P. (2000). Neurobehavioral changes in adolescence. *Current Directions in Psychological Science, 9,* 111–114.

Steinburg, L., & Cauffman, E. (1996). Maturity of judgment in adolescence: Psychosocial factors in adolescent decision making. *Law and Human Behavior, 20*(3), 249–272.

Steinberg, L., & Scott, E. S. (2003). Less guilty by reason of adolescence: Developmental immaturity, diminished responsiblity, and the juvenile death penalty. *American Psychologist, 58*(12), 1009–1018.

Steinburg, L., & Silverberg, S. (1986). The vicissitudes of autonomy in early adolescence. *Child Development, 57*, 841–851.

Stevens, A. A., Skudlarski, P., Gatenby, J. C., & Gore, J. C. (2000). Event-related fMRI of auditory and visual oddball tasks. *Magnetic Resonance Imaging, 18*(5), 495–502.

Stevens, D., Charman, T., & Blair, R. J. (2001). Recognition of emotion in facial expressions and vocal tones in children with psychopathic tendencies. *Journal of Genetic Psychology, 162*(2), 201–211.

Stone, V. E., Cosmides, L., Tooby, J., Kroll, N., & Knight, R. T. (2002). Selective impairment of reasoning about social exchange in a patient with bilateral limbic system damage. *Proceedings of the National Academy of Sciences of the United States of America, 99*, 11531–11536.

Strange, B. A., Henson, R. N., Friston, K. J., & Dolan, R. J. (2000). Brain mechanisms for detecting perceptual, semantic, and emotional deviance. *NeuroImage, 12*(4), 425–433.

Strawson, P. (1974). Freedom and resentment. In Strawson, *Freedom and resentment and other essays* (pp. 1–25). London: Methuen.

Street, S. (2006). A Darwinian Dilemma for Realist Theories of Value. *Philosophical Studies 127*, 109–166.

Stuss, D. T. (1991). Self, awareness, and the frontal lobes: A neuropsychological perspective. In J. Strauss & G. R. Goethals (Eds.), *The self: Interdisciplinary approaches* (pp. 255–278). New York: Springer-Verlag.

Stuss, D. T., Alexander, M. P., Lieberman, A., & Levine, H. (1978). An extraordinary form of confabulation. *Neurology, 28*, 1166–1172.

Stuss, D. T., Benson, D. F., & Kaplan, E. F. (1983). The involvement of orbitofrontal cerebrum in cognitive tasks. *Neuropsychologia, 21*, 235–248.

Sunstein, C. (2005). Moral heuristics. *Behavioral and Brain Sciences, 28*, 531–573.

Sutton, S. K., Vitale, J. E., & Newman, J. P. (2002). Emotion among women with psychopathy during picture perception. *Journal of Abnormal Psychology, 111*(4), 610–619.

Svavarsdottir, S. (1999). Moral cognitivism and motivation. *Philosophical Review, 108*(2), 161–219.

Swick, D., & Jovanovic, J. (2002). Anterior cingulate cortex and the Stroop task: Neuropsychological evidence for topographic specificity. *Neuropsychologia, 40*(8), 1240–1253.

Swick, D., & Turken, A. U. (2002). Dissociation between conflict detection and error monitoring in the human anterior cingulate cortex. *Proceedings of the National Academy of Sciences of the United States of America, 99*(25), 16354–16359.

Takahashi, H., Yahata, N., Koeda, M., Matsuda, T., Asai, K., & Okubo, Y. (2004). Brain activation associated with evaluative processes of guilt and embarrassment: An fMRI study. *NeuroImage, 23*, 967–974.

Tanaka, S. C., Doya, K., Okada, G., Ueda, K., Okamoto, Y., & Yamawaki, S. (2004). Prediction of immediate and future rewards differentially recruits cortico-basal ganglia loops. *Nature Neuroscience, 7*, 887–893.

Tangney, J. P. (2000a). Guilt. In A. E. Kazdin (Ed.), *Encyclopedia of psychology*. New York: Oxford University Press.

Tangney, J. P. (2000b). Shame. In A. E. Kazdin (Ed.), *Encyclopedia of psychology*. New York: Oxford University Press.

Tangney, J. P. (2002). Self-conscious emotions: The self as a moral guide. In A. Tesser, D. A. Stapel, & J. V. Wood (Eds.), *Self and motivation: Emerging psychological perspectives* (pp. 97–117). Washington, DC: American Psychological Association.

Tangney, J. P., & Dearing, R. L. (2002). *Shame and guilt*. New York: Guilford.

Tangney, J. P., & Fischer, K. W. (Eds.). (1995). *Self-conscious emotions: The psychology of shame, guilt, embarrassment and pride*. New York: Guilford.

Tekin, S., & Cummings, J. L. (2002). Frontal-subcortical neuronal circuits and clinical neuropsychiatry: An update. *Journal of Psychosomatic Research, 53*(2), 647–654.

Ten, C. L. (1987). *Crime, guilt, and punishment*. Oxford, Clarendon Press.

Thompson, R. A. (1998). Early sociopersonality development. In W. Damon & N. Eisenberg (Eds.), *Handbook of child psychology*. Vol. 3: *Social, emotional and personality development* (pp. 25–104). New York: Wiley.

Thomson, J. J. (1976). Killing, letting die, and the trolley problem. *Monist, 59*, 204–217.

Thomson, J. J. (1986). *Rights, restitution, and risk: Essays in moral theory*, (Ed.) W. Parent. Cambridge, Mass.: Harvard University Press.

Thomson, J. J. (1990). *The realm of rights*. Cambridge, MA: Harvard University Press.

Timmons, M. (1999). *Morality without foundations*. Oxford: Oxford University Press.

Tollhurst, W. (1998). Seemings. *American Philosophical Quarterly, 35*, 293–302.

Tomb, I., Hauser, M., Deldin, P. & Caramazza, A. (2002). Do somatic markers mediate decisions on the gambling task? *Nature Neuroscience, 5*(11), 1103–1104.

Tranel, D. (1994). Acquired sociopathy: The development of sociopathic behavior following focal brain damage. *Progress in Experimental Personality and Psychopathology Research,* 285–311.

Trevethan, S. D., & Walker, L. J. (1989). Hypothetical versus real-life moral reasoning among psychopathic and delinquent youth. *Development and Psychopathology, 1,* 91–103.

Trigg, R. (1970). *Pain and emotion.* Oxford: Oxford University Press.

Trivers, R. L. (1971). The evolution of reciprocal altruism. *Quarterly Review of Biology, 46,* 35–57.

Tuck, R. (1979). *Natural rights theories: Their origin and development.* Cambridge: Cambridge University Press.

Turiel, E. (1979). Distinct conceptual and developmental domains: Social convention and morality. In H. Howe & C. Keasey (Eds.), *Nebraska Symposium on Motivation, 1977: Social Cognitive Development, 25* (pp. 77–116). Lincoln: University of Nebraska Press.

Turiel, E. (1983). *The development of social knowledge: Morality and convention.* Cambridge: Cambridge University Press.

Turiel, E. (2002). *Culture and morality.* Cambridge: Cambridge University Press.

Turiel, E. (2006). Thought, emotions and social interactional processes in moral development. In M. Killen & J. Smetana (Eds.), *Handbook of moral development* (pp. 7–30). Mahwah, NJ: Lawrence Erlbaum Associates.

Turiel, E., Killen, M., & Helwig, C. (1987). Morality: Its structure, functions and vagaries. In A. Brandt & P. Rozin (Eds.), *Morality and health* (pp. 119–169). Chicago: University of Chicago Press; and in J. Kagan, and S. Lamb (Eds.), *The emergence of morality in young children* (pp. 155–243). Chicago: University of Chicago Press.

Turken, A. U., & Swick, D. (1999). Response selection in the human anterior cingulate cortex. *Nature Neuroscience, 2*(10), 920–924.

Unger, P. K. (1996). *Living high and letting die: Our illusion of innocence.* New York: Oxford University Press.

Valdesolo, P., & DeSteno, D. (2006). Manipulations of emotional context shape moral judgment. *Psychological Science, 17*(6), 476–477.

Vartanian, L. R. (2000). Revisiting the imaginary audience and personal fable constructs of adolescent egocentrism: A conceptual review. *Adolescence, 35*(140), 639–662.

Vecera, S. P., & Rizzo, M. (2004). What are you looking at? Impaired "social attention" following frontal-lobe damage. *Neuropsychologia, 42,* 1657–1665.

Veit, R., Flor, H., Erb, M., Hermann, C., Lotze, M., Grodd, W., & Birbaumer, N. (2002). Brain circuits involved in emotional learning in antisocial behavior and social phobia in humans. *Neuroscience Letters, 328*(3), 233–236.

Velleman, J. D. (1989). *Practical reflection.* Princeton, NJ: Princeton University Press.

Vitacco, M. J., Neumann, C. S., & Jackson, R. L. (2005). Testing a four-factor model of psychopathy and its association with ethnicity, gender, intelligence, and violence. *Journal of Consulting and Clinical Psychology, 73*(3), 466–476.

Vogt, B. A., Finch, D. M., & Olson, C. R. (1992). Functional heterogeneity in cingulate cortex: The anterior executive and posterior evaluative regions. *Cerebral Cortex, 2*(6), 435–443.

Volavka, J. (1999). The neurobiology of violence: An update. *Journal of Neuropsychiatry and Clinical Neurosciences, 11,* 307–314.

Waddington, C. H. (1975), *The evolution of an evolutionist.* Ithaca, NY: Cornell University Press; Edinburgh: Edinburgh University Press.

Waldmann, M., & Dieterich, J. (2007). Throwing a bomb on a person versus throwing a person on a bomb: Intervention myopia in moral intuitions. *Psychological Science, 18*(3), 247–253.

Walker, L. J., & Taylor, J. H. (1991). Family interactions and the development of moral reasoning. *Child Development, 62,* 264–283.

Walker, L. J., Hennig, K. H., & Krettenauer, T. (2000). Parent and peer contexts for children's moral reasoning development. *Child Development, 71*(4), 1033–1048.

Wallace, R. J. (1999). Moral cognitivism and motivation. *Philosophical Review, 108*(2), 161–219.

Watson, J. (1973). Investigation into deindividuation using a cross-cultural survey technique. *Journal of Personality and Social Psychology, 25,* 342–345.

Weiner, B., Graham, S., & Reyna, C. (1997). An attributional examination of retributive versus utilitarian philosophies of punishment. *Social Justice Research, 10,* 431–452.

Welkowitz, J., Ewen, R. B., & Cohen, J. (1991). *Introductory statistics for the behavioral sciences* (4th edn.). Philadelphia: Harcourt, Brace, Jovanovich College Publishers.

Wheatley, T., & Haidt, J. (2005). Hypnotically induced disgust makes moral judgments more severe. *Psychological Science*, *16*(10), 780–784.

Widiger, T. A., Cadoret, R., Hare, R. D., Robins, L., Rutherford, M., Zanarini, M., Alterman, A., Apple, M., Corbitt, E., Forth, A., Hart, S. D., Kultermann, J., Woody, G., & Frances, A. (1996). DSM–IV antisocial personality disorder field trial. *Journal of Abnormal Psychology*, *105*(1), 3–16.

Widom, C. S. (1977). A methodology for studying noninstitutionalized psychopaths. *Journal of Consulting & Clinical Psychology*, *45*(4), 674–683.

Wiggins, D. (1987). *Needs, values, and truth: Essays in the philosophy of value*. Oxford: Blackwell.

Wilkinson D., & Halligan, P. (2004). The relevance of behavioural measures for functional-imaging studies of cognition. *Nature Reviews Neuroscience*, *5*, 67–73.

Willey, L. H. (1999). *Pretending to be normal: Living with Asperger's syndrome*. London: Jessica Kingsley.

Williams, B. (1981). Internal and external reasons. Reprinted in B. Williams, *Moral Luck: Philosophical Papers 1973–1980* (pp. 20–39). Cambridge: Cambridge University Press.

Williams, B. (1995). Internal reasons and the obscurity of blame. Reprinted in B. Williams, *Making sense of humanity and other philosophical papers 1982–1993* (pp. 79–89). Cambridge: Cambridge University Press.

Williams, E. (2004). Who really needs a "theory" of mind? *Theory & Psychology*, *14*(5), 704–724.

Williamson, S., Harpur, T. J., & Hare, R. D. (1991). Abnormal processing of affective words by psychopaths. *Psychophysiology*, *28*(3), 260–273.

Wilson, T. D. (2002). *Strangers to ourselves: Discovering the adaptive unconscious*. Cambridge, MA: Harvard University Press.

Wittgenstein, L. (1958). *Philosophical investigations* (3rd edn., G. E. M. Anscombe, Trans.). New York: Macmillan.

Wood, J. N., & Grafman, J. (2003). Human prefrontal cortex: Processing and representational perspectives. *Nature Reviews Neuroscience*, *4*, 139–147.

Wood, J. N., Romero, S. G., Makale, M., & Grafman, J. (2003). Category-specific representations of social and nonsocial knowledge in the human prefrontal cortex. *Journal of Cognitive Neuroscience*, *15*, 236–248.

Woodworth, M., & Porter, S. (2002). In cold blood: Characteristics of criminal homicides as a function of psychopathy. *Journal of Abnormal Psychology*, *111*(3), 436–445.

Wrangham, R., & Peterson, D. (1996). *Demonic males: Apes and the origins of human violence*. Boston: Houghton Mifflin.

Wright, R. (1994). *The moral animal: Evolutionary psychology and everyday life*. New York: Pantheon.

Yamaguchi, S., & Knight, R. T. (1993). Association cortex contributions to the human P3. In W. Haschke, A. I. Roitbak, & E.-J. Speckmann (Eds.), *Slow potential changes in the brain* (pp. 71–84). Boston: Birkhauser.

Yang, Y., Raine, A., Lencz, T., Bihrle, S., LaCasse, L., & Colletti, P. (2005). Volume reduction in prefrontal gray matter in unsuccessful criminal psychopaths. *Biological Psychiatry, 57*, 1103–1108.

Yirmiya, N., Sigman, M. D., Kasari, C., & Mundy, P. (1992). Empathy and cognition in high-functioning children with autism. *Child Development, 63*(1), 150–160.

Young, L. J., & Wang, Z. (2004). The neurobiology of pair bonding. *Nature Neuroscience, 7*, 1048–1054 .

Young, L., Cushman, F., Adolphs, R., Tranel, D., & Hauser, M. (2006). Does emotion mediate the relationship between an action's moral status and its intentional status? Neuropsychological evidence. *Journal of Cognition and Culture, 6*(1–2), 265–278.

Young, S. N., & Leyton, M. (2002). The role of serotonin in human mood and social interaction. Insight from altered tryptophan levels. *Pharmacology Biochemistry and Behavior, 71*, 857–865.

Zak, P. J., Kurzban, R., & Matzner, W. T. (2005). Oxytocin is associated with human trustworthiness. *Hormonal Behavior, 48*, 522–527.

Zelazo, P., Helwig, C., & Lau, A. (1996). Intention, act, and outcome in behavioral prediction and moral judgment. *Child Development, 67*, 2478–2492.

Zimbardo, P. (2006), On rethinking the psychology of tyranny: The BBC prison study. *British Journal of Social Psychology, 45*(1), 47–57.

Zimbardo, P., Maslach, C., & Haney, C. (2000). Reflections on the Stanford prison experiment: Genesis, transformations, consequences. In T. Blass (Ed.), *Obedience to authority: Current perspectives on the Milgram paradigm* (pp. 193–237). Mahwah, NJ: Lawrence Erlbaum Associates.

Contributors

Abigail A. Baird
Vassar College

William D. Casebeer
Air Force Academy

Cordelia Fine
University of Melbourne and
Australian National University

Nathan A. Fox
University of Maryland

Uta Frith
University College London,
Institute of Cognitive
Neuroscience

Jordan Grafman
National Institutes of Health

Joshua D. Greene
Harvard University

Catherine A. Hynes
School of Psychology, University
of Queensland

Fátima Azevedo Ignácio
Cognitive Psychology, Instituto
Philippe Pinel

Richard Joyce
Australian National University
and University of Sydney

Jerome Kagan
Harvard University

Leonard D. Katz
Massachusetts Institute of
Technology

Jeanette Kennett
Center for Applied Philosophy and
Public Ethics, Australian National
University

Kent A. Kiehl
University of New Mexico and
The MIND Institute

Melanie Killen
University of Maryland

Daniel K. Lapsley
University of Notre Dame

Heidi Maibom
Carleton University

Victoria McGeer
Princeton University

John Mikhail
Georgetown University Law Center

Jorge Moll
National Institutes of Health &
CBNU, LABS-D'Or Hospital
Network

Shaun Nichols
University of Arizona

Ricardo de Oliveira-Souza
Universidade do Rio de Janeiro &
CBNU, LABS D'Or Hospital
Network

Mirella L. M. F. Paiva
National Institutes of Health

Adina L. Roskies
Dartmouth College

Jana Schaich Borg
Olin Neuropsychiatry Research
Center, Institute of Living

Katrina L. Sifferd
Dartmouth College

Walter Sinnott-Armstrong
Dartmouth College

Michael Smith
Princeton University

Mark Timmons
University of Arizona

Frédérique de Vignemont
Institut Jean-Nicod

Paul J. Whalen
Dartmouth College

Roland Zahn
National Institutes of Health

Index to Volume 1

Note: Figures are indicated by "f"; tables are indicated by "t," and footnotes by "n."

Index to Volume 2

Figures are indicated by "f"; tables are indicated by "t," and footnotes by "n."

Index to Volume 3

Figures are indicated by "f"; tables are indicated by "t," and footnotes by "*n.*"

induction, 72
infanticide dilemmas, 44, 89
inference
 and adolescence, 345
 and allocentrism, 278
 in children, 299, 322
 and ideals, 303
 of mental state (*see* mental states, of others)
 and moral judgments, 84, 182
 unconscious, 91*n*4
inferior colliculus, 310, 311
information-processing, 81
inhibition
 and basic emotions, 27
 brain region, 7, 329
 and temperament, 309, 317
 of violence, 276
innateness, 392
 See also internalism
insula
 and agency/intentionality, 10
 anger/indignation, 15
 and compassion, 16
 and disgust, 15
 and fairness, 54
 and guilt, 13
 and oddball effect, 12
 and somatic marker hypothesis, 330
intellect
 definition, 162
 and psychopathy, 120, 162, 168
intentionality
 and altruism, 308, 315
 brain regions, 10, 12, 160
 and guilt, 12
 and hedonism, 415
 and internalism, 184, 196
 and moral standards, 298
 and pride, 14
 and trolley/footbridge, 42
 See also double effect; ends; planning
interactional-socialization theory, 314

interalism
 and practical rationality, 179, 193, 211–215, 224*n*1, 225*n*6
internalism
 apology example, 393*n*6
 brain site, 178, 182–189, 192, 196–201, 221
 and ceteris paribus clause, 174, 179, 192, 195, 208–210, 217
 and conceptual rationalism, 380–385
 descriptions, 191–195, 205*n*1
 versus externalism, 173, 189, 193
 and folk concepts, 397–399
 and intention, 184, 196
 and necessity, 192
 non-naturalist, 180, 205*n*2
 and psychopathy, 180, 201–205, 381, 397
 simple motivational, 380, 382–385, 392*n*5, 393n6
 Smith (weak) version, 211–215, 225*n*6
 strict-motive version, 179–181, 207–211, 223, 225*n*6
 See also practical rationality
intuition(s)
 and conceptual rationalism, 380, 382
 conflicts, 89
 versus consequentialism, 70, 74–77
 and deontology, 91*n*3, 94–99, 116
 and evolution, 60
 justification principle, 402–404, 407*n*10, 421
 and moral judgment, 36, 67, 108, 396
 and psychopathy, 403–404
 and right *versus* wrong, 36, 63, 83
 source, 403, 407*n*10, 421
 and trolley/footbridge, 70, 84–87, 86f, 99, 106, 110
 See also moral grammar
investment game, 53
Ishikawa, S. S., 137, 166
item response theory analyses, 167
Izard, C. E., 347, 349

orbital frontal cortex
and awe, 16
and behavior change, 124
and compassion, 16
and disgust, 15
and embarrassment, 14
and gratitude, 16
and intentionality, 160
and moral judgment, 4
and oddball effect, 12
and psychopathy, 124–126, 136, 143, 146, 148, 364
and reward processing, 21
order
and autism, 239–245, 256n8, 262, 266–268, 279
in cosmos, 250–253, 261, 266–268, 287–289
maintenance of, 249
seeking *versus* creating, 266
and self-understanding, 261
ostracism, 369
other-conscious emotions, 2, 3t, 8
others
acknowledgment by, 297
and adolescents, 333–335
and autism, 235, 236, 263, 279
concern for, 307
and embarrassment, 27
emotions of, 8, 228, 255, 411, 416
ends of, 271
mental states, 7–10, 230, 239, 253, 299, 333
perspective, 334, 356, 389, 401–403
and pride, 14
and psychopaths, 236, 274
and self, 231, 234, 271, 312, 321, 416, 426
and uninhibited children, 318
well-being of, 251, 256n6, 307, 311–312
See also disinterested concern; empathy; third-party behavior

"ought"
versus "is," 72, 79n14, 371
metaethics view, 293n1
and moral error theory, 423
and obedience, 295n1
versus "want," 284
outcome assessment, 10, 11t, 13, 14, 15, 16
See also consequentialism; reward
outrage, 53, 55, 78n7, 358n3
oxytocin, 7

pain, 136
See also suffering
pantyhose experiment, 61
paralimbic system, 144–149, 147f, 160, 162, 165, 171
parasites, 155, 167
parents, 336
parietal lobes
and agency, 10
and cognition, 40
and emotion, 41
and moral dilemmas, 44–46
and psychopathy, 129, 141, 141f
and temperament, 311
peers
in adolescence, 333–338, 353, 355–357, 367
in military, 369
Peirce, C. S., 311
perfection, 298, 302
persistence
of moral judgments, 186, 198
and normativism, 206n4
personal fable, 333, 355
personality, 108
See also temperament
(im)personality
and charity, 47
and cognitive *versus* emotional, 106–108, 112
computer fairness study, 54

and perception, 403
and rationality, 389
relatives, 301, 303, 321
religion(s)
  Catholicism, 160
  and cosmic concern, 250, 287
  and love, 73
  and moral standards, 308
religiosity, 321
remorse
  apologies, 375, 386, 393n2, 393n6
  brain region, 186, 364
respect, 73, 95–97, 100
response-dependence, 75
responsibility, 364
retribution, 50, 70, 78n6, 98, 358n3
reward, 10, 21
Richler, J., 279
rightness, 357, 397
  See also wrongness
rights, 68, 74
Rilling, J., 54
risk-taking, 334, 338, 353
Ritov, I., 51
rituals, 287
Robinson, J. L., 348
Rogan, M. T., 363
Roper v. Simmons, 358n3
Roskies, A., 178–189, 190n7, 192, 193,
  207–215, 218, 220, 221, 224n2,
  225n4, 225n5, 225n6, 383, 385, 386,
  387
Ross, W. D., 94, 96, 101
Rozin, P., 56

sacrifice, 288
sadism, 269
  See also torture
sadness, 248
Sanfey, A., 54
Satin, 396, 422
satisfaction, 311–312
Savin-Williams, R. C., 338

Scanlon, T. M., 97, 98, 99, 100, 116,
  414, 415, 417n1
Schaich Borg, J., 159, 165–171, 166,
  168–170, 169, 171
Schelling, T., 48
schizophrenia, 120, 167
Schnall, S., 58
science, 67, 250, 307
scientific methodology, 19–21
Scott, E., 353, 354, 356
second-order representations, 329
self
  and agency, 245
  and autism, 238
  body state, 329–333
  deontologic view, 72–74
  diachronic awareness, 251, 261
  and enlightenment, 267
  and moral standards, 298
  and others, 231, 234, 271, 312, 321,
    416, 426
  and psychopaths, 176, 203, 235
  social position awareness, 303
  third-party perspective, 334, 356
  understanding, 261, 267, 288,
    299–305
self-characterization, 72–74, 297, 300,
  303–305, 312, 322
self-conscious emotions, 3t, 331–333,
  339, 346, 355
self-control. *See* behavior; inhibition;
  self-regulation
self-defense, 29
self-enhancement, 312, 321, 338
self-esteem, 9, 13, 14, 26
self-interest, 249, 270, 289, 307, 416
selfishness, 157, 390
self-organization, 237
self-reactive attitudes, 249
self-regulation, 27
Selman, R. L., 334, 335, 346
Semin, G. R., 27
sensation-seeking, 354